The Reagan Presidency

The Reagan Presidency

Pragmatic Conservatism and Its Legacies

Edited by W. Elliot Brownlee
and Hugh Davis Graham

 University Press of Kansas

Published by the University Press of Kansas (Lawrence, Kansas 66049), which was
organized by the Kansas Board of Regents and is operated and funded by Emporia
State University, Fort Hays State University, Kansas State University, Pittsburg State
University, the University of Kansas, and Wichita State University

Library of Congress Cataloging-in-Publication Data
The Reagan presidency: pragmatic conservatism and its legacies / edited
by W. Elliot Brownlee and Hugh Davis Graham.
   p. cm.
Includes index.
  ISBN 0-7006-1268-8 (alk. paper)
   1. United States—Politics and government—1981–1989.   2. Reagan,
Ronald—Political and social views.   3. Conservatism—United
States—History—20th century.   4. Pragmatism—History—20th century.   I.
Brownlee, W. Elliot, 1941–   II. Graham, Hugh Davis.
  E876.R4117 2003
  973.927—dc21   2003007158

British Library Cataloguing-in-Publication Data is available.

Printed in the United States of America

10 9 8 7 6 5 4 3 2 1

The paper used in this publication meets the minimum requirements of the American
National Standard for Permanence of Paper for Printed Library Materials Z39.48-1984.

To the memory of Hugh Davis Graham

Contents

Preface   ix

Introduction: Revisiting the "Reagan Revolution"   1
W. Elliot Brownlee

PART I: IDEAS AND RHETORIC

1. Ronald Reagan and the American Public Philosophy   17
   Hugh Heclo

2. Reagan and the Transformation of American Conservatism   40
   Ted V. McAllister

3. Reagan: The Soft-Sell Populist   61
   Terri Bimes

PART II: FOREIGN POLICY

4. Sticking to His Guns: Reagan and National Security   85
   Chester J. Pach, Jr.

5. Reagan and the Soviets: Winning the Cold War?   113
   Beth A. Fischer

6. Reagan, Euromissiles, and Europe   133
   Samuel F. Wells, Jr.

PART III: THE ECONOMIC AGENDA

7. Taxation   155
   W. Elliot Brownlee and C. Eugene Steuerle

8. Riding the Third Rail: Social Security Reform   182
   Martha Derthick and Steven M. Teles

9. The Welfare State   209
   Gareth Davies

10. Natural Resources and Environmental Policy   233
    Jeffrey K. Stine

PART IV: THE SOCIAL AGENDA

11. Failing the Test: Immigration Reform   259
    Otis L. Graham, Jr.

12. Civil Rights Policy   283
    Hugh Davis Graham

13. Mobilizing Women: The "Social" Issues   293
    Donald T. Critchlow

14. Federal Judgeships in Retrospect   327
    David M. O'Brien

Afterword: The Legacies of the Reagan Years   355
James T. Patterson

List of Contributors   377

Index   380

Preface

This book is the culmination of an interdisciplinary collaboration that Hugh Davis Graham launched in 1998 to help define and advance an agenda of historical research on the presidency of Ronald Reagan. Hugh hoped to promote what he described as a "second-generation" understanding of the history of the Reagan presidency. By that, he meant an understanding that would take into account the interpretations of the Reagan presidency by the first wave of its participants and observers, and then would move beyond to develop more seasoned historical judgments. To achieve this, Hugh adapted a model of collaboration he had developed successfully for studying the presidency of Jimmy Carter.*

In 1999, I joined Hugh as co-organizer of the project, and we subsequently called for scholars in history, political science, economics, and other disciplines in the humanities and social sciences to submit proposals for papers to be delivered at a conference at the University of California, Santa Barbara (UCSB). The strong response to the call enabled us to amass dozens of papers for the conference, which we convened in March of 2002. Among the participants was a group of scholars whom we had invited to write major essays on the history of the Reagan presidency. These scholars had attained distinction but generally had not yet written extensively on the Reagan years. Hugh and I eagerly looked forward to the results of their labors, particularly because we could not predict how their findings and interpretations would turn out.

One element of the research plan did not succeed as well as it had for the Carter project. Hugh and I had established the research schedule to take advantage of what we had assumed would be the opening in January 2001 of the policy-advisory documents within the collections of the Reagan Presidential Library. At that time, the twelve-year moratorium, set by the Presidential Records Act of 1978, on an exiting president's policy-advisory documents (restricted under the P-5 category of the act) was due to expire. Scholars participating in our conference would have, we thought, ample time to take advantage of the opening

---

*For the book that resulted from the Carter project, see Gary M. Fink and Hugh Davis Graham, *The Carter Presidency: Policy Choices in the Post–New Deal Era* (Lawrence: University Press of Kansas, 1998).

before the conference. In anticipation of the opening, we obtained the enthusiastic cooperation of archivists at the Reagan Library. They helped scholars request, within the framework of the Freedom of Information Act (FOIA), access to the documents that had P-5 restrictions. Fortunately, as it turned out, some documents of interest to our group of scholars were already opened, and others, unrestricted by P-5 or other provisions of the Presidential Records Act, opened up in response to FOIA requests. But the administration of George W. Bush slowed the release of P-5 documents and then issued Executive Order 13233, which limited access to the records of former presidents. These actions disrupted the research plans of scholars participating in the conference. Only on March 15, 2002, just a matter of days before our conference, did the Bush administration make a major release of the P-5 documents to which scholars had previously requested access.*

The conference, nonetheless, succeeded. The participants, who were primarily historians and political scientists, moved beyond the terms of debate that had prevailed in 1989. They employed multidisciplinary analysis. They took advantage of the perspective that the passage of time provides. They proved adept in exploiting primary sources that supplemented the resources of the Reagan Library. And they listened to each other. As the extensive press coverage of the conference suggested, the proceedings were not only stimulating but also extraordinarily civil, despite differing disciplinary, methodological, and ideological outlooks.†

The intellectual enthusiasm and civility that prevailed during the conference resulted largely from the example that Hugh Graham set for us. His approach to scholarly discussion was thoughtful, balanced, meticulous, often dryly ironic, and always respectful of divergent opinion. He passed away on March 26, 2002, just a little more than twenty-four hours before the opening of the conference, and our memories of him called us to the highest standards of our profession.

A great many people contributed to the conference and this book. The authors whose essays appear in this volume benefited from the colleagues who discussed earlier versions of the essays at the conference, and from the stimulation that the other conference papers provided. Important in supporting the con-

---

*On November 28, 2001, Public Citizen filed suit in federal court, on behalf of various plaintiffs, to overturn the executive order. Among the plaintiffs were the Organization of American Historians, the American Historical Association, the National Security Archive, the Reporters Committee for Freedom of the President, and presidential historians Stanley Kutler and Hugh Davis Graham.

†For some of the press coverage, see Nora K. Wallace, "Still a Great Divide on Legacy of Reagan Presidential Years," *Santa Barbara News-Press,* March 29, 2002; John Wildermuth, "Evaluating Reagan's Reign," *San Francisco Chronicle,* March 31, 2002; and Adam Clymer, "Rethinking Reagan: Was He a Man of Ideas After All?" *New York Times,* April 6, 2002.

ference were Ettore F. Infante and John H. Venable, former deans of the College of Arts and Science, Vanderbilt University; Henry Yang, the chancellor of UCSB; David Marshall, the dean of the Division of Humanities and Fine Arts within UCSB's College of Letters and Science; the chairs of UCSB's departments of history, political science, and economics: John E. Talbott, Lorraine M. McDonnell, and Rajnish Mehra, respectively; Bruce E. Cain, director of the Institute of Governmental Studies at the University of California, Berkeley; Alan Olmstead, chair of the All-UC Group in Economic History; and Floyd G. Brown, executive director of the Young America's Foundation: The Reagan Ranch. Leonard Wallock, the associate director of the Interdisciplinary Humanities Center (IHC), which was the lead sponsor at UCSB, was an inspired, creative, and calm champion of the conference from beginning to end. Andy Ross Sharp and Jeremy Tessmer, members of the IHC staff, created and maintained an excellent website. Jessica Chapman, a Ph.D. candidate in history at UCSB, proficiently managed local arrangements and kept the conference running smoothly. Michael A. Bernstein, Terri Bimes, John A. Douglass, Samuel F. Wells, and John Woolley assisted greatly in organizing the conference panels. At the Ronald Reagan Library, archivists Diane Barrie, Kelly Barton, Greg Cumming, Dennis Daellenbach, Mike Duggan, Sherrie Fletcher, Meghan Lee, Cate Sewell, Jenny Sternaman, and Lisa Vitt were consistently resourceful and hospitable. Fred Woodward, the director of the University Press of Kansas, offered the mix of wisdom, efficiency, and well-timed encouragement for which he is well known. Gil Troy read the entire manuscript and offered cogent advice on the structure of the book. Lou Cannon and Ted McAllister were especially important sources of insightful and generous advice.

The dedication expresses the gratitude of the contributors to Hugh Graham. Speaking for myself, the collaboration with him taught me a great deal about the meaning of professional dedication, and of personal courage.

W. E. B.

Introduction: Revisiting the "Reagan Revolution"

W. Elliot Brownlee

The presidency of Ronald Reagan (1981–1989) remains deeply controversial. Debate swirls around the same issues over which proponents and opponents of the so-called Reagan Revolution argued during the years of the Reagan presidency. Those who hold the most extreme positions agree on a central point: that there was, in fact, a "Reagan Revolution"—a set of fundamental shifts in national policy. They agree, as well, that those shifts had dramatic effects, for good or for ill.

Such controversy has followed other presidencies, but only the controversy over the meaning of the presidency of Franklin D. Roosevelt has persisted longer. Historians generally agree that Roosevelt did much that warranted sustained debate, even though very few now regard the New Deal as revolutionary. Roosevelt brought a long era of dominance by the Democratic Party, promoted recovery from the nation's most serious bout with unemployment, sponsored a limited welfare state of regulated capitalism, led an Allied victory in World War II, and initiated the postdepression and postwar restructuring of the world's economy.

Whether or not Reagan changed America and the world as much as Roosevelt did remains very much in dispute, but the extravagant claims that some proponents and opponents alike have made—that Reagan transformed both the domestic and world orders—help explain the extended nature of the arguments. The interpretive stakes are high. If it turns out that the Reagan presidency did, in fact, empower a conservative movement, bring an extended period of Republican ascendancy, promote the end of the nation's most serious bout with inflation, restructure tax, fiscal, and regulatory policy along neoconservative lines, rebuild American military power, preside over the destruction of the Soviet Union, and initiate a neoconservative restructuring of the world's political and economic relationships, then perhaps the Reagan presidency ought to join the Roosevelt presidency as the two that were most responsible for shaping America during the twentieth century.

While historical analysis of the Roosevelt administration is deep and rich, scholarship on the Reagan administration consists in the main of memoirs, studies by contemporary social scientists, and journalistic accounts. Much of this work is superb and is likely to remain important to later generations of historians. The insightful and candid memoirs of Martin Anderson, Martin Feldstein, Donald Regan, Paul Craig Roberts, and David Stockman, for example, will remain valuable places to begin in understanding Reagan's economic program.[1] The collection of essays edited by Larry Berman offers an excellent snapshot of how, toward the end of the Reagan presidency, leading political scientists assessed it.[2] And to take perhaps the best example of the accomplishments of the "first generation," Lou Cannon's splendid biographies of Ronald Reagan are likely to remain unequaled in the way in which they capture Ronald Reagan's personality.[3]

The passage of time, however, assists historians and political scientists. They can take advantage of the distance to understand the elements of continuity and discontinuity between previous and subsequent administrations, to place an administration's initiatives within long-run social, economic, and political developments, and to get a fix on the long-run consequences of an administration's political decisions and policy shifts. The passage of time also expands the possibilities for painstaking archival research—the staple in which historians specialize.

This book has resulted from an organized effort by an interdisciplinary group of scholars, primarily historians and political scientists, more than two decades after the beginning of the Reagan presidency, and more than a decade after its close, to take advantage of the perspective of time and opportunities for archival research in reaching an understanding of that presidency.

Most of the scholars focus their essays on important areas of national policy during the Reagan presidency. Within these topics, they explore the intentions, contents, and effects of the Reagan presidency. Although the topics they have developed do not provide a comprehensive survey of the policy agenda of the Reagan presidency, the contributors hope that the scope of this collection of essays is sufficiently broad to advance understanding of the history of the Reagan presidency.

The three scholars who launch the book, however, do not discuss an area of policy. These three focus instead on a crucial aspect of the topic of Ronald Reagan's leadership—the development and effect of his ideas. Modern political history has moved away from the presidential synthesis, but these essayists, along with most political historians, still believe that presidential leadership, including a president's ideas, must remain an important subject.

Hugh Heclo urges scholars to take Ronald Reagan's ideas seriously. Enough time has elapsed to make this possible, he suggests. "It is simply," Heclo writes, "that a better sense of historical proportion can arise as time rolls over the old quarrels and personal score keeping." Heclo writes that Ronald Reagan "was probably the only 20th century president whose political career was so thoroughly devoted to contesting for the public philosophy." Reagan's philosophy,

Heclo contends, constituted much more than "hackneyed slogans." It offered Americans "a sacramental vision" involving divine election that had sent America on a timeless mission to all mankind. The agenda flowed from this vision. Communism posed the external threat, while "modern government expansion represented the internal threat to America's consecrated mission of freedom." During the 1960s and 1970s, Reagan's public philosophy, Heclo claims, maintained "the sacramental vision as a living faith in the public mind rather than a dead tradition of antiquarian curiosity or ridicule."

Ted McAllister agrees with Heclo's assessment and sets Reagan's ideas in the context of the development of American conservatism and conservative ideas since the 1950s. McAllister associates Reagan's ideas during the 1960s with the "fusionism" of Frank S. Meyer, a conservative theoretician and a founding editor of *National Review*. Meyer's political philosophy, which attempted to resolve what McAllister describes as the "call to Return" with the "lure of Progress," provided Reagan with a middle-of-the-road intellectual position within the American right. During the 1970s, this position helped him assume leadership of the broad collection of groups that coalesced in a conservative movement. But Reagan, McAllister argues, had his preferences within the agenda of this coalition. He had more interest in Progress than in Return—and he emphasized a program of anticommunism abroad and neoconservative economics at home.

To these analyses of Reagan's public philosophy, Terri Bimes, in her essay, adds that Reagan owed a debt to Franklin Roosevelt and Harry Truman, who were early political heroes of Reagan. Bimes assesses Reagan's invocation of populist themes, particularly in his antigovernment messages. She suggests that Reagan adapted the "populist imagery" of Harry Truman and Franklin Roosevelt to his own agenda by replacing "greedy corporations" with the federal government as "the enemy of ordinary Americans." According to Bimes, Harry Truman may well have inspired Reagan's concept of "a citizen temporarily in public service." Although Bimes attends to the populist themes in Reagan's rhetoric, she reinforces the findings of Heclo and McAllister by discovering that Reagan toned down his populist rhetoric after the 1964 election. Rather than appeal to workers, farmers, and small business owners in terms of "their underdog economic status," Reagan tried to persuade "them to think of themselves in terms of their status as taxpayers, consumers, and as part of (the American family)." After his election, he limited his sharper populist appeals to his attack on government through budgetary and tax policies. In his major speeches and messages, which he aimed at national audiences, he moved away altogether from such appeals and sought to build consensus by invoking the kind of themes that Heclo discusses.

Taken as a group, these three essays significantly advance our understanding of how the Reagan presidency appealed powerfully to the American people, across party lines. They also help us see how Reagan's ideas helped focus the policies of his presidency. The essays in this book generally agree on the importance of this point. They find that whatever effectiveness Reagan had as a presidential leader was based on his strategic approach to policymaking—in other words, on his success in setting priorities. In his essay, Hugh Graham notes that Reagan's "core concerns," as revealed in his radio talks during the 1970s, "comprise a short list of topics—the global communist conspiracy, national defense and intelligence, international arms control, the growth of government, taxation, regulating free markets." Graham writes: "By concentrating his efforts on this short list, he achieved a surprising amount of what he attempted." In contrast, the policy agendas of Jimmy Carter and George H. W. Bush were, Graham argues, "long, complex, and lacked thematic coherence."

Reagan's priorities involved, as several of the essayists observe, the linkage of his two core programs of foreign policy and domestic economic policy. He believed, as Chester Pach puts it, "that the renewal of national power was essential to meet the dangers of international communism in an intensified Cold War," and that "rebuilding national strength—military and economic" must become the overarching goal of the administration. This construction of goals also represented pragmatic politics. As Ted McAllister notes, an emphasis on combating communism provided a powerful and practical means of uniting Reagan's diverse coalition of groups. And once the cold war had ended, as McAllister makes clear, maintaining conservative—and Republican—unity became a much more difficult chore.

Chester Pach and Samuel Wells identify the importance of Reagan's personal leadership in shaping the administration's foreign policy. At the same time, they acknowledge the importance of vigorous disagreements within the Reagan White House. The president's style, deliberate or not, Pach points out, involved encouraging members of his administration to struggle among themselves over how best to interpret and implement his national security goals. Wells criticizes this way of making policy. He writes: "In picking a team of senior officials who held quite divergent views on international affairs and in refusing to supervise closely or even to choose clearly between feuding advisers, like Shultz and Weinberger, Reagan created conditions for an inconsistent and error-prone— even scandal-prone—administration."

During 1983 and 1984, one of those struggles within the administration led the Reagan administration to shift away from hard-line policies toward the Soviet Union. Chester Pach, Samuel Wells, and Beth Fischer all agree on that. But our essayists disagree on the significance of the shift. According to Pach, it was less dramatic than both Fischer and Wells claim. Reagan, Pach argues, continued to put pressure on the Soviet Union by insisting on continued, significant increases in defense spending. And in 1983 he proposed his boldest national security program: the Strategic Defense Initiative (SDI). In contrast with advocates of the "Reagan Victory School," Pach does not argue that Reagan intended to use SDI to bankrupt the Soviet Union. But Pach stresses that Reagan, in his negotiations with Gorbachev, clung so stubbornly to his technological vision that he failed to reach his goal of a nuclear-free world. Finally, Pach notes the covert assistance that the Reagan administration provided to the Afghan resistance, and that the administration believed it had won a major victory when the Soviets withdrew in 1988.

At the end of his administration, Reagan believed that he had "followed his script and had done what he promised" (Pach's words) by restoring America's self-confidence and international reputation. But had he ended the cold war? In the division of labor within our volume, Fischer attempts to answer this question, and Wells takes up the related issue of the effect of Reagan's arms control negotiations. Fischer regards the end of the cold war as "a victory for the Reagan administration, but not in the sense that the Reagan victory school asserts." In other words, the Reagan administration did not bring down the Soviet Union, and the fall of the Soviet Union was not the key to peace. "The ending of the Cold War was a victory for both Reagan and Gorbachev," she writes, "because both leaders had sought peace."

Wells concurs. He reminds us that Reagan dreamed of a world free of nuclear weapons, and he believed in the power of personal relationships to resolve difficult issues. The Reagan-Gorbachev negotiations over arms control depended heavily on Reagan's desire for peace over security and arms control, and these negotiations, Wells concludes, paved the way for the end of the cold war. "While Reagan was not the largest force for change in this process," Wells adds, "he was an essential part and perhaps the only American political leader who could have made the concessions necessary to win Gorbachev's agreement."

At the top of the domestic side of the Reagan agenda for national renewal sat economic policy. And at the top of Reagan's economic agenda was reform of the welfare and regulatory state as it had evolved from the New Deal of Franklin Roosevelt through the Great Society of Lyndon Johnson. Four essays in the book analyze the intentions, accomplishments, and long-term effects of the Reagan presidency in the realm of economic reform.

The centerpiece of the Reagan economic agenda became his call in 1979 and 1980 for massive, across-the-board tax reductions. In our essay on Reagan's tax policies, Eugene Steuerle and I describe the proposed tax reductions as having two, closely linked supply-side goals. These were (1) stimulating economic activity through cuts in the tax rates of wealthy Americans and (2) controlling the size of government, which Reagan and his economic advisers believed wasted resources and impeded the growth of productivity. But we emphasize that the proposed reductions offered far more: significant tax relief to most Americans, who had experienced significant tax increases during the huge inflation of the 1970s. Thus, Reagan's original program of tax cutting contained a populist element—deep, across-the-board tax relief.

Reagan's tax program was, to a considerable extent, a product of his own political craftsmanship. Here, too, Reagan made a difference. From the 1970s through his years in the White House, Reagan consistently pushed for more tax cutting than even supply-side economists favored. Reagan looked for deeper tax cuts, ones that would benefit middle-class and even working-class Americans. In 1981, this impulse helped produce the deepest cuts in federal revenues since the aftermath of World War I.

Ronald Reagan's program of tax cutting in 1981 dominated his antigovernment program. Less important on his agenda at the time he came into office was the reform or reduction of entitlement programs.

Martha Derthick and Steven Teles make this point in their essay on Reagan's policies toward Social Security, the largest of all federal entitlement programs. Beginning in the 1960s, Reagan had expressed support for incorporating "voluntary" elements within Social Security, and during the 1970s economists like Martin Feldstein and Michael Boskin laid some groundwork for neoconservative reform. But Reagan moved cautiously. During the 1980 campaign, Reagan did not propose any clear program of reform and, in fact, promised, in a populist fashion, that he would not cut Social Security benefits. To propose either reductions in benefits or increases in Social Security taxes was inherently unpopular; either course meant identifying economic losers. Reagan was a conventional president in that he far preferred tax cutting, which involved only the identification of winners.

The economic circumstances of the late 1970s and early 1980s, however, required the federal government to address the fact that the Social Security system was running out of money. The White House had to offer some level of support for a combination of benefit reductions and tax increases. Reform would have to wait. By the time Reagan took office, congressional leaders were already deeply engaged in the difficult job of developing a finance package that would work both economically and politically. And the only feasible reforms were bipartisan—ones in which the two parties would share responsibility for administering bitter medicine. The Reagan administration engaged in the process and attempted to exert leadership. But as Derthick and Teles demonstrate, the administration proved inept, sponsoring a plan that included an early retirement provision with "harsh, immediate, and readily comprehensible effects." It opened the door for Speaker of the House Thomas P. O'Neill and the Democrats to paint the Republicans as the party that had broken a compact with the American people.

Derthick and Teles attribute the failure of the Reagan administration to a complex set of intertwined personal and institutional factors. They criticize budget director David Stockman for his arrogance in dealing with Congress, but they acknowledge that the surging deficit gave urgency to his cost-cutting efforts. They also fault the president himself for not paying enough attention to the details of the proposal. But they also recognize an inherent flaw "in the presidency as an institution for policy planning." They write: "It has a tendency to be torn between policy advisors who make recommendations to the president based on an overestimation of his power, and political staff who seek to distance their man from proposals bearing the possibility of political damage." In this instance, the result was that "Reagan embraced a policy proposal largely innocent of political calculation, and failed to put the full weight of his office behind it—policy adventurism combined with tactical timidity."

Ronald Reagan brought to the presidency views on welfare that were better developed than his ideas on Social Security. In his essay entitled "The Welfare State," Gareth Davies explains that during the 1960s and 1970s, Reagan had attacked the welfare system for subsidizing Americans who did not need or deserve it; for damaging the moral fiber of the recipients and the nation as a whole; for usurping powers reserved to the states; and for impeding the ability of capitalism to lift people out of poverty. These views on welfare reform were important to his presidential campaign on behalf of national economic renewal. Nonetheless, as was the case with Social Security, Reagan did not define a specific program for welfare reform during the campaign. But because certain welfare programs proved politically unpopular, Reagan was able to accomplish more than in the realm of Social Security. In particular, the Omnibus Budget Reconciliation Act (OBRA) of 1981 slashed poverty programs, especially Aid to Families with Dependent Children (AFDC) and food stamps.

Davies argues that the budget cuts of 1981 marked the high water of Reagan's assault on welfare. Whatever conservative victories against the welfare programs there were during the Reagan Revolution, they occurred during that brief revolutionary moment. In 1982, an effort to make another round of cuts in antipoverty programs failed in the face of the recession and rising concern among middle-class Americans that further cuts would be unfair. Also that year, a push toward the "New Federalism," which included moving AFDC and food stamps to the states, ran aground. Subsequent reversals in the 1982 elections led Reagan and his advisers to conclude that they had no popular mandate for welfare reform, and nothing that happened later changed their minds.

The moment for the most radical economic legislation of the Reagan Revolution may have passed in 1981, but the Reagan administration nonetheless went on to contribute to significant fiscal reform, as Eugene Steuerle and I explain in our essay. An important factor in the movement toward this reform was the huge deficit spending that the 1981 tax cuts helped produce. The deficit replaced inflation as the problem that had to be at the top of the economic agenda. Another factor was Reagan's personal resistance to hikes in tax rates; this slowed the process of deficit reduction and pushed the search for new revenues into the broadening of the tax base and, ultimately, the Tax Reform Act of 1986. The Reagan administration, led by Donald Regan, James Baker, and Richard Darman, used bipartisan cooperation and an enthusiastic Treasury to pick losers as well as winners and, in the process, reverse the regressive effects of the 1981 tax cuts. Reagan initially refused to take up base-broadening reform. But when he finally got behind it, he did so with enthusiasm. He discovered that championing the Tax Reform Act of 1986 once again allowed him to be a populist and to win broad public support for his administration. In contrast with 1981 and 1983, his populism was more traditional—that is to say, closer to that of Franklin Roosevelt. It was a call for defeat of special private interests who had sought out and won special favoritism within the tax code.

Derthick and Teles show us that the pattern was similar for Reagan's reform of Social Security. Tip O'Neill's success in embarrassing Reagan and Stockman over Social Security and the loss of a conservative majority in the House of Representatives in 1982 allowed White House chief of staff James Baker and his deputy Richard Darman to take control of the issue. They worked under the cover provided by the National Commission on Social Security Reform ("the Greenspan Commission") to collaborate with Democrats in crafting the Social Security Act Amendments of 1983. As in tax policy, Derthick and Teles argue that "program proprietors," or "system conservers"—rather than "partisans or ideologues"—had won a victory. The same could be said, too, of the Family Support Act of 1988, which Reagan signed. As Gareth Davies contends, this act owed more to the ideas of Senator Daniel Patrick Moynihan than to the agenda of Ronald Reagan. In the case of taxation, Social Security reform, and to some extent welfare reform, after the revolutionary moment of 1981 had passed, the pragmatism of the Reagan administration led it to undertake reforms that strengthened the economic instruments of the federal government that Reagan had inherited from the New Deal, Fair Deal, and Great Society.

Deregulation constituted another central element in Ronald Reagan's reform of the institutions of national government it had inherited. During the 1970s and through his 1980 presidential campaign, Reagan had denounced excessive regulation as an impediment to economic growth. Within a week of his inauguration, Reagan announced the creation of the Presidential Task Force on Regulatory Relief and the appointment of its chair, Vice President George H. W. Bush. But a comprehensive, systematic rollback of the regulatory apparatus of the federal government would have proven a daunting and dangerous task, and it is hardly surprising that neither the task force nor any other power center within the Reagan administration organized such an effort. But the Reagan administration, to some extent through the vigilance of the task force, no doubt slowed, at least for a time, the expansion of the regulatory state. This was so in the area of environmental policy, which Jeffrey Stine discusses in his essay.

Stine details how the Reagan administration launched an effort to roll back environmental regulation that it believed inimical to maximizing economic growth. To some extent, this element of the Reagan Revolution represented a shift of direction for the president. As governor, he had respected the popularity of environmental causes and had adopted a pragmatic approach to environmental politics. But after leaving Sacramento, Reagan, in the course of forging his presidential coalition and his program for national renewal, formed close ties with western conservatives like Paul Laxalt and Joseph Coors and discovered the neoconservative critique of environmental regulation. In the White

House, Reagan did not tackle the legislative base of environmental regulation, but instead employed what Stine calls "administrative fiat." This program of agency reorganization and the appointment of "like-minded loyalists in key positions within the federal bureaucracy" focused on weakening the Department of Interior, undersecretary James G. Watt, and the Environmental Protection Agency (EPA) under Anne M. Gorsuch. However, in this policy area as well, concern about Reagan's prospects for reelection led to a shift in direction. Environmentalist outrage and Democratic successes in 1982 forced the resignation in 1983 of both Watt and Gorsuch and their replacement with more moderate administrators.

Stine maintains that Reagan's environmental policy cut a deep, self-inflicted wound. The administration grossly underestimated, he argues, the depth of popularity of environmental causes and then offered up convenient targets, like James Watt, for the environmental movement, Democratic politicians, and dissident bureaucrats to shoot at. In the process, the administration energized the environmental movement. On this particular issue, Ronald Reagan's instincts for reading the American public failed him, and the Reagan Revolution turned out to be counterproductive.

The essays propose that in the realm of domestic economic reform, the most important, sustained accomplishment that emerged from the revolutionary moment of 1981 was the across-the-board reduction of income tax rates.[4] The true believers in the Reagan program of permanently slowing government, reforming welfare, and rolling back regulation found little to applaud in other policy areas, especially after 1981. In fact, much of what followed reinforced the welfare and regulatory state that had developed since the New Deal. But defeats that neoconservative economic interests suffered often energized them to press even more vigorously for their agenda after the close of the Reagan era. Martha Derthick and Steven Teles argue, for example, that the failure of "privatization" to gather traction during Reagan's reform of Social Security motivated neoconservatives to develop the approach that later captured the imagination of presidential candidate George W. Bush.[5] In addition, even when the Reagan administration failed to live up to the idealism of the Reagan Revolution, it sometimes indirectly stimulated later conservative successes. Gareth Davies makes this point by suggesting that Reagan's welfare policies "galvanized the states to become laboratories of welfare reform," and that Reagan's reelection victory convinced "new" Democrats like Bill Clinton to embrace a conservative position on welfare reform.

However limited the Reagan Revolution may have been as a program of economic reform, it was even more modest in its social realm. To some extent, this was a consequence of the power of economic neoconservatives and the Republicans' traditional corporate supporters, whose interests often ran against those of the groups that Ted McAllister describes as "traditionalists" or the "new right."

The effort to restrict immigration provides a good example of the conflict between factions within the Reagan coalition and of the relative weakness of the so-called new right. Otis Graham argues that the debate over immigration policy within the Reagan administration and the Republican Party was a contest between "two souls, one devoted to law-and-order and respect for the institutions of family, church and Nation, the other a more animated one steered not by those cautious and preservative instincts but by a libertarian, free-market, government-hating ideology." Ronald Reagan's "heart," however, Graham explains, was not with the cultural conservatives, some of whom wanted restriction of immigration and especially suppression of illegal immigration. Reagan came down on the side of the neoconservatives, who generally wanted to encourage immigration, and resisted what he saw as a campaign from within the federal bureaucracy "to make the government more intrusive." And, Graham argues, Reagan's lack of interest in suppressing illegal immigration led him to sign, in 1986, the bipartisan Immigration Reform and Control Act (IRCA). Graham regards the act as "a dismal and costly policy failure" because, in effect, it "kept the nation on the road the Democrats put them with the Immigration Act of 1965."

The Reagan administration also disappointed some cultural conservatives by failing to reverse the course of affirmative action policy. Hugh Graham relates how, in 1984 through 1986, Bradford Williams, assistant attorney general for civil rights, and Edwin Meese III attempted to jettison the minority preference policies inherited from the Carter administration. Meese won support for his position from the Domestic Policy Council but faced continuing opposition from the Labor Department bureaucracy, Secretary of Labor William E. Brock III, and several other cabinet members, including James Baker, George Shultz (who had been Richard Nixon's first secretary of labor), and Elizabeth Dole. These opponents worried about alienating minority and women voters and also large employers who did not want "to plunge into unknown legal waters" and "preferred hiring, under a diversity rationale, immigrant workers they found to be hard-working, low-cost, compliant, and resistant to union organizers." Thus, the failure to control immigration, Hugh Graham argues, became linked in its political consequences with the failure to reform affirmative action.

In the face of a badly divided White House, Meese kept the issue of affirmative action from reaching the desk of the president. Graham concludes that "being Reagan" in the affirmative action debate was less a case of "being disengaged, incurious, ill-informed, inconsistent" and more a case of "avoiding a bloody and possibly losing battle" over affirmative action, "saving your chits to cash in on the great, short-listed policy conflicts such as tax cuts and defense buildup."

To the forces of the new right, abortion was far more damnable than illegal immigration or the consequences of affirmative action. For the new right, it was the assault on abortion that provided the best test of Reagan's commitment to cultural conservatism.

In an essay that focuses on the issue of reproductive rights, Donald Critchlow emphasizes the importance of hostility to abortion, along with opposition to the Equal Rights Amendment and support for prayer in school, in helping Reagan, during the 1960s and 1970s, energize what Critchlow calls a "disheartened conservative movement." In the process of analyzing the importance of such issues to the development of the Reagan coalition, Critchlow highlights the importance of the Christian right and of women who held "traditional" values. These supporters read Reagan correctly. He was, according to Critchlow, a sincere supporter of right-to-life.

Critchlow finds no great tension within the White House over abortion between neoconservatives and the Christian right, as well as the other groups under the umbrella of the new right. During the revolutionary window of opportunity in 1981, when Reagan emphasized his economic agenda, the new right seemed to accept Reagan's priorities. And then, in 1982, Reagan vigorously supported the enactment of a constitutional amendment to overturn *Roe v. Wade*. The defeat of such a measure demonstrated that the most severe political problem that the new right faced was not internal division within conservative forces but, rather, the difficulty in winning bipartisan support for their program. Subsequently, Critchlow writes, "Reagan eloquently articulated the 'pro-life' position throughout his administration." Reagan did more than talk; he employed budgetary measures and administrative fiat to restrict government involvement in family planning. And he made key "pro-life" judicial and administrative appointments, including Richard Schweiker, Margaret Heckler, and Otis Bowen as secretaries of Health and Human Services. As a consequence of the loyalty of the Reagan administration to the core issues of groups within the new right, their loyalty to Reagan never failed.

The Reagan administration advanced the new right agenda primarily through the appointment of federal judges. In his essay, David O'Brien explains the appointment process and reflects on how Reagan shaped, in the longer term, the law and judicial practice. O'Brien agrees with Critchlow that it was in this arena that the Reagan administration advanced, most significantly, the traditionalist agenda. In the 1980 and 1984 elections, Reagan made it clear that he intended to appoint only federal judges who supported "traditional family values" and opposed abortion. He followed through on this promise with what O'Brien describes as "a more coherent and ambitious agenda for judicial selection than any previous administration." In the process, Reagan enhanced the power of the president in judicial selection and shaped the future of the federal bench by appointing almost half of the judges in the lower federal courts. At the level of the Supreme Court, however, Reagan enjoyed less success. He named three associate justices and elevated Justice Rehnquist to the chief justiceship. However, he still did not win a majority over to his Justice Department's positions on abortion, affirmative action, and other social issues.

O'Brien concludes that Reagan's judicial policy had two major effects. It moved "the Supreme Court and the federal judiciary in a decidedly more conservative direction." And, through his Office of Legal Policy and White House Judicial Selection Committee, Reagan "fundamentally changed the politics of appointing federal judges." Each of the presidents who followed Reagan, O'Brien observes, "gave greater priority and closer scrutiny to the appointment of federal judges than did Reagan's predecessors." And, at the same time, Reagan polarized the politics of selecting judges.

In the longer run, however, Reagan's support for the social agenda of the new right had a continuing effect on American politics and policy. As in the case of domestic economic policy, groups whom the hope of a Reagan Revolution had helped mobilize carried their issues forward into subsequent political battles. As they did so, the "moral conservatives," to use Donald Critchlow's term, set aside memories of slights or defeats within Reagan's White House. Critchlow writes that "their view of history placed Reagan as bold defender of their cause," and his "presidency imparted inspiration to carry their battle into the next millennium with the knowledge that Heaven's gates awaited them as onward soldiers for a better nation."

More generally, the Reagan presidency, through the symbolism of the "Reagan Revolution," and an imagined record of its conservative accomplishments, left a potent political legacy. As Lou Cannon has written, the force of such symbolism has contributed to Republican victories that produced "more Reagan Republicans in Congress today than when Reagan was in the White House," exerted "a rightward tug on the political system, creating the context for a Clinton presidency," and helped set the agenda for the George W. Bush administration. In Cannon's words, "Reagan casts a long shadow."[6]

The essayists in this volume tend to agree, however, that the intentions, accomplishments, and long-term effects of the Reagan administration were not as drastic as first-generation proponents or opponents of the Reagan Revolution maintain. As James Patterson puts the matter in his afterword: "To speak, therefore, of a 'Reagan Revolution,' or of an 'Age of Reagan,' seems excessive." Nonetheless, Patterson's estimate of the long-run influence of the Reagan administration is more modest than that of most of the contributors to this volume. They find the Reagan administration more successful in carrying out its core agenda, and see more significant long-run effects on conservative politics and policymaking than does Patterson.

Reconciling conflicting descriptions of Reagan's legacy must proceed cautiously. After all, the conflicts are over the *long-run* effects of a presidency that ended very recently by most historians' standards. As Patterson correctly warns, while scholars have reached a "fairly clear" consensus regarding "the substance of his [Reagan's] ideas, the nature of his personality, and the style of his leadership," they "are still too close to the Reagan years to reach assured judgments about his legacy." Suppose, however, that in the fullness of time, historians reach a consensus that the most important theme of the history of American politics in the twentieth century was the decisive force of conservatism. Then, the legacy of the Reagan presidency would seem larger than it does today, and might well establish Reagan, along with Franklin Roosevelt, as one of the two most influential presidents of the twentieth century.

NOTES

1. Martin Anderson, *Revolution* (San Diego: Harcourt Brace Jovanovich, 1988); Martin Feldstein, "American Economic Policy in the 1980s: A Personal View," in *American Economic Policy in the 1980s,* ed. Martin Feldstein (Chicago: University of Chicago Press, 1994), 1–79; Donald T. Regan, *For the Record: From Wall Street to Washington* (San Diego: Harcourt Brace Jovanovich, 1988); Paul Craig Roberts, *The Supply-Side Revolution: An Insider's Account of Policymaking in Washington* (Cambridge: Harvard University Press, 1984); and David Stockman, *The Triumph of Politics: How the Reagan Revolution Failed* (New York: Harper & Row, 1986).

2. Larry Berman, ed., *Looking Back on the Reagan Presidency* (Baltimore: Johns Hopkins University Press, 1989).

3. Lou Cannon, *President Reagan: The Role of a Lifetime* (New York: Simon & Schuster, 1991) and *Reagan* (New York: G. P. Putnam's Sons, 1982).

4. The essays focus on long-term, structural reforms. Of course, the Reagan administration's economic record includes important short-run measures and accomplishments. The most notable was the reinforcement of the Federal Reserve's aggressive invocation of monetary policy to suppress the forces of inflation. Ironically, as Eugene Steuerle and I point out, the success of the Federal Reserve contributed to the deficit problem that plagued the Reagan presidency.

5. My usage of the term "neoconservative" is somewhat broader than that of Ted McAllister. I lump both his "neoconservatives" and his "economic libertarians" together in this category. I include, as well, many Reagan economic advisers, like Martin Feldstein, who sought greater reliance on markets but were neither neoconservative, in McAllister's narrower usage, nor economic libertarians.

6. Lou Cannon, "'To the Best of His Ability': A Speech to the UCSB Conference on the Presidency," March 28, 2002. Important support for Cannon's point comes from the recent analysis by political scientists Earl Black and Merle Black. They find that Reagan's presidency was responsible for a realignment of white southern voters during the 1980s and "made possible the Republicans' congressional breakthrough in the 1990s." Earl Black and Merle Black, *The Rise of Southern Republicans* (Cambridge: Harvard University Press, 2002), 205.

PART I
Ideas and Rhetoric

1

Ronald Reagan and the American Public Philosophy

Hugh Heclo

A public philosophy has been usefully defined as "an outlook on public affairs which is accepted within a nation by a wide coalition and which serves to give definition to problems and direction to government policies dealing with them."[1] One may naturally object to the use of "the" in this essay's title, since there is certainly more than one American public philosophy. My view of the definite article in this case is parallel to what Alasdair MacIntyre has to say about a "tradition" that is alive and in good order. No one voice can yield "the" public philosophy; it is a set of contestations, or as MacIntyre puts it, "an historically extended, socially embodied argument, and an argument precisely in part about the goods which constitute that tradition."[2] Ronald Reagan was one of those rare political leaders in America who made powerful, unrelenting claims in the contestation that is the American public philosophy.

Pointing toward the historical, socially embodied side of things, a public philosophy implicates a philosophy of history. It gives meaning to the flow of events. Pointing toward "the good" entailed in the metaphysical side of things, it implicates civil religion and religion more generally. It asserts ultimate values transcending mere events. On both sides, a public philosophy draws us into the subject of storytelling. Exactly how all this happens will emerge in the course of considering the public ideas of Ronald Reagan. After the 1984 election—at the ostensible high-water mark of the conservative movement's influence—Ronald Reagan ignored the movement (indeed, infuriated movement leaders) by doing nothing to enact conservative social legislation and making arms control with the communists his main cause. In doing so, Ronald Reagan was not so much betraying conservatism as he was remaining faithful to his own larger vision. As we shall see, Kant's warning is appropriate: that considered in the

My thanks to Lou Cannon, Fritz W. Ermarth, and James Pfiffner for their extremely helpful comments on the first draft of this paper.

widest sense, nearly everything about human affairs is paradoxical, full of strange turns and unexpected patterns.[3]

REAGAN'S CLAIM ON THE PUBLIC MIND

Ronald Reagan is among that handful of American politicians, and a much smaller group of presidents, who have conducted their careers primarily as a struggle about ideas. When professors do this, it is called philosophizing; when a public figure does it, it is called being an ideologue. Reagan was a man of ideas born out of life experiences, even though he was not a thinker's idea of a thinker.

One could go further and say that Reagan was probably the only twentieth-century president whose political career was so thoroughly devoted to contesting for the public philosophy. To appreciate this significance, one must pay as much attention to Reagan's pre-presidential years as to his White House years. In that regard, Reagan belongs less to the twentieth century and more to the estimable company of Jackson, Madison, and Jefferson.

That last sentence will no doubt set many academic teeth on edge. For almost two generations, Reagan's more intellectually sophisticated critics in mainstream academia—and there have been a great many—have found it absurd to characterize Ronald Reagan as any sort of thinker, much less a figure in public philosophy. However, that is exactly what he was.

To be sure, Ronald Reagan did not engage the world of ideas in the intellectually sophisticated, abstract way of which academics approve. He did so as a public man seeking political power in the name of certain ideas. That he also became president is a very remarkable thing. At the risk of putting it too grandly, one might say that Ronald Reagan was devoted to advancing not just a political program, party, or even movement, but a philosophy of history. Reagan did this work in his political life by serving as narrator, a teller of many stories that all served to expound and defend what he regarded as the one American story. For almost forty years, sometimes explicitly and other times more indirectly, he taught it as a story with a point about things of ultimate importance.

By "philosophy of history," I am referring to what W. H. Walsh called the "speculative" (rather than the "analytic") view of man's historical existence, in brief, a set of claims about the underlying meaning and plot of that existence.[4] To call this work speculative is certainly not to suggest that it lacks practical political significance. Charles Frankel was a liberal contemporary with whom Reagan would have agreed on very little, but he accurately identified the practical value of viewing the public activities of someone like Reagan from this perspective: "A philosophy of history can be a way, at once, of making the social imagination more responsible by pinning it down to what is immovable, and of making it freer and more flexible by giving it a larger vision of human possibilities. It is a theory of how things get done in history, and of what men can make of history. As such, it is an implicit strategy of social action, and it can be a sober prelude to the development of a coherent social program."[5]

At its core, this is what Reagan's political existence was all about. He championed a particular philosophy of history and did so with remarkable success in the hurly-burly world of politics. This is why, despite all the inevitable compromises required of a working politician, despite his disinterest in managing details and the infirmities of advancing age, a generally coherent program always flowed out of Reagan's electoral contests. It is also why, on a human level, Ronald Reagan seemed to manage the unavoidable tension between philosophic conviction and political trimming with a certain graciousness and good conscience. He saw the latter slippages as something that was always secondary to and in the service of the former philosophical mission, his essential, enduring mission.

Of course, one can object that Reagan's ideas were nothing new. Many critics put the point more negatively: Reagan's so-called ideas were a rehash of simpleminded, jingoistic slogans that America had, or should have, outgrown a long time ago. To portray Reagan as an intellectually shallow, uncomprehending spokesman for outworn ideas—an "amiable dunce"—has been standard practice of his more severe critics, including some members of his own administration. "The man was more ancient ideologically than he was in years" was the contemptuous characterization by Reagan's ambitious young budget director, David Stockman.[6]

To this charge of Reagan as a mouthpiece for old-fashioned ideas, I offer three answers. First, to require something new in the world of ideas is too high a standard. Few, if any, Ivy League professors meet it. Second, to carry forward familiar ideas into a new context is to do an important work. It may even help hold people to sanity by exaggerating what they had neglected. Third, the burden of this essay is to show that there is much more to Reagan's claim on the public mind than hackneyed slogans. This is not a matter of trying to rehabilitate or celebrate the memory of anyone, at least not from my perspective. It is simply being willing to see what one sees, once history has rolled past old political quarrels and scorekeeping. As a leading social scientist from Reagan's generation, a distinguished intellectual of the left, recently put it to me from his sickbed, "We all underestimated Reagan."

THE SACRAMENTAL VISION

We should begin at the center of it all. In the years immediately after Reagan left the White House, "the vision thing" often became a meaningless slogan among political sophisticates. Possibly, it was music the tone deaf could not hear. Or perhaps not being able to reproduce the music, Washington insiders sought relief in wisecracks. In any event, the vision thing for Ronald Reagan was something far more than a mere rhetorical flourish or a contrived piece of political strategy. From Reagan's first to his last political utterances, God's unique relation to America was the central chord from which all else followed.

The secular orthodoxy favored in many intellectual circles made it difficult to take Ronald Reagan's motivating beliefs seriously. This is because his political career expressed a historical and philosophical worldview that was Christian in a very traditional American sense. The vision in his political philosophy stemmed from convictions rooted in the quiet piety of his mother, Nellie, and in young Reagan's conversion to a model of "practical" Christianity (as opposed to hypocritical churchliness). Religious convictions about America's meaning, reaching from deep in his youth and reaffirmed over time, lay at the heart of things for Reagan.[7] In one of his earliest semipolitical speeches, in June 1952, the forty-one-year-old Reagan, with a failing acting career, declared:

> I, in my own mind, have thought of America as a place in the divine scheme of things that was set aside as a promised land. It was set here and the price of admission was very simple; the means of selection was very simple as to how this land should be populated. Any place in the world and any person from those places; any person with the courage, with the desire to tear up their roots, to strive for freedom, to attempt and dare to live in a strange and foreign place, to travel half across the world was welcome here. . . . I believe that God in shedding his grace on this country has always in this divine scheme of things kept an eye on our land and guided it as a promised land for those people [who love freedom].

For Reagan it was not a matter of reforming or inventing anything new for America but of realizing a transcendent historical truth: "that this land of ours is the last best hope of man on earth."[8] In other words, there is a story in the heart of Americans' history, a story that they did not put there. Almost thirty-seven years later, President Reagan ended his farewell address to the nation with the same master theme. By now, Reagan could communicate the essential idea without even using the name "America":

> I've spoken of the shining city all my political life, but I don't know if I ever quite communicated what I saw when I said it. But in my mind it was a tall, proud city built on rocks stronger than oceans, windswept, God-blessed, and teeming with people of all kinds living in harmony and peace; a city with free ports that hummed with commerce and creativity. And if there had to be city walls, the walls had doors and the doors were open to anyone with the will and the heart to get here. That's how I saw it, and see it still.
>
> And how stands the city on this winter night? More prosperous, more secure, and happier that it was 8 years ago. But more than that: After 200 years, two centuries, she still stands strong and true on the granite ridge,

and her glow has held steady no matter what storm. And she's still a beacon, still a magnet for all who must have freedom, for all the pilgrims from all the lost places who are hurtling through the darkness, toward home.[9]

Intellectuals and political pundits often sneered at such language, sometimes suggesting that Reagan had simply absorbed the fantasies in World War II movies. However, Hollywood's patriotic romances were themselves echoing much deeper themes that were older than the Republic itself. Over the years, many Americans seemed to sense there was something sincere and important in Reagan's evocations of these themes. Deep was calling to deep.

More than a claim of American exceptionalism, Reagan recalled Americans to what can most accurately be described as a sacramental vision. The sacramental quality consisted in understanding the American experience to be set apart as something sacred, a material phenomenon expressing a spiritual reality. This theophanic view of the nation had at least three major facets.

Turned at one angle, this vision reflected the idea of divine election. God had chosen America as the agent of His special purposes in history. To be sure, the Calvinist language of election and predestination had long ago disappeared together with the Puritans, but Reagan carried forward a central remnant of the idea. The ever-recurring references to God blessing America served not only as supplication (or sometimes it seemed a demand) but also as the recognition of an accomplished fact and beatification of historical existence. Providence intended for America to be something special in the larger scheme of things. In this view, Reagan was echoing earlier generations of eminent historians. They could write without doubt or irony about the hand of God in American history.[10]

Seen from a second angle, the sacramental vision pointed out that the nation was not sanctified simply for its own sake. America undertook a mission charged with significance for all mankind. Reagan seemed to recognize in his farewell speech that through the years he might have overused Governor Winthrop's image of a shining "City on a Hill." Still, stripped of its excessive familiarity, the old Puritan's biblical metaphor caught the correct notion of a world watching the call and response between God and a chosen people. Winthrop's city on a hill came as the concluding application in a sermon about love. Set apart for a covenantal, marital closeness to God, this people would serve either as an elevating model or as a terrible warning for the rest of mankind. As Winthrop put it, "For we must consider that we shall be as a city upon a hill, the eyes of all people are upon us. So that if we shall deal falsely with our God in this work we have undertaken, and so cause Him to withdraw His present help from us, we shall be made a story and a by-word through the world."[11] While downplaying the threat of divine punishment, Reagan reassured Americans that the light shining on their nation implicated all humanity. A favorite story, repeated in radio addresses and his final Oval Office speech, finds a towering American ship such as the USS *Midway* rescuing a tiny boat of refugees adrift in the open seas. Reagan concluded with a quotation from Pope Pius XII and his own positive view: "'Into the hands of America God has placed the destiny of an afflicted mankind.' I think those young men on the *Midway* have reassured God that he hasn't given us more of an assignment than we can handle."[12] Reagan evoked the primeval theme of America as the rescuing redeemer nation. His final radio address to the nation ended on the same theme of an elect mission for untold others: "Whether we seek it or not, whether we like it or not, we Americans are keepers of the miracles. We are asked to be guardians of a place to come to, a place to start again, a place to live in the dignity God meant for his children."[13]

However, it is not just people but time itself that is redeemed by America. Viewed from this third angle, the sacramental vision sees an end to the wreck of history and the beginning of a new time. The ancient hold of recurrent time—a political life cycle of birth, growth, decay, and death—had been decisively broken in America. A new era had been born that would renew the world. Time was now getting somewhere. As Reagan put it in 1959, "In this land of ours occurred the only true revolution in man's history—the only revolution that did not just exchange one set of rulers for another. Ours was the only revolution that recognized man had the dignity and sacred right to determine his own destiny as an individual."[14]

In appealing to Americans in this way, Reagan gave political voice to a view of the nation that drew on deep historical sources as varied as Jonathan Edwards, Thomas Paine, and Hegel. Edwards saw America's spiritual awakening in 1740 and guessed, "'Tis not unlikely that this work of God's Spirit . . . is the dawning, or at least a prelude, of that glorious work of God so often foretold in Scripture, which in the progress and issue of it shall renew the world of mankind." In *Common Sense,* Paine urged America's revolutionaries that "we have it in our power to begin the world over again. A situation, similar to the present, hath not happened since the days of Noah until now. The birth day of a new world is at hand." In 1830 Hegel lectured his German students that in his own sweeping philosophy of history, "America is the land of the future, where in the ages that be before us, the burden of the world's history will reveal itself."[15] These were all different takes on the millennial vision of Christian time reckoning. Only now, the millennium had been brought down to Earth in one nation's destiny as a permanent new beginning. When Reagan spoke of America as a place for freedom-loving people to come to, he was not speaking simply about immigration. It was a place in a new time to which all people were being called. As he put it in 1980, "I believe it is our pre-ordained destiny to show all mankind that they, too, can be free without having to leave their native shore."[16] In his last speech to a major political gathering, Reagan said, "Emerson was right. We are the country of tomorrow. Our revolution did not end at Yorktown. More than two centuries later, America remains on a voyage of discovery, a land that has never become, but is always in the act of becoming."[17] Every dawn could be a great new beginning and every evening could bring men closer to that shining city upon a hill.

A divinely purposed nation, on a world-redeeming mission, breaking out of time into a millennial realm of endless becoming—this was a sacramental vision as old as any talk about the American Republic. Ronald Reagan carried it into a late twentieth century supposedly dominated by more modern, skeptical, and secularist notions.

Certainly, Reagan was not unique among politicians, and most of all presidents, in invoking the idea of a consecrated nation. However, to see only that similarity is to miss the point. Especially after the middle of the twentieth century, any political God-talk was on the defensive. It seemed an embarrassment to the spirit of the times. The new critical attitude of the 1960s readily caricatured the sacramental vision as little more than a series of hypocritical platitudes offered up by self-serving leaders to a gullible public. Leaders themselves seemed to invoke the old themes in an apologetic and pro forma manner. As Robert Bellah put it in 1973, "There was a profound failure of nerve at the top, an uncertainty as to the meaning and value of our institutions."[18] For all its positive accomplishments, the sixties mentality—shorthand for an array of confrontational views now sensitized by the oppressions of the past—went a long way in undermining respect for inherited values and beliefs. America's special mission in the world was unmasked as exploitation and oppression. The hand of Providence appeared as pompous nonsense in a world now seen to be ruled by the calculated exercise of power. At best, celebration of the American story in history was nostalgic naïveté. At worst, it was a ruse for co-opting people into the system's real exploitative agenda. Henceforth, all claims of traditional authority were suspect. Writing in the mid-1970s, Sidney Ahlstrom concluded the last revision to his magisterial *Religious History of the American People*. After eleven hundred pages, he found that the nation had reached a turning point that quite probably ended four hundred years of American history. The religious-mythic quality of the nation's saga had evaporated. Americans of all political persuasions now found it difficult to believe that the United States was still a beacon and blessing to other nations, and even less were they prepared to understand themselves as a chosen people. "In summary," Ahlstrom said, "one may safely say that America's moral and religious tradition was tested and found wanting in the sixties."[19]

For Reagan, with or without the sixties, there was no change. During his more than four decades of public life, Reagan continued to insist on the essential ideas that he had articulated in 1952. Once his political career was under way, Reagan's intellectually superior critics showed more than their usual ingenuity in missing the point. The important point is not that Reagan ever said anything fundamentally new, but that in the new context created by the sixties, Reagan continued to uphold something old. His effort helped pass on the sacramental vision as a living faith in the public mind rather than a dead tradition of antiquarian curiosity or ridicule. More than any other politician of the last half of the twentieth century, Reagan continued to speak the vision boldly and with deep personal conviction. For all their growing distrust of politicians, and not knowing it would be something they could draw upon in more difficult times of terrorism, many Americans seemed to sense that this was important work for Reagan to have done. His believing helped others remember what it was like to believe. Finally in 1994, as the former president publicly announced his personal descent into a mental abyss, his vision remained fixed on the eternal American sunrise: "I now begin this journey that will lead me into the sunset of my life. I know that for America there will always be a bright dawn ahead."[20] Reagan's commitment to the sacramental idea of America went beyond the intellect to a deeper part of personhood. This may go far to explain why Ronald Reagan always remained strangely distant from even his close acquaintances. He was mysterious in the way that a lover always remains private and analytically unreachable to outsiders looking in on the love bond.[21]

INNOCENCE AND STRENGTH

In 1927, sixteen-year-old Ronald Reagan wrote a story anticipating a form of terrorist attack against which twenty-first-century Americans would later learn to prepare. In this story, two lunatics planned to inject poison gas into a Washington, D.C., ventilation system. With hundreds of innocent citizens left dead and dying, the evildoers would be free to carry out their earthshaking plot: the sacking of the United States Treasury Building. A bankrupt America would be brought to its knees. In the end, two all-American boys from Yale saved the day.

Probably we should not make too much of anyone's high school compositions, but in Reagan's case, thematic continuity counts for much. The shining city always implied the counterpart presupposition of a surrounding world of darkness. Otherwise, there was nothing in which to shine. By its nature, the sacramental vision asserted a division between the consecrated and the nonconsecrated. More than that, the very fact of its exceptional mission meant that America was continually endangered. Its calling beyond time confronted a world of fully historical principalities and powers. Hence, the larger story Reagan taught about America always counterpoised the purity of the national calling with the threat of the surrounding darkness against which that calling must struggle.

By the mid–twentieth century, when Reagan was getting his political start, it had become academically popular to dismiss such views as an antimodern "paranoid style" in American politics advanced by the socially and economically dispossessed.[22] We now know that while this interpretation may have captured part of the picture, it was far too narrowly drawn. In declaiming the threat to the sacramental vision, Reagan was once again summoning up ideas at least as old as the Republic itself. As Gordon Wood has shown us, the ideas surrounding America's founding were suffused with Whig theories of corrupting conspiracies against freedom.[23] The cultural tide of evangelical Protestantism in the nineteenth century only expanded this theme. When Lincoln, who was neither evangelical nor paranoid, described his theory of a morally corrupt southern conspiracy during the 1858 debates with Stephen Douglas, ordinary Americans readily understood what he meant, and it propelled him to the leadership of the new Republican Party.

Reagan flirted with some of the language of internal conspiracy. His experiences with communist infiltration of motion picture unions and guilds in the 1940s left a lasting impression, not least of all because during this time, Reagan himself had been an innocent duped into fronting for communist groups.[24] When he subsequently became active in party politics during the late 1950s and early 1960s, Reagan occasionally raised muted suspicions. For example, in addressing conservative groups in 1959 about the dangers of expanding government in Washington, he observed that "in many cases the people in government were well-meaning, but aren't we justified in suspecting that there are those who have fostered the growth of government by deliberate intent and design?"[25] Still, the paranoid style was not really Reagan's style. What is most noteworthy, given the temptations of those times and Reagan's political inexperience, is how *little* Reagan focused on domestic conspiracy theories, in contrast to most of his contemporaries active in right-wing politics. By temperament as well as by conviction, Reagan seemed to find it difficult to ever think or speak ill of other Americans. It was in the larger outside world that America's mission was truly threatened by evil.

Reagan's focus on the external threat of hostile forces was not a matter of aberrational thinking. It was an inherent component of the vision, whereby the nation's "chosenness" stood over against outside powers of darkness. Of course, America could make mistakes, but they were the mistakes of innocence—trusting others too much, doubting itself, forgetting its calling, following false prophets. In Reagan's philosophy of history, American motives were essentially good because its mission in the world was essentially good. It produced (as he put it in 1952, at the height of McCarthyism) a distinctly "American personality" of open generosity and "the rich warm humor that comes from confidence in the belief in all that is good."[26] As Reagan's political career went on to blossom, secular academics and European sophisticates were galled, when not stupefied, by this self-righteous conviction about the purity of American motives.

It was the providential mission that made America innocent, but its goodheartedness also made it vulnerable. Thus, America had to be a wise innocent who knows to protect its mission with strength. For Reagan, there was nothing mysterious about evil. It despised the freedom that God intended for man. Again at the outset of his public life in 1952, he put it this way:

The great ideological struggle that we find ourselves engaged in today is not a new struggle. It's the same old battle. We met it under the name of Hitlerism; we met it under the name of Kaiserism; and we have met it back through the ages in the name of every conqueror that has ever set upon a course of establishing his rule over mankind. It is simply the idea, the basis of this country and of our religion, the idea of the dignity of man, the idea that deep within the heart of each one of us is something so God-like and precious that no individual or group has a right to impose his or its will upon the people."[27]

For Reagan this view of history meant a political career focused on the threat posed by communist powers. Clearly there is no reason anyone should have been surprised by President Reagan's "evil empire" speech on March 8, 1983. The Soviet press responded by accusing Reagan of harboring "a pathological hatred of socialism and communism." They were right about the hatred. Reagan saw communist states as simply the latest enemy on the offensive against the American idea of freedom, an enemy that needed to be defeated rather than accommodated. This is what he believed, and this is what he repeated for four decades. Critics found it a form of dangerous, all-or-nothing thinking, and in a sense they were right, too. However, Reagan's was not an unreflective or logically incoherent view, and it contained the possibility of major breakthroughs as well as major breakdowns between the United States and Russia.

Without going into detail, the major points are clear. For Reagan, the strength that American innocence required did not mean parity. This is because communist states were an inherently aggressive, expansionist force seeking to defeat freedom. The way of provoking such an enemy was through weakness, not strength. Peace had followed from U.S. military superiority, as after World War II, and it would do so again. Whether or not it was called superiority (and Reagan varied in using the term before different audiences),[28] his aim was invulnerability. This meant invulnerability not only to attack but also to any ultimatum that could force America to choose between surrender and destruction. The danger of being forced into such a choice was in fact one of Reagan's most recurrent themes.

Contrary to what some of his critics claimed, Reagan was quite open to negotiating mutual withdrawal from dangerous zones of confrontation between the two superpowers (as had occurred territorially in Austria in the mid-1950s and hopefully would occur with nuclear weapons in the future). The point is, he did not think enemies of freedom would agree to such breakthroughs in the absence of predominant American power. Because Reagan believed America had a real mission threatened by real enemies, foreign policy experts found him lacking in nuance. For Reagan, any middle ground of détente would only leave divisions in place between the United States and Russia in the vain hope that an implacable enemy would mellow and relax its hostility. Even worse, accommodation meant that the United States would lose its military edge at the same time the other side gained in strength from the strains we were taking off them. Rather than becoming less aggressive, the enemy would be encouraged to believe in their ability to catch up to and pass America. Then, realizing America would not allow itself to be conquered peacefully, the communist enemy would seek military superiority to impose the dreaded ultimatum of surrender or perish.

Crude as it sounds to some, Ronald Reagan believed America's mission in the cold war was victory, not mere survival. Essentially, Reagan thought the United States could live in peace with the Soviet Union, but only after the other side had given up. As Reagan put it in January 1977 to the man who would become the new president's national security adviser four years later, "Dick, my idea of American policy toward the Soviet Union is simple. It is this: 'we win and they lose.'" Thus commentators should not have been surprised that the new president predicted the demise of communism in one of his first major addresses after recovering from the 1981 assassination attempt.[29] He was simply summarizing the view he had explained in greater detail over twenty years earlier. Convinced that God had put America on the right side of history, Reagan calculated that the Russian foe was more likely to recognize the superiority of the American way of life if, far from accommodating them, we "let their economy come unhinged so that the contrast is apparent." Reagan's alternative way, as spelled out in 1963, was competition and victory "based on the belief (supported so far by all evidence) that in an all out race our system is stronger, and eventually the enemy gives up the race as a hopeless cause. Then a noble nation believing in peace extends the hand of friendship and says there is room in the world for both of us."[30] As these things go in world politics, it is not a bad description of what actually would occur a generation later.

THE NATION VERSUS THE GOVERNMENT

Reagan's advocacy of a predominant national defense was sharply compartmentalized from his no less vigorous distrust of Washington. One is left to ponder how such an ardent, indeed romantic, nationalist could at the same time be so disparaging of the national government.

One obvious answer is that Reagan believed that the central government had usurped the proper power of state governments on policy matters outside the sphere of national defense. The relentless flow of power to Washington was a favorite theme and the source of an unending supply of stories about excessive taxation, wasteful spending, overregulation, and bureaucratic blunders. In 1959, for example, Reagan recalled the time when citizens' main contact with the federal government was to buy a stamp at the post office. "Today," he said (before the Great Society of the sixties!), "there is hardly a phase of our daily living that doesn't feel the stultifying hand of government regulation and interference. We are faced with a collection of internal powers and bureaucratic institutions against which the individual citizen is absolutely powerless." In the 1970s and 1980s, the same concern led Reagan both as presidential candidate and as president to propose, without success, "a systematic transfer of federal authority and resources to the states" in areas of welfare, education, health care, housing, and economic development.[31]

Nevertheless, the heart of the matter for Reagan was not really federalism. It was government itself. To be sure, Reagan could never have been taken seriously as a contemporary American politician, much less a governor and president, if he had not believed in and used government. Moreover, government needed to be strong, not weak, in protecting freedom against the surrounding threats of disorder (hence, halfhearted government responses to urban riots, campus disruptions, and communist aggression in Vietnam were easy targets for Reagan's criticism in the 1960s). It was at a different, political-psychological level that Reagan could attack government as a constraining presence in people's lives and find a resonating public. Doing so tapped a current in the American mind that had never bent to the European idea of the state. In essence, Reagan portrayed the government as threatening the nation. This in turn went back to the original sacramental vision. Government threatens the nation because the nation is God's story of freedom meant for all persons. The hero of the story is the individual, a subcreator designed for freedom, a "maker" created in His image as Maker. The nation is all of these free individuals in free association, not isolation, and it is in this realm that true creativity and innovation arise. From here it was but a short step, and a step relished by Reagan's business supporters, to seeing the free market set against government collectivism as the true expression of the American way of life.

In the sense just discussed, the government could never truly represent the nation. As he put it in his first inaugural speech as governor, government should lead and listen but not lecture and rule. Now the idea of a government that does not rule might seem an odd thing. One could view as equally nonsensical Reagan's contention, this time in his presidential farewell address, that government should not tell the people what to do.[32] Such statements only make sense in the context of the larger and time-honored claims about the general relation between people and government. Moderns might object, but Reagan was simply being true to the Lockean tradition of American liberalism. The people were not in a contract with the government. Legitimate government was a created instrument of the people, lacking any independent existence even to be the contracting party with the people before they summoned it into being. It was the people who told the government what it was allowed to do, not the other way around. In notes jotted down to address a 1967 governors' conference, Reagan summarized his unchanging view: "We are faced with a choice; either we go back to this collective 'we' as the supreme power, with the 'state' it's [*sic*] agent—supremely powerful and unlimited in authority; Or we continue on the high road accepting man as a unique individual . . . a creature of the spirit with abilities and capacities . . . God given master of, not servant of, his own creation, the state."[33] In essence, Reagan as California's governor was carrying forward into the high tide of 1960s radicalism the grounding conservative argument that had come to life in the firestorm unleashed by the Whittaker Chambers/Alger Hiss controversy of the late 1940s.[34]

Hence, just as communist power represented the external threat, modern government expansion represented the internal threat to America's consecrated mission of freedom. Even when he held elective office, Reagan considered government to be as much a "them" as the communist foes were when he sat together with them in international negotiations. In a highly successful nationwide campaign speech in 1976, Reagan described his feelings about being governor of California: "I never in my life thought of seeking or holding public office and I'm still not quite sure how it all happened. In my own mind, I was a citizen representing my fellow citizens against the institution of government."[35]

REDISCOVERY AND LEADERSHIP

Given his worldview, the growth of government presented something of an explanatory problem for Ronald Reagan. As we have seen, he came of political age in a time when there was much talk in conservative circles about a leftist conspiracy behind the growth of government. But as we have also seen, while Reagan might toy with domestic conspiracy theories, he never seriously pursued them.

An alternative explanation would be that Washington was giving people what they wanted. If that were the case, Reagan's fellow citizens had lost their innocence and willingly traded their birthright of freedom for a mess of potage from Washington. Reagan then faced the problem of leading a debauched people, even if he dared not tell them so. What, then, was the explanation for such a dire threat to the sacramental vision? Answering that question gave form to Reagan's central idea of political leadership.

Reading through the maturing politician's public utterances over the years, one sees the nub of an explanation beginning to form, then grow, take rounded shape, and finally become the basis for the retiring president's farewell warning to the nation. Thus in 1959, General Electric's television spokesman questioned whether current government programs have really resulted from the demands of the people. "Isn't it true that government itself has dangled many programs before us with no mention of the ultimate costs or the loss in personal freedom?" Moreover, asked Reagan, are not government growth and its attendant "socialism through taxation" exactly what socialists like Rauschenbush, Norman Thomas, and Karl Marx have been planning for?[36]

By 1962, in a paid political broadcast endorsing Nixon for California's governorship, Reagan had dropped the questions about the puzzle. Conspiracy was muted (though present by indirection), and now the explanation moved toward inattention and drift:

> Now I don't believe in equating this Socialist desire and the Communist desire, that this equating should continue on to those many people who support the liberal welfare philosophy. I think one thing should be made plain. The overwhelming majority of our opponents do not knowingly and would not knowingly support a Socialist or Communist cause. I am convinced they are patriotic, they are sincerely dedicated to humanitarian ideals. I think it would be foolish and immoral to infer anything else. At the same time, I think it would be foolish to let them have their way without opposition. If someone is setting fire to the house, it doesn't make much difference whether he is a deliberate arsonist or just a fool playing with matches. Our friends seek the answer to all the problems of human need through government. Freedom can be lost inadvertently in this way. Government tends to grow; it takes on a weight and momentum in government programs that goes far beyond the original purpose that caused their creation.[37]

With the mid-1970s, Reagan's daily radio broadcasts and biweekly newspaper columns were reaching possibly twenty million Americans each week, and provided ever new opportunities to declaim the excesses of big government caused by inattentiveness and inadvertence. Growth was occurring within an insulated, permanent structure of government that citizens had carelessly allowed to develop and which citizens would have to stop. "Put another way, it's time we recognize the system has never let us down—we've let the system down now and then because we're only human."[38] In the major Oval Office speech launching his economic program in 1981, the president described at some length how "we forgot or just overlooked the fact that government—any government—has a built-in tendency to grow. We all had a hand in looking to government for benefits as if government had some other sources of revenue other than our earnings. Many if not most of the things we thought of or that government offered to us seemed attractive."[39] By the end of his presidency, Reagan could use the same logic to explain his whole political career: "But back in the 1960s, when I began, it seemed to me that we'd begun reversing the order of things—that through more and more rules and regulations and confiscatory taxes, the government was taking more of our money, more of our options, and more of our freedom. I went into politics in part to put up my hand and say, 'Stop.' I was a citizen politician, and it seemed the right thing for a citizen to do."[40]

For Reagan, the great task of political leadership was remembering and recovering. It was the ever-recurring work by which a people could regain a clear view and renewal of health. Although America was consecrated to break history's cycle of growth and decay, actually doing so required leaders and citizens who understood progress as an eternal return to truths that were both fixed and complete in their fullness. It was not, in Milton's fine phrase, a matter of "to be still searching what we know not by what we know, still closing up truth to truth as we find it."[41] Instead, the task of leadership was to inspire return. In this regard Ronald Reagan was not simply a conservative but a Tory in the spirit of Bolingbroke, who held that "all that can be done therefore to prolong the duration of a good government, is to draw it back, on every favorable occasion, to the first good principles on which it was founded."[42] It was in exactly these terms that Reagan understood the accomplishments of his political life. As he expressed it in his farewell address: "I know we always have [stood for freedom], but in the past few years the world again—and in a way, we ourselves—rediscovered it. . . . They called it the Reagan revolution. Well, I'll accept that, but for me it always seemed more like the great rediscovery, a rediscovery of our values and our common sense."[43] It was also within this same perspective that the retiring president framed his farewell warning to the nation. Ironically enough, it was a warning about memory loss.

For many years, Ronald Reagan had been accustomed to pointing out that America was only one generation away from the extinction of freedom. Now, Reagan left the stage warning in effect that it may be less than one generation from the extinction of the story. He welcomed the resurgence of patriotic feelings that had accompanied his eight years in office, but then came a darkening, almost un-Reaganesque tone: "This national feeling is good, but it won't count for much, and it won't last unless it's grounded in thoughtfulness and knowledge." What was needed, and lacking, was an informed patriotism. "Are we doing a good enough job teaching our children what America is and what she represents in the long history of the world?" For Reagan, a changed America was giving a negative answer to that question: "Younger parents aren't sure that an unambivalent appreciation of America is the right thing to teach modern children. And as for those who create the popular culture, well-grounded patriotism is no longer the style. Our spirit is back, but we haven't reinstitutionalized it." The consequence of continuing carelessness in passing on the sacramental vision lay at hand. "If we forget what we did, we won't know who we are. I'm warning of an eradication of the American memory that could result, ultimately, in an erosion of the American spirit. Let's start with some basics: more attention to American history and a greater emphasis on civic ritual." The recovery work of leadership would rest with the citizens, not Reagan. He even warned that it would rest with America's children calling a feckless adult generation to account. "And children, if your parents haven't been teaching you what it means to be an American, let 'em know and nail 'em on it. That would be a very American thing to do."[44]

We have now surveyed at least some of the major claims Ronald Reagan made on America's public philosophy. For too long, it was academically fashionable to dismiss his words as so much empty speech making with an admittedly persuasive style. True, Reagan's words were typically simple and direct, but they were not intellectually empty. His appeal to public thinking had form, logic, and historical substance. Indeed, as I have tried to argue, it had a philosophy of history that understood, in Simone Weil's term, "the need for roots."[45] Although political competition in America rarely descends into intellectual debate, Reagan's words spoke to a momentous contest of ideas that is nonetheless going on behind the scenes.

If that still seems to be claiming too much, we might consider Reagan from the other side of the ideological barricades, so to speak. Liberal opponents of Reagan over the years have harbored few doubts about the intellectual coherence and weightiness of their own case. When the liberal case (understood in its modern twentieth-century sense) is carefully and explicitly articulated, something impressive about Reagan emerges. One finds that his positions previously outlined offer a point-by-point rebuttal to that presumably sophisticated intellectual construct. We can take Charles Frankel and John Dewey as instances of the deliberate presentation of that modern liberal case.[46] Here there is space to frame only a small piece of the point/counterpoint structure of the argument, but the message should be clear enough: To move from one to the other is to cross real boundaries.

Proposition: Ideas we have inherited for interpreting our historical period are discredited. Old models and old ideals do not apply, if they ever did. Fixed patterns of traditional authority must give way to policies aimed at practical problem solving beneficial to human beings.

Reagan: Founding principles are the standard to which we must always return. These principles are eternal and complete, providing the basis on which traditional authority can maintain ordered freedom.

Proposition: Men can be trusted to choose their own values based on the use of reason in light of experience. Human experience itself is the sole ultimate authority. Religious beliefs are private affairs that should be without political significance.

Reagan: Men have been given the values to which they must be held accountable. Human experience is to be judged by its conformity to divine authority. Religious beliefs are the only foundation of legitimate political order.

Proposition: The world can be progressively redeemed by the human power of reform expressed creatively through specific government policies and programs. Such problem solving requires the extension of the activities of both the state and voluntary associations into new fields for the application of secular intelligence using experimentation and objective scientific knowledge.

Reagan: The individual is the only creative source of innovation. Human freedom is God's redemptive plan for the world, and government should never be more than man's servant to protect that freedom. However well-

meaning, government programs become a self-maintaining system of bureaucratic power and group privilege threatening freedom. Government's
social experiments most often produce unintended and counterproductive
consequences.

Proposition: America is the preeminent site for demonstrating modern
man's control over history and human destiny.
Reagan: God has chosen America as the preeminent instrument in history to realize His plan for human freedom in His image.

Proposition: Human suffering and misdeeds in the world are correctable
by discussion, the discovery of mutual interests, compromise, and enlight-
ened reform.
Reagan: Human suffering in the world is produced by the opposition of
evil to freedom and must be confronted with strength and a commitment to
victory.

Proposition: The problems liberalism confronts are political, not moral.
Reagan: Liberalism's political problems are moral problems.

CLARITY'S BLIND SPOTS

With the benefit of hindsight, Reagan now resembles a political force of nature
cutting through the cluttered sophistication of his times. He communicated well
with ordinary people not only because he spoke directly and simply but also
because he spoke from a fully finished perspective that needed only to be illustrated with any number of interesting facts, statistics, and stories. He could always explain to people what was happening to them in particular because he
was convinced he knew what was happening in general.

The price of such a completed vision was an incomplete field of view. With
Reagan, there could be no development in doctrine. By the term "development"
I do not mean an adaptation or compromise in the face of circumstances. As we
have seen, Reagan was quite capable of adjusting his message to different audiences and accommodating particular political realities. Neither is "development"
a matter of simply importing some outside idea to shore up a weakness in one's
case. What Reagan missed was an unfolding of ideas from within his worldview
to enlarge its promise. As G. K. Chesterton put it, "Development is the expansion of all the possibilities and implications of a doctrine, as there is time to
distinguish them and draw them out."[47] Because there could be no development
in doctrine, Reagan was left with gaping blind spots. I will mention four that
seem particularly important.

The first was the positive domestic role of national government, not for
bureaucrats but for Reagan's beloved individual. In his first radio commentary

after losing the 1976 nomination to President Ford, Reagan reflected on what he thought he had learned. He said that after nine months of campaigning, "my belief has been strengthened that if government would someday quietly close the doors; if all the bureaucrats would tiptoe out of the marble halls; it would take the people of this country quite a while to miss them or even know they were gone."[48] Unfortunately for their party, some Republican congressional leaders came to believe this version of Reagan's blind spot and walked off a cliff. Twenty years later, in the winter of 1995–1996, a beleaguered Democratic president was desperate enough to call their bluff with a government shutdown. The result was an easy reelection of Bill Clinton, an unfamiliar name of Lewinsky in the news, and the rest is history.

There is a saying that while Egypt built the pyramids, the pyramids also built Egypt. Reagan was right in his view that the American people built the government, but he could not see that they were continuing to build the govern-ment and in doing so were building what it meant for them to be a people. His explanation of government growth based on inadvertence, carelessness, and bureaucratic inertia was a partial truth masquerading as the whole. Government also grew to do things that people, in all their variegated ways, really wanted done. This positive, constructive role of constitutional government was pro-foundly and incurably lost on Reagan.

This first blind spot led into a second. Focusing on governmental threats to freedom, Reagan tended to be oblivious to equivalent threats posed by private power. This meant he consistently undervalued the importance of government regulation for the creation and maintenance of orderly markets. It meant neglect of collective standards for health, safety, environmental protection, and other social goals that could not be captured by valuations in the marketplace. In terms of the sacramental vision, it meant failing to appreciate the power of markets to devour individuals' freedom and the traditional values of their communities. Not least of all, it meant Reagan could be used to provide protective coloration for some selfish business interests that could have cared less about the shining city. Much the same can be said in the realm of foreign affairs, where Reagan's clear-eyed view of communism—as he put it, his willingness to see what he saw—blocked the view of a great deal of other evil.

Being an intelligent man, Reagan was aware of these things in a general sense and said so in a few of his speeches. However, they regularly fell outside the field of view for communicating his vision and the development of doctrine. All of this left Reagan vulnerable to history, when different times and circumstances might not have the goodness of fit with his fixed vision that was true in the 1980s. How-ever, that is simply to say that he was human and thus limited. Reagan had a win-ning way because his own foibles were also something he never doubted.

In the third place, Reagan remained impervious to the idea that American culture might be changing in fundamental ways. Earlier I tried to outline how Reagan's public philosophy represented a root and branch attack on secular liberalism, but the idea of such an attack is mine, not his. Reagan's enduring assumption was that when called back to the sacramental vision, Americans would respond out of a deeper culture that remained fundamentally fixed and intact. In that sense, the essential problem was a forgetting, and the essential task was a call to remembrance. Thus while Reagan fought against campus unrest and condemned leftist intellectual influences, he was never enthusiastic about ideas of a culture war, much to the frustration of some of his supporters. In a way, Reagan was oblivious to the sixties.[49] To embrace cultural conservatism seemed too much like being disillusioned and bitter about present-day America, too much like thinking ill of something he loved. If the sixties opened up a deep cleavage over American values, Reagan was not interested in noticing, unlike Richard Nixon, Pat Buchanan, Newt Gingrich, or even George Bush senior. From his earliest California political career onward, Reagan's faith in America's cultural soundness served him well by protecting him from identification with right-wing cranks, fringe groups, and political haters preoccupied with domestic enemies. But this faith was not a political pose or strategy. It was part of who Ronald Reagan always was.

Finally, I think it is fair to say that Reagan was unable to recognize that his faith and redemptive vision of America sailed dangerously close to idolatry, if not quite landing there. Missing from Reagan's view of the shining city was Winthrop's understanding that the brightness meant simply exposure. It could be for good or ill in the eyes of both God and the world. And if faithless, it would have been better to stay unchosen in history's shadows. That was good Puritan doctrine and more generally good Judeo-Christian doctrine. However, it was not Reagan's doctrine. There one finds an unqualified assertion of American goodness with only the barest sense of judgment looming in the background. For Reagan, the oversoul of the nation, intrinsically innocent, is assigned an ultimacy that seems indistinguishable from worship.

This became especially clear in the presidency's ceremonial services of national mourning. On numerous such occasions, Ronald Reagan prayed lost Americans into a civil religion heaven almost indistinguishable from that of Pericles' decidedly pagan funeral oration for Athens' fallen heroes. For example, with the death of 241 marines in the 1983 Beirut bomb attack, Reagan said, "I will not ask you to pray for the dead, because they're safe in God's loving arms and beyond need of our prayers. . . . They're now part of the soul of this great country and will live as long as our liberty shines as a beacon of hope to all those who long for freedom and a better world."[50] Likewise, American paratroopers killed in 1985, the *Challenger* astronauts in 1986, and the three dozen victims of a 1987 missile attack on the USS *Stark* were consigned to the arms of God as people who "made themselves immortal by dying for something immortal." Death in service of the nation was death in the service of the nation's God. Ipso facto, it was sufficient grounds for entering into the eternal heavenly presence of God.

A public philosophy, a philosophy of history, and a civil religion are not the same thing, but they can be closely related. For Ronald Reagan they were beginning to merge in the 1980s. Looked at in terms of civil religion, Reagan had begun by performing largely a prophetic role. He claimed to be the citizen politician prophesying against the solipsism and relativism of the sixties, against forgetfulness of first principles, against carelessness in drifting into internal and external dangers to those principles. In the 1980s he took on a more priestly role for the religion of the Republic. But in the end, and above all, he wanted Americans to remember who they are and what they represent for the future.

CONCLUSION

The Italian historian Benedetto Croce famously observed that all history is contemporary history. Certainly Ronald Reagan looks different after September 11, 2001, and the onset of America's war against "evildoers" than he did in the 1990s, when pundits made sport of "the vision thing." Since it is the only light at hand, we cannot escape seeing our subject in the light of the present, and tomorrow's interpreters of Reagan will have a different present.

Still, unlike most other twentieth-century American politicians, there will be a fixedness to Reagan that is somewhat immune to contemporary circumstances. This is because so much of his public presence subsisted in a story, the master narrative he had to tell about America into which all his other stories fit. The power of the story helped insulate him politically in his time and will probably do the same in the future. For it was, and will be, not simply the man but the power of the story that any critic has to overcome. This always threw his opponents on the defensive and drove them a little crazy. The story could only be overcome with another story, and thus they were always playing on Reagan's chosen ground. Democrats found that stories of class conflict, victimization, and the like could never quite measure up. Reagan's opponents in Moscow faced a similar problem. As the librarian of Congress, James Billington, put it, "The victory of American over Soviet values in the Cold War was essentially the triumph of a story over a theory."[51]

The point goes deeper. Looking at the elements of Reagan's story, we have found some very powerful features: the sacramental vision of a reality beyond or, perhaps better, within the obvious visible realm; innocence and its mission against evil; the struggle of a nation of individuals to escape from governmental attacks on their freedom; recovery and the regaining of clear vision for health; perhaps even the consolation that while humans may fall, God will assure that His plan comes right in the end. What is this we are hearing? Why does it seem to draw us? The match is not perfect but close enough to be worth noticing. Reagan's story resonates very strongly with the essential features—fantasy, recovery, escape, and consolation—that J. R. R. Tolkien identified in the "fairy-story."[52]

Have we therefore come this far with such an essay in order to spring a trap for ridiculing Reagan? Not at all. Of course, some will contend that Reagan did nothing more than project onto a complex reality a make-believe world of his own simple thinking. But what if it is the other way around? In that case, the power and joy of the fairy story would come from catching a sudden glimpse of the underlying reality and truth of things. Certainly that is the way Tolkien saw good fairy stories. The answer to "Is it true?" would then go far deeper than saying it was true for Reagan because he built a good story in his own little world. It would be true because Ronald Reagan caught a far-off gleam of authentic good news in the real world—a spark, if you will, from the shining city.

NOTES

1. Samuel H. Beer, "Encounters with Modernity" (unpublished manuscript, reproduced, Washington, D.C., 2002), 18. Professor Beer offered an insightful early account of Reagan's public philosophy in "Ronald Reagan: New Deal Conservative?" *Society* (January–February 1983): 40–44.

2. Alasdair MacIntyre, *After Virtue,* 2d ed. (Notre Dame: University of Notre Dame Press, 1984), 222.

3. Immanuel Kant, "What Is Enlightenment?" in *Internet Modern History Sourcebook,* <http://www.fordham.edu/halsall/mod/kant-whatis.html> (February 1, 2002).

4. W. H. Walsh, *An Introduction to the Philosophy of History* (London: Hutchinson, 1951), chap. 1, 9–28.

5. Charles Frankel, *The Case for Modern Liberalism* (New Brunswick, N.J.: Transaction Publishers, 2002), 7.

6. David A. Stockman, *The Triumph of Politics* (New York: Harper & Row, 1986), 49. The characterization of "amiable dunce" appears as a chapter title in Mark Hertsgaard's *On Bended Knee* (New York: Farrar, Straus & Giroux, 1988), one of many early and negative commentaries on Reagan's intellectual substance. See, for example, Haynes Johnson, *Sleepwalking through History: America in the Reagan Years* (New York: W. W. Norton, 1991). Assessments by leading academics have taken Reagan's conservative agenda more seriously, but have shown not so much a liberal as a secular bias in overlooking the religious grounding of Reagan's political ideas. See Paul Kengor, "Reagan among the Professors," *Policy Review* 98 (December 1999–January 2000): 15–27.

7. Writing from the White House in 1984, President Reagan acknowledged the "role model" he had found as a boy and ever since sought to follow in *That Printer of Udell's* (Harold Bell Wright, *That Printer of Udell's* [New York: A. L. Burt, 1903]). Letter of March 13, 1984, in the Dixon, Illinois, Public Library, cited in Paul Kengor, *God, Reagan, and the Evil Empire* (forthcoming). Kengor's is the best research to date on the relation between Reagan's religious views and his public career.

8. Davis W. Houck and Amos Kiewe, eds., *Actor, Ideologue, Politician: The Public Speeches of Ronald Reagan* (Westport, Conn.: Greenwood Press, 1993), 6.

9. Ibid., 327.

10. Robert Thompson, *The Hand of God in American History* (New York: Crowell, 1902). A generation earlier, throughout over forty years of revised editions of his monumental work, the nineteenth-century historian George Bancroft began by declaring, "It is the object of the present work to explain how the change in the condition of our land has been brought about; and, as the fortunes of a nation are not under the control of blind

destiny, to follow the steps by which a favoring Providence, calling our institutions into being, has conducted the country to its present happiness and glory." George Bancroft, *History of the United States,* vol. 1 (1834; reprint, Boston: Little, Brown, 1879), 3.

11. Governor John Winthrop, "A Model of Christian Charity," 1630. Reagan quotes this line verbatim, for example, in his August 7, 1978, radio address describing the ideological struggle between communism and America. Kiron K. Skinner, Annelise Anderson, and Martin Anderson, eds., *Reagan, In His Own Hand* (New York: Free Press, 2001), 14.

12. Radio address of June 1975, in ibid., 16.

13. Radio address of January 14, 1989, in Houck and Kiewe, *Actor, Ideologue, Politician,* 328.

14. "Business, Ballots and Bureaus," speech of May 1959, in ibid., 27.

15. Jonathan Edwards, "Thoughts on the Revival in New England" in *The Works of President Edwards,* vol. 3 (New York: Carter & Brothers, 1879), 313; Thomas Paine, *Writings,* vol. 1 (New York: Vincent Park, 1908), 118–19; Hegel, *Lectures in the Philosophy of History,* trans. J. Sibree (London: Henry Bohn, 1861), 90.

16. Speech to Veterans of Foreign Wars, August 18, 1980, in Skinner, Anderson, and Anderson, *In His Own Hand,* 486.

17. Speech to the Republican National Convention, August 17, 1992, in Houck and Kiewe, *Actor, Ideologue, Politician,* 334.

18. Robert Bellah, "American Civil Religion in the 1970s," in *American Civil Religion,* ed. Russell E. Richey and Donald G. Jones (New York: Harper & Row, 1974), 264.

19. Sidney E. Ahlstrom, *A Religious History of the American People* (New Haven, Conn.: Yale University Press, 1972), 1085. On this theme, see also 2, 1078, 1094.

20. Skinner, Anderson, and Anderson, *In His Own Hand,* 499.

21. Thus in 1988, Nicholas Lemann puzzled over the fact that, unlike other presidents, Reagan's tenure generated a spate of insider books from former White House aides that were calculated to be embarrassing and even outright antagonistic toward the president. As he rightly concludes, the lesser part of the explanation was because Reagan was not mean enough to fear or engaged enough to inspire respect from coworkers. Above all, the poisonous memoirs arose from aides learning that they were not really important to him. In terms of Reagan's vision, this was exactly right. Nicholas Lemann, "The Best Years of Their Lives," *New York Review of Books,* July 30, 1988, 5–6.

22. In addition to Richard Hofstadter's book by that title, see more generally Daniel Bell, ed., *The Radical Right* (New York: Doubleday, 1963).

23. Gordon Wood, *The Creation of the American Republic, 1776–1787* (Chapel Hill: University of North Carolina Press, 1969).

24. Ronald Reagan, with Richard G. Hubler, *Where's the Rest of Me?* (New York: Duell, Sloan & Pearce, 1965).

25. Houck and Kiewe, *Actor, Ideologue, Politician,* 20. For a later example of deploying the conspiracy theory, again emphasizing Russian-inspired duping of liberals, see Reagan's radio address, "The Suicide Lobby," March 13, 1978, in Skinner, Anderson, and Anderson, *In His Own Hand,* 139.

26. Houck and Kiewe, *Actor, Ideologue, Politician,* 7.

27. Ibid., 5.

28. For example, it was explicitly superiority in speeches of the late 1970s but not in talking points with Soviet foreign minister Gromyko in 1984. See Skinner, Anderson, and Anderson, *In His Own Hand,* 113, 496.

29. The conversation with Richard Allen is cited in Kengor, *God, Reagan, and the Evil Empire,* pt. 3, 26. In his May 17, 1981, commencement speech at Notre Dame, the president said, "The West won't contain communism, it will transcend communism. . . . It will dismiss it as some bizarre chapter in human history whose last pages are even now being written."

30. Skinner, Anderson, and Anderson, *In His Own Hand,* 442.

31. See speeches from 1959, 1975, and 1976 in Houck and Kiewe, *Actor, Ideologue, Politician,* 20, 144, 153.

32. The speeches emphasizing each of the two cited points from 1967 and 1989 are in Houck and Kiewe, *Actor, Ideologue, Politician,* 41, 324.

33. Skinner, Anderson, and Anderson, *In His Own Hand,* 443.

34. Both Reagan (who could quote passages from Whittaker Chambers's book *Witness* from memory) and the deep hostility of his liberal critics are incomprehensible outside the context of this moral and intellectual controversy. A valuable recent collection of readings from the time is in Patrick A. Swan, ed., *Alger Hiss, Whittaker Chambers, and the Schism in the American Soul* (Wilmington, Del.: Intercollegiate Studies Institute, 2003).

35. Houck and Kiewe, *Actor, Ideologue, Politician,* 152.

36. Ibid., 20.

37. Ibid., 28.

38. Skinner, Anderson, and Anderson, *In His Own Hand,* radio broadcast of December 22, 1976, 12. For other examples, see broadcasts of May 12, 1975, September 21, 1976, 294, 295.

39. Ibid., 488.

40. Speech of January 11, 1989, in Houck and Kiewe, *Actor, Ideologue, Politician,* 324.

41. John Milton, "Areopagitica" in *Great Books of the Western World,* vol. 32, ed. Robert M. Hutchins (Chicago: Encyclopedia Britannica, 1952), 405.

42. Henry Saint-John Bolingbroke, *Letters on the Spirit of Patriotism: On the Idea of a Patriot King.* Quoted in Stow Parsons, "The Cyclical Theory of History in Eighteenth Century America," *American Quarterly* 6 (summer 1954): 147.

43. "Farewell Address to the Nation," January 11, 1989, in Houck and Kiewe, *Actor, Ideologue, Politician,* 322–23.

44. Ibid., 326.

45. Simone Weil, *The Need for Roots: Prelude to a Declaration of Duties toward Mankind* (New York: G. P. Putnam's Sons, 1952).

46. Without citing chapter and verse, I take the subsequent propositions from Charles Frankel, *The Case for Modern Liberalism* (New Brunswick, N.J.: Transaction Publishers, 2002), originally published in 1955 as *The Case for Modern Man;* and one of Dewey's more accessible and concise statements, in Henry Goddard Leach, ed., *Living Philosophies: A Series of Intimate Credos* (New York: Simon & Schuster, 1931), 21–35.

47. G. K. Chesterton, *Saint Thomas Aquinas* (New York: Sheed & Ward, 1954), 13.

48. Skinner, Anderson, and Anderson, *In His Own Hand,* 236.

49. See Lou Cannon, *Governor Reagan: His Rise to Power* (working title; forthcoming).

50. This and the following quotations are taken from Richard V. Pierard and Robert D. Linder, *Civil Religion and the Presidency* (Grand Rapids: Academie Books, 1988), 282, 257.

51. James H. Billington, "The Impact of the Reagan Presidency on the End of the Cold War," *The Reagan Forum,* January 7, 1999, 7.

52. J. R. R. Tolkien, *Tree and Leaf* (Boston: Houghton Mifflin, 1965), 46 ff.

2

Reagan and the Transformation of American Conservatism

Ted V. McAllister

During the 1980 presidential season political pundits and scholars well understood Ronald Reagan. He was perhaps the most transparent politician of the modern era—a man of simple ideas possessing an uncomplicated personality. Yet, in the little over twenty years since, the actor-president has become enigmatic, a puzzle that drives scholars to distraction and even to very odd biographies.[1] Even Reagan's closest associates remain flummoxed.

But what is the cause of this confusion? The efforts of Reaganites to rehabilitate their leader—to challenge the dominant stereotypes of the president as a simpleton, as lazy, as a knee-jerk cold warrior—might lead them to exaggerate the complexity of Reagan. More important, scholars, or at least liberal scholars, have a difficult time understanding people and movements on the right. Here their challenges with Reagan fit a long-established pattern whereby liberal scholars explain or explain away right-wing movements as episodes of social pathology. Yet in recent years, scholars have taken these movements on the right more seriously.

Thankfully, this new openness to the complexity of conservatism has led to a fairly rich literature on the rise of the right since the 1950s, as well as an amazingly fair reassessment of the Reagan administration. Still, there is an interesting divide between conservative historians who tend to tell the story with an awkward tendentiousness and nonconservative historians who treat the subjects of the story as aliens and repair to their more comfortable categories of analysis—race and class—to explain them.[2]

So, I still find much confusion not only about Ronald Reagan but also about the larger movement that he came to symbolize. The problem is complicated further by the semantic quicksand that swallows all meaningful distinctions in American politics. The labels of American political life conceal more than they reveal, and the tendency is to organize ideas, programs, and policies around a simplistic "conservative–liberal" dichotomy.[3] But despite these procrustean labels, important and often subtle differences operate in both the world of ideas and the world of politics. The confusions about Reagan and the "conservative" movement are in no small part a function of the limitations of our political vocabulary. I seek here to tell a story of the rise of the American right with an eye to differentiating ideas and groups. Then I will attempt to place Reagan within this context before I offer some thoughts about the impact of his presidency on the movement. I must be brief and therefore very selective and often elliptical.

INTELLECTUAL ORIGINS

Conservative minds awaken when things they love appear threatened. Thus, a proper conservative philosophy emerges only in reaction, and the analysis that brings this philosophy to self-consciousness develops from a critique of offending change. One of the results of this disposition is that conservative movements emerge on an ad hoc basis, making more difficult any assessment of their relative strength. While it is clear that a particular version of conservatism emerged after 1945, it is also clear that the "founders" of this movement understood themselves to be heirs to a long and diverse body of sentiments, ideas, habits, and customs that have both European and American antecedents.

So, like all histories, we begin in the middle with men and women whose affections were well established and who found themselves, often reluctantly, reacting to many of the currents of their contemporary world. To understand this reaction we should recall the earth-shattering changes that have rocked the United States since the early 1930s. The depression made possible and popular the various innovations of the New Deal. For the first time Americans embraced, in some limited fashion, a welfare state. But perhaps more important were the changes brought about by the great patriotic war, during which the federal government aggrandized power to itself beyond anything imaginable by any previous generation. Nothing better symbolizes the moral problems associated with this expansion of federal power than the Manhattan Project, in which thousands of citizens labored on a massive secret project. Shockingly, these workers knew nothing of the purpose of their labor—they had ceded the moral responsibility of their work to the government. Of course, the Manhattan Project developed atomic weapons, the justification for which emerged out of the logic of total war. The United States, locked in mortal combat, had embraced the idea that the cause of victory justified the suspension of all moral restraints traditionally imposed on combatants. So, for conservatives like Richard Weaver, reflecting on the impact of the war, there was something symbolically important about the massive new power that the federal government used in such events as the bombing of Dresden and Tokyo, to say nothing of Hiroshima and Nagasaki. In reaction to these trends, these moral outrages, a small group of "conservative" thinkers began to articulate their vision of reality, drawing heavily on the resources that had already cultivated their affections and stocked their imaginations.[4] These resources were biblical, selective thinkers from ancient Athens and Rome, the great medieval churchmen, European Romantics of the early modern era, select founders of the American Republic, Tocqueville, the New Humanists, and the Southern Agrarians. In reaction to their times, drawing from this rich and diverse patrimony, conservative thinkers began to articulate a set of principles that together constituted a vision of reality. This vision I will label "conservative."

Conservatives are essentialists. A central distinction marks their thinking— that which exists must not be equated with that which is real. This emphasis upon a transcendent order is most compatible with a religious orientation, but it can extend so far as to embrace nontheistic Platonists like Irving Babbitt and some of the Straussians. Among the consequences of this essentialism is a healthy distrust of human reason. For conservatives, reason is a profoundly important but problematic virtue. On the one hand, it separates humans from all other earthly beings and gives humans a special dignity, but on the other hand, it also threatens to be their undoing, as it was for Eve. It is precisely because conservatives believe that reality extends beyond the world we experience directly that they fear unaided reason. Devotion to reason means accepting a reductionist view of reality, a view that leaves humans without any authoritative norms and thereby elevates humans to creators—authors of their own morality. What humans can know about the deeper reality that we inhabit, conservatives would tell us, is seen dimly and largely through what they call our "imagination." From holy writ to poetry, humans catch glimpses of a form beyond our ever-present shadowland. Employing a chastened reason in tandem with a well-furnished imagination allows us to develop norms that get worked out through generations of human experience and get encoded in traditions. Because we are morally blind without those traditions and without a well-furnished imagination, conservatives warn constantly about the dangers of "abstract" reason and of "ideologues" who seek to solve human problems without any reference to a transcendent order and authority.

Given these fears about the modern world, conservatives expressed concerns about almost any increase in federal power, especially if it came at the expense of local governments or other groups. Their gravest concern was that the complex, overlapping body of mediating institutions, like family, church, union, and local government, would be steadily stripped of their functions, leaving individuals bereft of any protections from the all-powerful state. They feared, moreover, that an excessive faith in democracy would lead to a tyranny of the majority, especially as the people lose their connections to the mediating institutions and turn to a powerful state for support. They feared any effort to impose equality. In short, conservatives affirmed a social order oriented around a faith in a higher authority, shaped by a long tradition of experience, buttressed by an emphasis upon good habits—and they stressed, especially, the delicate balance between order and freedom. These conservatives did not appeal to freedom as the highest good, but rather stressed the importance of local liberties, which implied a corporate understanding of human life. Behind all of this was a belief that as conservatives, they had a strong American tradition worthy of defense. Central to their understanding was a view of the American Revolution as a successful struggle to protect the local liberties of the British colonists and of the Constitution as a salutary document to encode this conservative objective in a new political context. The Revolution was, then, a necessary innovation to protect inherited liberties as well as natural rights.

The conservatives who fit this model are familiar to any scholar of American history—people like Russell Kirk, Richard Weaver, and the many people who wrote for *Modern Age.* Yet other thinkers on the right emerged in the fifties, also in reaction to their times. One of the most influential of these scholars was Friedrich von Hayek, whose book *The Road to Serfdom* (1944) warned of the creeping socialism of the New Deal. Most important about Hayek's argument, from the perspective of this story, are the moral imperatives of defending property rights, and of cultivating a society that allows individuals the freedom to choose with a minimum of government interference. While Hayek asserted the moral superiority of a free market and therefore the moral integrity of the free individual, he nonetheless grounded this freedom in a view of society that resonated with the more organic view suggested by the conservatives. Consider this illuminating quotation: "There probably never has existed a genuine belief in freedom . . . without a genuine reverence for grown institutions, for customs and habits and 'all those securities of liberty which arise from regulation of long prescription and ancient ways.' Paradoxical as it may appear, it is probably true that a successful free society will always in large measure be a tradition-bound society."[5]

Nonetheless, in the 1950s emerged the great fissure that would always threaten to divide any coalition of groups on the right. It matters greatly if one begins with an organic view of human life or an individualistic view. The tendency of the first is to look back to an inherited patrimony that gives direction to the present and a culture to preserve for posterity; the tendency of the second is to look forward to an ever better world made possible by the liberation of the individual. The American right is caught in a dialectical struggle between the primacy of the group and the primacy of the individual, between the call to Return and the lure of Progress.

But while there were divisions inherent in the movement, there were meaningful cords that tethered diverse elements into something approaching a coherent whole. Whittaker Chambers crafted the strongest cord in the 1950s with his stunning book, *Witness,* which not only helped make possible a powerful postwar conservatism but also gave it a particular coloring. It is hard to overstate the importance of *Witness* in shaping a conservative movement. Because Chambers so eloquently characterized the struggle with the Soviet Union as a cosmic war between two mutually exclusive faiths, communism and freedom, he gave justification to a life devoted to the destruction of communism. Nothing less than the fate of the Judeo-Christian civilization, which is to say Western civilization, was at stake in this titanic struggle for power. But the struggle was also a timeless one, emerging out of the Garden of Eden, between a vision of Man alone or of Man in relationship with God.

By so structuring his argument, Chambers called upon people to reject not only communism but also all efforts that would lead to a godless orientation. Moreover, since these two faiths warred in this way, one had to consider all communists (and perhaps all secularists) as implacable enemies who seek to undermine one's very civilization. Those influenced by Chambers would think of the cold war in primarily spiritual terms, which made compromise or accommodation intolerable. But equally important, Chambers's book would shape the language that gave form and direction to their thinking. Freedom became the charmed word of the right—a word without clear semantic location, which they uttered in fealty to a sort of reductive good. The right was filled with freedom fighters. This view of conflict between the forces of freedom and of communism (or secularism) fit well with Hayek's moral claims about the superiority of the free market and the dangers emerging from efforts to control or manage this market. Similarly, a reductive understanding of Chambers's book squared nicely with the small but vocal band of libertarians. Conservatives emphasized the greater complexity of Chambers's argument about freedom—freedom under God. The primary intellectual weapons of a conservative movement were now in the arsenal—the question was how best to employ them and toward what objective.

TOWARD A POLITICAL MOVEMENT

As a political movement, conservatism emerged in the 1950s and early 1960s out of a rather spirited struggle to blend these ideas into a common front and then translate them into political action. The story is a familiar one that need not detain us long here, except to emphasize how this political movement both depended upon the intellectual vitality of conservative thinkers and yet altered their beliefs to fit a political context.[6] In the fifties, political conservatives controlled neither party, though Robert Taft of Ohio led a powerful minority of fiscal conservatives who struggled with the liberal, corporate interests for control of the Republican Party. Under the popular rule of President Eisenhower, the conservatives would have to wait for a more opportune moment. Meanwhile, they prepared.

The battle for control over the Republican Party required the mobilization of a self-conscious conservative movement. By far the most important event in this mobilization was the founding of the *National Review* in 1955. The young and intellectually formidable owner, William F. Buckley, Jr., accomplished the nearly impossible by bringing together an eclectic and contentious group of editors and writers on the right under a single banner. Here was the rich variety of the emerging conservative movement, not only working to find a suitable and sustainable common cause but also working in the interstices of ideas and actions. In this electric environment, free from any party affiliation, enlivened by their position as challengers to a staid liberal orthodoxy, the editors of the *National Review* defined an amazingly coherent and politically viable conservatism. The so-called fusionism, a political philosophy most associated with Frank Meyer, would supply the necessary vital center of this emerging movement, supplying a praxis and establishing the boundaries for the movement.[7]

Meyer's fusionism was a brilliant blend of Progress and Return, of individual and group. Meyer tethered his political philosophy to the American founding, arguing that this philosophy recaptured the great principles worked out in the nation's genesis, in that halcyon historical moment when great men applied the greatest accomplishments of European civilization to the conditions of a new age. The founders had created a regime that inculcated virtue while tolerating great freedom, a regime that best exemplified ordered liberty. America had succeeded precisely as European civilization lost the balance in the great tension of Western civilization, beginning emblematically with the French Revolution. The advantages to this construction of history were manifold. It established a conservatism with roots reaching back to Genesis while still having a profoundly American cast. This story suggested that America saved European civilization even as Europeans were squandering their patrimony.

Equally important, this fusionist view of history contained a warning about an impending American fall if it followed the seductive ways of welfare liberalism. Meyer articulated a fighting faith that stressed the primacy of the individual and of individual choice, but only because this individual is formed in the context of social institutions like family, church, local community—all of which supply the individual with a strong moral foundation and which furnish the person with a strong sense of identity that rests upon the social and moral obligations owed to others. The expanding state threatens this moral economy by taking on the functions of the very mediating institutions that give shape and direction to the individual. For Meyer the freedom allowed in America is good only because it is necessary for genuine virtue, as virtue cannot be coerced. This construction of the individual, the group, and the state satisfied both libertarians and traditionalists, though traditionalists would see dangers in capitalism, and libertarians of the next generation would not be so enamored of virtue or of any governing vision of a transcendent order. But for the 1960s, this worked to create a common front and helped to cast into sharp relief the common enemy. Internally, liberalism, by which they meant the various justifications for expanding the welfare state, was the enemy for the reasons stated earlier. Externally, communism was the great threat, since communism was a godless and totalist faith whose adherents could brook no opposition in their struggle to impose their own messianic system on the world.

With this fairly simple articulation of a conservative philosophy, along with increasingly influential institutions to promulgate these beliefs, conservatives had something approaching a political agenda. They needed a party. During the 1960s, they wrested power from the eastern, liberal wing of the Republican Party with ideas. It was the ideas articulated by Meyers, Buckley, and a host of others that inspired the young idealists of the Young Americans for Freedom. It was fidelity to their strongly held beliefs that moved activists to mobilize a grassroots movement after the so-called Treaty of Fifth Avenue exposed that Richard Nixon was more interested in the politics of compromise than in the verities of the right.[8] It was a belief that ideas rather than interests should guide politics that led the movers and shakers of the conservative movement to target Barry Goldwater for their presidential candidate—a man whose most singular virtue was his candid if simplistic articulation of his basic beliefs.

A CHANGING COALITION

In a story told well in many other places, a new breed of political operatives emerged to generate and mobilize a grassroots movement—a group of believers who saw a future to which the guardians of conventional wisdom were blind. They succeeded in their coup of the Republican Party in 1964, with Barry Goldwater as their rather reluctant standard-bearer and with a party platform that embarrassed the old guard for its "extremism." But the extremism of 1964 would occupy the political center by 1980.[9] What happened in between is too complicated to address in any great detail, except to demonstrate how a new coalition evolved over those two decades and altered the movement.

During the sixties and seventies, new groups reacted to one or another of the developments in American politics and culture and, one by one, joined ranks with the movement that had evolved by 1964. Federal involvement in the civil rights movement, symbolized by the Civil Rights Act of 1964, to say nothing of the forced integration of southern society, brought a number of southern whites, long-standing Democrats all, to consider shifting parties.

By 1968 it appeared that white southerners were moving away from the Democratic Party, and while many were reluctant, the most conservative of them would land eventually with the Republicans. Meanwhile, a more amorphous set of grassroots movements began to stir, especially in the seventies. Reacting to various insults from the federal courts or the federal government, large numbers of what Nixon called the silent majority became politically vocal. They reacted to the federalizing of abortion, to court-imposed busing, to the Equal Rights Amendment (ERA), to pornography, and most important, to high taxes. Republican operatives had developed an aggressive and successful campaign to target people on issues that hit them directly or that violated their moral code. These "social conservatives," as many call them, were often suffering or fearing the recessions that afflicted the nation in the seventies. While they were mobilized in part because of these important issues, they were also feeling increasingly alienated from their society even as they feared that their great nation was nearing its nadir with economic woes on top of foreign policy disasters. The great accomplishment of the Republican Party in the seventies was to turn this strong but elusive feeling of estrangement against big government. These groups formed the populist wing of the Reagan coalition of 1980. They were the least attached to the deeper principles of the movement, but they possessed a strongly felt sense that as Americans, their great destiny was slipping away.

Akin to and overlapping this movement was the rise of the Christian fundamentalists, who operated with a strong if ill-defined sense that America had been formed as a peculiarly Christian nation and that it was part of God's providential plan. The fly in the buttermilk, however, was that everywhere these Christians looked, they saw moral decline. Divorce, abortion, the ERA, feminism, and numerous other changes seemed evidence enough of America having violated its covenant with God. While it is certainly true that their understanding of the founding and thereby the nature of the Republic differed from Meyer's fusionist history, they shared with the fusionists a declension story that involved, to one degree or another, the overweening power of the federal government.

Despite common cause between these elements of the "new right," as pundits have labeled these populists, and the old right as represented by the fusionist compromise, the differences were important and suggestive. The new right was in large part a product of political entrepreneurs who successfully tapped into long-undefined fears and worries with direct mail and by tirelessly constructing several activist organizations. The traditionalists were uncomfortable with the singularly political nature of these movements and their leaders who elevated the political above the social, the aesthetic, and the spiritual. The new right, moreover, was less interested in the free market or communism and more focused on using the federal government to redress the moral failings of the nation. The old right considered that the moral foundations of the nation must be nourished at the local level and usually by nongovernmental means.

More complicated was the evolution and impact of the neoconservatives.[10] The neoconservatives might best be described as liberals who reacted to the excesses of the Great Society and the new left liberalism. They were right-wing liberals. With origins among a small group of Jewish intellectuals and journalists, many with ties to the journal *Commentary,* these thinkers supported the civil rights movement but rejected the more radical calls for black liberation or for affirmative action. They tired of the youthful silliness of 1960s radicalism, and they became persuaded that the expensive and invasive government programs of the Great Society were ineffective at best and socially destructive at worst. In reaction to these currents, the neoconservatives developed a political philosophy as powerful and as simple as the earlier fusionist conservatism. First, they affirmed the great American experiment as the most noble in history. At its heart was the Declaration of Independence, which stressed natural rights and equality. The Constitution they venerated because it was a brilliant example of the science of politics, as exemplified by James Madison, who helped establish a regime that balanced interests as much as it stressed ideals. Neoconservatives emphasize these two elements of the American founding—its idealism and its successful compromises in light of the needs of practical politics. The ideals of natural rights (which belong to the individual qua individual) and of equality have played out in American history, with Lincoln standing as perhaps the tallest figure in the neoconservative pantheon for his reorienting America to its highest ideals as expressed in the Declaration. The civil rights movement, for them, was the final act in this drama to create a nation based upon these high principles: equality and natural right.

Here the differences between conservatives and neoconservatives concerning the nature of the regime are extremely important. For conservatives, equality is anathema and the Declaration of Independence, for all its venerable ideas, tends too much toward rational exuberance. Since conservatives rightly emphasize that there can be no formal distinction between equality of opportunity and equality of condition, they stress that a belief in equality, always a danger in a democracy, easily leads to efforts at social engineering. Neoconservatives, by contrast, argue for the greater moral claim of fostering a society that gives as many individuals as possible the opportunities and the means of improving their lives. Therefore, government efforts to provide public schooling, to supply a basic safety net, and to interfere in local and state governments to eliminate immoral inequalities before the law are all warranted and good. Underneath this division about equality is a fundamental disagreement about human nature, or at least a very different emphasis about human nature. Conservatives accept the corporate nature of humans and thereby stress individual obligations. Neoconservatives emphasize the glories of the individual freed to accomplish what she might and thereby stress individual rights. Conservatives stand in tension with neoconservatives in the same way that natural law stands in tension with natural right.

In foreign policy, the neoconservatives crafted a vision that effectively alienated conservatives from the rest of the right. Driven by their belief in the great American experiment of democracy and equality, neoconservatives suggest that the logic inherent in natural right obliges the United States to a form of imperialism. Unlike the more focused anticommunism of the 1950s and 1960s, this right-wing foreign policy borrowed from the long-standing liberal objective of making the world safe for democracy. In this way, neoconservatives stressed liberation from the past much more than recovering a threatened patrimony. Conservatives, who ranged from isolationists to solid cold warriors, could not endorse such an evangelical effort, since they considered American democratic culture to be a product of a long train of historical circumstances and therefore an inappropriate model for most other cultures.

One additional group deserves mention. We might call them economic libertarians. Unabashed capitalists, the new breed of libertarians tend to understand people in economic terms, as rational actors in a marketplace. For them the greatest ideal is freedom—a word they virtually scream. Freedom isn't a necessary condition for virtue, as it was for Meyer, but the only meaningful good a society can offer. Absent a governing idea of the social good, we are left with the individual who should be liberated to make her own choices with as little interference from any government as possible. Given this freedom in a context of a free market, people will make rational choices relative to what they want, which should not be dictated by any group.

These are the major groups, so far as I can tell, that composed the backbone of the Reagan coalition in 1980. In what sense was this movement conservative? It was certainly right wing. It is clear that the movement emerging out of the 1950s had important new contributors, and contributors who brought some necessary ingredients to the political success of the newly transformed Republican Party. They brought new money, and a great deal of it. They created numerous think tanks that concentrated on policy and activism. They brought a new political energy and a new style of grassroots politics that greatly strengthened the Republican Party in 1980. It is doubtful if Ronald Reagan would have won without them. But while they helped bring an end to the long dominance of the liberal, New Deal coalition, they did so by changing the "conservative" movement rather dramatically and, in the course of the Reagan administration, of redrawing the boundaries of the respectable right.

RONALD REAGAN

But before we turn to that part of the story, we must come to grips with this enigma—Ronald Reagan—and we must come to grips with him in light of this complex movement that made his presidency possible and that he in turn shaped. Mr. Reagan went to Washington much as Mr. Smith had gone in Frank Capra's depression-era film. In the film *Mr. Smith Goes to Washington,* we find a hardworking, patriotic citizen, called out of private life to serve in the far-off capital. Mr. Smith's first encounter with Washington, D.C., is something akin to a spiritual experience. He sees all the symbols of the great leaders, and especially the founders, whose colossal wisdom had established a new kind of nation based upon equality, individualism, and freedom—with a government that is beholden to the citizens rather than the other way around. The nation they birthed had grown great because its citizens—the real rulers—are good, decent, caring, hardworking, risk-taking, and forgiving. But Mr. Smith learns that the great ideals were threatened by a small buddy system of people who used the government for personal ends. The genius of Jefferson Smith was that in his naïve innocence, he understood that the role of government is to assist people to live their own lives. In Washington the innocent Smith was pitted against the so-phisticated and powerful who controlled much of the government and the media. Somehow, Smith exposed the corruption to his fellow citizens, and against them no cadre of interest peddlers could win. Smith had returned the capital to the people and had exposed the corrupt system. The message here is that the people can be trusted; it is the system that bears watching, the system that brings evil into the land.

This was very much a part of Reagan's self-understanding. He was an aver-age American called temporarily to politics to clean up government. Always the people could be trusted—this was an article of faith for the president that corresponded to his belief in the innate goodness of people. Perhaps this was an American characteristic, but it was hardly a conservative sentiment. Central to Reagan's vision of America was a belief that America was part of God's un-folding, progressive plan. Out of authoritarianism and corrupting forms of hi-erarchy, the American founding formed a pivot in history toward the greater moral objectives of freedom, equality, and individualism. Reagan rarely if ever reflected deeply on this trinity, but like so many of his beliefs, he held it tightly and seemed oblivious to any tensions or contradictions. His youthful imagina-tion was stocked with countless stories of the average Joe who worked hard, faced challenges with dogged determination, and because of his skills and his character, would eventually thrive in this free society. America at its best al-lows this person to succeed or fail on his own. America at its best fosters this sense of independence and self-reliance, but it also assists in ways that don't undermine these character traits. Most of the time this assistance comes from family, friends, and neighbors. When someone is hungry, they provide him with food or with a means of earning his food. If one's barn burns down, they rebuild it. Sometimes, however, America helps through the government. In spite of all of his rhetorical attacks on government assistance, there is nothing in Reagan's public record that suggests any problem with government assistance. Still, gov-ernment assistance must not damage the individualism and self-reliance so cen-tral to Reagan's vision of America. Government corrupts when it taxes at levels that hurt the entrepreneurial spirit or when governmental gifts lead to depen-dency. When he attacked big government, this is what he meant.[11]

Reagan's religious upbringing imbued him with a strong sense of God's providence and of individual destiny. Like so many Christians, Reagan lived in this great tension between human freedom and God's sovereignty, between human choice and God's plan. He could rest in the belief that God controls history while warning constantly of the great dangers of human decisions. He could believe in Armageddon while working to prevent it. However mysteri-ous Reagan's thinking is on this subject, it squares with countless other Ameri-cans, and it shaped his view of America's role in the world and even his personal place in history. America represents the future and thereby the model for the rest of the world. For him, America was a new beginning.

To defend America was to defend its ideas and its mission. Like so many of his generation, the experiences of World War II and the subsequent new role America was to play in a world of competing ideologies greatly shaped Reagan's understanding of America and the world. So far as I can tell, Reagan was never an isolationist. He accepted the new American role and embraced a mild form of democratic globalism—a belief in the need to fight for democracy and "freedom" (ill-defined) around the world. In all of these beliefs, Ronald Reagan was more attuned to the liberal center of American politics than to the emerging conservatism.

Reagan moved slowly toward the Republican Party and an intellectual attachment to fusionism in the 1950s and early 1960s. He read *National Review* and *Human Events,* which shaped his understanding and articulation of the issues. Perhaps his religious views made the conservative version of anticommunism more attractive than the liberal version. Reagan was influenced by *Witness,* especially by Chambers's description of two competing faiths, which suggested a greater cosmic and spiritual struggle behind the geopolitics. But it was probably his evolving beliefs about the dangers of liberal domestic policies that pushed him to the other side of the aisle. Among the many contributing factors to this change I would highlight two. First, as Reagan's income grew, he became more aware of how punishing high tax rates can be. Second, as he became a spokesman for General Electric, he worked systematically through his beliefs about the proper role of government in the economy.

By his famous 1964 speech,[12] the basic contours of his political agenda were in place and had become articles of faith. He warned that the great American experiment of self-government and "freedom" was at risk by a creeping socialism and a desire for security (as represented by a paternalistic government) over freedom. He identified the founding "idea" of the nation that "government was beholden to the people, that it had no other source of power"—an idea that is "the newest, most unique idea in all the long history of man's relation to man." The fundamental question at stake in the election of 1964, he stressed, was to choose self-government as the founders intended or to "confess that a little intellectual elite in a far-distant capital can plan our lives for us better than we can plan for ourselves." For Reagan, every policy issue must be answered relative to whether it is consistent with these principles of freedom. "We need true tax reform," he claimed, "that will at least make a start toward restoring for our children the American Dream that wealth is denied to no one, that each individual has the right to fly as high as his strength and ability will take him. But we can not have such reform while our tax policy is engineered by people who view the tax as a means of achieving changes in our social structure." America was the first place on Earth where the individual is free to do with his ability and his property what he wishes, and he is free to rule himself by his own lights. Government is, therefore, a protector of these basic freedoms rather than the means of acquiring other social goods. His was a philosophy more or less consistent with Meyer's fusionism, though leaning decisively more toward Hayek than toward Russell Kirk and the conservatives.

With these ideas, Mr. Reagan began his political career as governor of California. His leadership there is instructive, as he compromised on both economic and social policies. The tax burden for Californians went up, not down. He had a fairly progressive record on environmental policy, and he signed a liberal abortion bill. Reagan hadn't stopped believing in his philosophy, but he proved to be more flexible than his speeches would suggest, and he had a way of squaring these compromises with his philosophy. His philosophy appealed to those on the right, while his policies rarely threatened moderates. Somehow the tension was lost on Reagan. He left Sacramento with his public philosophy intact and prepared to fulfill his destiny. To this end, Reagan remained in public life giving numerous speeches and regular radio spots.

The recent publication of many of the scripts that Reagan wrote for radio illuminates much about this man and exposes something about why he became a man for his time.[13] In one address, entitled "Looking Out a Window," Reagan expresses his deep beliefs about the greatness of the American people and the dangers of "social engineers" and bureaucrats and elites of all sorts. He speaks of looking out his hotel window at the many cars going home from work, and he reflects on their individual lives. "Some of our social planners," he said, "refer to them as 'the masses' which only proves they don't know them. . . . They are not 'the masses,' or as the elitists would have it—'the common man.' They are very uncommon. Individuals each with his or her own hopes and dreams, plans and problems and the kind of quiet courage that makes this whole country run better than just about any other place on earth." He believed that—for him the people were "uncommon." Just like him, they were average but unique, courageous, and hardworking.

As he spoke to Americans in the mid- and late seventies, he addressed the failures and the peculiar challenges of the time. In each case, any failure was the result of government, not the American people. Taken together, his speeches set out a purpose for America, a purpose that springs from its divine mission and that calls for the people to retake their government. One of the great missions was to eliminate communism from the world, but without recourse to war. He warned of the need to avoid "Armageddon," but he minced no words in describing communism as a disease, a plague. "Communism is neither an economic nor a political system—it is a form of insanity—a temporary aberration which will one day disappear from the earth because it is contrary to human nature." Meanwhile, American foreign policy failures reflect the failure of nerve or the unwillingness of the foreign policy elites to fight for America's divine mission. Americans had been betrayed by their political leaders.

The domestic challenges facing America spring also from the perverse actions of government elites. They have imposed regulations that hurt the small entrepreneur, they have taxed the people too much, and they have decided that they are better able to guide the lives of Americans than are the people themselves. In short, Reagan warned about all manner of problems facing the nation, but he delivered this message with a clear sense of the cause (too much government) and with a very optimistic vision. Take back the government, and the great, uncommon, free people of America will return the nation to its former greatness.

In his campaign for president in 1980, these themes proved handy. In a time of economic dislocation, American prestige suffering from the aftermath of Vietnam, and the shame of Watergate still lingering, Reagan turned the anxiety of Americans against big government, much as Roosevelt had directed it against big business. The message made sense to many constituencies. Not only did Reagan retain the fusionist conservatives, but his populist, antigovernment message tapped the resentment of blue-collar workers suffering from global economic changes and worried about the preferential treatment given to minorities.[14] His message made sense to those who had come to fear government intervention through forced busing, or by federalizing abortion, even as he tapped the fears of Christians worried about moral decay. The neoconservatives were warmed by his emphasis on democratic globalism, and economic libertarians found his endorsement of supply-side economics much to their liking.

But how conservative was Reagan? One finds interesting tensions in his philosophy that make him hard to label finally. First, for all of Reagan's references to the past, he was much more interested in the future, in progress rather than conservation. Most of the stories he told, many of them set in earlier times but not historical, emphasized some character trait that he found important to the American spirit. His nostalgia for an imaginary past had little to do with history and everything to do with his mythic America, which if not fully realized is in the process of self-realization.[15] Few people have a greater faith in technology or in the power of science to solve problems than Reagan. Left free to explore, scientists would solve our pollution problems and medical challenges, and even, of course, eliminate the threat of nuclear war. Most interestingly, Reagan could invoke Thomas Paine more easily than Edmund Burke. Quoting the revolutionary, Reagan would emphasize that "we have the power to begin the world over again."[16] Truth be told, Reagan was more interested in new worlds than old ones, for he had a progressive and emancipatory view of history. In this way he stressed freedom as the great good. He did not stress virtue, since the people are by definition virtuous. Insofar as freedom led to other good things, he emphasized material prosperity and individual autonomy. Finally the goals of freedom, material prosperity, individual autonomy, and democratic equality are not for Americans only, but for the world. America was, therefore, the redeemer nation.[17]

As Reagan became president, he relied heavily on a language he developed in the 1950s and 1960s, but his philosophy was very much akin to the thinking of neoconservatives and economic libertarians, while his governing style emphasized moderation and compromise. He brought to the presidency a team of advisers dominated by centrist Republicans and an agenda with a few simple objectives. First, he would cut tax rates; second, he would extend the process of deregulation; third, he would terminate a number of unnecessary or harmful government programs while cutting many others; and finally, he would strengthen American military power as a means of protecting American interests and in an effort to win the cold war. One might add one other objective, which was tied to a large number of lesser objectives, which is the effort to alter the composition of the federal judiciary in such a way as to influence an array of social issues and redress the imbalance of power between the states and the federal government.

CONSERVATIVE WARS

Policy historians debate the success of his agenda, but I am more interested in how Reagan's agenda, and his means of accomplishing it, shaped the coalition that brought him to power. One notes at the outset that Reagan did not put the concerns of the social conservatives (the new right) in his legislative agenda.[18] Very early in Reagan's administration, the entrepreneurs of the new right complained that they had been forgotten. It is hard for me to see any evidence that the diverse people they mobilized for Reagan ever felt abandoned, however. More significantly, Reagan's administration depended heavily on the large and growing body of social scientific reports emerging from the think tanks, most of which leaned toward either neoconservatism or economic libertarianism. While Reagan himself kept to an old script, his advisers drew heavily from this body of ready-made policy positions.

As Reagan came to office, the inevitable struggle for power went very much against two groups: the new right (the social conservatives) and the traditionalist conservatives (those followers of Kirk who had been part of the fusionist articulation of conservatism a generation earlier). By the mid-1980s, it had become clear that the neoconservatives were the new power brokers of the movement as they moved to extend their influence not only to the expansive network of think tanks but also to important media outlets and, with their Straussian allies, some important academic strongholds. They used this position to redefine the respectable right, just as Buckley had done in his *National Review* two decades earlier. The so-called conservative wars in the journals gave expression to this battle, and a new vocabulary emerged with traditionalist conservatives described, tellingly, as paleoconservatives.[19] The labeling of conservatives as paleos suggested that a purging was afoot. By the end of the Reagan administration, the so-called conservative movement had largely cast out the conservatism that had been part of the fusionist compromise. Something more significant had happened: the center of politics had moved to the right, but in the process the acceptable political spectrum had been truncated. Socialists and left-wing liberals of the McGovern variety, along with traditionalist conservatives of the Russell Kirk variety, had all become politically irrelevant. The center of gravity now wavered between right-wing and centrist liberals—but liberals all.

But it might still be argued that beyond the power struggle for influence in the Reagan administration, conservatives (paleos) had reason to cheer the transformations that had taken place during the 1980s. Many have accepted the limits to conservatism in the United States and support most of the right-wing agenda in public. Still, it is far from clear if conservative principles have advanced in any meaningful way. If we return to the tension of the right between the primacy of the group versus the primacy of the individual, between the call to Return and the lure of Progress, we find that for the time being, the conservative emphasis has lost rather emphatically to the more emancipatory focus.

One might note that the relative decline of socialist tendencies in government and the greater emphasis upon the "free market" should gladden the heart of conservatives. It is true that conservatives emphasize the necessary relationship between property and freedom and they are inclined to prefer a free economy over a managed one. Yet they are not enamored with corporate capitalism or with the emerging consumer culture. In its contemporary manifestation, capitalism has emerged as an aggressively forward-looking, tradition-crushing—to say nothing of homogenizing—force. If near the heart of conservatism is a belief that change ought to be slow and should take place with due reverence to the principles invested in traditions, prejudices, and habits, then modern, global capitalism presents numerous problems. Rather than seeing capitalism as an altruistic force, as did some of the influential authors on the right, traditionalists worried that an emphasis on profits would encourage companies to treat employees like objects and that to the degree that the "market" became the model for describing human interactions, humans would take an increasingly reductive, materialist view. In such an environment, everything becomes a commodity and value becomes a term to describe worth in a market. For traditionalists this is dehumanizing, even as the obsession with change will efface the traces of culture that have emerged from generations of human experience.

Conservatives' concerns about modern capitalism is that it leads to alienation by encouraging people to forget their ancestors and to think not of their posterity. Capitalism works to maintain genuine liberty, conservatives stress, only if the society has taught its members to think of themselves and others as participants in a spiritual community. From the point of view of the conservative, the evolution from political man to economic man (or from the left to the right) is, therefore, hardly praiseworthy. If a society trains its members to love individual choice above social and familial obligations, to pursue their lives through rational calculations relative to personal desires, then it will produce moral idiots who are cut off from the very sources of the self that make possible both distinctive personality and meaningful liberty. In short, the conservative emphasis on restraint has lost to the seductive appeal of a materialist paradise. Liberal democratic capitalism works in America to create abundance beyond any previous generation's imagination. It supplies constant stimulation, constant diversions, so that people can not only forget their ancestors and their posterity, but dull the hunger in their own souls. If we have become economic creatures, pleasure-maximizing beings, then we have indeed discovered the best way to live. The clarion call of freedom makes sense in this context, but little else does.

Beyond the traditionalists, the movement goes on and, in some ways, has become part of the establishment. The failure of the Reagan administration to reduce the size of government, to limit its reach, to dramatically alter the tax burden, has left members of the movement with a sense of unfinished business. Unfortunately for them, they have no Reagan, no leader who can be all things to all people, and they tend increasingly to fratricidal struggles. For these people, Reagan is more important as symbol than as leader, and it has become fairly standard now for most groups in the Republican Party to call themselves "Reagan Republicans." As symbol, no political leader in the past fifty years has been so potent or so malleable. Reagan as symbol became more important for conservatives in light of his successor, George Bush, whose devotion to the cause was suspect from the beginning. His betrayal on the most central element of the Reagan agenda, taxes, undermined forever his credibility with the right wing of his party and nearly cost him the nomination in 1992.

Nonetheless, the victory in 1992 of the "new Democrat" Bill Clinton exposed how much Reagan had altered the political landscape even as the new president would help reinvigorate the right. Clinton won only because he sounded as though he had abandoned the liberalism of the older Democrats and embraced a new way, a third way between the old liberals and the old conservatives. His subsequent hard left in office—gays in the military, a massive health care plan—mobilized the various groups on the right for a counterattack. The stunning victory in the 1994 election by Republicans represented, to them at least, the Reagan agenda, part 2. Their famous "Contract with America" borrowed heavily and unashamedly from Reagan's speeches as it outlined an economic plan that aimed to get government off the backs of the people. Populism was back, but it came with a more combative tone and methods that a new generation of baby boomer conservatives embraced—a take no prisoners assault on their enemies.[20]

The new Republican majority in the House of Representatives was led by economic libertarians with support from a new breed of social conservatives who were waiting for the best time to turn the focus to their issues. At the point was Newt Gingrich, who marched to war with visions of a transformed nation, of a technological and information revolution that would alter American life and expand dramatically the power of individuals to control their lives. The right now joined the left in devotion to the great moral objective encapsulated in the word "empowerment"—they differed on means, not on ends. The power of this new political phalanx is best exposed by the degree that Clinton, threatened with political extinction in the upcoming election, moved to the right, co-opting the most popular parts of the Republican agenda. In the ensuing battles between the now "moderate" Clinton and the now "extremist" Republicans, which led to government shutdowns and other showdowns, Clinton won, but only because he adjusted to the new policy world created by Reagan. As Clinton ended his tenure in office, he could point to numerous successes that had once been the purview of those on the right.

The era of big government is over, claimed Clinton. But this is a matter of perspective. The goal of so many believers in the movement had been to defund the left, to rescind the Great Society and even the New Deal. That didn't happen. The nation, its government now wealthy enough to balance its budget while supporting its existing programs, had embraced a capitalist order along with a fairly strong government to protect its citizens from many of the vicissitudes of life.

But while the Republican Congress represented a political resurgence of the populist-libertarian wing of the Reagan coalition, other currents on the right were also strong. A new generation of neoconservatives, led by William Kristol, many of them influenced by Leo Strauss or Straussians, have shifted the emphasis in neoconservative circles toward virtue. Perhaps here some of the old conservative ideas still had a political forum. Struck by signs of cultural disintegration, from family breakdown to changing sexual mores to the cultural debris called "popular culture," these neoconservatives developed a decidedly nonpopulist position. For them there is no reason to believe that the people are virtuous or that they will use their freedom to do good. While many of them stress the old conservative answer of supporting the function of mediating institutions, they are generally more willing than the traditionalists to employ government to inculcate or support virtues. Neoconservatives believe in ideas, in the ideas of the founding, in the importance of an established and unchanging standard of right conduct, and in the moral obligation to spread these ideas at home and abroad.

It is hard to know how the tug of war between the economic populists and the virtue-oriented and elitist neoconservatives will shape the movement in the coming years. Is this a new stage in the old conservative dialectic? Most movement conservatives agree on the ongoing struggle to lower taxes and eliminate many federal regulations and programs, and they tend toward a belief in democratic globalism and thereby free trade and interventionist foreign policy. All of these doctrines were central to Reagan's agenda. But without a communist threat to help tie the factions to an overarching moral enterprise, the groups will likely fight each other nearly as much as they fight so-called liberals. Meanwhile, in a broader sense, politics has changed insofar as those in the center and those on the right have a more or less shared, if limited, objective—to liberate individuals to choose their own life with maximum flexibility and minimum interference. Politics is the struggle over the means of liberation. It is one of the paradoxical legacies of the "conservative" Reagan that he helped foster a forward-looking, individualistic, and freedom-loving political culture.

NOTES

1. Reagan has received a great deal of attention during the last decade. I have found the following the most useful: Lou Cannon, *President Reagan: The Role of a Lifetime* (New York: Public Affairs, 2000); Garry Wills, *Reagan's America* (Garden City, N.Y.: Doubleday, 1985); and William E. Pemberton, *Exit with Honor: The Life and Presidency of Ronald Reagan* (New York: Sharpe, 1998).

2. For many years, the only reliable accounts of the conservative movement came from self-proclaimed conservatives—the rest of the historical profession left the subject almost untouched. The first intellectual history, and still the best, is George Nash's *The Conservative Intellectual Movement Since 1945* (New York: Basic Books, 1976). In the world of politics, William Rusher's *The Rise of the Right* (New York: William Morrow, 1984) supplies a valuable insider's point of view on the emerging political movement. An eccentric but very valuable survey of the movement is Paul Gottfried's *The Conservative Movement,* rev. ed. (New York: Twayne Publishers, 1993). More recently the historiography of American conservatism has become more complex and nuanced. While a few well-established liberals have sought to understand the movement—such as Godfrey Hodgson's *The World Turned Right Side Up* (Boston: Houghton Mifflin, 1996)—most have come from young scholars seeking fresh subjects. Some of the more interesting are Mary Brennan's *Turning Right in the Sixties: The Conservative Capture of the GOP* (Chapel Hill: University of North Carolina Press, 1995) and Jonathan Schoenwald's *A Time for Choosing: The Rise of Modern American Conservatism* (New York: Oxford University Press, 2001).

3. This problem is deeper still. Most conservatives understand themselves relative to ideas, and they take as an article of faith that "ideas have consequences." They are not given to thinking of themselves as having an "ideology." Yet ideology is one of the key labels liberal historians apply to conservative beliefs. The categories of analysis liberal historians employ are alien to conservatives, which makes it difficult for liberal historians to understand conservatives as they understood themselves. Rarely do historians provide a precise definition of conservatism, and insofar as they attend to such definitional requirements, they do so exclusively within the context of political movements. Here the labels become "moderate," "conservative," and "extremist." Two problems plague this dominant strategy. First, for conservatives, politics is not the beginning or the end of the story, but should be placed in a larger intellectual and cultural context. Second, these labels provide absolutely no content, but they do carry a rhetorical wallop.

4. See, for instance, Richard Weaver, *Ideas Have Consequences* (Chicago: University of Chicago Press, 1948), 64–65.

5. Friedrich von Hayek, *The Constitution of Liberty* (Chicago: University of Chicago Press, 1960), 61.

6. Several works already mentioned cover this terrain. Note especially Rusher, *Rise of the Right;* Hodgson, *World Turned Right Side Up;* Brennan, *Turning Right in the Sixties;* and Schoenwald, *A Time for Choosing.* Another good source for this story is Lee Edwards, *The Conservative Revolution: The Movement That Remade America* (New York: Free Press, 1999). It is worth noting that while all of these are fairly narrow political histories—interested in political realignment—the ones written from self-proclaimed conservatives give noticeably greater space and emphasis to the intellectual roots of the movement (see Edwards and Rusher). Gottfried's book *(Conservative Movement),* however, is much more concerned with the clash of ideas within the movement—and, importantly, Gottfried is clearly the most conservative of these authors.

7. See Frank Meyer's essay "Freedom, Tradition, and Conservatism" in his *What Is Conservatism?* (New York: Holt, Rinehart & Winston, 1964) as well as his *In Defense of Freedom* (Chicago: Regnery, 1962).

8. Rusher, *Rise of the Right,* 87–127.

9. Few labels are as meaningless as "extremist." It made political sense for Lyndon Johnson to tar Barry Goldwater with the label, but for scholars to use it only leads to confusion. An otherwise fine book, Schoenwald's *A Time for Choosing* depends upon the category without ever giving it any meaningful semantic location. In this case, "extremism" has moved to the right of Goldwater, thereby exonerating the Arizonian of the label.

10. The secondary literature on neoconservatives is growing rapidly. I have found useful Mark Gerson, *The Neoconservative Vision: From the Cold War to the Culture Wars* (Lanham, Md.: Madison Books, 1996). J. David Hoeveler, Jr., *Watch on the Right: Conservative Intellectuals in the Reagan Era* (Madison: University of Wisconsin Press, 1991) is an excellent book on the internal coherence of conservatives. I disagree with Hoeveler's argument, however, as I emphasize divisions separating conservatives from neoconservatives.

11. Terri Bimes supplies a very helpful study of Reagan's populism in her essay, "Ronald Reagan and the New Conservative Populism," contained in this volume.

12. See Reagan's own analysis of this speech in *Ronald Reagan: An American Life* (New York: Pocket Books, 1990), 137–43. See also Wills, *Reagan's America,* 332–43.

13. Kiron K. Skinner, Annelise Anderson, and Martin Anderson, eds., *Reagan, In His Own Hand* (New York: Free Press, 2001).

14. Consult Bimes's essay, "New Conservative Populism," on Reagan's form of populism.

15. Wills, *Reagan's America.*

16. George Will made this reference famous. See his commentary "Fresh Start?" *Washington Post,* October 31, 1985.

17. For an excellent study of Reagan's public philosophy, consult Hugh Heclo's essay, "Ronald Reagan and the American Public Philosophy," contained in this volume. Heclo argues persuasively that Reagan was the most oriented toward a coherent and even consistent public philosophy of all our recent presidents. Heclo noted that "the important point is not that Reagan ever said anything fundamentally new, but that in the context created by the sixties, Reagan continued to uphold something old. His effort helped pass on the sacramental vision as a living faith in the public mind rather than a dead tradition of antiquarian curiosity or ridicule." Just so.

18. Many populists challenged the Reagan administration on social policies, but the most vigorous complaints came from Richard Viguerie, who complained about Reagan's tax policy. See Rusher, *Rise of the Right,* 313–14; Edwards, *Conservative Revolution,* 225–

41; and Gottfried, *Conservative Movement,* 97–117. For a good sampling of the populist's concerns, see Richard Viguerie, *The Establishment vs. the People: Is a New Populist Revolt on the Way?* (Chicago: Regnery Gateway, 1983); and David Brooks, "Please, Mr. Postman: The Travails of Richard Viguerie," *National Review,* June 20, 1986, 28–32.

19. The best single source for this story is Paul Gottfried, *Conservative Movement,* 142–66.

20. See Nina J. Easton, *Gang of Five: Leaders at the Center of the Conservative Crusade* (New York: Simon & Schuster, 2000), for an excellent analysis of the new style of baby boomer conservatives.

3

Reagan: The Soft-Sell Populist

Terri Bimes

Conventional wisdom suggests that Ronald Reagan was an unusually effective rhetorical leader. Dubbed the "Great Communicator," Reagan has been praised by both journalists and academic observers for his popular leadership skills. Despite this general agreement about Reagan's skills, there is less of a consensus on the nature and significance of his rhetorical leadership. To some, Reagan's rhetoric was marked by consensual appeals that unified the nation. For instance, Robert Dallek depicts him as a "soft sell" spokesman; Bert Rockman notes how Reagan used "dulcet tones" to mask the sweeping changes in government he was proposing; and Thomas Cronin remarks how Reagan resembles a Mr. Rogers, a president who explains policy in a "neighborly way."[1] To others, Reagan represents a populist agitator. In *The Populist Persuasion,* Michael Kazin characterizes Reagan's leadership as the culmination of the conservative capture of populism that began with Richard Nixon. In Kazin's view, Reagan drew upon the populist language coined in the nineteenth century by dramatically reinterpreting the meaning of the people and the special interests to fit his conservative agenda.[2] Similarly, author and columnist Richard Reeves describes Reagan as a populist crusader along the lines of Andrew Jackson, William Jennings Bryan, Franklin D. Roosevelt, and George Wallace.[3] Even one of Reagan's speechwriters highlights the populist tropes of the 40th president, depicting him as an Andrew Jackson of the 1980s.[4] This paper attempts to gauge the validity of these contrasting claims by tracing the development of Reagan's rhetoric from his early forays into political activism through his presidency, and by comparing Reagan's use of populism to his immediate predecessors and successors.

Reagan's populism emerged before his adoption of the conservative agenda of rolling back the national government. Campaigning for Harry Truman in 1948, Reagan attacked corporate greed, defended the common man, and attacked the Republican Congress for tax cuts that he and other Democrats charged were

I would like to thank Elliot Brownlee, Richard Ellis, Louis Fisher, and Bruce Miroff for their helpful comments. I also am grateful to the Institute of Governmental Studies at the University of California, Berkeley, for supporting this research.

skewed toward the wealthy. With his conversion to conservatism in the 1950s and early 1960s, Reagan successfully adapted the Democrats' populist imagery to his new political agenda. Although the national government replaced greedy corporations as the enemy of ordinary Americans, Reagan's rhetoric continued to evoke the populist understanding of politics as a battle between the people and the special interests.

As Reagan gained more political experience, however, he recognized the political risks posed by the populist jeremiad. Following Barry Goldwater's defeat in the 1964 election, Reagan called for fellow conservatives to tone down their remarks to the general public—advice that Reagan would heed himself throughout his presidency. A close observation of Reagan's presidential rhetoric thus reveals a two-pronged specialization strategy that helped him avoid charges of extremism. He generally reserved his populist appeals for a limited set of issues—relating to fiscal and tax policy—rather than risking such rhetoric with potentially explosive social and cultural issues. He also relied less on populist appeals in his major addresses to nationwide audiences than to campaign and narrower audiences. These two specialization strategies aided Reagan in brandishing his image as populist reformer, while maintaining his reputation as a soft-sell spokesperson.[5]

THE DEVELOPMENT OF REAGAN'S POPULISM

Reagan's rhetorical approach as president has its roots in the two main phases of his political life: the liberal Democratic phase that spanned his early support of Franklin Delano Roosevelt through the early 1950s and the more enduring conservative phase that marked Reagan's thinking throughout his career as an elected official. As a liberal Democrat, Reagan drew upon the Democratic tradition of populist appeals, adopting the themes of the citizen politician and class conflict in his own speeches. During Reagan's conservative phase, he shifted targets, but the populist form remained intact. Thus, both the liberal and conservative phases played important roles in the shaping of Reagan's presidential rhetoric.

The Reagan of 1948 differed dramatically from the Reagan of 1980. After World War II ended, Reagan seemed eager to establish his liberal credentials. In his own words, he was a "near-hopeless hemophilic liberal."[6] He joined several groups promoting humanitarian or liberal causes: the Americans for Democratic Action, the liberal American Veterans Committee, the Hollywood Independent Citizens Committee of the Arts, Sciences, and Professions (HICCASP), and briefly the World Federalists.[7] In the fall of 1948, Reagan campaigned for Hubert Humphrey for Senate and for Harry Truman for president. During the campaign, Reagan adopted populist themes that echoed Truman's fiery rhetoric. In a radio speech sponsored by the International Ladies Garment Workers Union, Reagan made a strong populist case for electing Truman over the Republican Thomas Dewey. He introduced himself as a concerned citizen: "This is Ronald Reagan. You may know me as a motion picture actor. But tonight I am just a citizen concerned about the national election next month and more than a little impatient with those promises Republicans made before they got control of Congress a couple of years ago."[8]

Reagan noted that Republicans had promised in the 1946 campaign to help boost the incomes of all citizens, but he charged that instead, "the profits of corporations have doubled while workers' wages have increased by only a quarter. . . . The small increase workers did receive was more than eaten up by rising prices." To emphasize the linkages between high corporate profits, Republican economic policies, and the suffering of ordinary Americans, Reagan contrasted the story of Smith L. Carpenter, a ninety-one-year-old retiree who had to return to work because he "didn't figure on this Republican inflation" eating up all of his savings, with that of Standard Oil of New Jersey, which "reported a net profit of $210 million after taxes for the first half of 1948, an increase of 70% in one year." In other words, Reagan concluded, "high prices have not been caused by higher wages, but by bigger and bigger profits."

He ended the broadcast by lambasting the Republican Congress for the "vicious" Taft-Hartley law that had "handcuffed" the labor unions, for the Gearhart bill which had "snatched away" Social Security benefits from nearly a million workers, and for passing a tax cut bill that would "benefit the higher income brackets alone; the average worker saved only $1.73 a week."

These passages underscore several elements of Reagan's rhetorical approach that would endure throughout his career, even as the specific targets of his populist appeals shifted with his political ideology. In the first passage, Reagan painted himself as an average citizen as opposed to a Hollywood actor. Reagan's use of the idea of the citizen politician fit well with Truman's depiction of himself as a Washington outsider. Notwithstanding his position as an incumbent president, Truman emphasized his citizen politician status in the 1948 campaign. In a public explanation of his running for office in 1948, Truman noted that he would have been "content to stay entirely clear of the White House" if it were not for the threat of a reversal of New Deal reforms by "reactionaries."[9] Later, in his administration, Truman remarked that he was just an "ordinary citizen of this great Republic of ours who has the greatest responsibility in the world."[10]

The idea of the citizen politician proved useful to Reagan throughout his political career. It not only defused charges that his years as an actor were inadequate preparation for governing, it also folded into the populist trope of the outsider fighting for the people against a corrupt political establishment. When presented with his gubernatorial rival's extensive record of governing experience and accused of not having any experience for the job, Reagan quipped, "The man who currently has the job has more experience than anybody. That's why I am running."[11] In his 1970 reelection bid for governor of California, Reagan campaigned as "a citizen temporarily in public service."[12] Years later, in his farewell address as president, Reagan explained his motivations for seeking political office: "Back in the 1960s, when I began, it seemed to me that we'd begun reversing the order of things—that through more and more rules and regulations and confiscatory taxes, the government was taking more of our money, more of our options, and more of our freedom. I went into politics in part to put up my hand and say, 'Stop.' I was a citizen politician, and it seemed the right thing for a citizen to do."[13]

Perhaps even more striking than Reagan's framing of himself as a citizen politician is his use of a populist jeremiad that sets the average American worker against greedy corporations and their servants in Congress. In doing so, Reagan tapped into an old Democratic theme dating back to Andrew Jackson and other nineteenth-century Democrats—one that was expressed intermittently by Franklin Roosevelt and brandished routinely by Truman.[14] Just as Democrat Andrew Jackson had attacked the Second Bank of the United States for making the "rich richer and the potent more powerful," Reagan charged that greedy corporations and their Republican allies were responsible for inflation that robbed ordinary Americans of their savings.[15] Though Reagan's beliefs about the causes of inflation changed dramatically as he moved to the right, he retained the same basic populist sense that politics was largely a struggle between ordinary Americans and a self-serving elite.[16]

Finally, the 1948 campaign speech also exhibited Reagan's belief that the job of a political leader is to restore fundamental values. By electing Truman, voters could prevent Republicans from eviscerating the liberal state and could instead safeguard the New Deal's accomplishments in bringing social justice to workers and retirees. Even as his political views changed, Reagan retained this understanding of executive leadership as an instrument to reinstate a just order that had been threatened by the depredations of special interests.

As has been documented by numerous scholars and journalists, Reagan's political views shifted in the 1950s.[17] As late as November 1950, Reagan campaigned for Helen Gahagan Douglas, the liberal representative contesting Richard Nixon for the California Senate seat. Less than a year later, Reagan addressed the Kiwanis International Convention in St. Louis, criticizing the national government for heaping undue taxes on motion picture industry workers. He warned the "average citizen" that if "they [the federal government] can get away with it there [Hollywood], it is aimed at your pocketbook and you are next."[18] In a collection of speeches published after his presidency, Reagan labeled this speech his "basic Hollywood Speech" and noted how it created the foundation for future speeches about governmental abuses. Where his 1948 radio address for Truman had depicted tax battles as a distributional fight between high-income individuals and ordinary workers, Reagan in the 1950s instead emphasized the conflict between all taxpayers and a greedy federal government.

Reagan vigorously polished these conservative populist themes during his stint as the spokesperson for General Electric from 1954 to 1962. During this time, Reagan hosted the television program *General Electric Theater* and toured the country as the company's "goodwill ambassador," traveling to over 135 GE plants across thirty-eight states and delivering what would become his basic political stump speech. He also became a popular speaker at Rotary Clubs, Chamber of Commerce dinners, and national conventions. As Lou Cannon describes, "The script that emerged from this corporate-sponsored odyssey was patriotic, antigovernment, anticommunist, and probusiness."[19] Touring America also brought Reagan closer to middle America. Reagan told Edward Langley that "when I went on those tours and shook hands with all of those people, I began to see that they were very different people than the people Hollywood was talking about. I was seeing the same people that I grew up with in Dixon, Illinois. I realized I was living in a tinsel factory. And this exposure brought me back."[20] In his biography, he tells how "he'd listen and they'd cite examples of government interference and snafus and complain how bureaucrats, through overregulation, were telling them how to run their businesses."[21] Gradually, Reagan shortened the part of his speech that focused on the mistreatment of Hollywood actors and spent more time "beating the bushes for free enterprise" and warning people about the "threat of government."[22]

By the end of the 1950s and early 1960s, Reagan was regularly pointing out to people the threat of communism "in their own backyards."[23] In a 1959 speech entitled "Business, Ballots, and Bureaus," Reagan sounded many of the same themes that he would draw upon as president. He assailed big government programs, including attempts to "socialize medicine," the progressive income tax, and even Social Security. He complained about the growing complexity of the tax code, noting how it had increased from "thirty-one words to four hundred and forty thousand words." And he criticized the permanent bureaucracy that was "beyond the reach of any ballot." But this speech is noteworthy in that it goes much further than Reagan's speeches as president in identifying the socialist threat as both an external and internal enemy. Reagan noted that in many cases, people in government were well meaning, but "aren't we justified in suspecting that there are those who have fostered the growth of government by deliberate intent and design?" As a consequence of the strong antigovernment messages employed in speeches like "Business, Ballots, and Bureaus," Reagan acquired a reputation among Democratic and labor groups for being a "right-wing extremist" and threatened to spoil GE's image as a middle-of-the-road company. In 1962, GE canceled the *General Electric Theater* because of falling ratings and concerns that Reagan was becoming too controversial to be its spokesperson.[24]

The cancellation of his GE contract did not temper Reagan's political oratory. Indeed, two years later, in a speech given on behalf of presidential candidate Barry Goldwater, Reagan cemented his image as an outspoken opponent of big government. This speech did not break new ground for Reagan, but rather drew upon the same 1950s themes, though supplemented with new statistics and folk stories to illustrate his argument. In "the Speech," as his advisers referred to it, Reagan attacked a long litany of government programs: Aid to Families with Dependent Children, farm aid, the disadvantaged youth program, urban renewal programs, the progressive income tax, and Social Security. His attacks on these governmental programs highlighted three central themes that would form the core of his conservative populism. He attacked big government for its cost and waste of the taxpayer's money. He lambasted the Democratic Party for pushing the country "down the road under the banners of Marx, Lenin, and Stalin." Finally, he criticized the "little intellectual elite," the "do-gooders," and the "government planners" who advocated the creation of a welfare state that stripped citizens of their freedom.[25] David Broder exclaimed that Reagan's 1964 speech was "the most successful debut since William Jennings Bryan electrified the 1896 Democratic convention with his 'Cross of Gold' speech."[26]

Nonetheless, after Lyndon Johnson's landslide victory over Goldwater, Reagan was one of many Republicans to reconsider the nature of their appeals to the public. In December 1964, Reagan issued an alert to the Republican community in the *National Review.* He cautioned conservatives to moderate their rhetoric—without sacrificing their policy principles—to counter the radical image that the Republican Party had acquired during the 1964 campaign. He explained that Republicans had lost because Democrats had been able to "portray us as advancing a kind of radical departure from the status quo." To counter such Democratic tactics, Reagan declared that "our job beginning now is not so much to sell conservatism as to prove that our conservatism is in truth what a lot of people thought they were voting for when they fell for the cornpone come-on. In short—time now for the soft sell to prove our radicalism was an optical illusion."[27]

With this article, Reagan signaled his realization that the antigovernmental populist themes that he and other Republicans had sounded during the Goldwater campaign needed to be refined and even toned down. To foster a broad electoral and legislative coalition, Republicans had to offer their conservative policy prescriptions with a rhetoric that defused charges of radicalism. Though Reagan would continue to draw upon populist appeals after 1964, he gravitated toward a strategy of rhetorical specialization, in which he generally reserved his more strident populist salvos for the purpose of mobilizing party loyalists, while tending to emphasize more consensual, soft-sell themes when addressing a broader audience. Furthermore, Reagan came to reserve his populist salvos for a limited set of economic issues, while using "softer," consensual appeals when discussing a wide range of other topics.

As Reagan prepared to run for the governor of California, his advisers worked hard to distance him from the radical fringe of the Republican Party. When Goldwater offered to help his campaign, Reagan wrote a note thanking the former presidential candidate for his support but carefully sidestepped the offer.[28] Once in the governorship, Reagan by no means dropped populism entirely. As Cannon aptly notes, Reagan still referred to the government as "them," and viewed himself as the protector of Californians against "welfare cheats, foul-mouthed student demonstrators, and ivory-tower leaders of the state's entrenched higher-education establishment."[29] Yet populism was only one element of Reagan's rhetorical approach. The signature theme of his governorship was the vision of "the creative society" in which government would play a positive role in solving the dilemmas of modern society in partnership with private initiatives. According to Reagan, while there needed to be safeguards on government largesse, government would "lead but not rule, listen but not lecture."[30]

In short, Reagan always retained a populist sensibility, even as he shifted political allegiances and even as he responded to the strategic problems posed by populist rhetoric. For him, politics consisted of a conflict between self-serving elites and ordinary Americans, and the president's job was to fight the elites and to restore the position and well-being of the general public. Given this view of politics, Reagan maintained an attachment to the populist Truman long after he came to reject many of the Democrat's policies. Reagan recalled in his biography that "I campaigned for Harry Truman, and to this day, I think Truman was an outstanding president. . . . He had a common sense that helped him get to the roots of problems; he stood up to the bureaucrats, and when he had a tough decision to make, he made it."[31] Like Truman, Reagan viewed himself as a commonsense leader capable of standing up to bureaucrats. But where Truman and other New Deal Democrats focused on corporate greed as the main target of their populist appeals, Reagan came to view big government, the Democratic Congress, and intellectual elites as the enemy of the people. These targets were linked together by the broader argument that wasteful, intrusive government is sustained by the combination of pork-minded Democratic members of Congress, demanding liberal interest groups and their associated clienteles, and out-of-touch elitist intellectuals. Where Truman, building on the successes of FDR, had sought to build a coalition of workers, farmers, and small business owners united by their underdog economic status, Reagan sought to win these groups' allegiances by persuading them to think of themselves in terms of their status as taxpayers, as consumers, and as part of "the American family."[32] Furthermore, Reagan also departed from Truman in forging a rhetorical strategy that simultaneously used populist appeals to mobilize his base, while deploying more consensual themes to build a broader electoral and legislative coalition.

REAGAN'S PRESIDENCY: A NEW POPULIST MOMENT?

With Reagan's convincing victory in the 1980 presidential election, the moment appeared ripe for the triumph of his brand of conservative populism on the national stage. In preparing his inaugural address, Reagan drew upon the blueprint of "the Speech" for inspiration, instructing his speechwriter, Ken Khachigian, to refer to it when writing the first draft.[33] Yet, the striking feature of Reagan's first inaugural address was how he toned down the more antagonistic themes from his earlier rhetoric and quickly moved toward consensual, unifying language. Reagan did not indict the Democratic Party for its alleged socialistic or totalitarian tendencies. He did not recommend reforming Social Security or cutting other specific governmental programs, and he never identified a specific enemy of "we the people." In a *New York Times* op-ed, William Safire described the inaugural address as really two speeches. The first speech, Safire noted, was "an FDR-style warning of economic peril, coupled with an attack on big Government as the source of our problem." In the second speech, Reagan shifted gears to emphasize more consensual themes, evoking "memories of patriotic fervor, national will, and individual sacrifice."[34] Retaining the same commitment to scaling back the size of government as in 1964, Reagan now attempted to reach moderates by adding a consensual, soft-sell approach to his earlier populist formula.

A content analysis of Reagan's rhetoric as president reveals that this hybrid strategy persisted well beyond his inaugural address.[35] Although Reagan continued to draw upon populist imagery, he limited his populism in two important ways. First, he generally reserved his populist appeals for a subset of issues. When discussing budgetary and tax policies, Reagan often framed his appeals in antagonistic terms, emphasizing the need to protect taxpayers by reducing the size of government. However, when discussing a range of other issues that potentially could be framed in populist terms—such as social and cultural issues or defense policy—Reagan instead opted for an inclusive, consensual rhetoric that belied charges of radicalism. Second, Reagan skillfully tailored his rhetorical approach to his audience. When he addressed a nationwide audience, Reagan accentuated his role as a unifying head of state and generally shunned populist appeals. By contrast, when campaigning for Republican candidates or when speaking to narrower, specialized audiences, Reagan made extensive use of populism. This bifurcated strategy allowed Reagan to appeal to blue-collar workers and disaffected Democrats, while defusing the charges of intolerance or extremism that had dogged Goldwater.

REAGAN'S POPULISM: CULTURAL OR ECONOMIC?

To understand Reagan's presidential rhetoric, one must first consider the difference between cultural and economic populism. Michael Kazin, a historian who studies the evolution of populism in American political history, argues that the conservative capture of populism in the 1970s and 1980s hinged on cultural appeals. According to Kazin, Republicans replaced the economic-based populism of such Democrats as FDR and Truman with a cultural populism in which the national government and liberal interest groups were attacked for undermining traditional values, for fostering disorder, and for promoting the interests of minorities.[36] Kazin's depiction of conservative populism is reasonably apt for Richard Nixon, particularly if one focuses on Nixon's use of his first vice president, Spiro Agnew, as a surrogate. Agnew traveled the country denouncing "permissivists," "avowed anarchists and communists," "elitists," the "garbage of society," "thieves, traitors, and perverts," and "radical liberals."[37] Agnew's explicit strategy was to achieve what he called a "positive polarization" of the electorate. In a 1971 speech describing his role in the 1970 elections, Agnew declared that "dividing the American people has been my main contribution to the national political scene since assuming the office of vice president. . . . I not only plead guilty to this charge, but I am somewhat flattered by it."[38] Nixon privately shared Agnew's hatred for the so-called Eastern Establishment, but his public remarks tended to be much more restrained than the rhetoric of both his vice president and his own private conversations.[39]

Reagan, who lacked Nixon's private anger, went further in limiting his populism to economic targets rather than cultural ones. Table 3.1, which lists the subjects of Reagan's populist appeals in his major addresses, shows that Reagan relied heavily on populist appeals when discussing economic matters, but rarely used these appeals when talking about cultural matters.[40] Reagan's most sustained use of populism coincided with two of his major economic initiatives: his 1981 budget battles and his 1985 push to reform the tax system. In 1981, armed with an arsenal of statistics and charts showing economic trend lines, Reagan charged that the "mass of regulations imposed on the shopkeeper, the craftsman, professionals, and major industry . . . is estimated to add $100 billion to the price of the things we buy and it reduces our ability to produce."[41] Reagan's use of statistics underscored that his main concern was with the economic impact of these policies, not their cultural ones. Reagan continued to draw upon populism in 1982 as budgetary issues remained near the top of the agenda, but his major speeches in 1983 and 1984 made scant use of populism (see table 3.1). In those years, Reagan's national addresses focused largely on defense and foreign policy, such as promoting his plans for toppling the Sandinista government in Nicaragua and justifying his policies in Lebanon and Grenada.[42] Where Reagan had used a total of twelve populist appeals in his formal and major addresses in 1981 and 1982, he employed just two in 1983 and 1984.

It was not until 1985, when Reagan once again launched a major economic initiative, that populism returned to prominence in his rhetoric. In his campaign to reform the tax structure, Reagan unleashed the fiercest populist appeals of his entire administration. Soon after his second inaugural address announced the beginning of a "Second American Revolution," Reagan charged that the present tax system was "un-American" and offered a plan that would "reduce tax burdens on the working people of this country, close loopholes that benefit

Table 3.1. Targets of Reagan's Populist Appeals in Major Addresses (based on hand coding)

	Date	Subject of Populist Appeals
Inaugural Address	January 20, 1981	Big government (elites and accountability)
Address to the Nation	February 18, 1981	Big government (cost and accountability)
Address to the Nation	April 28, 1981	Big government (cost)
Address to the Nation	July 27, 1981	Opponents of tax reform
Annual Message	January 26, 1982	Big government (cost and accountability)
Address to the Nation	April 29, 1982	Balanced budget amendment
Address to the Nation	August 16, 1982	Opponents of tax and budget legislation
Address to the Nation	October 13, 1982	Government spending
Address to the Nation	November 22, 1982	Strategic arms defense
Annual Message	January 25, 1983	Food stamps (cost)
Address to the Nation	January 25, 1984	Tax reform
Inaugural Address	January 21, 1985	Big government (cost and accountability)
Address to the Nation	February 6, 1985	Big government (cost)
Address to the Nation	April 24, 1985	Big government (cost, accountability, and elites), Amtrak, and farm subsidies
Address to the Nation	May 28, 1985	Tax reform
Annual Message	February 4, 1986	Big government (cost and accountability), education policy
Address to the Nation	February 26, 1986	Reform of defense appropriations process
Annual Message	January 27, 1987	Big government (cost), welfare system (cost and regulations)
Address to the Nation	June 15, 1987	Economic Bill of Rights
Annual Message	January 25, 1988	Big government (cost)

Note: Major addresses include inaugural addresses, state of the union (annual) messages, and other prime-time, nationally televised speeches.

a privileged few, [and] simplify a code so complex [that] even Albert Einstein reportedly needed help on his 1040 form."[43] As defined by Reagan, the Second American Revolution did not constitute a cultural crusade but an economic revolt against the Internal Revenue Service and government spending.

A primary beneficiary of this economic revolt would be the family. Reagan's lexicon defined family values more in economic terms than cultural or moral ones. Past governmental policies, he contended, had "betrayed families and family values"—not so much because they had espoused malevolent cultural values but because they had caused inflation and bracket creep. In discussing the benefits of his economic policies, Reagan observed that "for years inflation and taxes robbed the family of more and more of its livelihood—an economic factor, of course, but as I say, a moral factor, too."[44] In this regard, Reagan viewed his 1985 tax reforms as the "strongest profamily initiative in postwar history."[45]

After the enactment of tax reform in October 1986, as foreign policy matters again came to dominate the agenda, populism receded as a theme in Reagan's major addresses just as it had in 1983 and 1984 (see table 3.1). Indeed, throughout his presidency, when attention shifted away from economic issues, Reagan generally sought to project an image of the unifier, bringing the country together after a period of division.[46] Discussing civil rights in his 1982 state of the union message, Reagan remarked, "Our nation's long journey towards civil rights for all our citizens— once a source of discord, now a source of pride—must continue with no backsliding or slowing down."[47] Where Agnew had adopted a caustic approach in which specific groups of citizens—such as protesters and "permissivists"—were identified as the enemy, Reagan softened his populism by limiting it to economic issues in which big government played the role of an abstract enemy of the people.

By emphasizing the economic costs of big government rather than its cultural affinities, Reagan also linked his populism to that of FDR and Truman. These Democratic presidents had primarily defined the people in economic terms, using populist rhetoric to depict politics as a struggle between working people and greedy corporate leaders. For example, when fighting for new regulatory and redistributive policies in 1936, Roosevelt declared, "Our resplendent economic autocracy does not want to return to that individualism of which they prate. . . . Give them their way and they will take the course of every autocracy of the past—power for themselves, enslavement for the public."[48] Truman similarly conceived of the people in economic terms. In contrast to the economic autocrats and special interests, Truman identified "the people" as being "mostly made up of those who primarily work with their hands."[49] Reagan also often referred to "working men and women" and "working families" in his speeches. At several rallies in 1982, Reagan asked, "Will we create more jobs by going back to the policies that taxed working families like millionaires? Or is there a better way?"[50] However, when Reagan referred to workers, he was not pitting them in an economic struggle with corporations. His conservative agenda led him to drop the class rhetoric of Roosevelt and Truman, even as he appealed to citizens' economic interests. The key was to focus on the shared interests of a wide range of Americans—workers and businessmen, wealthy and middle class—victimized by the "bloated" federal government. For example, when Democrats attempted to frame his economic recovery program as benefiting the rich and hurting the poor, Reagan responded, "I don't believe it's the job of government to play to the politics of envy or division, to hand to Federal bureaucrats the right to redistribute our people's income in the hope of ushering in some great new utopia. Our economic program will try to help everyone."[51] He pledged that his economic plan would help wealthier Americans, the middle class, working Americans, entrepreneurs, small businessmen, and lower-income individuals. Thus, even as Reagan took a firm stand against class warfare, he appealed to citizens in terms of their ostensible economic interests.[52]

By framing his populism in economic terms, Reagan focused attention on the federal government, an overspending Democratic Congress, and allied liberal special interest groups as the source of America's troubles, while avoiding direct attacks on specific, identifiable classes or groups of Americans.[53] Considering the distinction between economic and cultural populism therefore illuminates the fortieth president's bifurcated image: when pressing his major economic initiatives in 1981, 1982, and 1985, Reagan relied heavily upon populism; when other issues came to the fore, however, he assumed the mantle of the consensual leader seeking to unify the nation.

REAGAN'S POPULISM: THE STRATEGY OF SPECIALIZATION

Just as Reagan limited his populist appeals to a subset of issues, he also employed a strategy of rhetorical specialization that helps to explain his split image as both populist agitator and soft-sell spokesman. With the exception of his efforts to promote his major economic initiatives, Reagan made only limited use of populist appeals in "official" forums, such as his inaugural addresses and state of the union messages. These occasions were primarily used to display the president as a unifying figure—the "soft-sell spokesman" of Robert Dallek. Throughout his term, Reagan reserved most of his populist appeals for other, less formal occasions.

In a content analysis of Reagan's presidential papers, this pattern becomes apparent.[54] Table 3.2 summarizes Reagan's use of populist appeals for each year for four categories of speeches: formal addresses, which consist of inaugural addresses and state of the union messages; other major addresses, which consist of prime-time televised addresses to a national audience; minor addresses, which consist of remarks about governmental affairs such as veto messages, addresses to economic interest groups and cultural groups, and Saturday morning radio addresses; and campaign speeches, which consist of nomination acceptance addresses, speeches to campaign rallies, and speeches on behalf of members of Congress and other elected officials. This table demonstrates that Reagan generally made only limited use of conflictual appeals during formal occasions. In nine inaugural and state of the union messages, Reagan chose to use only seven populist appeals.[55] In most of these cases, the appeals consisted of limited attacks on the "bloated federal establishment."[56] By contrast, Reagan made heavy use of consensual appeals during his formal, nationwide addresses. When talking about Social Security reform, he applauded the American people for their capacity to "pull together for the common good."[57] Reducing the size of the government even comes across as a largely consensual task: "Together we have cut the growth of new Federal regulations nearly in half."[58]

Table 3.2. Populist Appeals across Different Types of Messages during Reagan's Administration, 1981–1989 (based on CD-ROM coding)

	Inaugural Addresses and State of the Union Messages	Other Major Addresses to the Nation	Minor Addresses	Campaign Addresses	Total
1981	2	3	39	0	44
1982	0	7	69	12	88
1983	1	0	82	0	83
1984	0	1	50	37	88
1985	2	6	117	3	128
1986	1	2	82	10	95
1987	1	2	101	0	104
1988	0	2	55	34	91
1989	0	0	10	0	10
Total	7	23	605	96	731

Note: Major addresses include all prime-time, nationally televised addresses.

Though Reagan relied more on populist appeals in nationwide speeches that did not have the formal trappings of state of the union or inaugural addresses, he nonetheless tended to emphasize consensual themes rather than antagonistic ones. This is especially apparent when one compares these addresses with "the Speech" he gave for Goldwater. In the Goldwater speech, Reagan devoted a whole paragraph describing how a young mother on welfare attempts to abuse the system and then derides liberals for supporting such programs. In contrast, as president, Reagan took a more indirect approach in his major prime-time televised addresses. In his address to the nation on the economy, Reagan criticized the welfare system in the following terms: "In the past two decades, we've created hundreds of new programs to provide personal assistance. Many of these programs may have come from a good heart, but not all have come from a clear head—and the costs have been staggering."[59]

A further indication of the tempered nature of Reagan's populist appeals in his major addresses is that he often used them to reinforce his soft-sell approach. For example, in a 1982 address to the nation, Reagan expressed his frustration at special interest groups, which had painted him as an extremist. Reagan noted that these groups had charged that his "budget would deprive the needy, the handicapped, and the elderly of the necessities of life." According to him, these claims had no basis. Yet he avoided charges of bad faith on the part of his opponents, noting that "many of these people were sincere, well intentioned, but also misinformed."[60]

Although he used restrained rhetoric in his major addresses, Reagan burnished his image as populist repudiator of the old order in his minor speeches and in his campaign rhetoric (see table 3.2). He used populist appeals frequently at meetings of economic interest groups (173 times), party functions (79 times), and campaign fund-raisers and rallies (96 times). This record places Reagan near Truman in his reliance on populist appeals (see table 3.3). In these minor addresses, he often repeated the themes of "the Speech." In 1964, he had offered Americans a choice between going down to totalitarianism or up to individual freedom. As president, in a speech to the Conservative Political Action Conference, he gave his audience a choice between the same two alternatives: either "a drab, material-istic world where Big Brother rules by promises to special interest groups" or "a world of adventure where everyday people set their sights on impossible dreams, distant stars, and the Kingdom of God."[61] Speaking at the 1983 Annual Conven-tion of the American GI Forum, Reagan sounded a similar theme when he warned, "Don't let America sink back into the boredom and mediocrity of collectivism, into the politics of envy, protest, and special interests."[62]

Reagan's differential use of populist language in his nationwide and his minor speeches reveals a strategy of specialization, which has become increas-ingly common among presidents in the twentieth century. Although not dealing directly with populist rhetoric, other social scientists have observed a pattern in which politicians and presidents tailor their message to the partisan makeup of their audience. For instance, Aronson finds that when politicians are delivering a message to the party faithful, they are more likely to draw upon more extreme rhetoric than when addressing an audience of mixed loyalties such as in a na-tionwide address.[63]

In the nineteenth century, presidents did not have access to so many different venues for direct communication with the electorate. They were essentially lim-ited to inaugural addresses, state of the union messages, veto messages, and other formal communications of the White House.[64] Given the limited number of ven-ues in which to express presidential views directly to the public, nineteenth-century executives had to make the most out of their formal state communications. Thus, they had to play both the unifying role of the "chief of state" and the more divi-sive role of "prime minister" in their state of the union messages.

In contrast, twentieth-century presidents can afford to specialize. They are able to employ the inaugural and state of the union addresses to highlight their chief of state role, while using other venues to play a more political, prime ministerial role.[65] Reagan was clearly not the first president to rely on this strategy of specialization, but he was a particularly effective practitioner. Where Truman's populist salvos in the 1948 campaign dominated his image for the remainder of his term, Reagan was able to foster a broader coalition by attacking the abstract enemy of big government and refraining from an all-out attack on any specific governmental program or group of individuals. Conse-quently, he was still able to play the unifying role of consensual leader and head of state in his formal addresses. This specialization may explain why scholars have reached such divergent conclusions about Reagan, for he was both a con-sensual leader (in his official rhetoric) and a populist "agitator" (in his campaign speeches and minor addresses).

REAGAN'S POPULIST LEGACY

Reagan's use of populism demonstrated how this traditionally Democratic rhetoric could be appropriated for conservative ends. Reagan, however, was not the first Republican president to practice conservative populism. Richard Nixon, in particular, departed from past Republican presidents by repeatedly drawing upon populist appeals throughout his administration.[66] Table 3.3 demonstrates that Nixon was the first president after Truman to engage in a substantial number of populist appeals. Nixon made a total of 147 populist appeals as president—far short of Truman's 1,238 appeals—but more than his immediate predecessors. The evolution of conservative populism, however, was slow and uneven. Only 17 of Nixon's 147 populist appeals took place in major addresses. In addition, as noted earlier, Nixon contracted out his fiercest populist attacks to his vice president. Agnew's attacks on cultural and social issues did not become a part of the Reagan-era populist formula, which instead emphasized an economic critique of big government.[67]

Reagan's Democratic predecessor, Jimmy Carter, also attempted to cloak his presidency in populist symbolism. Carter famously chose to walk instead of ride down Pennsylvania Avenue after his inauguration and requested that "Hail to the Chief" not be played every time he entered a public place. The Georgia Democrat also used a fair number of populist appeals in his rhetoric,

Table 3.3. Number of Populist Appeals across Four Types of Messages, 1932–1993 (based on CD-ROM coding)

	Inaugural Addresses and State of the Union Messages (Formal)		Other Major Addresses		Minor Addresses	Campaign Addresses	Total
Roosevelt (FDR)	10	(.63)	10	(.34)	57	26	103
Truman	12	(1.50)	42	(1.82)	317	867	1,238
Eisenhower	3	(.30)	5	(.16)	34	22	64
Kennedy	0	(0)	1	(.09)	16	0	17
Johnson	0	(0)	2	(.13)	34	11	47
Nixon	6	(.75)	11	(.40)	110	20	147
Ford	1	(.33)	2	(.22)	109	44	156
Carter	3	(.33)	8	(.62)	196	18	225
Reagan	7	(.77)	23	(.61)	605	96	731
Bush	3	(.60)	6	(.50)	223	137	369
Clinton (1993 only)	0	(0)	5	(1.67)	125	0	130

Note: The average number of populist appeals per address appears in parentheses in the columns for inaugural addresses and state of the union messages, and for other major addresses. Major addresses include all prime-time, nationally televised addresses.

attacking both traditional Democratic targets, such as lobbyists for the wealthy, and newer, conservative targets, such as wasteful congressional spending. The populist mantle, however, did not fit easily on Carter, who approached his presidency through the lens provided by his engineering background. In the end, the mantra of his presidency, "no easy answers," conflicted with populist suspicions about experts.[68] Even Carter's populist assaults against wasteful government projects were framed in terms of the technical language of cost-benefit analysis.[69]

Reagan was considerably more successful than Carter in integrating populism into his leadership approach. Though Reagan relied at times upon statistics in unleashing his attacks on government, these statistics were presented in stark, easy-to-understand terms.[70] Furthermore, from his 1948 anecdote about the ninety-one-year-old Smith L. Carpenter who was forced back to work by "Republican inflation" through his final speeches as president, Reagan skillfully used stories about individual Americans to personalize his argument for his audience. By repeatedly referring back to his status as a citizen politician outside the Washington establishment, Reagan avoided the tension between expertise and populism that pervaded Carter's leadership.

Yet, Reagan's successful integration of populism into his rhetorical leadership did not necessarily set a blueprint for his Republican successors. Compared with Reagan, George H. W. Bush was more restrained in his use of populist appeals in his inaugural addresses, state of the union messages, and other major nationwide speeches (see table 3.3). Interestingly, Bush relied heavily on populist appeals in his minor speeches and especially in his campaign rhetoric. Indeed, in his four years in office, Bush actually employed slightly more populist appeals in his campaign remarks than did Reagan in his eight years in the White House. This extreme form of rhetorical specialization suggests an increasing disconnect between populism as a campaign strategy and populism as an element of a governing strategy. When he sought reelection and campaigned for Republican candidates, he often adopted a conflictual, populist approach. Bush, more than Reagan, needed to convince the base of the Republican Party that he was a true conservative. By sounding populist themes similar to Reagan's on the campaign trail, Bush attempted to establish his own conservative credentials. However, when he sought to gain support for enactment of his policies, Bush generally embraced a more consensual approach.[71]

The rise to the presidency of Bush's son, George W. Bush, also suggests both the limitations and the staying power of Reagan's populist legacy. When lobbying for his tax cut in 2001, Bush borrowed heavily from the Reagan conservative populist playbook, arguing that the "people" know how to spend their money better than "Washington bureaucrats."[72] In contrast, Bush's signature slogan of "compassionate conservatism" harkens back to the other side of

Reagan's rhetorical approach, that of the consensual unifier, the "soft-sell" spokesman. The question is: Which of these images will in the end dominate for Bush and future Republican presidents? In either case, Reagan will have left a significant mark on the rhetorical approach of his Republican successors.

NOTES

1. Robert Dallek, *Ronald Reagan: The Politics of Symbolism* (Cambridge: Harvard University Press, 1984, 1999), 32. Bert Rockman, "The Style and Organization of the Reagan Presidency," in *The Reagan Legacy: Promise and Performance,* ed. Charles O. Jones (Chatham, N.J.: Chatham House Publishers, 1988), 8. For Thomas Cronin quote, see Jack Nelson, "The Reagan Legacy," in *Beyond Reagan: The Politics of Upheaval,* ed. Paul Duke (New York: Warner Books, 1986), 111.

2. Michael Kazin, *The Populist Persuasion: An American History* (New York: Basic Books, 1995), 260–66.

3. Richard Reeves, "The Ideological Election," *New York Times,* February 19, 1984, sec. 6, 26. See also Jeffrey Bell, *Populism and Elitism: Politics in the Age of Equality* (Washington, D.C.: Regnery Gateway, 1992).

4. Peggy Noonan, *What I Saw at the Revolution: A Political Life in the Reagan Era* (New York: Random House, 1990), 143.

5. Populism, in this study, refers to a form of rhetorical appeal that pits the people against a corrupt special interest or minority (see Kazin, *Populist Persuasion,* 1, and Thomas Goebel, "The Political Economy of American Populism from Jackson to the New Deal," *Studies in American Political Development* 11 [spring 1997]: 109–48). This definition of populism as a political argument has the benefit of sidestepping debates over the substance of a populist appeal and whether or not a policy in fact harms the people. Political leaders are able to draw upon populist appeals to promote progressive, conservative, partisan, or personal agendas.

6. Ronald Reagan with Richard G. Hubler, *Where's the Rest of Me?* (New York: Duell, Sloan & Pearce, 1965), 139.

7. Lou Cannon, *Reagan* (New York: G. P. Putnam's Sons, 1982), 79.

8. Transcript taken from "Truman vs. Dewey: Excerpts from a 1948 Union Radio," *Talking History,* October 26, 2000, Segment 5, <http://www.albany.edu/talkinghistory/arch2000july–december.html> (February 12, 2003).

9. "Truman Talks About Why He Ran in '48," <http://www.trumanlibrary.org/whistlestop/study_collections/ 1948campaign/large/docs/ student_activities/sta8–1.htm> (February 12, 2003).

10. Harry Truman, "Remarks at a Dinner Given by the Chairmen and Directors of Federal Reserve Banks," January 16, 1950, *Public Papers of the Presidents of the United States* (Washington, D.C.: Government Printing Office, 1965), 114.

11. Lou Cannon, *President Reagan: The Role of a Lifetime* (New York: Public Affairs, 2000), 25.

12. Kurt Ritter and David Henry, *Ronald Reagan: The Great Communicator* (New York: Greenwood Press, 1992), 44–45.

13. Ronald Reagan, "Farewell Address to the Nation," January 11, 1989, *Public Papers of the Presidents of the United States* (Washington, D.C.: Government Printing Office, 1991), 1721.

14. See Terri Bimes, "The Metamorphosis of Presidential Populism" (Ph.D. diss., Yale University, 1999).

15. Andrew Jackson, "Bank Veto Message," *Compilation of the Messages and Papers of the Presidents* (New York: Bureau of National Literature, 1897), 1153.

16. Interestingly, Reagan's use of an individual citizen's story (in this case, the story of ninety-one-year-old Smith L. Carpenter) to personalize his argument also was a staple of his rhetoric as president. But in his state of the union messages, Reagan tended to use such stories to highlight consensual themes—such as the heroism of individual citizens—rather than as part of his populist appeals.

17. The sources of this ideological shift have been explored by Cannon, *Reagan,* 91–97; William E. Leuchtenburg, *In the Shadow of FDR* (Ithaca, N.Y.: Cornell University Press, 1983), 222–23; and Gary Wills, *Reagan's America: Innocence at Home* (Garden City, N.Y.: Doubleday), 257–58.

18. Ronald Reagan, *Speaking My Mind* (New York: Simon & Schuster, 1989), 21.

19. Cannon, *Reagan,* 67.

20. As reported by Cannon, *Reagan,* 94.

21. Ronald Reagan, *An American Life* (New York: Simon & Schuster, 1990), 129.

22. Reagan, *An American Life,* 129.

23. Reagan and Hubler, *Where's the Rest of Me?* 264.

24. Reagan, *An American Life,* 137. Cannon, *Reagan,* 96. As suggested by Gary Wills, General Electric may have also canceled the show because they were wary of an antitrust suit lodged by the Kennedy Justice Department that named the Screen Actors Guild from the time when Reagan was president as a co-conspirator.

25. As cited in E. J. Dionne, Jr., *Why Americans Hate Politics* (New York: Simon & Schuster, 1991), 204.

26. Stephen Hess and David S. Broder, *The Republican Establishment: The Present and Future of the G.O.P.* (New York: Harper & Row, 1967), 253.

27. Ronald Reagan, *National Review,* December 1, 1964, 1055.

28. Matthew Dallek, *The Right Moment: Ronald Reagan's First Victory and the Decisive Turning Point in American Politics* (New York: Free Press, 2000), 212.

29. Cannon, *Role of a Lifetime,* 30.

30. Ronald Reagan, "Inaugural Address," January 5, 1967, in *Actor, Ideologue, Politician: The Public Speeches of Ronald Reagan,* ed. Davis W. Houck and Amos Kiewe (Westport, Conn.: Greenwood Press, 1993), 40–46.

31. Reagan, *An American Life,* 133.

32. Truman defined the Democratic Party as "the great middle-of-the-road party—the party of the farmers and the workers and the small businessmen and the party of the young people." See "Speech at the State Fairgrounds, Raleigh, North Carolina," October 19, 1948, *Public Papers,* 824.

33. Cannon, *Role of a Lifetime,* 73–77.

34. William Safire, "The Land Is Bright," *New York Times,* January 22, 1981.

35. To operationalize populism in the content analysis, I chose key words that tapped into this conflictual notion of the people against a special interest and searched for these words in the presidential papers. The American Freedom Library (AFL) recently put the

messages and papers of presidents from the eighteenth, nineteenth, and twentieth centuries on CD-ROM. With the help of a research assistant, I then used Boolean searches for twenty-one populist words and phrases in the presidential papers. I searched for such words as "special interest," "interests of the few," and "elite." Within the AFL database, there is also a search function that permits searches of combinations of words within ten words of one another. Searches of this nature were done for "rich-poor," "few-many," and "private-public," among others. After a word or phrase was found in the database, the research assistant read the surrounding text to validate its usage (i.e., to make sure the phrase was used in an antagonistic manner) and also to examine the context itself (e.g., what institutions, class, or programs were being attacked). A full description of the methodology used in the content analysis is available at <http://socrates.berkeley.edu/~bimes>.

36. Kazin, *Populist Persuasion,* chap. 10.

37. As cited in James L. Sundquist, *Dynamics of the Party System: Alignment and Realignment of Political Parties in the United States,* rev. ed. (Washington, D.C.: Brookings Institution Press, 1983), 387.

38. "Divisive but Positive, Agnew Says of Himself," *Washington Post,* October 6, 1971, A2.

39. One example of Nixon's private hatred occurred in April 1971 in a White House meeting with Henry Ford II and Lee Iacocca. During a discussion about environmental protection, Nixon called consumer and environmental advocates "enemies of the system." "They're interested in destroying the system," he charged, while "I am for the system." This kind of rhetoric was rare in Nixon's formal addresses as president. (As cited in Tom Wicker, *One of Us: Richard Nixon and the American Dream* [New York: Random House, 1991], 515–16.)

40. Major addresses include inaugural addresses, state of the union messages, and other prime-time, nationally televised speeches. See Lyn Ragsdale, *Vital Statistics on the Presidency: Washington to Clinton,* rev ed. (Washington, D.C.: Congressional Quarterly, 1998). Prior to the onset of television, major addresses also include nationwide radio broadcasts.

41. Reagan, "Address Before a Joint Session of the Congress on the Program for Economic Recovery," February 18, 1981, *Public Papers,* 109.

42. See Ragsdale, *Vital Statistics on the Presidency,* 164–65.

43. Reagan, "Address to the Nation on Tax Reform," May 28, 1985, *Public Papers,* 678–79. Although Reagan criticized the tax system throughout his administration, his reforms actually strengthened the national government's capacity to collect taxes. See the essay by W. Elliot Brownlee and C. Eugene Steuerle, "Taxation," in this volume.

44. Reagan, "Remarks at a White House Briefing for Supporters of Welfare Reform," February 9, 1987, *Public Papers,* 116.

45. Reagan, "Address to the Nation on Tax Reform," May 28, 1985, *Public Papers,* 678.

46. This is not to say that Reagan's populism was bereft of cultural references. For example, Reagan extolled the values of "diligent toil, moral piety, and self-governing communities" as they sought to mobilize the "moral majority" against a corrupt "liberal establishment" (Kazin, *Populist Persuasion,* 246). During his eight years as president, Reagan also criticized "sophisticated circles" who opposed school prayer, but he did this only in minor addresses, not in any of his major addresses.

47. Reagan, "Address Before a Joint Session of the Congress Reporting on the State of the Union," January 26, 1982, *Public Papers,* 77.

48. Franklin D. Roosevelt, "Annual Message to Congress," January 3, 1936, *The Public Papers and Addresses of Franklin D. Roosevelt,* item 1 (Washington, D.C.: Government Printing Office, 1938).

49. Truman, "Rear Platform and Other Informal Remarks in Michigan and Ohio," September 6, 1948, *Public Papers,* 466.

50. Reagan, "Remarks at a North Carolina Republican Party Rally in Raleigh," October 26, 1982, *Public Papers,* 1388.

51. Reagan, "Remarks at the Republican Congressional 'Salute to President Ronald Reagan Dinner,'" May 4, 1982, *Public Papers,* 557.

52. Reagan's rhetoric also harkens back to Truman's in his repeated reference to his status as the sole representative of the "special interest group" of "we the people." Truman similarly depicted himself as "the people's lobbyist."

53. The special interests attacked by Reagan were rarely identified by name.

54. See footnote 34 above for a summary of the methodology used in the content analysis.

55. One potential concern about the content analysis methodology is that it is plausible that searching for specific terms leads one to miss populist appeals that use phrases that are omitted from the coding scheme. When Reagan's inaugural and state of the union speeches were coded by hand, a few additional populist appeals were found. These findings, however, did not change the general tenor of the results. Reagan made less use of populist appeals in his state of the union and inaugural speeches than in his minor addresses and campaign speeches. It is also worth noting that the appeals found through the hand-coding method tended to be focused on economic rather than cultural issues.

56. Reagan, for instance, said in his second inaugural address, "We must never again abuse the trust of working men and women, by sending their earnings on a futile chase after the spiraling demands of a bloated Federal Establishment," January 21, 1985, *Public Papers,* 56.

57. Reagan, "Address before a Joint Session of the Congress Reporting on the State of the Union," January 25, 1983, *Public Papers,* 103.

58. Reagan, "Address before a Joint Session of the Congress Reporting on the State of the Union," January 26, 1982, *Public Papers,* 73.

59. Reagan, "Address to the Nation on the Program for Economic Recovery," September 24, 1981, *Public Papers,* 833.

60. Reagan, "Address to the Nation on the Fiscal Year 1983 Federal Budget," April 29, 1982, *Public Papers,* 533.

61. Reagan, "Remarks at the Annual Conservative Political Action Conference Dinner," March 2, 1984, *Public Papers,* 289.

62. Reagan, "Remarks at the Annual Convention of the American GI Forum in El Paso, Texas," August 13, 1983, *Public Papers,* 1162.

63. Elliot Aronson, *The Social Animal* (San Francisco: W. H. Freeman, 1972), 70–71.

64. Nineteenth-century presidents did take advantage of partisan newspapers to persuade voters of their favored policies, but in many cases, their participation was concealed. See Mel Laracey, *Presidents and the People: The Partisan Story of Going Public* (College Station: Texas A&M University Press, 2002).

65. Lawrence W. Miller and Lee Sigelman, "Is the Audience the Message? A Note on LBJ's Vietnam Statements," *Public Opinion Quarterly* 42, no. 1 (spring 1978): 71–80.

66. Eisenhower, for example, according to Fred Greenstein (*The Hidden-Hand Presidency: Eisenhower as Leader* [Baltimore: Johns Hopkins University Press, 1982], chap. 1), styled himself as a hidden-hand leader, who studiously avoided "engaging in personali-

ties," and instead sought to use a consensual style that highlighted his role as chief of state rather than prime minister. Prior to Nixon, the sole Republican president who relied extensively on populism during his administration was Theodore Roosevelt, but Roosevelt used populism to promote his progressive reform agenda rather than on behalf of conservatism. Herbert Hoover made only limited use of populist appeals as president (Bimes, "Metamorphosis of Presidential Populism").

67. Nixon's political goal of appearing to be a moderate alternative to the Democrats likely limited his use of populism. To this effect, Nixon campaigned with the slogan "Bring Us Together" in 1968 and urged the country in his first inaugural address to tone down its "angry" and "bombastic rhetoric" (Richard Nixon, "Inaugural Address," January 20, 1969, *Public Papers of the Presidents of the United States* [Washington, D.C.: Government Printing Office, 1971], 2). These consensual slogans, while fitting in with his governing agenda, also helped moderate his public image from the 1950s as a zealous anticommunist crusader.

68. Stephen Skowronek, "Bill Clinton in Political Time" (New York: French-American Foundation, 1996), 24.

69. Carter's 1977 attack on water projects seemed an ideal opportunity for the new president to take on a populist stance against the corrupt influence of special interests. Although Carter pointed out that special interests would benefit from specific water projects, his primary focus centered on standards of efficiency and effectiveness. In a March 1977 letter to Congress, Carter explained his rationale for eliminating nineteen projects. Only two were singled out for their benefits to special interests; the other seventeen were eliminated based on economic, legal, and environmental criteria. Carter affirmed that his review process had been "objective, complete, and fair." His decision to delete these projects was motivated out of a "commitment to fiscal responsibility, environmental quality, and human safety." (Carter, "Water Resource Projects," March 16, 1977, *Public Papers of the Presidents of the United States* [Washington, D.C.: Government Printing Office, 1977], 454–55.)

70. Before becoming president, Reagan drew many of his statistics from *Reader's Digest*. His statistics as president had a similar quality. See Cannon, *Reagan,* 197.

71. The coding scheme in this paper focuses on identifying conflictual appeals. However, the additional methodology adopted in my book manuscript (Bimes, "Metamorphosis of Presidential Populism") includes hand coding each inaugural address and state of the union message, allowing one to assess directly the extent to which each president used consensual appeals. Using that coding scheme, I conclude that Bush made extensive use of consensual appeals and much more limited use of populist rhetoric. The book manuscript also provides a detailed discussion of the content of consensual appeals.

72. See George W. Bush, "Address of the President to the Joint Session of Congress," February 27, 2001,<http://www.whitehouse.gov/news/release/2001/02/2001028.html> (February 1, 2002). Also see George W. Bush, "Remarks by the President in Billings Montana Welcome Event," March 26, 2001, <http://www.whitehouse.gov/news/releases/2001/03/20010327.html> (February 1, 2002).

PART II
Foreign Policy

4

Sticking to His Guns:
Reagan and National Security

Chester J. Pach, Jr.

"I had an agenda I wanted to get done," Ronald Reagan explained soon after he left the White House. "I came with a script."[1] Parts of the script were familiar—opposition to "big government" and "high taxes" and a determination to diminish both. Also prominent on Reagan's agenda was fortifying national security. Reagan believed that U.S. strength and security had eroded during the 1970s, victims of insufficient vigilance, spending, and resolve. As a candidate for president in 1980, Reagan repeatedly called for the modernization of strategic and conventional forces that would give the United States the means to meet Soviet threats in many regions and on several levels. Most of the administration's main defense policies or programs Reagan had advocated as candidate. The principal exception was the Strategic Defense Initiative, although Reagan had occasionally discussed his discontent with mutual assured destruction (MAD) and his interest in finding an alternative.

Reagan wrote most of the script he brought to the White House. Recent openings of personal papers show that candidate Reagan read extensively about defense and national security matters, discussed these issues on trips to East Asia, Africa, and Europe, and frequently wrote about them. Between 1975 and 1979, Reagan drafted hundreds of scripts for a regular weekly radio program of political commentary. Many of them concerned national security, including the nuclear balance, arms control, defense spending, and new weapons systems. Once he became president, Reagan remained engaged with a wide variety of issues, as the presidential handwriting file at the Ronald Reagan Library reveals. He answered correspondence, wrote substantial drafts of his own speeches, and debated issues with correspondents. "Some in the media delight in trying to portray me as being manipulated and lead [*sic*] around by the nose," he wrote in a letter in May 1982, "but I'm in charge and my people are helping to carry out the policies I set."[2] Reagan did set policies, although they did not preclude strong, persistent, and even fundamental divisions among his advisers. Sometimes he made controversial choices, such as providing arms to Iran in the hope of securing the release of U.S. hostages in Lebanon, which produced sharp disagreements among top defense and foreign policy officials. Still, on national security matters, Reagan had a core set of beliefs or ideas, which he developed—sometimes at length—prior to his presidency and which guided his decisions once he entered the White House.

PRINCIPLES, POLICIES, AND PROPOSALS

The ailing economy may have been the voters' greatest concern in 1980, but Ronald Reagan also made restoring national security a central theme of his campaign. Many people remember the famous question that Reagan posed at the conclusion of his debate with Jimmy Carter. "Are you better off than you were four years ago?" he told people to ask themselves as they made their choice on election day. Yet that was only the first in a series of questions that called attention to what Reagan believed was declining U.S. international power and reputation as well as a weakening economy with high inflation, interest rates, and unemployment. "Is America as respected throughout the world as it was?" he also asked voters to consider as they made their decisions. "Do you feel that our security is as safe? That we're as strong as we were four years ago?" Rebuilding national strength—military and economic—was Reagan's most important goal.[3]

Reagan believed that the renewal of national power was essential to meet the dangers of international communism in an intensified cold war. In some ways, Reagan's campaign rhetoric resembled Carter's, after the president drastically revised his assessment of Soviet intentions in the wake of the Red Army's invasion of Afghanistan in December 1979. Yet Reagan had repeatedly warned about communist threats to U.S. security long before Carter's conversion. Antipathy toward communism was one of Reagan's core convictions. Reagan considered communism an abhorrent ideology, one that lacked moral legitimacy. It "is neither an economic or [sic] a political system—it is a form of insanity—a temporary aberration which will one day disappear from the earth because it is contrary to human nature," he told radio listeners in May 1975. Reagan also insisted that communists were completely unscrupulous. "They say that any crime including lying is moral if it advances the cause of socialism," he asserted. These criticisms anticipated Reagan's blunt condemnation of Soviet leaders at his first press conference after becoming president, when he declared that "the only morality they recognize is what will further their cause, meaning they reserve unto themselves the right to commit any crime, to lie, to cheat."[4]

What made the Soviets so dangerous, Reagan said frequently, was that they had carried out "the biggest military buildup in the history of man."[5] Reagan traced the origins of this military expansion to the Soviet retreat during the Cuban missile crisis; it aimed at ensuring, as one Kremlin official explained, that "never will we be caught like this again."[6] By the early 1970s, the Soviets had achieved strategic parity with the United States and even gained numerical advantages in land-based intercontinental ballistic missiles and submarine-launched ballistic missiles. Reagan deplored the end of U.S. strategic superiority, which he considered the ultimate guarantor of national security. He also found alarming Soviet increases in naval strength, tactical aircraft, and long-range bombers. He warned that these new conventional capabilities supported a Soviet "drive for dominance in the Middle East, the Indian Ocean, Africa and the South Atlantic" and threatened the "political independence of our allies and access for them, and us, to raw materials and the freedom of the seas."[7] During the campaign of 1980, he asserted that the Soviet Union had surpassed the United States in most measures of military strength. He also emphasized that the Soviets were spending far more than the United States on defense, even though their economy was considerably smaller.[8] The magnitude of the Soviet military effort and the efficiency of Soviet armaments industries were controversial subjects that divided intelligence professionals. So, too, were the purposes of this vast expansion of military capabilities.[9] Yet Reagan expressed no doubts about the Kremlin's objectives: the Soviets aimed at world domination on the basis of offensive military strength.[10]

Contributing to the Soviet surge in power, Reagan believed, was a weakening of U.S. resolve. Reagan maintained that Carter had "sacrifice[d] our technological lead" by canceling some sophisticated weapons, such as the neutron bomb—"the dreamed of death ray of science fiction"—and cutting the funding or delaying the deployment of others, such as the MX missile and the Trident submarine. He harshly criticized Carter's decision in 1977 to halt production of the B1 bomber. Although polls showed public approval for the president's action, Reagan reached a different conclusion.[11] "I've found, out in the country there is an unease on the part of the people about our *entire* defense posture and the cancellation of the B1 is kind of symbolic of that unease."[12] Reagan alleged that administration officials were not "telling us the truth" when they declared that the aging B52 was an adequate and less costly substitute for the B1.[13] In September 1979, he informed radio listeners about a correspondent for the *Washington Star,* who flew on a B52 mission and watched the crew wedge a tin can into the instrument panel to make unreliable navigation equipment function properly. The reporter, Arthur Hadley, worried that this "hunk of frazzled wires" was "our first line of defense." "America has never gotten in a war because we were too strong," Reagan declared in his debate with Carter. But weakness in the face of danger only invited aggression, he insisted. As important as strength, though, was determination. "Only by mustering a superiority, beginning with a superiority of the spirit," Reagan declared, "can we stop the thunder of hobnailed boots on their march to world empire."[14]

Reagan feared that Soviet leaders were thinking the unthinkable about nuclear war. He began warning in the mid-1970s that Soviet defense officials thought victory was possible in an all-out nuclear exchange. He drew on the writings of U.S. defense experts, some of whom had founded the Committee on the Present Danger in late 1976 to call attention to what they believed was the vulnerability of the U.S. strategic deterrent and the possibility of a disarming Soviet first strike.[15] In many ways, Reagan's thinking accorded with that of Harvard University historian Richard E. Pipes, who wrote in a highly influential article in *Commentary* magazine that the Kremlin's goals were "not deterrence, but victory; not sufficiency in weapons but superiority; not retaliation, but offensive action."[16] A prominent member of the Committee on the Present Danger, Pipes also served on the Central Intelligence Agency's Team B, a group of outside experts who believed that the government's National Intelligence Estimates had underrated "the intensity, scope, and implicit threat" of Soviet strategic programs.[17] Reagan summarized the threat starkly when he told the Veterans of Foreign Wars (VFW) in August 1980 that the Soviets "seek a superiority in nuclear strength that, in the event of a confrontation, would leave us with a choice of surrender or die." In several earlier radio commentaries, he discussed a speech that Leonid I. Brezhnev made to a secret meeting of communist leaders in 1973 in which the Soviet president predicted "a decisive shift in the correlation of forces" by 1985 so that "we will be able to extend our will wherever we need to." Brezhnev, according to Reagan, was faithfully following Lenin's dictum that "it would not matter if three-fourths of the human race perished; the important thing is that the remaining one-fourth be communist." Reagan also noted ominously that Brezhnev declared that "to tie one's hands in advance and to openly tell an enemy who is presently armed that we *will* fight him and when is stupidity."[18]

In view of his interpretation of Soviet strategic thinking, Reagan doubted that MAD was a reliable deterrent. Many times Reagan emphasized that there was no defense against nuclear war. Occasionally he lamented the abandonment of earlier programs aimed at providing defense against a missile attack. "We settled for something called mutual destruction," he wrote in September 1979. "Today there is reason to question that as an adequate defense." Yet it was by no means clear that Reagan ever placed much confidence in MAD. Instead he thought that U.S. nuclear superiority had provided the strongest guarantee of security. "Peace was never more certain," he declared, than "when we had the mightiest military force in the world and a monopoly on nuclear weapons." The overwhelming U.S. strategic advantage, he believed, had prevented a disaster during the Cuban missile crisis. Nuclear parity, he insisted, left the United States vulnerable. "No one denies that the Russians have assembled an offensive force of tanks, mobile artillery, support aircraft and armored personnel carriers on the Western front in Europe superior to our NATO forces," he explained to a radio audience in March 1978. "Until recently our deterrent was nuclear superiority. If the Soviets attacked Western Europe we could threaten Russia with nuclear destruction. That of course is no longer true." Restoring U.S. security required rebuilding U.S. defenses, perhaps even regaining strategic advantages. "We can have the strategic superiority we had in 1962 if we have the will," he insisted. The alternative was to have "our national leaders face the 1980s alone, with nothing but a broad smile and good intentions to protect us in our final days."[19] During the 1980 campaign, he told the VFW, "I've called for whatever it takes to be so strong that no other nation will dare violate the peace. If that means superiority, so be it."[20]

Reagan's prescription for strengthening U.S. security required avoiding SALT. The strategic arms limitations talks, in Reagan's view, had only sanctioned Soviet military advantages. During the late 1970s, Reagan launched a barrage of criticism against SALT. Experienced Soviet negotiators, he said, had "out traded" Carter administration diplomats, who wanted a treaty "simply for the sake of having" one. He insisted that Soviet concessions involved only U.S. weapons systems under development, while "our team" retreated on including existing Soviet weapons, such as the Backfire bomber, under treaty limitations. Even worse were "unilateral concessions"—such as cancellation of the B1 and the neutron bomb—which deprived U.S. negotiators of leverage at the conference table. The result, in Reagan's view, was that SALT II, which Carter and Brezhnev signed in June 1979, was a flawed agreement that allowed the Soviets to maintain all their strategic advantages.[21]

At times Reagan directed his criticism specifically at this treaty; at times, he suggested that arms control agreements—especially with the Soviets—were a bad idea. "The Russians don't keep their word," he stated categorically, and he cited former Secretary of Defense Melvin R. Laird, who wrote that the Soviets had "repeatedly, flagrantly, and . . . contemptuously violated the treaties to which we have adhered." Whether or not the Soviets kept their word, historical experience, Reagan insisted, showed that arms control agreements neither brought nor maintained peace. "One thing stands out sharply," he said in a radio broadcast in March 1978. "No nation which put it's faith in treaties but let it's [sic] military hardware deteriorate stayed around very long." Yet Reagan also said that he favored a verifiable agreement that called for equality in U.S. and Soviet nuclear strength and that diminished "the effect of nuclear weapons on world politics." Ultimately, he hoped for "a reduction of these nuclear weapons to the point that neither one of us represents a threat to the other." "I cannot, however, agree to a treaty—specifically, the SALT II treaty, which, in effect, legitimizes a nuclear arms buildup," he told the VFW at the beginning of the 1980 campaign. Indeed, a year earlier he wondered whether it would be worse to have "an unrestrained arms race which the U.S. could not possibly lose given our industrial superiority or a treaty (SALT II) which says that the arms race is over and that we have lost it."[22]

SALT exemplified what Reagan saw as fundamental problems with détente. The failures of détente during the 1970s were central to Reagan's thinking about national security. Sometimes he dismissed that strategy with a quip. "Détente—

isn't that what a farmer has with his turkey—until thanksgiving day?" he asked in one radio commentary. In another he used an analogy with a different animal. "To those who think 'détente' is working because things seem to be quiet right now," Reagan explained, "it's always quiet when you are feeding the alligator—when you throw him an arm or leg every now and then—when you drop Angola or Somalia over the side without much of a splash, when you kill the B1 and abort the MX missile. Under those circumstances . . . things are bound to be quiet—except for the munching and crunching."[23] Reagan considered détente at worst as tantamount to appeasement, at best as a misguided strategy that worked mainly to the advantage of the Soviets. He said Brezhnev had boasted that "we are achieving with détente what our predecessors have been unable to achieve using the mailed fist." When Kremlin officials warned that criticism of their human rights policies might harm Soviet-American relations, Reagan remarked to his radio listeners, "I don't know about you but I didn't exactly tear my hair and go into a panic at the possibility of losing détente."[24] Reagan only restated long-standing criticisms when he declared at his first presidential news conference in January 1981, "Well, so far détente's been a one-way street that the Soviet Union has used to pursue its own aims."[25]

Reagan proposed a different strategy based on strength and principle. Speaking to the Chicago Council of Foreign Relations in March 1980, he stressed that "we must have the unquestioned military ability to preserve world peace and our national security." Achieving these goals meant bolstering the U.S. strategic deterrent, maintaining a superior navy, improving readiness, and drawing on innovations in science and technology. Reagan proposed to use this strength to refurbish "our reputation with our allies" and to stand firmly against such threats as the expansionist designs of "the Moscow-Havana axis" in Central America. Yet as important as power was conviction, "a clear vision of, and belief in America's future." The "vacillation, appeasement and aimlessness" of recent years had taken a toll, as had "humiliations and symbols of weakness. . . . We apologize, compromise, withdraw and retreat; we fall silent when insulted and pay ransom when we are victimized." "The American success story used to be a shining example, something that other people aspired to. It was and can still be the American dream. But the world must see that we still believe in that dream." Rearmament, a rejuvenated economy, and renewed spirit were all essential components of Reagan's strategy for restoring U.S. strength.[26]

HOW MUCH IS ENOUGH?

"Defense is not a budget issue. You spend what you need." Although Reagan often repeated this aphorism, spending on military programs was indeed a critical budget issue during the Reagan administration's early months. The administration gave first priority to economic matters; polls consistently showed that the public considered high inflation, interest rates, and unemployment their most urgent concerns. Reagan and his chief advisers were determined to change the whole approach to fiscal and economic questions that had dominated Washington thinking for more than a generation. Yet critical to Reagan's unconventional goal of substantially cutting taxes while still balancing the budget was how much to spend on defense. Swift action was essential, since the president decided to capitalize on his overwhelming election victory and public support for action by formulating an economic program that he would announce on February 18 in a televised address.

The policymaker who was supposed to make the numbers add up was David Stockman, the new director of the Office of Management and Budget (OMB). Stockman considered himself a Reagan revolutionary, one who was ardent but somewhat naïve. Reared in "the truths of Christianity and Republicanism," he fell into "the clutches of campus radicalism" while attending Michigan State University in the 1960s, only to discover "that the left was inherently totalitarian." After this jolting experience with left deviationism, Stockman regained his ideological bearings and became an unwavering advocate of supply-side economics while working on the staff of the House Republican Conference and serving two terms as a representative from Michigan. As budget director, Stockman aimed at radical change—sweeping away "forty years' worth of promises, subventions, entitlements, and safety nets issued to . . . every component and stratum of society" and replacing it with "minimalist government." Achieving this purest form of the Reagan Revolution, the OMB director recognized, required "mortal political combat with all the mass constituencies of Washington's largesse."[27]

Stockman did not expect to do battle with defense advocates, since minimalist government would not prevail at the Pentagon. Raising defense spending in real terms—beyond the level of inflation—was one of Reagan's fundamental policy goals. Stockman embraced the president's objective and described himself as a defense hawk, a conviction that solidified after "watching the grim footage of the charred remains of the U.S. servicemen" who died in April 1980 during the failed attempt to rescue U.S. hostages in Iran.[28] It took Stockman and Secretary of Defense Caspar W. Weinberger less than a half hour when they met at the latter's Pentagon office on January 30 to agree on a plan for 7 percent real annual growth in defense spending over five years. They settled on that figure by splitting the difference between the 5 percent increases that the outgoing Carter administration had proposed and the 9 percent hikes that some members of Weinberger's staff favored. The secretary agreed to the compromise, although he considered it "lean" in view of "the disgraceful mess we're inheriting."[29]

Despite Weinberger's deprecating language, the Reagan administration accelerated a defense build-up that the Carter administration had begun. During his last two years in office, Carter asked Congress for increases in the defense budget of 5 percent and 6 percent, respectively. If he had won a second term, Carter planned to spend $1.27 trillion on defense during fiscal years 1982 through 1986, a figure that the Reagan administration increased by $184 billion. The actual or proposed increases in defense allocations during the last two years of the Carter administration constituted a reversal from Carter's earlier decisions to pare spending on many strategic weapons programs. Yet increased U.S.–Soviet tensions, especially after the invasion of Afghanistan at the end of 1979, and domestic criticism of the administration's national security policies encouraged Carter to support new strategic weapons systems, such as the MX missile and the Trident II submarine. Yet for Weinberger and Reagan, Carter remained the president who canceled the B1 and halted production of the neutron bomb. There were indeed substantial differences between Carter's and Reagan's defense policies, but Reagan administration officials tended to exaggerate them.[30]

Stockman and Weinberger should have spent less time criticizing the Carter administration and more checking their own figures, as their budget deal was all too casual and careless. As he sat in Weinberger's office, Stockman punched figures into a pocket calculator, while aides recorded the results on pieces of paper. Neither principal made decisions on the basis of detailed defense planning. As policymakers raced to put together the president's economic program, Stockman decided that an extensive review of defense spending would "blow out the White House circuits." After just ten days in office, Weinberger and his staff had only had time to designate a few items in the Carter administration's fiscal year (FY) 1982 defense budget for "get well" increases. Haste, improvisation, and expediency prevailed throughout the planning of Reagan's economic program, as policymakers rushed to meet the February 18 deadline. Translating percentage increases into dollar figures produced highly uncertain results, as Stockman relied on optimistic, multiyear projections of economic growth and inflation that were at best speculative, at worst the product of wishful thinking or political convenience.

When Stockman finally "took a hard look" at the defense figures several weeks later, he discovered that he had made a colossal error. To calculate the cost of the annual defense increases to which he and Weinberger had agreed, Stockman had started with FY 1982, the first full budget year of the Reagan administration, rather than FY 1980, the last of the Carter administration. By building on this higher base—one that included Carter's increases as well as Weinberger's "get well" additions—Stockman projected that defense spending would grow during FY 1980–1986 at an average annual rate of 10 percent. If Pentagon spending rose so drastically, Stockman knew that there would be no prospect of achieving a balanced federal budget by the end of Reagan's first term.[31]

Fixing this error proved to be far more difficult than Stockman ever imagined. Weinberger simply refused to concede that Stockman had miscalculated. Instead, he insisted that Pentagon planners needed every dollar for essential programs. Stockman resented Weinberger's resistance, especially since the secretary had himself been budget director during the Nixon administration and had earned the nickname "Cap the Knife" for his efforts to slash federal spending. Yet Weinberger, who had served as California's finance director while Reagan was governor and as a senior adviser during the campaign of 1980, appreciated how strongly the president supported higher defense spending, especially after the secretary announced in early March that the administration planned to commit $1.46 trillion to military programs during the next five years. "There must be no perception by anyone in the world that we're backing down an inch on the defense buildup," Reagan told his advisers in early August when Stockman proposed to hold the size of the military expansion to $1.33 billion to compensate for his error. "When I was asked during the campaign about what I would do if it came down to a choice between defense and deficits, I always said national security would come first, and the people applauded every time."[32] Recent public opinion surveys seemed to confirm Reagan's analysis. Richard B. Wirthlin, the president's pollster, found that despite widespread concern about the economy, 73 percent of the public favored "a tougher attitude" toward the Soviet Union and 64 percent preferred higher defense spending.[33]

Stockman's frustrations deepened as he realized that he was fighting a losing battle. As earlier projections for a "Rosy Scenario" of strong economic growth gave way to the reality of impending recession, Stockman warned of a budget deficit of at least $75 billion in FY 1984 and proposed defense savings that would eliminate $15 billion in red ink. Yet Weinberger did not yield. He resorted to a favorite tactic, which was to "take a position and never change."[34] At "showdown" meetings with the president, Stockman's adversaries completely outmaneuvered him. They insisted that his deficit projections showed a lack of faith in the president's tax and budget programs, which Reagan had only signed into law on August 13 and had yet to take effect. They also maintained that his "slower growth alternative" would impede the restoration of U.S. military strength. At one briefing, Weinberger showed Reagan "a blown-up cartoon" with figures that represented the supposed results of the OMB and Pentagon budgets. The former was "a four-eyed wimp . . . carrying a tiny rifle," while the latter was "G.I. Joe himself . . . all decked out in helmet and flak jacket and pointing an M60 machine gun." Reagan, who disliked such disputes, eventually mediated a settlement, but on terms that both he and Weinberger preferred. The solution called for a reduction in planned defense spending of $6 billion, less than 10 percent of the projected FY 1984 deficit. Stockman bitterly concluded that "the whole episode was a critical turning point . . . when I ceased to believe that the Reagan Revolution was possible."[35]

MEANS AND ENDS

Stockman complained that the Pentagon was spending not just lavishly but recklessly. He expected that the budget figures to which he and Weinberger agreed in January 1981 would change, as administration officials balanced "what we could afford and what we felt we needed." That reckoning never occurred. Instead, according to Stockman, the Pentagon bureaucracy absorbed every dollar "down to the last six-hundred dollar ashtray." Richard A. Stubbing, another OMB official, insisted that the "military services were stunned. . . . [They] simply went to the shelf and took off everything that had been on their wish lists, even low-priority items." As military budgets rose, congressional defense reformers also complained about waste and extravagant spending, but their most powerful argument was that the most expensive equipment was not the most reliable or effective—that more money did not necessarily buy more security.[36]

Yet however much waste or profligacy prevailed at the Pentagon, these defense programs still had broad objectives that reflected Reagan's long-standing views. Most important was building both strategic and conventional capabilities to meet the global challenge of the Soviet Union. Weinberger maintained that paying the bill for what he misleadingly called years of neglect required replacing all three elements of the nuclear triad—with a reinstated B1 bomber program, Trident submarines, and MX missiles. Nuclear strength, the secretary explained, was no substitute for conventional forces that could hold key positions in such vital regions as the Persian Gulf or blunt Soviet attacks in other critical areas. Weinberger announced, for example, that the navy would increase its size to six hundred ships, an increase of about 30 percent over its strength during the Carter administration. New thinking, the secretary declared, had to accompany new equipment. "The first change needed . . . is a clear recognition that we face adversaries with serious long-term goals incompatible with our own and that we must, therefore, undertake a sustained effort to increase the ability of the United States and our allies to protect our common interests and to deter the use of force."[37]

Yet there was more muddled than new thinking in dealing with the complexities of deploying the MX missile. Reagan saw the MX—a missile that could carry ten independently targeted warheads—as essential to closing what he and many other defense advocates called "the window of vulnerability," the possibility of Soviet missiles equipped with new and more precise guidance systems carrying out a disarming first strike against U.S. land-based missiles. The effectiveness of the MX in closing the alleged window depended on basing it so it would be less vulnerable than the Minuteman missiles, located in fixed silos, that the MX would replace. The Carter administration proposed a mobile system that shuttled the missiles among many possible launch sites. Even in the restricted form that Carter's secretary of defense, Harold Brown, eventually endorsed, this basing system was highly controversial, as it required considerable tracts of land in Utah and Nevada.[38]

Weinberger rejected a basing system that provoked political opposition in strongly Republican states and that included Senator Paul Laxalt of Nevada, a close friend of Reagan. Weinberger considered several other possibilities, including one known as DUMB—deep underground missile basing—that would embed the missile deep in the earth and then elevate it for launching. Eventually Weinberger decided on a limited deployment of MX missiles in existing, fixed silos, while proceeding with further studies of alternative basing systems. Reagan rather casually approved Weinberger's plan on September 28, 1981. The president and the secretary of defense announced their plans for the MX at a news conference four days later. When asked why the MX would be any less vulnerable than the Minuteman, Reagan replied, "I don't know but what maybe you haven't gotten into the area that I'm going to turn over to the Secretary of Defense."[39]

Weinberger encountered his own problems answering similar questions about the administration's MX basing proposal. Unable to overcome skepticism in Congress, Weinberger eventually endorsed a new plan, known as "Dense Pack." The MX missiles would be clustered together, and some would survive an attack because the incoming missiles would suffer from fratricide—the first exploding warhead would destroy those that followed. The problem with fratricide, though, was that it was a theory, untested and untestable, owing to limits on atmospheric nuclear explosions under the Limited Nuclear Test Ban Treaty of 1963. Many defense experts doubted that the Dense Pack system would work; the Joint Chiefs of Staff divided over endorsing the basing system; and many members of Congress were skeptical. Indeed, on December 7, 1982, the House of Representatives voted against the administration's request to fund the MX.[40]

Finally, the administration turned the question of MX basing over to the President's Commission on Strategic Forces. This bipartisan group included four former secretaries of defense, two previous secretaries of state, and two ex-directors of central intelligence. Brent Scowcroft, national security adviser during the Ford administration, chaired the commission. In April 1983, the Scowcroft commission recommended the deployment of MXs in fixed silos and argued that there was no risk in doing so, as the Soviets could not simultaneously destroy the missiles and the U.S. nuclear bomber fleet. The commission provided the political leverage that made possible congressional approval of the MX program. Yet the defense experts also maintained that the "window of vulnerability"—a major justification for the procurement of the MX—was no danger, after all.[41]

Military strength, including the MX, had a central role in the policy toward the Soviet Union in National Security Decision Directive 75 (NSDD 75), which Reagan approved in January 1983. The administration aimed at both resisting "Soviet imperialism" and diminishing its sources. The principal method of preventing "unacceptable behavior" was inflicting costs that exceeded gains. Doing so required modernization of U.S. strategic and conventional forces so that Soviet leaders understood that any attack would produce intolerable losses. Yet as important as U.S. power was the will to keep building it and to use it. "Sustaining steady, long-term growth in U.S. defense spending and capabilities—both nuclear and conventional— . . . is the most important way of conveying to the Soviets U.S. resolve and political staying power." Arms control should not interfere with "necessary force modernization plans." The Strategic Arms Reduction Talks (START) should aim at achieving "balanced, significant, and verifiable reductions to equal levels of comparable armaments."[42] During 1983 and 1984, the Reagan administration moved away from hard-line policies, such as those in NSDD 75, toward more moderate efforts to engage the Soviets. Yet even as that transition occurred, Reagan continued to insist that increased spending on strategic and conventional programs was essential to protect U.S. national security. This is precisely what Reagan had been saying about defense policy for years before he took office.

LEGACIES OF VIETNAM AND USES OF FORCE

Preventing "another Vietnam" was a powerful imperative that shaped public debate and official thinking about national security policy in the aftermath of that disastrous war. Yet there was sharp disagreement about what had gone wrong in Southeast Asia. Some people counseled against intervention in civil wars in Third World countries where U.S. interests were peripheral and limited involvement could lead progressively to the dispatch of combat troops.[43] For Reagan, however, avoiding "another Vietnam" had a very different meaning. Using power effectively, he asserted, required ridding "ourselves of the Vietnam syndrome," recognizing the "moral courage" of Americans who fought in Vietnam, and "never again . . . asking young men to fight and die in a war that our government is afraid to let them win."[44] Reagan's explanation, frequently repeated, offered solace to those who had trouble accepting defeat and who yearned for vindication of the U.S. war effort.[45] It became so popular that even the title character in the notorious film *Rambo, First Blood, Part II*, when asked to undertake a risky mission to rescue U.S. prisoners of war still in captivity in Southeast Asia, inquired, "Sir, do we get to win this time?"[46]

The most obvious possibility of "another Vietnam" was Central America, where revolution and civil war had attracted U.S. involvement and ignited controversy. In July 1979, Anastasio Somoza, the last ruler in a family dictatorship that had controlled Nicaragua since the 1930s, yielded power to the Sandinista National Liberation Front headed by Daniel Ortega. The Carter administration, which had hoped for a moderate alternative to both Somoza and Ortega, continued economic aid to the new government while trying to avoid pushing it farther to the left. The Carter administration also supported the conservative government of El Salvador in its war against the Farabundo Martí Front for National Liberation (FMLN). Reagan condemned both the "leftist" regime in Nicaragua and the "Marxist-totalitarian revolutionaries" in El Salvador. Behind the strife in both countries, he asserted, were Soviets and Cubans, who aimed at spreading their influence throughout Central America.[47]

Reagan's advisers divided over how to deal with what they interpreted as a threat to U.S. security and credibility. One of the most vociferous advocates of forceful action was Secretary of State Alexander M. Haig, Jr. Experience as a career military officer in Vietnam and as a staff member of the National Security Council (NSC) during the presidency of Richard M. Nixon persuaded Haig that Central America was where the Reagan administration should "draw the line" against communist expansionism. Doing so required going "to the source," which, Haig said, was Cuba. At a meeting of the National Security Council in March 1981, he told Reagan, "Just give me the word and I'll make that fucking island a parking lot." Pragmatic advisers, committed to achieving what was politically possible, reacted in horror. Michael Deaver, the president's deputy chief of staff, recollected that Haig's bellicosity "scared the shit out of me" and had the same effect on the president. Military action in Central America or the Caribbean, the pragmatists knew, would jeopardize congressional approval of the administration's tax and budget reforms as well as the proposed increases in defense spending. By the end of 1981, the administration had settled on the main outlines of its policies toward Central America—military and economic aid for El Salvador, covert logistical and training assistance to the contras to enable them to fight the Sandinistas. The covert support to the Nicaraguan counterrevolutionaries marked the beginning of policies that eventually became part of the Iran-Contra scandal.[48]

The divisions between hard-liners—such as Haig, CIA director William E. Casey, and ambassador to the United Nations Jeane Kirkpatrick—and pragmatists—including Deaver and chief of staff James A. Baker—persisted on many issues, including those involving the use of force. Partly they endured because of the president's distaste for making conclusive decisions and his preference for letting staff members with different opinions "work out the details." Sometimes, however, the "details" involved substantial, not just incidental, matters. Occasionally, the president's actions in fractious meetings were so inscrutable that aides tried to figure out whether a tilt of the head or a particular anecdote indicated approval of their position. Partly the cleavages continued because different factions disagreed over whether they were best serving the president by accomplishing as much as possible of his agenda or by faithfully adhering to what they thought were his basic principles.[49]

Yet Reagan may have had stronger views about sending troops to Central America than some of his advisers realized. Reagan understood that avoiding "another Vietnam" meant securing public support for any commitment of ground forces. Yet polls consistently showed that a majority of Americans were wary of U.S. involvement in Central America. A Gallup survey in March 1982, for example, revealed that 71 percent of the public opposed the dispatch of U.S. troops to El Salvador even if there was no other way to prevent an FMLN victory. Three years later, half of the people who knew that the Reagan administration was helping the contras preferred halting all aid, while 42 percent favored its continuation. And 59 percent predicted that it was "very" or "fairly" likely that Nicaragua could become another Vietnam. Reagan also privately criticized those Americans "far to the right" who would "have marched in the troops." Those zealots did not understand the "image in Latin America of the big colossus to the north sending in the Marines." "Those sonsofbitches won't be happy until we have 25,000 troops in Managua," the president complained, "and I'm not going to do it."[50]

The Reagan administration tried to avert the use of force during the Falklands crisis between Argentina and Great Britain. The British ruled the Falklands, but the Argentinians insisted that they had sovereignty over what they called the Malvinas. After a long dispute, Argentine marines occupied the capital city of Port Stanley at the beginning of April 1982. Haig flew between Buenos Aires and London, but his shuttle diplomacy produced only disappointment and frustration. He complained that Argentinian duplicity and bad faith hampered his efforts, but probably no negotiator could have found common ground in the antagonistic positions of the two governments. British forces reached the Falklands at the end of April and defeated the Argentinians within a month. The Reagan administration supported Great Britain with military equipment and intelligence. Although he had hoped for a peaceful solution, Haig eventually concluded that the British action had helped to dispel the "delusion" that Western democracies were "too soft, too decadent" to defend themselves.[51]

Reagan ruled out any U.S. military involvement in the Falklands, but he made a controversial decision to use U.S. Marines to help bring peace to Lebanon. Civil war had ravaged Lebanon since 1975; violence increased when the Palestine Liberation Organization (PLO) shifted its base from Jordan to Lebanon. In June 1982, Israeli forces invaded, and U.S. negotiator Philip Habib tried to stop the fighting. Reagan announced U.S. participation in a multinational peacekeeping force to bolster Habib's mediation efforts. The president made his decision at an awkward moment in July, just after Haig's resignation and before the new secretary of state, George P. Shultz, had taken over. Shultz eventually supported the U.S. military presence because he thought it provided diplomatic leverage. But Weinberger objected to putting U.S. forces into a volatile situation. Weinberger lost the argument, and U.S. Marines helped carry out an agreement to evacuate the PLO from Lebanon before themselves departing in mid-September.

Days later, Lebanon once more exploded. A bomb killed the Lebanese president-designate; Israeli forces moved back into West Beirut; and Lebanese militia slaughtered hundreds of Palestinian civilians while the Israeli troops took no action. The killings and turmoil persuaded Reagan to send the marines back to participate in a new multinational force that could help end "Lebanon's agony," restore "a stable government," and bring "a just and lasting resolution to the conflict between Israel and its Arab neighbors." Shultz and Weinberger clashed over the new deployment, the first of many disputes that defined the most significant cleavage between Reagan's national security advisers. Reagan expected that the marines would stay for only "a limited period." But a year later, they remained in Beirut, immersed in disputes between warring factions. At an NSC meeting on October 18, 1983, Weinberger warned that the marines were "sitting on a bull's eye" and recommended their redeployment to ships along the coast. Shultz dissented; the president agreed with him; the marines stayed.[52]

There was no disagreement—at least among the president's top advisers—about sending U.S. combat troops to Grenada in October 1983. Events in that small island nation in the Caribbean had long troubled Reagan. During the campaign of 1980, Reagan denounced the "totalitarian Marxists" who had seized power the previous year. The members of the New Jewel movement may not have exactly fit Reagan's description, but the government of Prime Minister Maurice Bishop had little respect for political freedoms or human rights. The presence of Cuban advisers, who were "training guerrillas for subversive action against other countries," provided confirmation, Reagan declared, of the aggressive designs of the Moscow-Havana axis of evil. Three years later, in a speech that most people remembered for the dramatic announcement of the Strategic Defense Initiative, Reagan once more warned about the "Soviet-Cuban militarization of Grenada." Cuban construction battalions, with financial support from the Kremlin, were building an airfield with a ten-thousand-foot runway, even though Grenada had no air force. "Who is it intended for?" the president asked ominously.[53]

A coup that deposed Bishop on October 13, 1983, threw Grenada into turmoil. The revolutionaries executed the prime minister, deported journalists, and announced an around-the-clock curfew enforced with an order to shoot violators on sight. These swift and convulsive events alarmed the members of the Organization of Eastern Caribbean States (OECS), who urgently requested U.S. intervention to restore order.

Even before the Reagan administration learned of the OECS action, a Crisis Preplanning Group, chaired by Robert C. McFarlane, considered the possibility of U.S. military action. McFarlane, who became the president's national security adviser during the crisis, worried about "a second Cuba at our doorstep, . . . the export of revolution to countries in South America, . . . [and] a serious challenge from Moscow." He apparently helped inspire the OECS request by issuing instructions to determine whether Grenada's neighbors "might be inclined to coordinate a call for assistance . . . that would legitimize our involvement."[54] CIA director William Casey saw an opportunity to solve a festering problem that had suddenly become acute. "Fuck it," he declared, "let's dump these bastards."[55]

Preliminary discussions also concerned dangers to about eight hundred U.S. medical students on the island. Shultz wrote that he and other administration officials, recalling the "searing memory of Tehran," believed that "conditions were ripe . . . for hostage taking." Reagan, too, worried about hostages, according to Shultz. But the president authorized intervention only when he learned about the OECS request for action in the early morning of October 22, after McFarlane awakened him during a golfing vacation in Augusta, Georgia. According to McFarlane, Reagan believed that at stake in Grenada was U.S. credibility and his "own commitment to the defense of freedom and democracy." The exact scope of the mission was still uncertain, but Reagan's decision indicated that he favored the rescue of potential hostages as part of a larger operation that would oust the revolutionaries and expel the Cubans. Available information shows that Reagan chose military action in Grenada twenty-four hours before he learned that a suicide bomber had killed 241 U.S. marines in their barracks in Lebanon.[56]

Unexpected criticism of the impending U.S. invasion came from Reagan's staunch ally, Margaret Thatcher. The prime minister expressed her disapproval directly and bluntly in several messages and telephone calls. The coup, she said, had brought "thugs" to power, but they had overthrown an unsavory government. Democracy had vanished when Bishop took control in 1979; the recent coup was "a change in degree rather than in kind." Thatcher also protested that U.S. officials had exaggerated what British intelligence saw as a "peripheral" Soviet interest in Grenada. The Cubans had a greater stake in the island and, perhaps, planned to use the new airfield to ferry troops to Ethiopia or Angola, countries in which they were already involved. Yet the main purpose of the new facilities, she insisted, was commercial—accommodating tourist flights. In addition, she worried that U.S. intervention would endanger, rather than protect, British and American nationals in a country that was a member of the Commonwealth. Finally, she was irked that Foreign Secretary Sir Geoffrey Howe, on the basis of preliminary information, had assured Parliament that there would be no U.S. military intervention. The British government, she feared, would look "at best, . . . impotent; at worst . . . deceitful." Aides who watched Reagan hold the telephone a few inches from his ear as he listened to the prime minister's outburst were baffled by Thatcher's failure to reciprocate U.S. support during the Falklands war. The prime minister, for her part, concluded that "frustrated anger" over the Beirut bombings accounted for the Reagan administration's actions in Grenada.[57]

Skeptical reactions also came from members of Congress and the news media. When Reagan informed congressional leaders hours before the beginning of the invasion, he faced opposition from some Democrats such as Speaker of the House Thomas P. O'Neill (D-Mass.), who resented being "informed but not consulted." Journalists complained about the military's refusal to transport them to Grenada and their subsequent exclusion during most of the fighting. Many doubted the official explanation that conditions on the island were too dangerous and suspected that the Pentagon was trying to manage the news so that scenes of casualties in Grenada so soon after the horrors of the terrorist attack on the marines in Lebanon would not produce popular disapproval of the operation.[58]

Representative Newt Gingrich (R-Ga.) urged Reagan to give a speech that would help both journalists and the public overcome their "state of shock." Neither, he believed, was "intellectually prepared" to "look beyond each crisis" and understand the dangers of a world in which the Soviets used "terrorists, spies and surrogates" to erode U.S. resolve and strength. Although he apparently drew on some of Gingrich's ideas and language, Reagan gave a much better speech than Gingrich proposed, one he wrote in large part himself. The president told the American people in his televised address on October 27 that "events in Lebanon and Grenada, though oceans apart, are closely related," as Moscow had encouraged and supported "the violence in both countries . . . through a network of surrogates and terrorists." Yet what probably affected more people than Reagan's insistence on the underlying Soviet challenge was the moving story of a hospitalized marine, so badly wounded in the Beirut attack that he could not speak, who grasped the hand of General P. X. Kelley, the marine commandant, and then scrawled the words "Semper Fi," shorthand for the marine motto. What also touched people was the arrival at Charleston Air Force Base, shown on live television, of the evacuated medical students. The first one who walked off the plane knelt and kissed the ground. Shultz declared, "Suddenly I could sense the country's emotions turn around. . . . I knew that we had won a clean sweep: on the ground in Grenada and in the hearts of the American people."[59] Grenada was a symbolic triumph, one that administration officials insisted demonstrated renewed strength and resolve.

Divisions continued in the Reagan administration about committing combat forces, even though the president and his top aides believed that they had won a victory in Grenada.[60] U.S. troops deposed the revolutionaries, ejected the Cubans, and quickly returned home after suffering few casualties. Shultz considered Grenada "a shot heard round the world," a clear indication that Reagan was "capable of action beyond rhetoric" and that "some Western democracies were again ready to use the military strength they had . . . built up over the years in defense of their principles and interests." Shultz doubted that force should be a last resort, however appealing the principle. Grenada, he believed, vindicated the view that it was "better to use force when you *should* rather than when you *must*," as delay might increase risks, in this case both to troops and civilians that they rescued.[61]

Weinberger reached very different conclusions, drawn more from the disaster in Lebanon than from the success in Grenada. The secretary consolidated his thinking in a speech on November 28, 1984, before the National Press Club about "The Uses of Military Power." He emphasized the range of challenges—such as wars of national liberation, terrorism, and covert action—that stopped short of direct attack on U.S. soil but could threaten national security. He thought troops should fight overseas only to protect vital U.S. or allied interests and only in pursuit of clear military and political objectives. Also essential was "a clear intention of winning," although Weinberger never addressed the complexities of determining the meaning of that goal. Success on the battlefield also required "reasonable assurance" of public and congressional support. And, finally, force should be a last resort, one that followed the exhaustion of diplomatic and political alternatives. These criteria, collectively known as the Weinberger Doctrine, did not prevent limited uses of force, such as the U.S. air strikes on April 14, 1986, against targets in Libya including the barracks of President Muammar Qaddafi in retaliation for terrorist attacks. Yet when it came to larger deployments of force, especially ground troops, the Weinberger Doctrine revealed that the legacies of Vietnam continued to affect administration thinking.[62]

REAGAN'S NOT-SO-MAD WORLD

The Strategic Defense Initiative (SDI) was Reagan's boldest and most controversial national security proposal. In a televised address about national defense on March 23, 1983, Reagan disclosed that he had "become more and more deeply convinced that the human spirit must be capable of rising above dealing with other nations and human beings by threatening their existence." He proposed to transcend this "sad commentary on the human condition" by finding a way "to save lives [rather] than to avenge them."

> What if free people could live secure in the knowledge that their security did not rest upon the threat of instant U.S. retaliation to deter a Soviet attack, that we could intercept and destroy strategic ballistic missiles before they reached our own soil or that of our allies?
>
> I know this is a formidable, technical task, one that may not be accomplished before the end of this century. . . . There will be failures and setbacks, just as there will be successes and breakthroughs. . . . But isn't it worth every investment necessary to free the world from the threat of nuclear war? . . .
>
> My fellow Americans, tonight we're launching an effort which holds the promise of changing the course of human history.

Reagan had fundamentally challenged conventional strategic thinking, and he presented his proposal in sweeping, visionary terms.[63]

Reagan had been interested in defensive systems for several years. A pivotal event occurred on July 31, 1979, when Reagan toured the headquarters of the North American Aerospace Defense Command at Cheyenne Mountain, Colorado. The visit made him keenly aware that "there is nothing we can do to prevent a nuclear missile from hitting us." Six weeks later, he wrote in a radio commentary that "there once was the beginning of a defense; an antiballistic missile system which we . . . bargained away in exchange for nothing," a depre-cating and inaccurate reference to the Antiballistic Missile Treaty of 1972. As candidate and president, Reagan occasionally met proponents of various defense systems and expressed interest, both for strategic and moral reasons, in their ideas.[64]

Reagan said that SDI would render "nuclear weapons impotent and obso-lete." Yet it is still not clear how thoroughly he embraced the idea of nuclear abolition before his famous speech.[65] Recently available documents offer some tantalizing hints. In May 1982, Reagan wrote to Ann Landers, after a staff member showed him a column that contained a letter from a reader—signed "Ter-rified in D.C."—who worried about a nuclear war. Such a conflict was "unthink-able," the president declared, and that was why "we must have a true verifiable reduction [in nuclear arsenals] leading to an eventual elimination of all such weapons." The staff of the National Security Council objected, and Reagan fi-nally signed a sanitized version of the letter without the sentence about his ulti-mate hope. This incident could have encouraged Reagan to be careful about revealing that he was thinking what some members of his staff considered the unthinkable. In any case, his correspondence more commonly explained that "our true ultimate purpose is arms reduction." As yet, there is no conclusive evidence that Reagan's thinking about strategic defense or nuclear abolition changed sig-nificantly in the months before the SDI speech or that the president got new information about any technological breakthrough, actual or anticipated.[66]

The president may have hoped that the announcement of the SDI would deflate public and congressional opposition to his defense program. The re-cession had diminished support for real, double-digit percentage increases in defense spending. A Gallup poll in January 1983 found that 45 percent of those surveyed believed that the government was spending "too much" on defense, while only 14 percent judged appropriations "too little" and 33 percent "about right." The nuclear freeze movement also had a strong influence on public and congressional attitudes. During 1982 and 1983, polls consistently showed that 70 percent of the American people believed that both the United States and the Soviet Union should immediately halt "the testing, production, and deploy-ment of nuclear weapons." The freeze appealed even to those who were wary of Soviet power, as many people thought that both sides had accumulated ar-senals that had exceeded any reasonable requirements of security. The House of Representatives barely defeated a freeze resolution in 1982, and proponents of the measure gained strength in that year's congressional elections. Freeze advocates also fortified opposition to the deployment, scheduled for late in 1983, of U.S. Pershing missiles in Europe. Reagan told members of Congress that a freeze would allow the Soviets to maintain their strategic advantages while removing incentives to agree to the 50 percent cuts in ICBMs that the administration had proposed in the strategic arms reductions talks. According to Stockman, Reagan planned the March 23 address to mobilize public pressure on Congress to continue the defense buildup and planned "a 'little surprise' in the speech that would leave all those defense cutters on the Hill swooning and gasping with admiration."[67]

SDI did not have those immediate effects. Instead, it produced a torrent of criticism for being technologically infeasible, a reckless dream, "Star Wars." Some of Reagan's advisers at first were cool to a proposal that they learned about only shortly before the president's speech, if they got advance notice at all. Yet Reagan continued promoting SDI, occasionally saying that it could be just a partial defense against a missile attack, more often imagining a leakproof shield, even if most experts considered such a hope highly unrealistic. Polls eventually showed public support for a program that promised protection against nuclear devastation. As Frances FitzGerald has suggested, Reagan "appropriated the rhetoric of the anti-nuclear movement" and sounded "like a man of peace."[68]

But Reagan apparently believed in what he dreamed. Aides supported SDI for a variety of reasons—as a bargaining chip, a way of inducing concessions from the Soviets on arms control, or a means of blocking U.S.–Soviet agreements that they considered unwise. Yet at the remarkable summit with Mikhail Gorbachev in Reykjavik in October 1986, Reagan clung stubbornly to his insistence that SDI research not be confined to the "laboratory," a stipulation that almost certainly would not have compromised its development. Shultz was stunned as Gorbachev laid "at our feet . . . concession after concession," culminating in the breathtaking proposal that both sides eliminate within ten years all their strategic nuclear weapons. Reagan had come stunningly close to his radical vision of a nuclear-free world, but he instead chose the dream of SDI.

IRAN-CONTRA SCANDAL

SDI produced controversy, but the administration's provision of arms to Iran to secure release of U.S. hostages and its illicit schemes to support the contras in Nicaragua produced a damaging scandal. When the Iran-Contra scandal became public in November 1986, Reagan's popularity plunged. The Gallup poll recorded that the public approved Reagan's handling of his job as president by a margin of more than two to one just before the scandal broke. But by early December, only a small plurality—47 percent to 44 percent—approved of the president's performance in office. And by late February 1987, Gallup found that those who disapproved outnumbered those who supported Reagan, 53 percent to 40 percent. Even more serious than the decline in the polls were the troubling questions about whether Reagan knew about the actions of his aides or whether he was capable of monitoring them. At times, he got obvious facts wrong, as when he declared during a press conference that no third country participated in transporting the weapons to Iran, even though White House Chief of Staff Donald Regan had already revealed Israel's involvement. More disturbing were the president's lapses of memory and the contradictory statements he made about his involvement. When Reagan testified before the Tower Board—the commission he appointed that consisted of Senator John Tower (R-Tex.), former Secretary of State Edmund Muskie, and Brent Scowcroft to investigate Iran-Contra—Reagan contradicted himself on basic issues. "I, for one, was shocked at what I was hearing," Tower declared. Reagan eventually abandoned his efforts to recall fundamentals of his involvement in the scandal. "The simple truth is, 'I don't remember—period,'" he wrote to the board.[69]

Despite extensive investigations by the Tower Board, select House and Senate committees, and special prosecutor Lawrence E. Walsh, it is still difficult to know Reagan's exact role in Iran-Contra. Determining what Reagan knew or did is hard, partly because of the president's contradictory statements and lapses of memory, partly because various aides tried to protect him, and partly because NSC staff member Oliver North shredded documents before investigators could secure them. Yet despite the gaps in information, Reagan sometimes did take a direct role or have specific knowledge of North's various schemes to supply the contras. Following the passage of congressional restrictions on U.S. military aid to the contras under the Boland amendments, the president told North to do what was necessary to maintain the Nicaraguan opposition "body and soul." Reagan was determined that the counterrevolutionaries whom he often called "freedom fighters" would not suffer when Congress halted military aid to the contras in 1984. North used a variety of shady or illegal expedients, including soliciting contributions from wealthy conservative donors and from other nations, including South Africa, Israel, and China. Reagan was aware of some of these third-party contributions, as he thanked King Fahd of Saudi Arabia in February 1985 for his support of the contras. Indeed, at a meeting on June 25, 1984, about third-party support for the contras, Reagan closed the discussion by stating, "If such a story gets out, we'll all be hanging by our thumbs in front of the White House." Yet after the scandal became public knowledge, Reagan made this remarkable statement to a group of newspaper editors on May 15, 1987: "As a matter of fact, I was very definitely involved in the decisions about support to the freedom fighters. It was my idea to begin with."[70]

Reagan was also deeply involved in his administration's provision of armaments to Iran. The Iran initiative apparently began as an effort to develop contacts with "moderates" who would be in a position to exercise considerable power once the aging Ayatollah Ruhollah Khomeini died. McFarlane especially was an advocate of developing those contacts, and an arms dealer, Manucher Ghorbanifar, with a dubious reputation claimed to be in a position to make the necessary liaisons. In early August 1985, Reagan approved the shipment from Israeli stocks of TOW missiles to Iran, with the United States to replenish the Israelis' supply. Reagan found attractive the possibility of opening a dialogue with Iranian moderates. But what was clearly closest to his heart was securing the release of U.S. hostages whom terrorists had seized in Lebanon. Reagan felt deeply the plight of the hostages. He also apparently worried about the political difficulties of another hostage crisis. In any case, he overrode the vehement opposition of Shultz and Weinberger, the latter of whom even warned the president about a criminal conviction owing to the embargo on arms shipments to Iran and restrictions on the retransfer of U.S. weapons in Israel's possession. Yet the deliveries of armaments continued into 1986, despite the president's public statements about not dealing with terrorists. Three hostages did gain their freedom, apparently through the intervention of the Iranian "moderates." But while the arms transfers occurred, three new hostages were seized.[71]

Once these unsavory transactions became known to the public, much of the investigation of the president's role centered on whether Reagan knew about "the diversion"—the use of profits from the Iranian armaments deals to support the contras. No incontrovertible evidence ever showed that Reagan did know about what North called the Iranian "contra-bution." John Poindexter, McFarlane's successor as national security adviser, testified that he never informed Reagan about the diversion. That the diversion was apparently North's "neat idea" that the president knew nothing about helped Reagan recover his popularity during 1987. So, too, did Reagan's willingness to "take full responsibility" for Iran-Contra, as he told the American people in a televised address on March 4, 1987. "My heart and my best intentions still tell me" that the administration "did not trade arms for hostages." Yet the president conceded that "the facts and the evidence tell me" that was precisely what happened. Yet what may have been most important was the reservoir of personal popularity on which Reagan could draw. Even while public disapproval of his handling of the presidency increased, Reagan remained personally appealing to a substantial majority of the American people. By July 1987, public approval of his presidency had risen to a favorable rating of 63 percent to 28 percent. Yet while the president did much to restore his reputation, troubling questions remained about an administration that violated laws to secure its national security objectives and that created covert capabilities designed to circumvent the normal processes of accountability.[72]

AIDING THE AFGHAN RESISTANCE

The provision of weapons to Iran at times intersected with another of the Reagan administration's covert operations, the provision of armaments to the Afghans who were resisting the Soviet invasion. Despite their deep differences, the United States and Iran had a common interest in countering Soviet domination of Afghanistan. The Iranian government opposed the establishment of a Soviet client on their eastern border. On several occasions during discussions of the transfer of U.S. weapons, Iranian and U.S. officials considered the possibility that the Iranians would provide a portion of the armaments to the mujahideen, the Afghan resistance. Available information does not reveal whether the Afghans ever received U.S. weapons from Iran. Ghorbanifar also raised the possibility of diverting some of the profits from the Iranian arms sales to the mujahideen. Again, documents that have so far been released do not reveal what happened to Ghorbanifar's suggestion.[73]

The Carter administration began supplying weapons to the mujahideen, either directly or through Pakistan. Carter's national security adviser, Zbigniew Brzezinski, explained that the covert U.S. aid aimed at ensuring "that the Soviets paid some price for their invasion." The Reagan administration hoped to make the Soviets feel real pain. The Carter administration spent about $30 million on arming the mujahideen during 1980. The Reagan administration allocated $625 million for weapons and training during its first three years. In March 1985, Reagan approved National Security Decision Directive 166, which called for a considerable expansion in aid to the mujahideen and that set as the ultimate goal the defeat of the Soviets in Afghanistan. After considerable debate, the Reagan administration began in 1986 supplying Stinger surface-to-air missiles, weapons highly effective in neutralizing low-altitude Soviet air power.[74]

The lack of substantial documentary evidence makes it difficult to determine how much the covert assistance contributed to the Soviet decision to begin withdrawing troops from Afghanistan in May 1988. Yet the Reagan administration invested heavily in the Afghan resistance and considered that it had won a substantial victory when the Soviets began their withdrawal. Shultz wrote that the Reagan administration's "support for people who fight for freedom had won out over the Brezhnev Doctrine of perpetual control by Soviets of territory they had seized. This was a new day and a major signal to restive Soviet satellites throughout the world."[75]

CONCLUSION

Ronald Reagan sometimes confounded expectations. No one anticipated in 1981 that Reagan would establish friendly relations with a Soviet leader and speak about the approaching end of the cold war. As Beth A. Fischer has shown in her essay in this volume, the Reagan administration revised its tough policies and instead pursued moderate efforts to engage the Soviets. In many ways, the results were stunning. In the felicitous phrase of John Lewis Gaddis, there was an "unexpected Ronald Reagan."[76]

Yet on some matters, including defense issues, there was also a remarkable consistency between what Reagan advocated as candidate and what his administration did. During Reagan's presidency, defense spending soared. Budget authority increased during the period 1981 through 1985 in real terms by over 9 percent; budget outlays grew by almost 7 percent before reaching a plateau. Reagan found it harder during the final years of his presidency to get the defense appropriations he requested with Democratic majorities in both houses in Congress, discontent over the Iran-Contra scandal, and improving relations with the Soviets. Yet still he asked Congress for substantial annual increases until the end of his presidency. Indeed, he vetoed the FY 1989 defense authorization bill, explaining that it moved "back toward the weakness and accommodation of the 1970s" and jeopardized negotiating leverage with the Soviets. Overall, however, Reagan found satisfaction in "overcoming years of weakness and confusion" by rebuilding defenses.[77] That strength, in conjunction with economic rejuvenation, he said in his farewell address, had restored "our morale" and international reputation. Reagan believed that he had followed his script and had done what he promised.

NOTES

1. Lou Cannon, *President Reagan: The Role of a Lifetime* (New York: Public Affairs, 2000), 771.

2. Letter, Reagan to Wright, May 18, 1982, folder 39; and letter, Reagan to Loeb, June 28, 1982, both in Series II: Presidential Records, 3/25/82 continued 7/26/82, Presidential Handwriting File, 1980–89, Ronald Reagan Library, Simi Valley, Calif.

3. *The Gallup Poll: Public Opinion, 1935–97* (Wilmington, Del.: Scholarly Resources, 2000), CD-ROM ed. 1980, 218–19; *New York Times,* October 29, 1980; William Schneider, "The November 4 Vote for President: What Did It Mean?" in *The American Elections of 1980,* ed. Austin Ranney (Washington, D.C.: American Enterprise Institute for Public Policy Research, 1982), 227–40; Burton I. Kaufman, *The Presidency of James Earl Carter* (Lawrence: University Press of Kansas, 1993), 205–7.

4. *Washington Post,* January 1, 1980; Kiron K. Skinner, Annelise Anderson, and Martin Anderson, eds., *Reagan, In His Own Hand* (New York: Simon & Schuster, 2001), 12, 60; *Public Papers of the Presidents of the United States: Ronald Reagan, 1981* (Washington, D.C.: Government Printing Office, 1982), 57. I have written out some of the abbreviations that Reagan used in his radio scripts (e.g., "military" instead of "mil." or "and" instead of "&").

5. *New York Times,* October 29, 1980. That language is from Reagan's remarks during his debate with Carter.

6. Skinner, Anderson, and Anderson, *In His Own Hand,* 83.

7. Ibid., 112. Reagan was quoting approvingly the conclusions of American Cause, a defense-advocacy public interest group.

8. Ibid., 82–84.

9. See, for example, NIE 11–3/8–76, December 1976; and B-Team Report, December 1976, both in Donald P. Steury, ed., *Intentions and Capabilities: Estimates on Soviet Strategic Forces, 1950–1983* (Washington, D.C.: Center for the Study of Intelligence, 1996), 339–90.

10. Skinner, Anderson, and Anderson, *In His Own Hand,* 110–13, 482.

11. Among those who had heard about Carter's decision to cancel the B1, 47 percent supported the president's action and 33 percent disapproved. *Gallup Poll,* 1978, 27.

12. Skinner, Anderson, and Anderson, *In His Own Hand,* 86, 102–4. A survey in April and May of 1978 showed public opinion almost equally divided—43 percent in favor, 44 percent opposed—about whether U.S. forces should be equipped with neutron bombs. On the question of defense spending, a survey in July 1977—the date closest to Reagan's comment in April 1978 about popular discontent with defense—showed that 27 percent thought defense spending too low, 23 percent too high, and 40 percent about right. *Gallup Poll,* 1977, 1064–66; 1978, 181–82.

13. The B52 had gone into service in the air force in 1955.

14. *New York Times,* October 29, 1980; Skinner, Anderson, and Anderson, *In His Own Hand,* 105–13.

15. Paul H. Nitze, *From Hiroshima to Glasnost: At the Center of Decision* (New York: Grove Weidenfeld, 1989), 352–54.

16. Charles R. Morris, *Iron Destinies, Lost Opportunities: The Arms Race between the USA and the USSR, 1945–1987* (New York: Harper & Row, 1988), 348–49; David Skidmore, *Reversing Course: Carter's Foreign Policy, Domestic Politics, and the Failure of Reform* (Nashville: Vanderbilt University Press), 149.

17. Steury, *Intentions and Capabilities,* 366.

18. Skinner, Anderson, and Anderson, *In His Own Hand,* 33–35, 117–19, 485.

19. Ibid., 84–85. Reagan was quoting former secretary of the air force Thomas C. Reed.

20. Ibid., 99–102, 480–83.

21. Ibid., 75–58, 85; *New York Times,* October 29, 1980.

22. Skinner, Anderson, and Anderson, *In His Own Hand,* 57, 62–63, 90–91, 484.

23. Ibid., 84. Reagan was again quoting Reed.

24. Ibid., 15, 118–19.

25. *Public Papers,* 1981, 57.

26. Skinner, Anderson, and Anderson, *In His Own Hand,* 471–79.

27. David A. Stockman, *The Triumph of Politics: Why the Reagan Revolution Failed* (New York: Harper & Row, 1986), 1–2, 8–9.

28. Ibid., 107; abstracts of evening news, ABC, CBS, NBC, *Vanderbilt Television News Archive,* April 27, 1980, <http://tvnews.vanderbilt.edu/cgi-bin/absdir.cgi (February 15, 2002).

29. Stockman, *Triumph of Politics,* 107–8.

30. Skidmore, *Reversing Course,* 44–51, 66–83; *Congressional Quarterly Almanac,* vol. 37, 1981 (Washington, D.C.: Congressional Quarterly, 1982), 192.

31. *Congressional Quarterly Almanac,* 108–9; Hedrick Smith, *The Power Game: How Washington Works* (New York: Ballantine Books, 1988), 384–85.

32. Stockman, *Triumph of Politics,* 273–74, 277–78; *Washington Post,* March 5, 1981.

33. Memorandum, Wirthlin to Reagan, June 18, 1981, folder 4, box 1, Presidential Handwriting File, Reagan Library; *Gallup Poll,* 1981, 119–23.

34. George P. Shultz, *Turmoil and Tradition: My Years as Secretary of State* (New York: Charles Scribner's Sons, 1993), 144.

35. Stockman, *Triumph of Politics,* 269–99; Caspar W. Weinberger, *Fighting for Peace: Seven Critical Years at the Pentagon* (New York: Warner Books, 1990), 66–67.

36. Smith, *The Power Game,* 384–85; Richard A. Stubbing, *The Defense Game: An Insider Explores the Astonishing Realities of America's Defense Establishment* (New York: Harper & Row, 1986), 374–75; Daniel Wirls, *Buildup: The Politics of Defense in the Reagan Era* (New York: Cornell University Press, 1992), 81–101.

37. Report of Secretary of Defense Caspar W. Weinberger to the Congress on the FY 1983 Budget, February 8, 1982, 10; report of Secretary of Defense Harold Brown to the Congress on the FY 1982 Budget, January 19, 1981, 154.

38. Cannon, *President Reagan,* 133–34.

39. Frances FitzGerald, *Way Out There in the Blue: Reagan, Star Wars, and the End of the Cold War* (New York: Simon & Schuster, 2000), 187–89; Cannon, *President Reagan,* 133–38; *Public Papers,* 1981, 879.

40. FitzGerald, *Way Out There in the Blue,* 189–91.

41. Ibid., 192–94.

42. NSDD 17, January 17, 1983, reprinted in Robert C. McFarlane, *Special Trust* (New York: Cadell & Davies, 1994), 372–80.

43. Chester Pach, "Television," in *Encyclopedia of American Foreign Policy,* 2d ed., ed. Alexander DeConde, Richard Dean Burns, and Fredrik Logevall (New York: Charles Scribner's Sons, 2002), 3 vols., 3:554–55.

44. Skinner, Anderson, and Anderson, *In His Own Hand,* 479

45. See, for example, letter, Reagan to Reverend F. Andrew Carhartt, March 12, 1982, folder 30, Series II: Presidential Records, 12/14/81–3/25/82, Presidential Handwriting File, Reagan Library.

46. *Rambo, First Blood, Part II,* TriStar Pictures, 1985.

47. Skinner, Anderson, and Anderson, *In His Own Hand,* 477, 485. For background of the revolutions in Nicaragua and El Salvador, see William M. LeoGrande, *Our Own Backyard: The United States in Central America, 1977–1992* (Chapel Hill: University of North Carolina Press, 1998), 3–51.

48. LeoGrande, *Our Own Backyard,* 80–86, 143–46; Cannon, *President Reagan,* 163.

49. FitzGerald, *Way Out There in the Blue,* 217–19, 265; Cannon, *President Reagan,* 122, 293–94.

50. *Gallup Poll,* 1982, 53–54, 1985, 70–73; Cannon, *President Reagan,* 291–92.

51. Alexander M. Haig, Jr., *Caveat: Realism, Reagan, and Foreign Policy* (New York: Macmillan, 1984), 261–302.

52. "Remarks and a Question-and-Answer Session with Editors and Broadcasters from Midwestern States," April 30, 1982, *Public Papers,* 1982, <http://www.reagan.utexas.edu/resource/speeches/1982/43082b.htm> (March 13, 2002); "Address to the Nation Announcing the Formation of a New Multinational Force in Lebanon," September 20, 1982, ibid., <http://www.reagan.utexas.edu/resource/speeches/1982/92082f.htm> (March 13, 2002); Cannon, *President Reagan,* 339–85; Weinberger, *Fighting for Peace,* 135–60.

53. Skinner, Anderson, and Anderson, *In His Own Hand,* 477; "Address to the Nation on Defense and National Security, March 23, 1983, *Public Papers,* 1983, <http://www.reagan.utexas.edu/resource/speeches/1983/32383d.htm> (March 13, 2002). For background on the political situation in Grenada, see Shultz, *Turmoil and Triumph,* 324–27, and Weinberger, *Fighting for Peace,* 101–6.

54. Robert C. McFarlane, *Special Trust* (New York: Cadell & Davies, 1994), 257–59; Bob Woodward, *Veil: The Secret Wars of the CIA, 1981–87* (New York: Simon & Schuster, 1987), 290.

55. McFarlane, *Special Trust,* 260–63; Woodward, *Veil,* 288–91.

56. Shultz, *Turmoil and Triumph,* 328–31; Weinberger, *Fighting for Peace,* 110–13; McFarlane, *Special Trust,* 260–63.

57. Margaret Thatcher, *The Downing Street Years* (New York: HarperCollins, 1993), 328–33; McFarlane, *Special Trust,* 265; Shultz, *Turmoil and Triumph,* 336.

58. Shultz, *Turmoil and Triumph,* 335; Pach, "Television," 3:555.

59. Memorandum, Gingrich to Duberstein, October 25, 1983, folder Sp 818–181858 [3 of 4]; White House Staffing memorandum and attachment, October 25, 1983, folder Sp 818–176132; draft presidential address, October 27, 1983, folder Sp 818–181858 [1 of 4]; draft presidential address, October 27, 1983, folder F224, series III: Presidential Speeches, Presidential Handwriting File, all in Reagan Library; "Address to the Nation on Events in Lebanon and Grenada," October 27, 1983, *Public Papers,* 1983, <http://www.reagan.utexas.edu/resource/speeches/1983/102783b.htm> (March 13, 2002); Shultz, *Turmoil and Triumph,* 339–40.

60. Polls showed that the American people agreed. By a margin of 59 percent to 32 percent, the public approved of Reagan's handling of Grenada. Lebanon produced a different conclusion, with only 34 percent approving and 52 percent disapproving the president's policies. *Gallup Poll,* 1983, 262–63.

61. Shultz, *Turmoil and Triumph,* 344–45.

62. Weinberger, *Fighting for Peace,* 433–45; Woodward, *Veil,* 444–46.

63. "Address to the Nation on Defense and National Security," March 23, 1983, *Public Papers,* 1983, <http://www.reagan.utexas.edu/resource/speeches/1983/32383d.htm> (March 13, 2002); Shultz, *Turmoil and Triumph,* 263.

64. Martin Anderson, *Revolution* (New York: Harcourt Brace Jovanovich, 1988), 81–97; Skinner, Anderson, and Anderson, *In His Own Hand,* 120.

65. For a thorough and provocative discussion of this subject, see Luther M. Boggs, Jr., "From Hollywood to Reykjavik: Ronald Reagan and Nuclear Abolition" (master's thesis, Ohio University, 1994).

66. Letter, Reagan to Landers and attachments, May 24, 1982, folder 40, and letter, Reagan to Kelly, May 21, 1982, and letter, Reagan to Spock, May 7, 1982, both in folder 36, all in Series II: Presidential Records, 3/25/82 continued 7/26/82, Presidential Handwriting File, 1980–89, Reagan Library; Wirls, *Buildup,* 144–47.

67. *Gallup Poll,* 1982, 94–95, 1983, 37; notes, meeting with bipartisan members of Congress on the nuclear freeze, March 15, 1984, folder 7, Series II: Presidential Records, 3/25/82 continued 7/26/82, Presidential Handwriting File, 1980–89, Reagan Library; Stockman, *Triumph of Politics,* 366–67; Wirls, *Buildup,* 147–54; FitzGerald, *Way Out There in the Blue,* 194–209.

68. *Gallup Poll,* 1985, 50, 255, 1986, 14; FitzGerald, *Way Out There in the Blue,* 255–64.

69. *Gallup Poll,* 1986, 255–63, 1987, 21, 41; Cannon, *President Reagan,* 613; William E. Pemberton, *Exit with Honor: The Life and Presidency of Ronald Reagan* (Armonk, N.Y.: M. E. Sharpe, 1998), 190–91.

70. Malcolm Byrne, "Ronald Reagan's Role in the Iran-Contra Affairs" (paper presented at the Conference on Ronald Reagan, University of California, Santa Barbara, March 29, 2002), 2–10; Peter Kornbluh and Malcolm Byrne, eds., *The Iran-Contra Scandal: The Declassified History* (New York: New Press, 1993), 82; Theodore Draper, *A Very Thin Line: The Iran-Contra Affairs* (New York: Touchstone, 1991), 570.

71. Byrne, "Ronald Reagan's Role in the Iran-Contra Affairs," 20; Pemberton, *Exit with Honor,* 178–82.

72. Byrne, "Ronald Reagan's Role in the Iran-Contra Affairs," 1–2; *Public Papers,* 1987, 208–11; *Gallup Poll,* 1986, 262–63, 1987, 151.

73. James Hershberg, "The War in Afghanistan and the Iran-Contra Affair: Missing Links?" *Cold War History* (forthcoming).

74. John Prados, *Presidents' Secret Wars: CIA and Pentagon Covert Operations from World War II through Iranscam* (New York: William Morrow, 1986), 362–67; Peter Schweizer, *Victory: The Reagan Administration's Secret Strategy That Hastened the Collapse of the Soviet Union* (New York: Atlantic Monthly Press, 1994), 212–14, 268–71.

75. Shultz, *Turmoil and Triumph,* 1094.

76. John Lewis Gaddis, "The Unexpected Ronald Reagan," in idem, *The United States and the End of the Cold War: Implications, Reconsiderations, Provocations* (New York: Oxford University Press, 1991), 119–32.

77. Wirls, *Buildup,* 36–37; *Public Papers,* 1988–89, 2:1013–14, 1718–23.

5

Reagan and the Soviets: Winning the Cold War?

Beth A. Fischer

What role did the Reagan administration play in ending the cold war? On the face of it, this is a rather straightforward question, and the answer presumably could be found by studying letters, memos, and discussions between the president, his advisers, and Soviet officials. However, appearances can be deceiving. As one ponders this question, a multitude of further questions and clarifications come to mind. For example, what were the goals of the United States' Soviet policy, and how did these change over time? This is the source of considerable debate. Some contend that the Reagan administration maintained a hard-line posture toward Moscow throughout its two terms in office, while others assert that the administration began seeking improved relations late in its first term.

There are broader questions, too. For instance, when exactly did the cold war end? Some contend it began to end with Mikhail Gorbachev's assumption of power in March 1985, while others might argue that it did not completely die until September 11, 2001. The date one chooses affects any assessment of the Reagan administration's role.[1] Related to the matter of when the cold war ended is an even more daunting question: what exactly *was* the cold war? This query alone has spawned a cottage industry among historians, for the way in which one defines the cold war affects the way in which one assesses its inception, its evolution, and its ending.

This essay does not seek to tell the whole story of how the cold war ended or to explain how U.S. foreign policy was made. Rather, it seeks to understand the role that the Reagan administration played in ending cold war hostilities. In keeping with the purposes of this book, this chapter will assume that the cold war began to end during President Reagan's second term, particularly after the November 1985 Geneva summit meeting.[2]

What role did the Reagan administration play in ending the cold war? Essentially, there are four schools of thought regarding the Reagan administration's role in ending the cold war.

The first perspective contends that the Reagan White House played virtually no role in ending the cold war. In this view, Soviet General Secretary Mikhail Gorbachev single-handedly brought about the end of the cold war, through his policy of "New Thinking." Gorbachev came to power seeking to reform the Soviet economy. He sought to devote more resources to domestic goods and infrastructure, and fewer resources to the Soviet military. Consequently, Gorbachev sought to end the costly arms race and the cold war that had spawned it. His policy of New Thinking therefore entailed a more conciliatory posture toward the West and a host of unilateral confidence-building gestures, such as a moratorium on the deployment of new intermediate-range nuclear missiles and a moratorium on nuclear weapons tests. Rather than focus on a bipolar world and its attendant competition, Gorbachev emphasized "common human values" and the manner in which all civilizations were threatened by the nuclear arms race, environmental degradation, and global disparities in wealth.[3]

In this view, Gorbachev's desire for domestic reform ultimately led to the end of the cold war. The Kremlin's decision to end the arms race led first to improved relations between Western Europe and Moscow and ultimately to an end to the forty years of hostility between the United States and the USSR. From this perspective, the Reagan administration was simply a passive actor that benefited from these changes in Soviet policy.

On the other end of the spectrum are those who contend that the Reagan administration brought about the end of the cold war by hastening (if not causing) the collapse of the Soviet Union. Sometimes called the "Reagan victory school," this group asserts that President Reagan's unprecedented military buildup and demonstrations of resolve forced the Soviets to capitulate the cold war.[4] The Soviets could not keep up with the Reagan administration's military expenditures or match U.S. technology. Consequently, Gorbachev was forced to become more conciliatory toward Washington. From this perspective, Gorbachev's unilateral efforts at disarmament were demonstrations of Soviet weakness—not, as Gorbachev argued, confidence-building measures intended to prove Moscow's benign intentions. The Soviet moratoria were acts of desperation, not determination. Moreover, in this view, Gorbachev's New Thinking in foreign policy was not a response to domestic needs, but rather an example of Moscow knuckling under American pressure.

Another variant of this school of thought contends that the Reagan administration was keenly aware of the fragile state of the Soviet economy during the 1980s and intended to push the USSR into bankruptcy. In this view, the White House supported covert aid to the mujahideen in Afghanistan and pursued the Strategic Defense Initiative (SDI) primarily to drain Soviet resources. SDI became the jewel in the crown of the United States' Soviet policy not because the administration really thought it would work, but because it wanted to goad Moscow into devoting massive amounts of resources into developing an SDI program of its own. According to this view, these policies and others forced the

Kremlin to conclude that it could no longer afford the cold war. Moscow had no option but to surrender.

The third school of thought turns this logic on its head. In this view, President Reagan's approach to the Soviet Union was an impediment to ending the cold war and may, in fact, have prolonged the conflict. Reagan's hard-line anticommunism, his belligerent rhetoric, and the military buildup that he initiated combined to make it more difficult for Gorbachev to pursue improved relations with the West. These scholars point out that Gorbachev faced a hard-line contingent within the Politburo that was deeply wedded to traditional Soviet policy toward the United States. These Soviet hard-liners saw the United States as an imperialist enemy that sought to weaken the USSR. Consequently, they were initially opposed to Gorbachev's policy of New Thinking, believing that Washington would perceive it as a sign of weakness and take advantage of the Soviet Union. The more belligerent Reagan acted, the more these Soviet hard-liners were convinced that Gorbachev was on the wrong course. Thus, they pressured him to abandon his reforms. From this perspective, then, Reagan's "get tough" posture had the unintended effect of supporting those Soviet hard-liners who favored a more antagonistic approach toward Washington. If Reagan hadn't been so belligerent, Gorbachev would have had more domestic support for his foreign policy reforms, and the cold war would have ended earlier.

Finally, there is the view that President Reagan and his administration played an important, albeit secondary, role in ending the cold war. While this argument has many different variations, the main point is that the administration engaged in critical ways with Soviet leaders, particularly during Reagan's second term in office.[5] While the president had avoided summit meetings and was hostile to the Soviets during his first term, by the early part of his second term, he had largely toned down his rhetoric and signaled an interest in improving relations. These changes in the U.S. approach cleared the way for the establishment of a personal rapport between Reagan and Gorbachev, five summit meetings in four years, and the conclusion of the intermediate-range nuclear forces (INF) treaty.[6] Therefore, U.S. actions were crucial in bringing the cold war to its peaceful conclusion.

Owing to space restrictions, this chapter cannot consider each of these perspectives in detail. Rather than attempting to discuss each in a superficial manner, the rest of the chapter will focus instead on one of the most widely cited schools of thought: that of the Reagan victory school. Given space restrictions, the emphasis will be on information that has been released relatively recently or that has not been widely circulated. Moreover, the evidence provided is meant to be illustrative rather than exhaustive.

There are important differences between the Reagan victory school and the other perspectives on the ending of the cold war. First, the Reagan victory school contends that the Reagan administration did not seek to improve relations with the Soviet Union, but rather to vanquish the Soviet Union. The intention was to win the cold war, not to resolve it. Second, the Reagan victory school understands the collapse of the Soviet Union and the end of the cold war to be synonymous. The other perspectives take a more nuanced view: the cold war began to draw to a close as one or both of the superpowers modified their foreign policies throughout the mid- to late 1980s. These other schools imply, therefore, that the cold war might have ended even if the USSR had not collapsed. Likewise, they imply that the cold war could have heated up if Gorbachev's successors had reverted to a more belligerent posture toward the West. A final difference is that the Reagan victory school seeks to determine who won or lost the cold war. The other perspectives focus instead on explaining the way in which the conflict was resolved.

THE REAGAN VICTORY SCHOOL

The Reagan victory school contends that the collapse of the Soviet Union was a victory for the Reagan administration because the White House had intentionally sought to vanquish its nemesis. Reagan had embarked on the largest peacetime military buildup in U.S. history, introduced the Strategic Defense Initiative, provided aid to those resisting Soviet influence, and had engaged in belligerent rhetoric toward Moscow for the purpose of forcing the Soviets to their knees. The dissolution of the USSR, therefore, was the ultimate victory.

To consider the validity of this perspective, one must break down the argument into its component parts. The rest of the chapter will focus on the following assertions:

1. The Reagan administration pursued a hard-line policy toward the Soviet Union throughout its two terms in office.
2. The Reagan administration intended to bankrupt the USSR.
3. Soviet "New Thinking" was a response to the Reagan administration's policy toward Moscow.
4. Soviet attempts to match the Reagan administration's military buildup caused the collapse of the USSR.

THE REAGAN ADMINISTRATION'S HARD-LINE POLICY

The Reagan victory school contends that the Reagan administration's hard-line policy forced the Soviet Union to capitulate the cold war. However, the Reagan administration pursued a hard-line policy only during its first three years in office. By January 1984, President Reagan was ardently pursuing a rapprochement with Moscow.

Upon entering office, Reagan officials contended that the Soviets were gaining the military advantage and asserted that the United States had to restore its comparative strength. Consequently, in 1981 Reagan proposed the largest peacetime military budget in U.S. history, increasing military spending by approximately 7 percent per year between 1981 and 1985. Defense expenditures would consume more than 30 percent of the federal budget during an era in which government spending was being slashed in all other sectors.[7] In addition, in 1983 the president unveiled the Strategic Defense Initiative, which he hoped would lead to a comprehensive defense against nuclear attack. President Reagan envisioned SDI as a "nuclear umbrella" that would protect Americans from nuclear annihilation. Initially, the Soviets vociferously opposed SDI. They argued that it not only violated the 1972 Antiballistic Missile (ABM) Treaty, but also threatened to launch an arms race in space. Consequently, SDI was the main thorn in superpower relations until early 1987, when the Soviets decided to shift the focus of superpower talks elsewhere.[8] Between 1981 and 1983, Reagan officials also engaged in belligerent rhetoric, calling the Soviet Union the "evil empire" and accusing the Soviets of imperialism, immorality, and terrorism.

However, the Reagan administration jettisoned its hard-line policy in 1984. On January 16, 1984, President Reagan delivered an address on superpower relations that unveiled important changes in U.S. policy.[9] Reagan sought to reassure Moscow of Washington's benign intentions and to establish a dialogue between the superpowers. "We must establish a better working relationship," Reagan declared, "one marked by greater cooperation and understanding." Cooperation and understanding would mitigate the chances of war, the president suggested. "Reducing the risk of war—and especially nuclear war—is priority number one. . . . We need to find ways to reduce—and eventually eliminate—the threat and use of force in solving international disputes."

Rather than focusing on the ideological competition between the United States and the USSR, as he had in the past, Reagan focused on what they had in common. "Neither we nor the Soviet Union can wish away the differences between our two societies and our two philosophies," he intoned. "But we should always remember that we do have common interests." Foremost among these common interests was the desire for peace.

In his address Reagan stressed that the United States posed no threat to Soviet security. "Our challenge is peaceful," he declared. "We do not threaten the Soviet Union. . . . Our countries have never fought each other; there is no reason why we ever should." This statement was a striking departure from the administration's earlier approach. Threats—both explicit and implicit—had been the very foundation of the earlier strategy. Moreover, in previous years Reagan administration officials had repeatedly dismissed the idea that Moscow could possibly feel threatened by the United States.[10]

During this speech, the president introduced a strategy for attaining cooperation and understanding between the superpowers. The first element of this strategy was the institutionalization of superpower dialogue. "We must and will engage the Soviets in a dialogue as constructive as possible," proclaimed the only president in forty years never to have met his Soviet counterpart. "High level consultations [should] become a regular and normal component of U.S.–Soviet relations." The aim of the dialogue would be to clarify intentions, minimize uncertainty, and ultimately, to avoid conflict. "We seek genuine cooperation, [and] cooperation begins with communication," he explained. "The fact that neither of us likes the other's system is no reason not to talk," the president reasoned. "Living in the nuclear age makes it imperative that we do talk."[11]

The second element of this new strategy was an increased emphasis on arms reduction. Reagan devoted a significant portion of his address to the need to "stop arms races around the world" and called upon the superpowers to "accelerate" efforts to conclude arms reduction agreements. "Nuclear arsenals are far too high," the president insisted. "My dream is to see the day when nuclear weapons will be banished from the face of the Earth."

Confidence-building measures were the third element of the new strategy. In his address, Reagan began calling for measures that could "reduce the threat and use of force . . . in regional conflicts." Rather than denouncing the Soviets' "expansionist" activities, as was his custom in the past, Reagan stated that the superpowers "should jointly examine concrete actions that we can both take to reduce U.S.–Soviet confrontation" throughout the world.

To underscore his sincerity, in December 1983 Reagan wrote a letter to Soviet leader Yuri Andropov in which he called attention to the cooperative tone of his upcoming address. "I continue to believe that despite the profound differences between our two nations, there are opportunities—indeed a necessity—for us to work together to prevent conflicts, to expand our dialogue, and to place our relationship on a more stable and constructive footing," Reagan wrote. "We do not seek to challenge the security of the Soviet Union and its people."[12] Since the president's letters to his Soviet counterparts were the only confidential channel of communication between the two capitals, the administration had hoped that this letter would underscore American intentions to improve relations.[13] After Andropov passed away six weeks later, Reagan immediately wrote a letter to his successor, Konstantin Chernenko, reiterating the same themes. "As I made clear in my January 16 address, I have no higher goal than the establishment of a relationship between our two great nations characterized by constructive cooperation," Reagan explained:

> Differences in our political beliefs and in our perspectives on international problems should not be an obstacle to efforts aimed at strengthening peace and building a productive working relationship. . . . Let me conclude by seeking to lay to rest some misunderstandings which may have arisen. The United States fully intends to defend our interests and those of our allies, but we do not seek to challenge the security of the Soviet Union and its people. We are prepared to deal with you in a manner that could establish

the basis for mutually acceptable and mutually advantageous solutions to some of our problems."[14]

President Reagan's January 16 address was not an anomaly. Rather, the president introduced lasting changes to the United States' Soviet policy. Throughout the next four years, Reagan officials continued to pursue a rapprochement with Moscow, both publicly and in their private interactions.[15]

What is noteworthy about the changes that were introduced in January 1984 is that the Reagan administration was clearly seeking to improve superpower relations—not to vanquish the Soviet Union. As National Security Adviser Robert McFarlane explained to reporters in a background briefing before Reagan's January 16 speech, "The fundamental purpose of the president's address will be to present in a clear and comprehensive manner his objective, which is to solve problems with the Soviet Union and to improve the state of this crucial relationship."[16] Jack Matlock, the director of Soviet affairs on the National Security Council (NSC) staff at the time, recalled, "The president's speech of January 16, 1984 set forward the parameters on which the cold war was eventually eliminated. What we envisioned at that time was a process which we hoped conceivably could end in the end of the cold war, but we couldn't be confident that it would."[17]

Matlock, who wrote the bulk of the January 16 address, has recollected that the administration thought an improvement in superpower relations might be years in the making:

At the time [January 1984] I said, "I don't see any way the present Soviet leadership is going to be able to respond, but we need to be on the record. At least when there are changes [in Soviet leadership] and they are prepared to engage, we should have a policy that is ready and which is directed at not doing them in." . . . Now, did we think they would say, "Hoorah, that's right, we're gonna do it?" Of course not. We were very aware of all of the suspicions and of the real problems. My own estimate at the time was that nothing would happen for a year or even two, but if we could keep steadily reiterating our [new policy] we would eventually engage the Soviets on it.[18]

At the time, Matlock was dismayed that the American press did not pick up on the new approach and attributed this oversight to the 1984 presidential election. "We told [the press] beforehand that this was serious and important, and we even briefed them beforehand, but this was a partisan time," he explained. "But the new approach kept going long after the election was over but many journalists didn't do their job. And then in 1987–88 the journalists were surprised and asking, 'How did we get to this point?' And I said, 'We told you in 1984 we were doing this!'"[19]

In sum, the suggestion that the Reagan administration pursued a hard-line policy toward the Soviet Union throughout its two terms in office is not supported by evidence. The White House jettisoned this policy in 1984—more than two years before the Soviets even began to reform and nearly eight years before the collapse of the USSR.[20] Consequently, it is inaccurate to argue that Reagan's hard-line policy forced the Soviet Union to surrender the cold war.

THE REAGAN ADMINISTRATION'S INTENT TO BANKRUPT THE SOVIET UNION

The Reagan victory school asserts that the Reagan administration intended to cause the collapse of the Soviet system.

President Reagan clearly believed that the Soviet system could not, in the end, survive. While he did not indicate that the collapse of the Soviet system was imminent, throughout the 1970s and 1980s he seemed to be thinking about such a geopolitical earthquake to a greater extent than many so-called foreign policy experts. "Communism is neither an economic or a political system—it is a form of insanity," Reagan asserted during a May 1975 radio address that he wrote himself. "[It is] a temporary aberration which will one day disappear from the earth because it is contrary to human nature."[21] In another address that year, Reagan contended that the Achilles' heel of the Soviet system was its economy. In this address, entitled "Russian Wheat Deal," Reagan agonized over whether American farmers should be allowed to sell their grain to the USSR. On the one hand, he explained, he believed in the value of a free market. Consequently, he felt that American farmers should be allowed to sell their goods wherever they could get the best price. On the other hand, he reasoned, there was also a national security issue. "If we believe the Soviet Union is hostile to the free world . . . then are we not adding to our own danger by helping the troubled Soviet economy? . . . Are we not helping a Godless tyranny maintain its hold on millions of helpless people? Wouldn't those helpless victims have a better chance of becoming free if their slave masters' regime collapsed economically?" Reagan concluded, "Maybe there is an answer. We simply do what's morally right. Stop doing business with them. Let their system collapse but in the meantime buy our farmers' wheat ourselves and have it on hand to feed the Russian people when they finally become free."[22] Two years later Reagan reiterated his view that the USSR could fall from within because it did not meet consumer needs. "The Soviet Union is building the most massive military machine the world has ever seen and is denying its people all kinds of consumer products to do it," he explained. "We might have an unexpected ally if citizen Ivan is becoming discontented enough to start talking back. Maybe we should drop a few million typical mail order catalogues on Minsk and Pinsk and Moscow to whet their appetites."[23]

Before becoming president, Reagan had also suggested that the arms race might ultimately bankrupt the Soviet Union. In a September 1979 radio address condemning the second Strategic Arms Limitation Treaty (SALT II), Reagan asked, "Which is worse? . . . An unrestrained arms race which the U.S. could not possibly lose given our industrial superiority, or a treaty [SALT II] which says that the arms race is over and that we have lost it." Reagan was not-so-implicitly suggesting, of course, that one way to win the cold war would be to step up the arms race.[24]

Reagan's personal views about the weakness of the Soviet system found their way into policy statements during his first term as president. "The West won't contain communism, it will transcend communism," Reagan asserted during a 1981 commencement speech. "It will dismiss [communism] as some bizarre chapter in human history whose last pages are even now being written."[25] During an address to the British Parliament the following year, the president predicted that "the march of freedom and democracy . . . will leave Marxism-Leninism on the ashheap of history."[26] "President Reagan just had an innate sense that the Soviet Union would not, or could not survive," recalled Secretary of State George Shultz after leaving office. "That feeling was not based on a detailed learned knowledge of the Soviet Union; it was just instinct."[27]

Clearly, some members of the Reagan administration—and the president in particular—believed the Soviet system to be weak and that it was necessary for the United States to place pressure on these weaknesses. However, this does not mean that the United States caused the collapse of the Soviet system or even that it intended to cause the collapse of the USSR, as the Reagan victory school asserts. Although the president personally believed that the USSR would ultimately fail, there is little to suggest that this was the goal of U.S. policy, even during Reagan's first term.

Reagan officials understood that the Soviet economy was weak, but there were disagreements within the administration regarding the larger significance of these problems. Many members of the administration dismissed Moscow's economic problems, finding it incomprehensible that the superpower could not overcome them. "Even in the beginning of the 1980s national security thinking was quite driven by the view that it didn't matter if the Soviet Union was totally chaotic, that it was so wealthy that it could go on forever. [This was] an underlying premise of détente," McFarlane explained in 1998. "Well, Reagan had a very different view. He didn't subscribe to that notion and instead believed that a more aggressive—well, that's the wrong word—a more energetic competition could impose such burdens as to bring down the Soviet Union. . . . However, many in his own Cabinet at the time didn't agree with him."[28] Douglas MacEachin, the director of the Office of Soviet Analysis in the CIA between 1984 and 1989, elaborates:

In the 1960s and 1970s the argument about the economic and societal problems of the Soviet Union provoked a sort of "so what?" kind of response. By the early 1980s, the virtually unanimous view was that this thing had reached a near critical point, although there was not unanimity on what would be done about it. . . . Basically two views existed [within the Reagan administration]. One was "Oh well, the old Stalinist methodology . . . will enable this thing to be kept in the box [i.e., under control]." Another argument was "Sooner or later it's going to have to be confronted by the political leadership, but when is not certain and the result is not certain." That was where we kind of stood on the eve of Gorbachev's election.[29]

Reagan officials recall that they recognized Moscow's economic difficulties and sought to place pressure on these weaknesses. However, they reject the notion that the administration was consciously seeking to bankrupt the Soviet Union. "We imposed costs [on the Soviet Union], and put pressure on them through the USIA [U.S. Information Agency] and so forth," McFarlane explained in 1995. "But 80 to 90 percent of what happened to the USSR was because Marxism was a dumb idea. At most the Reagan administration accelerated its decline by five to fifteen years."[30] Jack Matlock agrees that the White House did not aim to vanquish the Soviet Union. "I think we recognized the difficulties with the Soviet economy," Matlock recalled in 1998:

If you're going to negotiate, any rational negotiator tries to position things so your negotiating position will be advantageous. . . . There was no contradiction whatsoever in bringing pressure to bear on the Soviet system, particularly since we knew they needed to end the arms race [for domestic reasons]. . . . [But] I would say that none of the key players [in foreign policymaking] were operating from the assumption that we were going to do the Soviet Union in, or that the purpose of the pressure was to bring them down. . . . That's all thinking after the fact. Our goal was always to give the Soviets incentives to bring the Cold War to an end.[31]

Archival material overwhelmingly supports these recollections. For instance, on January 19, 1983, Secretary Shultz sent a memo to President Reagan outlining a plan for U.S.–Soviet relations during the coming year. The memo proposed a strategy for "an intensified dialogue with Moscow to test whether an improvement in the U.S.–Soviet relationship is possible." Shultz noted the "enduring features of U.S.–Soviet competition" and admitted that "there is no realistic scenario for a breakthrough to amicable relations with the Soviet Union. . . . If this dialogue does not result in improved U.S.–Soviet relations, the onus will rest clearly on Moscow; if it leads to actual improvement, all the better." Commenting on the health of the Soviet government, Shultz remarked, "To be sure, the Soviet system is beset by serious weaknesses. But it would be a mistake to assume that the Soviet capacity for competition with us will diminish at any time during your presidency."[32]

Shultz's remarks are significant for two reasons. First, they indicate that the administration's long-term goal was to improve superpower relations—not to vanquish the Soviet Union or to "win" the cold war. And second, the memo dismisses the idea that the United States was even capable of bankrupting the USSR.

Moreover, the Reagan administration did not pursue SDI for the purpose of bankrupting the Soviet Union, as some have charged. "I was present at many, if not most, of the discussions on [SDI]," Lieutenant General Edward L. Rowny explained in 1998. "As the archives are opened, I would be greatly surprised if you find any serious talk about [spending the Soviets into the ground] at all. I think it did come up once or twice in passing, but by and large, throughout the period, President Reagan's idea was 'Let's defend the people of the United States.'"[33] McFarlane's recollection supports this view. According to McFarlane, the United States pursued SDI for three reasons. First, Reagan considered mutual assured destruction (MAD) to be immoral and felt SDI was a more moral approach to achieving security. Second, the United States was trying to address a perceived strategic imbalance and believed a defensive system could offset Soviet advantages in land-based intercontinental ballistic missiles (ICBMs). And third, the administration believed it could redress this imbalance more cheaply by investing in its comparative advantage—technology—rather than by trying to match the Soviets "tank for tank, and ship for ship."[34] If there were an economic rationale to SDI, then, it was to reduce long-term costs for the United States.

In sum, although the president personally doubted the Soviet Union's long-term ability to survive, the White House was not actively seeking to bankrupt or to vanquish the USSR. The aim of the United States' Soviet policy was to improve superpower relations.

THE SOURCES OF GORBACHEV'S "NEW THINKING"

The Reagan victory school assumes that Gorbachev's "New Thinking" was nothing more than a response to the policies of the Reagan administration. In this view, Moscow began seeking better relations with the United States because it feared Reagan's military buildup and demonstrations of resolve. The Reagan victory school does not consider that there may have been other reasons for the change in Soviet foreign policy.

Former Soviet officials unanimously reject the notion that U.S. policy caused Soviet reforms and ultimately the collapse of the USSR. "Some Americans, especially those seeking to justify Reagan's enormous arms build up and tough foreign policy, still maintain that it was the principal cause of the disintegration of the Soviet Union," observed Anatoly Dobrynin, the Soviet ambassador to the United States from 1962 through 1986. "I cannot agree with that."[35] Soviet officials insist that New Thinking was a response to domestic problems within the USSR—problems that were evident decades before Reagan entered the White

House. As Gorbachev's foreign affairs adviser, Anatoly Chernyaev, explained in 1998:

> The decline of the Soviet Union became particularly noticeable when [Soviet leaders] made attempts to change some things in Khrushchev's time. It turned out that our society would not give way to reform. . . . We already sensed back in the 1960s that our society was in decline. It was obvious then that what was later called the Brezhnev period [of] stagnation—[was] both a correct name and an incorrect name because it was not stagnation, it was the gradual dying of our society.[36]

There were myriad reasons for this economic decline. "By the end of the 1970s . . . the Soviet economic system was no longer functioning," recalled Oleg Grinevsky, Gorbachev's ambassador-at-large:

> The economy was in a pitiful state. What were the main causes? . . . First of all, the system of planned economics turned out not to be efficient and the economy was slowly deteriorating. Secondly the military-industrial complex exerted an enormous burden upon the Soviet economy. There are different evaluations, but about 80% of industry, directly or indirectly, was tied into or working for the military-industrial complex. These non-productive expenses were a heavy rock that was truly depressing the economy. And the third factor was corruption. Terrible corruption was having a caustic effect upon our society year after year, and increasingly so.[37]

Chernyaev's colleague, Georgy Shaknazarov, adds two more factors to this list:

> The main cause of what transpired was not economic, but the falling behind of the Soviet Union technologically. . . . It was lagging in the area of computers and high technology. . . . But [there is] one more very important factor: management. Any economic system exists more or less successfully when it has resources, when it is provided with innovation, and when it has good management. We had gerontology, we had an old folks home.[38]

Even before Reagan came to office, Soviet leaders had concluded that there needed to be major changes in the Soviet economic system. The Soviet economy needed to be revived, and one way to achieve this would be to decrease military expenditures. In order to reduce defense spending, Moscow needed to end the arms race.[39] "Among the military, we were aware that the burden of military expenses that the Soviet Union was carrying had become intolerable for it," Soviet military scientist Vladimir Slipchenko observed in 1998. "A Gorbachev had to appear in the Soviet Union. If it was not Gorbachev, it could have been any other person, but a change in our country had to happen."[40] Shaknazarov concurs. "If there had been no Gorbachev another leader would have appeared," he asserts. "However . . . he was not the only person like this. . . . We had already as far back as the 1950s or 1960s, not only among dissidents, but also among our leadership, a sizeable group of people who were aware of the need for change and improvement. And they were all doing what they could, in their own way."[41]

Even though Gorbachev's colleagues disagreed on the proper policy toward the United States, there was broad agreement on the need to reduce arms spending. "It was not just Gorbachev who said that we were not going to spend as much as we used to," Chernyaev recalled:

> Look at his colleague, Ligachev, he was a conservative, right? A reactionary even, and yet he, at the most fierce zealous moment, would stand up, right in front of Gorbachev, and he would scream, "How long will our military-industrial complex keep devouring our economy, our agriculture, and our consumer goods? How long are we going to take this ogre, how long are we going to throw into its mouth the food of our children?" Even Ryzhkov, all who were located on the conservative side, everybody was against the arms race.[42]

Reagan's demonstrations of resolve may have had more of an effect within the United States than in the Soviet Union. The U.S. media fixated on President Reagan's 1983 assertion that the Soviet Union was the "evil empire" and the "focus of evil in the modern world." These phrases dogged Reagan for the remaining years of his presidency and beyond. Interestingly, former Soviet officials confess that they were not fazed by these remarks. Sergei Tarasenko, the principal policy assistant to Soviet Foreign Minister Eduard Shevardnadze, recalls that Soviet policymakers paid little attention to this name-calling. "I can only speak in partial representation of the Ministry of Foreign Affairs, the American division," Tarasenko explained in 1998. "Maybe it will seem strange to you, but frankly speaking, we didn't notice [the evil empire rhetoric much] because we were so accustomed to it. For many decades we called each other God knows what names. . . . In other words, this was normal, run of the mill rhetoric. We didn't think it was a big deal. On the other hand, our propaganda and our newspapers seized on this term and started getting upset about it. But on the political level . . . it did not play a role. It had an effect close to zero."[43] Chernyaev concurs. "I must say that among us, the international experts of the Central Committee [of the Communist Party of the Soviet Union], this term 'evil empire' . . . basically did not change anything of the moment. We could have expected anything from America, our main adversary . . . this label, this nickname, I don't think changed anything," Chernyaev recalls. "On the other hand, . . . for [some Soviet citizens] this term, ['evil empire'] and propaganda was perceived as punishment for what we did in Afghanistan. In other words, we felt that we deserved it. We were excusing Reagan."[44]

While it appears that Reagan's rhetoric had little effect on policymaking within the Politburo, his words were used by Soviet military leaders for their own ends. Vladimir Slipchenko, a leading military scientist at the time, recalled,

"The military, the armed forces, more than the politicians or the diplomats really, used [Reagan's] declaration. They used this statement as a reason to begin a very intense preparation inside the military for a state of war." Slipchenko recalls that Soviet military leaders used this rhetoric as an excuse to initiate "intense inspection plans," to conduct large-scale military exercises, and to begin planning "very new directions for war." "I would say that the military took advantage of this statement by Reagan and raised the level of military readiness during that period," Slipchenko explains.[45]

"I do not believe that the anti-Communist, anti-Soviet rhetoric, and the increase in the armaments and military power of the United States played a serious role in our decision making," Chernyaev reflected in 1998. "I think perhaps they played no role whatsoever. The United States is a colossal power, a military superpower, it was clear to us, but it was a constant. What was important was that we came to the realization that we needed to stop the arms race. . . . So, for us to end the arms race was an internal domestic problem. Whatever Reagan might do or not do, that did not change this fact."[46]

In short, the changes in Soviet foreign policy that Gorbachev introduced were a response to domestic needs and had their roots in internal discussions that preceded Reagan and SDI. New Thinking was not a response to Reagan's hard-line policy, but rather a response to long-term economic issues within the Soviet Union. The goal was to restore economic health. New Thinking was the medicine.

THE COLLAPSE OF THE USSR

The Reagan victory school also contends that Soviet attempts to match the Reagan administration's military buildup—and SDI in particular—proved more than the Soviet economy could bear. The result was the economic collapse of the USSR. By this logic, then, Reagan's arms buildup and SDI forced the Soviet Union into bankruptcy.

Certainly, the cold war played an important role in the decline of the Soviet economy. According to Chernyaev, nearly 80 percent of Soviet gross national product (GNP) went to military expenditures in the decades before President Reagan came to office.[47] While others may quibble with this figure, the bottom line is that the Soviets devoted a large percentage of their resources to defense spending over a long period of time. These expenditures took a toll on the health of the Soviet economic and political systems. By the time Reagan entered the White House, Soviet leaders had become keenly aware of the economic costs of the decades-long cold war. During the 1985 Geneva summit meeting, Gorbachev raised this issue with Reagan. Observing that the United States was in a recession, Gorbachev explained, "Studies in both countries have shown what, for example, Japan and the FRG [Federal Republic of Germany] have been able to do with little expenditure on the military. They have experienced an economic upsurge. . . . Scholars have shown that one job in the military sector is three times as costly as in the civilian sector," Gorbachev continued. "More jobs can be created if money is channeled into civilian areas. . . . The military is devouring huge resources."[48] The Soviet leader sought to convince Reagan that an end to the arms race would benefit the economies of both superpowers.

Owing to their realization that the arms race had been too costly, the Soviets did not seek to match the Reagan administration's increases in military expenditures. Throughout the 1980s, Soviet military expenditures remained more or less stable. While the U.S. military budget grew at almost 8 percent a year during the Reagan administration, the CIA estimated that Soviet military spending leveled off in 1975 to a growth rate of 1.5 percent a year and remained at that rate for a decade. Between 1985 and 1987, Soviet military spending grew at 4.3 percent per year, but this largely reflected an earlier decision to modernize the ABM system around Moscow. By 1988 Soviet defense spending was back down to 1980 levels.[49] The Soviets never attempted to match the increases in U.S. defense spending.

Moreover, although some from the Reagan victory school contend that SDI brought the Soviet Union to its knees, the Soviets never even bothered to mount their own SDI program. They conducted at least two studies to determine the feasibility of the Reagan administration's SDI program, and both concluded that a comprehensive shield was virtually impossible. One study concluded that even if the United States could build a shield that was 99 percent effective, sixty Soviet warheads would still be able to reach their targets. Since one nuclear explosion alone would cause unacceptable damage, the Soviets concluded that SDI was a "chimera."[50] They also determined that it would be considerably less costly to try to counter SDI than to match it. "We found over 200 alternative solutions [to SDI]," Slipchenko recalls. "We chose 20 to 30 of them to look at more closely. We evaluated our anti-SDI measures against a realistic SDI of the United States and found out that it would cost us about 10 per cent of what the Americans would have to spend on SDI. Then we were happy. Actually, we would have been quite glad if the Americans continued building SDI . . . because we realized that SDI could be fought very successfully—not by means of creating a similar system, but by way of creating means to overcome the system."[51]

Soviet officials also suspected that SDI was a hoax of sorts—a large-scale disinformation campaign aimed at goading the Soviets into wasting their resources. According to Aleksandr Yakovlev, Gorbachev's adviser and ally, some Soviet scientists advised the general secretary that SDI "was a fuss about nothing." "We suspect that this SDI is nothing but a bluff," they concluded.[52] (In September 1993, then Secretary of Defense Les Aspin acknowledged that while SDI had been a legitimate research program, there had been an accompanying "deception program" aimed at misleading the Soviets into massive defense outlays.[53])

According to Soviet officials, Gorbachev was opposed to SDI for political reasons rather than military reasons. Gorbachev was not opposed to SDI because he thought a comprehensive defensive shield was possible (none of the Soviets did). Rather, he opposed SDI because it undermined the ABM Treaty and the fundamental tenets of all previous arms control accords, and threatened the "militarization of space." Politically speaking, it would be more difficult for Gorbachev to pursue arms reduction if some of his Soviet colleagues believed the United States to be not only building up but also launching a new arms race in space. Soviet Foreign Minister Andrei Gromyko explained the Soviet position to Secretary Shultz during their January 1985 meeting in Geneva. "The United States reasons that the Soviet Union could also develop its own strategic defense. Then there would be two such systems, a Soviet one and a U.S. one," Gromyko reasoned. "But why have these systems at all? After all, one side has nuclear arms and the other side has them too, so although it is possible to . . . neutralize these weapons, why create a system to do so? Isn't it simpler just to eliminate nuclear weapons themselves?"[54] Gorbachev wanted to avoid the costly charade of SDI and focus on reducing existing nuclear arsenals. This, he believed, could restore the economic health of the USSR. "For Gorbachev, [domestic reform] was the main thing," Chernyaev explained. "To do this he needed to stop the arms race."[55] For a variety of reasons, then, the Soviets devoted minimal amounts of resources to countering Reagan's SDI program.[56]

In short, one cannot argue that the Reagan administration's military buildup bankrupted the Soviet Union because the Soviet Union never sought to match U.S. expenditures. Military spending continued at previous levels throughout the 1980s, and the Soviets chose not to invest in an SDI program of their own. "The increased Soviet defense spending provoked by Reagan's policies was not the straw that broke the back of the evil empire," explains Anatoly Dobrynin, Soviet ambassador to the United States. "We did not bankrupt ourselves in the arms race, as the Caspar Weinbergers of this world would like to believe. The Soviet response to Star Wars caused only an acceptable rise in defense spending. Throughout the Reagan presidency, the rising Soviet defense effort contributed to our decline, but only marginally, as it had in previous years. The troubles in our economy were the result of our own internal contradictions of autarky, low investment, and lack of innovation, as even Western economic specialists at the World Bank and elsewhere now believe."[57]

CONCLUSION

What role did the Reagan administration play in ending the cold war? One of the most widely cited arguments is that the administration won the cold war by hastening, if not causing, the collapse of the Soviet Union. The Reagan administration sought to vanquish its enemy and achieved victory when the Soviet Union ceased to exist at the end of 1991.

Archival evidence and oral testimony simply do not support this view. The Reagan administration abandoned its hard-line policy in January 1984 and began actively seeking better relations with Moscow. It is clear that the administration sought to improve superpower relations, not to destroy the Soviet Union. Moreover, key officials in the Reagan White House themselves reject the notion that the administration forced the collapse of the USSR or that they even intended such a feat.

However, the Soviet decision to seek an end to the arms race was based in part on the realization that defense spending had taken an unacceptable toll on the Soviet economy over the preceding four decades. The cold war had been costly. While Soviet economic reforms were not a response to the Reagan administration's policies per se, they were, in part, a response to forty years of cold war hostility. The Reagan administration's policies did not destroy the Soviet Union, but the cold war certainly played a role.

If the Reagan administration did not single-handedly win the cold war by forcing the collapse of the Soviet Union, then what role did the administration play, if any? Space limitations prevent a full discussion here, but some observations can be made, based upon the preceding discussion.

First, the preceding discussion casts doubt on the argument that the Reagan administration prolonged the cold war by pursuing a hard-line policy toward Moscow. The White House abandoned its hard-line policy in January 1984 and adopted a new policy aimed at improving superpower relations. In both public and private, Reagan officials sought to reassure Moscow of Washington's benign intentions and to seek new avenues for communication and arms reductions. Moreover, although some Americans were appalled at Reagan's use of the phrase "the evil empire" and similar sentiments, Soviet officials testify that this earlier, more belligerent tone had little effect on Soviet policymaking. Consequently, it seems unlikely that this rhetoric prevented an earlier conclusion to the cold war.

Second, the assertion that Mikhail Gorbachev single-handedly ended the cold war through his policy of New Thinking also appears extreme, if one takes into account the important changes in U.S. policy beginning in 1984. It is doubtful that the cold war could have ended as rapidly if the Reagan administration had continued to shun summit meetings and sincere arms talks, as it did during its first two years in office. While Gorbachev's policies were certainly crucial to the peaceful resolution of the cold war conflict, the Reagan administration's policies were also critical.

Finally, the ending of the cold war was a victory for the Reagan administration, but not in the sense that the Reagan victory school asserts. The victory was not that the Soviet Union collapsed, but rather that cold war hostility ended.

The ending of the cold war was a victory for both Reagan and Gorbachev because both leaders had sought peace.

NOTES

1. The reverse is also true: the factors that one assumes to be important in ending the cold war can determine the date one chooses for the ending of the cold war. A variety of dates have been proposed for the ending of the cold war. Some suggest that the Geneva summit meeting in November 1985 was the beginning of the end, while others propose that the introduction of glasnost and perestroika in the spring of 1986 paved the way for the dissolution of the Soviet Union and, therefore, the end of the cold war. Throughout 1989 several East European states that had been in the Soviet sphere of influence took major steps to open their borders and their political systems. On November 9, 1989, the Berlin Wall came down, which signaled to many that the cold war was drawing to a close. Alternatively, others have argued that the cold war ended on December 25, 1991, the day that the Soviet Union was officially dissolved.

2. The Geneva summit meeting was the first time that President Reagan had met with a Soviet leader. The main accomplishments of the summit were the personal rapport that was established between Reagan and Mikhail Gorbachev, and the agreement to hold two further summit meetings.

3. William D. Jackson, "Soviet Reassessment of Ronald Reagan, 1985–1988," *Political Science Quarterly* 113, no. 4 (winter 1998–1999): 623–24.

4. Authors who subscribe to this view include Richard Pipes, "Misinterpreting the Cold War," *Foreign Affairs* 74 (January–February 1995): 154–61; Caspar Weinberger, *Fighting for Peace* (New York: Warner Books, 1990); Robert Gates, *From the Shadows: The Ultimate Inside Story of Five Presidents and How they Won the Cold War* (New York: Simon & Schuster, 1996); and Peter Schweizer, *Victory: The Reagan Administration's Secret Strategy that Hastened the Collapse of the Soviet Union* (New York: Atlantic Monthly Press, 1994).

5. For examples of this view, see Beth A. Fischer, *The Reagan Reversal: Foreign Policy and the End of the Cold War* (Columbia: University of Missouri Press, 1997); Jackson, "Soviet Reassessment"; and Daniel Deudney and G. John Ikenberry, "Who Won the Cold War?" in Ikenberry, ed., *American Foreign Policy: Theoretical Essays,* 2nd edition (New York: HarperCollins, 1996), 625–36. Secretary of State George Shultz's memoirs, *Turmoil and Triumph: My Years as Secretary of State* (New York: Charles Scribner's Sons, 1993), can also be interpreted in this vein.

6. The five summit meetings were in Geneva (November 1985), Reykjavik (October 1986), Washington (December 1987), Moscow (May–June 1988), and New York (fall 1988).

7. Richard Halloran, "Reagan to Request $38B Increase in Military Outlays," *New York Times,* March 5, 1981, and William Kaufmann, *A Reasonable Defense* (Washington, D.C.: Brookings Institution Press, 1986), 25.

8. By 1987 the Soviets were convinced that SDI was technologically infeasible, and Gorbachev decided to shift his focus away from attempts to block the program and focus instead on gaining an arms reduction treaty.

9. Ronald Reagan, "The U.S.–Soviet Relationship," *Department of State Bulletin* 84:2083 (January 16, 1984), 1–4. Reagan officials sometimes refer to these initiatives as the "four pillars" because the president called for progress in four areas: bilateral relations, regional issues, human rights, and arms control. Members of the administration had been pushing for such a change in the United States' Soviet policy off and on throughout 1983. For more detail about this address and its consequences, see Fischer, *Reagan Reversal.* See also the remarks of Robert McFarlane and Jack Matlock, *Understanding the End of the Cold War, 1980–87: An Oral History Conference,* Brown University, May 7–10, 1998.

10. For example, see Reagan, Press Conference, May 21, 1982, *Weekly Compilation of Presidential Documents* 18, 714; and Shultz, *Turmoil and Triumph,* 464.

11. Of course, Reagan had been living in the nuclear age since taking office. Despite this, he had refused to take part in a summit meeting for the first three years of his presidency.

12. Reagan letter to Andropov, December 23, 1983. (Drafts dated December 19, 1983.)

13. The two sides had tried from time to time to establish an unofficial "back channel" for communications but were never able to do so. At one point the Soviets proposed that their ambassador to the United States, Anatoly Dobrynin, could serve this function, but the Reagan administration took this to mean that the Soviets wanted to communicate only through official channels. The administration wished to communicate through someone other than Dobrynin because they suspected he was not reporting their messages in full to Moscow.

14. Reagan letter to Chernenko, February 11, 1984.

15. Given space limitations, it is impossible to cite every instance in which these themes were expressed during Reagan's subsequent four years in office.

16. McFarlane briefing, January 1984, WHORM subject file SP 833 (Soviet/U.S. Relations, WH 1/16/84) 168687–194999.

17. Matlock, Brown Conference, 85. Matlock went on to become the U.S. ambassador to the USSR between 1987 and 1991.

18. Matlock, Brown Conference, 89.

19. Matlock interview with author, September 19, 1995.

20. Gorbachev came to power fifteen months after Reagan's January 16 address, but did not introduce perestroika and glasnost until mid-1986.

21. Kiron K. Skinner, Annelise Anderson, and Martin Anderson, eds., *Reagan, In His Own Hand* (New York: Free Press, 2001), 12. Skinner, Anderson, and Anderson have provided transcripts of Reagan's handwritten radio addresses that include all errors in spelling, punctuation, and grammar. For this chapter I have corrected such mistakes.

22. Skinner, Anderson, and Anderson, *In His Own Hand,* 31.

23. Reagan, "Soviet Workers," May 25, 1977, in Skinner, Anderson, and Anderson, *In His Own Hand,* 146–47.

24. Reagan, "Salt II," September 11, 1979, in Skinner, Anderson, and Anderson, *In His Own Hand,* 63. Reagan was quoting journalist Ben Stein.

25. Ronald Reagan, Commencement Address at Notre Dame, May 17, 1981, *Weekly Compilation of Presidential Documents* (WCPD) 17, 532.

26. Ronald Reagan, Speech to Members of the British Parliament, June 8, 1982, *Department of State Bulletin* (July 1982): 27.

27. As quoted in Schweizer, *Victory,* xiii.

28. McFarlane, Brown Conference, 32.

29. Douglas MacEachin, Brown Conference, 12–13.

30. McFarlane remarks in interview with author, July 7, 1995. His remarks about possibly accelerating the rate of the Soviet decline are subject to debate.

31. Matlock, Brown Conference, 86, 88.

32. George P. Shultz, "U.S.–Soviet Relations," January 19, 1983, memorandum to President Reagan.

33. Ed Rowny, Brown Conference, 63.

34. McFarlane, Brown Conference, 45–48.

35. Anatoly Dobrynin, *In Confidence: Moscow's Ambassador to America's Six Cold War Presidents* (New York: Times Books, 1995), 616.

36. Anatoly Chernyaev, Brown Conference, 8–9.

37. Oleg Grinevsky, Brown Conference, 14–15. For a more complete discussion of the decline of the USSR, see Jack Matlock, *Autopsy on an Empire* (New York: Random House, 1995), and Raymond Garthoff, *The Great Transition* (Washington, D.C.: Brookings Institution Press, 1994), among others.

38. Georgy Shaknazarov, Brown Conference, 26–27.

39. Former Soviet officials contend that there was a secondary reason for wanting to end the arms race: they wanted to repair the image of the USSR. They were concerned that the Soviet Union was viewed internationally as an aggressor that violated human rights. See remarks by Sergei Tarasenko and Anatoly Chernyaev, Brown Conference, 74–80.

40. Vladimir Slipchenko, Brown Conference, 25.

41. Shaknazarov, Brown Conference, 28.

42. Chernyaev, Brown Conference, 33.

43. Tarasenko, Brown Conference, 252.

44. Chernyaev, Brown Conference, 251.

45. Slipchenko, Brown Conference, 264–65.

46. Chernyaev, Brown Conference, 81.

47. Ibid.

48. Gorbachev, Geneva summit, November 19, 1985, Plenary Session 11:45–12:15.

49. Frances FitzGerald, *Way Out There in the Blue: Reagan, Star Wars, and the End of the Cold War* (New York: Simon & Schuster, 2000), 474–75.

50. One study was conducted by the Velikhov Committee, and the other study, which is quoted here, was conducted by "the military institutions of the USSR." Slipchenko, Brown Conference, 51–52. Grinevsky relates that Marshall Akhromeev called SDI "a chimera" (Brown Conference, 41). U.S. analysts had reached similar conclusions about the possibility of building a defense system that was 99 percent effective. See FitzGerald, *Way Out There in the Blue.*

51. Slipchenko, Brown Conference, 51–52.

52. Yakovlev, as cited in FitzGerald, *Way Out There in the Blue,* 411.

53. Garthoff, *Great Transition,* 516 n, R. Jeffrey Smith, "3 'Star Wars' Tests Rigged, Aspin Says; Scheme to Mislead Soviets Went Awry," *Washington Post,* September 10, 1993, A19; and Transcript of Secretary of Defense Les Aspin's press conference of September 9, 1993, *New York Times,* September 10, 1993.

54. Memorandum of Conversation, Second Shultz-Gromyko meeting, Geneva, January 7, 1985.

55. Chernyaev, Brown Conference.

56. See also Garthoff, *Great Transition,* 516–17.

57. Dobrynin, *In Confidence,* 617. Caspar Weinberger was Reagan's defense secretary from 1981 until November 1987. He favored a hard-line policy toward Moscow.

6

Reagan, Euromissiles, and Europe

Samuel F. Wells, Jr.

For the continent of Europe, the two most seminal events of the second half of the twentieth century were the end of the cold war and the creation of an integrated Europe through the evolution of the European Community into the European Union in 1993. In each important process, the critical transforming events occurred during the 1980s. During that vital decade, the principal actors in European affairs were Margaret Thatcher, François Mitterrand, Helmut Kohl, Ronald Reagan, and Mikhail Gorbachev. In the long road leading to the end of the cold war, the two main players were Reagan and Gorbachev. Their actions set the stage—unwittingly as it developed—for the fall of the Berlin Wall in 1989 and the collapse of the Soviet Union in 1991. But the leaders of the two superpowers played no significant role in the creation of an integrated Europe, although it is arguable that the reduction of cold war tensions was a necessary precondition for the process of integration to advance. This essay will try to explain how the United States under Ronald Reagan played such a large role in the end of the cold war but no substantial part in European integration.

THE REAGAN REVOLUTION

As president of the United States, Ronald Reagan posed a major problem for European leaders. His main objectives were to create a vigorous government in Washington and reassert U.S. leadership in the world. He wanted to reduce the size of government, cut federal regulations, and unleash the American economy to achieve a new level of growth and prosperity. A devoted anticommunist, he sought to rebuild U.S. military power and use it to resist the Soviet Union in all its adventures around the world. He brought to Washington a political program built on a few broad principles, and his operating style, established in eight years as governor of California, was to leave the design and implementation of policy to trusted aides.[1]

The fact that Reagan's cabinet members and top White House staff were of no single persuasion on international policy would prove a complicating factor for U.S. allies. The administration was composed of an odd mixture of conservative ideologues (National Security Adviser Richard Allen, Secretary of Defense Caspar Weinberger, Undersecretary of Defense for Policy Fred Iklé, Assistant Secretary of Defense for International Security Policy Richard Perle, and CIA Director William Casey) and pragmatists (Chief of Staff James A. Baker III, Secretary of the Treasury Donald Regan, and on European policy Secretary of State Alexander Haig). The triumvirate of top White House aides, Baker, and counselors Edwin Meese and Michael Deaver had planned for the National Security Council (NSC) staff under Richard Allen to be the main coordinating point for foreign policy issues, but within a year it was obvious, in the judgment of foreign policy specialist I. M. Destler, that the NSC was "the weakest since the Truman administration." Soon Allen was out, to be replaced in January 1982 by Judge William P. Clark, who had been chief of staff for Reagan as governor and knew all of the foreign policy principals in the new administration. Problems remained for European governments. Administration priorities were on domestic affairs. On international issues, unless foreign leaders shared the president's views or knew his top staff— and only Margaret Thatcher did—they would likely have a difficult time changing Reagan's mind or influencing his policies.[2]

In a recent interview about the role of the national security adviser, Robert McFarlane indicated that he would not "pretend President Reagan came into town with a foreign policy agenda on his mind." But he did come with a number of well-developed attitudes and aphorisms which would guide much of his early orientation on foreign policy. We have some sense of these attitudes in an extremely interesting new book based on the handwritten radio addresses that Reagan made in the 1970s for the most part. For example, in one radio address that he made in August 1978, he indicates his total opposition to a policy of détente with the quip: "détente—isn't that what a farmer has with his turkey—until Thanksgiving Day?"[3] In May 1977, in a radio talk on the Russians and what a threat they are to the United States and its way of life, he made the comment without any indication of where he got the idea that "apparently the Russians have a laser beam capable of blasting our missiles from the sky if we should ever try to use them, and apparently we had no inkling such a weapon was being added to their arsenal."[4]

FOREIGN POLICY GOALS

In international policy, senior officials of the Reagan administration uniformly agreed that their principal task was to respond to a series of challenges originating in Moscow. They believed that Soviet leaders were exploiting U.S. weakness and lack of political will in the aftermath of Vietnam and the oil shocks. The recently concluded hostage crisis in Iran was the latest evidence of this failure of American leadership. Based on a massive expansion of conventional and nuclear arms, the Soviet Union had increased the stakes in the cold war by its invasion of Afghanistan in December 1979. It threatened Western interests and international stability by its military support of terrorism and hostile regimes in the Middle East and the Horn of Africa. With the backing of Fidel Castro's Cuba, Moscow gave vital support to the socialist government of Nicaragua in its effort to overthrow elected governments in El Salvador and Honduras. In Europe the Soviets were threatening the security balance by their deployment of intermediate-range SS-20 missiles and the support of antinuclear movements among America's European allies.[5]

The Reagan administration responded to this perceived Soviet threat by a broad defense buildup and a new counteroffensive strategy. In his second month in office, Defense Secretary Weinberger submitted formal revisions to the budgets before Congress requesting an additional $7 billion for fiscal year (FY) 1981 and $26 billion for FY 1982. Taken together, these revisions in the budgets proposed by President Jimmy Carter projected a 10.1 percent real annual growth in obligational authority for the fiscal years 1981–1986, bringing defense spending to an average of 7 percent of gross national product (GNP). This new funding would expand procurement on the most advanced conventional and nuclear weapons, increase high technology research and development, and move toward the goal of the six-hundred-ship navy. In his annual report for 1982, Weinberger described his new strategy by saying the United States, if attacked, would respond with force "at places where we can affect the outcome of the war," striking at both political and military targets of sufficient importance to "offset" the original attack. This policy of horizontal escalation would require more military forces, especially for the navy.[6]

In the early Reagan years, international policy was driven more by defense policy than by diplomatic initiative. The administration provided aid to the government of El Salvador and covert support to the opponents of the Sandinista regime in Nicaragua. Massive assistance also went to the mujahideen in Afghanistan. Washington gave strong military and diplomatic support to Israel and launched an active campaign against terrorism around the world. Led by defense department officials, the administration placed additional limits on the transfer of military or dual-use technology and tried to restrict trade and credit for the Soviet bloc. U.S. officials encouraged the NATO (North Atlantic Treaty Organization) allies to implement the deployment of U.S. intermediate-range missiles in response to the Soviet SS-20s. Initially the administration moved slowly on arms control in the hope that the United States military buildup would show Moscow that it would have to make a clear choice between negotiating arms reductions or facing an arms race with the United States.[7]

EARLY RELATIONS WITH EUROPE

In its first months in office, while concentrating on developing its economic reform program and launching the defense buildup, the Reagan administration

took few significant international actions but did assess its main European partners. The president had a prior relationship with Margaret Thatcher from the
time when both were out of leadership positions, and more importantly, they
shared a conservative philosophy of minimal government and a strong foreign
policy based on national interests in a European environment dominated by
socialist governments with a firm commitment to détente. Thatcher would be
Reagan's first state visitor in February 1981, and she was received in Washington with great respect and high ceremony. Administration officials were skeptical about Helmut Schmidt in Germany, because his party seemed to have
deserted him on the deployment of intermediate-range nuclear forces (INF) and
his government appeared threatened in the forthcoming elections. In France the
new socialist government of François Mitterrand was viewed with even more
unease due to its left-wing economic program and the inclusion of four communist ministers. As the months passed, U.S. officials came to take a much more
positive view of Mitterrand when they understood how much he agreed with
U.S. policy toward the Soviet Union and on the need to fight European neutralism by deploying the INF missiles.[8]

The Reagan administration's early statements on the use of nuclear weapons
and the need to defer strategic arms control negotiations caused distress in most
European leaders. It was bad enough to have senior officials who had campaigned
against SALT II and European pacifism, but now these same individuals were
discussing nuclear demonstration shots in congressional testimony, and the president himself talked about a limited nuclear exchange in Europe with a group of
newspaper editors. Such remarks helped fuel the antinuclear demonstrations in
October and November of 1981 in Bonn, London, and Florence. Officials in each
of these countries expressed their dismay to Washington and asked for help in
winning public support for the INF missiles scheduled for deployment on their
territory.[9]

In deciding how to go to the negotiating table on INF, officials in the Reagan
administration underwent the first of what would be a long series of battles on
arms control and security issues between the Pentagon and the Department of
State. Leading the fight for the respective sides was Richard Perle for the Pentagon and Richard Burt for the Department of State. They ultimately came to
seize on a version of zero Western deployments in exchange for zero missiles
left deployed by the Soviets as their solution, but there were many variations
between their approaches. Perle proposed a zero missiles initiative that would
include both long- and short-range theater weapons, called in the debates "zero
only." Richard Burt responded with a "zero plus" proposal that would offer zero
on both sides for long-range missiles but included the flexibility to retain up to
one hundred launchers on each side. Ultimately President Reagan chose the
Pentagon's version because of its clear simplicity and the ease with which it could
be explained. This was to be zero pure and simple, which Richard Perle, as all
of those around him knew, hoped would prove unnegotiable.[10]

Working hard on the speech himself, President Reagan made a dramatic proposal for the elimination of all intermediate-range missiles in Europe with his "zero-option" proposal at the National Press Club on November 18, 1981. The essence of the president's proposal came in a single sentence: "The United States is prepared to cancel its deployment of Pershing II and ground-launched cruise missiles if the Soviets will dismantle their SS-20, SS-4 and SS-5 missiles." Experienced policymakers saw problems with this new proposal. Walter Slocombe, a senior arms control official in the Carter administration, said there were some in the new administration who hoped "the proposal is so brilliant that the Soviets will never accept it and that . . . it will stop" the negotiations. William Hyland, a specialist on Soviet policy and arms control, was concerned that the prospect of zero missiles would persuade vulnerable European governments to refuse to allow the preparation of missile sites to show the West's resolve. But many in Europe breathed easier when INF negotiations between U.S. and Soviet delegations opened in Geneva on November 30. These talks would drag on for over six years before the decisive intervention of the new Soviet leader Mikhail Gorbachev would lead to the signing of an INF treaty in December 1987.[11]

The imposition of martial law by the Polish government in December 1981 created a more serious problem in transatlantic relations. This, too, was a problem that a more adroit administration could have avoided if it were less concerned with sending a strong message to its allies about economic relations with the Soviet adversary. Arguing that the Soviet Union had forced the Polish government to suppress Solidarity with martial law, which we now know was done by Warsaw for its own reasons, the Reagan administration announced on December 29 a series of sanctions that were primarily aimed at restricting U.S. exports to build a natural gas pipeline from Siberia to Germany. The purpose of the sanctions was twofold: to delay the construction of the pipeline and, more importantly, to instruct the West Europeans on how dangerous it was to become dependent on Soviet energy supplies. European governments and press were shocked at the U.S. sanctions and argued against them using the logic of détente and the need to create mutual interests in trade and arms control. The pipeline debate became part of the agenda at the Versailles economic summit in June 1982, where a heated debate between Ronald Reagan and François Mitterrand produced an ambiguous deal for the United States not to push sanctions any further while the Europeans restricted credits to the Soviet Union. At a NATO summit in Bonn a few days later, this deal was neither clarified nor recorded, so that after the meeting Reagan and Mitterrand each gave different versions of what had been agreed. In a recent interview, Richard Burt, at the time director of the Bureau of Political-Military Affairs at the Department of State, said that the gas pipeline sanctions decision "was a total fiasco."[12]

Back at home Reagan received strong criticism from conservatives for not winning the support of the allies for pipeline sanctions. The president's top White

House staff decided to take a strong stand on the pipeline issue as a way of striking back at Secretary of State Haig, whom they blamed for not getting a better result in Europe. Judge Clark, the national security adviser, called a meeting of the NSC for June 18, when Haig had to be at the United Nations in New York. At this session the staff pushed through a set of expanded sanctions to include subsidiaries of U.S. firms operating abroad and European firms using technology under American licenses. This claim of "extraterritorial sanctions" brought a howl of protests from European capitals including a strong lecture from Mrs. Thatcher, who was in Washington for a visit shortly after the decision. The NSC action did produce the resignation of Alexander Haig, who was replaced by George Shultz. And, as Burt says, "we had a full-blown crisis within the alliance where even Reagan's natural allies like Margaret Thatcher were very distressed, very unhappy." George Shultz suddenly found himself inheriting this mess and, according to Burt, "he handled it in a great way. He got a dialogue started and listened to people and finally reached agreement with the French in which we were at least able, in lifting our sanctions, to get people to focus on the problem and began a dialogue on what the security consequences were of this kind of trade with the Soviets. But it was a difficult, prolonged process." As an official in the Elysée Palace in Paris put it, in order to maintain a generally cordial relationship with Washington, "a lot of water was put in the wine." But the memory remained of how little the Reagan administration seemed to know or care about European views on alliance unity or the value of détente as part of a balanced approach to the Soviet Union. The pipeline sanctions crisis also reflects the fundamental reality that Reagan administration policy for Europe was largely a derivative of the primary policy toward the Soviet Union.[13]

Some new information has recently come out concerning CIA estimates of Soviet strength and Soviet behavior and how these were used during the Reagan administration. These were published in a volume by the CIA under the title *CIA's Analysis of the Soviet Union, 1947–1991*, edited by Gerald K. Haines and Robert E. Leggett. These were discussed at a conference at Princeton University in March 2001 when further assessments were made of the validity and the use made of these assessments. An estimate of August 1982 evaluated the prospects for the Siberia–Western Europe natural gas pipeline. After reviewing the elements of technology involved and the likelihood that the Soviets would be able to get from other sources many of the things that the sanctions would deny them, the analysis concluded that the new export pipeline could probably begin functioning in late 1985 and reach nearly full volume in 1987, a delay of roughly one year as a result of the sanctions. On the negative side, it pointed out that the West Europeans needed the relatively low-priced Soviet gas and viewed the pipeline as creating employment for their citizens as well as a form of economic interdependence that would "lead to more responsible Soviet behavior." The analysis pointed out that the West Europeans are "deeply angry about the U.S. decision, especially the extraterritorial and retroactive features of the measures, which they regard as a serious infringement of their sovereignty." This estimate was quite accurate and essentially confirmed information contained in publicly available economic analysis. In many other ways, however, papers at the conference pointed out that during the Reagan years, the CIA was a key part of the process of overemphasizing most dimensions of the Soviet threat. At the conference, Raymond Garthoff, a longtime CIA military analyst, admitted that "there were consistent overestimates of the threat every year from 1978 to 1985." Douglas MacEachin, a thirty-two-year veteran and former deputy director, "identified the biggest single trap for intelligence estimates was Soviet intentions." He went on to say that the agency completely missed the extent to which the Soviet military industrial complex drove its own institutional growth and was motivated in part by its perceptions of American military strength. He said the agency overestimated the accuracy of Soviet missiles and the quality of their equipment. Other analysts pointed out that the CIA economic estimates had significantly exaggerated the economic well-being of Soviet citizens and were very slow to catch on to the fact that the Soviet Union was beginning to encounter serious economic problems from the early 1970s on. Fritz Ermarth, a former chairman of the National Intelligence Council, said that the agency's first paper indicating that the heavy level of military production was creating domestic stress on the system was produced only in the fall of 1985, a date that was "embarrassingly late."[14]

In the pipeline crisis and with other issues, Washington officials took little notice of signs of German dissatisfaction with U.S. and alliance policies or of a series of French initiatives to strengthen security cooperation with Germany. Disturbed by the rise of neutralism in Germany and the weak response in Bonn to the imposition of martial law in Poland, the French government had given strong support for the deployment of INF missiles in Germany, culminating in Mitterrand's dramatic speech before the Bundestag on January 20, 1983. France proposed a new security dialogue which was endorsed by Helmut Schmidt in February 1982 and reaffirmed by Helmut Kohl when he came to Paris on his first day as chancellor, October 4, 1982. The French government also revived the Western European Union as an instrument of enhanced security cooperation with a group of allies including Germany. And France created a new rapid intervention force, la Force d'action rapide (FAR), to signal French commitment on the Central Front in times of crisis. None of these steps received much attention in the upper levels of the Reagan administration, and at a Wilson Center meeting in October 1984, a senior defense official was openly dismissive of the military capabilities and significance of the FAR.[15]

For most of 1983, U.S. and allied diplomacy focused on deploying INF missiles and strengthening conventional defenses. The State Department under George Shultz's leadership concentrated on maintaining alliance cohesion and providing support for nations pledged to deploy the INF missiles, especially West Germany. As chancellor and head of the Social Democratic Party (SPD), Helmut Schmidt had proposed and been the principal advocate for INF deployment, but his party moved away from this position and toward antinuclear attitudes throughout the early 1980s. In advance of a major decision on missile deployment in the Bundestag, the SPD held a special party congress in Cologne on November 18, 1983. Despite Schmidt's strong defense of the alliance decision for missile deployment, the party delegates voted to reject the missiles by 386 to 14. An intense two-day missile debate consumed the Bundestag on November 21 and 22. The coalition government of Helmut Kohl's Christian Democratic Union (CDU) and Hans-Dietrich Genscher's Free Democratic Party (FDP) held firm, and the deployments won endorsement by 286 to 226. The Soviet Union walked out of the INF negotiations in Geneva in protest the next day. By the end of December, German defense officials announced that the first group of Pershing II intermediate-range missiles was operational at German bases.[16]

At the same time, the Reagan administration was pushing European allies to strengthen conventional defenses including a new operational doctrine of Deep Strike into enemy territory and increased European contribution to defense costs. Coming at a time of stagnant European economies, the demand for increased burden sharing was not well-received. To make matters worse, many in Europe questioned the need for improved conventional defenses. One widely read analyst, Josef Joffe, opposed high-technology conventional defense and preferred to rely on the strategy of Flexible Response. He argued that "the system has worked too well to be lightly abandoned in favor of reform-minded conventionalism. Nuclear deterrence in Europe has a track record, conventional defense has not, and four decades of ultrastability are an impressive argument for the status quo."[17]

Walter Schütze, a respected German specialist working in France, raised serious questions about the stability of Germany as the centerpiece of the alliance. The battle over the deployment of INF missiles, he believed, had broken the consensus on security policy and defense that had lasted for over twenty years. Contending that pressure on the Europeans to spend more, such as the Nunn amendment of 1984 called for, might well be counterproductive, he concluded:

> To put it in a simple way, people in Germany and in Western Europe are beginning to get fed up with being pushed around. By and large Germans are convinced that they do their fair share within the overall Western defense effort . . . and that, after all, better security cannot be bought by more armaments but by arms-control agreements with the other side. As Chancellor Kohl said in a recent Bundestag debate: "We want peace with less weapons!"[18]

THE CHALLENGE OF SDI

Reagan's views on nuclear weapons posed a large threat for all nations that were comfortable with the strategy of nuclear deterrence. On March 23, 1983, the president addressed the American people on national security and defense issues. After a lengthy review of the Soviet military buildup of the last twenty years and what his administration was doing to redress the inadequacies of U.S. defenses, Reagan offered to share "a vision of the future which offers hope." He raised the possibility of defending against missile attack and declared:

> Tonight, consistent with our obligations of the ABM Treaty in recognizing the need for closer consultation with our allies, I'm taking an important first step. I am directing a comprehensive and intensive effort to define a long-term research and development program to begin to achieve our ultimate goal of eliminating the threat posed by nuclear strategic missiles. This could pave the way for arms control measures to eliminate the weapons themselves. We seek neither military superiority nor political advantage. Our only purpose—one all people share—is to search for ways to reduce the danger of nuclear war.[19]

The president's appeal for a shield against ballistic missiles came as a surprise to almost everyone, and few took it seriously. This was a mistake. The need to eliminate the threat of nuclear weapons was one of Ronald Reagan's most strongly held beliefs. Combined with his unlimited faith in American technological ingenuity, this belief created a dream of a world freed from the terror of nuclear weapons. Many officials in the administration, like Deputy National Security Adviser Robert McFarlane, advanced the idea of missile defense hoping to trade it in negotiations with the Soviets for large cuts in numbers of weapons. But McFarlane and others who supported missile defense for tactical reasons would be disappointed. Reagan would not give up his dream of a nuclear-free world. As arms control expert Strobe Talbott told biographer Lou Cannon: Reagan "was a romantic, a radical, a nuclear abolitionist." The president's chief START negotiator, Lieutenant General Edward L. Rowny, declared privately in 1985: "People are in for a surprise. Reagan really wants to abolish nuclear weapons, and he is confident the people will support him against the arms control establishment."[20]

Richard Burt, who was completely absorbed in managing arms control consultations and negotiations on INF, was totally surprised by the president's announcement of SDI in March of 1983. Burt recalled: "My initial reaction was of a kind of unpleasant distraction because it appeared with so little consultation and so little preparation that it did disturb the alliance." He pointed out that the Germans were upset with the potential decoupling of the alliance and by the reduction of any sense of risk sharing that would be involved. But he went on to emphasize that "the people who reacted first and foremost and the strongest were the British. Mrs. Thatcher was upset and she probably did more than anyone to put a fence around SDI." This was really brought to completion when she got President Reagan to sign on to her list of agreed points during a meeting at Camp David.[21]

Although the Pentagon soon organized the missile defense efforts of the various services into the Strategic Defense Initiative (SDI) and would by the end of 1990 have spent $17 billion on the program, European reaction was limited to complaints about the president's speech undermining alliance strategic doctrine and public confidence in deterrence. Defense Secretary Caspar Weinberger propelled European political leaders into action when he wrote them on March 26, 1985, asking for their participation in SDI research and giving sixty days for a reply. In explaining the delayed reaction to SDI, a senior French diplomat declared, "We felt it was just another Reagan Sunday speech like those about the evil empire or school prayer. But when we realized that American generals were touring Europe with their checkbooks open ready to sign up our best technology firms, we knew we had to respond in a substantive way." European governments gave a mixed reaction to the proposed research cooperation. France, Germany, and Britain firmly let it be known that they had reservations about strategic innovations that undercut nuclear deterrence, but they all wanted to benefit from the new high-technology research. The French government insisted it would not endorse research participation, but quietly it allowed French companies to sign contracts for SDI-sponsored research.[22]

Led by France, Europe soon created several responses to the American SDI. In April 1985 the Mitterrand government announced the creation of Eurêka as a cooperative program of civilian technology research and development ranging from microelectronics and computers to advanced industrial turbines. This program would involve eighteen European nations in cooperative projects and would generate significant partnerships among firms in France, Germany, the Netherlands, and the United Kingdom. In another response, the European Council, meeting in June 1985, endorsed proposals to revive activity in the Western European Union (WEU). Franco-German defense cooperation also picked up with joint maneuvers involving 150,000 troops in 1986 and on the suggestion of Chancellor Kohl the creation of a Franco-German brigade the following year.[23]

The United States gave verbal support to expanded Franco-German defense cooperation as long as it did not detract from NATO. Assistant Secretary of State Richard Burt conveyed the message about protecting the uniqueness of NATO in unusually direct fashion in February 1985. Irritated by these European initiatives, the State Department let it be known that it saw no particular need to revitalize the WEU and it felt that cooperation in armaments could basically be done through the Eurogroup. Basically the United States government wanted the Europeans to improve their conventional defenses, pay more of the costs of NATO, and follow policies made in Washington for high-technology research, completion of the INF deployments, and the reduction of battlefield nuclear weapons as had been agreed. Privately, defense officials in the United States discounted Eurêka and the Franco-German brigade as largely exercises in symbolism, and events of the next fifteen years essentially proved them right.[24]

Arms control negotiations dominated the attention of the upper levels of the Reagan administration after 1985. This unanticipated result stemmed from the conjuncture of three very different sets of events. Ronald Reagan shifted the direction of his policy toward Moscow in January 1984. In a speech on January 16, the president moved beyond attacking the aggressive aims of the Soviet Union and began to focus on the threat of war. "Reducing the risk of war—and especially nuclear war—is priority number one," he asserted. Although his speech was largely discounted as election year rhetoric, Reagan from this point on was more conciliatory toward the Soviets, and against the advice of some of his hardline senior officials consistently pressed for arms reduction. Equally important was the fact that Mikhail Gorbachev came to power in Moscow in March 1985 and wanted to reduce the costs of military and foreign commitments in order to advance economic and political reform within the Soviet Union. At roughly the same time in the summer of 1985, the Reagan administration launched a secret program of arms sales to Iran and from the autumn of 1986 would be mired in the public disclosures of the Iran-Contra scandal until Congress issued a report from its joint hearings in November 1987.[25]

Gorbachev provided the spark for new negotiations in a linked set of separate Geneva negotiations on INF, START (Strategic Arms Reduction Talks), and defense and space issues beginning in March 1985. Numerous new proposals came from both sides, but hard-liners in each delegation prevented progress. In the hope of advancing through improved relations between leaders, Reagan and Gorbachev met for a series of meetings including two private sessions in Geneva between November 19 and 21, 1985. The two leaders discussed a wide range of issues, but Reagan's refusal to allow limitations on SDI blocked any advance on arms control questions. There was a glimmer of hope for future progress when at the end of their second private meeting on November 19, Gorbachev "appealed to the President to recognize the true signal he was conveying to him as President and to the U.S. Administration as a whole. The Soviet Union did indeed wish to establish a new relationship with the United States and deliver our two nations from the increasing fear of nuclear weapons."[26]

Reagan's personal assessment of the Geneva summit was contained in a breezy "Dear Murph" letter to fellow actor-turned-politician George Murphy. The president thanked the former senator for "that most generous review of my performance in Geneva. I must say I enjoyed playing the part and the show did have something of a happy ending." He went on to declare that Gorbachev "is a firm believer in their system. . . . At the same time, he is practical and knows his economy is a basket case." The United States, Reagan concluded, should convince Gorbachev that his country "will be better off if we make some practical agreements, without attempting to convert him to our way of thinking."[27]

After the Geneva summit, while American officials were debating what steps to take, Gorbachev again took the initiative and on January 15, 1986, proposed a set of actions that would result in the elimination of all nuclear weapons "by the end of 1999." This initiative included a provision for "the complete liquidation of Soviet and U.S. medium-range missiles in the European zone—both ballistic and cruise missiles—as a first stage on the path to freeing the European Continent of nuclear weapons." Soviet negotiators in Geneva showed some further flexibility in dropping their prior insistence on including British and French nuclear forces in the INF totals for the West. But they were unwilling to separate the INF terms from negotiations on START and SDI until Gorbachev again forced the pace by telling Senator Edward Kennedy during a visit to Moscow in February that an INF agreement was not linked to other issues. In numerous exchanges of views in the three negotiating groups in Geneva, it became apparent to U.S. officials that the Soviet representatives were much less interested in progress on INF than in blocking SDI. Seeking a way out of this deadlock, Max Kampelman, head of the U.S. delegation in Geneva, and Paul Nitze, special adviser to the president and the secretary of state on arms control, sought numerous routes to achieve "a grand compromise" on START and SDI by trading limitations on SDI for deep reductions in offensive strategic weapons. But this quest for a breakthrough initiative was thwarted at every step by a coalition of defense hawks led by Richard Perle.[28]

In September Gorbachev took another bold step to provide an "impulse" to the negotiations by proposing a small informal summit in Reykjavik, Iceland, in mid-October. The terms of his letter proposing this meeting and statements by Soviet officials in Moscow and in Geneva led American officials to believe that INF would be at the top of the Soviet agenda. In preparing the State Department for this meeting, Richard Solomon, director of the policy planning staff, wrote to George Shultz pointing out that the likely factors behind the Soviet initiative were the realization of Gorbachev and his team that the INF missiles were unnecessary, since their strategic weapons could cover all targets in Europe plus a desire to reduce tension between the Soviet Union and the United States. This did not mean their motives were totally positive, because Europeans had now ironically changed their attitudes from the early 1980s and were presently concerned that any significant reduction in missiles would leave them vulnerable to the superiority of Soviet conventional forces. Solomon concluded that Gorbachev's main agenda would be to advance a common European peace agenda which would focus on conventional arms control, INF, and chemical weapons disarmament.[29]

The small team of Americans went to Reykjavik prepared to discuss a wide range of arms control issues, hopefully to prepare for the conclusion of agreements at a summit in Washington by the end of the year. At Reykjavik negotiations occurred in two long, private meetings between Reagan and Gorbachev and in an experts working group that attempted to put details into the general agreed framework developed by the two leaders. Through many exchanges in the private meetings, Reagan asked for sharp reductions in strategic weapons but consistently defended SDI as a system the United States would share with other countries and which would help in their mutually agreed objective of the elimination of nuclear weapons. Gorbachev artfully pointed out the difficulties of a transition to lesser numbers of offensive weapons while building up defensive weapons. He showed that there would be a point in this transition when defense could overwhelm offense and make a first strike tempting to hawks on either side. The leaders reached agreement on the elimination of all strategic nuclear weapons within ten years and on the broad terms of an INF agreement. In the terms of the Memorandum of Conversation drafted by the American note taker, Gorbachev then declared that "it was time for the American side to make a move. . . . Gorbachev had heard it said that the President did not like to make concessions but he also recalled an American expression that seemed apt: 'it takes two to tango.' With respect to the major questions of arms control and nuclear disarmament, the two leaders were the only partners in sight. Was the President prepared to dance?" But Reagan was not ready to dance because he refused to accept the Soviet demand for a ban on testing weapons in space. Allied leaders in Europe were aghast that such a proposal would be discussed without any senior U.S. military officers present and without any consultation with NATO. They were not reassured that the deal had been blocked by the president's insistence on protecting SDI. Less than a month later, on November 4, the news broke that the United States had been selling arms to Iran in violation of its own loudly proclaimed arms embargo and using the profits to fund operations of the contras in Nicaragua, whose U.S. support had been terminated by the Congress.[30]

Over the next few months, as the White House staff prepared for multiple investigations of the Iran-Contra affair, those officials at the Defense and State departments who had been marginalized in the Reyjkavik negotiations resumed work with Soviet negotiators to try to generate a positive agreement. At the end of February 1987, Gorbachev broke a deadlock by agreeing to consider INF weapons separately from a package linking strategic forces and space weapons in a single proposal. Negotiators focused on INF issues for the rest of the year and signed a treaty on INF weapons on December 8, 1987, eliminating both long- and short-range INF missiles from Europe. Europeans were pleased to reduce Soviet nuclear weapons on their continent but were anxious that the Soviets retained a significant advantage in conventional arms. This anxiety was eased when a year later Gorbachev announced the start of large reductions in conventional forces in central Europe. This was followed in the Bush administration by agreement on the Conventional Forces in Europe Treaty in November 1990 and later by significant cuts in strategic weapons with the signing of the START I Treaty on July 31, 1991.[31]

WINDING DOWN THE COLD WAR

The end of the cold war developed largely through a series of Soviet-American negotiations, and the main agenda was security and arms control. At the center of the process was a new Soviet leader with a broad agenda for reforming his own society. Gorbachev came to power resolved to eliminate the security dilemma facing the Soviet Union: massive defense spending but decreasing security. While he developed his program of political and economic reform during 1985, he established an important and promising personal chemistry with Ronald Reagan at the Geneva summit. The solution to his security dilemma lay in a reduction of tensions with the United States, and by the spring of 1986 he felt comfortable moving toward this goal because he understood, as no prior Soviet leader had, that the United States posed no offensive threat to his country. Ronald Reagan shared the Soviet general secretary's belief in the power of personal relationships, and despite a long career of opposition to communism, he was concerned about the danger of nuclear war and came to believe he could reduce this threat through negotiations with Gorbachev.[32]

An assessment of how the Reagan-Gorbachev relationship worked to improve Soviet-American relations is contained in two memoranda by Anatoly Chernyaev, Gorbachev's top foreign policy adviser. In his suggestions for Gorbachev's speech to the Politburo on the Washington summit of December 1987, Chernyaev said: "We used the effect of Reykjavik very well. . . . The Americans wanted the treaty mostly for internal considerations—the coming Presidential elections. But also because without it we could not begin with START, and that issue is of immediate concern to the Americans." He goes on to suggest that Gorbachev make a statement about "the tactics of negotiating with Reagan, his incompetence. [The fact that] the real power rests with the group of Bush, Carlucci, and the others around them." The adviser comments that "from the point of view of Soviet-American relations, and through them—of world politics—direct contact with American society, through its most influential figures, is probably the most important issue right now." He closes by saying: "The main and decisive conclusion from the visit: everything depends on the success of perestroika. Perestroika is the major strike factor, the major force that can prevent war . . . [and turn] the entire global development toward peace and progress."[33]

At the session of the Politburo on December 17, 1987, Gorbachev used some of Chernyaev's ideas but chose to make other points in his own words and somewhat more sharply. He started his discussion by saying that the Washington summit built on the relationships established and the successes and failures of both Geneva and Reykjavik. One element of progress was that Reagan's characteristic tactic of accusing the Soviet Union and blaming all the troubles of the world on Moscow was less evident. "I told him: 'you are not a prosecutor, and I am not a defendant, you are not a teacher, and I am not a student. . . . Otherwise, it will not work.'" He declared that this "was the key moment in trying to find a common language: on equal terms, and business-like, each of us keeping the ideologies to ourselves." Gorbachev went on to tell the Politburo: "The summit in Washington also represented an important test of another fundamental idea of new thinking—namely, that its success and effectiveness depended on how things worked domestically, how perestroika was succeeding at home." He had been particularly impressed with the changed attitudes in Washington: "The friendly atmosphere, even enthusiasm to some degree, with which straight-laced Washington met us, was a sign of the changes that had begun to transpire in the West, and which meant that the 'enemy image' had begun to erode, and that the myth of the 'Soviet military threat' was undermined. It was very special for us. And it was noticed in the entire world." He concluded by saying that in Washington, we were prepared completely to use our previous overtures to the American leadership, "to literally incorporate the purely human factor into the big international politics. This is also an important element of new thinking. And it also produced its results. We felt that in Washington—maybe for the first time so clearly."[34]

These two very different men cooperated to set in motion a reduction of tensions and lower levels of arms that encouraged steps for freedom in Eastern Europe. The Reagan-Gorbachev negotiations over security and arms control from 1985 to 1988 prepared the way for the dissolution of East Germany and the fall of the Berlin Wall. While Reagan was not the largest force for change in this process, he was an essential part and perhaps the only American political leader who could have made the concessions necessary to win Gorbachev's agreement.

ECONOMIC POLICY AND EUROPEAN INTEGRATION

In the second big story of Europe's last fifty years, the growth of European integration, the Reagan administration played a very minor role. European foreign ministers and heads of government spent more of their time in the Reagan years dealing with economic issues including European Community affairs than on security, and by the latter half of the 1980s they were beginning to achieve important success. But in the United States, top Reagan administration officials dealing with international affairs devoted very little time to economic questions. International economic policy, including European Community affairs, was the mandate of a separate bureaucracy that involved part of the Commerce and State departments, the Treasury, the Office of the U.S. Trade Representative, a section of the Federal Reserve, and a small economics staff in the Executive Office of the President. Their work involved the European Community primarily over trade disputes and through preparation for the annual economic summits of the G-7. Issues related to the European Community were seldom on the agenda at cabinet or NSC meetings. This lack of attention is reflected in the memoirs of George Shultz as secretary of state covering the years 1983 through 1988. In a volume of 1,138 pages, Shultz has four entries on the European Community.[35]

In discussing the relationship between the Reagan administration and the European Community, Richard Burt made two broad points:

There are two things going on here. One is that to the extent that anybody worries about the EC, there was a strategic decision taken not to recognize it as a place to do business with the Europeans, because it was just easier and more profitable to work more bilaterally through the major capitals. In a sense we felt why recognize and give that institution status when the United States could more easily succeed in what it was trying to achieve by picking off these countries one by one. Because once you started focusing on the EU and the institutions in Brussels you are in a sense almost granting them character and standing.

The second factor is that frankly it is a matter of lack of understanding and a lack of attention, and I think that most senior decision makers in Washington (assistant secretaries and above) don't pay attention and know what is happening in the EU. [While the EU] is still fragmented and still chaotic and messy . . . , [it is an institution we have to take seriously. Unfortunately] we are always a little behind the power curve in understanding what is happening in terms of Europe.[36]

This trenchant evaluation of U.S. policy toward the European Community is almost as true today as it was in the 1980s.

The objectives of U.S. international economic policy in the 1980s were quite similar to those today. U.S. officials sought expanded trade, open markets, and increased GATT (General Agreement on Trade and Tariffs) coverage through completion of the Uruguay Round of negotiations for tariff reductions. With less certainty, they also worked to maintain relative currency stability and an improved fair, transparent rule of law for investment and multinational corporations.

Throughout the Reagan administration, officials in Washington voiced support for European economic integration while continuing to protect U.S. trade and investment interests. Given the preoccupation with arms control negotiations and Iran-Contra hearings, there was little top-level attention devoted to the Single European Act (a set of measures that would create a single internal market among member states by 1992) when it was adopted by the European Community in July 1987. A good statement of U.S. policy came at a Washington seminar on "Integration of the European Internal Market: Implications for Europe and the United States" in April 1988. After a description of the goals of the Single European Act and an estimate of its benefits to European economic growth, Paolo Cecchini, former deputy director-general for Internal Market and Industrial Affairs for the Commission of the European Communities, predicted that the new steps would also benefit foreign companies operating within the European Community and companies outside that would gain advantages from simplification of trade regulations. Responding to Cecchini's presentation, James M. Murphy, assistant U.S. trade representative for Europe and the Mediterranean, said the United States supported the current integration efforts and expected to benefit from increased exports, new access to sectors previously closed such as telecommunications and power-generating equipment, and decreased trade tensions. But Murphy expressed concern about the lack of transparency in European Community rule making, whether there would be new EC-wide quantitative import restrictions, and how the slogan "Europe for the Europeans" would affect U.S. multinationals operating within the European Community. In a restatement of official policy, Murphy concluded that the United States would continue to support European economic integration but would remain vigilant to protect American trade and business interests.

When American business leaders and economic specialists realized the Single European Act was moving toward creating a more efficient economy within the European Community, there were many fears expressed that "1992" would bring a fortress Europe. These anxieties ebbed in the years following the completed implementation of the Single European Act when U.S. exports to the then European Union doubled and its investment in Europe tripled. Similar patterns of inattention followed by high anxiety occurred after the implementation of the Maastricht Treaty in November 1993 and the European Monetary Union, which was phased in over the next nine years. One particularly recalls the alarmist predictions of economist Martin Feldstein, who suggested "the Euro means war." In fact it has been a quiet success.[37]

CONCLUSION

Ronald Reagan's personal role in his presidency was somewhat larger in setting the basic ideas and objectives of the administration than many observers felt at the time. For example, it was Reagan's own initiative to set significant limitations on nuclear weapons and to promote the concept and ultimately the program of the Strategic Defense Initiative. Yet in picking a team of senior officials who held quite divergent views on international affairs and in refusing to supervise closely or even to choose clearly between feuding advisers, like Shultz and Weinberger, Reagan created conditions for an inconsistent and error-prone—even scandal-prone—administration.

In terms of political and security policy for Europe, the Reagan team managed the dual-track arms control policy for intermediate-range missiles quite well once the State Department got the green light to proceed with negotiations. George Shultz and Richard Burt did a good job of smoothing over the bad feelings stemming from the pipeline sanctions and the way in which SDI was introduced, and established good and effective working relationships with their European counterparts. Prior to 1984, administration officials at the upper levels seemed to understand very little of what was going on in the Soviet Union and were setting themselves up for a series of surprises. They were rescued from even greater error by Mikhail Gorbachev, and the policy on balance was moderately successful in encouraging Gorbachev in a program of reforms which, some U.S. officials hoped, would be destined to go out of control. The Reagan-Gorbachev arms control negotiations led to an important set of agreements that reduced tensions and paved the way for the end of the cold war.

In terms of broad domestic and international economic policy, the administration's record is the least distinguished. The initial policies of tax cut and defense buildup created large deficits and led to a stalled economy until late 1982, which was further depressed by the savings and loan crises. But the restructuring of industry and a revival of consumer spending by the mid-1980s protected the administration from hard choices and larger mistakes. Reagan's two terms did leave significant potential problems for his successor George Bush in stagnating productivity and a long period of inattention to the changing nature and growing power of the European Community.

NOTES

1. I. M. Destler, "The Evolution of Reagan Foreign Policy," in *The Reagan Presidency: An Early Assessment,* ed. Fred I. Greenstein (Baltimore: Johns Hopkins University Press, 1983), 117–58; Helga Haftendorn, "Toward a Reconstruction of American Strength: A New Era in the Claim to Global Leadership?" in *The Reagan Administration: A Reconstruction of American Strength?* ed. Helga Haftendorn and Jakob Schissler (Berlin: Walter de Gruyter, 1988), 3–29.

2. Destler, "Reagan Foreign Policy," 118–28; Frances FitzGerald, *Way Out There in the Blue: Reagan, Star Wars, and the End of the Cold War* (New York: Simon & Schuster, 2000), 138–39.

3. Kiron K. Skinner, Annelise Anderson, and Martin Anderson, eds., *Reagan, In His Own Hand* (New York: Free Press, 2001), 12.

4. Skinner, Anderson, and Anderson, *In His Own Hand,* 34.

5. Haftendorn, "Reconstruction of American Strength," 5–7; Destler, "Reagan Foreign Policy," 129–36.

6. James W. Abellera, Roger P. Labrie, and Albert C. Pierce, *The FY 1982–1986 Defense Program: Issues and Trends* (Washington, D.C.: American Enterprise Institute, 1981), 4–9; Samuel F. Wells, Jr., "A Question of Priorities: A Comparison of the Carter and Reagan Defense Programs," *Orbis* 27 (fall 1983): 650–54; Caspar W. Weinberger, *Annual Report to the Congress* (FY 1983) (Washington, D.C.: Government Printing Office, 1982), I-15–I-16.

7. Wells, "Question of Priorities," 652–66; Haftendorn, "Reconstruction of American Strength," 11–13, 20–25.

8. Geoffrey Smith, *Reagan and Thatcher* (London: Bodley Head, 1990), 23–48; Samuel F. Wells, Jr., "The Mitterrand Challenge," *Foreign Policy* 44 (fall 1981): 57–61.

9. Strobe Talbott, *Deadly Gambits: The Reagan Administration and the Stalemate in Nuclear Arms Control* (New York: Alfred A. Knopf, 1984), 43–57.

10. Talbott, *Deadly Gambits,* 57–75.

11. Talbott, *Deadly Gambits,* 75–81 (quotations on 80); Miles Kahler, "The United States and Western Europe: The Diplomatic Consequences of Mr. Reagan," in *Eagle Resurgent?*

The Reagan Era in American Foreign Policy, ed. Kenneth A. Oye et al. (Boston: Little, Brown, 1987), 306–10; Destler, "Reagan Foreign Policy," 141–45; Smith, *Reagan and Thatcher,* 56–58.

12. In commenting on this essay at the Santa Barbara conference on March 29, 2002, Richard V. Allen declared that the Siberian pipeline was almost canceled but that back-channel negotiations broke down. Raymond L. Garthoff, *The Great Transition: American-Soviet Relations and the End of the Cold War* (Washington, D.C.: Brookings Institution Press, 1994), 546–51; Destler, "Reagan Foreign Policy," 146–51; Kahler, "The United States and Western Europe," 310–17; Smith, *Reagan and Thatcher,* 71–75, 95–99; Ambassador Richard R. Burt interview with author, Washington, D.C., May 7, 2001. For a discussion of the Polish crisis with documents from Polish and Soviet archives showing the Soviet Union had no intention of intervening, see "New Evidence on the Polish Crisis, 1980–1981," Cold War International History Project *Bulletin* 11 ("Cold War Flashpoints," winter 1998), 3–133.

13. Smith, *Reagan and Thatcher,* 99–106; Destler, "Reagan Foreign Policy," 146–51; Burt interview. For reports of continued threats of extraterritorial sanctions from Richard Perle, see Reginald Dale, "U.S. Threatens Technology Transfer Ban," *Financial Times,* May 17, 1983.

14. CIA analysis of the pipeline, 219; Steven Kotkin, "What They Knew, Not!: Forty-four Years of CIA Secrets," *New York Times,* March 19, 2001.

15. For a more detailed account of these issues, see Samuel F. Wells, Jr., "The United States and European Defence Co-operation," *Survival* 27 (July–August 1985): 158–68.

16. Garthoff, *Great Transition,* 551–53; Jeffrey Herf, *War by Other Means: Soviet Power, West German Resistance, and the Battle of the Euromissiles* (New York: Free Press, 1991), 202–14.

17. Josef Joffe, "Stability and Its Discontent: Should NATO Go Conventional?" *Washington Quarterly* 7 (fall 1984): 146.

18. Walter Schütze, "Prospects for Effective Conventional Defense in Europe: The Case of the Federal Republic of Germany: Problems and Trends," Working Paper no. 60, October 30, 1984, International Security Studies Program, Woodrow Wilson Center, Washington, D.C.; the Nunn amendment, introduced by Senator Sam Nunn (D-Ga.) on June 20, 1984, called for the United States to reduce its troop strength in Europe by almost 30 percent unless the other NATO allies honored prior commitments to spend more on strengthening their defense forces. The amendment was tabled after intense lobbying by the White House, but the message remained that many American political leaders wanted Europe to share a larger part of the defense burden. See Congressional Quarterly, *Congress and the Nation,* vol. 6, 1981–1984 (Washington, D.C.: Congressional Quarterly, 1985), 247.

19. Ronald Reagan, Address to the Nation on Defense and National Security, March 23, 1983, *Public Papers of the Presidents of the United States, Ronald Reagan, 1983,* book 1 (Washington, D.C.: Government Printing Office, 1984), 442–43.

20. Lou Cannon, *President Reagan: The Role of a Lifetime* (New York: Simon & Schuster, 1991), 318–33; Lieutenant General Edward L. Rowny, conversation with the author, May 28, 1985; Robert C. McFarlane with Zofia Smardz, *Special Trust* (New York: Cadell & Davies, 1994), 225–35.

21. Burt interview.

22. Samuel F. Wells, Jr., "Mitterrand's International Policies," *Washington Quarterly* 11 (summer 1988): 65–66; Cannon, *President Reagan,* 333 and 862 n. 122.

23. Wells, "European Defence Co-operation," 162–64; Kahler, "The United States and Western Europe," 322–24; Samuel F. Wells, Jr., "France and European Cooperation: Implications for United States Policy," *Atlantic Community Quarterly* 23 (winter 1985–1986): 382–85.

24. Wells, "European Defence Co-operation," 166.

25. Quoted in Beth A. Fischer, *The Reagan Reversal: Foreign Policy and the End of the Cold War* (Columbia: University of Missouri Press, 1997), 32–40; also see Beth Fischer's essay in this volume.

26. Strobe Talbott, *The Master of the Game: Paul Nitze and the Nuclear Peace* (New York: Alfred A. Knopf, 1988), 253–88; Memorandum, Ambassadors Kampelman, Tower, and Glitman to Secretary Shultz, November 14, 1985, Briefing Paper for President Reagan's Trip to Geneva, November 16–21, 1985, and Memorandum of Conversation, Reagan and Gorbachev Second Private Meeting, November 19, 1985, Declassified documents, "End of Cold War, Box 2," National Security Archive (NSA), Gelman Library, George Washington University, Washington, D.C.

27. Letter, Ronald Reagan to George Murphy, December 19, 1985, Handwriting File 371494, Ronald Reagan Library (RRL).

28. "Statement by M. S. Gorbachev," *Pravda,* January 16, 1986, English translation in "End of Cold War, Box 2," NSA; Talbott, *Master of the Game,* 289–303.

29. Richard Solomon to Secretary Shultz, October 8, 1986, "End of Cold War, Box 2," NSA.

30. Memorandum of Conversation between Reagan and Gorbachev, Reykjavik, October 12, 1986, "End of Cold War, Box 2," NSA; Talbott, *Master of the Game,* 314–26; FitzGerald, *Way Out There in the Blue,* 314–69; George P. Shultz, *Turmoil and Triumph: My Years as Secretary of State* (New York: Charles Scribner's Sons, 1993), 783–859, 901–24.

31. Garthoff, *Great Transition,* 555–58. In the midst of the Tower Commission investigation of the Iran-Contra affair, National Security Adviser Robert McFarlane attempted suicide on February 9, 1987. Cannon, *President Reagan,* 713.

32. Mikhail Gorbachev, *On My Country and the World* (New York: Columbia University Press, 1999), 171–72, 184–94; William C. Wohlforth, ed., *Witnesses to the End of the Cold War* (Baltimore: Johns Hopkins University Press, 1996), 16, 37, 49.

33. Ideas for Gorbachev's speech at the Politburo session, December 16, 1987, English translation, Papers of A. S. Chernyaev, Fond 2, Opis 2, Archive of the Gorbachev Foundation, Moscow, copy in "End of the Cold War, Box 2," NSA.

34. Anatoly Chernyaev's Notes from the Politburo Session, December 17, 1987, English translation, Papers of A. S. Chernyaev, Fond 2, Opis 2, Gorbachev Foundation, Moscow, copy in "End of the Cold War, Box 2," NSA.

35. Shultz, *Turmoil and Triumph,* 1150.

36. Burt interview.

37. Paolo Cecchini, "Integration of the European Internal Market: Implications for Europe and the United States" (unpublished meeting report, May 1988, Woodrow Wilson Center); Samuel F. Wells, Jr., "A New Transatlantic Bargain," *Washington Quarterly* 12 (autumn 1989): 56–57; Martin Walker, "Variable Geography: America's Mental Maps of a Greater Europe," *International Affairs* 76, no. 3 (2000): 459–74.

PART III
The Economic Agenda

7

Taxation

W. Elliot Brownlee and C. Eugene Steuerle

In 1981, President Ronald Reagan launched an attack on the American welfare state. The first and most significant blow in that attack was a massive cut in income taxes. It is on this 1981 tax cut that both the proponents and opponents of "the Reagan Revolution" often like to focus when remembering Reagan. But by 1985, Reagan had supported a series of base-broadening tax increases and embraced an approach to reform that would yield the Tax Reform Act of 1986 and strengthen the income tax system that he had challenged in 1981. This essay seeks to explain the origin and subsequent transformation of Reagan's tax policies.

REAGAN'S TAX IDEAS

The economic ideas that Ronald Reagan brought to tax policy had deep roots in his life and political career. He had a particularly long-standing concern with the progressive income tax. In the late 1940s, as a highly paid movie star, he paid taxes at a marginal rate of more than 90 percent. At roughly the same time, he went through a messy and expensive divorce, his career in films seemed to be waning, and he feared for his financial future. Lou Cannon, Reagan's foremost biographer, believes that Reagan expressed some of his frustration during this period by attacking the tax system and the Bureau of Internal Revenue (renamed the Internal Revenue Service in 1953), which he sometimes called "my senior partner." Cannon suggests that it was the tax issue "more than any other which signaled Reagan's drift from Democratic liberalism into Republican conservatism."[1]

During the 1950s, Reagan's denunciation of the income tax became a hallmark of the hundreds of speeches he gave at General Electric plants. His origi-

We are grateful to Anthony J. Badger, Leonard E. Burman, Gareth B. Davies, Andrew DeWit, Naohiko Jinno, Laura Kalman, Steve Sheffrin, and Sven Steinmo for their valuable comments on earlier versions of this essay.

nal focus was on the high rates of taxation on the largest incomes; he denounced the high marginal rates as debilitating to individual initiative. As he refined his talk, in what became known as "the Speech," he expanded his attack on the income tax to include not only its progressiveness but also its capacity to increase the size of government. In 1964, when he nominated Barry Goldwater for president, Reagan gave The Speech, including the tax message. In 1966, when he ran for governor of California, he gave the Speech again and again. When inaugurated, in 1967, he declared, "We stand between the taxpayer and the taxspender."[2]

During Reagan's eight years as governor, however, he did not get very far in acting upon his class analysis. After he left the governorship, he puzzled over what kind of new assault on the income tax might work. He consulted with his growing network of economic advisers, which included, most notably, Milton Friedman of the University of Chicago, and Reagan tested ideas through his weekly radio talks.[3]

During the late 1970s, Reagan discovered that dismal economic conditions were creating a breeding ground for a popular revolt against government and especially against the tax system. Rising postwar inflation interacted with the tax system to produce sharp tax increases. The "bracket-creep" in income tax rates often became "bracket-leap." At the extreme, some upper-middle-class people saw their marginal federal income tax rate almost double from 22 percent to over 40 percent, while their state and local income taxes were also growing much faster than their incomes. And it was not just the rich and middle class who were affected. Many lower-income people, especially those with dependents, had to pay income tax for the first time as the value of their personal and dependent exemptions and the effective tax-exempt level of income eroded. During this period, real estate values also rose rapidly, leading to large property tax increases relative to income. These increases added to the general unrest over taxation.

In response, in 1977, Reagan endorsed a measure designed to address "bracket-creep": the indexing of income tax rates for inflation.[4] In October of that year, Reagan went further by endorsing the deep cuts in income taxes—across the board by 10 percent every year, for three years—that Republican Jack Kemp had recently proposed. (These became known as the 10-10-10 tax cuts.)[5]

To some extent, Reagan's proposal represented traditional Republican tax cutting. Reagan remembered the high rates that had left him with almost nothing from additional work, and he consequently regarded a tax cut for the rich as an effective way of stimulating economic productivity. But Reagan's proposal also had a populist dimension. The proposal for major tax cuts offered significant economic relief to middle- and working-class Americans. Reagan emphasized, in particular, that the deep cuts would directly offset the harsh impact of inflation on standards of living for all income-tax payers.[6] At the same time, he recognized that the cuts would respect the widespread public support that progressive tax rates still commanded. Reagan stressed that his program of tax cuts would "keep the inc. [*sic*] tax progressive."[7] Reagan wished to forge a tax program whose combination of deep, across-the-board tax cuts and progressiveness would have broad popular appeal. Even though Reagan's message was antistatist, like Franklin D. Roosevelt, he sought to build a new political coalition of workers and consumers.

In 1977, Reagan also invoked a startling argument for dramatic cuts in taxes. The argument was that the cuts would actually reduce budget deficits and thus relieve the upward pressure on prices, including interest rates. This deficit reduction would occur, Reagan argued, because of the huge expansion of the tax base produced by American investors and workers invigorated by big cuts in tax rates. Thus, Reagan seemed to embrace what became the most controversial proposition of the "supply-side" argument for tax cuts: the tax cuts would not just stimulate productivity; they would also reduce deficits. Martin Anderson, a central economic adviser in Reagan's first term as president, later claimed that supply-siders were actually moderate in their views, arguing only that tax cutting "would *not lose as much revenue as one might expect*" [emphasis in original]. Anderson was correct for most supply-siders, especially among professional economists who leaned toward that view, but not all. But Reagan himself on occasion tended to express true belief in the extreme view, which implied almost no loss in revenues, even in the initial years. In the radio address in which he endorsed Kemp's program, Reagan declared that "economists like Paul McCracken . . . , Milton Friedman . . . , Arthur Laffer . . . , Allan Meltzer . . . , [and] Arthur Burns . . . have each made it clear that government can increase its tax revenues . . . by lowering the tax rates for business and individuals." The Kemp cuts, he said, "would reduce the deficit which causes inflation because the tax base would be broadened by increased prosperity."[8]

In 1978, Reagan found encouragement for his tax program in the stunning success of California's Proposition 13, which limited the property-tax rate to 1 percent of market value, restrained the growth in property assessments for existing home owners, and required a two-thirds majority in the legislature to enact any new taxes. The victory for Proposition 13 convinced Reagan that the time had now come to focus the movement to limit government around middle-class protests over taxes. Reagan carried the ideas of indexing and across-the-board cutting into the congressional elections of 1978 and then his presidential campaign. By August 1979, Reagan had a formal tax program for his presidential campaign. Martin Anderson, Reagan's economic coordinator, organized a proposal for "a program—of at least three years duration—of across-the-board tax cuts," and indexing "federal tax rate brackets, as well as the amount of exemptions, deductions, and credits."[9]

During his 1980 campaign for the presidency, however, Reagan never entertained any intention of reforming the federal tax system in a fundamental way. One nonstarter was replacement of the progressive income tax with a flat-rate tax, or with a compressed set of progressive rates, on a comprehensive base of income.[10] The broader a reformer could make the base of income by closing off loopholes—income tax deductions, exclusions, and credits—the lower would be the rate of taxation required. By the 1970s, base broadening, coupled with a compression of progressive rates, had won some support from economists, including both conservatives and liberals who saw a "win-win" opportunity in this combination. They envisioned tax reform packages that could remove favoritism toward certain forms of income or consumption, provide more equal treatment of those with equal incomes, and still maintain progressivity. In effect, tax reform could advance the goals of both equity and efficiency.

Reagan, however, had long been skeptical of the concept of "tax expenditures" and opposed to tax reform focused on their reduction. For example, in 1975, in response to that year's Congressional Budget Act, which called for an annual accounting of "tax expenditures," Reagan ridiculed loophole closing and suggested that closing the oil depletion allowance, which he described as "the showcase loophole," would save only a trivial amount of revenue. He asserted that "the truth is most of what our politicians call loopholes are the legit. [sic] deductions the working people depend on to keep their inc. [sic] tax from being more intolerable than it is."[11] Two years later, after President Jimmy Carter took up the cause of loophole closing, Reagan once again claimed that very few of the deductions taken by taxpayers benefited the rich. In July 1979, Reagan said that the term "tax expenditures" was "the new name government has for the share of our earnings it allows us to keep. You and I," he said, "call them deductions." "All told," he concluded, "our rich . . . Uncle Sam has an eye on about $170 billion that we think is ours."[12]

By the late 1970s, discussions among tax experts over the complex issues surrounding tax expenditures had become quite sophisticated. We have no evidence that Reagan followed the nuances of the tax expenditure debates, and Reagan personally made relatively little use of personal tax shelters.[13] But Reagan's position on this issue made sense in terms of his general approach to tax policy, his political philosophy, and his economics. He detested *any* new taxes or tax increases, which is what eliminating tax preferences probably sounded like to him. In addition, as a conservative, he ought to have been suspicious of base-broadening reform; in the ways many at the time proposed it, such reform was likely to produce significantly higher rates of taxation on the rich. After all, President Carter and other liberals supported "tax expenditure" reform because they were interested in closing tax loopholes for the rich in order to make the income tax more progressive and increase its revenue capacity.

Some of Reagan's economic advisers may have cautioned him about the economic risks of undertaking reform of tax expenditures. Many conservative economists, including Norman Ture and Paul Craig Roberts, who advised Jack Kemp, approved of the way in which many tax expenditures favored investors and savers, who were concentrated in higher income brackets. These economists often embraced this favoritism as a way of offsetting what they regarded as the penalties that the income tax imposed on saving. They argued, for example, that the income tax penalizes savers by taxing twice income earned and saved while taxing only once income earned and spent, and that the income tax taxes capital income twice—at both the corporate and the individual level. To redress this imbalance, conservative economists often wanted to lower further the effective tax rate on capital income and supported the adoption of new tax expenditures favoring capital. Some conservative economists might have welcomed, in principle, a tax reform package that included broadening the tax base in exchange for lower tax rates. But liberal politicians displayed slight interest in rate reductions, and in any case, framing such a package would have required identifying losers as well as winners—an enterprise rarely attractive even in populist political campaigns. Consequently, Reagan's economic advisers do not seem to have presented to him the policy option of base broadening coupled with rate compression, and Reagan did not expand the populism of his presidential campaign into a war on tax expenditures.[14]

The way was wide open for corporate lobbyists who were eager to expand tax breaks for capital income. During the summer of 1980, they succeeded in inserting a huge tax expenditure into the Reagan program. Their leader was Charls Walker, whose firm represented dozens of industrial clients—members of the traditional Republican elite—who had enormous investments in plant and equipment. Walker, with the support of economists who wanted to lower the effective tax rate on capital income, persuaded the Republican platform committee to propose a dramatic increase in the allowances to corporations and individuals for depreciation of tangible assets. The proposal became known as "10-5-3," which was shorthand for the three new depreciation lifetimes for structures (ten years), equipment (five years), and light vehicles (three years). To pay for 10-5-3, Reagan's platform committee dropped entirely the proposal to index the individual income tax, which was of much greater benefit to labor income and income of the middle class.[15]

THE ECONOMIC RECOVERY TAX ACT OF 1981

When Reagan won the Republican nomination in 1980, his campaign staff quickly turned to the analysis and drafting of tax legislation. Reagan intended to make tax reduction the first major victory for the Reagan administration's domestic program. But as Reagan and his staff wrestled with the details of the legislation, they had to cope with the major complication that tax cutting would increase budget deficits. The advisers disagreed among themselves as to the extent of the deficits. But most agreed that there indeed would be deficits and that unless contained, the deficits would put pressure on capital markets, possibly raise interest rates, and undermine public confidence in Reagan's program.

Reagan's personal views heavily shaped how the administration implemented its campaign platform. A few weeks after Reagan's acceptance speech, his economic advisers met with him, and most, including Alan Greenspan and Charls Walker, advised Reagan that he ought to go slower and take five, rather than three, years to implement the 10-10-10 tax cuts. They had two goals in mind. First, they wanted to reduce the deficits. Second, they wanted to protect the proposed cuts in the tax on capital. They were less interested in the very large share of across-the-board cuts that would go to middle-income and upper-middle-income workers than in reductions in the tax on capital. The supply-side economists among them also believed that the primary economic stimuli from the individual reductions would come from cutting the top rates, and that the large reduction in the bottom and middle rates would have little economic stimulus effect. All the advisers believed they might be able to have their cake and eat it, too—a tax cut on capital income *and* a lower deficit effect—because the tax cut on capital would be cheaper in terms of tax revenues than the across-the-board cut.

When Reagan's economic advisers had made their case and warned him about the deficits, he replied, "I don't care." Walker remembers that they all "nearly fell out of their chairs." Reagan had turned out to be the most extreme populist in the room. The president wanted to cut everyone's taxes, regardless of whether or not any particular economic theory supported him, and regardless of whether or not the cuts worsened the deficit. The president got his way and stayed with the 10-10-10 formula. In general, the president, more than many of his advisers, wanted deep cuts in income taxes, and he did not want the cut focused on businesses and the highest income individuals. His goal was to exploit broad popular support for a tax cut, pave the way for other policy initiatives, and produce a more profound realignment of voters.[16]

Reagan and his supply-side advisers—Martin Anderson, Paul Craig Roberts, and Norman Ture, for example—may have had another reason for supporting the deep tax cuts. They may have actually *wanted* higher initial deficits in order to restrain spending, as Senator Daniel Patrick Moynihan once suggested. David Stockman, director of the Office of Management and Budget, denied that, and his memory of what was said in the councils of government seems to have been accurate.[17] But Stockman may not have fully understood Reagan's intentions nor have known how much weight others gave to this approach as at least a secondary consideration. After all, conservatives and liberals would generally agree on the simple point that spending is easier when revenues are available than when they are not. Reagan said as much on February 5, 1981, in a national address. He invoked one of his homilies to justify going forward with a tax cut before trying to moderate or roll back spending: "Well," he said, "we can lecture our children about extravagance until we run out of voice and breath. OR we can cure their extravagance simply by reducing their allowance."[18]

At first, Reagan's deep tax cuts encountered serious trouble in Congress. But in March 1981, the assassination attempt on the president intervened. It had the effect of increasing popular support for the president and, by extension, whatever program he wanted. Congress found the pressure irresistible. Moreover, Democrats believed they could make Reagan take responsibility for the large deficits that were almost certain to follow. And veteran leaders knew that they would have opportunities to raise taxes in the future. Russell Long, chair of the Senate Finance Committee, recalled that before the Reagan years, he "had voted for large tax cuts and for needed tax increases."[19]

Long and his Democratic colleagues in Congress abandoned caution and launched a frenzied bidding war with Republicans. Together, the two parties decorated their "Christmas tree" bill with a spectacular array of tax shelters. In the bidding, Congress also restored the very expensive indexing of tax brackets. Reagan's crusty and forthright secretary of the Treasury, Donald Regan, told Treasury staff: "My favorite part of the tax bill is the indexing provision—it takes the sand out of Congress's sandbox." To help pay for the enlarged scope of the tax cuts, Congress did pare some reductions in tax rates. The 10-10-10 formula became 5-10-10, providing for a 23 percent, rather than a 27 percent, net reduction in the tax cuts for individuals. And Congress delayed indexing until 1985. Proponents argued that indexing would sustain the tax cuts in outer years, but Congress enacted the delay to move many people back into higher tax brackets and thus reduce future deficits. The Economic Recovery Tax Act—ERTA— became law in August 1981.[20]

DEFICITS AND THE TAX EQUITY AND FISCAL RESPONSIBILITY ACT OF 1982 (TEFRA)

A recession and reduction in inflation rates, however, were already under way, and they quickly undercut revenues. On the day after Reagan had presented his tax and economic program to the nation, Secretary of the Treasury Regan testified before the House Budget Committee and presented what became known as "Rosy Scenario." At the time he predicted high real rates of income growth and a drop in the rate of inflation from 11 percent in 1981 to 4 percent in 1986. But the actions of Paul Volcker's Federal Reserve Board and the recession of 1981–1982 meant that both real income and inflation declined. Both declines reduced real revenues—the former because of lower real growth and the latter because of less bracket-creep—well below what Rosy Scenario had forecast.

Meanwhile, Reagan also pushed substantial increases in defense spending. This added to the deficits that followed ERTA, and they turned out to be the largest, relative to the size of the economy, that the federal government had ever run in peacetime. By fiscal 1984, the deficit had grown to 5.0 percent of gross domestic product (GDP) from 2.8 percent in 1980.[21]

During the immediate aftermath of its 1981 legislative successes, the Reagan administration had to face the prospect of political embarrassment in 1982 (an election year) over surging deficits and the upward pressure of those deficits on long-term interest rates and the stock market. The political pressure was bipartisan; it included conservatives in the capital markets and supporters of cuts in tax rates who had counted on reduced expenditures to help pay for those changes.[22]

After the passage of ERTA, the only way for the president to have stayed with both the tax cuts and defense buildup, and to have contained the damaging deficits, would have been to tackle the large, and continuing, growth in mandatory entitlement spending. A few in the White House understood this and were enthusiastic about the prospect, but many were not. In any case, entitlement reform was a slow process, not one that was easily engaged, and not one that could have an immediate, significant impact on the budget.[23]

The embarrassment over deficits led to a search for tax options, including ones that would derail some of the provisions that Congress had added when decorating the ERTA "Christmas tree." But the president resisted. "Almost everyone in the White House joined in the work of tax raising," Stockman recalled, "except for the guys who wore the Adam Smith ties and, unfortunately, the guy who had to sign the tax bills."[24]

One way of increasing taxes would have been to restore some of ERTA's cuts in individual tax rates. Supporters of this option included many who had a strong supply-side concern with the highest individual rates (or favored consumption taxes) but had less concern with rates below the top. But Reagan himself blocked this course of action. What Reagan's staff began to consider instead was relying on the less visible and less universal forms of tax increases—cuts in tax expenditures—in other words, cuts in the complex array of tax deductions, tax exemptions, and tax credits that riddled the tax code.[25]

In 1981, after the adoption of ERTA, Reagan resisted dramatic reductions in tax expenditures, but he concluded that tax increases were politically necessary and even attractive. Some of his advisers convinced him that congressional leaders would deliver three dollars of expenditure cuts in return for every dollar in tax increases. And, the president clearly preferred reductions in tax expenditures to increases in rates. So in September 1981, less than two months after the passage of ERTA, the Reagan administration quietly proposed not "tax increases" but "revisions in the tax code to curtail certain tax abuses and enhance tax revenues." At the same time, the Reagan administration worked more closely with the tax-writing committees of Congress, particularly the Senate Finance Committee under Robert Dole. Meanwhile, within Reagan's inner circle of advisers, the power of Chief of Staff James A. Baker, who was the most concerned about deficits, grew, while the influence of Edwin Meese, who had the strongest reservations about tax increases, waned. And as the process of increasing taxes unfolded in 1982, a number of supply-siders at Treasury—in particular, Paul Craig Roberts and Norman Ture—left the administration.[26]

During the summer of 1982, when the loophole closing encountered resistance in Congress from conservative Republicans, Reagan became more open in his advocacy and began, for the first time, to adopt the language of the base-broadening tax reformers. In one of his longest speeches to the nation on economic affairs, the president emphasized that the legislation would promote "simple fairness" for "every American, especially those in lower-income brackets" by "closing off special interest loopholes.[27]

The outcome of Reagan's leadership and the bipartisan cooperation was the Tax Equity and Fiscal Responsibility Act of 1982 (TEFRA). This act, which Congress passed in August 1982, imposed the first major tax increase during an election year in peacetime since 1932. TEFRA reduced some of the tax benefits for investment, thus beginning a reversal of the move that ERTA had begun toward a zero or even negative tax rate on income from physical capital.

THE SEARCH FOR NEW REVENUES AND THE BEGINNINGS OF REFORM

During the autumn of 1982, the search within the White House and Treasury for new revenues broadened in scope. The recession of 1981–1982 added to everyone's worries about the deficits and their effects on capital markets. The loss of conservative Republican seats in the 1982 congressional elections, along with polls that pointed to loss of public confidence in the economic stewardship of the Reagan administration, focused minds on deficit reduction. The assistant secretary for tax policy, John (Buck) Chapoton, worked especially closely with congressional staff to develop deficit reduction options. Within the White House, Richard Darman, Baker's deputy chief of staff and key adviser for economic matters, floated a variety of ideas, including delaying and reducing indexing and postponing the defense buildup.[28]

In the late months of 1982, interest in deficit reduction turned to the Social Security system, where there was serious fiscal trouble because Social Security seemed inadequate to support rising levels of benefits. In 1981, the Reagan administration had taken political hits for early cost-cutting initiatives and then abandoned attempts to develop solutions within the White House. In December 1981 Reagan signed an executive order creating the National Commission on Social Security Reform. In the autumn of 1982, the commission reported its recommendations, and in December, under the pressure of the looming deficits, the president decided to support the recommendations.[29]

The most radical income tax option that came under discussion in the White House during the last half of 1982 was the adoption of a "flat tax." In its extreme form, such a tax would have eliminated all deductions, exemptions, and credits and replaced the progressive tax structure with a single, low rate of tax. It also would have, in effect, converted the income tax into a tax on consumption while maintaining some progressivity by providing a credit or exemption against the first dollars of tax.[30]

Between mid-1981 and June 1982, members of Congress, including both Democrats and Republicans, had introduced about a dozen bills designed to introduce versions of a flat tax. Meanwhile, members of the Treasury staff had aroused Secretary Regan to think about moving toward a flatter tax as an expansion of TEFRA's cutting of tax expenditures. In May of 1982 he told the Ways and Means Committee that he was intrigued by the flat-tax concept. Later that month, Senator Robert Dole, the chair of the Finance Committee, announced that he would hold hearings on the tax, and the press reported that Senator Bill Bradley would soon join with Congressman Richard A. Gephardt in sponsoring legislation that would provide for a tax with flatter rates coupled with a surtax on higher incomes that would replace the top rate of 50 percent with a rate of 28 percent.[31]

Over the Christmas holidays in 1982, during a round of golf, Secretary of State George Shultz pressed the idea upon the president who, according to David Stockman, saw classic supply-side possibilities.[32] "By the eighteenth hole," Stockman wrote, "the President was convinced this was a way to reduce the deficit without increasing taxes." In Stockman's account, the president pressed the idea on Treasury secretary Regan and Attorney General Edwin Meese as a way of both lowering taxes and immediately reducing the deficit. "Soon," Stockman recalled, "everyone around the White House was talking flat tax." Darman recalled that by January 1983, a "faction . . . favored proposing radical tax reform, replacing the progressive income tax with either a flat tax or a consumed income tax that would exempt net savings and investment from any tax at all."

Stockman, Darman, and Martin Feldstein, the chair of the Council of Economic Advisers from 1982 to 1984, however, all had reservations about moving quickly toward a flat tax. They worried about versions that would increase deficits even further. They questioned the supply-side assumptions of a swift payoff in increased revenues that seemed to drive the president's interest in tax cutting. "They don't actually believe this mumbo-jumbo, do they?" Feldstein asked Stockman after a meeting in which the president pushed the flat tax.

Stockman and Darman developed an alternative plan, which Stockman later described as "perfectly disingenuous." They would accept the supply-side argument and assert that the flat tax, when adopted, would yield economic productivity gains of approximately $50 billion per year (about 1 percent of GNP). Then they would argue for the adoption of a "placeholder" tax—a temporary increase in income taxes—to raise this amount of revenue until the flat tax took hold, perhaps in 1986 or even later. "By hook or by crook I was going to put $50 billion in new revenue into the budget," Stockman recalled.

In early January they made their case within the White House. Secretary Regan accepted the concept of the placeholder tax but argued that its adoption should wait until 1986 when, presumably, the economy would be out of recession. He argued, further, that the administration should wait to submit legislation for the placeholder tax until Congress had agreed on the three-for-one budget cuts. Meanwhile, Baker and Darman began to get cold feet as they contemplated the political fallout from radical reform along flat-tax lines—reform that would require, for example, repeal of the deduction of interest payments on home mortgages. In addition, the president may have begun to worry about the possibility that the flat tax might increase taxes for "poorer taxpayers," in Secretary Regan's words.[33] In January, as Stockman recalled, "Shultz's original flat tax idea was packed off to Siberia, in this case a 'deep study mode' at Treasury with a view to 'broadening, simplifying and reforming the income tax.'"

The "placeholder" tax, however, remained in the tax program. The chances of its enactment were, Stockman recalled, "about as likely as an invasion of Martians." But the president was not necessarily convinced of this and, in any case, he hated to even appear to be asking for tax increases. "Oh darn, oh darn," he complained, as he signed the 1983 budget submission for fiscal 1984, which included the placeholder tax. "I had never seen him look so utterly dejected," Stockman later wrote.

On January 25, 1983, in his state of the union address, President Reagan called for not only the adoption of the recommendations of the Social Security Commission but also the provision of what the president now called "stand-by" tax authority. Reagan declared that "because we must ensure reduction and eventual elimination of deficits over the next several years, I will propose a stand-by tax." Reagan followed this declaration with the statement, stunning to some, that "we who are in government must take the lead in restoring the economy." Darman has written that with these two statements, the president "formally abandoned the supply-side principle" and revealed the truth that "the power of the Reagan Revolution's official fiscal policy was spent." However, the president had not yet given up on the idea that cuts in taxes could generate larger revenues. And Reagan had always believed in the responsibility of government for economic stability. What he had rejected was the Keynesian formulation of that responsibility; what he continued to favor was countercyclical monetary policy coupled with the stimulation of productivity through tax cuts.

REFORM OF SOCIAL SECURITY

During 1983, efforts to adopt a standby tax floundered. Technical analysis by Treasury and congressional staff raised daunting issues, and political assessments by both Republicans and Democrats in Congress identified problems with an on-again, off-again tax that would rise when the economy slowed. For his part, the president believed that Congress failed to engage in serious reduction of the deficit through expenditure reduction. Consequently, he refused to advance tax legislation. The movement for Social Security reform, however, bore fruit. A bipartisan Congress permanently reduced Social Security benefits, accelerated a previously scheduled increase in rates of payroll taxation, and expanded the tax base through the taxation of benefits. Once again, Reagan took the position that he was not increasing taxes. The rate increase he accepted was already scheduled to take place in 1990. So he argued that earlier administrations, not his, had increased the Social Security tax rate, and he was merely advancing the timetable. And he concluded that the broadening of the tax base through the taxation of benefits amounted to just a reduction in net benefits.[34]

ENTHUSIASM FOR REFORM OF THE INCOME TAX

In late 1983, as Reagan and his advisers prepared for the state of the union address, they returned once again to the possibility of raising taxes to reduce the deficits. Baker, Stockman, Darman, and Feldstein resumed their campaign for a standby tax and had support outside the White House from Bob Dole. Feldstein lavished praise on the president for his earlier tax cutting, but he forecast continued deficits and emphasized the "very strong link between deficits and inflation." Darman suggested the appointment of a deficit commission. But the president, reinforced by the Treasury secretary and the President's Economic Policy Advisory Board, was adamant in opposition to both ideas. The president made no reference to tax increases in his 1984 state of the union address. He did, however, take up the possibility of tax reform.[35]

During the preceding year, 1983, Secretary Regan had been paying increasing attention to the adoption of a flat tax or significant broadening of the income base. To lead the Treasury analysis, he had on hand John E. (Buck) Chapoton, the assistant secretary for tax policy, and Charles McLure, the deputy assistant secretary for tax policy. Regan later described McLure as "one of the main authorities on flat taxes." Under Chapoton and McLure was a staff that could develop a proposal for fundamental tax reform. The Treasury's tax policy staff, usually ignored in the development of campaign proposals, turned out to be not quite as remote as Siberia.[36]

Over the course of 1983, Regan had grown increasingly enthusiastic about such reform. He appreciated the virtues of making the tax system more economically efficient. His years on Wall Street as a broker predisposed him to favor tax reform that would remove tax shelters that drew investment capital away from more productive activities. He recalled that he had "chafed under laws that gave the banking industry tax breaks that brokerage firms were denied" and stressed that "when the same concept is extended to entire industries, the results" are "absurd." He was opposed to "industrial policy," whether it came through regulation or through tax expenditures. Moreover, the Treasury secretary had become intrigued by the prospect of further cuts in marginal rates of income taxation. He understood that in the face of the budget deficits, base broadening provided the only means to pay for them.[37]

In December 1983, during a meeting in which the president and his advisers were preparing for the 1984 state of the union address, secretary Regan seized his moment.[38] He began by shocking the president with the news that in 1982, the president's personal secretary had paid more federal taxes than General Electric, Boeing, General Dynamics, and fifty-seven "other big companies" combined. The president, according to Don Regan, did not believe him, but the Treasury secretary persisted: "The time has come to do something fundamental about the tax system. It's too complicated, it's grotesquely unfair, and it's a drag on the economy because it discourages competition." The president finally seemed to yield. "I agree, Don," he said. "I just didn't realize that things had gotten that far out of line." The secretary of the Treasury believed he had his marching orders "to go full steam ahead with a proposal to overhaul the entire federal structure so as to purge it of inequities, plug its loopholes, and lower the rates for individual taxpayers."

Ronald Reagan, in fact, was still not convinced. Nor were Reagan's other close advisers. Baker and Darman preferred to focus on deficit reduction, and they questioned the politics of serious base-broadening reform. However, Baker was worried that Democratic presidential candidate Walter Mondale might base his campaign on tax issues, especially if Reagan and Congress had to raise taxes again. Mondale might, Baker believed, run against Reagan's tax increases, past and future, and at the same time, with the support of Senator Bill Bradley, pick up the banner of tax reform that Jimmy Carter had dropped. So, Baker concluded, taking up the mantle of tax reformer might prevent the Democrats from out-flanking Reagan with a powerfully attractive domestic issue.[39]

Reagan, therefore, laid the groundwork for possibly playing, once again, the role of tax reformer. In his state of the union speech, the president said that he was "asking Secretary of the Treasury Don Regan for a plan . . . to simplify the entire tax code so all taxpayers, big and small, are treated more fairly." But few took the president seriously. When he said he was not asking for the plan to be delivered until after the election, in December 1984, almost a year later, the Democratic side of the audience broke out in peals of laughter.[40]

THE DEFICIT REDUCTION ACT OF 1984 (DEFRA)

After the state of the union address, during much of 1984, Baker, Darman, Stockman, and Feldstein returned to the business of trying to marshal support for deficit reduction efforts. They still had to face the supply-side obsession of the president. In January, over a lunch, Reagan told Feldstein and Stockman: "There has not been one tax increase in history that actually raised revenue. And every tax cut, from the 1920s to Kennedy's to ours, has produced more." Feldstein immediately dashed off a brief history of tax revenues before and after tax increases and concluded that "*every* increase in tax rates was followed by a rise in tax revenue" [emphasis in original]. For good measure, Feldstein looked at the huge tax increases during World War II and concluded: "There is no evidence that the rising tax rates were incompatible with increased real GNP."[41] In March, Feldstein went on to argue that tax increases were now necessary to prevent continuing deficits from crowding out new capital formation. He told the president that he needed to persuade "financial investors and others that you are committed to move the economy toward a balanced budget."[42]

The arguments that Feldstein mobilized may have had some impact. In March, the president, once again, agreed hesitantly to a series of modest loophole closings. Congress rejected most of these, but the president approved those that Congress substituted; in July he signed the Deficit Reduction Act of 1984 (DEFRA, rhyming with TEFRA). Thus, Reagan took another step backward from its dramatic measure of 1981. Taken together, TEFRA and DEFRA raised revenues on the average of $100 billion per year at 1990 levels of income. Increases this big had never been enacted except during major wars.[43]

After the passage of DEFRA, Baker and Darman considered developing an even larger tax increase—one that Darman described as a "big fix." They may have discussed an increase amounting to as much as 2 percent of GDP, and contemplated heavy taxation of consumption. But they faced the hostility of the president to tax increases that were both large and regressive. Moreover, when Reagan signed DEFRA, he concluded that he had been, in the words of David Stockman, "badly double-crossed" by the Democrats. They had not, Reagan concluded, delivered on the three-for-one spending cuts that they had promised in 1982 for the TEFRA tax increases. For the rest of his administration, Reagan became even more rigidly opposed to significant tax increases.[44]

THE TAX REFORM ACT OF 1986

During 1984, meanwhile, public opinion became a factor. Congressional debates over DEFRA raised awareness of the extent to which loopholes had perverted the tax code. So did intense newspaper advertising for tax shelters designed for people of all income levels. And a wide variety of well-publicized studies showed that many corporations with significant income paid little or no taxes. Among these studies was that of a public interest lawyer, Robert McIntyre, a protégé of Ralph Nader. McIntyre, who worked for a labor-funded organization called Citizens for Tax Justice, combed the annual reports of 250 of the nation's largest companies and discovered that over half of them had paid no federal income tax in at least one year between 1981 and 1983. Public confidence in the fundamental fairness of the federal income tax was rapidly eroding, and public opinion began to push Reagan toward base broadening.[45]

Tax reform, nonetheless, did not become a central issue in the 1984 campaign. During the summer, the president's advisers worried that Walter Mondale might propose what Darman described as a "soak-the-rich-end-the-unfair-loopholes-and-hit-the-big-corporations-plan" for reducing the deficit. They worried that the president would be caught between a Mondale initiative and Republican supply-siders who wanted him to rule out any tax increase. But Mondale decided against running as a tax reformer, and he never specified how he would raise taxes. He thereby allowed the Republicans to present a united front.[46]

The Treasury, meanwhile, accelerated its work on tax reform. During the first half of 1984, the Treasury staff had focused on the framing of DEFRA. Even after its passage, some staffers believed that they should concentrate principally on preparing the regulations required to implement DEFRA; they argued that political support within the White House and Congress for comprehensive reform was highly uncertain and that the Treasury always faced mandates for studies that exceeded the Treasury's capacity to produce them. But with Secretary Regan's support, Buck Chapoton, Ronald Pearlman, who replaced Chapoton as assistant secretary, and Charles McLure gradually shifted the attention of the staff to tax reform. C. Eugene Steuerle, who had come back to the Treasury in March 1984, after a year away, became the economic staff coordinator of the Project for Fundamental Reform. He organized the staff work around more than twenty modules, each focused on a key issue. As the staff completed them, Chapoton or Pearlman, accompanied by McLure, took them to meetings with Secretary Regan for discussion and approval.

Regan accepted several strategies that Steuerle, McLure, Chapoton, Pearlman, and the tax policy staff had recommended for structuring the Treasury study. The first was to defer consideration of consumption taxes by concentrating on special exceptions that might be present in both types of tax systems (for example, employee benefits and some itemized deductions). This prevented an internal Treasury debate over consumption taxation from destroying the momentum required to piece together an elaborate study of reform.

The second operating principle was to structure the reform proposal to be roughly neutral in both its revenue and distributional effects. The goal was to step outside of the kind of rancorous debates over tax cutting, deficits, and progressivity that had thrust aside attention to issues of economic efficiency and the equal treatment of people in roughly the same circumstances. These debates had derailed early attempts, such as in the early 1960s, at base-broadening reform.

The third strategic principle was to establish a conservative-liberal compromise over lower rates and a broader base. An important part of this strategy was to forge an alliance between "family conservatives" and the antipoverty liberals. Steuerle's earlier research had shown that the erosion of the personal exemption not only pushed the poor into the tax system but also discriminated most against families with children because their personal and dependent exemptions were, relative to their income, worth the most. He pointed out, as well, that ERTA had failed to offset the impact of earlier inflation on the poor and families with children. The president had, in fact, already committed himself to addressing this problem. In 1982, when the results of Steuerle's research had appeared, one of the president's advisers, Bruce Chapman, had brought the research results to his attention, and the president then announced his desire to increase the dependent and personal exemption.[47]

The fourth strategy was to be inclusive. The reform package would not spare any powerful interest groups. This would enable policymakers to see just how much rate reduction they might accomplish, and it would prevent one group from arguing that it, too, deserved special protection because others had it.

The fifth strategy was to lay out in detail how Congress and the Treasury would implement base-broadening reform. Steuerle won approval to go beyond the kind of studies that the Treasury had often produced in early years. These studies were well received but often wound up shelved in library stacks rather than embedded in legislation. The Treasury would, instead, prepare a "how-to" manual that would prevent critics from dismissing the study as a mere academic exercise that had left out the all-important, real-world details.

As the Treasury developed the ambitious program of reform, Secretary Regan, with the support of the president, protected his staff. He shielded them from members of Congress seeking to expand or protect tax expenditures, from the inquiring eyes of the press, and from the interventions of other members of the administration. Concern about details of the plan possibly leaking to the press, and thus embarrassing Reagan, reinforced the secrecy.[48] The Treasury "thinkers," Regan recalled, "had absolute freedom of thought, speech and action; political considerations were irrelevant. They were to disregard every factor except fairness, simplicity, and efficiency."[49]

The Treasury experts appreciated the protection, and they developed a powerful sense of mission: that of offering to the nation an income tax system that would be economically rational and would, at the same time, respond to the drumbeat of populist complaint and help restore the confidence of Americans in their tax system and their government. By the time of the 1984 elections, they had completed and submitted to Secretary Regan a far-reaching set of proposals known as "Treasury I." This plan implemented the theory of comprehensive income taxation, attacked "tax-code socialism" and "industrial policy in the tax code," attempted to index everything for inflation, and proposed elimination of the investment tax credit and restoration of longer depreciation schedules in exchange for lower rates of corporate taxation and lower tax rates on individual investors.[50]

Immediately following the 1984 elections, Secretary Regan presented Treasury I to the president. He was bemused. The threat from Mondale had ended, and Reagan was now worried about opening a major offensive against loopholes and taking on the traditional Republican elites who had benefited from the loopholes. After the briefing, which lasted for nearly two hours (the longest period that the secretary of the Treasury had spent with the president), Reagan still failed to make a firm commitment. But he did give the secretary permission to release the report to the public after Regan pointed out that it was already leaking to the press.[51]

After release, the study commanded wide attention. At first, retreat seemed to be in the air as interest groups loudly protested. Even Secretary Regan stated that "it was written on a word processor" and could easily be changed.[52] But White House staffers began to notice that Treasury I was receiving enthusiastic publicity as well. And the positive responses were bipartisan. Most of the conservative and liberal press gave the report rave reviews, and support emerged from both conservative and liberal think tanks, including the American Enterprise Institute as well as the Brookings Institution.[53] Meanwhile, savvy advisers like Baker and Darman began to realize that tax reform, which was clearly winning popular support, might fill a void in the presidential agenda. Major domestic policy initiatives had languished after 1981, except for the rather painful political actions in DEFRA, TEFRA, and Social Security reform, for which Congress had provided most of the leadership. But still, the president had not signed on. Then, in January 1985, Baker, the White House chief of staff, and Secretary of the Treasury Regan swapped jobs.

The reasons for this job swap remain something of a mystery. But whatever the reasons, the swap put Regan in position to push the president harder on tax reform. And Baker and Darman, who accompanied Baker to Treasury as deputy secretary, seemed clearly to have been attracted by the possibility of putting their mark on a historic tax reform. They had concluded that broad-based tax reform, coupled with even lower tax rates, would help the Republican Party adapt to the structural shifts associated with the growth of industries focused on finance, knowledge, technology, trade, and entertainment. They turned their formidable political skills to the task of what they regarded as domesticating Treasury I. They turned it into Treasury II, a document that was less pure but had a greater chance of enactment.[54]

Regan, Baker, and Darman finally persuaded the president to endorse the principles of Treasury I, which he did in his state of the union message of January 1985. By May the president had met with his staff and personally reviewed each key provision of Treasury II. While Reagan was not aware of many of the technicalities, the proposal did have an ingredient necessary to win his support—a further lowering of the top tax rate. And the president was now eager to assume the role of tax reformer. Reagan and his administration had become more interested in promoting unsubsidized competition and promoting tax equity than in protecting traditional corporate bureaucracies and the other beneficiaries of loopholes.[55]

On May 28, 1985, Reagan announced his tax proposals for "fairness, growth, and simplicity" in a nationally televised speech. The speech appealed to both the spirit of enterprise capitalism and a sense of tax justice—tax justice rooted not in the vertical equity of progressive taxation but in the horizontal equity of a tax that provided uniform treatment to broad categories of taxpayers. His proposal would, he said, "free us from the grip of special interests." He was proposing reduced tax rates "by simplifying the complex system of special provisions that favor some at the expense of others." There would be "one group of losers in our tax plan—those individuals and corporations who are not paying their fair share, or for that matter, any share. These abuses cannot be tolerated. From now on, they shall pay a minimum tax. The free rides are over." The president followed with an open letter to Congress, which struck the same themes. He told Congress that "we face an historic challenge: to change our present tax system into a model of fairness, simplicity, efficiency, and compassion, to remove the obstacles to growth and unlock the door to a future of unparalleled innovation and achievement."[56]

The president then barnstormed around the nation and pounded away at the same points. At times he became tangled in the specifics of his proposal.[57] But he stayed on the high ground of tax justice and galvanized audiences. The White House was delighted with the polls, and the president relished the applause. Don Regan recalled that the president's triumphant speaking tour restored his confidence in his own popularity.[58] The proposal seemed to give Reagan's second term a point of focus, just as ERTA had done for the first term. Moreover, both ERTA and Treasury II were quite consistent in the president's mind with his primary goal of rate reduction.

Over the months that it took for the tax bill to crawl through the legislative process, the president's radio messages and speeches continued to drum up public support for tax fairness. Whoever wished to attack Treasury II had to invoke principles more compelling than those of the president. The leaders of the tax-writing committees—Dan Rostenkowski, chair of Ways and Means, and Robert Packwood, chair of Senate Finance—each, in turn, decided that they had to transform themselves and become advocates of horizontal equity and the kind of economic efficiency that results from lowering rates in exchange for a broader base. The momentum was such that neither wanted to take the blame for the failure of reform.

Reagan played the role of reformer well. He accepted the horizontal equity and efficiency goals and articulated them clearly. He used the media effectively to express those goals, explain the reform program, and generate popular support for it. And in working with Congress, he reached out to Democratic leaders to provide a bipartisan foundation for reform. On October 22, 1986, the president signed the Tax Reform Act of 1986 into law.[59]

The reform act (1) reduced individual tax rates across the board, (2) lowered the marginal rate at the highest incomes from 50 percent to 28 percent,[60] (3) increased personal exemptions and standard deductions, taking six million poorer Americans off the tax rolls, (4) expanded the earned income tax credit to provide a major increase in the "negative" income tax to millions of poorer Americans, (5) increased capital gains taxes for those at the highest incomes from 20 percent to 28 percent, (6) reduced the top corporate rate from 48 percent to 34 percent, and (7) slashed tax expenditures, particularly those applying to businesses or investment. (For example, it repealed the investment tax credit.) For the first time since World War II, a major piece of tax legislation picked not only winners but also a significant number of losers. The losers in 1986 were the many individuals, corporations, and industries for which the loss of preferences was greater than their gains from the reduction of the top rates. The biggest losers were those who sold tax shelters and some traditional Rust Belt industries. The oil industry emerged with its deductions relatively unscathed, largely because of the intervention of Baker and Vice President George Bush.[61] But in fact, those companies benefiting from large deductions actually lost because lower rates made their deductions less valuable. Among businesses, the biggest winners were investment bankers, high-tech industries, service industries, and some multinationals. The Tax Reform Act of 1986 helped finance cuts in individual income taxes by raising corporate taxes by nearly $120 billion over the next five years, although the net increase in effective rates on capital income was fairly small because of an offsetting drop in personal tax rates.[62]

In his memoirs Reagan declared: "With the tax cuts of 1981 and the Tax Reform Act of 1986, I'd accomplished a lot of what I'd come to Washington to do."[63]

CONCLUSION: THE LEGACY

The Reagan administration had, in fact, made the most significant changes in the tax system since World War II. And some of the important changes have proved remarkably durable.

First, income tax rates have remained significantly lower. Under the Bill Clinton administration, the top marginal rate increased to about 40 percent (before it fell again, under the administration of George W. Bush), but even this rate was still substantially lower than the 70 percent level in place before ERTA. Lower rates may well have increased voluntary compliance with the tax code, and they have certainly reduced the value of the special deductions and exclusions that remained in the tax code after 1986. The lower rates, however, did not mean that the tax system became more regressive. In fact, the net effect of the tax policies of the Reagan Revolution was to leave tax progressivity and average rates essentially unchanged.[64]

Second, the business tax expenditures have remained close to the lower levels achieved by the Tax Reform Act of 1986. The act reversed the growth of tax expenditures, which had surged during the 1970s and then continued to grow in the early 1980s, increasing (by one measure) from 6 percent of GDP to

8 percent of GDP in just the five years between 1980 and 1985. Between 1986 and 1990, however, tax expenditures declined to less than 6 percent of GDP, and tax expenditures to business declined by two-thirds. Individual—but not business—tax expenditures crept up during the George H. W. Bush and Clinton administrations.[65]

The Tax Reform Act of 1986, reinforced by falling inflation rates, has been most effective in closing shelters involving partnerships that borrowed heavily to purchase tax-preferred assets. But the act only modestly reduced complexity in some areas. The tax-rate and tax-base differentials that remained were smaller, but skillful lawyers and accountants have seized on many of them and have learned how to exploit them with increasing effectiveness.[66] A new wave of sheltering and arbitrage has resulted. This wave illustrates how daunting is the task of setting up any tax system that would be immune to new forms of exploitation. But the wave also points to the need for an expansion of, rather than a retreat from, the accomplishments of the Tax Reform Act of 1986. Ironically, the Reagan tax reforms strengthened the political foundation of the income tax system that was initially the major target of the Reagan Revolution. The reductions in the highest rates and the reduction in tax expenditures enhanced support for the federal tax system among those who appreciated that Reagan's tax reforms reduced both the inefficiencies resulting from very high rates and the economic distortions arising from favoritism for one type of capital over another. In addition, the continuing progressivity of the federal tax system helped maintain middle- and lower-class support for it. As a consequence, the Reagan tax policies have made it more difficult for critics of the income tax to make an appealing case on behalf of its abandonment. And in the future, the successes of the Reagan administration in promoting horizontal tax equity may turn out to provide some inspiration, and popular support, for renewed attacks, as needed, on special privilege within the tax code.

NOTES

1. Cannon also suggests that Reagan hated all taxes in a deep, visceral way. See Lou Cannon, *President Reagan: The Role of a Lifetime* (New York: Simon & Schuster, 1991), 90–92, and Cannon, *Reagan* (New York: G. P. Putnam's Sons, 1982), 235–37.

2. This was language that John C. Calhoun would have recognized. In *A Disquisition on Government,* Calhoun wrote "the necessary result" of taxation is to place "tax-payers and tax-consumers . . . in antagonistic relations" because "every increase is to enrich and strengthen the one, and impoverish and weaken the other." John C. Calhoun, *A Disquisition on Government and a Discourse on the Constitution and Government of the United States* (New York: D. Appleton, 1854), 21.

3. Reagan and Friedman became mutual supporters in 1973 after Friedman accompanied Governor Reagan on a barnstorming tour of California in an unsuccessful campaign on behalf of Proposition 1, a measure that would have amended the state constitution to

limit state spending. (The measure said nothing about limiting taxes.) Milton and Rose Friedman, *Two Lucky People: Memoirs* (Chicago: University of Chicago Press, 1998), 389. On Friedman's influence, see Martin Anderson, *Revolution* (San Diego: Harcourt, 1988), 172–73. On the importance of the radio talks, see Kiron K. Skinner, Annelise Anderson, and Martin Anderson, eds., *Reagan, In His Own Hand* (New York: Free Press, 2001).

4. Ronald Reagan, "More About Taxes, January 19, 1977," and "Indexing, June 15, 1977," in Skinner, Anderson, and Anderson, *In His Own Hand,* 273–74. Reagan was following the lead of a number of economists, including Martin Feldstein of Harvard University and William Fellner of the American Enterprise Institute. Reagan was also watching California, which led the nation in debating and adopting indexing. See "Comments" by Murray Weidenbaum, Martin Feldstein, and Russell Long in "Tax Policy, Summary of Discussion," in *American Economic Policy in the 1980s,* ed. Martin Feldstein (Chicago: University of Chicago, 1994), 228.

5. Ronald Reagan, "Taxes, October 18, 1977" in Skinner, Anderson, and Anderson, *In His Own Hand,* 274–77. As Lou Cannon has suggested, Reagan's endorsement of the Kemp formula came early, fully two years before Reagan (according to Martin Anderson) endorsed Kemp's specific plan as part of a deal to win Kemp's support for Reagan's presidential bid. See Cannon, *Reagan,* 236–37, and Anderson, *Revolution,* 162–63. The total tax cut proposed was a bit smaller than the 30 percent that Kemp and Reagan touted. Because the tax cut program would apply each 10 percent cut to a successively lower rate of taxation, the net tax proposed was about 27 percent. More precisely, the net tax cut percentage, pt, was: $pt=1-[(1-.1)x(1-.1)x(1-.1)]$.

6. Reagan was correct about the direction of the tax relief that a rate reduction would offer to those suffering from inflation, but he did not mention the fact that a rate reduction offered a great deal more relief from the effects of inflation to the wealthy than to the poor. An individual who, previous to inflation, had no income tax burden might now begin to pay taxes because of inflation. But a 27 percent tax would pare back only about one-fourth of his increase in taxes. In contrast, someone with almost all of her income in the top tax bracket would have little income subject to "bracket-creep" but would still get a 27 percent cut in taxes.

7. Ronald Reagan, "Taxes, October 18, 1977" in Skinner, Anderson, and Anderson, *In His Own Hand,* 277.

8. Ronald Reagan, "Taxes, October 18, 1977" in Skinner, Anderson, and Anderson, *In His Own Hand,* 274 and 277. (I have spelled out some of the abbreviations that Reagan used in his original radio scripts.) Reagan's commitment to the extreme version of supply-side economics appears to have come more than two or three years earlier than the briefing on the Laffer curve, by Arthur Laffer, that David Stockman and others believed marked Reagan's conversion just before his 1980 victory in the New Hampshire primary. In 1976, in a newspaper column, Reagan suggested that the tax cuts of presidents Harding and Kennedy had produced increased revenues. Sidney Blumenthal claims that at a dinner in 1977, Reagan told Arthur Laffer that he supported supply-side economics. In 1976 and 1977, Reagan may have been reading Jude Wanniski's *Wall Street Journal* editorials promoting Laffer's ideas. See Sidney Blumenthal, *The Rise of the Counter-Establishment: From Conservative Ideology to Political Power* (New York: Random House, 1986), 166–67 and 190–96, and David Stockman, *The Triumph of Politics: How the Reagan Revolution Failed* (New York: Harper & Row, 1986), 258. On the role of Wanniski's editorials,

see Paul Craig Roberts, *The Supply-Side Revolution: An Insider's Account of Policymaking in Washington* (Cambridge: Harvard University Press, 1984), 27–30, and Anderson, *Revolution,* 148–52.

9. See Anderson, *Revolution,* 113–21; the quotation is from page 117.

10. Another nonstarter for Reagan was a federal consumption tax, like a VAT. Reagan may have understood and been sympathetic to the economic case for consumption taxation, but was probably aware that some Democrats had begun to smile on VAT forms of consumption taxation as a means for painlessly expanding the welfare state. And he also may have been aware that an important source of Republican support—the small-business community—was hostile to a VAT. A third nonstarter was the head tax or, in the term more common in the United States, a poll tax. Supply-side economics pointed logically toward them, but they were alien to American political culture. We do not know whether or not Margaret Thatcher, whose later proposal of a small head tax contributed to her political downfall, ever discussed head taxes with Reagan. On the supply-side logic of poll taxes, see C. Eugene Steuerle, *The Tax Decade: How Taxes Came to Dominate the Public Agenda* (Washington, D.C.: Urban Institute, 1992), 40.

11. Ronald Reagan, "Tax Loopholes, May 1975" in Skinner, Anderson, and Anderson, *In His Own Hand,* 268–70.

12. Ronald Reagan, "Tax Expenditures, July 27, 1979" in Skinner, Anderson, and Anderson, *In His Own Hand,* 283–84.

13. For Ronald Reagan's 1981 federal income tax return, see the website of Tax Analysts, <http://www.tax.org/THP/Presidential/reagan81a.htm>.

14. Both Paul Craig Roberts and Norman Ture had advised Congressman Jack Kemp and in 1975, in that capacity, provided him with a "supply-side basis" for a bill designed to promote capital formation through tax subsidies to investment. Roberts, *Supply-Side Revolution,* 31.

15. On the role of Charls Walker, see Jeffrey H. Birnbaum and Alan S. Murray, *Showdown at Gucci Gulch: Lawmakers, Lobbyists, and the Unlikely Triumph of Tax Reform* (New York: Random House, 1987), 16–18; Timothy J. Conlan et al., *Taxing Choices: The Politics of Tax Reform* (Washington, D.C.: Congressional Quarterly, 1990), 96; and Cathie J. Martin, *Shifting the Burden: The Struggle over Growth and Corporate Taxation* (Chicago: University of Chicago Press, 1991), 47.

16. Charls Walker, "Summary of Discussion," in *American Economic Policy in the 1980s,* 224–25.

17. In 1986 and again in 1994, David Stockman denied that the deficits were deliberate. See Stockman, *Triumph of Politics,* 267–68, and "Comments by David Stockman, Summary of Discussion: Tax Policy," in *American Economic Policy in the 1980s,* 287.

18. Ronald Reagan, "Economic Speech—Address to the Nation, February 5, 1981," in Skinner, Anderson, and Anderson, *In His Own Hand,* 490.

19. Max L. Friedersdorf, "Meetings with Representatives John J. Duncan, Bill Archer, and Bill Frenzel," March 26, 1982, ID #04366, Presidential Briefing Files, Ronald Reagan Library (RRL). Russell Long remembered, in particular: "We had twice repealed and subsequently reenacted the investment tax credit." Russell Long, "Tax Policy," in *American Economic Policy in the 1980s,* 221.

20. For the quotation of Regan, see Kevin D. Hoover and Steven M. Sheffrin, "Causation, Spending, and Taxes: Sand in the Sandbox or Tax Collector for the Welfare State?" *American Economic Review* 82 (March 1992): 225. The president's legislative study had

come to support the shift to 5-10-10 as a means "of deficit reduction and acceptance of selected other tax reduction proposals necessary to achieve a political majority." See "Meeting of Legislative Strategy Group," May 12, 1981, folder Economic/Budget Policy 5/81, OA 10972, Craig Fuller Files, RRL.

21. Martin Feldstein, "American Economic Policy in the 1980s: A Personal View," in *American Economic Policy in the 1980s,* 47–48.

22. In 1981 and 1982, Paul Volcker played an important role behind the scenes by lobbying the administration, particularly Secretary of the Treasury Regan, to reduce deficits in return for some monetary ease. Donald T. Regan, *For the Record: From Wall Street to Washington* (San Diego: Harcourt Brace Jovanovich, 1988), 178. Within the administration, Alan Greenspan defended the Federal Reserve and argued that "at root, our problem is that the markets believe that the Federal deficit will continue to hemorrhage, inducing the Federal Reserve to create excessive money supply growth and hence inflation." Alan Greenspan, untitled enclosure, February 1, 1982, folder "Briefing Book for Long-Range Planning Meeting, Camp David, February 5, 1982 (2)," Box 1, Richard G. Darman Files, RRL.

23. On the lack of focus within the White House on the growth in entitlement spending, see Stockman, *Triumph of Politics,* 161–62.

24. Comments by David Stockman, "Summary of Discussion: Tax Policy," in *American Economic Policy in the 1980s,* 276. For opposition within the White House to tax increases, see Richard S. Williamson to James A. Baker et al., "Tax Increase Issue," November 2, 1981, folder Economic/Budget Policy 11/81 (2), OA 10972, Craig Fuller Files, RRL.

25. Regan, *For the Record,* 179.

26. Regan, *For the Record,* 176–84. See also Stockman, *Triumph of Politics,* 356; Feldstein, "American Economic Policy in the 1980s," in *American Economic Policy in the 1980s,* 51; and Edwin Meese III, *With Reagan: The Inside Story* (Washington, D.C.: Regnery Publishing, 1992), 142–47. For Stockman's and Meese's later evaluations of how the three-for-one deal turned out, see note 44 below. On the support of the Reagan administration for a bipartisan approach, see Donald T. Regan to Dan Rostenkowski, July 12, 1982, folder Tax Issues (3), and Kenneth M. Duberstein, "Meeting with Senator William Roth," August 10, 1982, folder Tax Issues (4), OA 14862, Frederick McClure Files, RRL.

27. "Text of the Address by the President to the Nation," August 16, 1982, folder Tax Issues (4), OA 14862, Frederick McClure Files, RRL. On the administration's efforts to highlight the base-broadening elements in TEFRA, see "Fact Sheet, The Equity and Fiscal Responsibility Act of 1982," folder Tax Issues (3), OA 14862, Frederick McClure Files, RRL.

28. Richard G. Darman, "Key (Abstract) Elements of Program," attachment to Legislative Study Group Agenda, December 13, 1982, Economic/Budget Policy 12/82, OA 10972, Craig Fuller Files, RRL.

29. On the early initiatives, see the essay by Martha Derthick and Steven M. Teles in this volume. In December 1982, the president followed the advice of his staff. Darman wrote to the president that his "legislative and political advisers (along with Dick Schweicker and Dave Stockman)" recommended that the president should "try to work with the Commission to get as good a deal as possible—not withstanding the fact that any bi-partisan solution will be short of what you would have wished." Richard G. Darman, "Note for the President, Subject: Social Security," December 16, 1982, folder Social Security Commission, box 5, Richard G. Darman Files, RRL.

30. Even in the extreme version, therefore, the tax was a two-rate tax, with the first rate equal to zero.

31. On congressional interest in the flat tax in 1982, see "Flat-Rate Tax Advanced as Radical Cure for Problems of Existing Revenue System," *Congressional Quarterly* (June 5, 1982): 1331–34.

32. The following discussion of deliberations within the White House in late 1982 and 1983 draws upon the consistent recollections of David Stockman and Richard Darman. See Stockman, *Triumph of Politics*, 355–65, and Richard Darman, *Who's in Control: Polar Politics and the Sensible Center* (New York: Simon & Schuster, 1996), 118–19.

33. Donald Regan's recollections point to the president's concern about the loss of progressiveness in the flat tax. See Regan, *For the Record*, 198. His recollections are consistent with his comments in "Interview of Donald T. Regan by Alan Murray of the *Wall Street Journal*, Anne Swardson of the *Washington Post*, and Peter Kilborn of the *New York Times*," July 9, 1986, folder Tax Reform 1985 (4), OA 14862, Frederick McClure Files, RRL. In this interview Regan said that the administration had had reservations about a flat tax because it "would increase taxes for a heck of a lot of people."

34. See Steuerle, *Tax Decade*, 61–64. For Martin Feldstein's effort to explain the "standby" tax to the president, see Feldstein, "Memorandum for the President: Standby Tax," August 3, 1983, folder Memos to the President (Eyes Only), October 18, 1982–July 5, 1984 (5), Martin Feldstein Files, RRL.

35. On the Dole proposal of a contingency tax and the reaction to it within the administration, see Donald T. Regan, "Memorandum for the Honorable James A. Baker, Jr.: Dole Tax Proposal," October 17, 1983, folder Issues (1), Box #8, and James A. Baker III Files, RRL; Jonathan Fuerbringer, "Reagan Sees Contingency Tax Plan," *New York Times*, December 13, 1983. For Feldstein's praise for the president's tax cutting, see Martin Feldstein, "Memorandum for the President: Success at Reducing Taxes and Spending," October 13, 1983, folder Memos [see n. 34] (4), "Memorandum for the President: Tax Cuts Since 1981," January 3, 1984, folder Memos (2), and "Memorandum for the President: Cut in Tax Rates since 1960s," January 4, 1984, folder Memos (2). For Feldstein's linkage of deficits and inflation, see Martin Feldstein, "Memorandum for the President: Deficits and Inflation," January 8, 1984, folder Memos (2), OA 9815, Martin Feldstein Files, RRL. For overviews of the preparations for the 1984 state of the union address, see Stockman, *Triumph of Politics*, 374–75; Regan, *For the Record*, 196–201. The President's Economic Policy Advisory Board (PEPAB) consisted of outside economists, including Milton Friedman, William Simon, and others who had held economic-policy positions in earlier administrations. On the role of the PEPAB, see Anderson, *Revolution*, 265–71; Friedman, *Two Lucky People*, 391–95; and Roberts, *Supply-Side Revolution*, 210. Edwin Meese described Friedman as "a particular favorite of the president." Meese, *With Reagan*, 127.

36. "Interview of Donald T. Regan by Alan Murray of the *Wall Street Journal*, Anne Swardson of the *Washington Post*, and Peter Kilborn of the *New York Times*," July 9, 1986. In that interview, Regan could not remember Charles McLure's name. "What was the guy's name that we hired at Treasury?" Regan asked.

37. Regan, *For the Record*, 207; "Interview of Donald T. Regan by Alan Murray of the *Wall Street Journal*, Anne Swardson of the *Washington Post*, and Peter Kilborn of the *New York Times*," July 9, 1986.

38. The following account, including the quotations, is based on Secretary Regan's recollections. See Regan, *For the Record*, 193–203. The specific briefing meeting in December 1983 when Regan made his case to the president is unclear. But the meeting would have

included at least Baker, Feldstein, and Stockman. During the years he served in the Treasury, Regan never met alone with the president. See Regan, *For the Record,* 142.

39. On Baker's political concerns, see Feldstein, "American Economic Policy in the 1980s: A Personal View," and Russell Long, "Summary of Discussion, Tax Policy," in *American Economic Policy in the 1980s,* 20 and 226; Conlan et al., *Taxing Choices,* 48–49.

40. Regan, *For the Record,* 202–3.

41. Martin Feldstein, folder Memos [see n. 34] (2), OA 9815, "Memorandum for the President: Tax Rates and Tax Revenue," January 10, 1984, Martin Feldstein Files, RRL. The recollection of Reagan's statement at lunch is Stockman's. Stockman, *Triumph of Politics,* 374.

42. For Feldstein's advocacy of tax increases to reduce the deficits, see Martin Feldstein, "Memorandum for the President: Deficit Reduction Package," March 16, 1984, folder Memos (1). Feldstein expressed this same view vigorously in a letter to Jack Kemp and forwarded a copy of the letter to President Reagan. See Feldstein to Kemp, March 28, 1984, and Feldstein to Ronald Reagan, March 28, 1984, folder Memos (1), OA 9815, Martin Feldstein Files, RRL.

43. For an overview of the tax increases, see Steuerle, *Tax Decade,* 64–69.

44. For the quotation of Richard Darman, see "Commentary by Charls Walker, Summary of Discussion, Tax Policy," in *American Economic Policy in the 1980s,* 232. In his recollections of this episode, Darman implies that he continued to consider further deficit reduction after the passage of DEFRA. See Darman, *Who's in Control,* 124. For Reagan's conclusion that the Democrats had "reneged on their (TEFRA) pledge," see Ronald Reagan, *An American Life: The Autobiography* (New York: Simon & Schuster, 1990), 314–15. While Edwin Meese supported TEFRA at the time, he later described the compromise as "the greatest domestic error of the Reagan administration." See Meese, *With Reagan,* 147. David Stockman, however, has described the notion that the Democrats failed to deliver on their side of the bargain as the "big lie" of the supply-siders. See David Stockman, "Budget Policy," in *American Economic Policy in the 1980s,* 271–72.

45. For a description of the growing public awareness of tax shelters for individuals and corporations in 1984, see Birnbaum and Murray, *Showdown at Gucci Gulch,* 11–13.

46. In July, Richard Darman outlined a message on taxes and tax reform for the president to use in response to Mondale. Richard G. Darman to Richard Wirthlin, "Tax Strategy," July 26, 1984, James A. Baker III Files, folder Dick Darman's File, Box 7, RRL. Baker's staff then developed "talking points" for the president, and Peggy Noonan drafted a radio address, which Reagan delivered on August 4. "Talking Points Re. Taxes" and "Presidential Radio Talk: Taxes," August 4, 1984, folder Issues (2), Box 8, James A. Baker III Files, RRL. After George Bush and the president appeared to disagree publicly on whether or not the administration might consider tax increases, Baker went up to Reagan's Santa Barbara ranch with political strategist Stuart Spencer to craft a nuanced position. On August 9 Baker asked the president for his comments on a statement, which the White House released on August 12. See Baker to Mr. President, August 9, 1984, including undated, handwritten notes which appear to be Baker's regarding the mountaintop meeting with Reagan, and "Statement of the President," August 12, 1984, folder Issues (2), Box #8, James A. Baker III Files, RRL. For a description of the ranch meeting, see Peter Goldman et al., *The Quest for the Presidency, 1984* (New York: Bantam Books, 1985), 252–54. On the worries of the White House advisers about pressure from supply-siders,

see Anonymous, "Memorandum: Darman and Hopkins Tax Memos," July 30, 1984, folder Issues (2), Box #8, James Baker Files, RRL.

47. In a personal letter to C. Eugene Steuerle, dated July 28, 1985, Bruce Chapman, director of the White House Office of Planning and Evaluation, wrote: "Had I not read your paper . . . I would have missed what became the core argument for the family initiative which I had urged on the President, and which he adopted—and there never would have been a Presidential decision to double the personal exemption in the tax code. Regardless of the fate of the tax bill this fall, the tax exemption portion, I predict, will survive—and it's all due to your insightful analysis." Files of C. Eugene Steuerle.

48. Among those whom Regan kept out of the process were the members of the Council of Economic Advisers (CEA). William Niskanen, who became acting chair of the CEA in July of 1984, recalled that he "asked Regan to allow me to participate in these reviews." Regan told him "bluntly that no one outside Treasury would be informed about the developing plan until after the election." The Treasury, Niskanen noted, had "an effective monopoly within the administration over the formulation of tax policy." William Niskanen, *Reaganomics: An Insider's Account of the Policies and the People* (New York: Oxford University Press, 1988), 87.

49. Regan, *For the Record,* 206.

50. On the process for drafting Treasury I, and its provisions, see Steuerle, *Tax Decade, 1981–1990,* 102–14.

51. For a description of the briefing, see Cannon, *President Reagan,* 566.

52. Regan, *For the Record,* 283.

53. On the cheering by economists, see Conlan et al., *Taxing Choices,* 68–69.

54. In 1996, Darman recalled that before leaving the White House for the Treasury, he had put tax reform on the "top of the domestic list" and that this "made Treasury an exciting and attractive opportunity for me as well as Baker." See Darman, *Who's in Control,* 139–40.

55. On the president's review of the administration's tax reform measure, see Alfred H. Kingon to the President, "Cabinet Affairs Briefing—Tax Simplification," April 23, 1985, ID #231828; "Meeting on Fundamental Tax Reform, April 23, 1985," ID #271493SS; "Meeting on Fundamental Tax Reform, April 24, 1985," ID #271493SS; "Meeting on Fundamental Tax Reform, April 30, 1985," ID #2714933SS; James A. Baker, "Fundamental Tax Reform" [summary of proposals of April 23, 24, and 30], undated, ID #2171560PD; James A. Baker to the President, "Fundamental Tax Reform" [review of changes made in April meetings], undated ID, #2719493SS; James A. Baker to the President, "Fundamental Tax Reform" and attachments [decision memoranda following April meetings], undated, ID #271493SS; James A. Baker to the President, "Tax Reform (Supplement to Decision Memos)," May 10, ID #271493SS; James A. Baker to the President, "Fundamental Tax Reform" [list of required decisions], undated, ID #271493SS; James A. Baker to the President, "Fundamental Tax Reform," May 23, 1985 [outline of the president's "guidance" on May 21], ID #271493SS. All of the memos cited in this note are in FI010-02, WHORM: Subject File, RRL. The final version of the administration's proposal, approved by the president, had the higher rate structure of Treasury I, the larger tax expenditures of Treasury II, and at least two major tax expenditures that had not appeared in either version: retention of the depletion allowances for the oil and gas industry and a cut in the rate of capital gains taxation. On the meetings in April and May, see also, Jeffrey H. Birnbaum and Alan S. Murray, *Showdown at Gucci Gulch,* 89–93.

56. "The President's Tax Proposals to the Congress for Fairness, Growth, and Simplic-

ity," Summary, May 1985, folder Tax Reform 1985 (3), OA 14862, Frederick McClure Files, RRL; "Address by the President to the Nation," May 28, 1985, folder Tax Reform (5), OA 17746, Beryl Sprinkel Files, OA 17746, RRL. Ronald Reagan to the Congress of the United States, May 29, 1985, folder Tax Reform 1985 (3), OA 14862, Frederick McClure Files, RRL.

57. For example, on June 19, when he met with businessmen in Mooresville, Indiana, Reagan hesitated when someone asked him how his proposal would simplify the tax code. He said, "Wow," and turned to Donald Regan for help in answering. David Hoffman, "President Postpones Tax Blitz," *Washington Post,* July 4, 1985.

58. Regan, *For the Record,* 286.

59. On the congressional deliberations, see Birnbaum and Murray, *Showdown at Gucci Gulch,* 96 ff., and Conlan et al., *Taxing Choices,* 84 ff.

60. There was, however, a 33 percent "bubble." This 33 percent rate applied at high (but not the highest) income levels until the individual paid an effective rate of 28 percent on all income. At that point, the 28 percent kicked back in again.

61. The crucial meeting in which George Bush defended the oil industry was on May 21. Birnbaum and Murray, *Showdown at Gucci Gulch,* 94. On May 23, the president initialed his approval for the changes favoring the oil industry. James A. Baker III to the President, "Fundamental Tax Reform" [outline of the president's "guidance" on May 21], May 23, 1985, ID #271493SS, FI010-02, WHORM Subject File, RRL.

62. The increase in corporate taxes can be misleading, however. Many corporations, including IBM and General Motors, favored the reform because they believed that they would profit from being in the competitive, lower-rate environment. Moreover, the effective rate of tax on investment depends on the combination of corporate and individual rates, and this effective rate increased only slightly, mainly through compromises made after Treasury I, on the way to enactment.

63. Ronald Reagan, "Remarks by the President at the Signing Ceremony for Tax Reform Legislation," October 22, 1986, folder Tax Reform 1985 (4), OA 14862, Frederick McClure Files, RRL; Reagan, *An American Life,* 335.

64. The Congressional Budget Office has regularly published estimates of the effective federal tax rate on families in various income categories. Their 1990 estimates showed that in 1980 and 1991, the effective tax rates for the five quintiles of the income distribution from lowest to highest were as follows: 8.4 percent (1980), 8.5 percent (1991); 15.7 percent (1980), 16.7 percent (1991); 20.0 percent (1980), 20.7 percent (1991); 23.0 percent (1980), 22.9 percent (1991); and 27.3 percent (1991), 26.8 percent (1980). This calculation includes Social Security payroll taxes as well as the federal income tax. The average rate for all families barely budged between 1980 and 1991, declining from 23.3 percent to 23.1 percent. The top 1 percent experienced only a modest drop, from 31.8 percent to 28.9 percent. For details, see C. Eugene Steuerle, *Tax Decade,* 194–96.

65. Eric Toder, "The Changing Composition of Tax Incentives, 1980–1999," Urban Institute (March 1999), chart I.

66. For analysis of the new wave of tax shelters, see C. Eugene Steuerle, "Economic Perspective: Defining Tax Shelters and Tax Arbitrage," *Tax Notes* (May 20, 2002): 1249–50. Much of the complexity of the tax code reflects a desire to limit tax preferences and to measure income more accurately. For a discussion of such complexity, see Charles E. McLure, Jr., "Reagan's Tax Policy," in *Looking Back on the Reagan Presidency,* ed. Larry Berman (Baltimore: Johns Hopkins University Press, 1990), 163–64.

8
Riding the Third Rail:
Social Security Reform

Martha Derthick and Steven M. Teles

The constitutional prerogatives of the legislative branch would have to be, in effect, suspended. Enacting the Reagan Administration's economic program meant rubber stamp approval, nothing less. The world's so-called greatest deliberative body would have to be reduced to the status of a ministerial arm of the White House.
—David Stockman, *Triumph of Politics*

The real power of the purse, the power to spend or not spend, lies with Congress.
—Martin Anderson, *Revolution: The Reagan Legacy*

During Ronald Reagan's administration, Social Security began to emerge, for the first time since its founding in the mid-1930s, as a leading fault line of partisan politics. In part the reason for this lay within the program, the costs of which were now being fully—and unpredictably—revealed. But in addition to the tensions rising inescapably with costs, under Reagan partisanship was exacerbated by the administration's misjudgments, prominently including a failure to comprehend the gravity and political force of the government's promises to payroll taxpayers. Ill-conceived proposals to reduce Social Security that the administration announced in the spring of 1981 brought a savage Democratic counterattack and made Republican politicians vulnerable on the issue for decades to come. The administration's attempt to limit the damage, which led it to acquiesce in 1983 in legislation that solidified the existing program, rather than put matters to rest ironically energized disillusioned conservatives outside of the

We would like to thank the following for help with locating and interpreting source material: Kelly Barton, Edward Berkowitz, Larry DeWitt, Pat Dilley, Mike Duggan, Steve Entin, Aldona Robbins, and John Trout.

administration, who set to work on a newly bold and challenging Republican strategy of privatization.

Public officials who bore responsibility for the program all felt compelled to take action in 1980 and 1981, as the Reagan presidency was beginning to take shape. In the 1970s, Social Security had begun to run into serious financial trouble, the result both of enacted changes—the indexing of current benefits, along with a badly designed formula for indexing—and of the erratic performance of the economy. In 1977, Congress had attempted to repair the program's finances with increases in both the wage base (the amount of a worker's earnings subject to taxation) and the tax rate. This fix was supposed to keep revenues and expenditures in balance for at least thirty-five years, but in fact it was proving insufficient after only three, to the distress of congressional leaders of the program, who saw it as their duty to sustain public confidence in Social Security. Double-digit inflation was causing benefits to soar, tied as they now were to the cost of living, while high unemployment and low wage growth—indeed, in 1979 and 1980 a *decline* in wages—were causing payroll tax returns to fall short of predictions, resulting in annual program deficits on the order of $3 billion to $4 billion. In 1979 the report of the trustees of the Social Security trust fund, a government document that analyzes the financial condition of Social Security, warned of a fragile balance between revenues and expenditures in the immediate future. Still more alarming, the report for 1980, issued in mid-year, said that the trust fund for old-age and survivors' insurance would be exhausted late in 1981 or early in 1982 and called for "early attention by the Congress."[1]

Thus jolted, Congress members, study commissions, and policy analysts were groping for solutions as Reagan prepared to take office.[2] Already in the air were such proposals as taxing benefits, which both parties rejected in their 1980 platforms; raising the normal retirement age above sixty-five, which organized labor strongly opposed; or revising the COLA (cost-of-living adjustment) to make it less liberal, a change that had support from academic analysts across the political spectrum. Nevertheless, although there was a sense of urgency in Washington, the situation did not admit of easy fixes. Some combination of benefit reductions and tax increases would be required, against the preferences of politicians and their constituents.

The Reagan administration's intentions for Social Security were unclear. On one hand, Reagan was known to be unsympathetic to the program. He had criticized Social Security on the lecture circuit in the early 1960s, and in his nationally televised speech on behalf of Barry Goldwater in 1964, the speech that catapulted him to national prominence, he had spoken of introducing "voluntary features" into it.[3] He thought that people should have the choice of providing for their own financial security in retirement rather than having to submit to the coercion of a government program. Also, the promises on which Reagan ran—to reduce taxes and domestic spending but to increase spending for defense—necessarily implied a critical examination of the government's most expensive domestic program. The Republican platform in 1980 pledged cryptically to restore Social Security "to its original purpose," and conservative intellectuals were working on critiques of it, as in essays by the Harvard economist Martin Feldstein, who would become Reagan's second chairman of the Council of Economic Advisers (CEA), and the Stanford economist Michael Boskin.[4]

On the other hand, against all this, Reagan during the campaign had promised not to cut benefits. Charged by his opponent, Jimmy Carter, with wanting to make Social Security voluntary, Reagan denied having said that. Haunted by Goldwater's large loss to Lyndon Johnson in 1964, which was generally thought to be attributable in part to criticism of Social Security, Reagan and his advisers treated the subject cautiously, the advisers living in fear that he would forget himself and hold forth on it spontaneously.[5] Just what the administration would do was not clarified by an eleven-member task force on Social Security that Reagan appointed in September 1980.[6]

The administration quickly fell victim to its own internal contradictions. In what many analysts, including both journalists and administration insiders, have judged to be its first big blunder, it advanced a Social Security proposal that called for deep and immediate cuts in benefits for early retirees—that is, persons who voluntarily chose to retire with reduced benefits between the ages of sixty-two and sixty-four, rather than wait for full benefits at the normal retirement age of sixty-five.[7] This proposal touched off a furious reaction in Congress, and the fury soon also engulfed an earlier administration proposal to eliminate a statutory provision for a minimum benefit.

Although members of both parties overwhelmingly repudiated the administration—with the Senate voting 96 to 0 against the cut in early retirement benefits and the House voting 405 to 13 against the proposal on the minimum benefit—Democrats under the leadership of Speaker Thomas P. O'Neill were able to turn the administration's mistake to a partisan advantage that they exploited for years to come. They would continue to portray Republicans as the party that "wants to cut your social security benefits," a strategy that eventually would silence Republican officeholders on the subject. It was O'Neill who called Social Security the "third rail" of American politics because to touch it was to die.[8] It was mainly O'Neill, capitalizing on the ineptitude of the Reagan administration, who in the 1980s decisively turned it into the third rail, overturning a tradition of bipartisanship that had been developed in the House Ways and Means Committee during the 1950s and 1960s.[9]

Our account will explore the origins of the administration's blunder; the administration's subsequent attempt to recover from it, which culminated in a law of 1983 that confirmed the existing program, contrary to conservative preferences; and the development of a distinctive conservative position on Social Security after 1983 that was better articulated and promoted to the public than anything offered by the Reagan administration.

CUTTING SOCIAL SECURITY

Led in the matter mainly by Office of Management and Budget director David Stockman, who was spearheading the administration's attempt to reduce domestic spending, the administration made three large strategic errors in regard to Social Security in the opening half of 1981. It acted as if it did not need the cooperation of Congress. At least nominally, it pursued an ambitious goal: "dewelfarizing" the program—that is, removing unearned benefits and redistributive features from it—although it had not secured agreement on any such principled reform even among its own members and ideological allies. And it violated the norm of promise keeping, which is central to policymaking for a public retirement program in a democracy.

Arrogance. "Basically I screwed up quite a bit on the way the damn thing was handled," Stockman told William Greider of the *Washington Post.* "I was just racing against the clock. All the office things I knew ought to be done by way of groundwork, advance preparation, and so forth just fell by the wayside. . . . Now we're taking the flak from all the rest of the Republicans because we didn't inform them."[10]

But it wasn't an "office thing" that Stockman had overlooked. It was a *constitutional* thing, fundamental and commonsensical—that Congress is a coordinate rather than subordinate branch, with broad powers over taxing and spending. This failure to consult at a critical moment was only the climactic event in a pattern of disrespect for the legislature that was evident in Stockman's behavior throughout the spring.

In regard specifically to Social Security, there was, first and foremost, a rebuff to leaders of the president's own party in the Senate, which was under Republican control for the first time since 1954. Pete Domenici of New Mexico, chairman of the Budget Committee, told the administration in March that he had eleven Republican and five Democratic votes, more than two-thirds of the committee, for a proposal that would revise the formula for cost-of-living increases and save $10 billion in the immediate budget and $25 billion by the fifth year.

With conflicting motives, the administration leaped to kill this proposal. James Baker, Reagan's politically astute chief of staff, feared the political consequences of cutting Social Security; Stockman concluded that the senators were trying to protect other domestic programs that he wished to attack while he saved Social Security for later and grander use. With both advisers, the president journeyed to Capitol Hill to explain his position.[11]

Several senators besides Domenici tried to argue with the president—William Armstrong of Colorado, Slade Gorton of Washington, Rudy Boschwitz of Minnesota, and John Tower of Texas, with Armstrong, who was chairman of the Social Security subcommittee of the Finance Committee, making the strongest case. "We're not talking about a cut," he said, meaning that no current benefits would be cut, only prospective ones. "We have a unique bipartisan opportunity. It will save more money than almost any other single action we can take over the next four or five years, and we really hope you'll reconsider this advice to us, Mr. President." But Reagan insisted that he could not renege on a campaign promise, and the senators reluctantly acceded to presidential leadership at this early stage in the administration.[12]

This meeting helped spread the misleading impression that the administration intended to spare Social Security, a message that was spread initially when it largely escaped Stockman's first round of proposed reductions and Reagan promised in a speech to Congress on February 18 that the social safety net would be preserved.[13] Stockman all the while, following a strategy of procrastination and preemption, was saving it for use in a third round of cuts, the "true heavy lifting . . . of the Reagan fiscal revolution." The big middle-class entitlement programs, beginning with Social Security but including also Medicare and the federal government's retirement pensions, would produce the "future savings to be identified" that the president's initial budget submission promised.[14] This was the famous "magic asterisk" that Stockman invented and Howard Baker named. Others in the administration, including Reagan's three principal advisers—James Baker, Edwin Meese, and Michael Deaver—were not deliberately colluding with Stockman in this plan, merely hoping to find that there would be enough magic in fraud, waste, and abuse to avoid having to attach Social Security to the asterisk.

A second congressional initiative came in early April from J. J. (Jake) Pickle, who was newly installed as chairman of the Social Security subcommittee of the Ways and Means Committee and dedicated to rapid restoration of the program's finances. Supported by a very able staff, Pickle had been holding hearings and markups with the aim of producing a bill. He kept in touch both with the subcommittee's ranking Republican, William Archer, and with staff of the Social Security Administration (SSA), who attended the markups and assisted with cost estimates. Released by Pickle in his own name, the bill had bipartisan backing. It would have gradually raised the normal age of eligibility for retirement from sixty-five to sixty-eight, starting in 1990 and completing the change by 2000.[15]

Stockman feared this proposal on the arrestingly perverse ground that it had too much congressional support. It had become "everyone's favorite Social Security reform fetish," with backing from such staunchly conservative Republicans as Barber Conable and Archer in the House and Armstrong in the Senate.[16] Increasingly desperate for savings in order to keep a balanced budget within reach—his aim was now an added $44 billion per year—Stockman needed a plan that would save more money sooner. After the Pickle bill was announced, the administration began to focus on preparing a proposal.

Not that the administration had previously been idle. In February, Secretary Richard S. Schweiker of the Department of Health and Human Services (HHS) formed a work group on Social Security, headed by Undersecretary David Swoap. Before long the group was enlarged to include representatives also from the departments of Treasury and Labor, the White House Office of Policy Development (OPD), OMB, and the CEA. At the SSA, staff members began preparing options papers under the direction of Lawrence H. Thompson, associate commissioner for policy, with the aim of draft legislation by early April.

Seeking cooperation with members of Congress or common ground on Social Security issues, even with Republicans, was not part of the administration's strategy in these early months. Stockman in particular treated Social Security as a tool of the administration's economic program and Congress as a tool of the administration.

Conceptual Ambition without Consensus. As the administration approached office, conservative intellectuals had developed a critique of Social Security without, however, having settled on a plan that might meet tests of both principle and politics. Clues to the administration's possible intentions nevertheless may be gleaned from the work of Boskin, who emerged at this time as the articulator of a conservative position on Social Security. He served on the Reagan task force on Social Security, and he contributed an essay on the subject to a volume of brief policy analyses assembled at the Hoover Institution, a California-based conservative think tank, prior to Reagan's taking office.

Boskin argued that three types of problems plagued Social Security: adverse incentives to save and invest; a long-range funding deficit of "stunning proportions"; and charges of unfair treatment from many groups in the population, particularly working women who resented the benefits that nonworking women received as dependent spouses. Among his proposals for reform were: gradually increasing the normal retirement age to sixty-eight over several decades while preserving the option of early retirement with reduced benefits; shifting redistributive features gradually into income support programs financed with general revenues rather than the payroll tax; and opening up "more ways in which individuals can prove that they have provided for their retirement, either privately or publicly." He urged beginning promptly on fundamental reform, but also stressed that changes must be gradual because many individuals had made retirement plans and that capital markets had adjusted to current expectations.[17] Boskin was not an intimate of Reagan, and his recommendations should be read as a guide to what some conservative intellectuals were hoping for rather than anything to which the administration was committed.

Stockman's opening rounds of cuts in February and March 1981 consisted of the relatively easy cases, "cats and dogs," that were pulled off the shelf at OMB or out of the budget proposal that he and Representative Phil Gramm of Texas, then still a Democrat, had put together when Stockman was in Congress.[18]

One early target was student benefits, which had been authorized in 1965 for eighteen- to twenty-two-year-old dependents or survivors of retired, disabled, or deceased workers if they were enrolled in postsecondary schools. Both the Ford and Carter administrations had proposed to eliminate student benefits, which by 1981 cost $2 billion a year.[19]

Another target was the "regular" minimum benefit. Historically, Social Security had provided for a minimum monthly payment, designed in 1935 (at $10) as an administrative convenience, to avoid issuing checks for trivial, quixotic amounts. Congress raised the minimum frequently, and eventually this produced windfalls for persons, such as federal government employees, who were covered primarily by other pension programs but secured enough covered employment to qualify for Social Security benefits as well. In 1972, partly on the urging of Social Security commissioner Robert M. Ball, Congress authorized a new form of benefit, the "special" minimum, for persons who had paid into the system for at least ten years. It was meant to protect long-term but low-wage workers, such as agricultural or domestic employees. Ball anticipated that this would make it possible to eliminate the regular minimum, and in 1977 Congress took a tentative step in that direction by freezing it at $122 a month. With a fixed size, it would gradually cease to have effect. The Reagan administration would have ended it immediately while preserving the special minimum.[20]

Other proposals of February and March were: imposition of a "megacap" for disability benefits, designed to assure that such benefits from all public sources, including workers' compensation, not exceed the recipient's prior net earnings; tying eligibility for disability benefits more closely to recent work; elimination of an automatic lump-sum death payment of $255, except where a spouse existed to receive it; and ending the use of Social Security trust funds to pay for vocational rehabilitation services for disabled beneficiaries. The savings from these proposals were estimated variously at $25.6 billion to $36.8 billion for 1982 through 1986, though even the higher of these two figures would have left a deficit of $74 billion for the five-year period, based on a "worst-case" set of economic assumptions that Thompson had prepared and Stockman elected to use.[21] This mixed bag of budget proposals certainly did not constitute a coherent program of Social Security reform.

Coherence was not attained either in April as the work group sought to fashion a proposal by selecting elements from the "monkish texts"—Stockman's phrase—of the SSA staff. Sometimes the work group met at HHS as staff members of the various member agencies, but it also brought department and agency heads together in cabinet-level meetings in the Roosevelt Room of the White House or in the Old Executive Office Building adjacent to the White House. Several meetings occurred in April and May. In the first week of May, as pressure to reach a result intensified, the group met on three successive days.

Three different sets of goals and interests emerged in these meetings. The members from HHS, led by Schweiker, were in a hurry to produce a result that would be reassuring to the public. In his confirmation hearings before the Senate Finance Committee in early January and again before Pickle's subcommittee on February 19, Schweiker promised prompt action. Social Security, he said, was his top priority. As a former member of both the House and Senate, he was sensitive to Congress's desire to affirm the financial integrity of Social Security and keep the public's confidence.[22]

Within HHS, the dominant figure as of early April, displacing the Carter administration's Thompson, was the deputy commissioner for programs, Robert J. Myers, who was new to the Reagan administration but far from new to policymaking for Social Security. As a young actuary, fresh out of college, Myers had been present at the creation of the program in the mid-1930s, and he was the SSA's chief actuary between 1947 and 1970. After resigning that position over policy differences with Commissioner Robert Ball and perhaps in disappointment at not being named by the Nixon administration in Ball's place, he had remained active as a frequent consultant to study commissions, advisory councils, and congressional committees, being helpful especially to Republicans who needed a source of expert advice. Myers was himself more dedicated to the program than to any political party, and his leading proposal was wholly traditional. He wanted to bolster the program's finances by extending coverage to all new federal government employees as of June 1, 1982, and to all state and local government employees, new and incumbent, as of January 1, 1984. Enlarging coverage was historically a way of bringing fresh revenues into the system, more effective in the short term than the long, because eventually there would also be added benefit obligations. But in this case, the SSA also expected a long-term improvement in the financial condition of the system. Because federal government employees had clung to their own pension system, and state and local governments had been free to participate in Social Security or not, public employees constituted a last frontier for expanded coverage.

A second position was that of the Treasury Department's supply-side economists, led by Paul Craig Roberts, assistant secretary for economic policy, and his deputy Stephen J. Entin, who in turn was supported by a career civil servant with expertise in Social Security, Aldona DiPietro. They were reluctant to endorse any Social Security proposal in the spring of 1981 for fear that it would stir up a fight in Congress and jeopardize a tax cut, which was their overriding goal. Nonetheless, within the work group they argued for contracting the program in the long run by indexing promised benefits to prices rather than to wages, which normally rise faster than prices. In their view, this would turn the program into a floor of protection on top of which individuals could construct private savings, rather than allowing it to continue to grow as the major source of retirement income. In the short run, they counseled the use of inter-fund borrowing, because the trust funds for disability and health insurance were for the time being better financed than that for old-age and survivors' insurance. "We believe we should do as little as possible in the short run," Entin advised Secretary of the Treasury Donald Regan.[23] Besides fearing that short-run cuts would give insufficient notice to the victims and be inflammatory in Congress, they also feared a larger than necessary buildup of the trust funds. William Niskanen, an economist who represented the CEA, was allied with them.

These opposing forces largely canceled each other. There was enough opposition to expanding the program to prevent any increase in coverage—a decision that in the end was rendered by the president himself. However, Myers prevailed in opposing price indexing, which he argued was a delusion because Congress was likely to deviate from it in order to enact larger increases ad hoc.[24] Swoap and the administration's new commissioner of Social Security, John A. Svahn, held firm in support of Myers despite appeals from Entin and Niskanen in a private meeting.[25]

The mutual destruction achieved by the forces of expansion versus the forces of contraction enhanced the power of the third main participant, Stockman, whose overriding goal was to balance the government's budget within the next five years. Stockman was in any case the dominant figure in domestic policymaking at this time, and within the work group he had support from Martin Anderson of OPD. With staff support from his politically appointed associate director for health and income maintenance programs, Don Moran, and a veteran career member of OMB, David Kleinberg, Stockman was searching for ways to achieve the largest possible savings with the greatest possible speed. From the menu prepared by HHS, Stockman seized cuts in benefits for early retirees. Among four packages that HHS had offered, two contained reductions in early retirement benefits. One package would have reduced them by 5 percent, whereas another would have done so by 10 percent. Nothing HHS put forth sanctioned the 25 percent cut that became part of the administration's proposal.

Myers would later complain that Stockman's position on early retirement was driven entirely by budgetary considerations: "[OMB] figured out how much money they wanted to save and worked their way back from that. . . . It came out that their goals would be met if people retiring at age 62 got benefits of only 55 percent of what they would get at 65. . . . The 55 percent was just drawn out of the air."[26] Myers argued to Svahn that this should not be done, at least not right away, but Svahn, a veteran of the Reagan gubernatorial administration in California and a loyalist, declined to put up a fight. "'Look, they're running the show,' he said of Stockman and his collaborators in budget cutting. 'We can argue, but they're running the show.'" If HHS had a large influence on the agenda, OMB had an even larger one on the outcome.

Schweiker might have been able to kill the deep cut within the work group but for the fact that in the context of the Reagan administration's budget politics of 1981, even a deep cut could be seen as relatively moderate—and essential to achieving the $75 billion to $100 billion in savings that the work group had agreed on as a goal. In January, as Reagan took office and the budget cutting began, Stockman had proposed eliminating early retirement benefits altogether, but had backed down when Schweiker protested that this was too radical—it would never pass Congress.[27]

In determining the size of the package, Stockman and HHS were perversely allied, HHS wishing to use pessimistic assumptions in order to get the biggest possible fix for the program, Stockman wishing to get the biggest possible fix for the budget overall. The fact that the administration was using worst-case assumptions to design its Social Security proposals while touting more optimistic economic assumptions to promote its tax cut would contribute to the intense anger that arose later in Congress.

The final session on Social Security, the culmination of the work group's work, was a one-hour meeting with the president on May 11. In the proposal presented to the president, the cut in early retirement benefits did not stand out. It was one of two items under the euphemistic heading "changes to encourage work between 62–65." There are several explanations for the general failure at this time to recognize the blunder the group was about to commit.

From the start of the planning effort, HHS officials had thought of themselves as acting cautiously because they avoided what they termed "big-ticket" items. They did not propose to raise the normal age of retirement, or revise the COLA formula, or immediately cover all federal employees. In a covering memorandum to the president, Schweiker claimed that the group had been able to solve both the short- and long-run financial problems of Social Security "without resorting to extremely controversial items." The recommended package contained "technical changes" only, and reduced benefits only on a "prospective basis." Only one item, the president was told, would affect current beneficiaries. This was a proposal to change the date for automatic increases under the COLA from June to September.[28]

Although the memorandum to the president did not say as much, it was true that cutting early retirement benefits was not controversial per se, given widespread agreement among policymakers that workers should be encouraged to remain in the workforce longer. Within the Ways and Means Committee, Richard Gephardt, a Missouri Democrat who would become a leading liberal member of the party, had proposed gradually increasing the reduction in benefits for early retirees from 20 percent to 30 percent starting in 1983 and concluding in 1990.[29] Pickle's bill would have begun to reduce early retirement benefits in 1990, allowing them to drop for sixty-two-year-olds to 64 percent of the full benefit by 2000. It was the size and immediacy of the administration's reduction that would make it so controversial in Congress.

A third explanation is that the administration, Stockman most of all, was in a euphoric state, not conducive to caution or clear thinking. It is no coincidence that the administration's critical decision on Social Security followed by only a few days a triumphant vote in the House of Representatives, where not a single Republican defected and sixty-three Democrats voted for the administration's budget bill.[30] Obsessive in pursuit of budget reduction, Stockman had deluded himself that it could be forced upon Congress with an exercise of presidential power seemingly bestowed by the results of the 1980 election and augmented by Reagan's oratory, support from conservative Democrats in the House of Representatives, and procedural legerdemain (the inventive use of reconciliation) in the budget process. Speaking of the severe cut in early retirement benefits, Stockman later admitted that "I just hadn't thought through the impact of making it effective immediately."[31]

Finally, both Stockman and Schweiker believed that Pickle's commitment to producing a bipartisan bill augured well for success. "They want to take to the Hill a substantial list of benefit reductions with major short run savings in 1983 and 1984 to help balance the unified budget in 1984," Entin explained to Undersecretary Norman Ture. "They believe Representative Pickle is in a hurry to mark-up a bill; that he is receptive to additional cuts; that he will act in a bipartisan spirit; that he will delay mark-up one more week but no longer." The danger, Entin presciently added, was that the cuts might be so unpopular that the Democratic leadership would scuttle "Mr. Pickle's supposedly bipartisan effort."[32]

No doubt, the president should have been more inquisitive. Even sympathetic accounts of Reagan as a decision maker, such as that provided by Anderson, do not portray him as critical in the face of choices presented by staff members—and this was a man only six weeks away from a serious assault on his life. Perhaps a more astute chief executive, less damaged by a bullet in his pulmonary cavity and more versed in the details of policy, would have thought to ask how the magical result described to him—a set of technical changes that would solve all the financial problems of Social Security, short-term and long-term, without controversy—could have been achieved. If it was so easy to fix Social Security, why hadn't someone else done it, or why hadn't the administration proposed doing it earlier instead of shying away from the subject?

No one at the presentation dissented. Treasury, defeated in the work group and in any case not the lead agency, was silent. Secretary Regan stayed away from the meeting and sent Ture instead in order to minimize involvement and avoid being tarnished by the disaster that Treasury staff sensed was impending.[33] The minutes of the meeting say that Schweiker "urged quick action because his discussions with Congressman Pickle and his former colleagues in the Senate convinced him that there is a 'window of opportunity' to get Congressional action with little partisan criticism." They also say that "David Stockman urged quick action because of budgetary considerations."[34]

The plan was not a sweeping attack on unearned benefits or redistributive features of the program, despite Stockman's later claim that these were high among his goals. The savings achieved were estimated at $46.4 billion for the five years 1982 through 1986, which, when added to the budget proposals of February and March, would have produced a total savings of $81.9 billion. Only two provisions, which together accounted for $4.8 billion in savings, were described in the administration's press release as reductions in welfare elements. The smaller of the two provisions would have eliminated benefits for the children of early retirees, an added attack on early retirement. The other would have capped family benefits for recipients of retirement or survivors' insurance. Under existing law, benefits for families of retired or deceased workers could exceed a worker's net take-home pay. A maximum designed to prevent this had been enacted for disability insurance in 1980, and the plan would have extended such a limit to retirement and survivors' insurance.

The biggest single block of savings—$21.9 billion—came from tightening eligibility for disability benefits by increasing the waiting period from five to six months, requiring a prognosis of twenty-four rather than twelve months' duration, requiring a "medical only" determination of disability that would exclude vocational factors, and requiring thirty quarters of coverage out of the last forty instead of twenty out of forty.

The saving from reducing early retirement benefits was also large, estimated at $17.6 billion over five years.[35] Since 1961 all workers had had the option of retiring as early as age sixty-two with a reduction in benefits of up to 20 percent. By the early 1970s, more than half of retirees were choosing to retire prior to the "normal" age of sixty-five, and the proportion was rising. By 1977 it had reached 60 percent. Early retirement was prevalent in particular among industrial workers, whose occupations had been physically punishing. It was the prompt and large potential for savings here that made the change so attractive to Stockman—and, correspondingly, made it so dangerous politically.

Although the administration's press release described the plan as redirecting "social security to its original purpose," an echo of the Republican platform, and Stockman claimed that it reversed "45 years of Social Security history," it was on the whole a modest step backward.[36] Its apparent virtue was that it improved the program's finances without raising taxes or reducing benefits for current recipients—except that the latter virtue was delusory. The cut in benefits for early retirees came so soon—on January 1, 1982—as to be tantamount to an attack on current beneficiaries, as anyone could see who paused to look.

Still lacking a powerful rationale, the program lacked support even from the administration that produced it. Within hours of the president's approval, it was on its way to being disowned by the White House. It was announced on May 12 by Schweiker rather than the White House because James Baker and his deputy, Richard Darman, who perceived a political hazard in it, tried to put distance between Reagan and the decision he had just made.[37]

Starkly manifest at this moment was a flaw inherent in the presidency as an institution for policy planning. It has a tendency to be torn between policy advisers who make recommendations to the president based on an overestimation of his power, and political staff who seek to distance their man from proposals bearing the possibility of political damage. The consequence in this case was that Reagan embraced a policy proposal largely innocent of political calculation and failed to put the full weight of his office behind it—policy adventurism combined with tactical timidity.

Promise Breaking. Reagan's campaign promise not to cut benefits, seemingly confirmed by early indications that the administration would interpret that promise strictly, contributed to the furor that ensued. More fundamentally at issue, however, was the nature of the promise historically embedded in the program. Reluctant to cut benefits at all, administrators of Social Security and members of Congress implicitly were developing at this time a shared agreement that, if cuts were to be attempted, they should be gradual and remote in time. Citizens should not be deprived of benefits that they were currently receiving or were imminently expecting to receive. This norm grew both out of the nature of a retirement program and out of the imperatives of electoral politics.

In Congress, the May 12 proposal provoked rage—not so much for the sum total of its contents or the policy direction allegedly embodied in it, which the legislature did not seriously debate, but for the early retirement provision, with its harsh, immediate, and readily comprehensible effects. As an HHS fact sheet helpfully pointed out, guaranteeing publicity, a low-income worker expecting to retire at age sixty-two on January 1, 1982, would get $163.90 a month in benefits instead of the $247.60 on which he or she had been counting. A worker retiring at the maximum benefit level would get $310.50 a month instead of $469.60. Among Democrats, who knew a political windfall when they saw one, the rage was mostly feigned, whereas among Republicans it was the real thing.

"To save the House, [Speaker Thomas P.] O'Neill needed an issue," his biographer writes, "and Social Security promised to be one."[38] At a press conference on May 13, O'Neill read a prepared statement, charging the administration with a breach of faith. "For the first time since 1935 people would suffer because they trusted in the Social Security system," he said. Asked by a reporter if the Reagan plan was a political mistake, O'Neill replied: "'I'm not talking about politics. I'm talking about decency. It is a rotten thing to do. It is a despicable thing.'"[39]

Within two days, Stockman knew he was in deep trouble. At a breakfast with House Republicans, the conservative Carroll Campbell of South Carolina, a confirmed Reagan supporter, "lit into me like a junkyard dog." "'You absolutely blind-sided us with this Social Security plan,' he seethed. 'My phones are ringing off the hook. I've got thousands of sixty-year-old textile workers who think it's the end of the world. What the hell am I supposed to tell them?'" Campbell went on to say that most of the package was sound. "'But you've screwed it up completely by making the early retirement reduction effective immediately. That's going to bring the whole thing down in flames.'"[40]

On the Senate side, a staff member for the Republicans warned a counterpart in the administration that the early retirement provision, alone in the package, was a "real clinker." He had supposed that the administration included it only as a bargaining chip, but incredulously concluded, after a briefing from Commissioner Svahn, that "you're all serious about it." He characterized the proposal as "unreal" in that it would require "older people planning to retire next year to bear the brunt of [the] short-term social security crisis."[41]

In the Senate, Daniel P. Moynihan of New York, who was the ranking Democrat on the Social Security subcommittee of the Finance Committee, sponsored a resolution condemning the "breach of faith with those aging Americans who have contributed to the Social Security System and have planned for their retirement upon the promise of a specific level of Social Security income." Moynihan explained later that this was the Democrats' "best issue with the new president. . . . This was my responsibility and our moment."[42]

The resolution failed by only one vote, with two Republicans, William Roth of Delaware and Lowell Weicker of Connecticut, joining the Democrats in support of it. The Senate then unanimously passed a Republican substitute, offered by Robert J. Dole, chairman of the Finance Committee, that promised not to "precipitously and unfairly reduce early retirees' benefits." This was on May 20. After a brief and halfhearted attempt to defend the administration's proposal, the White House backed off and began referring to the plan on background as Schweiker's folly. On May 21, Reagan sent the Congress a letter appealing for "statesmanship of the highest order" and pledging the administration's help in launching "a bipartisan effort to save Social Security."[43] But it was too late for bipartisanship.

Once the Democrats achieved an advantage with Social Security, they pressed it relentlessly. On the defensive throughout the spring, they were now enabled to counterattack. "The ball has been lofted to us," Representative Tony Coelho, chairman of the Democratic Congressional Campaign Committee, said. "We've taken it, and we're running with it. . . . We're not going to fumble it."[44]

The conflagration of May over cutting early retirement benefits spread in June to elimination of the regular minimum benefit. This matter could easily be made to seem simpler than it was. Most members of Congress, let alone the general public, did not grasp the difference between the regular and special minimums, and could therefore be led to believe that the administration's proposal was an attack on the poor.

The Ways and Means Committee, under Democratic control, agreed in the spring to eliminate the regular minimum, but only for future beneficiaries. It adhered to the principle of protecting all current beneficiaries from reductions. The Finance Committee, more accommodating to the administration, agreed to eliminate the minimum for current recipients but authorized benefits under Supplemental Security Income (SSI), a means-tested program financed with general revenues, to compensate the needy among them.

In a series of complicated maneuvers in the House in June, a pro-administration conservative coalition prevailed on this issue, so that the House version of the budget reconciliation bill concurred with the Senate Finance Committee. But the House leadership fought back outside of the budget process. On July 21,

Majority Leader James Wright sponsored a resolution urging that "necessary steps be taken to insure that Social Security benefits are not reduced for those currently receiving them." Wright explained that he intended this to encourage House conferees on the reconciliation bill to deviate from their instructions, or, failing that, to commit the House to adopting separate legislation that would reverse the contents of the budget act.[45] With Social Security advocacy groups demonstrating on the Capitol steps, the House passed this resolution 405 to 13, and ten days later passed a bill to amend the Omnibus Reconciliation Act of 1981 so as to restore the regular minimum benefit to all current recipients.

More than the administration's proposed cut in early retirement benefits, elimination of the minimum benefit raised the issue of de-welfarizing Social Security, inasmuch as the administration defended its cut by arguing that needy persons could apply for SSI instead. Republicans were beginning to rationalize de-welfarization as a way to relieve Social Security of costs that could more properly be borne by other programs. To Democrats, that was a red flag. They celebrated Social Security as creators of the program always had, for saving the elderly from the indignity of having to go on welfare. Representative Pickle deplored "a Government action that on purpose would ask someone at this stage of life to choose between dignity and welfare. It breaks a faith and a promise made for over 40 years."[46]

Once again the administration backed down, in the face of a Democratic position that, by protecting the benefits of current beneficiaries, tightly wedded principle to political expediency. In September, Reagan urged Congress to restore the regular minimum benefit for current recipients with low incomes. "It was never our intention," he said, "to take this support away from those who truly need it."[47] In December, Congress restored the regular minimum benefit for all current recipients. The Democrats had taught the Republicans a lesson in promise keeping.

CUTTING THE COSTS OF TRYING TO CUT SOCIAL SECURITY

Stockman would eventually conclude that the punishing defeat in Congress in May marked the end of any effort to arrest the growth of Social Security. "The centerpiece of the American welfare state had now been overwhelmingly ratified and affirmed in the white heat of political confrontation," he wrote after leaving office.[48] But the outcome, enacted by Congress in the spring of 1983, was more subtle and complicated than that. Although the Reagan administration suffered a serious defeat, the politicians whom Stockman's book treats with such contempt did incorporate in the law a significant long-run reduction in Social Security benefits, by raising the normal age of retirement to sixty-seven. After further describing the Democrats' rout of the Reagan administration on Social Security, we will conclude by briefly exploring how that happened.

Stockman in the summer of 1981 continued to hope that Reagan could rescue the administration's plan by giving a televised speech in its defense. The president himself for a time harbored such a hope and nearly incorporated a plea for the proposal in a speech of late July in which he made the case for a tax cut. He omitted Social Security from that speech only after receiving a written appeal to do so from Howard Baker and Robert Michel, the Republican leaders in the Senate and House.[49]

Again in the fall, after the tax cut had been enacted, Reagan considered mounting a public appeal on Social Security and in early September drafted a speech for that purpose. Stockman and Darman were pushing a "fall offensive" that would attempt new spending reductions or deferral of the large tax cuts that Congress had approved, so alarmed were they by deficits now foreseeable. Reagan read his draft to Baker and Michel. He said that he was worried about the system's solvency. He thought younger people were afraid that they would not get their benefits. He argued that the May reforms were fair and would save money.[50]

When he was done reading, Baker responded, "I think that's an awful good speech. But I don't think you'd better make it because we can't pass that thing." Instead, in the speech that he actually delivered on September 24, which covered a range of economic subjects, the president settled for a tepid defense of the administration's Social Security plan and proposed, at Baker's suggestion, the creation of a task force, to be composed of members chosen in equal numbers (five each) by Baker, Speaker O'Neill, and the president. This task force would be charged to come up with a plan that would assure the fiscal integrity of Social Security.[51] It was a stark admission of the administration's failure to establish leadership of policymaking on this subject, and an acknowledgment of the power of Congress in the constitutional system. It was also an admission of the persistent autonomy, or at least special status in policymaking, of Social Security. "This is an issue apart from the economic reform package," Reagan said in the September speech, in sharp contrast to the administration's actual behavior four months earlier.

If President Reagan was a big loser in Social Security politics in 1981, others were legislative committees with responsibility for the program. Most of the leaders of these committees—chairmen of Ways and Means in the House and Finance in the Senate and of their Social Security subcommittees—clung to the hope that they would be able to frame legislation that would restore the program to fiscal health. When Schweiker announced the administration's proposal, Speaker O'Neill's political aide, Kirk O'Donnell, called the Ways and Means staff and was told that Dan Rostenkowski, the committee chairman, and Pickle, as subcommittee chairman, "were playing down the controversy because they felt a fiduciary responsibility, as good Democrats, to work with the White House to make Social Security solvent." "'Danny doesn't want to play politics with it,'" O'Donnell reported to the Speaker. But O'Neill did. O'Neill "saw the Reagan administration overreaching and at that point he just jumped on it."[52]

In the fall, Dole as Finance Committee chairman hoped to take a major bill into a conference with the House and reach a "quiet agreement" on both the short-term and long-term financing of Social Security. "If he could just sit down with Pickle and Rostenkowski, Dole felt sure he could reach an agreement," according to Paul Light. Dole, like Pickle, would have raised the retirement age.[53] However, by the fall the Democratic leadership—O'Neill and Rules Committee chairman Richard Bolling—had told Pickle that there was to be no Social Security legislation in the current Congress, and told Jim Shannon, a Social Security subcommittee member and protégé of O'Neill, to sabotage a bill if necessary. Shannon recalled later, "Pickle wants to write the bill. Danny agrees. We're Democrats. We're responsible. But Kirk [O'Donnell]'s view is that Social Security is all we got. I had to spend a year throwing sand in the gears."[54]

Although Social Security's legislative leaders were unable to act in 1981, they did agree to set a short deadline for acting. In mid-December, two days before the end of the session, they resolved the issue over the minimum benefit and authorized the Old-Age and Survivors (OASI) trust fund to borrow from the trust funds for disability and health insurance until December 31, 1982. Inter-fund borrowing was a possible response to the impending deficit in the OASI fund, which was expected to run out of money in late 1982 or early 1983. On the initiative of Representative Conable, the conference forswore inter-fund borrowing as a substitute for a more durable solution. With this decision, the legislative committees held their own feet—and those of all members—to the Social Security fire.[55]

On December 16, 1981, President Reagan signed an executive order creating the National Commission on Social Security Reform, appointed the members, and set December 31, 1982, as a deadline for its report, which he hoped would be bipartisan and realistic, and would put Social Security on a "sound financial footing"—a tall order at this point.[56] Known informally as the Greenspan Commission for its chairman, the conservative economist Alan Greenspan, the commission was too riven by partisan and ideological differences to produce a plan, besides being hampered by a legal requirement that it act publicly. Yet it eventually provided cover for productive negotiations between the administration and its Democratic opponents.

By the end of 1982, the administration was desperate for a settlement, fearing that if anything went wrong with Social Security, the president would be blamed. Moreover, it had been weakened by the November election, in which the Democrats gained 26 seats in the House, giving them a majority of 269 to 166. This deprived the administration of both its conservative majority in the House and the prospect of winning the House any time soon. Both sides believed that Social Security had been critical to this outcome.[57] A "well-positioned lobbyist" told White and Wildavsky: "By the time the November election was over, Baker, Darman and that crowd were in charge of the issue. . . . It was clear that they would take their own grandmothers off Social Security to get a deal with the Democrats. They were in the trough of a depression, the President's popularity was at bottom, they had lost their House majority, and they wanted it *done*, behind them!"[58]

Behind the scenes in December, the administration made overtures to two Democratic members of the commission, Senator Moynihan and Robert Ball, with whom it thought it could work. As the new session of Congress opened, Moynihan made an overture on the Senate floor to his colleague Dole, who in turn engaged Representative Conable. After a couple of preliminary meetings in Dole's office, a rump version of the commission began meeting secretly with representatives of the administration, first in the recreation room of James Baker's residence and later at Blair House, across Pennsylvania Avenue from the White House. Besides Baker, the members of the administration were Stockman, Darman, and Kenneth Duberstein, the White House's legislative liaison officer.[59]

Ball was the chief negotiator for the Democrats, superior in expertise and experience to everyone else. A veteran of three decades in the SSA and eleven years (1962–1972) as its commissioner, at the end of which President Nixon sought his resignation, he had devoted his life to building the Social Security program. O'Neill had named him to the commission and now trusted him to define the Democrats' position in consultation with the Speaker's office. "'Bob didn't make a move that we weren't aware of,'" according to Jack Lew, a staff member for O'Neill.[60] He wanted to present to the Congress a package on which O'Neill and Reagan had agreed.

The negotiating group acted with extreme urgency because the trust funds would be exhausted within a few months. It concentrated on averting the impending crisis, calculating that a quick infusion of funds would sustain the program until the 1990s, when relief would come from demography. Persons born during the Great Depression, a narrow cohort, would be retiring then. Aided by two extensions of the commission's life—one to January 15, another to January 20—the clandestine inner group and then the commission arrived at a "consensus package" to recommend to the Congress. Twelve of the fifteen commission members joined the consensus, with three conservatives—Archer, Armstrong, and Joe D. Waggoner, Jr., a former Democratic member of Congress from Louisiana—in dissent.

The two most remunerative items in the package, not coincidentally yielding $40 billion each between 1983 and 1989, involved changes in the timing of benefits and taxes. The next cost-of-living adjustment to benefits, scheduled for July 1983, would be delayed until January 1984, and all subsequent COLAs would be timed to the calendar year rather than the fiscal year. Scheduled tax rate increases were to be accelerated. A rate set in law for 1985 would take effect instead in 1984, and part of an increase scheduled for 1990 would take effect in 1988, with the added provision—a concession to organized labor—that individual taxpayers could offset the payroll tax increase for 1984 with a deduction from their income taxes.

A smaller amount—$30 billion—would be realized from taxing the Social Security benefits of high-income persons, an important policy change. Since the 1940s, benefits had been exempt from income taxation as a result of an IRS ruling that Ball had long wanted Congress to overturn. As both a tax increase and a benefit reduction, the measure was exquisite in its ambiguity. Both parties had opposed such a tax in their 1980 platforms. This endowed it with neutrality, and, perversely, with political utility.

Another major change, which the president had earlier opposed and which still was opposed by organized labor—extending coverage to new employees of the federal government as of January 1, 1984 (and incidentally also to employees of nonprofit organizations)—was expected to realize $20 billion. The tax on self-employed persons would be increased from 75 percent to 100 percent of the combined employer-employee rate, which would yield $18 billion in payroll tax revenues (because self-employed persons would be allowed to deduct half of their payroll taxes as a business expense on their income tax returns, the government would lose general revenues from this change). Another $18 billion would be realized from an accounting gimmick: the Social Security trust funds would be credited with a lump-sum payment as compensation for uncashed Social Security checks and the cost of certain wage credits for military service.

This package did not suffice, however, to take care of the long-term deficit, about a third of which remained. This meant that Congress was still left with a politically difficult choice. Seven of the commission members, a plurality, recommended that the remaining deficit be met by a gradual increase in the age of normal retirement. Another five members, the most liberal in the commission, preferred to meet it with an increase in tax rates, with an income tax credit to be given to employees for their share of the increase. General revenues would have been used to meet the deficit.[61] Presumably, this choice would precipitate a partisan fight, with congressional Republicans favoring an increase in the retirement age and Democrats favoring the tax increase, although Pickle's having sponsored a retirement age increase introduced an element of uncertainty.

In a surprise to the Democratic leadership, which did not make this a party vote, the House voted 228 to 202 to raise the retirement age. The Social Security Act amendments of 1983, on which Congress completed action in April, raised the normal age of retirement gradually to sixty-seven by 2027, less of a change than Pickle had proposed two years earlier but still a significant contraction of the program. This was the largest single improvement in the program's long-run financial condition that Congress enacted in 1983, much larger than the taxation of benefits, which was next in magnitude.[62] An accomplishment of Pickle, it was at the last minute aided by the distraction of organized labor, which was more interested in killing the extension of Social Security to federal government employees than in defeating an increase in the retirement age.[63]

THE SYSTEM CONSERVED

Critics of Congress typically claim that it is adept at handing out good things to its constituents but is unable to enact reductions in programs that are either very broadly popular, as is Social Security, or supported by well-organized interests, as is also true of Social Security, which has historically been supported by organized labor and more recently also by the American Association of Retired Persons and other lobbies of older Americans. But in the Social Security Act amendments of 1983, Congress voted to reduce benefits through taxation in the near future and to raise the normal age of retirement in the remote future—gradually to sixty-six by 2009 and sixty-seven by 2027. Congress continued to permit early retirement at age sixty-two, but the reduction for early retirement would be increased from the current 20 percent to 25 percent by 2009 and 30 percent by 2027. These were significant reductions—milestones in policymaking for Social Security, which until then had followed a seemingly inexorable path of expansion. They at least raise the possibility, without proving, that if the administration had allowed Congress to take more of the lead in 1981, the result would have been more to the president's liking than what emerged. Recall that Pickle's original bill would have completed a change in the normal retirement age from sixty-five to sixty-eight by 2000, and would have increased the reduction in benefits for early retirees from 20 percent to 36 percent, also by 2000. Such an approach would also have been less damaging to the Republican Party and the tradition of consensual policymaking.

It might be claimed that the foregoing history proves that Republican politicians cannot initiate reductions or that they make the attempt only at extreme peril. The tax on benefits originated with a Democrat, Ball, who did not hold elective office, and the increase in the retirement age came from a veteran Democrat who held a safe seat; Pickle represented Texas' Tenth District, consisting of Austin and its growing suburbs, which was historically Democratic but had voted for Reagan in 1980. Both measures then secured bipartisan backing in the legislature.

On this point, however, the history of 1981–1983 is inconclusive. So ill-conceived and inept was the administration's proposal of May 1981 that one cannot say with certainty that a Republican proposal more carefully framed and presented, after due consultation with Congress, would not have had more success. The administration's instant confession of error, indicated by the White House's decision not to announce the proposal, vitiates it as a test of Republican strength or strategies. The Reagan administration did, after all, succeed in eliminating student benefits and also in prospectively eliminating the regular minimum benefit. The act of 1983, however, was not a product of presidential leadership, and in fact the presidential leadership that was incompetently undertaken in 1981 arguably led to an outcome that took longer, damaged Reagan's political momentum, and was less in keeping with his ideological preferences than congressional initiatives would have been had the administration been willing from the outset to seek alliances in Congress.

The 1983 amendments were a defeat for Republican critics of Social Security, of whom the president had initially been supposed to be one. Ball regarded the outcome as the supreme accomplishment of his career.[64] Besides averting a fiscal meltdown and strengthening the program with changes that he favored, such as covering federal employees and taxing benefits of the well-to-do, the Greenspan Commission report contained a resounding repudiation of what everyone took to be the Reagan ideological agenda:

> The members of the National Commission believe that the Congress, in its deliberations on financing proposals, should not alter the fundamental structure of the Social Security program or undermine its fundamental principles. The National Commission considered, but rejected, proposals to make the Social Security program a voluntary program, or to transform it into a program under which benefits are a product exclusively of the contributions paid.[65]

Within the House, even after addition of the Pickle amendment, sixty-nine conservative Republicans voted against the 1983 amendments. In the Senate, the conference bill passed fifty-eight to fourteen, with the most conservative Republicans dissenting and many members absent.

Among political actors, the ultimate victors in this two-year battle were what one of us, in an earlier study of Social Security, called "program proprietors."[66] They were also Douglas Arnold's "coalition leaders," searching for the terms on which a coalition in support of Social Security legislation could be built.[67] In this case, they included the Republican congressional leaders Baker and Michel, who helped deflect the president away from defense of his controversial package and toward a commission, an ad hoc creation that they were able to adapt to their purpose. In the end, they had the cooperation of an administration that felt under great pressure to satisfy public expectations of system conservation—or pay the consequences in a partisan war that it was losing. A member of the Reagan administration told White and Wildavsky that "once we stopped being revolutionaries and started being system conservers, it was a tremendous accomplishment."[68]

Rebuffed first by the Reagan administration in the spring of 1981 and then by O'Neill in the fall and throughout the campaign season of 1982, system conservers nonetheless persisted in an effort to devise legislation that could pass Congress with bipartisan support, keep the program viable, reinforce the public's expectation that promised benefits would be paid, and also keep policymaking mostly within the durable framework of trust fund financing, which presumed a balance of payroll tax revenue and benefit expenditures. Afterward, it was frequently claimed—both by President Reagan upon signing the law and by scholars who studied the settlement—that "the system worked." If so, it worked because a set of system conservers, as distinct from partisans or ideologues, was present to make it work.

ALTERED POLITICS

It might be supposed that after their experience of 1981 through 1983, Republicans in Congress would have chosen to leave Social Security strictly alone. Yet the party's fiscal conservatives in the Senate, hoping to combat the government's large budget deficit, soldiered on with an effort to reduce the program's cost.

In 1985, with Republicans still in control of the Senate, Dole as the new majority leader and Domenici still as Budget Committee chairman tried to balance the budget with the help of a one-year COLA freeze, along with elimination of some minor domestic programs and tying defense spending to the rate of inflation. Believing that they had support from the president, Dole and Domenici waged a hard fight and achieved a forty-nine to forty-nine tie for their proposal on the floor by bringing ailing Senator Pete Wilson of California into the chamber on a gurney to cast the tying vote. Vice President George W. Bush then broke the tie to give the Republicans a victory.

However, House Republicans under a new minority leader, Trent Lott, were absolutely opposed to the COLA freeze, which was the centerpiece of the Senate proposal, and the president, in a tête-à-tête with Speaker O'Neill, cut a deal to drop the freeze but maintain the Senate's level of defense spending, which the Democratic majority in the House would have preferred to reduce. Dole and Domenici, who had taken the risk of putting nearly all of the party's senators on record in favor of the freeze, were enraged and embarrassed.[69]

In the election of 1986, Republicans lost the Senate, giving up the seats of seven incumbents while House Republicans held their ground. Again, as in the House election of 1982, the result was widely interpreted as the price of the Republicans' attempt to reduce Social Security. "The message was unmistakable," a Republican staff member in the Senate later wrote, "and it was seared into the consciousness of the Republican Party: Social Security is the one area of spending that you must not touch, no matter what."[70] After two costly defeats in midterm elections, Social Security had finally been confirmed for the Republicans as the "third rail" of American politics, just as O'Neill had said.

Yet if the partisan fury after 1981 and the losses of 1982 and 1986 ultimately had a paralyzing effect on Republican politicians, they galvanized conservatives outside of Congress, who were angered and frustrated by the act of 1983. It was now up to them to frame a strategy for "real reform" as distinct from the false reform that the administration had acquiesced in.[71] They reached for alternatives far from the program's existing structure.

Just as supply-siders complained about the "root canal economics" that characterized mainstream Republican support for balanced budgets, other Republican intellectuals began to develop a similar approach to Social Security. First, Republicans should hold existing and most prospective beneficiaries of the program harmless. Second, reforms should be sold as increasing the retirement income of current workers, not as painful but necessary reductions in order to maintain program solvency. Third, in order to open up political space for considering large-scale alternatives, the program would have to be brought into doubt by questioning the reality of the trust fund and the reliability of the government's promises. Fourth, new waves of citizens should be connected to private financial markets through expanded IRAs and 401(k) plans.

What all these strategies did was to invert the Stockman approach to Social Security reform—and yield proposals that no doubt were more consistent with the actual preferences of Ronald Reagan. Rather than pushing for painful changes in the present, they opted for the promise of pleasurable benefits in the future. Rather than attacking the program head-on, they worked around the edges and cut away the foundations from below. In the aftermath of Reagan, conservatives searched for ways to turn the politics of Social Security from blame avoidance to credit claiming, and in the process open up room for the party to reenter the debate with the hope that it could invert the closed, executive-centered politics of 1981 and gain politically from a public hearing of its ideas. The presidential campaign of George W. Bush in 2000, in which the candidate embraced "privatization" of Social Security, was a culmination of this strategy, with ironic roots in a conservative administration's twenty-year-old miscalculation.

NOTES

1. *1979 Annual Report of the Board of Trustees of the Federal Old-Age and Survivors Insurance and Disability Insurance Trust Funds,* 96th Cong., 1st sess., H. Doc. 96-101, 54; *1980 Annual Report of the Board of Trustees of the Federal Old-Age and Survivors Insurance and Disability Insurance Trust Funds,* 96th Cong., 2d sess., H. Doc. 96-332, 56–57. On the role of the trust fund in policymaking for Social Security, see Eric M. Patashnik, *Putting Trust in the U.S. Budget: Federal Trust Funds and the Politics of Commitment* (Cambridge: Cambridge University Press, 2000).

2. See, for example, *Social Security in America's Future,* Final Report of the National Commission on Social Security (March 1981). Formation of this bipartisan, nine-member commission was provided for by Congress in 1977, with instructions to conduct a complete study of Social Security.

3. The speech on behalf of Goldwater appears in *A Time for Choosing: The Speeches of Ronald Reagan, 1961–1982* (Chicago: Regnery Gateway, 1983), 39–57, and Ronald Reagan, *Speaking My Mind: Selected Speeches* (New York: Simon & Schuster, 1989), 22–36. Reagan criticized Social Security also in his lecture-circuit speeches of the 1960s, some of which are preserved in the Ronald Reagan Library (RRL). See also the discus-

sion of Reagan speeches from the 1960s and 1970s in Max J. Skidmore, *Social Security and Its Enemies* (Boulder, Colo.: Westview Press, 1999), 88–93.

4. An example of Martin Feldstein's work is "Toward a Reform of Social Security," *The Public Interest* 40 (summer 1975). For citations of Boskin, see below, n. 17.

5. Lou Cannon, *President Reagan: The Role of a Lifetime* (New York: Simon & Schuster, 1991), 243.

6. We have been unable to locate a copy of the task force report. A draft of the report recommended changes in the formulas for calculating initial benefits and annual cost-of-living increases, as well as mandatory coverage of all federal government employees. Edward Cowan, "Drive on Social Security Deficits Being Mounted by Congressmen," *New York Times,* January 2, 1981, A1 and A11.

7. William Niskanen calls the administration's Social Security proposal of May 1981 its "major domestic policy mistake . . . an extraordinary political misjudgment." *Reaganomics* (New York: Oxford University Press, 1988), 38. Cannon calls it a "calamity." *Role of a Lifetime,* 251. Reagan himself cited it when Laurence Barrett, at the end of 1981, asked if there was anything he would have done differently in the first year. *Gambling with History: Reagan in the White House* (New York: Penguin Books, 1984), 158.

8. George Hager and Eric Pianin attribute the phrase to O'Neill in *Mirage* (New York: Times Books, 1997), 142.

9. On the consensual mode in Ways and Means, see Martha Derthick, *Policymaking for Social Security* (Washington, D.C.: Brookings Institution Press, 1979), 43–47.

10. William Greider, *The Education of David Stockman and Other Americans* (New York: E. P. Dutton, 1982), 45.

11. There is a detailed account of this meeting in Cannon, *Role of a Lifetime,* 244–48. See also David Stockman, *The Triumph of Politics: Why the Reagan Revolution Failed* (New York: Harper & Row, 1986), 160–62. All citations of Stockman's book are to the hardcover edition. A paperback edition with different pagination came out later. It also had a less polemical subtitle: *The Inside Story of the Reagan Revolution.*

12. On Domenici's deference to presidential leadership from December 1980 through August 1981, see Richard F. Fenno, Jr., *Pete Domenici and the Reagan Budget* (Washington, D.C.: Congressional Quarterly, 1991), 48–57.

13. Stockman, *Triumph of Politics,* 130, 162; "President Reagan's Economic Proposals," *Congress and the Nation, 1981–1984,* vol. 6 (Washington, D.C.: Congressional Quarterly, 1985), 1039.

14. Stockman, *Triumph of Politics,* 124–25.

15. *Congressional Record,* 97th Cong., 1st sess., vol. 127, 1981, 7176 ff.

16. Stockman, *Triumph of Politics,* 184.

17. Michael J. Boskin, "Social Security and the Economy," in *The United States in the 1980s,* abridged ed., ed. Peter Duignan and Alvin Rabushka (Reading, Mass.: Addison-Wesley, 1980), 155–69. An earlier version of the essay appeared in Boskin, *The Crisis in Social Security* (San Francisco: Institute for Contemporary Studies, 1977).

18. Hedrick Smith, *The Power Game: How Washington Works* (New York: Ballantine Books, 1988), 353–54.

19. Research Notes and Special Studies by the Historian's Office, Research Note #11: The History of Social Security "Student" Benefits, 2001, <http://www.ssa.gov/history/studentbenefit.html> (June 17, 2002).

20. Edward D. Berkowitz, *Robert Ball and the Politics of Social Security* (tentative title) (Madison: University of Wisconsin Press, forthcoming), which cites as sources both a manuscript by Ball and Office of the Chief Actuary, Social Security Administration, *History of the Provisions of Old-Age, Survivors, Disability, and Health Insurance, 1935–1996,* SSA Publication Number 11-11515 (Washington, D.C.: Government Printing Office, 1997), 5. See also Robert J. Myers with Richard L. Vernaci, *Within the System: My Half Century in Social Security* (Winsted, Conn.: ACTEX Publications, 1992), 10–11.

21. The lower figure appears in John A. Svahn, "Omnibus Reconciliation Act of 1981: Legislative History and Summary of OASDI and Medicare Provisions," *Social Security Bulletin* 44 (October 1981): 3–24, at 6. The higher figure is in a fact sheet that HHS distributed on May 12, 1981, along with the administration's Social Security proposals of that date. See below, n. 34.

22. U.S. Senate, *Nomination of Richard S. Schweiker,* Hearing before the Committee on Finance, 97th Cong., 1st sess., 1981, 12; U.S. House of Representatives, *Social Security Financing Issues,* Hearings before the Subcommittee on Social Security of the Committee on Ways and Means, 97th Cong., 1st sess., serial 97-3, 1981, 215–20.

23. Memorandum for Secretary Regan from Steve Entin, "Short- and Long-run Social Security Options," April 17, 1981, in Derthick's files.

24. Memorandum, Robert J. Myers to John A. Svahn, "The Mirage of Price Indexing—INFORMATION," April 17, 1981, in Derthick's files.

25. Paul Craig Roberts, *The Supply-Side Revolution: An Insider's Account of Policymaking in Washington* (Cambridge: Harvard University Press, 1984), 268–72.

26. Myers with Vernaci, *Within the System,* 20.

27. Our source for the claim that Schweiker successfully resisted OMB at this point is Patricia E. Dilley, currently a professor of law at the University of Florida but then a Social Security budget examiner in HHS, who supplied us with confirmation in HHS budget documents. See also Joseph White and Aaron Wildavsky, *The Deficit and the Public Interest: The Search for Responsible Budgeting in the 1980s* (Berkeley: University of California Press, and New York: Russell Sage, 1989), 103–4, which describes OMB's proposal and retreat without, however, crediting the retreat to Schweiker. On the goal agreed to by the work group, see Stockman, *Triumph of Politics,* 184.

28. Memorandum to the President from Richard S. Schweiker, May 11, 1981, in Social Security file folder OA 9589, Robert Carleson Files, RRL. This memorandum is not signed, which raises the question of whether it actually went to the president, but there is evidence in secondary accounts that it did. Stockman, *Triumph of Politics,* 187.

29. "Report of Markup of OASDI Legislation, Committee on Ways and Means, Subcommittee on Social Security, April 6, 1981," staff document in file, "1981 Leg, W&M, Spring 1981," in MR [Mary Ross]-70, Office of Historian, SSA headquarters.

30. Barrett, *Gambling with History,* 154.

31. Stockman, *Triumph of Politics,* 190. Martin Anderson recalls, however, that the work group did discuss whether the cut should take effect right away. Telephone interview with Derthick, August 9, 2002.

32. Memorandum for Undersecretary Ture from Steve Entin, "Social Security," May 7, 1981, in Derthick's files.

33. Roberts, *Supply-Side Revolution,* 274–75.

34. Minutes, Cabinet Council on Human Resources, May 11, 1981, WHORM subject file, ID# 026567CA, RRL.

35. Our account of the proposal is derived from an HHS press release of May 12, 1981, entitled "Statement of HHS Secretary Richard S. Schweiker," with an attached fact sheet of eight pages that summarize the provisions and the SSA's analysis of savings. This document is contained in a file, "Early 1981 Admin Docs," MR [Mary Ross]-70, at SSA headquarters.

36. The quotation from Stockman is from *Triumph of Politics,* 187. Myers derides this remark, saying that "the cutbacks and rollbacks involved . . . were not all that philosophically momentous. If they had been, I would have cashed in my chips, resigned, and gone public on the issues." At the end of the year, Myers did resign, complaining that OMB "(and especially its civil service employees) develops policy without regard to the social and economic aspects of the Social Security program—and even the political aspects." Myers with Vernaci, *Within the System,* 11, 26–27.

37. Stockman, *Triumph of Politics,* 188–90. In his memoir, Edwin Meese, who was the president's principal policy adviser, with responsibility for overseeing OPD, makes the extraordinary claim that the administration's Social Security plan was leaked rather than officially announced. This flies in the face of the fact that the plan was put forth in a press release of the Department of Health and Human Services and defended by Schweiker in a press conference. Edwin Meese III, *With Reagan: The Inside Story* (Washington, D.C.: Regnery Gateway, 1992), 105–6.

38. John A. Farrell, *Tip O'Neill and the Democratic Century* (Boston: Little, Brown, 2001), 579.

39. Farrell, *Tip O'Neill and the Democratic Century,* 572.

40. Stockman, *Triumph of Politics,* 190.

41. Mike Batten to Ann Fairbanks, "Administration's Proposed Changes on Social Security," May 15, 1981, File Folder Social Security OA 9589, Robert Carleson Files, RRL. Schweiker, appearing on May 28 before Pickle's subcommittee, did indicate a willingness to compromise on the cut in early retirement benefits. U.S. Congress, House of Representatives, *Social Security Financing Recommendations,* Hearing before the Subcommittee on Social Security of the Ways and Means Committee, 97th Cong., 1st sess., serial 97-17, 1981, 18.

42. Daniel Patrick Moynihan, *Came the Revolution: Argument in the Reagan Era* (New York: Harcourt Brace Jovanovich, 1988), 18.

43. Stockman, *Triumph of Politics,* 191–92; "Letter to Congressional Leaders on the Social Security System," May 21, 1981, *Public Papers of the Presidents of the United States: Ronald Reagan, 1981* (Washington, D.C.: Government Printing Office, 1982), 450.

44. *Congressional Quarterly Weekly Report* (August 1, 1981): 1379.

45. *Congressional Record,* 97th Cong., 1st sess., vol. 127, 1981, 16637–38.

46. *Congressional Record,* 97th Cong., 1st sess., vol. 127, 1981, 16642.

47. "Address to the Nation on the Program for Economic Recovery," September 24, 1981, in *Public Papers,* 835.

48. Stockman, *Triumph of Politics,* 193.

49. White and Wildavsky, *Deficit and the Public Interest,* 176–77. Reagan had announced in advance, in letters hand-carried to the congressional leaders of both parties, that he would address Social Security, and Senator Moynihan's televised response to the speech on behalf of the Democratic Party took up that subject, even though Reagan in the meantime had dropped it. Moynihan, *Came the Revolution,* 27; Reagan to Thomas P.

O'Neill, Jr., Robert H. Michel, Howard H. Baker, Jr., and Robert C. Byrd, July 18, 1981, in WHORM subject file, WE 007 (Social Security), case file 019963, RRL.

50. Smith, *Power Game,* 359–60. This is our only source on this meeting among Reagan, Baker, and Michel.

51. *Public Papers,* 835–36. Dan Crippen, who was Baker's legislative assistant at the time, confirms Hedrick Smith's claim that the commission was Baker's idea. Deeply concerned about the rise of partisan conflict over Social Security, Baker hoped to arrest it. Crippen interview, June 28, 2002.

52. Farrell, *Tip O'Neill and the Democratic Century,* 572.

53. Paul Light, *Artful Work: The Politics of Social Security Reform* (New York: Random House, 1985), 134–35.

54. Farrell, *Tip O'Neill and the Democratic Century,* 581. Light nonetheless claims that Pickle made one last serious attempt at legislation late in 1981, offering a package in Ways and Means that was defeated, eighteen to fourteen, with Pickle on the Republicans' side of the vote. *Artful Work,* 135.

55. "Congress Clears Interim Social Security Bill," *Congressional Quarterly Weekly Report* (December 19, 1981): 2503–4; *Artful Work,* 136–37.

56. Executive Order 12335, "National Commission on Social Security Reform," and "Appointment of the Membership," December 16, 1981, in *Weekly Compilation of Presidential Documents,* vol. 17, no. 51 (December 21, 1981): 1371–94. Both documents are reproduced as Appendix A in *Report of the National Commission on Social Security Reform* (Washington, D.C.: Government Printing Office, 1983).

57. *Congress and the Nation, 1981–1984,* 9, and *Artful Work,* chap. 13. Redistricting may have had more to do with the result than Social Security, but on Capitol Hill, Social Security was perceived as critical.

58. White and Wildavsky, *Deficit and the Public Interest,* 312.

59. *Artful Work,* chap. 15, and telephone interview with Daniel P. Moynihan, August 2, 2002.

60. Farrell, *Tip O'Neill and the Democratic Century,* 601.

61. *Report of the National Commission on Social Security Reform,* 2–3 and 2–4.

62. John A. Svahn and Mary Ross, "Social Security Amendments of 1983: Legislative History and Summary of Provisions," *Social Security Bulletin* 46 (July 1983): 44.

63. For more detail, see White and Wildavsky, *Deficit and the Public Interest,* 324, and *Artful Work,* 210–11. For the point about organized labor, we are indebted to Robert Ball, letter to Derthick, August 7, 2002.

64. Berkowitz manuscript (see n. 20).

65. *Report of the National Commission on Social Security Reform,* 2-2. Some of the conservative members attached additional views.

66. Derthick, *Policymaking for Social Security.*

67. R. Douglas Arnold, *The Logic of Congressional Action* (New Haven, Conn.: Yale University Press, 1990).

68. White and Wildavsky, *Deficit and the Public Interest,* 322–23.

69. There is a detailed account of these events in Hager and Pianin, *Mirage,* 131–45.

70. Charles P. Blahous III, *Reforming Social Security* (Westport, Conn.: Praeger, 2000), 19.

71. Peter J. Ferrara, ed., *Social Security: Prospects for Real Reform* (Washington, D.C.: Cato Institute, 1985).

9
The Welfare State

Gareth Davies

Ronald Reagan's attitude to social welfare policy was straightforward and remained essentially unchanged during three decades in political life. His legacy
to the American welfare state is more complicated. Judged from 1989, it looked
unimpressive: after a stirring beginning, he achieved hardly any of his policy
objectives. Yet by 1996 something that looked a lot like a Reagan welfare revolution had materialized, following enactment of the Personal Responsibility and
Work Opportunity Reconciliation Act (PRWORA), which abolished the Aid to
Families with Dependent Children program (AFDC). Did "the end of welfare
as we know it" mark some kind of post-presidential achievement for Reagan?[1]
If so, what forces had the fortieth president helped to set in motion? If not, what
forces had earlier combined to deny him the glory?

Reagan's approach to the welfare state was underpinned by a number of
propositions. First, the federal government had a duty to protect the "truly needy":
this had been the purpose of the New Deal, which he had supported as a young
man. Second, most additional social spending during the period since the 1930s
had been directed at Americans who did not need or deserve it, such as the
Chicago welfare mother whose depredations featured so strongly in his 1976
presidential bid. Third, such spending had frequently damaged its recipients,
eroding their family life, work ethic, and self-respect. Fourth, it had also damaged the nation as a whole, undermining those virtues that made America unique,
such as the pioneer spirit and the habit of voluntary giving. Fifth, most federal
spending on the poor was not only unwise but also unconstitutional, usurping
powers reserved to the states and the people. And sixth, poverty could be eliminated, if only capitalism—a universally efficacious and just economic system—
were liberated from the leviathan state.[2]

I should like to acknowledge the valuable responses of Martin Anderson, Edward Berkowitz,
Elliot Brownlee, Lou Cannon, Robert Collins, Martha Derthick, Peter Germanis, the late
Hugh Davis Graham, Christopher Howard, Desmond King, Lawrence Mead, James Patterson,
and Alex Waddan to earlier versions of this paper.

When they were first adumbrated by Reagan, in "the Speech" that he delivered as a lecturer for General Electric between 1954 and 1962, some of these propositions were unexceptionable, but in toto they placed him on the ideological fringes of American politics, accompanied as they were by a seeming paranoia about government. Certainly, when he warned Americans contemplating a vote for Lyndon Johnson in 1964 that they would be taking "the first step into a thousand years of darkness," their response was not overwhelming. Most Americans, after all, possessed great faith in their government, were optimistic about their nation's future, and felt well-disposed toward LBJ's new "Great Society" program.[3] However, by the time that Reagan arrived in the White House, the Great Society was seen as a colossal failure, the long postwar boom had come to a juddering halt, and popular confidence in government had plummeted. According to one poll series, only 22 percent of Americans had distrusted the federal government in 1964, but by 1980 this had risen to 73 percent.[4] On the one hand, the fact that social spending had continued to expand during the 1970s in the face of this loss of confidence indicated that shrinking the welfare state would be no easy task and suggested the limits to popular conservatism. But on the other hand, that expansion may also explain why three-fifths of Americans now believed that their country spent "too much" on welfare, compared with only 44 percent as recently as 1974.[5] At any rate, Reagan had just won forty-four states, an ever-more-conservative Republican Party controlled the Senate, new rightists possessed the same kind of brio and self-belief that had characterized Great Society liberals at the start of the new president's political career, and "the Democrats," according to Tip O'Neill, "were demoralized, discredited and broke."[6] Finally, some way had to be found of paying for the massive arms buildup that had begun under Carter and which enjoyed widespread support in 1981. If the task of shrinking the American welfare state would not be easy, then surely the auguries were better now than at any time in the past half-century.[7]

To judge from the panegyrics of his admirers and the philippics of his detractors, it seems that Ronald Reagan must indeed have succeeded in eviscerating the welfare state. Martin Anderson and Edwin Meese are among the hagiographers, celebrating a wide-ranging Reagan Revolution, while the detractors include the historian Michael Katz, whose book *The Undeserving Poor* is subtitled *From the War on Poverty to the War on Welfare* and who finds that conservatives "triumphed easily in the early 1980s."[8] Just four months into the new administration, Representative Carl Perkins (D-Ky.) was already grieving for the Great Society: "I've worked for years for the welfare of the people, and now I'm seeing practically everything dismantled."[9] His colleague, Les Aspin (D-Wis.), told constituents that "welfare is due for the ax," while "Medicaid is to be chopped down."[10] And, writing in the *New York Times,* Steven Roberts reported a wider feeling of "sheer anger and frustration" among Democrats unable to stop a "wrecking ball" that threatened to "shred the fabric of social legislation woven over the last generation."[11] Depressed already by the first round of spending reductions, Robert Greenstein, speaking for the Project on Food Assistance and Poverty, gloomily predicted that future cuts would "be far more excruciating than what has already been done."[12]

In the light of these comments, it is surprising to record that nearly every welfare reform initiative that President Reagan attempted between Greenstein's September 1981 prediction and the end of his presidency failed to achieve its objectives. The "New Federalism" proposal of 1982 came to nothing, efforts to cut back on Social Security, disability benefits, and child nutrition programs stimulated a forceful backlash, not much came of an effort to convert categorical programs into block grants, a bid to encourage voluntary giving fizzled, and the *Up from Dependency* report of 1986 failed to generate an anticipated transformation in AFDC. Given that post-1981 record of disappointment, any claim that Reagan presided over a "revolution" must rest heavily on the reforms of that first year. How severe were the cuts implemented as part of the Omnibus Budget Reconciliation Act (OBRA)? And to what extent did these measures result in long-term changes to the American welfare state?

ASSESSING OBRA

Whether or not there was a Reagan Revolution, there was at least a revolutionary moment during the first six months or so, when defenders of the welfare state were on the run, overwhelmed by the president's popularity and by the widespread sense that excessive government spending lay at the heart of the nation's inflationary crisis. Richard Darman—deputy chief of staff and a leading moderate in the administration—would later note that OBRA and the simultaneous 23 percent reduction in income tax (over three years) "were the largest single spending control bill and the largest single tax reduction bill in the history of the American republic."[13] Cuts in AFDC deprived around 400,000 recipients of benefits and reduced payments to a further 279,000, saving the Treasury an estimated $1.2 billion during the next year. Following a decade of explosive growth, the food stamps program was cut back by even more than President Reagan had requested, with one million recipients losing benefits and federal savings estimated at $6 billion over three years. Even some strong supporters of the welfare state were heard acknowledging the need for cutbacks and admonishing those who resisted every change.[14] Speaker O'Neill, not part of that group, nevertheless did little to fight the president's legislation, "convinced" as he recalled in his memoir "that if the Democrats were perceived as stalling in the midst of a national economic crisis, there would be hell to pay in the midterm elections."[15]

The spending cuts were largely made in response to short-term economic exigencies and consequently motivated more by a desire to save money wherever the political resistance was weakest than by an integrated vision for welfare reform. Their immediate impact on the poor was substantial. James Storey calculated that 60 percent of 1981 savings in social spending came in antipoverty programs, even though such programs made up only 18 percent of federal income maintenance expenditure: while Social Security was essentially inviolate, spending for AFDC declined by 16.3 percent and food stamp cuts amounted to 18.6 percent.[16]

From the vantage point of the mid-1980s, this round of cuts seemed to have marked the point at which federal welfare spending had ceased to grow. Per capita welfare spending by the federal government (in constant 1984 dollars) increased from $55 in 1965 to $116 in 1970, and peaked at nearly $275 at the point of Reagan's arrival in the White House, before falling back to $241 in 1984, despite the high poverty and unemployment rates of Reagan's first term.[17] After a half-century of virtually unbroken expansion, this seemed an important accomplishment for Reagan. From a subsequent vantage point, however, it seems relatively insignificant because during the second half of the 1980s, federal spending on welfare would start to climb again. Reversing itself as Democratic strength in first the House and then the Senate grew, and defying Reagan, Congress liberalized food stamps, AFDC, and Medicaid (especially the latter).[18] Accordingly, by the time Reagan left office, federal welfare spending was higher than in 1980. And whereas during the recession of the early 1980s, welfare spending had declined, during the downturn of the early 1990s it escalated so dramatically that by 1995 it was 67 percent higher in real terms than at the end of the Carter presidency.[19] In terms of overall welfare spending, the OBRA cuts of 1981 seem less significant today than does the administration's subsequent loss of influence over Congress.

Edward Berkowitz and Nathan Glazer highlight a second consequence of OBRA that may be somewhat more important: it put a definitive end program to the negative income tax (NIT)/guaranteed income debate of the previous decade.[20] The NIT approach was designed to take families out of poverty and dependency by providing new work incentives. The most comprehensive attempt at initiating one, President Nixon's Family Assistance Plan, had foundered, but interest in subsidizing the earnings of low-income families did leave two legislative legacies: the "$30 and a third" rule of 1967 (which allowed welfare recipients to keep a portion of their welfare benefits when they took paid employment) and the 1975 Earned Income Tax Credit (EITC), an NIT for low-income workers. Many Nixon-era conservatives found the NIT approach congenial: it promised to reduce welfare dependency and promote the work ethic, and it proposed to do so via market mechanisms and straightforward cash transfers rather than through the tarnished "service strategy" (education, training, community action) that Great Society liberals favored. Nixon may have thought that he was being a conservative when he reminded Americans that "the government . . . has no less of an obligation to the working poor than to the nonworking poor."[21]

But from the vantage point of Reagan conservatives during the early 1980s, it seemed that the NIT approach, far from attacking dependency, simply extended it to the working poor. And in any case, Reaganites—unlike the Nixon Republicans whom Governor Reagan had battled a decade earlier (on which, see the following discussion)—doubted that *any* federal government program could play a positive role in liberating the dependent poor. That was the job of American capitalism. The administration's success in curtailing the $30 and a third rule was an important victory for that point of view (unpopular at the time, the source of some puzzlement, enacted because of the sheer momentum of the early Reagan presidency) and a defeat for those who looked to the federal government not simply to help those unable to work (the Reagan position) but to engineer paths to self-sufficiency for the wider dependent population.[22]

However, as with OBRA's spending cuts, one should not make too much of the demise of the NIT approach. For one thing, its decline had begun during the Carter years, with the failure of the 1977 Program for Better Jobs and Income. For another, while the $30 and a third program was curtailed, the EITC survived, even though the formidable David Stockman—director of the Office of Management and Budget, and principal architect and champion of OBRA—had combatively declared that "we just don't accept the assumption that the Federal Government has a responsibility to supplement the income of the working poor."[23] Indeed, it did more than survive; in 1986, 1990, and 1993 it was greatly enlarged. One of the biggest beneficiaries of federal antipoverty policy during that period, in other words, was the group that Reagan's followers felt should not be receiving any funds from Washington: the working poor.[24] More consequential than OBRA's cuts in spending was the boost that it gave to workfare. President Reagan's advisers on social welfare policy included a number of men who had served him in a similar capacity during his governorship. Back then, their emphasis had been on confining welfare to the truly needy by requiring able-bodied recipients to work off their benefits. Now, arriving in Washington, Robert Carleson, David Swoap, and John Svahn remained confident that state "workfare" programs rather than income disregards provided the key to reducing rolls.[25] With the passage of OBRA, they won two significant successes: states were permitted to launch Community Work Experience Programs (CWEP), and the waivers from federal AFDC regulations that had been permissible since 1962 under section 1115 of the Social Security Act were broadened to encourage workfare.

An attempt to *mandate* state workfare experiments failed, but by 1987 the General Accounting Office could identify as many as sixty-one programs operating in thirty-eight states, indicating that this was not a consequential reverse. Reductions in federal aid, the 1981–1982 recession, and concern about a new urban "underclass" combined to increase state interest in new ways of reducing welfare rolls; what Richard Nathan termed "new-style workfare"—designed to rehabilitate the dependent poor and not simply to deter loafers—became increasingly attractive.[26] Evaluations of some of these programs undertaken by the Manpower Demonstration Research Corporation (MDRC) during the mid-1980s found their impact on earnings and dependency "promising—although not dramatic." Impressed (perhaps overly so), a bipartisan assortment of governors and legislators embraced the idea of welfare reform, resulting in passage of what seemed at the time to be the landmark Family Support Act of 1988.[27]

Pierson rightly describes this series of events, originating with OBRA, as "a classic process of policy feedback." Another "policy feedback" connects OBRA to the *1996* reform: in 1987, the Reagan administration granted the waivers under revised section 1115 that helped to set in motion a second wave of state-level reformist activism that would culminate a decade later in passage of PRWORA. We will return to these delayed consequences of OBRA toward the end of the essay. First, however, we need to examine why the aspect of OBRA that had initially seemed most portentous—the cutbacks in welfare spending—turned out to be so evanescent.

An early hint of troubles ahead came in September of 1981.[28] Responding to severe cuts that Congress had approved in the child nutrition program, the Department of Agriculture (USDA) issued regulations allowing participating schools to shrink meal sizes and dilute their nutritional content. Finding voices that had been muted or ineffective during the recent traumatic round of tax and expenditure reductions, Democrats and lobbyists for the poor discovered the "fairness issue." Lou Cannon, in his superb biography of Reagan, argues that Democrats "usually wound up saying too little about his ignorance and too much about his supposed lack of compassion for the poor and dispossessed," a "caricature" that was "not convincing to a majority of white Americans."[29] Similarly critical, Michael Katz argues that liberals during this period "failed to weave together a fresh defense of the welfare state."[30] However, even if it won few elections, and even if it failed to constitute a positive new approach to antipoverty policy, the fairness issue did help embattled Democrats to weather the initial period of revolutionary fervor and derail the administration's subsequent welfare agenda. In this case, the Washington-based Food Research and Action Center mounted a fierce campaign focusing on the patent absurdity that the USDA would now permit schools to count tomato ketchup as a vegetable. In a much-publicized event on September 24, Senate Democrats sat down to what they contended would be a typical meal under the new regime: "meat and soybean patty, a few french fries, ketchup, one slice of white bread, and three-fourths of a glass of milk."[31] The very next day, engulfed by a tidal wave of media criticism and ridicule, Reagan backed down, reportedly ascribing his setback to "bureaucratic sabotage" by agency officials intent on derailing budget cuts.[32]

In itself, this was a trivial if embarrassing reverse for an administration that had been experiencing extraordinary political success since the assassination attempt of March 30, 1981. However, it opened a period during which Reagan was increasingly on the defensive for two other, much larger, reasons that had powerful implications for the future politics of social policy. First, the nation was entering a sharp economic recession marked by mounting unemployment and job insecurity, increasing poverty, and a liberalization in public attitudes toward the poor.[33] The idea started to gain ground that administration cuts had powerfully contributed to the new poverty and did not care. By April of 1982, according to one poll, only 30 percent of Americans felt that Reagan's policies were fair to the poor, while 62 percent considered them unfair.[34] Later that same month, Bill Moyers, a former aide to Lyndon Johnson, presented a CBS documentary, *People Like Us,* that poignantly described the direct impact of the previous year's cuts on four individuals: a cerebral palsy victim from Ohio whose disability benefits had been cut off; a New Jersey working mother who had to quit her job so that her unwell son could qualify for Medicaid benefits; a teenage girl from Wisconsin who had suffered two strokes; and a priest from Milwaukee who administered a food program for the poor.[35]

Second, the child nutrition flap coincided with the elevation of the deficit issue that was to be so central to the politics of the rest of the decade. We are accustomed to thinking of it as having "defunded the left," but the fact that the deficit was being widely blamed on a massive defense buildup and an extravagantly irresponsible tax cut made many Republicans, as well as Democrats, reluctant to support cuts aimed at the poor, who had already suffered disproportionately under the first round of spending reductions. When CBS and the *New York Times* asked Americans to indicate their preferred approach to deficit reduction, 59 percent favored reducing the scale of the previous year's tax cut, 49 percent endorsed cuts in defense spending, but only 29 percent wanted reduced antipoverty spending. Indeed, the last-named option was the least popular among every demographic group polled, including Republicans, conservatives, the rich, and those who felt they had benefited from the president's economic program.[36] Responding to this mood, Senator Robert Dole (R-Kans.)—who had skillfully stewarded OBRA through the Senate—noted acerbically that "somebody else is going to have to start taking a hit besides welfare recipients." Another powerful Republican senator, Pete Domenici of New Mexico, chair of the Budget Committee, warned that tax hikes were the only answer. And House Republican leader Robert Michel of Illinois warned the president that his troops, including such staunch conservatives as Trent Lott (R-Miss.) and Dick Cheney (R-Wyo.), were "paranoid on the subject of further spending cuts."[37] Even supply-side guru Arthur Laffer was reputedly critical of the antipoverty impact of the administration's policies.[38]

With the benefit of hindsight, this crucial period, from the fall of 1981 through the spring of 1982, could plausibly be presented as having marked the end of the Reagan Revolution in social policy. To some extent, this was also glimpsed at the time: the departure from the administration of such influential Reagan conservatives as Lyn Nofziger and Martin Anderson (the "conscience of the administration" according to Meese but the "keeper of the sacred scrolls" according to a less reverential cabinet member[39]); the weakening of Meese's position within the governing troika (Meese, James A. Baker, Michael Deaver); and the seemingly strengthened position of such moderates as Vice President Bush, Chief of Staff Baker, Darman, and Craig Fuller all seemed to signal a drift to the center. Meanwhile, Ronald Reagan's reduced popularity (see table 9.1) diminished the likelihood that he would be able to force through a second round of cuts.

In *The Triumph of Politics,* David Stockman presents this series of reverses as marking the point at which the Reagan Revolution was derailed: his purpose had always been "to force down the size of the domestic welfare state to the point where it could be adequately funded with the revenues available after the tax cut," but this objective now fell victim to the strong inertial tendencies of the American political system.[40] It is hard to know how much importance to attach to this judgment, not least because of the difficulty of establishing how committed the Reaganites were to Stockman's ambitious program. Some evidence suggests that they sought only to modify the growth of social spending, other evidence hints at a desire to cut the welfare state back to 1970 levels (i.e., before EITC, Supplemental Security Income, and the massive expansion of food and nutrition programs), some indications suggest a desire to repeal the Great Society and restore the lean New Deal welfare state, and in its more radical moments the administration appeared keen on repealing parts of the New Deal, too.

There is no value in trying to establish which of these four approaches represented the "true" Reagan agenda, for the impression of consistency thus achieved would be misleading. In any case, one does not need to do so to see that Stockman exaggerated the impact of the crisis of late 1981 through early 1982 on the White House's thinking. While the 1983 budget may not have contained cuts of the magnitude that he had desired, it is more surprising how *little* the administration changed course in response to this initial deterioration in its political standing. A lot of that was due to Ronald Reagan. Defiantly resisting the entreaties of almost all his advisers, his second budget avoided an increase in excise taxes, made only the most minimal adjustments to Caspar Weinberger's defense budget, and placed the principal burden for deficit reduction on a fresh round of cuts in Medicaid, AFDC, and the food stamps program. Recognizing the force of the fairness issue but retaining his customary sunny optimism and

Table 9.1. Ronald Reagan's Approval Rating (by percentage): Selected Months, 1981–1984

	5/81	9/81	12/81	5/82	10/82	2/83	8/83	10/83	11/83	1/84
Approval	68	60	51	44	42	37	42	47	53	52
Disapproval	21	29	39	46	48	54	47	43	31	38

Source: *Gallup Poll: 1981,* 110, 190, 266; *Gallup Poll: 1982,* 105, 238; *Gallup Poll: 1983,* 17, 146, 214, 249; *Gallup Poll: 1984,* 23.

ideological self-confidence, Reagan sought to show that cuts in social spending were part of a positive vision for national renewal whose principal beneficiaries included the poor.

Reagan's effort to present his economic recovery program as a conservative War on Poverty had three aspects. First, he went on the offensive with an argument that he had been honing for two decades, namely that government spending and economic mismanagement were responsible for poverty. The true believers of the Conservative Action Committee were told that it was their political enemies whose "policies drove up inflation and interest rates, and their policies stifled incentive, creativity, and halted the movement of the poor up the economic ladder." "It's time for us to find out," he continued, "if two of the most dynamic and constructive forces known to man—free enterprise and the profit motive—can be brought to play where government bureaucracy and social programs have failed."[41] And second, he argued that federal spending on the poor had crowded out private sector giving, with similarly damaging effects. Both of these arguments were on display when Reagan accepted an award from the National Conference of Christians and Jews in March of 1982: "There's more to brotherhood than government-inspired and administered charity. In recent years, too many of us have tended to forget that government can't properly substitute for the helping hand of neighbor to neighbor. And in trying to do so, government has, to a great extent, brought on the economic distress that mires us down in recession."[42]

This emphasis on voluntarism was strongly supported by conservative activists such as Holly Coors. She detected among conservative religious leaders a crusading ambition to help the poor, and when she had written to the president early on in his presidency to urge White House leadership, he had responded warmly, telling her of his own recent conversations with "two prominent ministers" who "believe the churches should become more involved replacing government as the dispenser of charity."[43] Now, under pressure to show his compassion for the poor, Reagan made public his enthusiasm for this radical idea, unveiling a task force on private sector antipoverty initiatives and proclaiming to the National Alliance of Business that "with the same energy that Franklin Roosevelt sought government solutions to problems, we will seek private solutions." The nation's "deep spirit of generosity," subverted by government spending, would be reflected in "a torrent of private initiatives that will astound the advocates of big government."[44]

Antigovernment activists concerned by the recent departure of such allies as Anderson, Nofziger, and Richard Allen from the administration, and by its reluctance to engage such controversial social issues as abortion and prayer in schools, were presumably pleased by this initiative. Congressional Republicans worried by the fairness issue seem to have been less impressed. With crucial midterm elections at stake, vulnerable GOP legislators were increasingly anxious to distance themselves from what journalist David Broder termed the "moral meanness" of the administration, and more generally from a president whose ratings were now even lower than those that the hapless Jimmy Carter had endured at a similar stage.[45] In stark contrast to the previous year, the administration won only 25 percent of the spending cuts that it had requested. New efforts to reform AFDC were turned back, and further severe cuts in the food stamps program were modified, thanks in part to the opposition of Dole, who mordantly observed that his party had "already got an image across the country of harpooning the poor" and did not need to make the problem worse.[46]

In 1982, however, the main social welfare initiative was neither the push for voluntarism, nor the budget, but rather a third proposal, the "New Federalism." This sought to devolve AFDC and food stamps to the states, in return for the federal government assuming responsibility for the Medicaid program (the latter was an effort to contain its costs and to make the package attractive to the states). *Pace* Stockman, for whom the Reagan Revolution was now dead, this "swap" was the most radical effort at welfare reform to be attempted during the Reagan presidency, inasmuch as it sought to repeal not just Great Society federal entitlements (food stamps) but also part of the bedrock New Deal welfare state (AFDC).

Devolving welfare to the states was, like voluntarism, a project dear to Reagan's heart and one of the things that set his crowd apart from mainstream conservatives. In 1976, his campaign against Gerald Ford had featured a plea that "for the sake of the people we are trying to help and for the taxpayers welfare should be administered at the state and local level without the benevolent hand of Washington laying a finger on it." In response, Ford had denounced his challenger as "unrealistic" and "irresponsible."[47] Five years on, Richard Darman, worried by the administration's unpopularity, believed that a debate about federalism would provide "the lift of a driving dream" (an infelicitous phrase lifted from Nixon) and a helpful respite from grimness.[48]

But, as with the voluntarism initiative, the New Federalism came to nothing, and its failure serves to emphasize how ideologically and institutionally isolated the Reaganites were after that initial period of triumph. One might have expected governors who had for years been complaining of burdensome federal regulations to have thought warmly of the proposal, but it turned out that what they wanted in 1982 was administrative autonomy combined with the full *federalization* of all income maintenance programs. When Reagan proposed instead that they should assume sole responsibility for funding one program that *was* fully federal—food stamps—they were bemused. And although he promised that they would not lose out financially, they did not believe him.[49]

It is less surprising that federal legislators should have rejected the idea of the swap. For one thing, they were institutionally resistant to ceding power to the states (this resistance was even somewhat evident in 1996). For another, Republicans worried by the fairness issue insisted that certain basic minimal national standards be retained. Even so, one is struck by the fierceness with which the chairman of the subcommittee charged with evaluating the New Federalism program reacted to it. Describing the proposal as "baloney" and "about the thinnest dodge I've ever seen," Senator David Durenberger (R-Minn.) associated it with the voluntarism gambit and posed what he presented as "the big question of this election year: Does this administration—does my party—care about the poor? Is the 'new federalism' a smoke screen for a repeal of the New Deal? Is private sector initiatives a fig leaf to cover a lack of compassion?"[50]

In the elections that followed, the Democrats made twenty-six gains in the House, and among their victims were fourteen Republican freshmen who had been elected on Reagan's coattails. Senate losses were avoided only because Republican senators in tight races—Durenberger, John Chafee (R.I.), and Lowell Weicker (Conn.)—persuaded unhappy voters of their political independence. Neither fact augured well for the future of the Reagan Revolution. This is not to say that the Democrats had the political initiative—they still struggled to furnish attractive leaders or a positive message, and had clearly benefited from an essentially negative verdict by the electorate—but they did now have the power to rein in Reagan. As we have seen, the president had initially responded to political challenge with boldness and defiance, resisting those who counseled political moderation and seeking to impart new momentum to his antigovernment credo. But after 1982 he seemed to lose interest.

RETREAT FROM REFORM: 1983 TO 1986

During the middle four years of the Reagan presidency, remarkably little happened in the area of domestic legislation (the Social Security amendments of 1983 and the 1986 tax bill are the obvious exceptions). In terms of antipoverty policy, a few trial balloons were floated—vouchers in education and housing, for example, and block grants—but they were proposed with little energy and with no palpable presidential direction. The last hurrah for serious spending cuts was the 1984 budget, which proposed an 8.5 percent cut in food programs and new restrictions on AFDC eligibility. But the administration got nowhere because the Republican-controlled Senate preferred the budget prepared by the House of Representatives' Democratic majority. The reasons for policy failure are by now familiar, but what was new was the White House's failure even to fight for conservative initiatives. This seems to have reflected two factors. First, Reagan continued to shed key conservative advisers, while some of those who remained lost influence at the expense of more moderate and pragmatic appointees.[51]

The first big sign of a decisive shift came in the fall of 1982, when Reagan threw his weight behind a $98.2 billion tax hike, a move that he had refused to countenance at the start of the year and which Meese would later regard as the biggest political blunder of his two terms.[52] By the end of 1983, when a weakened Meese left the White House for the Department of Justice, the ascendancy of the pragmatists was more or less complete. Darman, a beneficiary of this development, notes that "from the inside it seemed increasingly clear that, when forced to choose, the President was willing to risk alienating his right flank in order to strengthen his political viability in the broad American middle."[53]

The second factor leading to a more cautious presidential strategy was the approach of the 1984 presidential election. While the Democrats looked far from formidable, Reagan remained politically vulnerable until the end of 1983 (see table 9.1). The key to his reelection lay not in the issues (on which his positions were largely unpopular), but rather in avoiding issues and emphasizing his personality, which most Americans found agreeable.[54] This elevation of short-term politics over ideology became a marked theme of the second half of Reagan's first term. When Democrats proposed a $4.5 billion jobs package whose philosophy was diametrically opposed to his own, he equably lent his support. And the White House responded to a series of petty but embarrassing public relations reverses on the hunger issue with an unbroken series of capitulations.

Hunger became a sensitive political issue early in 1983, symbolizing the hardship and insecurity that a deep recession was inflicting upon millions of Americans. In Detroit—where unemployment stood at 21 percent—four hundred thousand were receiving emergency food aid, in Newark a food program administrator described hunger as a "national epidemic," and nationally, visits to soup kitchens were up 50 percent from the previous year. On Independence Day, twenty activists led by Mitch Snyder, head of the Washington-based Community for Creative Non-Violence, began a fast designed to force the federal government to release surplus commodities to the poor. Responding to news stories such as these, the U.S. Conference of Mayors declared a national food emergency, while congressional subcommittees launched high-profile investigations that strongly recalled the McGovern hearings of the late 1960s.[55]

Faced with this bombardment, the White House was occasionally defiant. President Reagan professed himself "perplexed," noting that spending on food and nutrition programs was still vastly greater than a decade ago and that all Americans whose income was less than 130 percent of the poverty level were eligible for free food stamps. He suspected mismanagement, fraud, or poor distribution. Indiscreetly, Attorney General Meese went further, telling reporters that he did not "know of any authoritative figures that there are hungry children" but did have "considerable information that people go to soup kitchens because the food is free and that's easier than paying for it."[56]

Defiance, however, was politically unwise. Reagan's and Meese's remarks each generated a stream of negative publicity. Responding to Reagan's puzzlement, Tip O'Neill exploded, "I don't know where he's been," charging that poor people were going hungry because "one particular conservative Republican has led a nationwide campaign of ridicule against America's nutrition programs."[57]

More generally, the administration yielded, aware that it no longer possessed the ideological initiative and thinking (wrongly, as it turned out) that a tough battle for reelection lay ahead. Two weeks after the start of Mitch Snyder's protest, a White House staffer warned Meese and Baker that it had now made the network news, that administration officials were about to be grilled by a House subcommittee, and that "this issue is rapidly becoming a Democratic attack point." In his view, a "proactive" response was imperative "in order to avoid a further deterioration of the administration's fairness perception."[58]

Just one day later, and on the same day that the House voted 408 to 15 not to accept any more cuts in food programs, Reagan announced a "no-holds-barred study" of the hunger problem, conceded Snyder's demand that free commodity distribution to the poor be resumed, and indicated a willingness to contemplate "more funding." By way of further indication of the administration's solidarity with the poor, Secretary of Agriculture John Block announced that his family had been living on a food stamp budget for a week. Pleased to report that the budget had kept them well fed, he nevertheless allowed that "it's impossible to really appreciate the plight of the poor" and that in a typically sultry Washington August, he had regretted not being able to cool down with beer and ice cream.[59]

One should not exaggerate the importance of this series of events, irritating and discomfiting as it undoubtedly was for the White House. By the end of 1983, the economy was rebounding, so was the nation's collective morale, and Reagan's fortunes revived just in time. In November 1984, he carried forty-nine of the fifty states, secured 59 percent of the vote, and became only the second modern Republican (after Richard Nixon in 1972) to win a majority of the blue-collar vote. But while the fairness issue did not damage him in electoral terms, the 1981–1982 recession had surely helped to undercut the ideological force of what remained of his presidency. Having won with a campaign that "managed to bypass conventional substance altogether" (as Darman records with evident distaste), Reagan lacked the kind of mandate for change that he had received from his narrower victory in 1980.[60] To gauge how much had changed, one only has to consider those few occasions on which social issues penetrated the feel-good haze. One could, for example, cite the two occasions when anti-poverty campaigns by the resourceful and politically savvy Mitch Snyder succeeded in winning fresh concessions from the White House.[61] Perhaps more arresting, however, was the moment in October's vice presidential debate when George Bush countered Geraldine Ferraro's effort to exploit the fairness issue by insisting that "spending for food stamps is way, way up under the Reagan administration. AFDC is up under the Reagan administration." One only has to imagine the same (wildly inaccurate) claim having been advanced as an administration selling point during the first eighteen months or so of the Reagan presidency in order to measure how thoroughly the revolution had been vanquished.[62]

WELFARE REFORM IN THE SECOND TERM

The second term policy initiative that had the greatest impact on the poor was undoubtedly the 1986 Tax Reform Act, which removed six million low-income workers from income tax liability.[63] Christopher Howard explains that "removing low-income workers from the income tax rolls was one of four unconditional requirements Reagan made of any tax reform bill." Reflecting the continued salience of the fairness issue, presidential adviser Mitch Daniels hoped that the reform would "erase the cartoon of our party as defender of the rich and privileged."[64] That it was effected in substantial part by expanding the EITC— to which the Reaganites were adamantly opposed—illustrated anew the ascendancy of the pragmatists within the administration (the tax bill was put together largely by James Baker and Richard Darman, from their new base at the Treasury Department).

The second major event was the signing by President Reagan, right at the end of his tenure, of the Family Support Act of 1988, widely heralded at the time as the most important welfare reform measure in half a century. This was the culmination of a debate about dependency that had percolated up from the states, led by such different political types as governors Mario Cuomo (D-N.Y.), Bill Clinton (D-Ark.), and Tommy Thompson (R-Wis.) and by a similarly ecumenical group of academics (from David Ellwood on the left to Lawrence Mead on the right). Much attention focused on the new "consensus" that appeared to underlie the debate, at whose heart lay a new willingness by liberals to contemplate work requirements, and by conservatives to spend additional federal money on antidependency measures.

Ronald Reagan provided momentum to the issue in four ways. First, it was federal cuts and the 1981 OBRA waivers that galvanized the states to become laboratories of welfare reform by mid-decade (a striking development, given how uninterested the governors had been in the New Federalism initiative). Second, it was Reagan's smashing reelection triumph that led leading centrist Democrats—including Clinton, Governor Charles Robb (Va.), and Senator Al Gore (Tenn.)—to distance themselves further from the old liberal faith and embrace conservative stances on crime, law and order, defense, and welfare. Third, Reagan's 1986 state of the union address had lent new energy to the debate. And fourth, of course, he signed the 1988 bill.

That said, the bill that Reagan signed owed comparatively little to his agenda and much more to the ideas of Senator Moynihan, who received the lion's share of the political credit. Whereas the administration had insisted that welfare legislation be budget neutral, the bill that Reagan signed was projected to cost an additional $3.3 billion over five years (a roughly 10 percent increase in the cost of AFDC). Whereas Charles Hobbs, chair of the president's Low Income Opportunity task force, had demanded that the states be released from federal micromanagement, the final bill was more notable for a series of *new* federal obligations: the AFDC–Unemployed Parent program was made mandatory, and states were required to meet new standards in the areas of training, health care, and transportation. Whereas congressional liaison official William Ball had insisted that a minimally acceptable bill require work of all able-bodied recipients whose youngest child was over six months old, the Family Support Act (FSA) featured only the most nugatory work requirement.[65]

Why did Reagan not get his way? And why did he sign a bill whose principal features had been privately denounced as "abominable" by aides such as Ball and Hobbs?[66] The FSA, after all, seemed to fit a well-established tendency by welfare state builders to "misuse conservative terminology and expand liberal programs," the very tendency that had led, by incremental steps, to what conservatives saw as America's bloated welfare state.[67] Throughout 1987 and much of 1988, Reagan's welfare specialists had been arguing that no bill at all would be preferable to Moynihan's cunningly expansive measure.

A number of points are relevant. First, as throughout the Reagan years, conservative Republicans in Congress—and especially senators—were not particularly enamored of his social agenda and were institutionally inclined both to compromise and to preserving their authority over the states. Hobbs reported in one memo that no Republican on the Senate Finance Committee "even supports much less is willing to lead an effort in behalf of the president's initiative," while GOP staffers such as Bob Dole's Sheila Burke were "much closer to Moynihan's draft" than to the administration position. Prospects for the committee endorsing "any . . . welfare reform we could accept," he reported, "are slim to none, and slim is packing his bags. . . . In short, if in the present circumstances we were to undertake negotiations with Moynihan and the Senate Finance Republicans, we would be on one side of the table, and all of them would be on the other."[68]

The reluctance of Senate Republicans to support their president also reflected a number of historically specific factors. In November of 1986, weeks before Hobbs unveiled his package, the Democrats had regained control of the Senate. And just one day later, Reagan's political standing suffered a still more wounding—indeed, shattering—reverse, when news broke of the administration's illegal arms sales to Iran. By the end of the month, when the illegal diversion of the proceeds to the contra guerrillas in Nicaragua was discovered, the administration was in free fall: the *New York Times* reported the sharpest one-month decline in presidential popularity in history: from 70 percent to 46 percent. Lou Cannon vividly portrays the shattering impact of all this on Reagan, reporting that the seventy-six-year-old president—already laid low by prostate surgery, from which he was recovering only slowly—was "overwhelmed by the realization that he had lost the trust of the American people."[69] Already semidetached from day-to-day politics in the aftermath of some damaging staffing changes—chroniclers generally agree that Donald Regan was a poor chief of staff[70]—he was certainly neither able nor inclined to provide leadership on what must have seemed the entirely trivial issue of welfare reform. Neither were Republican leaders keen to align themselves more closely with White House initiatives during this period.

For conservatives who cared passionately about welfare reform, this presidential inattention and loss of momentum must have been deeply frustrating. When, after a brief round of appearances to boost the program, Reagan lapsed back into inactivity, Hobbs let his frustration show, complaining to the new chief of staff, Howard Baker, that the proposals were "dwindling rapidly in the absence of any recent visible evidence of the president's commitment to his initiative." He had "neither . . . talked about it publicly, nor met with [the governors] to renew their interest." Moynihan had taken full advantage.[71]

Reference to Baker brings us to one factor that may explain why Reagan signed a measure that was so offensive to some on the right. Assigned the formidable task of restoring the administration's public standing and congressional relations, he succeeded in part by cultivating friends on the Hill whom Regan had disdained. A pragmatist by temperament—Darman describes him as "chronically moderate"[72]—he was also close to Moynihan and seems to have been the subject of a concerted lobbying campaign from his former Senate colleague: in one memo, Moynihan waxed nostalgic about "a young feller from Tennessee" who had sponsored considerably more expansive welfare legislation back in 1978. Additional pressure on Baker came from Republican governors John Sununu (N.H.) and Lamar Alexander (Tenn.), both of whom were committed to compromise.[73] At that point, the archival trail runs dry: there is nothing in the Reagan library to indicate Baker's response to these entreaties. However, since Reagan signed a bill with provisions largely opposed by his welfare specialists and ideological compadres at the Heritage Foundation, it seems plausible that Baker succeeded in appealing to that side of Reagan's makeup that had always been prepared to compromise and accept half a loaf.

This presents an opportunity to mention an aspect of Reagan's political personality that, perhaps more than anything else, singles him out as being an unusual conservative. Pondering the unhappy fate of "his" economic program, David Stockman concluded that Reagan "had no business trying to make a revolution because it wasn't in his bones." Allowing only that the president "leaned to the right," the OMB director discovered that his boss "was a consensus politician, not an ideologue."[74] However, this verdict is challenged by the sheer evangelical, right-wing radicalism of the welfare agenda that he commended to the nation in 1981 and 1982, and is more generally insupportable in the light of the fascinating glimpses that his recently published radio addresses from the late 1970s afford. Invariably, they show him cleaving to the most conservative political stance that one could take while remaining within the bounds of respectable politics.[75]

What is remarkable about Reagan is the way his fervent ideology clashed with his equable temperament—how willing he was to compromise in order to make modest advances toward his agenda. In other words, he was a pragmatic ideologue.

How many of his ideological soul mates—hostile to the progressive income tax, wishing that the Social Security program could be made voluntary, fixated on "welfare queens," favoring the abolition of farm subsidies, devoted to *Human Events* and *National Review*—would have forged good working relationships with Robert Moretti (Democratic speaker of the California Assembly during his governorship), shared Irish jokes with Tip O'Neill, spoken warmly of Franklin Roosevelt, or appointed pragmatists James A. and Howard Baker to be their chiefs of staff? Reagan had the fixity of belief of the true believer, but not the attitude toward political compromise that typically goes with such intensity.

Also relevant to understanding Reagan's willingness to sign a measure that some fellow conservatives viewed as anathema may have been a characteristically cheerful belief that it did indeed comport with his beliefs. After all, while its compulsory workfare component was small, it was stronger than any previous measure.[76] Moynihan had given Howard Baker the political arguments over a year before Reagan applied his signature, and one assumes that they would have had particular appeal in October of 1988, when Reagan was presumably thinking beyond his recent troubles to his vice president's forthcoming election and to his own place in history: "If the president signs this bill he can legitimately claim to be the president who presided over the biggest tax reform in half-a-century, negotiated real arms reductions with the Russians, and transformed the welfare system."[77]

CONCLUSION: THE REAGAN WELFARE LEGACY TWO DECADES ON

Eight years later, Bill Clinton also had an election on his mind when he signed a much more comprehensive welfare reform bill, one that ended the federal entitlement to welfare, replacing AFDC with a block grant, and that imposed a five-year lifetime maximum on eligibility for "temporary assistance to needy families" (TANF, the successor to AFDC). PRWORA in a sense highlights the comparative limits of Reagan's reformist legacy, which after all explains why comprehensive welfare reform was still on the agenda in the mid-1990s. Moreover, scholars trying to make sense of the later measure have characteristically emphasized short-term and immediate explanations: Clinton's desire to prove himself a New Democrat, Dick Morris's penchant for triangulation, a recent precipitous rise in welfare rolls, a proliferation of newly influential right-wing pressure groups and media outlets, a shift to the right in public attitudes toward welfare and government more generally, and the coming to power in the House of Newt Gingrich and in Congress of the first Republican majority in over forty years. In all of these ways, the environment was much more conducive to radical reform now than at any time in the Reagan years after the first six months.[78]

One could take a different line, however, and argue that 1996 saw the final triumph of a slow-burning Reagan Revolution. Arguably, that revolution had begun as far back as the early 1970s, when Governor Reagan made welfare reform the central issue of his second term and struggled tenaciously with Nixon's White House and Elliot Richardson's Department of Health, Education, and Welfare (HEW) for the right to pursue radical experiments in workfare. At that time, the momentum in welfare policy had been toward nationalization of benefits and eligibility standards, and Reagan had seemed to be merely tilting at windmills, but his doggedness did win him federal approval for an unprecedentedly large state experiment, while his opposition to Nixon's Family Assistance Plan helped derail the cause of federalization.[79] Four years later, Reagan again made the welfare issue central to his challenge from the right. Neither his pursuit of a partly invented Chicago welfare mother nor his ideas for devolution won him the nomination, but they did provide an airing for ideas that had few other spokesmen in the mid-1970s, and they were ideas that had somewhat greater appeal by the end of the decade, as antiwelfare and antigovernmental feeling attained new intensity.

How might Reagan's presidency be made to fit this version of events? On the face of it, nothing after the first few months of his first term sustains the notion of a building momentum for Reaganite reform: from the evidence presented earlier, it seems that the president gave up on radical reform after the poor reception of the New Federalism initiative and withdrew from the fray, leaving Bill Clinton and Newt Gingrich to compete for the crown of welfare revolutionary a decade or so later. But this may seriously understate Reagan's contribution to the debate of the 1990s. For one thing, although this essay has emphasized opposition success in first curtailing and then reversing the cuts of 1981, it is also true that Reagan's popularity (except during the first term recession) and his trouncing of Walter Mondale in 1984 altered the Democratic Party in ways that made radical welfare reform possible. Martin Anderson's 1988 claim that Reagan had presided over a revolution rested in part on the grounds that it was now "largely irrelevant" who won the forthcoming election because "prospects are nil for . . . big, new social welfare programs."[80] The expansion of the *old* social welfare programs during the late 1980s and early 1990s might seem to diminish the importance of that assertion. But in another sense it looked quite prescient in the aftermath of Clinton's 1992 campaign and his signing of PRWORA, a measure that would have appeared outlandishly right wing had it been proposed a decade earlier. (The principal author of FSA, Senator Moynihan, described the 1996 measure as "the most brutal act of social policy since Reconstruction."[81])

For another thing, CWEP and the extensions of waiver authority legislated in 1981 precipitated state-level actions that in turn stimulated the important federal legislation of 1996. In *Whose Welfare?* (1996), Steven Teles portrays the congressional debate of 1987–1988 as little more than a sideshow. While it was receiving all the publicity, a little-noticed White House agency created by Reagan in 1987, the Low Income Opportunity Advisory Board, was granting New Jersey and Wisconsin far-reaching waivers that had previously been rejected by the Department of Health and Human Services, and whose subsequent granting lent new encouragement to governors interested in welfare reform.[82] During the successor presidency of George Bush, the waiver process continued to gain momentum; R. Kent Weaver refers to "tremendous ferment in the world of ideas and in the states." And with AFDC caseloads having shot up from 10.9 million in 1988 to 14.4 million in 1994, there was particular interest in harsh measures (family caps, time limits) that had "not [been] on policymakers' horizons" in 1988, when the emphasis had been on training and transitional entitlements.[83] By the time that PRWORA was enacted, twenty-five states had already used waivers granted by Reagan, Bush, and Clinton to end the entitlement status of AFDC.[84]

What overall lesson should the scholar seeking to establish the Reagan welfare legacy derive from this evidence? A closer examination of PRWORA than is possible here would probably tend to accent the uniqueness of the political environment that made far-reaching welfare reform possible in 1996, together with a dramatic radicalization in the Republican Party that took place well after Reagan's departure from the White House.[85] Certainly it would be ahistorical to claim that the policy legacy of 1981 to 1989 made the legislative outcome of 1996 somehow inevitable. However, by the same token it would be bad history to conclude from the lack of immediately visible policy success after 1981 that Reagan's social policy legacy was unimportant. Some of the evidence presented here suggests that while Reagan did not make the "ending of welfare" *inevitable,* he did make it *possible.* Accordingly, the Reagan Revolution in welfare policy looks a lot more substantial today than it did in 1989.

NOTES

1. William Clinton pledged to "end welfare as we know it" on the campaign trail in 1992. See Steven M. Teles, *Whose Welfare? AFDC and Elite Politics* (Lawrence: University Press of Kansas, 1996), 131.

2. For an introduction to Reagan's social philosophy, containing most of these elements, see "A Time for Choosing," television address in behalf of Senator Barry Goldwater, October 27, 1964, in *Ronald Reagan Talks to America,* ed. Richard Scaife Mellon (Old Greenwich, Conn.: Devin-Adair, 1983), 28. See also the recently collated radio addresses that Reagan composed for the O'Connor network between 1975 and 1979, and especially those delivered in April 1975 (n.d.), and on December 22, 1976, January 19, 1977, July 6, 1977, and January 9, 1978, in Kiron K. Skinner, Annelise Anderson, and Martin Anderson, eds., *Reagan, in His Own Hand: The Writings of Ronald Reagan That Reveal His Revolutionary Vision for America* (New York: Free Press, 2001), 389–95.

3. Reagan quote from "A Time for Choosing," in Mellon, *Reagan Talks to America,* 28. On the overall mood of optimism that prevailed at this time, see James T. Patterson, *Grand Expectations: The United States, 1945–1974* (New York: Oxford University Press, 1996).

4. They were responding affirmatively to the assertion that "you cannot trust the government to do right most of the time." See Seymour Martin Lipset and William Schneider, *The Confidence Gap: Business, Labor, and Government in the Public Mind,* rev. ed. (Baltimore: Johns Hopkins University Press, 1987), 17.

5. Scott Keeter, "Public Opinion and the Election," in Gerald Pomper et al., *The Election of 1996: Reports and Interpretations* (Chatham, N.J.: Chatham House Publishers, 1997), 112.

6. Thomas P. O'Neill, *Man of the House* (London: Bodley Head, 1987), 338.

7. For poll data, see Pomper et al., *Election of 1996,* 112.

8. Michael B. Katz, *The Undeserving Poor: From the War on Poverty to the War on Welfare* (New York: Pantheon Books, 1989), 139.

9. Perkins was longtime chair of the House Education and Labor Committee. *New York Times,* May 20, 1981, 22.

10. Aspin newsletter cited by John A. Farrell, *Tip O'Neill and the Democratic Century* (Boston: Little, Brown, 2001), 557.

11. *New York Times,* May 23, 1981, 10; and May 29, 1981, 13.

12. *Congressional Quarterly Weekly Report* (September 26, 1981): 1840.

13. Richard Darman, *Who's in Control? Polar Politics and the Sensible Center* (New York: Simon & Schuster, 1996), 70.

14. See Senator Carl Levin (D-Mich.), quoted in *New York Times,* March 11, 1981, B5.

15. O'Neill, *Man of the House,* 344.

16. Cited by Nathan Glazer, *The Limits of Social Policy* (Cambridge: Harvard University Press, 1988), 55–56.

17. Welfare is here defined as AFDC, Supplemental Security Income, Medicaid, food stamps, surplus food, social services, and work-training programs. Figures computed from tables 576 ("public aid" in constant dollars) and 573 (federal "public aid" spending as a percentage of total public spending on welfare), *Statistical Abstract of the United States: 1987* (Washington, D.C.: U.S. Department of Commerce, 1987), 340–42. The 1981 figure is approximate because the data for federal spending as a percentage of total welfare spending come from the previous year.

18. For food stamps and AFDC, see Paul Pierson, *Dismantling the Welfare State? Reagan, Thatcher, and the Politics of Retrenchment* (New York: Cambridge University Press, 1994), 118. For Medicaid, see Jean Donovan Gilman, *Medicaid and the Costs of Federalism, 1984–1992* (New York: Garland, 1998). Ironically, the annual budget reconciliation process, which had made helped to make spending *cuts* possible in 1981, helped to make *increases* in social spending possible later in the decade. Because of the deficit, Reagan could not afford to veto these omnibus measures, even when they expanded Medicaid and food stamps (as was the case every year from 1984).

19. Per capita federal spending on welfare (definition as in note 17) in constant 1995 dollars was $380.8 billion in 1980, $355.8 billion in 1985, $418.9 billion in 1990, and $635.8 billion in 1995. Computed from table 598, *Statistical Abstracts: 2000,* 378.

20. Glazer, *Limits of Social Policy,* 44–54; Edward D. Berkowitz, "Changing the Meaning of Welfare Reform," in *Maintaining the Safety Net: Income Redistribution Programs in the Reagan Administration,* ed. John C. Weicher (Washington, D.C.: American Enterprise Institute, 1984), 23–42.

21. Christopher Howard, *The Hidden Welfare State: Tax Expenditures and Social Policy in the United States* (Princeton: Princeton University Press, 1997), 66.

22. Reflecting the same philosophy, the administration also changed AFDC eligibility rules to exclude families whose gross income exceeded 150 percent of the state's need standard. See Sheldon Danziger, "Budget Cuts as Welfare Reform," *American Economic Review* 73 (May 1983): 67.

23. Pierson, *Dismantling the Welfare State?* 126. The contrast to the preceding quote by Nixon is instructive.

24. A full treatment of this topic lies beyond the scope of this essay. See Howard, *Hidden Welfare State,* chaps. 3 and 7; Michael B. Katz, *The Price of Citizenship: Redefining the American Welfare State* (New York: Henry Holt, 2001), chap. 11; and Dennis Ventry, "The Collision of Tax and Welfare Politics: The Political History of the Earned Income Tax Credit, 1969–99," *National Tax Journal* 53 (December 2000): 983–1026.

25. On their role, see *New York Times,* April 26, 1982, B8.

26. These were "work-*to*-welfare" rather than "work *for* welfare" programs, for the most part, and not what Reaganite purists meant by "workfare."

27. Much of the material in this paragraph is drawn from Katz, *Undeserving Poor,* 225–28.

28. A still earlier one, centering on Social Security reform, had come in May and is treated by Martha Derthick and Steven Teles elsewhere in this volume.

29. Lou Cannon, *President Reagan: The Role of a Lifetime,* 2d ed. (New York: Public Affairs, 2000), 440.

30. Katz, *Undeserving Poor,* 139.

31. *Congressional Quarterly Almanac: 1981* (Washington, D.C.: Congressional Quarterly, 1982), 498.

32. *New York Times,* September 26, 1981, 1. Reagan's deep distrust for the federal bureaucracy resurfaced some six months later, when reporters asked about anecdotal evidence of hardship generated by budget cuts. The president charged that "there are those out there in government employ who will, if possible, sabotage and deliberately penalize some individual who actually is not supposed to be penalized in order to get a story indicating that the programs are not working." See Question and Answer session with reporters, February 8, 1982, in *Public Papers of the President: Ronald Reagan: 1982* (Washington, D.C.: Government Printing Office, 1983), vol. 1, 119. See also his remarks in Bloomington, Minn., same day, ibid., 136.

33. Unemployment rose from 7.1 percent in 1980 to 9.7 percent in 1982. The proportion of Americans living in poverty increased from 13 percent in 1980 to 15 percent in 1982. See U.S. Congress, House of Representatives, Committee on Ways and Means, *Overview of Entitlement Programs: 1991 Green Book* (Washington, D.C.: Government Printing Office, 1991), 510, 1138. On the liberalization of public attitudes toward the poor during the 1980s, see Hugh Heclo, "Poverty Politics," in *Confronting Poverty: Prescriptions for Change,* ed. Sheldon Danziger, Gary Sandefur, and Daniel Weinberg (Cambridge: Harvard University Press, 1994), 402; and R. Kent Weaver, Robert Y. Shapiro, and Lawrence R. Jacobs, "Trends: Welfare," *Public Opinion Quarterly* 59 (winter 1995): 606–27.

34. Poll dated April 3, 1982. *Gallup Poll: 1982* (Wilmington, Del.: Scholarly Resources, 1983), 58.

35. *Washington Post,* May 19, 1982, A23; May 2, 1981, C1 and C3.

36. *New York Times,* March 19, 1982, 9.

37. Stockman, *Triumph of Politics,* 304; Darman, *Who's in Control?* 97.

38. Howard, *Hidden Welfare State,* 146.

39. *Washington Post,* February 12, 1982, 23. The name of the cabinet member was not recorded.

40. Stockman, *Triumph of Politics,* 304.

41. *Public Papers,* 1982, 1:228.

42. Speech given March 23, 1982, ibid., 1:359–61.

43. Handwritten postscript to letter, Ronald Reagan to Holly Coors, June 25, 1981, White House Office of Records and Management (WHORM) document 019592, subject file WE, Ronald Reagan Library (RRL), Simi Valley, Calif.

44. Speech given October 5, 1981, *Public Papers of the President: Ronald Reagan: 1981* (Washington, D.C.: Government Printing Office, 1983) vol. 2, 883–87.

45. *Washington Post,* January 20, 1982, A23. After thirteen months in office, only 47 percent of Americans approved of Reagan's performance, compared with 49 percent approval for Carter at the same stage. See *Gallup Poll,* 1982, 41.

46. *Washington Post,* June 12, 1982, A4.

47. Reagan's speech, dated January 22, 1965, is reprinted in Skinner, Anderson, and Anderson, *In His Own Hand,* 460. For Ford's response, see Timothy Conlan, *New Federalism: Intergovernmental Reform from Nixon to Reagan* (Washington, D.C.: Brookings Institution Press, 1988), 182.

48. Ibid., 184.

49. On the New Federalism, see Conlan, *New Federalism,* and Berkowitz, "Changing the Meaning of Welfare Reform," 34–35.

50. *Washington Post,* July 13, 1982, A4.

51. Ed Rollins, communications director throughout the first term, noted that "every single day Ed Meese was in that White House he lost power or gave up power. Every single day Jim Baker was in that White House he accumulated power—or Dick Darman accumulated power." Cannon, *Role of a Lifetime,* 152.

52. Edwin C. Meese III, *With Reagan: The Inside Story* (Washington, D.C.: Regnery Publishing, 1992), 147.

53. Darman, *Who's in Control?* 115.

54. Remarkably, even when Reagan's approval rating dropped to 47 percent, in February of 1982, 70 percent of Americans continued to approve of Reagan as a person. *Gallup Poll,* 1982, 41.

55. *New York Times,* March 1, 1983, 14; June 17, 1983, 26; May 25, 1983, 18; June 16, 1983, 17; June 17, 1983, 26; August 4, 1983, 16; August 3, 1983, B4. Katz claims that this was the time when "poverty once again became an important political issue" for the first time since the 1960s. Katz, *Undeserving Poor,* 126.

56. *New York Times,* December 15, 1983, B13.

57. *New York Times,* August 4, 1983, 16.

58. Memorandum, Lee Verstandig to James Baker and Edwin Meese, August 1, 1983, document OA10513, James A. Baker Files, RRL.

59. *New York Times,* August 3, 1984, B4; *Public Papers of the President: Ronald Reagan: 1983* (Washington, D.C.: Government Printing Office, 1984), vol. 2, 1118–1119; *New York Times,* August 5, 1983, 8.

60. Darman, *Who's in Control?* 141.

61. See *New York Times,* April 2, 1984, D14; and November 10, 1984, 15. On Snyder, see Victoria Rader, *"Signal through the Flames": Mitch Snyder and America's Homeless* (Kansas City, Mo.: Sheed & Ward, 1986).

62. *New York Times*, October 12, 1984, B7.

63. William Pemberton, *Exit with Honor: The Life and Presidency of Ronald Reagan* (Armonk, N.Y.: M. E. Sharpe, 1998), 145.

64. Howard, *Hidden Welfare State*, 232 n. 20, 145.

65. For the administration's agenda, I rely on Low Income Opportunity Working Group, *Up from Dependency: A New National Public Assistance Strategy* (Washington, D.C.: Government Printing Office, 1986), and memorandum, William Ball to Howard Baker, June 23, 1987, WHORM 497670, WE, RRL. For a description of the FSA, see *New York Times*, September 27, 1988, 30.

66. See memorandum, Charles Hobbs to Howard Baker, July 2, 1987, in Daniel Crippen Files, OA16099, RRL. See also an unsigned report (possibly written by Ball), titled "Lamar Alexander's Suggestions to Howard Baker on Welfare Reform," n.d. but July 1987, WHORM 509842, WE 10, RRL.

67. The quote is from an internal Heritage Foundation memorandum, Stuart Butler to Ed Feulner, July 1, 1987, copy in Judith Duggan Files, OA 10591, RRL.

68. Memorandum, Hobbs to Baker, July 2, 1987.

69. Only 14 percent of Americans accepted as accurate Reagan's initial explanation for his administration's actions, and 57 percent felt that Iran-Contra was more serious than Watergate. See Cannon, *Role of a Lifetime*, 639, 608. Reagan underwent three cancer operations in 1986 and 1987.

70. Reagan's friend and ally, Senator Paul Laxalt (R-Nev.) saw Regan, with his imperious disdain for Congress, as a "damn nuisance," while liaison aide Max Friedersdorf was "embarrassed" by the chief of staff's approach and found "sickening" the "obsequious yes men" who surrounded Regan. See Jane Mayer and Doyle McManus, *Landslide: The Unmaking of the President, 1984–1988* (Boston: Houghton Mifflin, 1988), 39–45. See also Cannon, *Role of a Lifetime*, 495–501. For Donald Regan's defense, which focuses on the role of the First Lady, see Regan, *For the Record: From Wall Street to Washington* (San Diego: Harcourt Brace Jovanovich, 1988).

71. Memorandum, Hobbs to Baker, July 2, 1987. For Reagan's initial round of activity in behalf of his proposal, see memorandum, Dennis Thomas to Donald T. Regan, February 3, 1987, in David Chew Files, OA14171, RRL.

72. Darman, *Who's in Control?* 183.

73. Letter, Moynihan to Baker, July 6, 1987, WHORM document 516187, subject file WE010, RRL. On Sununu, see memorandum, Joe Wright to Ken Duberstein et al., May 31, 1988, in Charles Greener Files, OA18138, RRL. On Alexander, see "Lamar Alexander's Suggestions."

74. Stockman, *Triumph of Politics*, 9.

75. See Skinner, Anderson, and Anderson, *In His Own Hand*.

76. See Desmond King, *Actively Seeking Work: The Politics of Unemployment and Welfare Policy in the United States and Great Britain* (Chicago: University of Chicago Press, 1995), chap. 5.

77. Letter, Moynihan to Baker, August 5, 1987, in Nancy Kennedy Files, OA18188, RRL. Vice President Bush came out strongly in favor of Moynihan's welfare reform bill in July of 1988, making it hard for Reagan to wield his veto pen, despite subsequent warnings that he was willing to do so. Jonah Edelman records that in trying to broker agreement with Congress, OMB deputy director Joseph Wright was influenced by Reagan's more "politically oriented White House officials," who felt that an election year veto must

be avoided at all costs. See Edelman, "The Passage of the Family Support Act of 1988 and the Politics of Welfare Reform in the United States" (D.Phil., Oxford University, 1995), 239–40, 251.

78. On PRWORA, see R. Kent Weaver, *Ending Welfare As We Know It* (Washington, D.C.: Brookings Institution Press, 2000); Benjamin Ginsberg and Martin Shefter, *Politics by Other Means: Politicians, Prosecutors, and the Press from Watergate to Whitewater*, rev. ed. (New York: W. W. Norton, 1999), 62–77; Timothy Conlan, *From New Federalism to Devolution: Twenty-Five Years of Intergovernmental Reform* (Washington, D.C.: Brookings Institution Press, 1998), 272–92.

79. The Nixon tapes afford some vivid insights into the relationship between Nixon and Reagan: for example, a vexed John Mitchell waxing sarcastic about "our dear governor from California" and asking, "What do we do to get him to quieten down?" and a weary Nixon complaining that "we are trying like the devil to cooperate there, but it's not easy I can assure you." See telephone conversation between John Mitchell and John D. Ehrlichman, November 12, 1971, Nixon presidential tapes, chronological series 2, 14–85; and conversation between Mitchell and Richard Nixon, November 17, 1971, chronological series 2, 15–4, Nixon Presidential Project, National Archives, College Park, Md. At HEW, Richardson viewed Reagan and the ideologues on his staff with irritation and a certain lofty condescension. His papers include transcripts of conversations that he had about the California workfare proposal with Ehrlichman, Mitchell, and Reagan during 1971 and 1972. See Richardson Papers, boxes 129–31, Library of Congress, Washington, D.C. See also various items in papers of John D. Ehrlichman, box 58, Nixon Project.

80. Martin Anderson, *Revolution* (San Diego: Harcourt Brace Jovanovich, 1988), 438.

81. James T. Patterson, *America's Struggle against Poverty in the Twentieth Century* (Cambridge: Harvard University Press, 2001), 238.

82. Teles, *Whose Welfare?* 123–30.

83. Weaver, *Ending Welfare,* 102, 3.

84. Anne Marie Cammisa, *From Rhetoric to Reform? Welfare Policy in American Politics* (Boulder, Colo.: Westview Press, 1998), 106–7.

85. On the latter point, see Ginsberg and Shefter, *Politics by Other Means.* Contrasting the limited objectives of Reagan with the radicalism of Newt Gingrich's GOP, they present George Bush's tax hike and a deep hostility to Clinton as the key factors underlying a new generation of right-wing activism during the 1990s. Right-wing foundations and religious groupings that had lacked political influence during the 1980s played a vital role in the welfare reform debate of the following decade.

10
Natural Resources and Environmental Policy
Jeffrey K. Stine

Policies relating to natural resources and the environment never received high priority during the Ronald Reagan presidency except to the extent that they advanced the administration's broader political objectives of reducing the overall size of the federal government and diminishing industrial regulation. Reagan's philosophical approach to natural resources and environmental policy diverged substantially from that of the Nixon, Ford, and Carter administrations. The legislation passed since the late 1960s had represented a bipartisan consensus that stressed, on the one hand, ever greater regulation, and, on the other, increasing conservation. The Reagan administration sought to move government in a different direction by placing increased emphasis on economic growth and production and less emphasis on environmental regulations.[1]

Toward this end, Reagan sought to expand the reliance on market forces and lessen the role of the federal government. This structural framework, he contended, would meet more of society's needs, without causing undue harm to the natural environment and public health. Shifting federal priorities and direction in this manner, however, provoked considerable controversy and political outrage from the environmental movement and many political leaders. Nevertheless, the administration's efforts rarely effected long-term change, primarily because of the White House's essential political strategy. Rather than using a legislative approach, Reagan relied on "administrative fiat"—reorganizing federal agencies; significantly reducing or reallocating money and personnel; altering, withdrawing, or weakening the enforcement of federal regulations; and placing like-minded loyalists in key positions within the federal bureaucracy. As Resources for the Future analyst Paul R. Portney observed: "There is a price to pay for inattention to legislative change . . . subsequent administrations can

The author is grateful for the research assistance provided by Morton I. Goldman and Jessica S. Sanders and for the criticism and suggestions from W. Elliot Brownlee and Marcel C. LaFollette.

more easily reverse policies pursued through administration action alone." "Fundamental change," Portney added, "is much more likely if an administration takes the time to work closely with Congress in redirecting policy," something that the Reagan administration consistently avoided.[2]

REAGAN'S EARLIER RECORD

To understand Reagan's approach, as well as the anger with which his environmental policies were greeted, it is useful to consider his earlier actions as governor of California. His tenure in Sacramento, from 1967 to 1975, overlapped with the coming of age of California's environmental movement. Although Reagan personally enjoyed the outdoors—especially the time he spent with family and friends at the various ranches he owned over the years—he never held conservation and environmental protection as causes to be championed. Buoyed by the rejuvenating experiences at his isolated and spacious properties in the Santa Monica Mountains north of Los Angeles (in the 1950s and 1960s) and the Santa Ynez Mountains northwest of Santa Barbara (after 1974) and informed by his travels throughout the West, Reagan came to view the country as enjoying a superabundance of land, beauty, and natural resources. His perspective came to parallel pro-development factions in the West that chafed at government regulations, on the one hand, while seeking government assistance in gaining access to public resources, on the other.[3]

Nevertheless, as governor of a state renowned for the relative strength of environmental values among its citizenry, he attempted to steer a middle-of-the-road course. Like Jimmy Carter, who had governed the state of Georgia from 1971 to 1975, Reagan was among the cohort of governors in office when the first big wave of federal environmental legislation took effect, and these experiences undoubtedly influenced his later views. Reagan's gubernatorial terms were highlighted by legislation associated with coastal zone protection and air and water pollution control. He also signed into law the wide-ranging California Environmental Quality Act. Reagan's fiscal conservatism and antagonism toward large federal projects led him to oppose the U.S. Army Corps of Engineers' massive Dos Rios Dam, which had been proposed for the middle fork of the scenic Eel River and which had attracted vigorous opposition from conservation organizations.[4]

As governor, Reagan clearly understood the sentiments of many Californians, even if he did not share the depth of their social concerns. Much like President Nixon on the national level, Governor Reagan did not personally initiate efforts to protect the environment, yet he did not stand in the way of others, so long as their proposals did not unduly burden the business sector. In the area of water resources development policy, Reagan often sided with environmentalists in their opposition to newly proposed projects, albeit for different reasons.[5]

When he vacated the governor's mansion in 1975, Reagan also left behind the associations he had forged with various pro-environment advisers in Sacramento. During the remainder of the decade, Reagan's views on natural resources and the environment came to be increasingly influenced, as his biographer Lou Cannon observes, by "his pro-development friends in business and industry" who opposed in principle federal environmental regulations and preservation programs.[6]

During the 1980 presidential campaign, Reagan stressed his desire to reduce the size of the federal government and to tame the inflationary economy that had plagued the nation throughout the Carter years. He promised Americans that he would cut taxes, limit federal domestic spending, and increase military expenditures. He also pledged to reduce the regulatory burden placed upon business and to transfer appropriate federal responsibilities to state and local government. Such emphases worked against assigning high priority to environmental values, and, to the extent that Reagan discussed natural resources and environmental policy at all during the campaign, he placed it within the framework of his political philosophy.[7]

As it turned out, the environment never really emerged as a major campaign issue for any of the principal candidates. Following the Democratic and Republican primary conventions, the Carter and Reagan campaigns both relegated environmental and natural resources questions to a minor role. In the face of rampant inflation and soaring interest rates, Reagan made the economy his top priority, emphasizing the incumbent's weak record. Carter focused his campaign on personal qualities, stressing his own honesty and integrity, and, by implication, casting doubts upon Reagan's trustworthiness. These campaign strategies, in fact, reflected the findings of leading pollsters, who continually showed voters failing to list natural resources and the environment among their top ten concerns.[8]

Reagan's decisive victory led the new administration to declare that it had received a mandate from the people, who thereby endorsed his call for a thorough reorientation of public policy.[9] The new administration assumed that the mandate extended to environmental policy and moved forward accordingly.

SETTING A NEW COURSE

The election sobered the environmental movement, confronting them with a new political landscape apparently hostile toward their core values. Lewis Regenstein of the Fund for Animals commented that "I feel as though I've got one foot in the grave and the other on a banana peel."[10] Such fears deepened during the first months of Reagan's presidency, as the administration announced its selections for key environmental posts, moved to slash budgets and personnel at the Environmental Protection Agency (EPA), and gutted the Council on Environmental

Quality. Environmental regulations across the board appeared threatened, as the administration seemed to be declaring that environmental protection and economic growth were incompatible.[11]

To accomplish its goals, the administration focused special attention on two agencies: the Department of the Interior and the EPA. Although authority to execute environmental policy also resides within the programs of several departments and independent agencies, including the Tennessee Valley Authority, U.S. Army Corps of Engineers, Department of Agriculture, Department of Commerce, and Department of Energy, the Interior Department, created in 1849, has served as the central player in management of the nation's natural resources, accumulating through the years a complex patchwork of duties and constituencies. Some of these responsibilities were preservationist in orientation, but some were developmental, resulting in internal bureaucratic tensions and competing public expectations. By 1981, the department's preservationist side encompassed the National Park Service, Fish and Wildlife Service, and Wilderness Area activities, while the developmental side included the Bureau of Reclamation, Bureau of Mines, Bureau of Land Management, and U.S. Geological Survey.

The nomination of James G. Watt as secretary of the Interior brought Reagan strong support from the right wing of the Republican Party, especially from those in the West. Watt, who was the founding director of the politically conservative, "wise use" Mountain States Legal Foundation, had brazenly pushed forward elements of Reagan's pro-industry and antiregulation political philosophy. His high profile, confrontational style, and often extreme official actions had also attracted media coverage and made him an obvious target for environmental groups. As a personality, he proved easy to ridicule, dislike, and even despise, and he came to symbolize what was widely perceived to be the administration's environmental insensitivity. He thus served as a lightning rod for the White House, keeping environmental criticism from touching Reagan directly, at least during the opening months of his presidency.[12]

Watt's leadership at Interior mirrored the tactics being employed throughout the administration: rather than pursue a legislative approach, Watt appointed loyalists to key agency positions, reassigned internal priorities, and used the agency's budget to shape policy.[13] When describing his emphasis on recruiting and promoting like-minded civil servants within the department, he explained: "I will build an institutional memory that will be here for decades."[14]

Reagan had entered office determined to give his cabinet secretaries a large voice in governing the nation, and he pursued that intent by establishing a system of cabinet councils. Questions of energy, environment, and natural resources fell under the Cabinet Council on Natural Resources and Environment, whose chairman pro tempore was the secretary of the Interior.[15] Heading this cabinet council expanded Watt's influence over environmental policy concerns that transcended individual executive branch agencies, allowing him to cast his shadow over the EPA and the departments of energy and agriculture. Watt's impact on the EPA was also magnified by the EPA's lack of cabinet status, which resulted in the omission of that agency's administrator from the council.[16]

When Watt disclosed his first bundle of policy directives in the spring of 1981, there was an avalanche of protests. Particularly galling to conservationists was Watt's moratorium on new land acquisitions for the national parks, his push to open up more federal land to mining and logging, the program to increase offshore oil and gas leases, and the proposal to turn regulation of strip mining over to the states. Watt also opposed the creation of urban national parks, advocated putting a hold on the listing of new endangered species, promoted accelerated oil and gas leasing in Alaska, and reoriented the Land and Water Conservation Fund.

Watt replaced the Carter-era directors of every Interior Department agency except for one: the National Park Service. There he left in place Russell E. Dickenson, a career parks administrator selected by Watt's predecessor, Cecil Andrus, in 1980. During his confirmation hearing, Watt told the Senate that he wanted to keep Dickenson as a sign of his intention to professionalize Park Service leadership; he did not add that he had gotten to know Dickenson when they had worked together at Interior during the Nixon administration, or that Dickenson already had agreed wholeheartedly with Watt's desire to freeze the acquisition of new park lands.[17]

Watt's retention of Dickenson may have soothed the anxieties of some Park Service employees, but it did little to reduce the growing waves of protest. Watt's dealings with the national parks ran into effective congressional resistance. Arguing that the Park Service had grown too quickly, he sought to reprogram money intended for land acquisition and use those funds to upgrade and repair roads and hotels within existing parks. Congress, however, put the money back into the agency's park acquisition budget.

As Watt continued with various programmatic shifts, environmental activists became more outraged. In July 1981, the National Wildlife Federation (NWF)—the nation's largest (at 4.5 million members) and most politically conservative environmental organization—called for Watt's dismissal, something already being pushed by the smaller, more politically liberal Sierra Club and Wilderness Society. The NWF, which had never before lobbied a president to dismiss a federal appointee, argued that, while Watt was paying "lip service to environmental protection, he is working to undermine or circumvent many of our basic environmental protection laws."[18]

Watt also drew fire from those opposed to offshore oil development. During his 1980 presidential campaign, Reagan called for acceleration of oil exploration under the nation's coastal waters. Once installed as secretary, Watt quickly moved ahead with that plan. One of his first proposals was to designate 111 tracts, totaling 5,100 acres, in the Santa Maria Basin off the San Luis Obispo County coast, and he later called for the lease of over 150,000 acres farther north. While national environmental organizations opposed Watt's proposal for Outer Continental Shelf lease sales in northern California, the strongest reactions came from the state's elected officials and congressional delegation, who complained that the administration's heavy hand on this matter contradicted Reagan's campaign promise to delegate more responsibilities to state and local government. In March 1981, a bipartisan group of California members of the House of Representatives wrote to ask Reagan to reconsider the proposed sale.[19] The state of California, along with nineteen local governments and several environmental groups, also challenged Watt's decision in federal court. On July 27, 1981, Federal District Judge Mariana Pfaelzer blocked the oil leases, ruling that the Reagan administration had violated the Coastal Zone Management Act of 1972, which gave the authority to prohibit such drilling if it conflicted with the state's coastal management plan.[20]

Watt's five-year coastal oil and gas leasing program proposal was also challenged in July 1982 in the U.S. Court of Appeals by the states of Alaska and California and seven environmental organizations. In October, the court ruled in favor of the plaintiffs, ordering the Interior Department "to give greater weight to 'environmental and social costs' in carrying out its offshore leasing program."[21] Watt announced another plan in July 1982 to develop almost a billion acres on both coasts. When twenty-eight members of Congress wrote to complain, the secretary responded that "it is much easier to explain to the American people why we have oil rigs off our coast than it would be to explain to the mothers and fathers of this land why their sons are fighting on the sands of the Middle East as might be required if the policies of our critics were to be pursued."[22]

Environmental organizations quickly made political hay from such controversies. The Sierra Club, for example, used a "remove James Watt" theme for its 1982 membership drive. As executive director Michael McCloskey stated in his membership invitation letter, "Unless you and I act immediately, we will surely see the destruction of lands needed for our national parks, the invasion of our irreplaceable wilderness lands, and the demise of habitat for our nation's wildlife." He described the club's successful "Dump Watt" campaign and announced a new, similar "Replace Watt" petition being circulated: "As soon as we have the signatures of 1,000,000 more friends—people like you—we will again take the REPLACE WATT petitions to Washington," he said. "Imagine the effect a total of *two million* signatures will have on the Congress, the press, and on President Reagan. Nothing of this magnitude has occurred in recent years in the conservation movement!"[23]

The resulting increased revenues enabled environmental organizations to build up their professional staffs to unprecedented levels. Ironically, the controversies raised by Reagan's appointees created a context in which environmental concerns gained a firmer footing as part of the public discourse in America.

Environmentalists were not the only group to find a silver lining in the controversial Watt. Within political circles, many Democrats came to regard the

Interior secretary as highly useful to their forthcoming election campaigns. As one journalist observed at the time, while Democrats were publicly calling for Watt's resignation, they privately "believe they have more political profit to make by having him remain in office."[24] An aide to House Speaker Thomas P. O'Neill, Jr., reportedly stated that "Watt is the best thing we have going for us."[25]

With the upcoming 1984 presidential election influencing political considerations within the Reagan administration, Watt began to be seen as a potential political liability. Nationwide polls indicated that Watt was widely considered to be too extreme and would harm the president's chances at reelection, even though he continued to enjoy strong support from conservative Republicans and many westerners.

When Watt resigned from office on October 9, 1983, the editors of the *New York Times* suggested that it was Watt's "indiscretions, not his—or Mr. Reagan's—policies, that did him in."[26] Rafe Pomerance, president of Friends of the Earth, told reporters that "the most positive thing that happened under Watt was the reaction to the Reagan Administration's assault on America's natural heritage."[27]

All eyes now turned to Reagan, watching to see whom he would nominate for Watt's replacement. Would he select someone to carry forth the changes initiated by his first Interior secretary? Reagan surprised nearly everyone by selecting his national security adviser, William P. Clark. Clark was a longtime confidant of Reagan, having served as his gubernatorial troubleshooter in California. He was someone the president thought he could trust to straighten out the controversies at Interior, while keeping the agency's basic policy orientation in line with the administration's.

Just as Clark had had little foreign policy experience prior to being named national security adviser, he had little background on environmental and natural resources issues. Representatives of various environmental organizations were quick to pick up on this, and they rained criticism on Reagan for his choice. Environmental Policy Institute president Louise Dunlap told reporters, "It is most significant that Judge Clark has been assigned to the most controversial issues. This appointment shows the White House understands they are in deep political trouble over the environmental issue." Wilderness Society executive vice president William Turnage called the appointment "a tragedy," adding that "the President clearly doesn't care about the environment and has delivered another insult to the environment." Even House Republican Leader Robert H. Michel of Illinois called Clark's nomination "incredible and baffling."[28] The *New York Times* editorialized about Clark's lack of qualifications but concluded that he was likely to "take less extreme positions on fundamental questions like how fast to exploit oil and coal resources on public lands. The Administration may recognize such moderation as the best politics of all."[29]

THE ENVIRONMENTAL PROTECTION AGENCY

The other locus of controversy was a newer organization, the Environmental Protection Agency, established in 1970. At Interior, the Reagan administration sought to open up federally owned natural resources to private sector development. With regard to environmental policy, the goal was to diminish regulatory programs and to transfer federal responsibilities to the states. The agenda for the EPA carried a lower priority for the administration, and this was reflected in the slower pace of making appointments to the agency. It was also reflected in the appointment of ideologically aligned appointees with little relevant professional experience, people disinclined toward strict enforcement of the EPA's regulations.

Reagan's top two EPA appointments, for example, had neither Washington experience nor deep knowledge of the scientific, regulatory, or political aspects peculiar to environmental policy. Anne M. Gorsuch, who became EPA administrator, was a Colorado-based attorney whose environmental experience came primarily from her activities as a conservative member of the Colorado state legislature. John Hernandez, who was a New Mexico engineering school dean with minimal managerial and government track record, was appointed deputy director. Because Gorsuch and Hernandez did not assume office until the spring, the EPA was left to drift without new leadership for the first three months of Reagan's presidency, at precisely the time the new administration was setting the course for its environmental policy. Reagan's other appointments to the EPA did little to raise public confidence; most had worked for or represented large corporations or had little knowledge and experience directly related to their areas of oversight within the agency.[30]

The Reagan administration's guiding political philosophy, which decried excessive government regulation, clashed with the values expressed in the federal statutes underpinning the EPA and ran counter to the belief systems permeating the agency's professional staff. The agency's new political leadership—which demonstrated laxity in their desire for strict enforcement of the agency's regulations, an open affinity toward corporations seeking reduced government oversight, and complicity in dealing with Office of Management and Budget officials working to slash the EPA's budget—seriously damaged morale within the agency. In April 1982, one journalist recounted the Washington truism that "the best way to neutralize an operation with high visibility and public appeal, such as EPA, is not to kill it outright—that is politically unwise—but to appoint hostile, uninspired, or incompetent managers and then let nature take its course."[31]

No issue brought greater trouble to the EPA during the Reagan years than the agency's toxic waste cleanup program. The Comprehensive Environmental Response, Compensation, and Liability Act of 1980, which had created the Superfund program, had been signed into law shortly before the end of the Carter presidency. Superfund—which was a program designed to locate, investigate, and clean up the nation's worst hazardous waste sites, using funds obtained from the polluting industries—was considered one of Carter's crowning environmental accomplishments.[32] The program's implementation, however, took place under Reagan. Beginning in the fall of 1982, the EPA found itself embroiled in a prolonged and highly visible controversy surrounding the management of toxic wastes.

In October 1982, the chairman of the House Energy and Commerce Committee's Investigations Subcommittee, Representative John D. Dingell, issued a subpoena to the EPA for documents to assist the subcommittee's investigations of alleged cover-ups of sweetheart deals with corporate toxic polluters and lax enforcement of its toxic waste cleanup program. The subcommittee believed that these actions demonstrated a pro-business bias, as well as a deliberate skirting of the law. In November, the House Public Works Committee's Investigations and Oversight Subcommittee also served Gorsuch a subpoena requesting documents on the toxic waste cleanup program—again, to assist its investigations of alleged EPA mishandling of the toxic waste cleanup funds.

Reagan instructed Gorsuch to refuse to provide the requested documents, invoking executive privilege and claiming that his administration had classified these documents as "enforcement sensitive." On December 16, 1982, the House of Representatives voted 259 to 105 to cite Gorsuch in contempt for failing to deliver subpoenaed documents.[33] This vote set an important precedent. Until then, no cabinet-level official had ever been held in contempt of Congress. It also placed the Congress in direct and public confrontation with the White House. Soon, there were six concurrent House committee and subcommittee investigations of the EPA's management of toxic wastes.

These hearings provided a visible forum for agency critics and added to the negative news coverage accompanying the discovery, in late 1982, of high levels of dioxin in Times Beach, Missouri. Dioxin, a chemical by-product from certain herbicide and germicide production, had been connected to kidney, spleen, liver, and bladder diseases in laboratory animals. Concern that it might also be highly toxic to humans was heightened by its presence in the herbicide Agent Orange, which was being linked to health problems of some Vietnam War veterans.[34]

The dioxin at Times Beach was traced to a now-defunct chemical plant elsewhere in Missouri, which had produced dioxin as one of its waste products. Sludge from the plant had been recycled with waste oil in a mixture that was sprayed on unpaved roads to control dust, including on the dirt roads of Times Beach.[35] When the nearby Meramec River flooded in December 1982, the Centers for Disease Control found alarmingly high levels of dioxin along the town's roadsides and beneath its streets and issued a health advisory. The state of Missouri advised residents not to return to their flood-damaged homes until after the contamination was cleaned. Memories of the chemical ground contamination at Love Canal in New York were still fresh. Critics questioned the EPA's management of its toxic waste program, eventually pressuring the agency into a federal buyout of Times Beach properties and voluntary relocation of residents.[36]

Controversies like this dogged Gorsuch throughout her relatively brief tenure, and she submitted her resignation to the president on March 9, 1983. In her formal letter of resignation, she claimed that her departure was "essential to termination of the controversy and confusion generated over Congressional access to certain EPA documentary materials,"[37] and it was clear that the White House wanted to slow congressional opposition to its policies. When announcing the administrator's resignation, Reagan added that he would be releasing all the documents subpoenaed by the House of Representatives. What the president did not say was that the White House had reached an agreement with the Investigations Subcommittee whereby those files involving ongoing EPA enforcement litigation would not be made public unless a majority of the subcommittee voted to release them. Moreover, upon such a vote, the subcommittee was to hear further argument from the EPA before issuing any final decision to make them public—a decision that would rest fully with the subcommittee.[38] In explaining the sustained criticism of his administration, Reagan quipped to reporters, "I sometimes suspect that the lobbyists for the environmental interests feel that they have to keep their constituents stirred up or they might not have jobs anymore." Asked about his views of these critics, Reagan replied: "Well, there is environmental extremism. I don't think they'll be happy until the White House looks like a bird's nest."[39]

The White House clearly viewed Gorsuch's departure as an opportunity for the administration to combat the political problems swirling around its environmental record, to move beyond the president's denouncement of his critics as extremists, and to strike a more conciliatory note by appointing an EPA administrator with an established record in environmental protection. Reagan's selection for the new EPA head, William D. Ruckelshaus, thus represented a striking departure from the earlier appointments. Ruckelshaus, a moderate Republican, had led the agency at its creation in 1970. Reagan assured the nation that "Bill Ruckelshaus will have direct access to me on all important matters affecting the environment. I've also authorized him to conduct an agency-wide review of the personnel and resources to insure that the EPA has the means it needs to perform its vital function." Reagan noted that, as governor of California, he had worked with then EPA administrator Ruckelshaus, whom he had found to be competent, tough, and fair. "Now, I'm proud of my environmental record as Governor of California, and I deeply believe that this administration has done a good job over the past 2 years," he added. "But I also believe that we can do better, and that after the dust settles and the country sees Bill Ruckelshaus at work in the EPA, our people will recognize that this administration's commitment to a clean environment is solid and unshakeable."[40]

Watt, who by virtue of his chairmanship of the Cabinet Council on Natural Resources and Environment was the White House's point person on such matters, told reporters that Ruckelshaus would enjoy a higher status within the White House than his predecessor, including treatment as a cabinet-level officer, extended access to the president, greater freedom of action, and permission to appoint his own senior staff at the EPA (a privilege Watt said had been denied Gorsuch). Watt stressed that the controversy that had raged at the EPA over the past three months had sensitized the Reagan administration to the need to restore public confidence in the EPA, as well as in the administration's overall environmental and natural resources policies. Watt insisted, however, that the administration did not intend to change the trajectory of its overarching policies, especially as they impacted at the Department of the Interior (although Watt himself would be forced to resign within six months).[41]

By the time Ruckelshaus was sworn into office in May 1983, the controversy over Times Beach and the EPA's toxic waste cleanup program had subsided. The next storm of protest surrounded acid rain, a highly contested matter associated with the upcoming renewal of the Clean Air Act. The media found the wrangling over acid rain made to order, because the debate pitted midwestern concerns against those of eastern states, in a way that proved divisive within both political parties. It also had international dimensions, as Canada began to protest environmental damage in its homeland that had been traced to airborne discharges from U.S. coal-fired power plants. Anticipating the need for the White House to navigate this political minefield, Reagan used Ruckelshaus's swearing-in ceremony to assign the new EPA administrator the task of conducting a thorough review of the acid rain debate.[42]

Ruckelshaus formed his own task force to determine and summarize what scientists currently knew about the causes and effects of acid rain and to develop a set of policy options for reducing the output of precursor emissions (such as switching fuels at power plants, coal washing, and abatement technologies). This group met with leading researchers and periodically briefed the White House Office of Policy Development, which maintained that too little was known about acid rain to justify increased federal restrictions on sulphur and nitrogen emissions and that the best course of action in the short term was therefore to increase federal research expenditures. Martin Smith of the Office of Policy Development acknowledged his colleagues' philosophical aversion to increasing sulphur and nitrogen control programs because of the economic burden it might place on certain economic sectors, but he warned that "it should be noted that the absence of any additional control program to date has been controversial and has resulted in negative publicity for the Administration."[43]

The White House recognized that acid rain stood as an intractable and highly controversial environmental policy concern. If Ruckelshaus did too little—or was perceived to be restricted in what he was allowed to do—criticism of the administration would probably worsen.[44] The situation was exacerbated by the Democratic presidential candidates, most of whom were adopting strong stands on countering the threat of acid rain, and by the Canadians, who continued to press the White House for greater action. Both factors kept the administration's waffling on the acid rain question in the news, further fueling the ongoing criticism of Reagan's commitment to environmental protection.[45]

Despite these external pressures, the high priority that Ruckelshaus and his staff placed upon addressing acid rain, and the months of debate within the White House, the administration sided with industry. In early 1984, Reagan called for additional funds for research into the causes and effects of acid rain and ways to control it, but failed to propose any program to curb the pollutants associated with it. Ruckelshaus had favored a mandatory control program aimed at coal-burning electric generating plants, so Reagan's decision came as a strategic defeat for the EPA administrator.[46]

THE 1984 PRESIDENTIAL CAMPAIGN

The most public of Reagan's attacks on environmental protection came during the first two and a half years of his presidency. As the controversies surrounding the EPA and the Department of the Interior worsened and as the criticism from environmental organizations grew more strident, Reagan and his advisers began to worry about the potential impact on his bid for reelection.[47]

The leaders of the nation's major environmental organizations were also cognizant that these issues had risen in priority for the campaign. One irony of the Reagan administration was the unparalleled boon it provided to the nation's environmental and conservation organizations, revitalizing their missions and increasing their memberships and financial contributions. Philip Shabecoff of the *New York Times* called it a potential "watershed for environmentalism in the United States." Drawing from his experience as a seasoned environmental journalist, Shabecoff argued that "for the first time, the environment as an issue emerged, if only temporarily, as a dominant feature on the nation's political landscape. It was an issue that captured and held the public's attention for weeks and preoccupied the Government at its highest levels."[48]

The enhanced political sensitivities associated with the growing anticipation and preparation for the president's reelection campaign made the pinch of environmental criticism all the more acute, especially as the administration's detractors gained greater purchase within Congress and the news media.[49] Things became so heated—with the EPA administrator and twenty other senior politically appointed officials at the agency resigning in the spring, and Interior Secretary Watt continuing to attract nearly constant media scrutiny—that the environment remained a front-page story throughout most of 1983.

In March 1983, Andy Pasztor of the *Wall Street Journal* reported that "the White House is trying to project a new image as a tougher foe of polluters, hoping to limit the political fallout enveloping the Environmental Protection Agency."[50] The shift in Reagan's stance on natural resources and environmental policy was not so much a reconsideration or reorientation of the administration's basic priorities, but an acknowledgment of practical political realities. Some modest compromises and a softening of Reagan's image—made clear by a variety of deliberate messages relayed by the news media—seemed the least that was necessary if the White House was to repair its relations with Congress and deny Reagan's Democratic opponents a potentially explosive campaign issue.

On June 11, 1983, Reagan devoted his weekly five-minute radio address to a defense of his administration's environmental policy. Claiming that his environmental record had been distorted by critics, he said America was growing "more healthy and more beautiful each year." He said he favored "a sound, strong environmental policy that protects the health of our people and a wise stewardship of our nation's natural resources."[51] Rather than helping to quiet the discord surrounding his administration's policies, Reagan's radio address merely stirred the coals of controversy, providing an opportunity for his environmental critics to get their views restated in the media, as they countered his claims with harsh assessments of his record on wilderness issues, national parks, natural resources development, and air and water quality.[52]

Perhaps because he was confident that voters who placed the environment at the top of their list of political concerns would cast their support to him, Walter Mondale did not ride that issue hard in the 1984 campaign. During his televised debate with Reagan on October 7, for example, Mondale totally eschewed the opportunity to criticize the president's record on natural resources and the environment, choosing instead to question Reagan's political and economic sensibilities.[53] Mondale was correct in his assumption, as three out of four voters claiming the environment was a key concern for them voted for Mondale. The problem was that these voters represented only 4 percent of those who went to the polls.[54] Americans cared about the environment, but other matters eclipsed those concerns in the election, in part because the administration had successfully cooled the controversy that had raged under Gorsuch and Watt in 1983.

The Office of Management and Budget's (OMB) mid-December 1984 review of the EPA's fiscal year 1986 budget request must certainly have troubled Ruckelshaus. With the election over and another four years to carry out its agenda, the White House now appeared far less worried about appeasing environmental interests. Among the OMB's cost-saving proposals was consolidation of the agency's ten regional offices into seven and the agency's thirty-one laboratories into seven regional ones. The OMB asked Congress to freeze the interagency acid rain research program at its current level of $63 million and ignored Ruckelshaus's request for $224 million for EPA's research and development program, trimming that amount by 31 percent.[55]

WATER RESOURCES, ENVIRONMENTAL GOALS, AND THE REAGAN APPROACH

After the stormy early years, the Reagan administration attempted in various ways to assuage the environmental movement. The March 1985 appointment of William Penn Mott, Jr., to be director of the National Park Service, for example, appeared to signal a softening on issues associated with national parks and recreation. Mott, who was a nationally acclaimed parks administrator and the former director of the California Department of Parks and Recreation under Governor Reagan, came to Washington brimming with ideas of how to revitalize the Park Service. Although he succeeded in raising hopes among park enthusiasts, Mott found his bolder reforms tightly limited throughout his term by his superiors within the Department of the Interior.[56]

Reagan's conservative fiscal policy was one area that often brought him in harmony with the environmental community, although they reached their common ground via very different paths. Environmentalists, for example, typically oppose new water resources development projects because of the harm they inflict upon rivers and wetlands, while the Reagan administration's advocacy of higher user fees—which were intended to force the beneficiaries of federal projects to pay a larger share of the costs—effectively slowed down such development and accomplished the same goal. Water policy reform had ranked high among President Carter's environmental objectives.[57] The Reagan administration also desired such reform, but with the intention of reducing waste, promoting only economically justifiable projects, and increasing the amounts the projects' beneficiaries pay for construction and maintenance, rather than for any ecological, aesthetic, or recreational reasons.

Deliberations into how the administration would oversee federal water projects began at the initial meeting of the Cabinet Council on Natural Resources and Environment in March 1981. A special water policy task force was created, its members eventually concluding that the technical and policy reviews of water projects by the Water Resources Council were too diffuse and that its function should be returned to the OMB, which offered greater leverage in enforcing compliance to common standards. To enact this change, Reagan issued an executive order repealing President Carter's executive order of January 1979.[58]

The Reagan administration's water policy appeared more paradoxical than that for any other natural resource. Environmental groups generally cheered the advocacy of state and local cost sharing for new navigation and irrigation projects. However, the White House did not extend this philosophy to projects already under way, no matter how large the federal percentage of sponsorship and no matter what the project's benefit-cost ratio. The administration's support for these works helped it avoid the type of negative reaction drawn by Carter when he had inaugurated his "water projects hit list" while still holding out for future reforms.

Despite the expectations of many western politicians that Reagan would be a strong advocate for restoring federal support of water projects, the president was also slow to approve new construction starts. In June 1983, Assistant Secretary of the Army for Civil Works William R. Gianelli testified before the Water Resources Subcommittee of the Senate Committee on the Environment and Public Works, stating that the administration was considering requiring the states and local interests to contribute 35 percent of the cost of all new federal water projects built by the Army Corps of Engineers and the Bureau of Reclamation. His comments spurred western politicians to lobby James Watt. On June 17, 1983, Watt responded with a letter to the subcommittee's chair, Senator James Abdnor, in which he said cost sharing would not be determined by a fixed formula but on a case-by-case basis, according to ability to pay. He also assured the chairman that any formal cost-sharing provisions would have to win congressional approval.[59]

The White House tended to look favorably upon new water projects proposed by the Bureau of Reclamation for the western states, where Reagan had received such strong political support. Outside the West, however, Reagan proved himself far more sympathetic to Carter's earlier approach, insisting upon high user fees and increased cost sharing by local and state governments. Most of these flood control, navigation, and conservation projects were administered by the Corps of Engineers and the Department of Agriculture's Soil Conservation Service.[60]

The Coastal Barrier Resources Act of 1982, for example, attempted to limit development of the nation's barrier islands located off the Atlantic and Gulf of Mexico coasts. The law did this by prohibiting most new federal expenditures and financial assistance for development on these islands and their associated aquatic habitat. In this respect, by curtailing federal subsidies for the development of coastal barriers, the White House sought to link its fiscal policy with its natural resources policy. Environmentalists could applaud this approach, as it promised to slow the development of these ecologically important resources, even though they preferred more aggressive government prohibitions on development rather than a reliance on market mechanisms. Nevertheless, this was one area where the administration offered a viable alternative in the area of environmental policy.[61]

The Reagan administration's management of wetlands—those landscapes (such as swamps, marshes, and bogs) that share characteristics of both aquatic and terrestrial habitats—was another area of environmental policy where it achieved mixed results. Prior to the passage of the Federal Water Pollution Control Act amendments of 1972, which initiated an Army Corps of Engineers permit program under its section 404, the federal government's policies with regard to wetlands had typically involved programs to assist with their filling and draining, not their preservation. That responsibility had been left to the states and to individual landowners. Such an approach had proved ineffective, however, in stemming the nationwide loss of resources now acknowledged to play essential roles in fish and wildlife habitat, water quality enhancement, recreation, moderation of floods and droughts, and buffering the effects of storms and tides. By the 1970s, the area encompassed by the forty-eight contiguous states had lost approximately half of its wetland resources since European settlement and was continuing to lose these dwindling resources at a significant clip, often to multiple small infillings.[62]

The corps's 404 permits, however, proved controversial. Many landowners and developers resented the requirement to obtain federal permission to alter their properties. As the nation's largest engineering organization and its oldest developmentally oriented agency, the corps resisted expanding its new authority beyond traditional navigable watercourses, but environmental values were shifting public opinion, and the federal courts increasingly ruled in favor of government regulation.[63]

This approach to wetlands management ran counter to the basic philosophy of the Reagan administration, which instinctively preferred to return to pre-1972 conditions of a smaller federal role and greater reliance upon the state and market forces. Wetlands policy, however, which affected hunters as well as hikers, represented an area of bipartisan environmental concern, one that ran both broad and deep.

When the Presidential Task Force on Regulatory Relief addressed the corps's 404 permit program, it considered such political issues carefully. From the regulatory perspective alone, section 404 seemed ripe for change. As the task force announced in an August 12, 1981, press release, the 404 program "involves the issuance of permits for the discharge of dredged and fill materials into U.S. waters. Current problems include the time required to obtain a permit, overlapping interagency responsibilities, and a lack of specificity in program objectives. For example, the processing of controversial permit applications averages 271 days."[64] And yet, other voices counseled for moderation.

In dealing with the corps's regulatory program, the Reagan administration again opted not to follow a legislative approach, working instead more quietly and (to the extent it was able) stealthily by using administrative tools. Secretary of the Interior Watt was expert in this approach, yet there were some areas where he longed to pursue a more resilient legislative course. And wetlands proved such an area. As chairman of the Cabinet Council on Natural Resources and Environment, Watt was engaged with policy development and guidance on this issue across the board, including the regulatory program of the Corps of Engineers. Within the Department of the Interior, however, Watt found the question of wetlands loss and protection of special interest because of the responsibilities of the department's Fish and Wildlife Service. Determined to shift the government's approach in this area, Watt appointed a private sector advisory group, which he titled Protect Our Wetlands and Duck Resources (POWDR). The advisers were asked to develop a wetlands protection program that would function without federal subsidies.[65]

Together with Watt's Department of the Interior staff, the POWDR advisory task force worked on the initiative for eight months, while Watt himself labored on behalf of the bill within the White House. By March 1983, Watt had revised the proposed legislation to the point where Reagan and his top advisers were willing to sign off on it. The POWDR system called for wetland parcels of five acres or more to be managed for their fish, wildlife, and water purification benefits. Within this system, the federal government would be precluded from expending any funds for purposes other than enhancing these benefits (for example, federal funds could not be used to subsidize the filling and draining of critical wetlands, with certain exceptions relating to national defense, maintenance of existing public roads and facilities, and certain energy activities). Key to this system was its voluntary nature: landowners could elect to include their wetlands in the system, but if they did not, they were not forbidden to develop their property (although they would not receive any federal assistance for so doing). The proposed act would also extend the Wetlands Loan Act for ten years, would amend the Land and Water Conservation Act to fund grants to states for wetlands conservation, and would provide the Migratory Bird Conservation Fund with additional revenues by allowing the secretary of the Interior to require a permit (either a federal duck stamp, which was required of hunters, or a single-visit permit) for entrance into a select number of National Wildlife Refuge System units, by doubling the price of federal duck stamps, and by allocating duties on imported guns and ammunition to the fund.[66] The signing ceremony associated with Reagan's transmittal of the bill to Congress—where Senator John Chafee and Representative Edwin Forsythe had agreed to introduce the bill—was said by White House staffer Craig to provide "an opportunity for the President to receive *positive* identification and visibility in the area of environmental policy."[67]

Critics declared that Watt's proposal was far less dramatic than he claimed and in fact would do little to address the most significant causes of wetlands destruction: conversion of wetlands for farming and the destruction of wetlands by water resource development projects and federal highway construction. The bill also exempted wetlands damaged by oil and gas exploration and left out a whole category of wetlands that were of profound importance to migratory waterfowl, the prairie potholes of the upper Midwest.[68]

The administration's wetlands bill failed to attract the necessary support in Congress, in part because of the opposition voiced by the major environmental organizations. During the next Congress, Chafee championed an alternative wetlands proposal that received the strong backing of the environmental and conservation communities, as well as bipartisan congressional support. Chafee's bill—the Emergency Wetlands Resources Act—incorporated some of the recommendations of the White House, such as instituting entrance fees at select national wildlife refuges. However, it broke with the administration in a number of its provisions, such as abandoning the White House's desire to earmark the import duties on arms and ammunition toward the operation and mainte-nance of the National Wildlife Refuge System and allocated only 30 percent (rather than the 100 percent advocated by Reagan's staff) of the entrance fees toward the same cause. In an action meant to increase cooperation among local, state, and federal governments in wetlands conservation, the bill required the states to include wetlands in their comprehensive outdoor recreation plans, which the National Park Service administered.[69] These differences proved tolerable to Reagan's cabinet officers, who recommended the president's approval of the legislation.[70] Reagan concurred with his advisers' recommendations and signed the Emergency Wetlands Resources Act into law on November 10, 1986.

CONCLUSION

Environmental and natural resources policy did not stand alone as a major policy objective of the Reagan administration—it was essentially embedded in and shaped by larger policy concerns. Perhaps because of this circumstance and despite high hopes to redirect federal programs, Reagan failed to achieve fun-damental reforms in this area.[71]

Much of the lack of long-term change can be attributed to the adminis-tration's decision to follow an administrative rather than legislative tack, but several other factors played a role. One was the administration's failure to com-prehend the depth of public concern for environmental quality and amenities. Among the reasons that environmental policy has remained a visible part of American politics, according to R. Shep Melnick, is that "the public now ex-pects the federal government to protect it from a wide variety of hazards."[72] Thus, while Reagan's push to limit the size of the federal government had broad ap-peal, Americans also now regarded the protection of human health from envi-ronmental hazards as an important federal function.

Another major factor limiting Reagan's influence was the successful media and public relations efforts of environmental organizations, which made reinforce-ment of Americans' concern for the environment a keystone of their activities. By providing contradictory interpretations of the administration's actions and supplying colorful quotations and protests, they helped to keep the issue on the front page. The media attention, in turn, helped create a climate of opinion that constrained Reagan's reforms, primarily by triggering and sustaining active con-gressional resistance to White House policies and encouraging career bureaucrats to resist the radical reorientation of their agencies. Taken together, the public and Congress proved highly effective in moderating the administration's influence. Reagan's attempt to maneuver around existing environmental laws and soften the enforcement of the protection measures put in place during the 1960s and 1970s was thus ultimately thwarted by deep-seated public support for such protection and by subsequent administrations with different priorities.

Asking how the Reagan administration justified "such a radical departure from the bipartisan consensus that had characterized environmental policies throughout the 1970s," political scientist Michael E. Kraft concluded that "the president and his aides cited the 1980 election results: the new agenda's legitimacy was based to a considerable extent on the presumed mandate that Reagan had received with his landslide victory." Kraft noted that Reagan and his advisers "seriously misjudged the public's commitment to environmental policy." He then paraphrased William Ruckelshaus's acknowledgment made after his installment as EPA administrator in 1983: "It had confused, he said, the public's wish to improve the way environmental and public health programs were administered with a desire to change the goals of the programs themselves. When it attempted to change some of those goals through deregulation, this caused the 'perception' that the administration was hostile to environmental programs."[73] It was only in 1983, after the mounting controversies with the EPA, that the administration softened its approach. This kinder and gentler attitude toward environmental matters lasted through the 1984 presidential election, but then slackened.

In many ways, Reagan managed to politicize and polarize environmental policy to an extent unseen at the national level since environmental legislation became a major area of concern under President Nixon. The Reagan administration also helped to reenergize the environmental movement, giving it an enemy against which the major groups could rally their troops, thereby greatly expanding their membership and financial base and allowing them to become far more politically and legally active.

Although the Reagan administration failed to transform the nation's environmental and natural resources policy, it did contribute to a political climate more receptive to market-oriented approaches to such issues, including expanded use of environmental mediation, conservation easements, and public-private sector partnerships. The Reagan administration also contributed to a short-term trend toward centrist environmental positions in national politics, as demonstrated in the 1982 midterm elections, when the political saliency of environmental policy rose. This trend continued during Reagan's second term in office, when moderate Republicans gained stronger voices and no doubt contributed to the position embraced by Vice President George H. W. Bush in the 1988 presidential campaign, when he declared that he wanted to become the nation's "environmental president."[74]

NOTES

1. For general discussions of the bipartisan nature of environmental policy, see Dennis L. Soden, ed., *The Environmental Presidency* (Albany: State University of New York Press, 1999).

2. Paul R. Portney, introduction to *Natural Resources and the Environment: The Reagan Approach,* ed. Paul R. Portney (Washington, D.C.: Urban Institute Press, 1984), 10. See

also Robert F. Durant, *The Administrative Presidency Revisited: Public Lands, the BLM, and the Reagan Revolution* (Albany: State University of New York Press, 1992).

3. See Lou Cannon, *President Reagan: The Role of a Lifetime* (New York: Simon & Schuster, 1991), 526–30.

4. For a brief assessment of Governor Reagan's environmental record, see Daniel J. Balz, *Ronald Reagan: A Trusty Script* (Washington, D.C.: Capitol Hill News Service, 1976), 2, 7–8; Lou Cannon, *Reagan* (New York: Putnam, 1982), 350–54; and Cannon, *Role of a Lifetime,* 530. For a sampling of the environmental concerns in California, see Ed Salzman, ed., *California Environment and Energy: Text and Readings on Contemporary Issues* (Sacramento: California Journal Press, 1980); Carolyn Merchant, ed., *Green Versus Gold: Sources in California's Environmental History* (Washington, D.C.: Island Press, 1998); and Samuel P. Hays, *Beauty, Health, and Permanence: Environmental Politics in the United States, 1955–1985* (New York: Cambridge University Press, 1987).

5. For President Nixon's stance on environmental and natural resources policy, see J. Brooks Flippen, *Nixon and the Environment* (Albuquerque: University of New Mexico Press, 2000).

6. Cannon, *President Reagan,* 530. For examples of Reagan's thinking on matters relating to natural resources and the environment during the 1970s, see Kiron K. Skinner, Annelise Anderson, and Martin Anderson, eds., *Reagan, In His Own Hand* (New York: Free Press, 2001), 307–8, 313–16, 318–41.

7. See John D. Leshy, "Natural Resource Policy," in Portney, *Natural Resources and the Environment,* 13.

8. See Michael E. Kraft, "A New Environmental Policy Agenda: The 1980 Presidential Campaign and Its Aftermath," in *Environmental Policy in the 1980s: Reagan's New Agenda,* ed. Norman J. Vig and Michael E. Kraft (Washington, D.C.: Congressional Quarterly, 1984), 44; Constance Holden, "The Reagan Years: Environmentalists Tremble," *Science* 210 (November 28, 1980): 988–89; and Raymond Tatalovich and Mark J. Wattier, "Opinion Leadership: Elections, Campaigns, Agenda Setting, and Environmentalism," in Soden, *Environmental Presidency,* 156–57.

9. For the question of mandates in presidential elections, including how Reagan reacted to his victories in 1980 and 1984, see Patricia Heidotting Conley, *Presidential Mandates: How Elections Shape the National Agenda* (Chicago: University of Chicago Press, 2001); and Kraft, "A New Environmental Policy Agenda."

10. Lewis Regenstein quoted in Holden, "The Reagan Years," 988.

11. For an early assessment of this trend, see Constance Holden, "Public's Fear of Watt Is Environmentalists' Gain," *Science* 212 (April 24, 1981): 422.

12. For a highly sympathetic biography, see Ron Arnold, *At the Eye of the Storm: James Watt and the Environmentalists* (Chicago: Regnery Gateway, 1982). For a hypercritical view of the Interior Department under Watt, see Jonathan Lash, Katherine Gillman, and David Sheridan, *A Season of Spoils: The Reagan Administration's Attack on the Environment* (New York: Pantheon Books, 1984), 215–97.

13. For comments on Watt's administrative approach, see Arnold, *At the Eye of the Storm,* 137.

14. Philip Shabecoff, "Nearing Complete Renovation of Interior Department Rules," *New York Times,* January 23, 1983. For more on Watt's "centralized planning" criticism, see "Watt Says Foes Want Centralization of Power," *New York Times,* January 21, 1983.

15. For a summary of Reagan's use of cabinet councils, see James P. Pfiffner, *The Strategic Presidency: Hitting the Ground Running* (Chicago: Dorsey Press, 1988), 58–64.

16. See Marc K. Landy, Marc J. Roberts, and Stephen R. Thomas, *The Environmental Protection Agency: Asking the Wrong Questions* (New York: Oxford University Press, 1990), 248.

17. See Lance Gay, "U.S. Parks Director Calls System Too Big," *Washington Star,* February 1, 1981.

18. NWF president Jay Hair quoted in Philip Shabecoff, "Wildlife Unit Asks Watt's Ouster," *New York Times,* July 15, 1981.

19. See letter, Don H. Clausen et al. to Ronald Reagan, March 18, 1981, NR006 (019001–030000) folder, box 22, WHORM subject file NR, Ronald Reagan Library (RRL).

20. See memorandum, Douglas D. Anderson to Secretary [Donald Regan], April 19, 1982, folder 1, box 128, Donald T. Regan Papers, Manuscript Division, Library of Congress (Regan Papers); minutes, Cabinet Council on Natural Resources and Environment, April 29, 1982, same folder; letter, Dianne Feinstein to Reagan, May 6, 1982, NR006–01 Naval Petroleum Reserves (018955–080000) folder, box 30, WHORM subject file NR, RRL; and Robert Lindsey, "U.S. Oil Lease Sale in Coast's Waters Blocked in Court," *New York Times,* July 28, 1981.

21. "Watt Is Slowed on Oil Leasing," *New York Times,* October 11, 1982.

22. Watt quoted in "Watt Unleashes Oil Explorers, to Some Dismay," *New York Times,* July 25, 1982. For an extended critique of Watt's plan, see Deni Greene's editorial, "To the Beaches! Oil Rigs Are Coming!" *New York Times,* July 19, 1982.

23. Form letter, Michael McCloskey to Dear Friend, n.d. (probably early 1982), Reagan Anti-Environmental Program: Miscellaneous Articles and Materials/box 1 folder, box 99, William Hoppen Papers, Manuscript Division, Library of Congress.

24. Philip Shabecoff, "Questions Arise Not Just over Watt's Words," *New York Times,* October 2, 1983.

25. Quoted in Shabecoff, "Questions Arise."

26. "What James Watt Said—and Did," *New York Times,* October 11, 1983.

27. Quoted in Philip Shabecoff, "Many Are Divided on Watt's Legacy," *New York Times,* October 12, 1983.

28. Dunlap, Turnage, and Michel quoted in Philip Shabecoff, "Environmental Groups Angered by Reagan Choice for Interior Job," *New York Times,* October 14, 1983. Clark's environmental critics did not mention his earlier role—as Governor Reagan's chief of staff—in supporting Norman (Ike) Livermore as director of resources. A Sierra Club member and avid outdoorsman, Livermore proved to be an effective pro-environmental force in Sacramento. See Lou Cannon, *Ronald Reagan: The Presidential Portfolio* (New York: Public Affairs, 2001), 63–64.

29. "To Interior, a One-Way Secretary," *New York Times,* October 15, 1983. See also John B. Oakes, "Clark's Low Wattage," *New York Times,* October 18, 1983.

30. See Robert W. Crandall and Paul R. Portney, "Environmental Policy," in Portney, *Natural Resources and the Environment,* 62; Landy, Roberts, and Thomas, *The Environmental Protection Agency,* 247; Joel A. Mintz, *Enforcement at the EPA: High Stakes and Hard Choices* (Austin: University of Texas Press, 1995), 40–59; and Richard N. L. Andrews, *Managing the Environment, Managing Ourselves: A History of American Environmental Policy* (New Haven, Conn.: Yale University Press, 1999), 257–61.

31. Steven J. Marcus, "Reagan's EPA: The New Fuddyduddyism," *Technology Review* 85 (April 1982): 11.

32. See Jeffrey K. Stine, "Environmental Policy during the Carter Presidency," in *The Carter Presidency: Policy Choices in the Post–New Deal Era,* ed. Gary M Fink and Hugh Davis Graham (Lawrence: University Press of Kansas, 1998), 194.

33. Fifty-five Republicans voted against the administration, while four Democrats opposed the citation. See Philip Shabecoff, "House Charges Head of E.P.A. with Contempt," *New York Times,* December 17, 1982.

34. See Robert Reinhold, "Missouri Now Fears 100 Sites Could Be Tainted by Dioxin," *New York Times,* January 18, 1983.

35. See Robert Reinhold, "Missouri Dioxin Cleanup: A Decade of Little Action," *New York Times,* February 20, 1983.

36. For a summary of events compiled by the White House's Office of Policy Development staff, see memorandum, Martin L. Smith to Roger B. Porter, June 27, 1983, chronological June 1983 folder, OA 12160, Martin Smith Files, RRL (Smith Files).

37. Anne McGill Burford to Ronald Reagan, March 9, 1983, reprinted in "Texts of Mrs. Burford's Letter of Resignation and the President's Acceptance," *New York Times,* March 10, 1983. On February 20, 1983, Anne Gorsuch married Robert Burford and changed her name.

38. See Raymond Bonner, "Inquiries on E.P.A. in Congress Go On, Panels' Chiefs Say," *New York Times,* March 11, 1983.

39. "Remarks and a Question-and-Answer Session with Reporters on Domestic and Foreign Policy Issues," March 11, 1983, in *Public Papers of the Presidents of the United States, Ronald Reagan, 1983,* vol. 1 (Washington, D.C.: Government Printing Office, 1984), 389.

40. "Remarks and a Question-and-Answer Session with Reporters on the Nomination of William D. Ruckelshaus to Be Administrator of the Environmental Protection Agency," March 21, 1983, in ibid., 421.

41. Philip Shabecoff, "Watt Says Status of Ruckelshaus at E.P.A. Surpasses Predecessor's," *New York Times,* March 23, 1983.

42. For a detailed summary of the White House's treatment of the acid rain question, see memorandum, Martin L. Smith to Edwin L. Harper, June 10, 1983, chronological June 1983 folder, OA 12160, Smith Files. For earlier White House debates over the Clean Air Act reauthorization, see memorandum, Danny J. Boggs to Legislative Strategy Group, July 8, 1981, chronological July 1981 (2 of 2) folder, box 4126, Danny Boggs Files, RRL (Boggs Files).

43. Memorandum, Martin L. Smith to Edwin L. Harper, June 10, 1983, chronological June 1983 folder, OA 12160, Smith Files.

44. Memorandum, Martin L. Smith to Edwin L. Harper, June 8, 1983, chronological June 1983 folder, OA 12160, Smith Files.

45. See memorandum, William H. Megonnell to the (Edison Electric Institute's) Steering Committee of the Clean Air Act Issue Group, May 23, 1983, chronological June 1983 folder, OA 12160, Smith Files.

46. See Andy Pasztor, "Reagan to Request Added Funds to Probe Acid Rain but Won't Seek Pollution Curbs," *Wall Street Journal,* January 25, 1984; and U.S. Environmental Protection Agency, Office of Public Affairs, press release, February 1, 1984, Environmental Protection Agency (4 of 7) folder, OA 10198, Lee L. Verstandig Files, WHORM staff files, RRL.

47. See, for example, James Nathan Miller, "What Really Happened at EPA," *Reader's Digest* 123 (July 1983): 64.

48. Philip Shabecoff, "Politics and the E.P.A. Crisis: Environment Emerges as a Mainstream Issue," *New York Times,* April 29, 1983. See also Andy Pasztor, "Reagan Policies Spur Big Revival of the Environmental Movement," *Wall Street Journal,* August 9, 1982; and Philip Shabecoff, "Environmentalism Back in Spotlight as Activists and Administration Battle," *New York Times,* September 19, 1982.

49. For an indication of the White House's concern about the mounting negative press coverage of the administration's environmental record, see minutes, Cabinet Council on Natural Resources and Environment meeting, February 9, 1983, CCNRE February 9, 1983 folder, OA 12582, Randall E. Davis Files, RRL (Davis Files).

50. Andy Pasztor, "White House Acts to Change Image on Environment," *Wall Street Journal,* March 11, 1983.

51. "Radio Address to the Nation on Environmental and Natural Resources Management," June 11, 1983, in *Public Papers,* 1983, 1:852–53.

52. For the response of environmental leaders to Reagan's radio address, see Steven R. Weisman, "Reagan, Assailing Critics, Defends His Environmental Policy as 'Sound,'" *New York Times,* June 12, 1983.

53. See "Debate between the President and Former Vice President Walter F. Mondale in Louisville, Kentucky," October 7, 1984, in *Public Papers of the Presidents of the United States, Ronald Reagan, 1984,* vol. 2 (Washington, D.C.: Government Printing Office, 1987), 1450.

54. See Cannon, *President Reagan,* 526.

55. Memorandum, Martin L. Smith to John A. Svahn, December 12, 1984, chronological December 1984 folder, OA 12160, Smith Files.

56. See Michael Frome, *Regreening the National Parks* (Tucson: University of Arizona Press, 1992), 39, 44, 104; Peter Schrag, *Paradise Lost: California's Experience, America's Future* (New York: New Press, 1998), 49; and John C. Miles, *Guardians of the Parks: A History of the National Parks and Conservation Association* (Washington, D.C.: Taylor & Francis, 1995), 305–6. For efforts to undercut Mott's proposal to reintroduce wolves into Yellowstone National Park, see letter, Dick Cheney to Donald P. Hodel, August 20, 1987, NR002 Natural Resources: Fish, Wildlife (532601–536000) folder, box 10, WHORM subject file NR, RRL.

57. For an overview of Carter's environmental policy concerns and actions, see Stine, "Environmental Policy during the Carter Presidency," 179–201.

58. See memorandum, Danny Boggs to Kenneth Cribb, October 7, 1981, chronological October 1981 (3 of 4) folder, box 4126, Boggs Files.

59. See William E. Schmidt, "Cost Sharing for Water Projects in West Is Studied," *New York Times,* June 19, 1983.

60. See Leshy, "Natural Resource Policy."

61. For discussions of this approach within the White House, see memorandum, James G. Watt to the President, September 21, 1981, chronological October 1981 folder, box 4126, Boggs Files; and memorandum, William Clark to Cabinet Council on Natural Resources and Environment, n.d. (prepared for the July 9, 1984, meeting of the council), CCNRE July 9, 1984, folder, OA 12582, Davis Files.

62. See Ann Vileisis, *Discovering the Unknown Landscape: A History of America's*

Wetlands (Washington, D.C.: Island Press, 1997); and Jeffrey K. Stine, *America's Forested Wetlands* (Durham, N.C.: Forest History Society, forthcoming 2004).

63. See Jeffrey K. Stine, "Regulating Wetlands in the 1970s: U.S. Army Corps of Engineers and the Environmental Organizations," *Journal of Forest History* 27 (April 1983): 60–75.

64. "Existing Regulations to be Reviewed," part of a set of material released at Vice President Bush's press conference on August 12, 1981, attached to memorandum, Jim Miller to Members of the Presidential Task Force on Regulatory Relief, August 12, 1981, folder 2, box 165, Regan Papers.

65. Memorandum, Craig L. Fuller to Frederick J. Ryan, March 16, 1983, NR004 (073001-075000) folder, box 17, WHORM subject file NR, RRL.

66. See "Protect Our Wetlands and Duck Resources Act of 1983: Summary of Major Provisions," undated typescript, NR004 (072001-073000) folder, box 17, WHORM subject file NR, RRL; and "Watt Proposes Wetlands Bill," *New York Times,* March 27, 1983.

67. Memorandum, Craig L. Fuller to Frederick J. Ryan, March 16, 1983, NR004 (073001-075000) folder, box 17, WHORM subject file NR, RRL.

68. See Cass Peterson, "Sinkholes in Wetlands Bill," *Washington Post,* March 16, 1983; "Watt Proposes Wetlands Bill," *New York Times,* March 27, 1983; and Russell W. Peterson, "Watt's Wetlands Fraud," *Audubon* 85 (May 1983): 4.

69. See Margaret N. Strand, "Federal Wetlands Law: Part III," *Environmental Law Reporter* 23 (June 1993): 10363.

70. See memorandum, James C. Miller III to the President, November 5, 1986, NR002 (426501-427000) folder, box 10, WHORM subject file NR, RRL; and Strand, "Federal Wetlands Law," 10363.

71. For an assessment of Reagan's inability to modify significantly the structure of environmental regulation in the United States, see George Hoberg, *Pluralism by Design: Environmental Policy and the American Regulatory State* (New York: Praeger Publishers, 1992), 169–94; and Michael E. Kraft, "U.S. Environmental Policy and Politics: From the 1960s to the 1990s," *Journal of Policy History* 12, no. 1 (2000): 28–29.

72. R. Shep Melnick, "Risky Business: Government and the Environment after Earth Day," in *Taking Stock: American Government in the Twentieth Century,* ed. Morton Keller and R. Shep Melnick (New York: Cambridge University Press, 1999), 158. See also Everett Carll Ladd and Karlyn H. Bowman, *Attitudes toward the Environment: Twenty-Five Years after Earth Day* (Washington, D.C.: AEI Press, 1995).

73. Kraft, "A New Environmental Policy Agenda," 29–30.

74. See Glen Sussman and Mark Andrew Kelso, "Environmental Priorities and the President as Legislative Leader," in Soden, *Environmental Presidency,* 141.

PART IV
The Social Agenda

11

Failing the Test:
Immigration Reform

Otis L. Graham, Jr.

Nobody dast blame this man. You don't understand: Willy was a
salesman. . . . He's a man way out there in the blue, riding on a smile
and a shoeshine.
—from Arthur Miller's *Death of a Salesman*

There is no clear "conservative" position on the immigration problem, and
no "conservative" solution.
—from Charles Heatherly, ed., *Mandate for Leadership* (1981)

On the morning of September 11, 2001, one of the hidden and shockingly high
costs of America's immigration policies was put on the books and harshly illu-
minated. Now the public understood what a few immigration policy critics and
specialists had warned about for years. Our porous borders and governmental
abandonment of virtually all interior immigration controls had allowed terrorists to glide easily in and out of the country for periods of their choosing, as
they contemptuously trained in this affable society for their deadly suicide missions against it.

The national security hazards posed by America's broken immigration system could now be added to a long list of defects. By the 1990s, three decades of
research and analysis, along with immigration-driven social change, had made
it clear that the costs of America's immigration regime, the illegal and also
the legal flows, were economically, politically, and socially very high.[1] In its
1996 report the congressionally mandated Commission on Immigration Reform, chaired by former congresswoman Barbara Jordan, found current immigration trends inimical to the national interest and urged cutting the volume of
legal immigration by almost half, changing the criteria for admission to more
closely reflect national needs, and taking serious steps to contain illegal entry.[2]
President Clinton accepted and weakly endorsed these findings. Nothing was

done in any of these directions. The Brookings Institution in 2000 gathered a panel of historians and political scientists to reflect upon the federal government's greatest achievements and failures since World War II, and it ranked controlling immigration as second among the top five failures.[3]

Who was responsible for this extended failure? The blame must be generously apportioned, starting with the liberal immigration reformers who delegitimized the old and designed the new system that Lyndon Johnson signed into law in 1965. Then there are those—they came from both parties, from business, from religious and ethnic groups, from the academy—who defended the indefensible status quo over the years, denounced as racists and xenophobes those who were critics and reformers, and tirelessly worked for four decades to make American immigration policy and practice more expansive, and existing or proposed controls weaker.

Where does Ronald Reagan's government come into the story? He was the chief executive when the first opportunity for reform came. It is important who was first, for where large-scale immigration is concerned, there is often not a second reform opportunity at all, or as favorable a time. When immigration builds to mass levels, it generates political constituencies inside the host country who are dedicated to keeping the doors open so that relatives, or a cheap labor force, continue to enter. It also establishes networks of communication and aid that create momentum, from immigrant-sending countries to immigrant-receiving, from—in the modern world—south to north.

Looking back, there seem to have been few occasions on which the post-1965 system might have been successfully challenged and reformed toward lower numbers, toward a different system of selection, and the maintenance of effective border and interior controls. The first came in the early 1980s, with Reagan in the White House. If that moment was lost and that effort failed, immigration momentum and political dynamics would put immigration reform farther out of reach during any subsequent reform opportunities, with immense consequences for the future.

THE POST-SIXTIES SURGE OF IMMIGRATION AND THE CALL FOR REFORM

Those who threw out the national origins system in 1965 and liberalized U.S. immigration law had repeatedly assured the public that they were making no changes that would result in larger numbers or a shift in source countries. But they had done both. Source regions shifted from Europe to Latin America and Asia. Annual totals of legal immigration, which had averaged 178,000 (with considerable yearly fluctuation) over the duration of the national origins system of the 1920s, rose to 400,000 by 1973 and to 600,000 by 1978, reaching 1 million by 1989. An unknown number of illegal aliens—the official estimate in the 1980s was 200,000 to 500,000—were thought to be entering the country annually, while apprehensions along the two-thousand-mile Mexican border reached .5 million by 1970 and topped 1 million by 1977—an "invasion," in the word of Leonard Chapman, commissioner of the Immigration and Naturalization Service (INS). The impression of a border out of control was enhanced across the 1970s by bursts of refugee landings from Cuba and Haiti, over 550,000 refugees from Southeast Asia following American withdrawal from Vietnam in 1974, and a large flow of migrants asking asylum from civil wars in El Salvador and Guatemala.[4] The large numbers arriving outside the rules generated a resurgence of restrictionist sentiment. All polls reported national majorities in favor of lower immigration, and critics built a strong case that immigrants undercut natives in labor markets, fueled unwelcome population increases with resultant pressures on resources and environment, and burdened social services—and an unknown but substantial number of them were illegal.[5]

President Ford in 1976 created a task force that recommended sanctions on employers and a limited amnesty, but it was his last year in office. Jimmy Carter, acknowledging that "illegal immigration was reaching a crisis stage," sent Congress a similar legislative proposal in late summer of 1977, urging penalties on American employers for hiring illegal aliens and temporary legalization for those in the country over five years.[6] Sensing political danger in both action and inaction with respect to the broken immigration system, Congress took a familiar way out. In 1978 it asked the president to establish the Select Commission on Immigration and Refugee Policy (SCIRP, or the Select Commission) to assess the immigration policy of the United States in its entirety.

The Select Commission was chaired by Notre Dame president Theodore Hesburgh, who had become quite concerned about illegal immigration. The commission report came on March 1, 1981, as the new Reagan administration moved in. Noting that public opinion was opposed to current high levels of immigration, both legal and illegal, SCIRP recommended "closing the back door" of illegal entry in order to shore up support for the legal flow, in which it saw net advantages though "there are limits to the ability of this country to absorb immigrants in much larger numbers effectively" and certain changes should be made. The central policy thrust was that the "jobs magnet" for illegals must be cut off by imposition of penalties on their American employers.

This required some reliable method of identification, and Hesburgh was able to rally a precarious 8–7 majority for what Jimmy Carter had first broached: a new secure worker identification card rather than relying upon existing documents. As for the estimated three million illegals already in the country, an amnesty was preferred to "mass deportation," framed as the only choices. But the commission voted unanimously that the amnesty was to be delayed until Congress was satisfied that "appropriate enforcement mechanisms have been instituted." The bargain was conditional. First things first.[7]

RONALD REAGAN: RELUCTANT PLAYER

Immigration reform was not a Reagan sort of issue. Like other Americans born on the eve of World War I (born 1911), he matured and took on his political outlook in the midcentury decades (and, in Reagan's case, in small-town Illinois settings) when large-scale immigration and the public issues it raised had been ended by the restrictionist reforms of the 1920s, supplemented by depression and war. One is thus not surprised to find nothing on immigration in Reagan's autobiography, *Where's the Rest of Me?* (1965).[8] As California governor for eight years (1966–1974), he continued the state's political tradition of ignoring immigration despite its impact on the Golden State, since it was a federal responsibility and the state had governmental problems of its own.[9] A recent book that is said to uniquely illuminate Reagan's core beliefs on the eve of his presidency has recently been constructed out of analysis of his radio commentaries from 1976 to 1980. The range of his interests was narrow, and immigration was not among them.[10] His two terms in office did not change this. The effort to contain the illegal immigration flow, embodied in the long battle over what would be called the "Simpson-Mazzoli" legislation, is not even mentioned in Reagan's memoir focused on his presidency, *Ronald Reagan: An American Life* (1990), or in his weekly presidential radio addresses.[11] It must mean something that he was not alone in this. His aides in their own memoirs, his biographers, and those writing on his presidency, either because they all took their cues from him as to what was important about his political career, or because they shared his instinct to avoid or ignore this awkward subject, almost universally have nothing at all to say about immigration or immigration policy. Their indexes do not have a place for it, and chief immigration reformer Senator Alan Simpson is rarely even mentioned.[12]

We should not conclude from all this that Reagan did not have an orientation, a place in his mind and a rhetoric, on the matter of immigration. His was the simplistic, sentimentalist, Statue of Liberty conception so widely shared among assimilated Americans of his day who could not remember when immigration had been a problem. In one of the few references to immigration in his published state papers covering his eight years in office, Reagan displayed in 1984 the then-dominant language of diversity celebration when he told an audience of naturalizing immigrants that immigrants "enlivened the national life with new ideas and new blood" and "enrich us" with "a delightful diversity."[13] And he closed his farewell address in 1989 with reference to the "shining city on a hill," a "city with free ports . . . and the doors were open to anyone with the will and the heart to get there."[14]

But immigration control for Reagan had no attraction as an issue appropriate for policymaking or (as Reagan usually preferred) policy unmaking. The issue was fundamentally at odds with Reagan's entire political purpose and temperament. He was interested in shrinking the (nonmilitary parts of the) government, and here was an issue in which the government he was about to lead was widely charged with incompetence, with not doing enough, and on an issue of law and public order with a natural resonance among Republicans. Presidential leadership in this area could only mean making the government more effective and possibly even larger. This was not Reagan terrain. As he told reporter Lou Cannon, "I have always talked generally on one subject—the growth of government."[15] And he did not like gloomy anything, or talk of limits.

Yet, just as he took office, a presidential commission reported with recommendations for sweeping policy change, and editorials in the nation's major newspapers were overwhelmingly supportive. Congressional action of some sort was sure to follow, and the executive branch had no choice but to participate energetically in the framing of laws it would be expected to enforce.

THE REAGAN ADMINISTRATION STARTS UP THE ROAD TO REFORM

Accordingly, five days after SCIRP reported, a Reagan memo announced the appointment of the cabinet-level Task Force on Immigration and Refugee Policy, chaired by Attorney General William French Smith and asked to report by May.[16] This has the look of leadership and certainly reflects Smith's personal views that illegal immigration must be curbed. But Smith was not in the White House inner circle. Historian Nicholas Laham describes the White House as "wary on the subject," which for the new administration had "only a marginal priority," to understate the matter.[17] Nonetheless, the issue of immigration reform must be engaged. Laham argues that "the Reagan administration operated within the prevailing consensus on this issue . . . viewing legal immigration as good, and illegal immigration as bad." This consensus was said to derive from "the experts" and to be shared by Congress.[18] This summary is a mixture of the banal and the misleading. Politicians, fearful of offending ethnic voters, invariably saluted legal immigration as "good for America." This had been the tone of the opening pages of the Hesburgh Commission report, which had nonetheless found legal immigration in need of changes. There existed even at this early stage in the era of post-1965 mass immigration a sizable critique of the legal immigration regime—its principles of selection, overall numbers, and especially the disarray in refugee and asylum policy, following the 1980 Mariel boatlift from Cuba which had stirred up much public resentment and dismay.[19] It is quite misleading to say that the Reagan administration moved amid a consensus that legal immigration reforms were off the table.[20] As for illegal immigration, no one in Congress openly defended it, but there was a range of views on how seriously to take it, and on the policy options. Here a sort of potential "bargain" had emerged, as both the Carter administration and the Hesburgh Commission had linked employer sanctions with an amnesty for illegals long in the country. Still, the Reagan administration, like Congress, had some hard choices to make, including the SCIRP position that there must be a delay on any idea of amnesty until illegal immigration was under control. The six years required to resolve the issue do not testify to "consensus." Interest groups were sharply divided, and the public mood unpredictable and unfocused. Presidential leadership, or lack of it, would matter.

Some of these choices had to be faced quickly, as congressional leadership on the issue had suddenly emerged. The Senate Subcommittee on Immigration was chaired after the Republican victory in 1980 by Alan Simpson (R-Wyo.), newly elected in 1978 but a respected Wyoming figure who had served on the Select Commission and made it clear he intended to produce legislation.[21] Romano Mazzoli (D-Ky.) chaired the House Subcommittee on Immigration and shared with Simpson both cordial personal relations and the intention to carry the issue of immigration reform to a legislative result. Both men were somewhat more restrictionist than the Hesburgh Commission majority, voting in that body to reduce legal immigration as well as fashion a remedy for illegal immigration.

Simpson sought a meeting with the president in May 1981, prior to Reagan's scheduled meeting with Mexican president Lopez Portillo, in order to urge the administration to keep American options open on immigration and to explain Simpson's own goals.[22] The meeting hinted at the relationship ahead. Reagan and his top officials, including the attorney general, were there. But the meeting lasted only fifteen minutes, and Reagan, as instructed, listened to Simpson's views and limited himself to a broad promise of cooperation as the legislative process went forward.[23] Congress was conceded the lead in immigration reform, though Simpson, in the words of a White House staffer in a memo to Reagan, had "indicated his willingness to 'carry the administration's water' on this issue."[24] They carried different water, as it turned out.

Simpson sensed from his early contacts with White House aides that cooperation with the Reagan White House was shaky, so he and Senator Walter D. Huddleston (D-Ky.), gathered fifty-one senators from both parties as signatories to a letter to Reagan declaring that both legal and illegal immigration numbers were too high, as public opinion polls confirmed. The president would, they were sure, be prepared to make "difficult and painful" rather than "easy short-term decisions" in the face of mounting immigration pressures.[25]

One important bias appeared to shape the task force's deliberations from the start. In the words of one White House staffer assigned to the task force, "the President is himself a firm believer in a high degree of freedom in immigration."[26] This aide, Francis Hodsoll, sensed not only that the president was temperamentally uninterested in (if not philosophically opposed to) border control, but also that he and others in the administration underestimated the public's irritation at large illegal alien and refugee flows. Hodsoll's memos reminded participants of the agitated state of public opinion through citation of poll results and evidence of sizable congressional reform sentiment.[27]

But top White House staff were pushing in another direction. A memo from White House Chief of Staff James A. Baker and Counselor to the President Edwin Meese to Reagan on June 3 concluded that "immigration is a no-win" issue. They framed the issue as one of political points to be won or lost, with no larger national implications that should guide the administration. The numbers of illegal as well as legal immigrants were rising, and the public perceived this as a large national problem. But "immigration enthusiasts" in the United States, along with the Mexican government, would fiercely resist restriction. The Baker-Meese memo to Reagan did not attempt to reach any conclusion as to the national interest, a phrase they never used. The question for a new administration was framed as one of political feasibility and implications. To veer toward either side would be politically divisive and costly. The administration could not endorse the status quo but in moving toward reform must find "a middle ground." One part of a formula for a middle position might well be to offset—politically—an employer sanctions feature with a new guestworker program, easing the pressures for illegal entry and at the same time pleasing southwestern growers and the government of Mexico.[28] They must have known that Reagan had expressed interest in guestworkers from Mexico in an interview with Walter Cronkite on March 3.

On July 1, 1981, the twenty-six-page task force report went to Reagan. For those familiar with the Hesburgh report, the Reagan task force had narrowed the agenda. It virtually ignored legal immigration but for two problems festering within U.S. refugee policy—what to do about the 135,000 Cuban and Haitian refugees that came during the Mariel boatlift of 1980, and the provision of welfare benefits to refugees. Fundamental questions about overall numbers and priorities for selection, as well as proposals to reform the floundering INS, all engaged by the Hesburgh Commission, were not addressed.[29] Issues surrounding illegal immigration dominated the report and generated internal divisions that were unresolved by July 1. The task force had reached agreement to make a large part of the problem of illegals simply disappear through an amnesty making them legal, though the details of this were in dispute. And it agreed to make more future illegals disappear by admitting them as legal guestworkers in agriculture. But there was no final agreement on the proposed employer sanctions provision, let alone whether it should be enforced through a national identity card or system.

In July the president presided over at least one cabinet meeting to resolve intra-administration differences.[30] While all cabinet meeting minutes have not been opened for research, Assistant to the President for Policy Development Martin Anderson has provided in his memoir an account of this crucial July cabinet meeting where the immigration reform project inside the administration was emasculated (in Anderson's view, cleansed of a very bad idea). At this meeting Attorney General Smith presented the task force proposals, including the idea inherited from the Select Commission of "an improved Social Security

card" to help employers determine legal residency. After the mention of an identification card—we are not sure of the attorney general's actual wording—there
was silence. Then Anderson, in his account, rallied the real Reagan antigovernment faithful, suggesting that it would be cheaper to "tattoo an identification
number on the inside of everybody's arm." Secretary of the Interior James Watt
at once pointed out that this brought to mind the biblical "Mark of the Beast."
The image of Nazi concentration camps was in the air. Reagan was aroused and
made his contribution. "Maybe we should just brand all the babies," he smil-
ingly proposed, getting into the swing of bad analogizing.[31]

Whatever happened in this July meeting, it was effectively the end of the
administration's receptivity to beginning the national experiment with a single
counterfeit-resistant identifier. Getting wind of the decision, the *Washington Post*
criticized the cabinet for abandoning the "new and less easily forged Social
Security card" and declared that "the test of any administration's determination
to confront the problem seriously becomes a willingness to devise some national
identifier," as recommended both by the Select Commission and the attorney
general's task force. "The cosmetic substitute of requiring workers and employers
merely to sign a piece of paper . . . is meaningless. . . . Only the president himself can rescue [this] . . . critical component." The newspaper was not alone in
sensing a pivotal issue and turning point. "Sanctions won't work without it [the
national identity card]," Simpson immediately declared, promising to restore
the essential element in hearings. "We'll consider everything but tattoos."[32]

The president did not rescue this component. The Justice Department on
July 30 put forward the administration's immigration proposals.[33] The president simultaneously issued a short statement of his own.

If observers had expected a conservative government to shift the policy
options toward firmer law enforcement while condemning liberal laxity, they
were surprised. The administration, Attorney General William French Smith
declared on July 30, agreed that there were problems: "Current laws and enforcement procedures are inadequate—particularly with regard to illegal aliens
and mass requests for asylum." Illegal immigrants "are creating problems for
themselves, as well as for the country." But the administration's proposals opened
the borders more than firming them. The principal ones were (1) sanctions on
employers *knowingly* hiring illegals, enforced through reliance on existing documents (the administration "explicitly opposed" a national identity card or system); (2) an "experimental" guestworker program admitting up to fifty thousand
Mexicans to work in sectors of agriculture where it appeared that American labor
was unavailable; and (3) a grant of amnesty for illegals in the country prior to
January 1, 1980.[34]

Reagan's own short message could have been written by liberal Ted Kennedy.
He began with the ritual incantation that "our nation is a nation of immigrants"
that would always welcome more to our shores. But the "Cuban influx to Florida"
required more effective policies that will "preserve our tradition of accepting

foreigners to our shores, but to accept them in a controlled and orderly fashion . . . consistent with our values of individual privacy and freedom."[35]

The attorney general, who from the first had been the strongest and, it sometimes seemed, the only restrictionist voice in the administration's top leadership, adopted a slightly firmer tone in his testimony on July 30 before a joint meeting of the immigration subcommittees of the House and Senate. He opened with the ritual salute to immigration, which has "overwhelmingly enriched" America, and made the odd comment that the president "believes we must modestly expand the opportunities for legal employment to reflect the reality of America's attractiveness to much of the world." Then: "We have lost control of our borders," he said, with three million to six million illegals in the country and one-quarter to a half million more arriving each year. Remedies must include increases in INS budgets, sanctions on employers, a guestworker program for Mexican agricultural labor, and an amnesty.[36] The questions from the Hill legislators were perfunctory, no one noting the crucial decision not to make the amnesty conditional upon effective controls on illegal immigration. The initiative would now shift to Congress, which had just been handed by the new administration a softer, more expansionist version of the Hesburgh recommendations, with a new "experimental" guestworker program added, along with a regime of employer sanctions built upon a legally weak and fraud-vulnerable worker eligibility verification process. Economist Vernon Briggs of Cornell justifiably characterized the Reagan proposals as "far more timid" than those of the Select Commission.[37] A key role had been played by Anderson and other White House aides who used Reagan's past record and rhetoric to resist what they considered a federal bureaucratic campaign to make the government more intrusive.[38]

In *The Congressional Politics of Immigration Reform,* James Gimpel and James Edwards argue that a political opportunity may have been lost at this early stage. Immigration issues, formerly without clear partisan configuration, had, under the pressure of the mass refugee and illegal alien flows of the late 1970s, taken on in the early Reagan years a partisan alignment. Some Republican politicians, formerly with no interest in or position on immigration, found that flows of Third World immigrants expanded the welfare state and angered their constituents who faced growing local social welfare costs. In this view, a restrictionist Republican complaint issue was emerging, but the Reagan administration, in 1981, had not recognized it.

IRCA: THE LONG ROAD TO PASSAGE, 1981 TO 1986

The administration's brief period of leadership had taken the form of a retreat, and it would now stand mostly on the sidelines. "The focus on immigration reform definitely shifted to Congress and remained there," wrote Thomas Maddox.[39] On March 17, 1982, Simpson and Mazzoli introduced the Immigration Reform and Control Act (IRCA). Unlike the Reagan proposals, they offered a comprehensive reform of both legal and illegal immigration law. On the legal side, they proposed a firm ceiling on the overall numbers, a shift toward skills and away from family reunification, and elimination of the fifth preference for brothers and sisters of U.S. citizens, the source of so-called chain migration enlarging the total numbers. But proposals to deal with illegal immigration immediately attracted the most attention and conflict. The strategy, Simpson liked to say, rested on "a three-legged stool": improved border enforcement, penalties for employers who hired undocumented workers, and a counterfeit-resistant national identification card verifying eligibility to work.[40]

Employer sanctions was hardly a new idea. The House had twice passed employer sanctions bills, first proposed by liberal Senator Paul Douglas in the mid-1950s because of his long-standing concern for American workers. Hispanic organizations stridently warned of discrimination in the workplace, and in response liberal legislators added an amnesty into the package as a potential trade. During the legislative struggles of 1982 and 1983, the administration generally backed Simpson. Smith expressed concerns about the budgetary consequences of the amnesty as proposed, said nothing about making it conditional upon effective controls, and suggested moving the qualifying date back to 1976 to reduce the numbers and cost.[41] Privately, he implored Reagan's top staff for more vigorous White House involvement.[42]

The Senate passed a complex package as the Simpson half of IRCA in 1982. But in the House it became entangled in multiple objections and delays. Speaker "Tip" O'Neill resisted a vote on the measure despite an appeal by the White House. Time ran out on the Ninety-seventh Congress.[43]

Simpson pushed essentially the same package through the Senate in May 1983, by an impressive 76–18 majority. Public opinion polls were running consistently and strongly in favor of Simpson's key idea, employer sanctions.[44] The House version moved out of committee and appeared headed toward the floor in early October, when Speaker O'Neill announced that he would not allow the bill to come to the floor in 1983. He offered three reasons: the Hispanic caucus opposed it, he could find "no constituency" for it, and he had been told that the president intended to veto the legislation to curry political favor with Hispanic voters in the 1984 elections.[45]

The reaction included much anger at, in Mazzoli's words, "the Speaker's abrupt, unnecessary, thoroughly unfounded action," and criticism of the whip hand over the Democratic Party apparently held by a small group of Hispanics.[46] Taken aback by the outcry and reassured by Simpson that the president would not veto any bill acceptable to both houses in 1984, O'Neill a month later promised that the full house could take up the measure. In House Rules Committee hearings in June, the departments of Labor, Agriculture, and Justice, along with the Office of Management and Budget (OMB), took different positions, presumably with White House knowledge or approval.[47] On June 20 a dramatic vote of 216–211 registered House approval of H.R. 1510. The outcome was in doubt to the end. The package included employer sanctions, a guestworker program for agriculture, and an amnesty for those in the country prior to 1982.[48] Immigration "reform" had moved ahead, but to many it looked like immigration expansion and facilitation. Politicians on all sides seemed to care most about claiming credit or assigning blame. Speaker O'Neill claimed that it is "a Reagan bill more than anybody else's," and the president in a press conference said it was long overdue, though Robert Pear of the *New York Times* reported that "administration officials have not been active or outspoken in pushing the bill this year."[49]

Presidential politics continued to complicate the picture. At the Democratic National Convention in July, under Hispanic delegates' pressure, nominee Walter Mondale promised to do what he could to kill Simpson-Mazzoli: "We're going to fight it, we're going to beat it!" The Reagan White House declared the House version "unacceptable," due to the fiscal costs of the amnesty.[50] The conference committee began work in September after the nominating conventions and could not bridge all the differences. For the third year in a row, immigration reform expired in Congress.[51]

At this point, the package of compromise measures called "Simpson-Mazzoli" or "immigration reform" had no clear identity. Two well-known historians took diametrically opposite views, Oscar Handlin of Harvard lamenting the defeat of "the most liberal measure . . . in 90 years," and Richard Wade of the City University of New York happy that legislation "identical with the restrictionist legislation of the 1920s" had failed. The *New York Times,* while editorially deploring "the death of a humane idea," reported that analysts could not agree on whether the principal message of the bill was "come in" or "keep out."[52]

So the Simpson-Mazzoli marathon, one of the most complex legislative struggles of recent years and a case study in modern policy paralysis, resumed in 1985. Simpson reintroduced the legislation with a few changes, most notably making the amnesty contingent on proof of sanctions' effectiveness as attested by a presidential commission. This time, the administration was more supportive of Simpson, though it still did not speak with one voice. The new attorney general, Edwin Meese, and INS commissioner Alan Nelson both praised the Simpson version of the legislation, though Meese did not express support for amnesty conditionality and Nelson did.[53] The administration (and Simpson, who said of the growers' lobby that "their greed knows no bounds") objected (unsuccessfully) to an expansion of a large guestworker program proposed by Senator Pete Wilson (R-Calif.).[54] The Senate measure passed 69–30 on September 19. Simpson grumbled openly at the concessions forced on him, and the administration was said to be ambivalent on the whole package, for different reasons.[55] It was late, and the House, stronghold of opposition to guestworkers, did not complete work before the end of the session. Throughout 1985 and into 1986, the deteriorating Mexican economy pushed rising numbers of illegals northward, and several California politicians called for troops at the border. Reagan's commissioner of the INS, Alan Nelson, reported "the greatest surge of people in history across our southern border."[56]

As the idea of immigration reform entered its fifth year, it had narrowed its target to illegal immigration and appeared to be frozen in a "bargain" structure (employer sanctions traded for amnesty and guestworkers) that generated internal disagreement and endless wrangling, without producing a majority coalition. The chance that 1986 might bring agreement on a new immigration policy seemed darkened in the first month, as the Reagan administration's internal divisions on immigration became exposed—again. A preliminary draft of the 1986 CEA (Council of Economic Advisers) report was leaked to the press and was found to conclude that illegals do not take American jobs and that excluding them from our labor markets would cost the nation a loss of output. This leak provided additional evidence that "the Reagan administration is of two minds about immigration reform," the *Economist* observed.[57] Congressman Peter Rodino (D-N.J.), dean of immigration legislators who had emerged in 1986 from a prolonged lethargy, demanded that the president clarify his own views. After a February *New York Times* editorial urging the president to back the legislation, Reagan met in March with key members of Congress to express support for legislation to stop the flow of illegal aliens.[58] The media that spring carried many statements—by Rodino, Father Hesburgh, the *New York Times* editorial board—that if reform did not come now, the growing restrictionist mood in the country would force tougher measures and outflank years of work on a moderate solution. But the House was a swamp of disputes, and in September Rodino declared the bill dead, blaming Republicans. The *New York Times* blamed both political parties and urged the president to "intervene . . . to put partisan Democrats on the spot."[59] Attorney General Meese urged the House to vote. Congressman Charles Schumer and others led negotiations over another package, with gloomy results. For their part, the outmanned restrictionist forces, led by the Federation for American Immigration Reform (FAIR), an organization of environmentalist and population limitationists formed in 1978, were deeply dissatisfied with a 1986 "reform" package so riddled with concessions that it appeared to be actually expansionist, and debated whether they should declare defeat rather than victory.

Suddenly, the White House announced that Reagan would meet with Soviet leader Mikhail Gorbachev in Iceland in mid-October, providing more time for congressional action on a number of matters. The leadership of the long-stalled immigration reform struggle suddenly mobilized. The house passed IRCA by a vote of 230–166 on October 9. "I guess we just jump-started a corpse," Simpson commented.[60] The bill was now so expansionist—riddled with amnesties, loaded up with a program for agricultural workers allowed to become citizens and vacate the program for more foreign laborers, all traded for an unenforceable ban on hiring illegal workers—that Republicans in the House had voted 105–62 against it.[61] A conference report was ready in four days, and both Houses ratified by October 17. The media reported that the administration had misgivings. Simpson and Rodino sought to reassure Reagan that everybody had misgivings, and Mazzoli declared the result "the least imperfect bill we will ever have before us."[62] Reagan signed the legislation on November 6, 1986.[63]

ASSESSMENT OF IMMIGRATION REFORM UNDER REAGAN

The outstanding features of the Immigration Reform and Control Act of 1986 were, in broad outline: making it unlawful to hire those illegally in the country, enforceable through employer acceptance of a range of existing documents; offering an "amnesty" for aliens who entered illegally but had resided continuously in the United States before January 1, 1982, who now could apply for permanent resident alien status and, eventually, citizenship; expanding the existing H-1 agricultural guestworker program and creating a new guestworker program by granting permanent resident alien status to up to 350,000 agricultural workers, with a "replenishment" foreign labor force if the original workers left the farm sector.[64] The problems on the legal immigration side that had been highlighted by the Hesburgh Commission were left for another day.

In a brief message on signing IRCA, Reagan called "this landmark legislation . . . an excellent example of a truly successful bipartisan effort . . . to control illegal immigration. . . . Future generations of Americans will be thankful."[65] Few others knowledgeable about the problem declared victory. Simpson, ever the realist, had little to say. "Nobody's certain it's going to work," said Representative Schumer (D-N.Y.), "so if it doesn't work we'll have to go back to the drawing board."[66] IRCA, commented FAIR's Roger Conner, "could be the turning point in regaining control over our nation's borders, or it could turn into an immigration disaster" if sanctions were not enforced and further measures to reduce legal immigration did not follow.[67]

The skeptics were right. IRCA was a dismal and costly policy failure. Arrests at the border did drop somewhat in 1987, as prospective border crossers waited to see if "El Norte" was serious about controlling illegal entry. By 1990 arrests were at pre-IRCA levels and rising. Employers continued to hire illegals, since IRCA was built around a huge loophole that had been pointed out repeatedly: documentary proof of eligibility to work was easily counterfeited. As historian David Reimers concluded in a book published at the end of the century: "It might appear that it [IRCA] was a restrictive law, but Congress failed to provide for an effective system to keep out undocumented aliens. It thus turned out to be a rather generous amnesty traded for employer sanctions" without teeth.[68] "To no one's surprise," wrote Harvard sociologist Christopher Jencks in a 2001 review of several end-of-century books on American immigration, "the new rules against hiring illegal aliens proved unenforceable. . . . [IRCA] failed because it did not offer employers a simple, reliable way of determining workers' legal status, . . . [so] IRCA's only enduring legacy was the amnesty," the law "a victory for the expansionists."[69]

These judgments came at the end of the century, when the law Ronald Reagan signed in 1986 could be seen in a larger and longer perspective. The "Reform and Control Act" reformed, but not toward control. When the Census Bureau analyzed the 2000 census, it released the estimate that 8.7 million illegal aliens now resided in the United States, suggesting an annual flow of 400,000 to 500,000. This was a devastating verdict on IRCA, signed and praised by Ronald Reagan.[70] And those who warned that one amnesty invites others were confirmed in the summer of 2001 when U.S. and Mexican presidents Bush and Fox pressed, without opposition, the idea of another large amnesty and new guestworker program.

The 9/11 attacks ended such talk, at least for a time. "If a Mexican day laborer can sneak across the border, so can an Al Qaeda terrorist," wrote Steven Camarota of the Center for Immigration Studies, noting that three of the September 11, 2001, airplane terrorists had been illegal aliens, and the INS had no information on several others who turned out to be in violation of immigration law.[71]

REAGAN AND IMMIGRATION REFORM

America's immigration policy disarray is not, of course, attributable only to the fumbling architects of IRCA, of whom Reagan was only one. But presidents play large roles, and Reagan was in the White House during one of the only two occasions in the last three decades of the century in which illegal immigration so vexed the national mind that not only was serious "reform" intensely discussed, but a legislative result was produced. The only historian to undertake a book-length assessment of Reagan and IRCA, Nicholas Laham, concludes that the administration's deliberations during the task force and after were "crippled" by "mistaken or unproven assumptions" provided to them by the community of experts, who at that time thought and wrote that illegal immigration brought economic benefits. Scholars like Vernon Briggs, George Borjas, and Barry Chiswick were even then arguing the opposite, but they could not get Reagan's or his advisers' attention. So the administration took a soft position, which was a "mistake," Laham thought. IRCA turned out to be "a dismal failure," and "the blame for the failure of employer sanctions must be assigned to the Reagan administration." In Laham's view, Smith, Meese, and others made "dishonest and deceitful statements" to the public and Congress, since they, and Reagan himself when he signed IRCA, "knew these provisions would fail." But they preferred a symbolic victory over a workable system because of ideological objections to federal invasion of privacy and the anticipated costs of a national worker identification card. "Reagan must assume a substantial share of the blame" and "failed to provide leadership."[72]

Laham offers no alternative scenario for what that leadership might have achieved, so I will offer one, in order to probe the possibilities. The assumption must be that, with Reagan communicating his full support for the hard choices to "fix" the immigration problem, we get a far better Simpson-Mazzoli, and probably earlier. Recalling that Simpson and Mazzoli in 1981 and 1982 proposed to reform both legal and illegal immigration, the Smith task force could have helped "carry Simpson's water" by addressing at least the most glaring of the flaws in legal immigration that were vexing the public at this time of unprecedented refugee and asylum pressures from the Caribbean and Central America. James Gimpel and James Edwards present evidence that many conservative Republicans in Congress had recently come for the first time to see refugee flows and illegal immigration as "redistributive policy," bringing into the country large numbers of impoverished and unskilled foreigners who would swell the welfare rolls. Broad immigration reform appeared ripe to become a popular Republican issue.[73] By implication, a case can be made that the Reagan administration squandered the available political and policy opportunities. A strong stand against amnesty would have had considerable support in Congress and, more important, with the public.[74] If this fight is made, and it seems that the Democrats in the House (whose edge in that chamber was 243–192 in 1981–1983 and 269–165 in 1983–1985) can block any legislation without an amnesty commitment, the White House reinforces Simpson's basic leanings, insisting that the amnesty be narrowed and made conditional on proof of border and entry control, and that employer sanctions are backed by a secure worker identification card for use at the point of hire. The three-legged stool. If this package cannot clear the House before the 1984 election, the president makes the obstructionism and expansionist leanings of Tip O'Neill, Walter Mondale, and the Democrats an issue before an electorate strongly supportive of effective border and workplace controls. The immigration issue is injected into national electoral politics, where it belonged. The president is reelected, and with this mandate, effective reform comes in 1985. More important, the Republican Party would have chosen the right, and the winning, voice on immigration, marginalizing its open border wing. This scenario implies that not only a public policy improvement but also a political opportunity was lost.[75]

This scenario is not immune to skepticism. Even if we heroically imagine Reagan in such a leadership role on an issue he disliked, we must reckon with the deeper forces at work upon the American political system. Immigration analyst David North first pointed out what has subsequently become a matter of gloomy consensus: Democracies in the West demonstrably cannot cope with the massive immigration pressures that began to build globally in the 1960s and 1970s and which promise for at least another century to wash uncontrollably from south to north as impoverished and overpopulated societies send their surplus populations to the developed world. Politicians in the West, most especially in the United States, fear to make immigration restriction an issue, lest the name-calling and backlash of a swelling pool of ethnic voters cost more than is gained from the diffuse approval of an ambivalent and ill-informed public.[76]

In this perspective, the enfeeblement of immigration policy and enforcement in face of these pressures is and will continue to be widespread in all countries in the West and has deep roots. The U.S. case, as always, is congruent if a bit different. If there is one policy area in U.S. governmental life that is regularly and more than all others encumbered by irresolution and incompetence, it is immigration. For immigration policymaking in America is emotionally entangled in the special irrationalities born out of (misremembered and mythical) history, pride at the image of asylum, and the conflicting claims of homeland loyalty and contemporary ethnicity. Americans' outlook on immigration, even, for many, on illegal immigration, has been aptly called "ambivalent romanticism," in the words of Michael Teitelbaum and Jay Winter.[77]

And along with these confused sentiments among the general public there are rational special interests at work to keep the borders and entry points open to those with or without official permission to enter. Our political institutions elevate interest-group claims over the more diffuse concerns of the larger public, giving an advantage to the intense and well-financed lobbies for pliable, cheap labor or more kinsmen to augment group power.

In view of these and other factors making for policy irresolution and a pervasive liberality and avoidance, how much leadership on immigration reform can we expect from presidents? Senator Simpson and William French Smith, two serious reformers in the battles of the early 1980s who knew that public opinion was behind them, repeatedly complained then and later about the multiple sources of their extended frustration. As loyal Republicans, they left Ronald Reagan entirely off their list of troublemakers, and it is substantial without him. Simpson was especially scathing about his daily antagonists, the defenders of the broken, discredited, open-border status quo. They included the unprincipled boss of the House Tip O'Neill, liberal Democrats in the House, and Ted Kennedy in the Senate who responded spinelessly to a bizarre lobbying coalition of membership-less and Ford Foundation–funded Hispanic ethnic lobbying organizations running under the "civil rights" flag, big western growers, religious leaders, immigration lawyers, and the ACLU. And Simpson's allies were scarce. The many and militant patriotic societies, veterans' groups, and the firmly restrictionist labor movement who massed behind immigration control in the first decades of the century had either failed to show up or proven irresolute as players in the battles over Simpson-Mazzoli. FAIR's scant twenty-five thousand national members were "nice people, but they have no troops," in Simpson's words.[78]

Even this brief summary conveys the impressive difficulties in the way of gaining control of an unusual invasion, by people who mostly wanted (at least for one generation) to work cheap. From the 1960s to September 10, 2001, many people seem to have reluctantly accepted North's proposition that in democracies and especially in America, border and interior enforcement of immigration limitations was a good idea backed by majorities but nonetheless was an impossible dream. Now, after 9/11, the mood is, at least for the moment, different. The security of the nation is the government's first business, and its legitimacy is on the line. The media now convey a broad consensus that regaining control of the borders is technologically and politically a live option. If it becomes so, it may alter our historical perspective.

After September 11, 2001, when we revisit Ronald Reagan's presidency, immigration reform must have a different look and importance. Reagan's chief law enforcement officer, the attorney general, felt—as did much of the Republican electorate and most of the general public—that, in the words of the Republican senator from Wyoming, "widespread flouting of our Nation's immigration laws leads to a disrespect for our laws and institutions in general."[79] This is the conservative position, and it requires combating that lawbreaking with, among other things, a secure identification system for all immigrants and possibly all Americans. A similar conservative position is opposition to an "amnesty" for illegal aliens, a setting aside of law that rewards lawbreakers and permits forgiven criminals to butt in line in front of millions of people following the earlier rules. These are the hard choices that realism—another conservative attribute—requires and that public opinion supported when Simpson-Mazzoli was debated. And Ronald Reagan called himself a conservative.

But a key to the outcome was that he was not, and neither were thousands of Republican operatives Reagan brought to Washington and installed in places where they could implement his revolution. The Republican Party had two souls, one devoted to law and order and respect for the institutions of family, church, and nation, and the other a more animated one steered not by those cautious and preservative instincts but by a libertarian, free-market, government-hating ideology. For the latter, "immigration reform," in the meaning of control, had never been on their agenda, but they quickly understood that it meant strong government somewhere. So with religious conviction they moved quickly from a total lack of interest in the subject to vigorous opposition. As a result, throughout the five-year immigration reform episode, reporters found themselves noting that the administration "was not of one mind" and kept sending mixed signals. But the libertarian wing had very early won the key victory at a meeting with Reagan in July 1981, when in an emotional moment the president, under prompting, ridiculed the very idea of adequate documentation of national identity. The *Wall Street Journal* editorial writers had won, without needing their desired constitutional amendment, "Let There Be Open Borders."

The "struggle for the soul of the Republican Party" did not last long because Ronald Reagan's heart was not with the conservatives but with the rightist ideologues. Indeed, the reality was more startling. He swam comfortably in a sea of liberalism. Yale law professor Peter Schuck has argued that the 1980s produced two (IRCA and the 1990 immigration law) expansionist policy changes despite much public sentiment in the opposite direction, because of the contribution of the "role of ideas." But when he names them, it is clear that he uses a relaxed definition of "ideas" and has in mind several sentimentalisms: the genuflection to "diversity," universal humanitarian principles of human rights, a muddled notion that global free labor markets offer a sort of economic free lunch, and the idea that national sovereignty is obsolete. Schuck finds these sentiments among policy elites, the media, judges, church leaders, and other activists. But Ronald Reagan could mouth these sentiments with the best of them and never smelled their distinctive ideological odor or glimpsed their implications.[80]

Apart from Reagan's political values, he was an uncommonly passive leader because of the limitations of his intellect and curiosity. His outlook had been formed years earlier, and, in the words of one historian, "when the subject was not supply-side economics or the military budget . . . he left its resolution to others." His aide Donald Regan made the revealing observation that "President Reagan essentially never told anyone what to do."[81] The Tower Commission inquiry into the Iran-Contra episode depicted the president, in the summary of the *New York Times,* as "a confused and remote figure . . . gliding gracefully across the national stage with an optimistic smile."[82]

So it came about that President Reagan, and those who shared his gut-level sentiments that immigration policy should be decided with reference to the same core beliefs in weak and frugal government and sunny California optimism, had kept the nation on the road the Democrats put them on with the Immigration Act of 1965. That road amounted to what Christopher Jencks has recently called "a vast social experiment of the kind that Republicans normally detest." Noting (to his apparent surprise and dismay) that by reasonable projections, the U.S. population may be propelled by immigration to exceed five hundred million or about twice the current total by 2050, Jencks sees this experiment with mass immigration as aimed inexorably toward a crowded and troubled United States contributing rising pollution loads to the global environment and struggling with a faltering assimilation process.[83] Others stress the possibility that mass immigration amounts to an unannounced reshaping of the nation's ethno-racial composition and, inevitably, culture. Decades of mass immigration from Latin America and Asia, with increasing flows from the Middle East, have actually generated a vigorous discussion of "the National Question," such as we have not heard since Teddy Roosevelt's era a hundred years ago.

Liberal Democrats, whose mission in our system is to launch social experiments, sent down the rails this parallel-track experiment in the 1960s but without formal announcement. Then they fought off intermittent and ill-focused efforts by (some) conservative Republicans in the eighties and nineties to question and slow it. Conservative Ronald Reagan, in a moment of critical reassessment and decision, lined up with the liberals, on the "keep the experiment going" side. His historical reputation should reflect this.

NOTES

1. For a lucid review of recent literature, see Christopher Jencks, "Who Should Get In?" *New York Review of Books,* pt. 1 (November 29, 2001), pt. 2 (December 20, 2001). For a summary of the state of the immigration debate at end of century, see Otis L. Graham, Jr., "The Unfinished Reform," in *Debating American Immigration 1882–Present,* ed. Roger Daniels and Otis L. Graham (Lanham, Md.: Rowman & Littlefield, 2001), 89–105.

2. U.S. Commission on Immigration Reform, *Becoming an American: Immigration and Immigrant Policy* (Washington, D.C.: U.S. Commission on Immigration Reform, 1997), and *U.S. Immigration Policy: Restoring Credibility* (Washington, D.C.: U.S. Commission on Immigration Reform, 1994).

3. Paul C. Light, *Government's Greatest Achievements: From Civil Rights to Homeland Security* (Washington, D.C.: Brookings Institution Press, 2000). The failures were devolving responsibilities to the states, immigration control, simplifying taxes, expanding urban mass transit, and renewing poor communities. The top achievement was rebuilding Europe after World War II.

4. Vernon Briggs, Jr., *Mass Immigration and the National Interest* (Armonk, N.Y.: M. E. Sharpe, 1992), 120–33, 151; Daniels and Graham, *Debating American Immigration,* 152–59.

5. For a brief account of the "New Restrictionism," see David M. Reimers, *Unwelcome Strangers: American Identity and the Turn against Immigration* (New York: Columbia University Press, 1998), chap. 3; and Otis L. Graham, Jr., "Illegal Immigration and the New Reform Movement," FAIR Paper #2, 1980.

6. Briggs, *Mass Immigration,* 154.

7. Select Commission on Immigration and Refugee Policy, *U.S. Immigration Policy and the National Interest* (Washington, D.C.: Government Printing Office, March 1, 1981). For an outsider's view, see the oral history by Roger Conner, FAIR Tenth Anniversary Oral History Project. January 27, 1989, 64–68, in the Gelman Library, George Washington University. Fuchs's view is presented in *The American Kaleidoscope: Race, Ethnicity, and the Civic Culture* (Hanover, N.H.: University Press of New England, 1990), 250–52.

8. Ronald Reagan with Richard G. Hubler, *Where's The Rest of Me?* (New Rochelle, N.Y.: Conservative Book Club, 1965).

9. Robert Lindsey, "California Rehearsal," in Hedrick Smith et al., *Reagan the Man, the President* (New York: Macmillan, 1992).

10. Kiron K. Skinner, Annelise Anderson, and Martin Anderson, eds., *Reagan, In His Own Hand* (New York: Free Press, 2001).

11. Ronald Reagan, *An American Life: The Autobiography* (New York: Simon & Schuster, 1990). In the memoir Reagan remarked that fear of a larger "flow of illegal immigrants who . . . were already overwhelming welfare agencies and schools in some parts of our nation" was one of his reasons for fighting communism in Central America, a public issue that *was* important to him (473). And he recalled that when Gorbachev had chided him on

proposals in the United States to build a fence on the Mexican border, he had replied that building a fence to stop people who wanted to join our society "was hardly the same thing as building the Berlin Wall" (698). There is no mention of immigration in Fred L. Israel, ed., *Ronald Reagan's Weekly Radio Addresses: The First Term,* vol. 1 (Washington, D.C.: Scholarly Resources, 1987).

12. There is no reference to immigration issues in the memoirs by Edwin Meese III, George P. Shultz, Donald T. Regan, David Stockman, and Michael Deaver. The sole exception among memoirists is, unsurprisingly, William French Smith. In his 1991 memoir he gave the issue extended treatment, claiming in the end that they had fixed the problem in 1986. See his *Law and Justice in the Reagan Administration: The Memoirs of an Attorney General* (Stanford: Hoover Institution Press, 1991), 193–201. There is no mention at all of immigration issues in the Reagan biographies and presidential studies by Lou Cannon, Edmund Morris, Ronnie Dugger, Bob Schieffer and Gary P. Gates, Deborah H. and Gerald S. Strober, William F. Pemberton, and Robert Dallek. Dinesh D'Souza, in *Ronald Reagan* (New York: Free Press, 1997), touches the issue only in one paragraph. There is no mention of immigration issues in the leading studies of Reagan's presidency by Haynes Johnson, Laurence I. Barrett, John L. Palmer, Sidney Blumenthal, and Thomas Byrne Edsall.

13. "Remarks at Naturalization Ceremonies in Detroit, Michigan, October 1, 1984," *Public Papers of the Presidents of the United States: Ronald Reagan, 1984* (Washington, D.C.: Government Printing Office, 1985), 1394–95. See also his radio address on the Centennial of the Statue of Liberty, July 5, 1986 (*Public Papers,* 1986, 924–45), and remarks on awarding the Presidential Medal of Freedom, January 19, 1989, in which he said "if we ever closed the door to new Americans, our leadership in the world would soon be lost" (*Public Papers,* 1989, 1751–53). For another Reagan speech deploying the myth of the Statue of Liberty as "a woman holding a torch of welcome. . . . She represents our open door," see Reagan's remarks in Shanghai, China, April 30, 1984, in Emil Arca and Gregory J. Pamel, eds., *The Triumph of the American Spirit: The Presidential Speeches of Ronald Reagan* (Detroit: National Reproductions Corporation, 1984), 40–42.

14. *Public Papers,* 1989, 1722.

15. Lou Cannon, *President Reagan: The Role of a Lifetime* (New York: Simon & Schuster, 1991), 20. One organization with an intense interest in the new president's views, FAIR, did turn up two brief comments in the 1980 campaign that reveal much about Reagan's basic outlook on both legal and illegal immigration. When asked by a reporter what he thought of the Hesburgh Commission report, he apparently was not familiar with it and simply gave the California growers' answer to any question about immigration: "We ought to have a worker program where they could have visas to come up here and work, and then they could go home at the end of the period." Then, in Texas, in response to a reporter's question: "The way to solve the problem of the undocumented aliens was to give them all documents" (Conner oral history, 70).

16. Memorandum, Ronald Reagan to the Attorney General et al., March 6, 1981, box 3, Francis M. Hodsoll Files, OA12739, Ronald Reagan Library (RRL).

17. Briggs, *Mass Immigration,* 155; Nicholas Laham, *Ronald Reagan and the Politics of Immigration Reform* (Westport, Conn.: Praeger), 1.

18. Laham, *Ronald Reagan,* 6–7.

19. See Michael Teitelbaum, "Right versus Right: Immigration and Refugee Policy in the United States," *Foreign Affairs* (fall 1980), pp. 21–59.

20. Useful anthologies capturing the contemporary debate are Nathan Glazer, ed., *Clamor at the Gates: The New American Immigration* (San Francisco: Institute for Contemporary Studies, 1985), and David E. Simcox, ed., *U.S. Immigration in the 1980s: Reappraisal and Reform* (Boulder, Colo.: Westview Press, 1988).

21. On Simpson's immigration involvement, see Mary Elizabeth Brown, *Shapers of the Great Debate on Immigration: A Biographical Dictionary* (Westport, Conn.: Greenwood Press, 1999), 247–60.

22. Simpson had earlier been busy acquainting the White House with his "rather conservative" views as a SCIRP member. See Simpson staffer Richard Day to Frank Hodsoll, March 16, 1981, box 2, Hodsoll Files, Immigration and Refugee Policy Development file, RRL.

23. Laham, *Ronald Reagan,* 36–41.

24. "Suggested Talking Points for Meeting with Senator Alan Simpson," cited in Laham, *Ronald Reagan,* 41.

25. Walter D. Huddleston and Alan K. Simpson to Ronald Reagan, July 8, 1981, box 2, Hodsoll Files, RRL. This letter was FAIR's idea, according to FAIR director Roger Conner. See Conner oral history, 71.

26. Memorandum from Francis M. Hodsoll to Martin Anderson, May 4, 1981, Hodsoll Files, box 16, RRL.

27. Hodsoll was not alone in reading public and congressional opinion as increasingly restrictionist and requiring an administration response. See White House aide Charles P. Smith, "Immigration Policy Opportunities," March 14, 1981, box 1, Jan W. Mares Files, RRL, and a lengthy memorandum from the director of the National Security Council, Richard V. Allen, commenting on the Baker-Meese briefing of the president, discussed in Laham, *Ronald Reagan,* 88–96. On public opinion polls on a variety of immigration options, 1980 to 1981, see Kenneth Lee, *Huddled Masses, Muddled Laws: Why Contemporary Immigration Politics Fails to Reflect Public Opinion* (New York: Praeger, 1998), 7–9, 21–31. For the task force, see Thomas R. Maddox, "The Reagan White House and the Task Force on Immigration, 1981" (paper delivered at the Ronald Reagan Conference, Santa Barbara, Calif., March 27, 2002).

28. Memorandum, James A. Baker III and Edwin Meese II to Ronald Reagan, June 3, 1981, box 2, Hodsoll Files, RRL. See also Laham, *Ronald Reagan,* 78–88.

29. See Jason Juffras, *Impact of the Immigration Reform and Control Act on the Immigration and Naturalization Service* (Santa Monica: RAND Corporation, 1991), 10–11.

30. The *Washington Post* reported that four cabinet meetings were devoted in July to discussion of the Smith task force proposals, and historian Nicholas Laham writes that there were three (*Washington Post,* July 19, 1981, A19; Laham, *Ronald Reagan,* 106). The newspaper's count must be too high, and Laham's count may be an incorrect reading of the disorganized Hodsoll files. The confusion may arise from the administration's fast-changing system of "cabinet councils" made up of only a part of the cabinet. Martin Anderson's memory of only one full cabinet discussion of the task force's recommendations is probably correct.

31. Martin Anderson, *Revolution* (New York: Harcourt Brace Jovanovich, 1988), 272–77. Several versions of the idea of a worker identification card of some sort remained in discussion in the Cabinet Council on Legal Policy into 1982, but soon the administration's dislike of any hint of "a national identity card" hardened. See Cabinet Council on Legal Policy, Agenda of April 16, 1982, "Arguments for and against National Identity Cards," Edwin Meese Files, OA 11841, RRL.

32. "Card Tricks," *Washington Post,* July 21, 1981; Simpson quoted in Charles Babcock, "Migrant Policy Said to Benefit Western Bosses," *Washington Post,* July 19, 1981, copies in WHORM subject file, Task Force on Immigration and Refugee Policy, RRL.

33. "Report of the President's Task Force on Immigration and Refugee Policy," July 1, 1981, box 10, Hodsoll Files, RRL; Department of Justice, "U.S. Immigration and Refugee Policy," July 30, 1981, Hodsoll Files, RRL.

34. Department of Justice, "U.S. Immigration and Refugee Policy," July 30, 1981, Hodsoll Files, RRL.

35. "Statement on United States Immigration and Refugee Policy," *Public Papers of the Presidents of the United States: Ronald Reagan, 1981* (Washington, D.C.: Government Printing Office, 1982), 676–77. Liberal professor Lawrence Fuchs of Brandeis, former executive director of SCIRP, wrote the White House that "the overall tone is good," but "without a secure means of identification" the proposal will be "marginally effective." Lawrence Fuchs to Frank Hodsoll, August 28, 1981, Hodsoll Files, Box 5, RRL.

36. "Testimony of William French Smith, Attorney General, before the Senate Subcommittee on Immigration and Refugee Policy and the House Subcommittee on Immigration, Refugees and International Law," July 30, 1981, Hodsoll Files, Box 5, RRL.

37. Briggs, *Mass Immigration,* 154.

38. See Maddox, "Reagan White House," 30. Anderson had allies in White House counsel Fred Fielding and pollster Richard Wirthlin.

39. Maddox, "Reagan White House," 29–30.

40. *Congressional Quarterly Almanac,* 97th Cong., 1st sess., 1981, 422–24.

41. Memorandum from William French Smith to Cabinet Council on Legal Policy, April 20, 1983, Edwin Meese Files, OA 9945, RRL.

42. William French Smith to Jim Baker, Chief of Staff, June 10, 1982, Michael Uhlmann Files, OA 9445, RRL.

43. *Congressional Quarterly Almanac,* 97th Cong., 2d sess., 1982, 405–10; James G. Gimpel and James R. Edwards, *The Congressional Politics of Immigration Reform* (Boston: Allyn & Bacon, 1999), chap. 4.

44. This was evident in all the Gallup polls of the 1980s. See, for example, George Gallup, Jr., *The Gallup Poll: Public Opinion 1984* (Wilmington, Del.: Scholarly Resources, 1985), reporting that 75 percent of Americans in 1984 thought it should be illegal to employ a person without papers, and 20 percent disagreed; among Hispanics the proportions were 56 percent to 33 percent (250 to 52).

45. *Congressional Quarterly Almanac,* 98th Cong., 1st sess., 1983, 287.

46. Mazzoli quoted in Smith, *Law and Justice,* 218.

47. Aristide Zolberg, "Reforming the Back Door: The Immigration Reform and Control Act of 1986 in Historical Perspective," in *Immigration Reconsidered,* ed. Virginia Yans-McLaughlin (New York: Oxford University Press, 1990), 324.

48. *Congressional Quarterly Almanac,* 98th Cong., 2d sess., 1984, 229–36.

49. "House Moves Briskly on Immigration Law Change," *New York Times,* June 17, 1984, 4:1; Robert Pear, "Bill on Aliens," *New York Times,* April 22, 1984, 1:1.

50. Mondale quoted in *Congressional Quarterly Weekly Report* (July 21, 1984): 1733; Robert Pear, "Chief Sponsor Moves to Rescue Immigration Bill," *New York Times,* August 4, 1984, 24.

51. Robert Pear, "Conferees on Alien Bill Again Fail to Compromise," *New York Times,* October 10, 1984, A22; Robert Pear, "Amid Charges, Immigration Bill Dies," *New York Times,* October 12, 1984, A16.

52. Zolberg, "Reforming the Back Door," 323–26; Robert Pear, *New York Times,* October 12, 1984, A16.

53. Laham, *Ronald Reagan,* 198–200.

54. "Action Starting on Immigration Legislation," *Congressional Quarterly Weekly Report* 43 (July 20, 1985): 1421.

55. Zolberg, "Reforming the Back Door," 328–29; Robert Pear, "Immigration Bill Still at Sea," *New York Times,* May 4, 1985, 4:5.

56. Philip Shenon, "Startling Surge Is Reported in Illegal Aliens from Mexico," *New York Times,* February 21, 1986; Peter Applebome, "Surge of Illegal Aliens Taxes Southwestern Town's Resources," *New York Times,* March 9, 1986, 1:2.

57. *The Economist,* February 1, 1986, 22.

58. Robert Pear, "Reagan Agrees to Press for Immigration Bill," *New York Times,* March 12, 1986, A12.

59. Editorial, "To Control Aliens, Control Partisans," *New York Times,* September 29, 1985, A14.

60. Quoted in Peter Schuck, "Politics of Rapid Change: Immigration Policy in the 1980s," in Marc Landry and Martin A. Lewin, eds., *The New Politics of Public Policy* (Baltimore: Johns Hopkins University Press, 1995), 60.

61. Robert Pear, "Conferees on Bill Pressing to Reconcile Differences," *New York Times,* October 11, 1986, 1:9.

62. Zolberg, "Reforming the Back Door," 335.

63. "Remarks on Signing the Immigration Reform and Control Act of 1986," November 6, 1986, *Public Papers,* 1981, 1521–22.

64. Congressional Quarterly, *Congress and the Nation, 1985–86,* vol. 7 (Washington, D.C.: Congressional Quarterly, 1990), 717–23. As Vernon Briggs points out, there was not one amnesty in IRCA, but four. One was for illegals who had been in the country since January 1, 1982, one for "Special Agricultural Workers," one for Cubans and Haitians, and one moving forward the registry date, which allows the attorney general to adjust the status of long-term illegals (Briggs, *Mass Immigration,* 160–61).

65. *Public Papers of the Presidents of the United States: Ronald Reagan, 1986* (Washington, D.C.: Government Printing Office, 1987), 1521–22.

66. Mary Thornton, "Immigration Changes Are Signed Into Law," *Washington Post,* November 7, 1986, A3.

67. *FAIR Immigration Report,* November 7, 1986.

68. David Reimers, *Unwelcome Strangers,* 27. On IRCA as a "toothless tiger," see Barry Chiswick, "Immigration Reform and Control Act," in *U.S. Immigration Policy Reform in the 1980s,* ed. Francisco Rivera-Batiz (Westport, Conn.: Greenwood Press, 1991).

69. Jencks, "Who Should Get In?" pt. 2, 100. See the longer web version at <www.nybooks.com/articles/14942>. For an early prediction that IRCA would disappoint due to flaws in the method of enforcement and the institutional weakness of the INS, see Michael C. LeMay, *From Open Door to Dutch Door: An Analysis of U.S. Immigration Policy Since 1820* (New York: Praeger Publishers, 1990), 146–51. The dollar cost of the amnesty, direct (social services) and indirect (services to workers displaced by foreign workers, plus

services provided to children of amnesty recipients), brought the cost to U.S. taxpayers over ten years to $78.7 billion, according to David Simcox, "Measuring the Fallout: The Cost of the IRCA Amnesty after Ten Years," *CIS Backgrounder,* May 1997.

70. Center for Immigration Studies, "Census Bureau: Eight Million Illegal Aliens in 2000," October 24, 2001.

71. The Census report can be read at <http://www.census.gov/dmd/www/ReportRec2.htm>.

72. Laham, *Ronald Reagan,* 8, 16, 23–28, 202–19.

73. Gimpel and Edwards, *Congressional Politics,* 132–34, 143–44, 153.

74. Ibid., 137–38.

75. The party platform statements on immigration were sharply different. The Democrats said, "Our first priority must be to protect the fundamental human rights of American citizens and aliens" and made it clear that the rights of Americans they were concerned about were Hispanics who might be discriminated against under employer sanctions. The Republican tone was quite otherwise: "We affirm our country's absolute right to control its borders." *Congressional Quarterly Weekly Report* 42 (July 21, 1984): 1768, (August 25, 1984): 2109–10.

76. David North, "Why Democratic Governments Cannot Cope with Illegal Immigration" (paper delivered at the International Conference on Migration, Rome, March 13–15, 1991) (Paris: OECD, 1991).

77. *A Question of Numbers* (New York: Hill & Wang, 1998), 145. For the misuses of history, see Otis L. Graham, Jr., "Uses and Misuses of History in the Debate over Immigration Reform," *Public Historian* 8 (spring 1986): 41–64.

78. Alan Simpson, conversation with Otis L. Graham, San Diego, California, August 15, 1985.

79. *Congressional Digest* 62 (August–September 1983): 214, 218.

80. Schuck, "Politics of Rapid Change." Reagan's liberal instincts on immigration stand in sharp contrast to those of a real conservative he was said to admire, Margaret Thatcher. In the 1976 speech that earned her the label "the Iron Lady," Thatcher remarked that she could well understand why "people are really rather afraid that this country might be rather swamped by people with a different culture." Kenneth Harris, *Thatcher* (Boston: Little, Brown, 1988), 80–81. For Reagan as a liberal, see Ted V. McAllister, "Reagan and the Transformation of American Conservatism," this volume.

81. Thomas S. Langston, *Ideologues and Presidents: From the New Deal to the Reagan Revolution* (Baltimore: Johns Hopkins University Press, 1992), 67.

82. Steven Roberts, "Inquiry Finds Reagan and Chief Advisers Responsible for 'Chaos' in Iran Arms Deals," *New York Times,* February 27, 1987, 1.

83. Jencks, "Who Should Get In?" pt. 2, 96–97.

12
Civil Rights Policy
Hugh Davis Graham

Owing to author illness, this paper is posted as a synopsis of the events, evidence, and argument for the panel discussion of civil rights policy in the Reagan presidency. The synopsis will be presented and the discussion guided by Professor John David Skrentny, whose research in historical sociology I have frequently acknowledged for strengthening my own work on affirmative action and immigration policy.[1] Although civil rights policy properly includes an expanding universe of categories beyond black-and-white race relations, space limits this paper to the traditional black-and-white dyad exclusively, and the case study approach confines it to one illuminating conflict.[2] The synopsis begins with a summary describing the failure of an internal drive by leaders of the Republican Party's traditional conservative wing during 1984 through 1986 to persuade President Reagan to strike down minority preference policies. To achieve this, Reagan would rewrite the affirmative action executive order to bar the use of statistical enforcement remedies (e.g., percentages and ratios showing minority underutilization).

This campaign failed, and its failure dismayed cultural conservatives in the Republican Party. The postmortems produced a journalistic and scholarly consensus identifying the reasons for failure and the lessons taught. This synopsis presents a brief narrative describing the failed campaign, followed by a summary of four explanations commonly adduced to account for the failure. Three additional forces are then identified to account for the defeat of the campaign against race-conscious affirmative action. They help account for the surprising passivity of President Reagan's storied role as the "Great Communicator" in the conflict and the growing defense of affirmative action in the American corporate community since the 1970s.

With the exception of minor editorial changes, this essay appears exactly as Hugh Davis Graham submitted it on February 25, 2002, for the International Conference on the History of the Reagan Presidency, Santa Barbara, California.

THE CAMPAIGN TO REWRITE THE AFFIRMATIVE ACTION
EXECUTIVE ORDER

The drive to revise Executive Order 11246 was led by William Bradford Reynolds, assistant attorney general for civil rights, and supported by Edwin Meese III, White House counselor during Reagan's first term and, after February 1985, Reagan's attorney general. In January 1984, Reynolds, frustrated by the unwillingness of Labor secretaries Raymond J. Donovan (1981–1985) and, after April 1985, William E. Brock III to abandon minority preference policies inherited from the Carter administration, launched a major campaign to revise the executive order.[3] Meese, who chaired the Domestic Policy Council of the cabinet, won support for revising the executive order from secretaries Donald Hodel (Interior), William J. Bennett (Education), John Herrington (Energy), and OMB director James C. Miller III.

Leading the cabinet-level opposition to rewriting Executive Order 11246 was Labor secretary Brock, whose department had risen in authority and esteem since 1965 largely on the strength of its status as the government's lead agency in contract compliance. Joining Brock in defending the affirmative action status quo within Reagan's cabinet were secretaries George Shultz (State), James Baker (Treasury), Margaret Heckler (Health and Human Services), Elizabeth Dole (Transportation), and Samuel Pierce (Housing and Urban Development).[4] Brock's resistance stemmed partly from within the Labor Department bureaucracy, where the rights revolution of the 1960s and 1970s, by adding the Office of Federal Contract Compliance (OFCC) in 1965 and the Occupational Safety and Health Administration (OSHA) in 1970, had transformed a once-feeble mission agency into a powerful, two-fisted engine of social regulation. Shultz, as Nixon's first Labor secretary, had led the campaign to adopt the Philadelphia Plan.[5] Dole and Heckler had political ties to organized women's groups; Pierce, the lone African American in Reagan's cabinet, was attentive to urban constituencies.

Resistance in Reagan's cabinet to changing the executive order had political as well as bureaucratic origins. It reflected Republican uneasiness over attacking affirmative action, reinforced by the reluctance of the nation's large employers to plunge into unknown legal waters.[6] The Associated General Contractors and the Chamber of Commerce supported Reynolds and his conservative battalion in the campaign for color-blind nondiscrimination enforcement. But the National Association of Manufacturers supported Brock. Big business, strongly Republican and supporting deregulation elsewhere, preferred the known routines of underutilization analysis and minority hiring requirements to the unknown perils of reverse discrimination lawsuits. Employers with affirmative action plans approved by the Equal Employment Opportunity Commission (EEOC) and the OFCC, equally binding their business competitors, were protected from lawsuits filed by white workers like Brian Weber.[7]

At a cabinet meeting on October 22, 1985, Brock mounted a stout defense against the revisionists. He argued that the Labor Department's goals were not quotas, that enforcement abuses inherited from the Carter years were being corrected administratively, and that a political war over affirmative action would damage Republicans in the 1986 and 1988 elections. Meese, a supporter of cabinet government, was unwilling to take directly to the president an issue on which his cabinet was so deeply divided. Nor was White House chief of staff Donald Regan, a former Wall Street executive who screened President Reagan from the entire dispute. In March 1986, Reynolds released a report documenting alleged quota requirements from Labor Department correspondence with contractors. This, however, only stiffened the resistance of Brock and his allies, who resented such intramural attacks from the Justice Department. When Congress recessed for the 1986 elections (in which the Democrats recaptured the Senate), Reynolds's campaign was dead.[8]

THE STANDARD ACCOUNT

With only one significant exception, most book-length studies of civil rights policy in the Reagan administration have been written by conservative scholars who deplore the failure of the Meese-Reynolds campaign.[9] This literature describes a standard account that emphasizes the vulnerability of split coalitions in a separation-of-powers system, wherein it is easier to block policy initiatives than to achieve them. The standard account emphasizes four such divisions or splits during the 1980s, all of them widely discussed by contemporary journalists and political commentators. One split divided Republicans within the GOP tent, setting traditionalist, family-values conservatives against libertarian-minded entrepreneurs. A second split, mirroring the first, divided Reagan's cabinet. A third divided the business community itself, setting small business, Chamber of Commerce interests and needs against those of the National Association of Manufacturers and the Fortune 500 companies.

Finally, there was the intensifying party split. By tradition, the civil rights coalition was bipartisan in Congress, ably led by the Leadership Conference on Civil Rights, which threatened Republican critics with a racist label. In the voting rights extension of 1982, the civil rights coalition ignored White House proposals and expanded voting rights to provide for "majority minority" electoral districts—a form of affirmative action in voting rights designed to elect minority candidates, most of them Democrats by political tradition. In 1985, the Leadership Conference claimed to have signed commitments from 69 senators and 180 House members willing to block legislatively any agency attempting to gut affirmative action remedies inherited from the Carter administration. Collectively, the dangers posed by widening these divisions supported pragmatist Republican views that a fight over affirmative action offered far more in losses than gains for the Republican Party in the Reagan presidency.

REAGAN'S LOW PRIORITY FOR CIVIL RIGHTS REFORM

Nonetheless, Reagan's conservative civil rights critics remained puzzled by his inability, or unwillingness, to rewrite the executive order, even after reelection in 1984. Nicholas Laham, in the first book-length study of Reagan's civil rights policy to use documents in the Reagan Library, called Reagan's presidential behavior on affirmative action "confused, contradictory, inconsistent, and ultimately unprincipled."[10] Severe judgments such as Laham's reflect an assumption that Reagan placed a high priority on returning civil rights policy to the principles stipulated in the bipartisan Civil Rights Act of 1964. As Reagan told audiences during his campaign against Jimmy Carter in 1980, "We must not allow the noble concept of equal opportunity to be distorted into federal guidelines or quotas which require race, ethnicity, or sex—rather than ability and qualifications—to be the principal factor in hiring or education."[11] This passage indubitably reflected Reagan's personal beliefs about rewarding individual merit and opposing group rights and minority preferences. But the words themselves were crafted by a speechwriter.

A more revealing barometer of Reagan's social and political priorities is provided by the handwritten scripts of his radio commentaries in the 1970s. Between 1975 and 1979, Reagan gave more than one thousand daily radio broadcasts, more than two-thirds of which he wrote himself. In 2001 a book, based on these scripts and edited by Kiron Skinner, Annelise Anderson, and Martin Anderson, was published under the title *Reagan, In His Own Hand.*[12]

Reagan wrote the radio scripts on long yellow pads and edited them quite capably—he was a well-schooled grammarian. He was also an intelligent man whose command of the facts and circumstances surrounding issues he deeply cared about was considerably stronger than his critics, and even some of his supporters, generally assumed. Reagan's ability to mix fact with fancy should not blind critics to the cogency of his core beliefs, given the assumptions and principles that underpinned them. *In His Own Hand* provides a corrective to underestimating Reagan in two ways. First, Reagan's core concerns, which dominate *In His Own Hand,* comprise a short list of topics—the global communist conspiracy, national defense and intelligence, international arms control, the growth of government, taxation, regulating free markets. These areas dominated Reagan's presidential agenda during 1981 through 1989. By concentrating his efforts on this short list, he achieved a surprising amount of what he attempted. Unlike Carter or Bush (senior), whose policy agendas were long, complex, and lacked thematic coherence, Reagan confined his attention to a short list of high-priority items.

Second, civil rights topics as traditionally understood are scarcely visible in *In His Own Hand.* The index contains no listings for civil rights, affirmative action, race, minorities, immigration, quotas, the NAACP, the *Bakke* decision. Reagan's opposition to race-conscious remedies in affirmative action programs was vague and abstract. Unlike Nixon, who was a keen student of the structure and function of government agencies as well as a shrewd student of their politics, Reagan was remarkably incurious about organizational structures and their consequences. As a two-term governor of the country's largest state, Reagan remained a crude Weberian on the politics of bureaucracy. Routinely he ordered senior appointees heading bureaucracies he saw as Democratic boondoggles (for example, the departments of Energy, Education, the Environmental Protection Agency) to dissolve their agencies. Reagan was self-disciplined and attended to his homework in areas important to him, areas that included keeping physically fit as an actor, committing text to his extraordinary memory, and later, as an elected government official, studying the briefing books on certain vital issues in foreign policy and international arms control. In areas falling outside the small cluster of high-priority issues that interested him, however—and civil rights policy fell outside the central cluster—Reagan soothed the faithful with his moving rhetoric, but little taxed his energy beyond offering these symbolic stroking measures.

AFFIRMATIVE ACTION AND AMERICAN CORPORATE MANAGEMENT

Reagan's personal style of political leadership constituted one of three forces insufficiently explored in the literature that shaped his presidency's civil rights policy, and hence its legacy, in surprising directions. Reagan, by sharing Nixon's ambivalence about affirmative action, in effect validated liberal claims in the 1980s that a conservative policy should preserve the race-conscious policies that Nixon had established and Carter had expanded (in both cases with considerable assistance from the federal courts).

The second force was grounded not in the peculiar attributes of individual leadership but in the broad corporate development of American business management. During the 1970s, American firms and business schools accommodated to the "rights revolution" by professionalizing the field of employment relations. Traditional personnel departments, with their emphasis on testing, hiring, and training, were transformed by the "human resources" model of personnel management. Emphasizing employee rights as well as employer needs, it integrated and institutionalized business practices in affirmative action, safety, health, and benefits.

Corporate counsel, seeking to avoid an anticipated flood of "reverse discrimination" lawsuits like the *Bakke* case (falsely, as it turned out), advised firms to negotiate affirmative action plans with the EEOC. The advice of corporate counsel coincided with human resources professionalization. Increasingly during the 1970s, human resources departments policed employee rights protections enacted by Congress. This grew beyond hiring and promoting racial and ethnic minorities, women, older workers, the handicapped, and Vietnam veterans, to include protecting employees from safety and health risks (OSHA, passed in 1970) and safeguarding employee benefits (Employee Retirement Income Security Act, ERISA, passed in 1974). Typically, corporate vice presidents of human resources were themselves members of protected groups. Large employers capable of providing this growing array of services, including their heavy reporting burden with regulatory agencies, were thereby advantaged over small employers. Little wonder that affirmative action was supported by the National Association of Manufacturers (NAM) but not by the Chamber of Commerce.[13]

AFFIRMATIVE ACTION AND IMMIGRATION

The history of affirmative action is rich with irony, as session chairman John Skrentny has notably observed.[14] Perhaps none is so painful to the sponsors of minority preference policies as the accumulating evidence that these policies, while benefiting the minority middle class, not only failed to benefit the black underclass but significantly harmed them. The failure to assist poor blacks occurred partly for familiar reasons: the minority underclass was too poorly organized and educated to take advantage of race-conscious benefits such as contract set-aside programs and university admissions preferences. The harm occurred chiefly because the return of mass immigration in the 1970s lowered wages and workplace opportunities for all low-skilled native workers in America, among which blacks were themselves a minority.[15]

By the 1980s, Reagan's ambivalence about affirmative action provided no effective counterweight to the splits within his government, especially the growing business preference for hiring immigrants. The failure of the Reagan administration to curb significantly both race-conscious affirmative action and mass immigration was seen by corporate America as crucial to survival and expansion in a globalizing economy where success rewarded low labor costs, weakened union movements, and credible corporate options of outsourcing, downsizing, and moving offshore.[16]

How did affirmative action mesh with mass immigration in this process? Briefly, the Nixon administration, anxious to deny that affirmative action threatened racial quotas, stressed the importance of minimalist, "good faith efforts" in achieving a nondiscriminatory work force. Corporate America interpreted this, largely successfully, to validate the "diversity" rationale that underpinned the shift to the human resources paradigm. In practical terms, this meant massive hiring of Latino and Asian workers in preference to native blacks. By 1979 these trends so angered EEOC chairwoman Eleanor Holmes Norton that the EEOC sued a series of firms in Chicago, seeking a federal court ruling requiring employers to hire according to racial and ethnic proportionality. Norton won in the trial courts but lost in the courts of appeal, where by the late 1980s, conservative, antiregulationist judges appointed by Reagan were gaining majorities on the federal bench.[17]

Similarly in the 1980s, corporate America opposed immigration restriction and worked successfully with expansionist groups, chiefly Latino, to gut enforcement provisions in the Immigration Reform and Control Act of 1986 (IRCA). Employers preferred hiring, under a diversity rationale, immigrant workers they found to be hardworking, honest, low-cost, compliant, and resistant to union organizers. These attributes were especially found in the growing pool of illegal immigrants, which by the turn of the century had reached eight million to nine million. By 2000, thirty-five million immigrants had come to America, twenty-seven million of them from Latin America or Asia, and hence eligible as members of protected classes for affirmative action programs and benefits.

THE REAGAN LEGACY IN CIVIL RIGHTS POLICY

From the perspective of the turn of the century, the Reagan administration had largely failed in its efforts to win a conservative turnaround in civil rights policy in the executive and legislative branches. By the end of the 1980s, for example, Congress routinely expanded minority set-aside requirements in the massive federal procurement budgets, and federal agencies administering the programs worked closely with leaders of the civil rights coalition, as they had in the Carter years—and as they would again in the Clinton years. Reagan's legacy survived only in the federal judiciary, where the *Croson* decision in 1989, and *Adarand* in 1995, signaled a shift to narrow conservative margins at the Supreme Court level in cases involving minority preference programs. But even here, the conservative Rehnquist court practiced a cautious constitutional minimalism. The *Croson* standard held not that the Constitution was color-blind and that racial preference programs were unconstitutional per se, but only that race-conscious remedies must be remedies of last resort, narrowly tailored to correct documented instances of discrimination.

"Let Reagan be Reagan," cried "movement" conservatives in the 1980s. They sought a Reagan Revolution to return government to the bedrock principles of the founders—in this case to the principle of equal individual rights rather than to group rights. But Reagan *was* being Reagan. In fields such as civil rights policy, which did not make Reagan's short list of crucial import, this meant being occasionally persuasive, but more often being disengaged, incurious, ill-informed, inconsistent. Or, to credit a remarkably successful politician who won important contests far more often than he lost, "being Reagan" in the affirmative action debate meant avoiding a bloody and possibly losing battle, saving your chits to cash in on the great, short-listed policy conflicts such as tax cuts and defense buildup. Whichever Reagan was the real Reagan, the result was a passive and inattentive president in the affirmative action debate. And when these traits were combined with the incipient splits in the Republican Party and its constituencies, the result was defeat in the inside-the-Beltway politics of interest group bargaining. There the well-organized forces of the civil rights coalition worked effectively with corporate lobbies to protect the Carter administration's affirmative action programs, including a "diversity" rationale that permitted massive hiring of immigrants from Latin America and Asia, and to pass an immigration control law in 1986 against hiring "undocumented" immigrants that was unenforceable from the start.

From the perspective of the twenty-first century, what is new about this story is the role of mass immigration, a phenomenon unknown in America since before World War I. In the 1980s, growing immigration on balance strengthened the civil rights coalition in its defense of affirmative action. By the turn of the century, however, immigration was weakening the heart of the affirmative action rationale. Affirmative action for immigrants made no sense, critics said. Who was an official minority in America, and why? Rising rates of intermarriage were producing millions of native Americans of mixed-race or -ethnic parentage who objected to federal census forms requiring that one line of their parentage be rejected. In the aftermath of the battle over the census forms for 2000, civil rights officials warned that minority preference programs as they had been implemented in the past are increasingly vulnerable to court challenge—for example, barring eligibility for affirmative action benefits to Americans with "ancestry" from Iran, Morocco, Palestine, or Egypt, as is done in the Small Business Administration's minority contract set-aside program. On the other hand, what is the public policy rationale for allowing affluent Asian American entrepreneurs to dominate the federal government's largest minority set-aside program in the nation's largest state, California?[18] Reagan's short-circuited rewriting of the executive order, by papering over the accumulating problems of logical incoherence in affirmative action's race-conscious rationale, allowed them to proliferate and worsen.

In revising our understanding of civil rights policy in the Reagan presidency, we thus need to study not only the behavior of the senior officials whose documents dominate the Reagan Library, but also the behavior of business interests, whose corporate archives are typically closed, and especially the renewed phenomenon of mass immigration in America. Ironically the immigrant wave, welcomed by civil rights leaders in the 1970s and 1980s, has sped the unraveling of the affirmative action programs that the civil rights coalition and corporate interests sought successfully to protect during the Reagan years.

NOTES

1. See, for example, John David Skrentny, ed., *Color Lines: Affirmative Action, Immigration, and Civil Rights Options for America* (Chicago: University of Chicago Press, 2001).

2. I have explored civil rights policy in the Reagan presidency more broadly in three publications that are based primarily on research in the Reagan Library: Hugh Davis Graham, "The Storm over Grove City College: Civil Rights Regulation, Higher Education, and the Reagan Administration," *History of Education Quarterly* 38 (winter 1998): 407–29; idem, "The Politics of Clientele Capture: Civil Rights Policy and the Reagan Administration," in Neal Devins and Davison M. Douglas, eds., *Redefining Equality* (New York: Oxford University Press, 1998), 103–19; idem, "The Surprising Career of Federal Fair Housing Law," *Journal of Policy History* 12 (spring 2000): 215–32.

3. James C. Miller to Orrin G. Hatch, September 14, 1981, White House Office files (WHORM), HU 012, ID #034700, Ronald Reagan Library (RRL); Augustus F. Hawkins to the President, October 16, 1984, WHORM PE 002-01, ID #248938, RRL; William Bradford Reynolds to Mayor W. Wilson Goode, December 12, 1985, WHORM HU 010, ID #327919, RRL; Ralph G. Neas to Members of the Press, "Update on the Executive Order on Affirmative Action," February 15, 1986, Leadership Conference on Civil Rights Papers (LCCRP), Manuscript Division, Library of Congress.

4. *Newsweek,* December 30, 1985; Daniel Seligman, "It Was Forseeable," *Fortune,* July 22, 1985; Gary L. McDowell, "Affirmative Inaction," *Policy Review* 48 (spring 1989): 32–37.

5. Hugh Davis Graham, *Civil Rights and the Presidency* (New York: Oxford University Press, 1992), 150–69.

6. Mel Bradley to Jack Svahn, October 23, 1984, WHORM PE 002-01, ID #248938, RRL; Memorandum, John G. Roberts to Diana G. Holland, April 10, 1986, WHORM PQ 341000, RRL.

7. Daniel Seligman, "Affirmative Action Is Here to Stay," *Fortune,* April 19, 1982; Anne B. Fisher, "Businessmen Like to Hire by the Numbers," *Fortune,* September 16, 1985; Steven A. Holmes, "Affirmative Action Plans Are Part of Business Life," *New York Times,* November 22, 1991.

8. Ralph Neas press release, October 22, 1985, LCCR Papers; Howard Kurtz, "Meese, Brock Set Hiring-Plan Talk," *Washington Post,* February 15, 1986; Kurtz, "Reynolds Seeks Affirmative Action Change," *Washington Post,* March 29, 1986; Memorandum, Robert M. Kruger to Peter J. Wallison, April 7, 1986, Kruger Files, folder RMK/Affirmative Action—Reply to Inquiries, OA 18389, RRL.

9. Books by conservative scholars critical of President Reagan's civil rights record include Abigail M. Thernstrom, *Whose Votes Count? Affirmative Action and Minority Voting Rights* (Cambridge: Harvard University Press, 1987); Robert R. Detlefsen, *Civil Rights under Reagan* (San Francisco: Institute for Contemporary Studies, 1991); Raymond Wolters, *Right*

Turn: William Bradford Reynolds, the Reagan Administration, and Black Civil Rights (New Brunswick, N.J.: Transaction Publishers, 1996); and Nicholas Laham, *The Reagan Presidency and the Politics of Race* (Westport, Conn.: Praeger, 1998). For a critical assessment of Reagan's record written by a civil rights lawyer, see Norman C. Amaker, *Civil Rights and the Reagan Administration* (Washington, D.C.: Urban Institute Press, 1988).

10. Laham, *Reagan Presidency and the Politics of Race,* 126.

11. Quoted in McDowell, "Affirmative Inaction," 32.

12. Kiron K. Skinner, Annelise Anderson, and Martin Anderson, eds., *Reagan, In His Own Hand* (New York: Free Press, 2001). As pre-presidential papers, the Reagan scripts are not presidential documents controlled by the National Archives. Reagan's handwritten scripts were discovered by Hoover Institution researcher Kiron Skinner among the pre-presidential papers, 1921–1980, in the Reagan Presidential Library in Simi Valley, California, in the 1990s.

13. Lauren B. Edelman et al., "Legal Ambiguity and the Politics of Compliance: Affirmative Action Officer's Dilemma," *Law and Policy* 13 (January 1991): 73–97; Erin Kelly and Frank Dobbin, "How Affirmative Action Became Diversity Management," *American Behavioral Scientist* 41 (April 1998): 960–84.

14. John David Skrentny, *The Ironies of Affirmative Action* (Chicago: University of Chicago Press, 1996).

15. Network job recruiting, especially among Spanish-speaking workers, additionally drove many black workers from low-skilled jobs, such as construction and hotel services, they had previously held. Philip Martin, "Network Recruitment and Labor Displacement," David E. Simcox, ed., *U.S. Immigration in the 1980s* (Boulder, Colo.: Westview Press, 1988), 67–91; Roger Waldinger, *Still the Promised City? African-Americans and New Immigrants in Postindustrial New York* (Cambridge: Harvard University Press, 1996).

16. For evidence and citations supporting arguments offered in this synopsis that corporate America found both affirmative action and mass immigration vital for prospering in a globalizing economy, see Hugh Davis Graham, *Collision Course: The Strange Convergence of Affirmative Action and Immigration Policy in America* (New York: Oxford University Press, 2002).

17. Ibid., 157–60.

18. Hugh Davis Graham, "Affirmative Action for Immigrants? The Unintended Consequences of Reform," in *Color Lines: Affirmative Action, Immigration, and Civil Rights Options for America,* ed. John David Skrentny (Chicago: University of Chicago Press, 2001), 53–70.

13
Mobilizing Women:
The "Social" Issues
Donald T. Critchlow

The decade of the 1970s in America presents the historian with a puzzle. The puzzle is this: Social commentators depicted, I believe accurately, this period as a time when Americans turned inward, becoming narcissistic, obsessed with their physical and mental well-being, given to new diets, physical fitness, faddist therapies, and spiritualism. In this new mood of turning inward, emotions and intuitions, rather than the rational and the intellectual, were celebrated. One estimate was that there were five thousand encounter groups in New York City alone. Writing in 1976, Jerry Rubin, once a student radical, wrote that from 1971 to 1975 he underwent EST, Gestalt therapy, bioenergetics, rolfing, massage, jogging, health foods, tai chi, and Esalen.[1] "Trust your feelings, Luke," was the advice given in the climactic moments of *Star Wars* (1977), and the young Skywalker obediently shut his eyes and put his faith in the Force. "Trust your feelings," as journalist David Frum observes, expressed the spirit of the age.[2]

Coinciding with this heightened sense of "self," however, were demands for extending group rights and liberation for women, racial minorities, and homosexuals. These demands often culminated in social protest, at times quite violent. In the drive for equality, conventional culture, established institutions, and customary social roles came under attack.

Yet, in the midst of this turn inward and the extension of group rights, American politics had shifted politically to the right, culminating in the election of Ronald Reagan, an avowed conservative, in 1980. How is the historian to explain this paradox in which the culture appeared to reject traditional values concerning religion, the family, gender roles, and individual rights (as opposed to group rights), and yet elect a candidate who seemed so out of sync with the culture? And, at the same time that Ronald Reagan was elected, Republicans gained control of the Senate, taking many seats that liberal Democrats had held.

This essay posits that key social issues including abortion, the equal rights amendment (ERA), and prayer in school played an integral role in Reagan's election and the rightward shift in American politics. These social issues mobilized traditional-minded women to become involved in politics on a grassroots level to oppose ERA and abortion, while supporting legislation or a constitutional amendment to allow prayer in public schools. This mobilization activated a disheartened conservative movement and laid the foundation for the election of Ronald Reagan in 1980. The grassroots campaign that emerged over these social issues showed Republican Party operatives that Roman Catholics (traditionally aligned with Democrats) and nonaligned evangelical Christians could be won over to the GOP. This mobilization of the pro-life and anti-feminist right created what later became known as the gender gap (i.e., the difference in voting patterns between white men and women). The real gap, however, was not between men and women, but between single white women, who tended to vote Democratic, and white men and married women who tended to vote Republican.

Thus rests another paradox within the decade of liberation—if you will, a paradox within a paradox: While the culture appeared to accentuate personal liberation, and group rights were extended to ethnic minorities and women, traditional women provided a catalyst for political change from the right. The age of liberation manifested, for want of a better term, a dialectical negation of progressive liberation—the mobilization of right-wing women. If this was the age of liberation, it was equally the age reaction.

Yet, while the 1980s further sharpened differences between the left and right in American politics, social issues ultimately led to tensions within the conservative movement itself. As a result, divergence occurred between economic and social conservatives, the Christian coalition and the anti-abortion movement, and debates within the anti-abortion movement itself. These disagreements within the right revealed the limits of the Reagan Revolution. The debate over social issues, especially reproductive rights, showed all too clearly that the right was hardly the monolith it was viewed to be by many of its opponents.

American culture has historically manifested pronounced moralist attitudes, but the "social issues"—abortion, prayer in school, and the equal rights amendment—gave these attitudes particular salience during the 1970s, a decade of reduced expectations.[3] The somber realities of perceived declining economic competitiveness and lessened geopolitical influence led large numbers of voters to reject the liberalism of Franklin D. Roosevelt's New Deal. Americans placed less confidence in the ability and the advantages of government to redistribute resources, promote egalitarianism, and guarantee basic social provisions as part of the universal rights of citizenship.[4] With this erosion in confidence in government, liberalism was no longer assured of its political base.[5] A declining economy exacerbated differences among constituencies, especially within the working class.[6] The universalistic ethos of the modern welfare state and the social vision of New Deal liberalism came under heavy criticism in an economy experiencing stagflation and a society undergoing racial and ethnic tensions.[7] In this context, women who upheld traditional family and religious values were compelled to activism by the emergence of social issues that they perceived as an attack on what they held dear—God, church, country, and family.

What is most striking about this conservative resurgence was how quickly this turnabout came, given the disarray of conservative Republicans in the late 1960s. At the Republican convention in Miami in 1968, many conservatives rallied behind Ronald Reagan for the GOP nomination.[8] Senator Strom Thurmond (R-S.C.) and Republican activist Phyllis Schlafly played critical roles in holding the GOP right from wholesale desertion to Reagan.[9] At the same time, Reagan's strategy of hoping for a deadlocked convention played into the hands of a skillful campaign by Nixon for the nomination. Nixon won the nomination, but large numbers of conservatives continued to distrust him. Once in office, Nixon did little to reassure his conservative base and, as a consequence, conservatives were soon complaining that Nixon had forgotten who had elected him. Conservatives found that they did not like either Nixon's foreign policies or his domestic agenda. In short, they grew to despise Nixon, arguably even more than did Nixon's enemies on the left.

Long before some scholars such as Joan Hoff reassessed the Nixon domestic program as "progressive," conservatives were denouncing Nixon as a liberal dressed in conservative clothing.[10] Nixon's Family Assistance Plan (FAP), his wage and price controls, and the growth of federal domestic expenditures all bitterly disappointed conservatives.[11] Social expenditures under Nixon rapidly increased, even though he had campaigned on the promise to "clean up the welfare mess."[12] By 1975 social services financed by the federal government were on their way to having universal coverage, not only for the poor but for the middle classes as well. By the time Nixon left office, social expenditures totaled approximately $338.7 billion, which covered an estimated 72.7 percent of all social welfare expenditures in the nation. Nixon's imposition of wage and price controls in 1971 frustrated conservatives even further.

Nixon's foreign policy proved even more disturbing to conservatives. His appointment of Henry Kissinger, a longtime associate of Nelson Rockefeller, was taken as an insult by conservatives. Moreover, it did not take long for conservatives to blame Nixon for prolonging the war in Southeast Asia and then negotiating a peace that in effect sold our South Vietnam ally down the river. Although conservative organizations such as the Young Americans for Freedom had held patriotic rallies to support the war, privately many conservatives thought Vietnam was a mistake that played into the hands of the Soviet Union, which was rapidly building its nuclear arsenal.[13] If things were not bad enough for conservatives, the opening of relations with mainland China led conservative activists to denounce the Nixon administration in language usually reserved for their liberal opponents.[14] The Kissinger-written SALT treaties of 1972 (along with subsidized grain shipments to the Soviet Union) led to open denunciations of Nixon by conservatives. Feelings were so high that U.S. Representative John

Ashbrook of Ohio challenged Nixon in the 1972 primaries and William Rusher, publisher of the *National Review,* tried unsuccessfully to form a third party. By the time Nixon resigned from office in 1974, the conservative movement was in disarray and on the defensive.

Matters did not get any better when Gerald Ford succeeded to the presidency.[15] Ford picked Nelson Rockefeller as his vice president and retained Kissinger as his secretary of state—two appointments that cost Ford heavily among GOP conservatives. Moreover, Ford continued Nixon's policies toward the Soviet Union and mainland China.[16] On domestic policy, Ford sought to hold down federal spending and taxes and to prevent the expansion of government, but he faced a Democratic majority in both houses of Congress so huge that theoretically the Democrats could override any veto without a single Republican vote. Because of Watergate, Democrats gained 46 seats in 1974 and controlled the House 290 to 145; in the Senate, they picked up 4 seats, adding to their already large majority. Ford vetoed more bills than any president since Harry Truman, but any credit he might have received from conservatives for his fiscal restraint was diminished by his continuation of the "Rockefeller-Kissinger" foreign and defense policies they despised.

Yet in this period of discouragement, stirrings among grassroots activists marked the beginning of a revival of the right. The mobilization of female conservative activists proved critical to this conservative resurgence. This resuscitation of the conservative movement came to be labeled the "new right."[17] Critical to the new right was its capacity to raise money for political causes through direct mailing and its emphasis on moral issues—the so-called social issues. Postwar conservatives had long lamented the decline of traditional values and Christian morality in America, but what gave these moral issues poignancy in the 1970s was changing gender relations, the emergence of the feminist movement in the late 1960s and early 1970s, and the Supreme Court's decision to legalize abortion. These social issues brought Protestant evangelicals into the conservative movement.[18] The first indication of the potential of mobilizing Protestant evangelicals to the conservative cause came when evangelical Christian women joined grassroots campaigns against abortion and the equal rights amendment. As this occurred, an alliance was formed between traditional Roman Catholic conservatives and newly mobilized evangelical Protestants.[19]

Thus, central to revival of the right in the 1970s were two issues—abortion and the ERA. Efforts to liberalize abortion laws began on the state level in the late 1960s, which in turn stimulated the rise of the anti-abortion movement. The emergence of the feminist movement at this same time added to the momentum to repeal state laws restricting abortion. Under the slogan My Body Belongs to Me, feminists began staging speak-outs, street theater, and other demonstrations in favor of abortion, adding to the groundswell for the repeal of abortion laws.[20] Hawaii became the first state to repeal its law, thereby permitting hospital abortions of "nonviable" fetuses.[21] New York followed with legislation that removed all restrictions on abortions performed in the first twenty-four weeks of pregnancy. Signed into law by Governor Rockefeller in 1970, this measure gave New York the most liberal abortion law in the nation. Alaska and Washington passed similar legislation, while thirteen other states allowed abortion to preserve the life of the woman or protect her physical or mental health. In another twenty-nine states, abortion remained unlawful except when it was necessary to save the life of the mother.[22]

In opposition to this movement, anti-abortion activists organized on the grassroots level. During the fight over legalized abortion in California, groups such as the Right to Life League and Mothers Outraged at the Murder of Innocents (MOMI) organized to lobby against a bill introduced in the California legislature. Although under heavy pressure from these local activists, as well as from Roman Catholic James Francis Cardinal McIntyre of Los Angeles, Governor Ronald Reagan signed the act into law in 1967.[23]

The hierarchy of the Catholic Church supported the anti-abortion movement as it emerged in the late 1960s, but the impetus for the movement came from local activists who organized on the local level without official Church support. These local organizations often mirrored the unique character of their individual leaders.[24] Women played critical roles in these organizations, as both leaders and foot soldiers.[25] Most of these early activists were Roman Catholics, although a number of the most prominent female leaders were Protestants, including Dr. Mildred Jefferson, an African American Harvard University–trained physician in Massachusetts; Dr. Carolyn Gerster in Arizona; Judy Fink in Pennsylvania; and Marjory Mecklenburg in Minnesota. In mid-1971 the National Right to Life Committee (NRLC), funded by the National Conference of Catholic Bishops, was established as a national coordinating organization to provide material and information to local and state organizations.

As the election of 1972 approached, Nixon sought to direct this growing anti-abortion movement to the Republican Party.[26] George Wallace's dramatic showing as a third-party candidate convinced Nixon that the northern ethnic Catholic vote—the backbone of the Democratic Party in urban areas—was vulnerable.[27] Further evidence of this vulnerability was revealed when James Buckley, the brother of William Buckley, editor of the conservative *National Review*, won the Senate seat in New York running on a third-party ticket, the Conservative Party, against two liberals. Nixon felt the key to winning the Catholic vote lay in his support of parochial schools and in opposing abortion.[28]

In May 1972, Nixon issued a public statement condemning "unrestricted abortion policies." He declared, "I consider abortion an unacceptable form of population control. In my judgement, unrestrictive abortion policies would demean human life." Shortly afterward, Nixon released a letter he sent to Terence Cardinal Cooke of New York supporting his campaign to repeal the recently passed New York abortion law, enacted by Republican governor Nelson Rockefeller.[29] The *Roe v. Wade* Supreme Court decision the following year changed all this, but in the meantime, Nixon's "Catholic strategy" paid off. That November, Nixon captured 60 percent of the Catholic vote, 59 percent of the working-class vote, and 57 percent of the union household vote.

The Supreme Court's decision in *Roe v. Wade* transformed American politics, polarizing the electorate and the two major political parties. On the federal level, opponents of abortion in Congress sought to repeal *Roe* through the enactment of constitutional amendments and to prevent federal funding of abortion. On the state level, anti-abortion groups undertook efforts to limit legalized abortion through restrictive abortion regulations. By early 1976, more than fifty different constitutional amendments to ban or limit abortions had been introduced in Congress. At the same time, anti-abortion congressional leaders sought to withdraw federal funding for abortions under the Medicaid program unless these operations were deemed "medically necessary."[30]

While battles raged in Congress, fights on the state level proved even more intense. Thirty-eight states by 1990 had adopted a labyrinth of regulations restricting abortion.[31] As a result, each state became a battleground between pro-abortion and anti-abortion activists for the hearts and minds of the electorate and state legislators. Anti-abortion activists, usually led by women, often won in the political arena by drawing support from districts with heavy Catholic populations. The courts became centers of political struggle. Court rulings, however, left neither side totally satisfied, and each ruling seemed to aggravate both sides.[32] Abortion intensified divisions within the Republican Party while polarizing both parties.

The anti-abortion wing of the Republican Party believed that Gerald Ford could not be trusted on the abortion issue. Within weeks of Ford's presidency, his wife, Betty Ford, announced her support of abortion by telling the press that she would advise her daughter to have an abortion if necessary. She also announced her support for the equal rights amendment. Furthermore, Ford's vice president, Nelson Rockefeller, had signed the bill legalizing abortion when he was governor of New York.[33] Nonetheless, Ford tried to finesse the issue by taking a moderate stance on abortion. When Representative Henry J. Hyde (R-Ill.) successfully placed a rider to an appropriations bill banning federal funding for abortions for any reason, the Senate countered with a similar measure, adding the critical qualifier that federal funds could be used to save a woman's life. Finally, after a series of intense conference meetings, an agreement was reached to reconcile the two versions of the bill that accepted less restrictive language. When the bill reached Ford's desk, he vetoed the measure. Congress overrode Ford's veto, thereby restricting federal funds for abortion. Congressional opposition to abortion led Ford to support a constitutional amendment to allow individual states to regulate abortion policy. Moreover, when the amendment was challenged in the courts, Ford instructed his solicitor general, Robert H. Bork, to file an amicus curiae with the Supreme Court in support of the Hyde amendment.[34]

Meanwhile, Ford encountered a grassroots revolt over the issue of the equal rights amendment, which had passed Congress with more than the two-thirds required for constitutional amendments.[35] Congress gave the ERA until 1979 for thirty-eight states to ratify the amendment. The amendment simply stated, "Equality of rights under the law shall not be denied or abridged by the United States or by any State on account of sex," and that Congress shall have the power to enforce provisions of this article.[36]

The amendment passed the Senate in March 1972 with a vote of 84–8. Attempts by Senator Sam Ervin (D-N.C.) to modify the amendment to exclude issues of the military draft and combat, marital and family support, privacy protections and exemptions, and homosexuality failed, but they set the stage for debates in the states. The very day that the Senate passed the ERA, Hawaii became the first state to ratify, followed in the next few days by Delaware, Nebraska, New Hampshire, Idaho, and Iowa. By early 1973, twenty-four states had ratified the ERA.[37]

By late 1973, however, ERA proponents had lost control of the ratification process. Longtime Republican Party activist Phyllis Schlafly started a movement called Stop-ERA, declaring that the ERA meant the drafting of women into the military (remember, America was just emerging from the Vietnam War), the taking away of statutory rights of wives and mothers, and the federalizing of laws that were perceived as properly in the jurisdiction of the fifty states.[38] This anti-ERA movement spread like a wildfire among traditional women.[39] Schlafly entered the ERA fight as an experienced organizer with a network of supporters throughout the country.[40] Few political observers believed the forces for defeating the ERA stood much of a chance. In fact, leaders of the National Organization of Women (NOW), ERAmerica, and other supporters of the ERA at first dismissed Schlafly and her grassroots crusade. Three more states ratified in 1974, one in 1975, and another in 1977, bringing the total to thirty-five states of the necessary thirty-eight. At this point, the ERA came to an abrupt halt. Meanwhile, five states rescinded their previous ratification of the ERA. By 1976, ERA proponents were taking Schlafly seriously, admitting that they had failed to win over the average homemaker.[41] Simply put, Schlafly outmaneuvered her opponents.[42]

At first, Schlafly drew support from her network of conservative Republican women across the country, but as the movement gained strength, she effectively reached out to bring average women who had not been previously involved in politics. As the movement gained momentum, however, Schlafly tapped into a new constituency that had not been previously involved in politics—fundamentalist Christian groups.[43] Most of these women were mothers, but their church activities had given them skills in public speaking and in converting unbelievers. Equally important, these women brought an evangelical enthusiasm to the cause.

Gerald Ford and his wife, Betty, actively lobbied for the ERA, leading Schlafly at one point to picket the White House.[44] The 1976 Republican platform endorsed the ERA, but it was clear that rebellion in the ranks was rising against the Republican establishment.[45] Ronald Reagan rode this resurgence by challenging Ford for the Republican nomination.[46] Ford narrowly won the nomination, but he was deserted by the right.

In the presidential campaign of 1976, both Ford and Democratic Party presidential nominee Jimmy Carter wanted to treat the abortion issue gingerly. The Republican Party platform declared, "The question of abortion is one of the most difficult and controversial of our time." The platform went on to say that the party urges "a continuance of the public dialogue on abortion and supports the efforts of those who seek enactment of a constitutional amendment to restore protection of the right to life for unborn children."[47]

The abortion issue proved even more divisive for the Democrats. At the convention, Carter clashed with feminists over the abortion plank, finally reaching a compromise that declared the party's opposition to any attempt to overturn legalized abortion. Nonetheless, Carter disavowed the platform, categorically declaring that "abortion is wrong."[48]

Ford's moderate position on abortion left the anti-abortion wing of his party discontented, while Carter's moderate stance left the women's movement unhappy.[49] In the end, Carter narrowly won the election with 49.9 percent of the popular vote to Ford's 47.9 percent. Carter swept the South, drawing evangelical Christians to the Democratic Party. He believed that Betty Ford's strong pro-abortion views and Gerald Ford's ambivalence on abortion had helped the Democrats win the White House.

Once in office, Carter sought to placate feminists by appointing Midge Constanza, a pro-abortion feminist, to his White House staff. Furthermore, he actively campaigned for ratification of the ERA, personally phoning state representatives in key states to back the amendment.[50] Still, many feminists accused Carter of not doing enough to support the ERA. Eleanor Smeal, president of the NOW, blamed Carter for failing to apply political pressure on Democrats in key state legislatures where the ERA was being considered for ratification.[51] Even though the Democratic-controlled Congress extended the deadline three years to 1982, the ERA fell dead when Florida, Missouri, Oklahoma, North Carolina, and Illinois refused to ratify the amendment. It was clear by 1980 that Phyllis Schlafly and the grassroots right, now called the "pro-family" movement, had won.

Carter's relations with the women's movement were further embittered over his stance on the abortion issue. In 1977, the Supreme Court ruled in *Harris v. McRae* that the congressional restrictions on funding for abortion through Medicaid did not violate a woman's constitutional right to secure an abortion. When Carter bluntly endorsed the decision, feminists within his administration revolted, leaving his administration deeply divided.[52] Relations did not improve when Carter signed legislation that banned federal funds for abortions except to protect the life of a mother or in cases of rape and incest.[53]

Witnessing the success of Schlafly's ability to mobilize evangelical Christians in the fight against the ERA, Republican Party activists believed that this vote could be harnessed in support of the party by tying social issues such as school choice, abortion, and prayer in schools to long-standing Republican causes—free market economics and hard-line defense and foreign policy. These conservative operatives brought their political skills into the congressional election of 1978 by employing the abortion issue as a wedge that separated liberal Democratic congressional representatives from their more socially conservative constituents. Democrat after Democrat went down in defeat. Similarly, liberal Republicans who had waffled on the abortion issue and had supported the ERA joined the list of the defeated, including Charles Percy in Illinois and Clifford Case in New Jersey.[54]

The emergence of the pro-family movement, consisting of evangelical Protestants and Catholics whose allegiance had been to the Democratic Party, plus the revitalized conservatives in the Republican Party, set the stage for the 1980 election.[55] Reagan's time had come. During the Republican primaries, Reagan focused on the economic failures and foreign policy debacles of the Carter administration. At the same time, he reassured his right-wing base in the party that he was one of them on social issues by advocating a constitutional amendment to prohibit all abortions except when necessary to save the life of the mother. Reagan attacked the "cultural elite" for its betrayal of traditional family values, including prayer in schools and abortion.

While the general campaign focused primarily on economic and foreign policy issues, Reagan's commitment to the conservative social agenda assured him of the support of the new mobilized Christian right and traditionalist women. Anti-abortion activists rallied at the grassroots level as the 1980 election approached. Typical was the call issued by the National Pro-Life Political Action Committee in its September 1979 newsletter that declared "1980 Elections Start Now!" The Pro-Life Political Action Committee reported that it had sent fourteen "specially selected" men and women from campaign staffs to a weeklong training school run by the Committee for the Survival of Congress to learn "every aspect of political management."[56]

Conservative women also emerged to play a role at the Republican convention in Detroit in 1980, when Stop-ERA activists successfully removed the ERA from the Republican platform, where it had been a fixture since 1940, and inserted a plank calling for an anti-abortion constitutional amendment. By boldly linking economic and social issues into a populist attack on federal bureaucrats, out-of-touch politicians, and an arrogant cultural elite, Reagan overwhelmed Carter at the polls, receiving 51 percent of the vote to Jimmy Carter's 41 percent.

In the election, Reagan took advantage of the fact that nearly two-thirds of married women (but fewer than half of single women) tend to vote. Exit polls showed that women for the ERA gave Carter only 63 percent of their vote, while women opposing the ERA overwhelmingly supported Reagan, 69 percent to 31 percent.[57]

Moreover, Republicans gained thirteen Senate seats, winning control of the Senate for the first time since 1952 and only the third time since Hoover's defeat. In the House, Republicans gained thirty-three seats, depriving House Speaker Tip O'Neill of working control of the chamber. Republican candidates for the Senate and House ran essentially even with Reagan nationwide.[58]

Once in office, however, Reagan placed cultural issues on the back burner in order to pursue his agenda of tax cuts, budget reduction, and deregulation.[59] Even while doing so, however, he continued to use strong anti-abortion rhetoric that encouraged abortion opponents.[60] Still, he wanted to maintain support of this significant grouping within the conservative movement. His staff continued to remind him that "these people could help a great deal in providing grass roots support for your economic program."[61] As a consequence, when Reagan spoke at the annual dinner of the Conservative Political Action Conference, a prominent umbrella group in the conservative movement, he declared, "Because ours is a consistent philosophy of government, we can be very clear: We do not have a social agenda, separate economic agenda, and a separate foreign agenda. We have one agenda." To drive home the point, he added, "Just as surely as we seek to put our financial house in order and rebuild our Nation's defenses, so too we seek to protect the unborn."[62]

Meanwhile anti-abortion activists pursued their agenda in the U.S. Senate when five major pieces of anti-abortion legislation were introduced, including the Garn amendment (S.J. Res. 17); the Grassley amendment (S.J. Res. 18); the "paramount" or Helms amendment (S.J. Res. 19); and the fourth and fifth, the human life statute (S. 158) and the Hatch human life federalism amendment (S.J. Res. 110). The legislative proposals showed the strength of the anti-abortion movement, but also reflected political differences within the movement.[63]

Senator Jesse Helms (R-N.C.) proposed a constitutional amendment that stated that human life begins at conception and that fetuses are legal "persons" protected by the Fourteenth Amendment. The Helms amendment, called the paramount amendment, read as follows: "The paramount right to life is vested in each human being from the moment of fertilization without regard to age, health, or condition of dependency." This was considered the "most hardline" of the amendments.[64] Doubtful about the constitutionality of the Helms amendment, Senator Orrin Hatch (R-Utah) drafted another constitutional amendment to return abortion policy back to the state legislatures. Hatch's proposal was procedural and not substantive, but won the support of the National Conference of Catholic Bishops. As a consequence, the anti-abortion movement split over the Helms and Hatch amendments.[65]

While anti-abortion and pro-abortion groups mobilized their supporters, the bills had become deadlocked in Congress. The Senate Judiciary Separation of Powers Subcommittee, chaired by John P. East (R-N.C.), approved Helms's amendment (S. 158) by a 3–2 vote on July 9, 1981. (At the hearings, six pro-abortion activists were arrested and later convicted for disrupting the hearings.) At Hatch's request, East's committee delayed full committee action until the Hatch proposal was acted upon. On December 16, the Senate Judiciary Constitution Subcommittee approved Hatch's proposal by a 4–0 vote. As a result, the Helms and Hatch amendments appeared before the Senate in September.

The Hatch proposal won the support of the National Conference of Catholic Bishops, the NRLC, and the National Pro-Life Political Action Committee. Other anti-abortion groups including the March for Life and the Life Amendment Political Action Committee opposed the bill, calling it "nothing short of a sellout of the principles that have motivated the pro-life movement."[66]

In an effort to unify the anti-abortion forces, Senator Mark Hatfield (R-Oreg.) introduced S. 2372, which permanently banned federal funds for abortions unless the life of the mother was endangered, but also stated that "unborn children who are subjected to abortion are living members of the human species." When the Supreme Court agreed to review five cases from Ohio, Missouri, and Virginia involving state and federal restrictions on abortion, the emotions within the Senate intensified.[67]

The debate on abortion began August 16, 1982, when Helms and his allies proposed to tack anti-abortion and voluntary school prayer legislation onto a debt limit bill. This was supported by the Republican majority leadership. Immediately Senator Robert Packwood (R-Oreg.) launched a filibuster against the bill by reading from historian James Mohr's *Abortion in America.* After parliamentary maneuvering, Packwood lost and then regained control of the floor to continue his filibuster. Finally, on September 8, Reagan stepped directly into the fray when he urged Senate Majority Leader Baker to close the debate and vote on Helms's abortion bill.

Pressure for Reagan to intervene came from grassroots activists as well as within his administration. Morton Blackwell, a longtime conservative activist serving in the White House, captured the mood of the anti-abortion movement when he wrote Elizabeth Dole in the White House Liaison Office in August, "Until now the President has avoided personally urging specific actions on the matter of abortion. . . . He has not urged legislators to vote for or against any particular measure." He warned, however, that "this policy has caused a great deal of concern among grassroots right-to-life activists. . . . Thus we are at a critical moment in the relationship between the President and the prolife activists. . . . If the President fails to take specific steps to obtain cloture in the Senate on Senator Packward's filibuster, that failure will be read as a betrayal."[68] Acting upon Blackwell's suggestion, Elizabeth Dole called for President Reagan to support a cloture vote on the Helms amendment. By September 2, the White House staff had drafted a letter under the president's signature to be sent to Majority Leader Baker and to key Senate leaders calling for a vote on cloture. This presidential statement had been carefully vented with major Catholic organizations, including the Knights of Columbus, the Catholic Daughters of America, and key Catholic bishops.[69]

In an open letter to the NRLC, Reagan declared: "One can tiptoe around principles so long." This was followed by a confidential letter to nine Republican senators, urging them to support cloture of the filibuster led by Robert Packwood (R-Oreg.).[70] The White House staff worked to mobilize pro-life organizations to lobby on behalf of cloture and the Helms bill. With President Reagan's active intervention, pro-life activists, both inside and outside the White House, felt optimistic that they were going to win the vote in the Senate. Blackwell believed that "this is a very winnable fight," while Douglas Johnson, legislative director of the NRLC, predicted victory.[71] The White House staff also called key senators shortly before the vote.[72] The effort was to little avail. After two unsuccessful cloture votes, on September 15 Orrin Hatch made a surprise announcement that he was withdrawing his constitutional amendment. This was a sign the fight was over. Shortly afterward, another cloture motion to end the filibuster failed, 50–44, ten votes short of the three-fifths required. At that point, Senator S. I. Hayakawa (R-Calif.) made a motion to table the Helms amendment, which passed, 47–46.[73] This became the last serious attempt within the Reagan administration to enact a constitutional amendment to overturn *Roe.*

Reagan's commitment to the anti-abortion amendment was, as his biographer Lou Cannon notes, sincere.[74] Nonetheless, he invested few political resources in the issue—another point made by Cannon, although with some exaggeration. Surely, after the 1982 failure to pass a constitutional amendment, the Reagan administration did not place abortion at the top of its policy agenda. Still, this does not mean, as Cannon suggests, that the administration's interest in reproductive rights was primarily rhetorical and not substantive.[75] Cannon maintains that the Reagan administration took a "pragmatic" view of abortion.

Reagan's stance against abortion was more than just a product of political calculation. By appointing anti-abortion advocates into his administration, he assured that abortion would be placed on the policy agenda. Such appointments were good politics, but this does not mean that Reagan acted only out of political gain. By supporting an anti-abortion agenda, even a limited one, Reagan and his staff knew that this position carried political costs, especially among single women. Reagan strategists noted the "gender gap" among unmarried women in the 1980 returns. Nonetheless, the Reagan administration pursued a limited program of restricting government involvement in family planning whenever possible. This also entailed supporting "pro-life" judicial appointments.

Following the defeat of the Helms amendment, Reagan's ability to reshape federal family planning policy was limited. This had become apparent at a January 22, 1982, meeting with pro-life leaders in the cabinet room with top administration officials to plan a strategy on behalf of the Helms amendment and other legislation. At the meeting, as Morton Blackwell observed, "there were a number of cases where it became clear that the Administration could not take pro-life steps" under the law. As a consequence, the administration met with anti-abortion leaders again that April to discuss support for the Helms amendment as well to discuss incremental changes in the law.[76]

Whatever political calculation Reagan brought to the abortion issue, pro-abortion and feminist activists nevertheless accused Reagan of waging war on women.[77] This suggests that Reagan's policies were more than symbolic sops to keep his right-wing base in order. Although a constitutional amendment overturning *Roe* failed in the Senate, Reagan eloquently articulated the pro-life position throughout his administration, and this was more than just a sop to the anti-abortionists. At the very outset of his administration, Reagan met with anti-abortion leaders to discuss ways of altering federal policy not just on abortion but also on sex education, family planning, and world population control. Reagan and Budget Director David Stockman met with anti-abortion activists who presented them with a white paper outlining how $3.9 billion a year could be saved by scrapping most of the government family planning, birth control, sex education, teenage counseling, and world population control programs.

Reagan subsequently chose Dr. C. Everett Koop, a Philadelphia surgeon, evangelical Christian, and anti-abortionist, as surgeon general in charge of programs administered by the Centers for Disease Control, the Population Research Center, and the National Institutes of Health. Although Koop's service as surgeon general severely disappointed the anti-abortion movement—leading members to conspicuously boycott his retirement dinner—at the time of his appointment he was seen as an anti-abortion appointment.

In addition, he appointed Marjory Mecklenburg, president of American Citizens Concerned for Life, to head the Office of Adolescent Pregnancy Programs, which gives grants to aid teenage mothers and counsels them on birth control. In addition, a number of other appointments within the administration were made to people with well-known anti-abortion credentials, including Gary Bauer, Morton Blackwell, Dee Jepsen in the Public Liaison Office, and Michael Uhlmann in the attorney general's offices.

Most important, Reagan also named Richard Schweiker—one of the first supporters of a pro-life amendment—to head the Department of Health and Human Services. Schweiker began an investigation of Planned Parenthood for several violations of federal law. This investigation placed Planned Parenthood on the defensive, although in the end no violations were discovered.

Following Schweiker's resignation in 1983, Reagan appointed Margaret Heckler to succeed him. She was an avid and longtime opponent of abortion. She would be succeeded by Otis R. Bowen, the former governor of Indiana, in 1985. As head of Health, Education, and Welfare, (HEW), Bowen sought to limit access to abortion and contraceptives. He lobbied Congress to revise the Public Health Services Act to limit abortion services and counseling at clinics receiving federal funds. Rebuked by a Democratic-controlled Congress, he sought to go around them by announcing the Public Health Service Act, which banned funding to organizations that performed or counseled abortion. This administrative fiat became known as the "gag rule."

Reagan also supported the refunding of the Adolescent Health Services and Pregnancy Prevention and Care Act as the Adolescent Family Life Act in 1981, sponsored by Senator Jeremiah Denton (R-Ala.).[78] This reconstructed program required the active involvement of religious groups in family planning; prohibited federal funds to any organizations (such as Planned Parenthood) involved in abortion or counseling services; mandated that providers emphasize adoption; and instructed providers to encourage premarital abstinence. By 1985 this program was spending nearly $15 million on fifty-nine demonstration projects to discourage teenagers from engaging in sexual activity.

Also, in the first year of his administration, Reagan cut family planning funds under Title X by nearly 25 percent. At the same time, the Department of Health and Human Services issued a regulation prohibiting family planning clinics supported by Title X funding from providing any information about abortion—even neutral information. Although Congress subsequently increased the funding for Title X programs in 1983 and 1984, this action restored funding only to 1981 levels.[79] A review of federal family planning programs during Reagan's first term provides an overview of federal family planning budgeting and reveals the effects of Democratic Party congressional victories in 1982 and 1984, which blocked further cuts in family planning services (see table 13.1).

These figures illustrate the Reagan administration's inability to undertake significant cuts in family planning programs after Democrats regained control of Congress in 1984.[80] Nonetheless, Reagan appointees aggressively pursued an agenda aimed at restricting federal involvement in family planning and downsizing programs whenever they could. Much of this was done through administrative fiat, only to be overturned by Congress or the courts.[81]

Reagan believed that control of the federal bench and the Supreme Court was critical to sustaining the anti-abortion agenda.[82] Reagan shared the conservative belief that the federal courts had become too activist and by doing so, had undermined the separation of powers between the legislative function and the judiciary function. As one Reagan official declared, "Roe was just a dramatic example of a system of judging that had run badly off the rails."[83] During his two terms in office, Reagan appointed over three hundred judges to the federal bench. Although Justice Department officials denied that they imposed an "ideological litmus test" on candidates, Reagan's critics did not believe them.

Reagan's record of appointments on the Supreme Court proved mixed from the point of view of his anti-abortion wing of the party. Reagan's first nominee to the Supreme Court, Sandra Day O'Connor, in 1981, drew opposition from anti-abortion groups because of her earlier support of a family planning bill in Arizona that would have replaced existing state law banning abortions. Further-

Table 13.1. Expenditures for Federal Family Planning Services, FY1981–1985

	FY81	FY82	FY83	FY84	FY85
Family planning services	$161,671,000	$124,800,000	$124,088,000	$140,000,000	$142,000,000
Adolescent family life program	—	$11,033, 000	$13,404,000	$14,918,000	$14,716,000
Population research center	$76,830,000	$80,277,000	$86,209,000	$90,776,000	$104,950,000
Maternal and child health block grant	$454,393,000	$373,750,000	$478,000,000	$399,000,000	$478,000,000
Special supplemental food (WIC)	$927,040,000	$934,080,000	$1.160	$1.3	$1.5

Source: Congressional Quarterly Almanac, 1984, 466–67.

more, in the early 1970s, as a representative in the state legislature, O'Connor had signed a statement calling for population control in the United States.

The opposition by anti-abortion activists to the O'Connor nomination came in the first year of Reagan's administration. Reagan was able to placate many of these activists by his subsequent intervention on behalf of the Helms amendment in 1982. Nevertheless, some conservative/anti-abortion activists remained distrustful of Reagan's commitment to the social issues.

The anger that the O'Connor nomination elicited led White House official Morton Blackwell, serving as the liaison within the conservative movement, to meet with Paul Weyrich, Connie Marshner, and Dick Dingman, as well as fifty other leaders of the conservative and pro-family organizations. Following the meeting, Blackwell informed the White House that these leaders opposed O'Connor's nomination and that there was a growing consensus among these groups that the president and his senior advisers "don't think this coalition contributed significantly to his election." Furthermore, conservatives were angry over a Justice Department memo by Kenneth W. Starr that said O'Connor had "never had any disputes or controversies" with Dr. Carolyn Gerstler, a Phoenix physician and former president of the NRLC. This "cover-up" was likened by anti-abortion movement leaders to "Judge Harold Carswell's failure to reveal his past segregationist views."[84]

Reagan immediately sought to prevent a brush fire in the ranks of social conservatives. In a widely circulated letter to grassroots conservatives, Reagan explained that when O'Connor was a state senator in Arizona, she opposed a spending bill to which the state house had attached an amendment preventing university hospitals from performing abortions. This, Reagan said, was unconstitutional under Arizona law because an amendment needed to pertain to the subject of the original bill.[85] In the meantime, Reagan politely refused to meet with Dr. Gerstler because of "his schedule."[86] O'Connor easily won the appointment to the Court as its first female justice. As a justice, O'Connor shifted the legal foundation for regulating abortion away from the trimester approach of *Roe* to the doctrine of "undue burden."[87]

Nonetheless, the O'Connor nomination and the subsequent failure to pass either the Hatch or Helms amendments left pro-life activists disappointed in the Reagan White House. As Gary L. Bauer, working in the White House, wrote to presidential political strategist Edwin Harper in late 1982, "I believe all of us, including myself, have underestimated the expectations that existed for some action on abortion among the right-to-lifers." Fearing alienation of this activist core, Elizabeth Dole in the Public Liaison Office urged that the administration develop an aggressive strategy of keeping the "pro-family" movement on board in the Reagan Revolution. As the administration began to look at the approaching 1984 election, White House strategists determined that it would be "necessary to obtain approximately the same Catholic ethnic vote in the northeast industrial belt and in the border states" as the Reagan campaign had in 1980.[88]

Extensive studies were undertaken to develop a Reagan "Catholic strategy" for the 1984 election.

As part of this strategy, the Reagan administration courted the pro-life and Catholic vote, delicately seeking to "mend fences" with the bishops and the U.S. Catholic Conference. Differences over Reagan's defense buildup, his policy toward Nicaragua, and his cuts in social expenditures had created tensions between the Reagan administration and the Catholic hierarchy. In pursuing this strategy, the Reagan administration arranged to invite key bishops to a series of state White House dinners, including Milwaukee archbishop Rembert Weakland to the German state dinner. Weakland was chairman of the Bishop's Committee on Economic and Social Justice, which was drafting a pastoral letter on unemployment and social welfare.[89]

At the same time, the administration sought to ensure that its base in the pro-life movement would remain solid. As part of this strategy, the administration decided to have Reagan write an article for the anti-abortion periodical *Human Life Review,* reaffirming his pro-life position. By March 1983, Justice Department lawyer Michael Uhlmann, working with a team of speechwriters, had drafted such an article. This article was designed to encourage supporters in the pro-life movement, but also to counter an impending pastoral letter from the National Conference of Catholic Bishops calling for a "nuclear freeze" on the development of weapons. The bishops sought to make pro-life and nuclear freeze a package, but the editors at *Human Life Review* promised to publish Reagan's article before the pastoral letter, in order, as Uhlmann said, "to frame the pro-life issue in our terms rather than the political opposition's."[90]

When this article appeared, and with its later republication as a booklet, *Abortion and the Conscience of the Nation* (1984), Reagan eloquently proclaimed his pro-life position by comparing the *Roe v. Wade* decision to the Dred Scott decision (1857), which had denied freed slaves their rights as citizens.[91] In late January 1983, Reagan also addressed by telephone the annual pro-life rally, which had drawn over one hundred thousand grassroots anti-abortion marchers to Washington. Before the rally, Reagan met with top rally leaders to thank them for their support of the Helms amendment and, while reaffirming his support for a human life amendment, to emphasize that the critical fights in the future would be on federal funding of abortions and cutbacks in federal family planning programs.[92]

Reagan easily won election to a second term, solidifying his support among Roman Catholics and within the anti-abortion movement. In his second term, the Reagan administration continued to maintain its anti-abortion policies, although a Democratic-controlled Congress restrained Reagan initiatives.

The most concerted attempt to overturn *Roe* came in 1985 when Charles Fried became solicitor general. In *Thornburgh v. American College of Gynecologists and Obstetricians* (1986), Fried argued that the privacy doctrine should be upheld but that abortion law should be decided by state legislatures. The Court did not accept Fried's argument, but four justices dissented from the majority decision.[93] Reagan continued to press the appointment of pro-life judges on the Supreme Court, although with mixed success.[94]

Within the administration, pro-life political appointees pressed to restrict abortion funding, usually against fierce opposition from within the administration and outside reproductive rights advocate groups. Most notable in this regard was the firing of Jo Ann Gasper, deputy assistant secretary to population affairs at the Department of Health and Human Services (HHS), for refusing to award a $300,000 training grant to the Planned Parenthood Federation of America (PPFA) in early 1987 because of a determination that it was an abortion advocate. This policy decision was announced at a White House meeting with anti-abortion leaders and greeted with great enthusiasm. Nonetheless, Secretary Otis Bowen, fearing a backlash from pro-abortion activists, ordered Gasper to rescind the order. Gasper told Bowen that her deputy, a civil servant, would sign the grants if so ordered, but Bowen insisted that Gasper issue the grants under her signature. After months of controversy, Bowen fired Gasper on July 2, 1987. Bowen had reacted to pro-abortion advocate groups, but was surprised to discover an avalanche of protest letters coming from the anti-abortion side. This episode occurred in the midst of the Iran-Contra scandal, but it was reported that more than one hundred thousand letters—more mail than the Iran-Contra scandal generated—flooded into the White House protesting the firing of Gasper.

Already under pressure from the Iran-Contra scandal, the White House responded immediately. Gasper was placed in the Department of Education under Secretary William Bennett, while the White House ordered Bowen to appoint Nabors Cabaniss to fill the position as deputy assistant secretary for population affairs. Cabaniss had been an aide of Jesse Helms and Jeremiah Denton and was Gasper's former deputy. Bowen was conspicuously absent at the White House ceremony introducing Cabaniss.[95]

Gasper's firing caused other rifts within the administration. In response to protests over Gasper's removal from HHS, Reagan ordered Surgeon General Koop to issue a finding as to whether abortion medically harmed women. A month later, Koop declared that the research evidence on the medical effects of abortion were inconclusive. Although this was taken by pro-abortion advocates as a declaration in their favor, Koop's position was only that more research needed to be done on this issue. Nonetheless, this left anti-abortion advocates angry at Koop, who would now be seen as having caved in to pro-abortion pressure.[96]

Nonetheless, the Gasper episode led to more positive results for anti-abortion groups. In response to political pressure, Reagan instructed Bowen to translate Gasper's ruling into regulatory policy.[97] At the same time, the White House threw support behind Capitol Hill efforts to ban all public-supported abortion in the

District of Columbia, unless determined necessary to save the life of the mother. Anti-abortion groups greeted this legislation as a huge victory.[98]

Yet, Reagan also learned that relations with the anti-abortion movement, a single-interest group, created its own difficulties. The Grove City bill was a case in point. After vetoing the bill in 1988, Reagan sought to rally conservatives to his support. Yet, because the bill contained an anti-abortion amendment, key anti-abortion groups such as the NRLC refused to side with Reagan, declaring its neutrality on the issue.

The battle over the bill began when Grove City College, a four-year liberal arts institution in Pennsylvania, became embroiled in a dispute with the federal government when it refused to file an assurance of compliance with Title IX, barring discrimination on the basis of sex. In *Grove City College v. Bell* (1984), the Supreme Court ruled on behalf of the school, declaring that only the school's financial aid program was covered by Title IX of the 1972 education act. This decision meant that the entire educational institution, Grove City College, could not be forced to comply with Title IX. As a consequence of the ruling, the Department of Education's Office of Civil Rights was forced to end or restrict dozens of antidiscrimination lawsuits.

Civil rights proponents pressed Congress to enact legislation to reverse the high court's ruling by stating specifically that all colleges and universities, private and public, receiving any federal aid were barred from discrimination. Led by Senator Edward Kennedy (D-Mass.), legislation was proposed to overturn the Grove City ruling. The proposed legislation met with strong opposition in the Republican-controlled Senate, as well as the Catholic Church hierarchy, which said the legislation would broaden abortion rights by forcing university hospitals to perform abortions in compliance with nonsexual discrimination legislation. In order to pass the legislation in the Senate, its supporters agreed to the inclusion of an amendment put forth by John Danforth (R-Mo.) exempting abortion from the legislation. Lowell P. Weicker (R-Conn.), Bob Packwood (R-Oreg.), and Howard M. Metzenbaum (D-Ohio) unsuccessfully opposed the amendment. In the end, Congress passed S-557, although it was formally opposed by the National Organization for Women and drew little enthusiasm from civil rights groups because of the Danforth amendment. At the same time, Christian conservative groups criticized the bill as well because of its restrictions on religious institutions.[99]

Declaring that the measure would "diminish substantially the freedom and independence of religious institutions in our society," Reagan vetoed the bill when it reached his desk.[100] In a carefully outlined strategy developed by White House aides Gary Bauer and Dinish D'Sousa, the administration sought to rally conservative opposition to the bill.[101] The White House sent out a mass mailing to pro-life activists across the country, consisting of a letter from William B. Allen of the U.S. Commission on Civil Rights, suggesting that the Danforth amendment to the Grove City bill would require the courts to strike that provision from the act. Douglas Johnson, legislative director of the NRLC, wrote a two-page hand-delivered letter loudly protesting this tactic. "We strongly object to these attempts," he declared, "which are contrary to the interests of the pro-life movement."[102] The NRLC had swung behind the Grove City bill because of its abortion exemption, which "emphatically rejected anti-abortion policies as a form of sex discrimination."[103] With the anti-abortion movement and the Catholic Church hierarchy behind the bill, the Senate overrode Reagan's veto and it became law.

Throughout his two terms in office, Reagan's domestic program focused primarily on fiscal and economic policy, not social policy. No doubt, relations between his administration and social conservatives at times became strained. Indeed, early in Reagan's presidency, Richard Viguerie and the *Conservative Digest* publicly attacked Reagan for backing away from conservative principles, leading Reagan to privately write John Lofton, editor of the publication: "I believe that the July *Conservative Digest* is one of the most dishonest and unfair bits of journalism I have ever seen."[104] Nonetheless, in both presidential elections, Reagan won Catholic swing voters as well as evangelical Christians, many of whom had been mobilized in the Stop-ERA fight and the struggle over abortion. Moreover, he had actively pushed anti-abortion policies, even while confronting a Democratic Congress. This support of the anti-abortion agenda came with political costs.

The media and feminists continued to tout the "gender gap," claiming that women were less likely to vote for Reagan and for Republicans identified with a conservative social agenda. This voting gap, however, was not a gap between women and men but between single women and married women.[105] Thus, as single women voted overwhelmingly Democratic, married women overall voted Republican. These social changes created the sharp ideological polarization around moral issues that characterized the Reagan era. Social issues enabled conservative Republicans through Ronald Reagan an opportunity for political realignment; yet, a cultural and political chasm had been opened, ensuring further political acrimony with no end in sight.

In this way, Reagan had inspired anti-abortion activists and social conservatives in their moral crusade against what they perceived to be a culture in decline. Yet, within the context of a growing gender gap, many Republicans sought to shift the party away from an emphasis on moral issues, toward economic and defense issues. Inevitably, these two agendas created political tensions within the Republican Party and the conservative movement itself. The differences simply were not over "political pragmatism" versus "moral absolutism" (economic and defense conservatives brought a moral fervor to these issues as well). For moral conservatives, victory did not just mean political power. To their battle they brought a moral certainty that often did not allow for ready political compromise. Reagan had imparted much to their struggle, but the moral crusade against liberal culture had taken firm root in local communities and state legislatures, as female grassroots conservative activists continued to mobilize on the national level. Whatever ambivalence they might have felt at times during Reagan's administration, grassroots conservatives forgot past ambivalence on both their and the administration's part. Their view of history placed Reagan as bold defender of their cause. His presidency imparted inspiration to carry their battle into the next millennium with the knowledge that Heaven's gates awaited them as onward-marching soldiers for a better nation.

NOTES

1. Jerry Rubin, *Growing Up at Thirty Seven* (Philadelphia: M. Evans, 1976).

2. David Frum uses *Star Wars* as an example of how feelings turned inward in *How We Got Here: The Seventies—the Decade that Brought You Modern Life, for Better or Worse* (New York: Basic Books, 2000). Also on the 1970s, see Bruce J. Schulman, *The Seventies: The Great Shift in American Culture, Society, and Politics* (New York: Free Press, 2001).

3. There is an extensive literature on the importance of religion and moral concerns in American politics extending back to the early Republic. For example, see Richard Carwardine, *Evangelicals and Politics in Antebellum America* (New Haven, Conn.: Yale University Press, 1993); and Nathan O. Hatch, *The Democratization of American Christianity* (New Haven, Conn.: Yale University Press, 1989). On the persistent historical role of religion and moral concerns, see Furio Colombo, *God in America: Religion and Politics in the United States,* trans. Kristin Jarratt (New York: Columbia University Press, 1984); Robert L. Kelley, *The Cultural Pattern in American Politics: The First Century* (New York: Knopf, 1979); Mark Noll, *One Nation under God? Christian Faith and Political Action in America* (San Francisco: Harper & Row, 1988); and Gary Wills, *Under God: Religion and American Politics* (New York: Simon & Schuster, 1990).

4. John R. Hibbing and Elizabeth Theiss-Morse, eds., *What Is It about Government That Americans Dislike?* (Cambridge: Cambridge University Press, 2001).

5. The decline in confidence in government, public institutions, and political leaders is evidenced by a huge body of survey data. Especially useful in discussing citizen distrust of government are essays found in Hibbing and Theiss-Morse, *What Is It about Government?* Also useful are Joseph Cappella and Kathleen Hall Jamieson, *Spiral of Cynicism* (New York: Oxford University Press, 1997); Stephen C. Craig, *The Malevolent Leaders: Popular Discontent in America* (Boulder, Colo.: Westview Press, 1993); E. J. Dionne, *Why Americans Hate Politics* (New York: Simon and Schuster, 1991); Benjamin Ginsberg and Martin Shefter, *Politics by Other Means: The Declining Importance of Elections in America* (New York: Basic Books, 1990); John R. Hibbing and Elizabeth Theiss-Morse, *Stealth Democracy: Americans' Belief about How Government Should Work* (Cambridge: Cambridge University Press, 2002); and James Morone, *The Democratic Wish: Popular Participation and the Limits of American Government* (New York: Basic Books, 1990). In addition, there is an important monographic literature on this subject.

6. This point is explored, among other places, in Thomas Byrne Edsall and Mary D. Edsall, *Chain Reaction: The Impact of Race, Rights, and Taxes on American Politics* (New York: Norton, 1991).

7. Discussion of the universalistic welfare state and its critics can be found in Michael B. Katz, *The Undeserving Poor: From War on Poverty to War on Welfare* (New York: Pantheon Books, 1989); Neil Gilbert, *The Enabling State: Modern Welfare Capitalism* (New York: Oxford University Press, 1989); Edward Berkowitz, *America's Welfare State: From Roosevelt to Reagan* (Baltimore: Johns Hopkins University Press, 1991); Lawrence M. Meed, *Beyond Entitlement: The Social Obligations of Citizenship* (New York: Free Press, 1986); and Marvin Olasky, *Renewing America's Compassion* (New York: Free Press, 1996).

8. Even before Nixon's election in 1968, conservatives in the Republican Party expressed anger in what they perceived as appeasement with the Soviet Union and the federal involvement in civil rights. For example, Robert Dresser, a Rhode Island attorney and major contributor to the GOP, expressed this alienation when he wrote in early 1966 to General Lucius Clay, chairman of the Republican National Finance Committee, to tell him he was not contributing any more money to the party until it stopped its drift to the left. He declared, "I have been a significant donor to the Republican party, but I refuse to give any more money unless . . . the [GOP] support for the Nuclear Test Ban Treaty ends; the support for Civil Rights and Voting Rights ends; and support of foreign aid to communist countries ends." Robert Dresser to General Lucius D. Clay, Republican National Finance Committee, January 10, 1966, Clarence Manion Papers, box 46, Chicago Historical Society.

9. A detailed discussion of this convention and divisions among conservatives over Nixon's nomination can be found in Phyllis Schlafly, "Phyllis's Confidential Notes on the Republican National Convention, Miami Beach, Florida, August 1968," Schlafly Kingmaker folder, Eagle Forum Office Files.

10. Joan Hoff, *Nixon Reconsidered* (New York: Basic Books, 1994).

11. Nixon's support of the Family Assistance Plan, in effect a guaranteed national income proposal (although first proposed by libertarian Milton Friedman in *Capitalism and Freedom* in 1962), drew heavy opposition from conservatives. By 1971 this proposal was all but dead in Congress, only to be replaced by the two other programs: the supplemental security income program and the food stamps program.

12. Having campaigned in 1968 on the promise to address the "welfare mess," Richard Nixon unveiled in August 1969 his Family Assistance Plan (FAP). FAP called for the consolidation of current welfare programs into a guaranteed annual income. This proposal ran into opposition in Congress from liberals and conservatives. Excellent studies of FAP are found in Vincent J. Burke and Vee Burke, *Nixon's Good Deed: Welfare Reform* (New York: Columbia University Press, 1974); Kenneth M. Bowler, *The Nixon Guaranteed Income Proposal: Substance and Process in Policy Change* (Cambridge: Ballinger Publishing, 1974); and Daniel P. Moynihan, *The Politics of a Guaranteed Income: The Nixon Administration and the Family Assistance Plan* (New York: Random House, 1973). An excellent discussion of Nixon's social policies is found in Hoff, *Nixon Reconsidered*.

13. The pro-war activities of Young Americans for Freedom are discussed in John Andrew, *The Other Side of the Sixties: Young Americans for Freedom and the Rise of Conservative Politics* (New Brunswick, N.J. : Rutgers University Press, 1997); and Gregory L. Schneider, *Cadres for Conservatism: Young Americans for Freedom and the Rise of the Contemporary Right* (New York: New York University Press, 1999).

14. Writing of Nixon's China policy, conservative radio commentator Clarence Manion told Eugene Lyons, a longtime foe of communism, "This is madness, of course, but it reveals that Nixon is a politician first, statesman second, and 'anti-communist' also ran." Clarence Manion to Eugene Lyons, April 19, 1971, Clarence Manion Papers, box 46, Chicago Historical Society. For Nixon's opening with China, see Jim Mann, *About Face: A History of America's Curious Relationship with China from Nixon to Clinton* (New York: Knopf, 1999).

15. On the Ford presidency, see James Cannon, *Time and Chance: Gerald Ford's Appointment with History* (New York: HarperCollins, 1994); John Robert Greene, *The Presidency of Gerald Ford* (Lawrence: University Press of Kansas, 1995). See also A. James Reichley, *Conservatives in the Age of Change: The Nixon and Ford Administrations* (Washington, D.C. : Brookings Institution Press, 1981).

16. Poignant criticisms of Ford's foreign policy from a right-wing perspective are found in Phyllis Schlafly and Chester Ward, *Ambush at Vladivostok* (Alton, Ill.: Pere Marquette Press, 1976); and Schlafly and Ward, *Kissinger on the Couch* (New York: Pere Marquette Press, 1974). For a broad overview of conservative criticisms of U.S. policy toward the Soviet Union, see Richard Gid Power, *Not without Honor: The History of American Anticommunism* (New Haven, Conn.: Yale University Press, 1998).

17. The "new right" was hardly "new" in terms of its ideology or leadership. Both the movement and its leaders of this "new" political formation had deep roots in the conservative movement that had appeared first in the grassroots anticommunist movement in the 1950s and the Goldwater campaign in 1964. New right leaders such as Phyllis Schlafly, Howard Phillips, and Paul Weyrich had been involved in the anticommunist movement and the Goldwater movement long before the new right arrived on the political scene. If the ideology of the new right was not exactly new, however, its ability to raise funds through computerized direct mailing was.

18. There is a plethora of studies on the new right and the Christian right. Especially useful are Clyde Wilcox, *God's Warriors* (Baltimore: Johns Hopkins University Press, 1992); Wilcox, *Onward Christian Soldiers? The Religious Right in American Politics* (Boulder, Colo.: Westview Press, 1996); and Steve Bruce, *The Rise and Fall of the New Christian Right* (New York: Oxford University Press, 1988). Also, see Steve Bruce, Peter Kivisto, and William H. Swatos, Jr., *The Rapture of Politics* (New York: Transaction, 1995); Matthew Moen, *The Christian Right and Congress* (Tuscaloosa: University of Alabama Press, 1989); Robert Liebman and Rother Wuthnow, *The New Christian Right* (Hawthorne, N.Y.: Aldine Publishing, 1983); and David Bromley and Anson Shupe, *New Christian Politics* (Macon, Ga.: Mercer, 1984). For the new right, see Alan Crawford, *Thunder on the Right* (New York: Pantheon Books, 1980).

19. As Richard Carwardine explains in his superb *Evangelicals and Politics in Antebellum America* (New Haven, Conn.: Yale University Press, 1993), at the center of Protestant evangelicals' concerns with the decline of Christian morality in the antebellum period was a deep fear of Roman Catholics, especially German and Irish Catholics who were flooding into America in the early nineteenth century. This fear, as shown in David H. Bennett, *The Party of Fear: From Nativist Movements to the New Right in American History* (Chapel Hill: University of North Carolina Press, 1988), continued into the late nineteenth century. Bennett in his discussion of the new right does not develop fully this profound transformation in the moral conservative tradition that brought Roman Catholics and Protestant evangelicals together in the new right of the 1970s.

20. There are many excellent accounts of the emergence of the feminist movement in these years. For example, see Jo Freeman, *The Politics of Women's Liberation* (New York: McKay, 1975); Barbara S. Rothman, *Woman's Proper Place* (New York: Basic Books, 1978); and Leila Rupp and Verta Taylor, *Survival in the Doldrums* (New York: Oxford University Press, 1987).

21. A good study of abortion reform law in Hawaii is Patricia G. Steinhoff and Milton Diamond, *Abortion Politics: The Hawaii Experience* (Honolulu: University Press of Hawaii, 1977). A feminist perspective on family planning and abortion is offered by Linda Gordon, *Woman's Body, Woman's Right: Birth Control in America* (New York: Grossman, 1976). Also useful is Kristin Luker, *Abortion and the Politics of Motherhood* (Berkeley: University of California Press, 1984). The abortion reform movement on the state level before *Roe* is discussed by David Garrow, *Liberty and Sexuality: The Right to Privacy and the Making of Roe v. Wade* (New York: Macmillan, 1994). An abortion reform perspective is found in Lawrence Lader, *Abortion II: Making the Revolution* (Boston: Beacon Press, 1973).

Other discussions of the politics of abortion can be found in Barbara Hinkson Craig and David M. O'Brien, *Abortion and American Politics* (Chatham, N.J.: Chatham House, 1993); Raymond Tatalovich and Byron W. Daynes, *The Politics of Abortion: A Study of Community Conflict in Public Policy* (New York: Praeger Publishers, 1981).

A good history of the anti-abortion movement is called for. A good beginning is made in Keith Cassidy, "The Right to Life Movement," in *The Politics of Abortion and Birth Control in Historical Perspective,* ed. Donald T. Critchlow (University Park, Pa.: Penn State University Press, 1996). Also important is Suzanne Staggenborg, *The Pro-Choice Movement: Organization and Activism in the Abortion Conflict* (New York: Oxford University Press, 1991). Useful for understanding the abortion debate on the state level is Robert J. Spitzer, *The Right to Life Movement and Third Party Politics* (New York: Greenwood Press, 1987); and Faye D. Ginsburg, *Contested Lives: The Abortion Debate in an American Community* (Berkeley: University of California Press, 1989). Two journalistic accounts are found in Andrew H. Merton, *Enemies of Choice: The Right to Life Movement and Its Threat to Abortion* (Boston: Beacon Press, 1981); and Connie Paige, *The Right to Lifers: Who They Are, How They Operate, Where They Get Their Money* (New York: Summit Books, 1983).

22. Craig and O'Brien, *Abortion and American Politics,* 51–58.

23. Merton, *Enemies of Choice,* 43–45.

24. The first permanent state anti-abortion group was organized in Virginia; the Illinois Right to Life Committee formed the following year. Minnesota Citizens Concerned for Life, which attracted a membership of ten thousand by 1973, became a model for other state groups. Paige, *Right to Lifers,* 58–60.

25. Who were these women anti-abortion activists? In many ways they mirrored their counterparts in the pro-abortion movement, although with some important social differences. Both the National Right to Life Committee and the National Abortion and Reproductive Rights Action League (NARAL), the leading pro-abortion organization, drew largely from white, suburban, middle-aged, college-educated women. The majority of both organizations, NARAL and NRLC, were women (78 percent and 63 percent, respectively); most were married (55 percent of NARAL's members, compared with 87 percent of NRLC's members); most were college educated (with 46 percent of NARAL having an advanced postgraduate degree, compared with 32 percent of NRLC's members). What

separated these two groups was religious affiliation. The great majority of NRLC's membership were Roman Catholic (70 percent, or about two and one-half times the proportion of the general population), while Roman Catholics composed only 4 percent of the pro-abortion activists. NARAL's membership was 17 percent Jewish, about eight times the proportion of the general population. Few of the NRLC's members were Jewish.

The composition of abortion and anti-abortion activists is found in Donald Granberg, "The Abortion Activists," *Family Planning Perspectives* 13, no. 4 (July–August 1981): 157–63.

Interestingly, although not surprisingly, 93 percent of NARAL's members supported the equal rights amendment, while only 9 percent of NRLC's members supported it. Similarly, 95 percent of NARAL's members approved of women having an equal role with men in business, industry, and government, but the great majority of NRLC's members (71 percent) approved this as well.

Traditional women upheld the importance of motherhood in raising children, which they placed as the primary role of mothers, but this did not preclude a belief that women should not enter the workforce or that women should not be discriminated in the workplace. Peter Leahy, "The Anti-Abortion Movement: Testing a Theory of the Rise and Fall of the Social Movement" (Ph.D. diss., Syracuse University, 1975). On the Catholic role in the abortion issue, see Mary T. Hanna, *Catholics and American Politics* (Cambridge: Harvard University Press, 1967). See also Constance Balide, Barbara Danziger, and Deborah Spitz, "The Abortion Issue: Major Groups, Organizations, and Funding Sources," in *The Abortion Experience*, ed. Howard J. Osofsky and Joy D. Osofsky (Hagerstown, Md.: Harper & Row, 1973), 496–529; Kenneth D. Wald et al., "Evangelical Politics and the Status Issue," *Journal for the Scientific Study of Religion* 28, no. 1 (1989): 1–15. Bruce, *Rise and Fall of the Christian Right,* argues against status as an explanation for understanding the new Christian right.

Furthermore not all anti-abortionists were politically conservative. From the outset, the NRLC included "progressive" forces such as Prolifers for Survival, a group formed in 1971 by a feminist advocate who preached nuclear disarmament and anti-abortion, and Feminists for Life, organized by Pam Circa, counselor for sexual assault victims working in the district attorney's office in Milwaukee, Wisconsin. These "progressive" anti-abortion women are explored in Paige, *Right to Lifers,* 58–60.

26. Thomas Littlewood, *The Politics of Population Control* (Notre Dame, Ind.: University of Notre Dame Press, 1977). Also see John H. Kessell, *The Domestic Presidency: Decision-Making in the White House* (North Scituate, Mass.: Duxbury Press, 1975).

27. Although Dan Carter overstates the importance of the race issues in the reemergence of conservatism in the 1970s, he provides a discussion of the Wallace influence on Nixon's political strategy in *George Wallace, Richard Nixon, and the Transformation of American Politics* (Waco, Tex.: Markham Press, 1992); and *The Politics of Rage: George Wallace, the Origins of New Conservatism, and the Transformation of American Politics* (New York: Simon & Schuster, 1995).

28. His staff, which was overwhelmingly Protestant, urged Nixon to remain silent on the abortion issue, but during the contentious Democratic Party primary in 1972, Hubert Humphrey gained ground on his rival George McGovern by attacking him for being soft on marijuana, abortion, and amnesty for those who had avoided the draft. Although McGovern eventually won the Democratic nomination, Nixon saw an opportunity to continue Humphrey's characterization of McGovern as a wild liberal while at the same time

staking his claim to the Catholic vote by opposing abortion. Nixon's so-called Catholic strategy needs further scholarly exploration, but insight into this strategy is found in Littlewood, *Politics of Population Control,* 107–32; and Theodore White, *The Making of the President* (New York: Atheneum Publishers, 1973), 51–52; 242–44.

Nixon's appeals to Catholics were expressed in Richard Nixon, "Statement about Policy on Abortions at Military Base Hospitals in the United States," April 3, 1971, *Public Papers of the Presidents of the United States: Richard M. Nixon, 1971* (Washington, D.C.: Government Printing Office, 1972), 500; and "Remarks at the Annual Convention of the National Education Association in Philadelphia, Pennsylvania, April 6, 1972," in *Public Papers of the Presidents of the United States, Nixon 1972* (Washington, D.C.: Government Printing Office, 1974), 243–44.

An analysis of the New York election is found in "The New York Campaign," *National Journal* (November 28, 1972): 1676–78. Although dated, useful in understanding the 1968 campaign are White, *Making of the President,* and Michael Barone, *Our Country: The Shaping of America from Roosevelt to Reagan* (New York: Free Press, 1990), 436–53.

29. When the irate Rockefeller phoned the White House to complain about the statement, Nixon's presidential aide John Ehrlichman told New York governor Nelson Rockefeller that "we have always tried to pass the abortion issue on to the states and we intend on continuing this policy." He added that the Nixon administration did not want to make the abortion issue a federal problem. For the administration's relations with the Rockefeller brothers, John D. Rockefeller III and Nelson Rockefeller, see John Ehrlichman, "Office Notes, May 5, 1972, phone call to Nelson Rockefeller," John Ehrlichman Papers, box 6, National Archives.

30. Federal abortion policy is discussed by Karen O'Connor in *No Neutral Ground? Abortion Politics in an Age of Absolutes* (Boulder, Colo.: Westview Press, 1996); and Craig and O'Brien, *Abortion and American Politics.*

31. Craig and O'Brien, *Abortion and American Politics,* 76–96. Also, for insights into state abortion laws, see *Abortion 1974–75: Need and Services in the United States, Each State and Metropolitan Area* (New York: Alan Guttmacher Institute, 1976).

32. An excellent account of Supreme Court rulings is found in Gerald N. Rosenberg, *The Hollow Hope: Can Courts Bring About Social Change?* (Chicago: University of Chicago Press, 1991), 173–201.

33. Nelson Rockefeller's nomination to the vice presidency was opposed by four Roman Catholic bishops who testified against him at his nomination hearings before Congress. See Paige, *Right to Lifers,* 63. For a discussion of Nelson Rockefeller's role in the abortion debate in New York while he was governor, see Donald T. Critchlow, *Intended Consequences: Birth Control, Abortion, and the Federal Government* (New York: Oxford University Press, 1999).

34. The politics of the Hyde amendment and the appropriations bill presents an interesting example of strange bedfellows coming together for their own interests. Representative Bella Abzug (D-N.Y.), a strong supporter of abortion rights, voted to overturn Ford's veto because of her commitment to maintain spending levels in the appropriations bill. Anti-abortion congressmen such as Hyde voted to overturn the veto on anti-abortion grounds, even though he was a fiscal conservative. An understanding of the politics of the Hyde amendment in this period is provided by Joyce Gelb and Marian Lief Palley, "Interest Group Politics: A Comparative Analysis of Federal Decision Making," *Journal of Politics* 41 (May 1979): 362–92, especially 375–77.

35. There is an extensive literature on the ERA fight. Especially good discussion of the ERA debate is David E. Kyvig, *Explicit and Authentic Acts: Amending the U.S. Constitution, 1776–1995* (Lawrence: University Press of Kansas, 1996); Janet K. Boles, *The Politics of the Equal Rights Amendment: Conflict and the Decision Process* (New York: Longman, 1979); and Jane J. Mansbridge, *Why We Lost the ERA* (Chicago: University of Chicago Press, 1986). The following discussion of the ERA draws heavily from Mansbridge, but is informed by archival research in the ERAmerica Papers in the Library of Congress. This collection offers a detailed and rich record of the strategy, tactics, and changing perceptions of the proponents of the equal rights amendment. In addition, this discussion utilizes research in the Phyllis Schlafly Papers, located in the Eagle Forum office in Clayton, Missouri. The Schlafly Papers include twenty-plus filing cabinet drawers of anti-ERA material. This collection is currently closed to researchers, although the author received special permission to undertake research in this collection.

36. The ERA was first proposed in Congress in 1923, backed by Alice Paul and her militant National Women's Party. The amendment, however, ran into immediate opposition from a coalition of Progressive organizations and union women concerned that the amendment would have made unconstitutional the protective legislation for women workers that had been supported by socialists and social reformers like Florence Kelley. Kelley, head of the National Consumers League, denounced the amendment as "topsy-turvy feminism." In 1940, the Republican Party revitalized the ERA by placing it on the party's platform. Republicans continued on record in support of the amendment in the 1950s during the Eisenhower administration. In the 1960s, however, support for the ERA shifted to the feminist movement with the formation of the National Organization for Women (NOW), which gave the ERA first place on its Bill of Rights for Women. In 1971, with NOW's support, Representative Martha Griffiths (D-Mich.) pushed the ERA through the House, which passed the amendment by a vote of 354–23.

37. This history of the ERA draws heavily from Mansbridge, *Why We Lost the ERA,* 8–20.

38. Detailed arguments against the ERA are found in the *Phyllis Schlafly Report* from 1972 to 1982. Schlafly's first articulation of her opposition to the ERA appeared in "What's Wrong with 'Equal Rights' for Women?" *Phyllis Schlafly Report* (February 1972). She followed this with a more detailed criticism of the ERA in "The Fraud Called the Equal Rights Amendment," *Phyllis Schlafly Report* (May 1972). Also of importance in understanding the legal opposition to the ERA is Paul Freund, "The Equal Rights Amendment is Not the Way," *Harvard Civil Rights–Civil Liberties Law Review* (March 1971).

39. A good study of conservative women in this period is found in Lisa McGirr, *Suburban Warriors: The Origins of the New American Right* (Princeton, N.J.: Princeton University Press, 2000). See also Rebecca Klatch, *Women of the New Right* (Philadelphia: Temple University Press, 1987); Sara Diamond, *Roads to Dominion: Right-Wing Movements and Political Power in the United States* (New York: Guilford Press, 1995); and Elinor Burkett, *The Right Women: A Journey through the Hearts of Conservative America* (New York: Scribner, 1998).

The tradition of women as moral reformers is found in an extensive literature on the subject. For the purpose of this essay, especially useful are Jane Dehart, "Gender on the Right: Meanings behind the Existential Scream," *Gender and History* 3 (autumn 1991); Zillah R. Eisenstein, "The Sexual Politics of the New Right," *Feminist Theory* 7 (spring 1982); Kathleen M. Blee, *Women of the Klan: Racism and Gender in the 1920s* (Berkeley: University of California Press, 1991); and Leonard J. Moore, *Citizen Klansmen: The Ku Klux Klan in Indiana, 1921–1928* (Chapel Hill: University of North Carolina Press, 1991). Of particular value for understanding the role of women in public life in the nineteenth century are Mary P. Ryan, *Cradle of the Middle Class: The Family in Oneida County, New York, 1790–1865* (Cambridge: Cambridge University Press, 1981); Ryan, "The Power of Female Networks: A Case Study of Female Moral Reform in Antebellum America," *Feminist Studies* 5 (1979); Barbara Leslie Epstein, *The Politics of Domesticity: Women, Evangelism, and Temperance in Nineteenth Century America* (Middletown, Conn.: Wesleyan University Press, 1981); Ruth Bordin, *Woman and Temperance: The Quest for Power and Liberty, 1873–1900* (Philadelphia: Temple University Press, 1981); Lori Ginzberg, "'Moral Suasion Is Moral Balderdash': Women, Politics, and Social Activism in the 1850s," *Journal of American History* 73 (1986); Karen Blair, *The Clubwoman as Feminist: True Womanhood Redefined, 1868–1914* (New York: Holmes & Meier Publishers, 1980); Kathryn Kish Sklar, "Hull House in the 1890s: A Community of Women Reformers," *Signs* 10 (1985); Paula Baker, "Domestication of Politics: Women and American Political Society, 1780–1920," *American Historical Review* 89 (1984); Ellen Carol DuBois, *Feminism and Suffrage: The Emergence of an Independent Women's Movement in America, 1848–1869* (Ithaca, N.Y.: Cornell University Press, 1978); and Susan Lebsock, "Women and American Politics, 1880–1920," in *Women Politics, and Change in Twentieth-Century America,* ed. Louise Tilly and Patricia Gurin (New York: Russell Sage Foundation, 1990).

40. As author of *A Choice Not An Echo,* a campaign book that had played a critical role in winning the Republican nomination for Barry Goldwater in 1964, she carried into the ERA campaign a national reputation. Moreover, she brought to the campaign grassroots organizing skills not found among her opponents. She had run for Congress in 1952, and served as president of the Illinois Federation of Republican Women from 1960 to 1964, and later as vice president of the national federation from 1964 to 1967. Following a bitter election fight for the presidency of the National Federation of Republican Women (NFRW) in 1967, she withdrew from the organization and began a monthly national publication, the *Phyllis Schlafly Report.* Many of the women who had supported her in the NFRW election quickly joined the crusade to stop the ERA. Carol Felsenthal, *The Sweetheart of the Silent Majority: The Biography of Phyllis Schlafly* (Garden City, N.Y.: Doubleday, 1981).

41. The view that women's groups had failed to connect with "homemakers" is found in Bonnie Cowan to Jane Wells (national coordinator, ERAmerica), March 19, 1976, ERAmerica, box 1, Library of Congress, Washington, D.C.

42. With a relatively hierarchical chain of command centering on Phyllis Schlafly, coalitions were formed in key battleground states, where conservative women were already active, especially in Illinois, Schlafly's own backyard. The *Phyllis Schlafly Report* provided her supporters with a steady stream of arguments against the ERA while providing information to local activists and handouts to be distributed to state legislators. Because Schlafly became the central spokesperson against the ERA, opponents, often amateurs, had to face an experienced and articulate debater. Her background in politics enabled her to know which legislators to lobby, how to dress, how to speak before the camera, how to form alliances with legislators, and which legislators to target with campaign contributions through her Stop-ERA political action committee. Mansbridge, *Why We Lost the ERA,* 135–38 and 173–78.

43. A useful study of anti-ERA activists is found in David Brody and Kent Tedin, "Ladies in Pink: Religion and Political Ideology in the Anti-ERA Movement," *Social Science Quarterly* 57 (March 1976): 72–82.

44. See "Will the Real Jerry Ford Please Stand Up?" *Phyllis Schlafly Report* (September 1974).

45. Schlafly discusses the fight over the ERA in the 1976 Republican convention in "ERA and the Republicans," *Phyllis Schlafly Report* (September 1976).

46. In 1975, polls showed Ford well ahead of Reagan, but Reagan's strength increased rapidly. Ford swept the first primaries in New England and then handily carried Florida, but in North Carolina Reagan rebounded by pounding on the Panama Canal issue, declaring, "We built it, we paid for it, and we're not going to give it back." American nationalism and a repudiation of the Nixon-Ford-Kissinger foreign policy won North Carolina for Reagan, saving what had been a faltering campaign. By the time of the national convention, the GOP was severely divided. A succinct account of the 1976 election is found in Barone, *Shaping of America,* 544–45, 548–51, 556–58.

47. Both the Democratic and Republican planks on abortion are quoted in full in O'Connor, *No Neutral Ground?* 73.

48. Carter had won the Iowa primary by mobilizing evangelical voters by proclaiming he was a "born-again" Christian, one that opposed abortion. After his victory in the Iowa primary, he qualified his anti-abortion stance by declaring that while he was personally against abortion, he was opposed to a constitutional amendment overturning *Roe.* For an excellent discussion of Carter's straddling the abortion issue during the campaign of 1976, his presidency, and the campaign of 1980, see Steven Hayward, *The Age of Reagan: The Fall of the Old Liberal Order* (Roseville, Calif.: Forum, 2001), 495–97. Tensions between Carter and pro-abortion feminists are discussed in O'Connor, *No Neutral Ground?* 73–75.

49. When Carter and Ford avoided the abortion issue during the campaign, Ellen McCormack, a New York housewife running on the Right to Life party ticket, injected it into the 1976 election. Her campaign attracted considerable media attention and elevated the abortion issue by waging a graphic television campaign that included spot ads showing a fetus being aborted. Spitzer, *Right to Life Movement,* 50–59; O'Connor, *No Neutral Ground?* 71–73.

50. His wife, Rosalyn, joined the ERA campaign as well, traveling to states to support the amendment. Key state representatives were singled out with special treatment through invitations to visit the White House, where they were wined and dined. This direct intervention by the president, however, backfired; many representatives resented the added pressure placed on them by the president, who had involved himself in local affairs. Paul Scott, "White House's ERA Problem," *Washington New Intelligence Syndicate,* June 27, 1979, in ERA Topic Files, Schlafly Office Files, Eagle Forum; White House, "President's Advisory Committee for Women, Monday, May 14, 1979," *Weekly Compilation of Presidential Documents,* vol. 5, no. 19, 789–843; Jack Germond and Jules Witcover, "Battle for ERA May Be Finished," *Newark Star Ledger,* December 9, 1978, in ERA Office Files, ERA Democrats, Eagle Forum Office.

51. Carter's problems with the feminist movement were further complicated by his strained relations with his National Advisory Committee on Women. Carter had formed the National Advisory Committee on Women on June 22, 1978. By November, the committee, chaired by former New York Democrat Bella Abzug, was ready to meet with Carter to lay out their plans for the ERA fight, but when they learned that they had been allotted

only fifteen minutes for the meeting, it was canceled and then rescheduled to last thirty minutes on January 12. The committee had prepared a ten-page memorandum to be given to the president, "The First Eighteen Months: A Status Report of the Carter Administration Action on International Women's Year Resolutions." The committee also had prepared a report to be released to the press after the meeting, but it was leaked on January 11, much to Carter's aggravation. When the meeting finally came, all hell broke loose when Carter told Abzug that he disliked her "confrontational style." Sharp words were exchanged on both sides. After the meeting, Abzug met with the press to express her dismay with Carter. Within moments after the press conference, she was summoned to the office of presidential aide Hamilton Jordan, where she was requested to resign. Meanwhile, Carmen Delgado Votaw, cochair of the committee, was detained by Carter and informed of the action to remove Abzug. When the committee reassembled, twenty of the forty members decided to resign. Carter accepted the resignations and appointed Marjorie Bell Chambers, a Republican and feminist from New Mexico, to serve as temporary chair. Later, Carter claimed that the mail had run two to one in his favor for firing Abzug, but clearly his relations with the women's movement had soured. "Washington Report of the National Advisory Committee for Women, January 20, 1979," in Office Files, ERA Office Files, National Advisory Committee on Women. This report was sent to Phyllis Schlafly by an unknown supporter.

52. For divisions within the Carter administration, see Joseph Califano, *Governing America: An Insider's Report from the White House and the Cabinet* (New York: Simon and Schuster, 1981).

53. *Congressional Record, House,* 95th Cong., 2d sess., 1978, 17266–74. See also Craig and O'Brien, *Abortion and American Politics,* 128; and "Family Planning, Crib Death Funds Authorized," *Congressional Quarterly Weekly Report* 36 (August 5, 1978): 2063–65.

54. Michele McKeegan, *Abortion Politics: Mutiny in the Ranks of the Right* (New York: Free Press, 1992), 1–23; and Michael Margolis and Kevin Neary, "Pressure Politics Revisited: The Anti-Abortion campaign," *Policy Studies Journal* 8 (spring 1980): 698–716.

55. Michael Johnston, "The 'New Christian Right' in American Politics," *Political Quarterly* 53, no. 2 (April–June 1982): 181–99.

56. Campaign staffers selected from anti-abortion candidates included Representative Robert Dornan (R-Calif.); Representative Dan Quayle (R-Ind.), who was challenging Senator Birch Bayh; Representative Charles Grassley (R-Iowa), running against Senator John Culver; and Representative Steve Symms (R-Idaho), up against Senator Frank Church. In addition, pro-life political activists from Louisiana, Pennsylvania, Oregon, Connecticut, Oklahoma, Wisconsin, and Massachusetts were sent to school to make them into "prolife political experts to help bring them over the top next November." See "1980 Elections Start Now!" *Pro-Life Political Reporter* 1 (September 1979): 4, in Dee Jepsen Papers, box I, Ronald Reagan Library (RRL).

57. For mobilization of the new right, see Pamela Johnston Conover, "The Mobilization of the New Right: A Test of Various Explanations," *Western Political Quarterly* 36 (December 1983): 632–49; Carol Mueller, "In Search of a Constituency for the 'New Religious Right,'" *Public Opinion Quarterly* 47 (summer 1983): 213–29; and Clyde Wilcox and Leopoldo Gomez, "The Christian Right and the Pro-Life Movement: An Analysis of Sources of Political Support," *Review of Religious Research* 31, no. 4 (June 1990): 380–88.

MOBILIZING WOMEN 323

The Carter administration's failure to win support among feminists left many in the administration bitter. Shortly after the 1980 Democratic convention, in an interview with the *Washington Post,* Anne Wexler, a senior assistant to Carter, declared: "The spokespeople for women in this [ERA] campaign ended up being the people who are in the forefront of the feminist movement. And I don't think their politics are very sophisticated." She added, "I thought that the way the women's leadership at the Democratic National Convention approached the issue of the ERA was about as wrong as anything that I've seen. What they did was say, 'We're going to punish you if you are not for us,' rather than 'We will reward you if you are.'" "Reflecting on Feminism, Politics, and the Democratic Party," *Washington Post,* December 9, 1980, in ERA Office Files, ERA Democrat, Eagle Forum Office.

58. Gillian Peel, *Revival and Reaction: The Right in Contemporary America* (New York: Oxford University Press, 1984).

59. Lou Cannon, *President Reagan: The Role of a Lifetime* (New York: Simon and Schuster, 1991), 112.

60. For an excellent legislative summary of congressional action on abortion, see Edward Keynes, "Abortion," in *The Encyclopedia of the United States Congress,* vol. 1, ed. Donald C. Bacon, Roger H. Davidson, and Morton Keller (New York: Simon and Schuster, 1995), 1–2. Also Edward Keynes, *The Court vs. Congress: Prayer, Busing, and Abortion* (Durham, N.C.: Duke University Press, 1989); and Laurence Tribe, *Abortion: The Clash of Absolutes* (New York: Norton, 1990).

61. Letters urging Reagan to meet with anti-abortion leaders are seen in Orrin G. Hatch to the President, May 28, 1981; William L. Armstrong to Honorable Edwin Meese III, May 29, 1981, Morton Blackwell Papers, box 8, RRL.

62. Presidential Papers of Ronald Reagan, 1981, "Conservative Political Action Conference, March 20, 1981," 327–28, in box 1, abortion folder, Elizabeth Dole Papers, RRL.

63. An excellent legislative summary of congressional actions on abortion is found in Keynes, "Abortion," 1–2. Also useful on the Reagan administration and the social issues is Keynes, *The Court vs. Congress.*

64. For an evaluation of these amendments, see "Five Proposals for Protection of the Unborn," *Family Policy Insights,* November 4, 1981, in box I, Dee Jepsen Papers, RRL.

65. Timonth Noah, "The Right-to-Life Split," *New Republic,* March 21, 1981, 7–9; also, *Congressional Quarterly Weekly Report* (December 19, 1981): 2526. For an overview, although it should be read cautiously, see Craig and O'Brien, *Abortion and American Politics;* and McKeegan, *Abortion Politics,* 1–23.

66. For a succinct summary of the abortion legislation, see "Anti-Abortion Measures Begin to Advance," *Congressional Quarterly Almanac,* 97th Cong., 1st sess., vol. 37, 1981, 425–26; and "Senate Kills Abortion, School Prayer Riders," *Congressional Quarterly Almanac,* 97th Cong., 2d sess., vol. 38, 1982, 403.

67. The five cases included *Akron Center for Reproductive Health v. City of Akron; City of Akron v. Akron Center for Reproductive Health; Planned Parenthood of Kansas City v. Ashcroft; Ashcroft v. Planned Parenthood of Kansas City;* and *Simpoulous v. Virginia.*

68. Morton C. Blackwell to Elizabeth Dole, August 20, 1982, Abortion File, box 1, Elizabeth Dole Papers, RRL.

69. Elizabeth Dole to Edwin Harper, August 31, 1982, Edwin Harper to Elizabeth Dole, September 7, 1982, Abortion File, box 1, Elizabeth Dole Papers, RRL.

70. See "Draft Letter, President Reagan to Key Senators," August 31, 1982; and Morton C. Blackwell to Elizabeth Dole, draft letter, September 1, 1982, in Abortion File, box 1,

Elizabeth Dole Papers, RRL. Also *Congressional Quarterly Weekly Report* (September 4, 1982): 2202, also quoted in Craig and O'Brien, *Abortion and American Politics,* 145.

71. Morton C. Blackwell, "Analysis of First Cloture Vote," September 9, 1982, Douglas Johnson to Morton C. Blackwell, September 13, 1982, in Abortion 2 File, box 1, Elizabeth Dole Papers, RRL.

72. See Kenneth M. Duberstein and Ed Harper, "Recommended Telephone Call to Senator Slade Gorton; Senator William Cohen; Senator Malcolm Wallop; Rudy Boschwitz; Alan Simpson; David Durenberger; and Mark Hatfield," September 8, 1982, Abortion 2 File, box 1, Elizabeth Dole Papers, RRL.

73. "New Right Defeated on Abortion," *Washington Post,* September 16, 1982, 1.

74. Cannon, *Role of a Lifetime,* 812; also Cannon, *Reagan* (New York: Putnam, 1982), 128–32.

75. He notes that none of his White House chiefs of staff wanted Reagan to become involved in the issue. This pragmatism was apparent in his appointment of James Baker as his chief of staff. Edwin Meese, appointed attorney general, expressed personal and policy views on abortion that were generally regarded as "middle of the road." Cannon recalls Meese in California expressing concern that restrictive abortion laws encouraged the birth of unwanted children who were often abused and neglected. Lyn Nofziger, Reagan's aide in California and key political strategist in Washington, had urged Reagan to sign the permissive abortion legislation in California because he believed in a woman's right to have an abortion. Similarly, Nancy Reagan avoided the issue, but many believed she was sympathetic to the abortion rights view. Cannon, *Role of a Lifetime,* 812.

76. Unknown author, "Meeting for April 17, 1982, with Prolife Leaders," Prolife File, box 8, Morton Blackwell Papers, RRL.

77. This perspective is expressed in McKeegan, *Abortion Politics,* 1–23; and Tanya Melich, *The Republican War against Women: An Insider's Report from Behind the Lines* (New York: Bantam, 1998).

78. See O'Connor, *No Neutral Ground?* 81–111.

79. Nadine Cohodas, "Federal Abortion Alternatives Cut by Reagan Administration," *Congressional Quarterly Weekly Report* (November 17, 1984): 2949–55.

80. These cutbacks in family planning programs outraged activists. Planned Parenthood Federation in New York City ran a full-page newspaper ad featuring a diaphragm floating through the galaxy. "When it comes to birth control, our technology isn't space age," the caption read. Quoted in Cohodas, "Federal Abortion Alternatives Cut," 2949–55.

Reagan's cut in Title X funds was challenged in court but upheld in *Rust v. Sullivan* (1991). See also "U.S. Supreme Court Upholds Title X Ban on Abortion Information," *Family Planning Perspectives* 23, no. 4 (July–August 1991): 175–81.

81. Of particular interest in this regard was the Baby Doe regulation, issued by HHS under Bowen on Reagan's instructions following the death of a newborn infant with Down's syndrome in Bloomington, Indiana. Following surgery to correct a detached esophagus, nourishment was withheld from the infant. The HHS issued a notice to all hospitals that received federal financial assistance under Medicare and Medicaid, reminding them that it was unlawful to discriminatorily withhold medically indicated treatment from handicapped children. On May 18, 1982, HHS issued an order that this was in violation of section 504 of the Rehabilitation Act of 1973. On April 14, 1983, Judge Gerhard Gesell of the U.S. District of Columbia Court declared that this final rule was invalid because HHS improperly failed to provide for public comment. The Supreme Court upheld the decision

in *Bowen v. the American Hospital Association* (1986) in a 5–4 decision, declaring that parents can instruct hospitals to deny nourishment.

Betty Lou Dotson, HHS, "Notice to Health Care Providers," May 18, 1983, in Prolife File, Box 7, Morton Blackwell Papers.

82. Steve Alumbaugh and C. K. Rowland, "The Links between Platform-Based Appointment Criteria and Trial Judges' Abortion Judgments," *Judicature* 74, no. 3 (October–November 1990): 153–62.

83. Charles Fried, *Order and Law: Arguing the Reagan Revolution—A Firsthand Account* (New York: Simon & Schuster, 1991), 58.

84. Morton Blackwell to Elizabeth H. Dole, "Conservative Organization Reaction to Sandra O'Connor Nomination," July 8, 1981, Conservative File, box 2, Elizabeth Dole Papers, RRL.

85. Ronald Reagan to Mrs. Marie Craven, August 3, 1981, Prolife File, box 8, Morton Blackwell Papers.

86. Tricia Rodgers to Anne Higgins, September 14, 1981, Conservative File, box 2, Elizabeth Dole Papers.

87. In her first major abortion case on the Court, Justice O'Connor joined dissenters in *Akron v. Akron Center for Reproductive Health, Inc.* (1983), which struck down most restrictions on abortion that had been legislated by the Akron City Council. In her dissent, O'Connor noted that *Roe* was "on a collision course with itself" because the trimester approach was "unworkable" in light of changing medical technology that lengthened viability. She echoed U.S. Solicitor General Rex E. Lee's amicus brief, which asserted that the test for state regulation for abortion should rest on the principle of "undue burden." This marked an important shift in the Court's thinking on the subject. O'Connor, *No Neutral Ground?* 94–102; and McKeegan, *Abortion Politics,* 173–91.

88. Found within the Reagan Library collections is a rich body of memorandums, studies, and exchanges concerning the Catholic vote in the approaching 1984 and 1988 elections, as well as specific election studies of various ethnic Catholic groups. See, for example, Thomas Patrick Melady to Michael A. McManus, "Comments on Obtaining the Catholic Ethnic Vote in 1984" (no. 59); Draft, "The Administration's Catholic/Ethnic Strategy" (n.d.), 2; Draft Paper, "Administration's Catholic/Ethnic Strategy" (n.d.), Catholic Strategy File, box 7, Marian Bell Papers; and "The Catholic Vote and the Republican Party (A Comprehensive Look)" (n.d.), Catholic Strategy File, box 8, Morton Blackwell Papers.

89. Linas to Faith Whittlesey, "Invitations to Catholic Bishops for State Dinners," September 14, 1983, Catholic Strategy File, box 7, Morton Blackwell Papers.

90. Michael M. Uhlmann to Edwin L. Harper, "Article for the President to Publish in Human Life Review," March 22, 1983; and Morton Blackwell to Faith Ryan Whittlesey, March 28, 1983, Pro-Life File, box 7, Morton Blackwell Papers.

91. Ronald Reagan, *Abortion and the Conscience of the Nation* (New York: T. Nelson, 1984).

92. Elizabeth H. Dole, "Meeting with Pro-Life Leadership," January 20, 1983; Elizabeth Dole to Ed Meese, January 24, 1983, Abortion 8 and 9 Files, Dee Jepsen Papers; and "Meeting with National Leaders of Pro-Life Movement," National Pro-Life File, box 7, Morton Blackwell Papers.

93. Fried, *Order and Law,* 77–81.

94. When Chief Justice Warren Burger, one of the members of the majority in *Roe,* retired, Reagan appointed Associate Justice William H. Rehnquist as chief justice and then nominated noted conservative Antonin Scalia to the Court. Shortly afterward, following

the retirement of Justice Lewis F. Powell in June 1987, Reagan nominated Judge Robert H. Bork, a well-known conservative and vociferous critic of the privacy doctrine position, in relation to abortion. This nomination unleashed the wrath of liberals in the Senate, feminists, and abortion advocates. Following a bitter fight in the Senate, Bork's nomination was defeated in a vote of 58–42. Reagan then turned to Judge Anthony Kennedy, who won Senate confirmation after he assured the Senate that he accepted a constitutional right to privacy. Herman Schwartz, *Packing the Courts: The Conservative Campaign to Rewrite the Constitution* (New York: Scribner, 1988).

95. Jo Ann Gasper, interview with author, September 3, 2001; "Anti-Abortion War Resumed by Reagan," *Washington Times,* July 31, 1987, A1, 12.

96. Robert M. Patrick, "Kemp Withdraws as 'Salute' to Dr. Koop Fans Controversy," *Lifeletter* 4 (1987): 1–2.

97. Press Release, "Remarks by the President in Briefing for Right to Life Leaders," July 10, 1997, Abortion File, box 1, Gary Bauer Papers, RRL.

98. For example, see Douglas Johnson, National Right to Life Legislative Director, to Board of Directors and State Offices, "Enactment of Prohibition on Funding of Abortions by the Government of the District of Columbia," October 5, 1988, Pro-Life File, box 1, Marian Bell Papers.

99. "Senate Showdown Set for Grove City Bill," *Action Line, Christian Action Council Newsletter* 11, no. 4 (June 5, 1987): 1.

100. This description of the legislation draws heavily in organization and language from "Grove City Bill," *Congressional Quarterly Almanac,* 100th Cong., 2d sess., vol. 44, 1988, 763–67. Kennedy's leadership in enactment of the legislation is found in "Edward M. Kennedy to Dear Colleague Letter," March 16, 1988, copy in Grove City File, box 7, Marian Bell Papers.

101. Dinesh D'Sousa to Gary Bauer, "Civil Rights Restoration Act," February 10, 1988; and "Civil Rights Restoration Act of 1987: Potential for Disaster," in Grove City and Pro-Life material, box 7 and box 1, Marian Bell Papers.

102. Douglas Johnson to Rebecca Range, Director of White House Public Liaison, March 10, 1988; and William B. Allen to Ronald R. Reagan, March 3, 1988, Abortion File, box 1, Gary Bauer Papers.

103. National Right to Life Committee, Press Release, "NRLC Proclaims Landmark Victory as House Joins Senate in Stripping Abortion Rights from Title IX Sex Discrimination Law," March 2, 1988, in Abortion File, box 1, Gary Bauer Papers.

104. In the handwritten draft, Reagan added, "not excepting Pravada and Tass that I have ever seen." Richard Darman, reviewing the draft letter, convinced Reagan to delete the phrase. Ronald R. Reagan to John Lofton, July 30, 1982, draft, Ronald Reagan to John Lofton (n.d.), box 3, Presidential Handwritten File, series II, Presidential Records, RRL. I want to thank historian Robert Collins for calling attention to this exchange.

105. This divide reflected the shifting relationship between the sexes and a cultural divide produced, in part, by changes in gender relations. Economic prosperity allowed increasing numbers of Americans to feel free not to have children and even to remain or become unmarried. The proportion of women working outside the home increased to about 55 percent by the middle 1980s. At the same time, beginning in 1967, the divorce rate shot up, reaching 50 percent of all marriages dissolving by the year 2000.

14
Federal Judgeships in Retrospect
David M. O'Brien

Federal judges are "Ronald Reagan's best legacy." That view of Reagan's presidential counselor Fred Fielding was widely shared by those who served in the Department of Justice (DoJ).[1] Even the administration's critics agree that Reagan's judicial appointees had a profound impact on the composition of the federal judiciary with major consequences for the direction of the federal courts.[2] Reagan appointed close to half of all lower court judges, more than any other previous president (see table 14.1). Nor has any president, other than Republican president Dwight Eisenhower, filled a greater percentage of the federal bench since Democratic president Franklin Roosevelt's (FDR) record of naming 80 percent of a much smaller federal judiciary. In addition, Reagan made four appointments to the Supreme Court. Numbers are only part of the story, however. Federal judgeships, at all levels, never had greater political symbolism or higher priority for a presidency.

Federal judgeships were campaign issues for the Republican Party in the 1980 and 1984 presidential elections. Reagan pledged to appoint only those supportive of traditional family values and opposed to abortion and past judicial activism. Even more important, behind the campaign rhetoric and political symbolism, Reagan's administration had a more coherent and ambitious agenda for judicial selection than any previous administration. Indeed, judges were viewed as instruments of presidential power and a way to ensure the president's legacy. Through the appointment of federal judges, as Attorney General Edwin Meese III once put it, the administration aimed "to institutionalize the Reagan revolution so it can't be set aside no matter what happens in future presidential elections."[3]

FEDERAL JUDGESHIPS AS SYMBOLS AND INSTRUMENTS OF PRESIDENTIAL POWER

Before discussing why the Reagan administration restructured the federal judicial selection process, how it did so, and with what consequences for the federal

327

Table 14.1. Number of Judicial Appointments from Roosevelt (FDR) to Reagan

	Roosevelt (FDR)	Truman	Eisenhower	Kennedy	Johnson	Nixon	Ford	Carter	Reagan
Supreme Court	9	4	5	2	2	4	1	0	4
Circuit courts	52	27	45	20	41	45	12	56	78
District courts	137	102	127	102	125	179	52	202	290
Total	198	133	177	124	168	228	65	258	372

judiciary, it is perhaps helpful to place the administration's approach to appointing federal judges within a broader historical context. Obviously, presidents differ in their priorities and more or less delegate when picking judges. They also enjoy more or less influence depending on the level of a judicial vacancy—whether it is on the Supreme Court, appellate court, or federal district court—and depending on whether they face a Senate controlled by the opposition party.

Presidents tend to weigh four broad considerations in selecting federal judges: the professional competence of potential candidates; personal patronage and rewarding party faithful and supporters; "representative" factors, such as a nominee's home state and geographical balance on a court, as well as the religion, race, ethnicity, and gender of potential nominees; and finally, potential candidates' ideological and legal policy or jurisprudential positions. Each of these factors has, arguably, been given different weight or priority during different presidencies, and as a result there are, at least, three models of presidential selection of federal judges.

First is the "classic Democratic model" of rewarding party faithful with federal judgeships as political patronage. Looking back, it seems fair to say that Democratic presidents Franklin D. Roosevelt, Harry Truman, John F. Kennedy, and Lyndon Baines Johnson paid, particularly with respect to Supreme Court nominees, primary attention to (1) personal patronage and rewarding party faithful, with (2) some (but not very great) consideration given to professional competence, and (3) occasionally symbolic representation. FDR, for instance, gave weight to geography and religion, as did LBJ in replacing Jewish Justice Arthur J. Goldberg with his close personal friend, Jewish Justice Abe Fortas, as well as when appointing the first African American, Justice Thurgood Marshall. Beyond rewarding friends and party faithful, and thus inviting charges of cronyism, these Democratic presidents gave little consideration to pursuing their administrations' policy agenda through the appointment of federal judges. Indeed, some of their judicial appointees, particularly in the lower federal courts, actively opposed their public policies.[4]

By contrast, Republican presidents Dwight D. Eisenhower and Gerald R. Ford, along with Democratic presidents Jimmy Carter and Bill Clinton, pursued what might be termed a "bipartisan approach" to judicial recruitment. They emphasized, first and foremost, their nominees' professional competence. Some, but not overriding, attention was given to rewarding party faithful, along with some consideration of symbolic representation of race and gender on the federal bench. But none of these presidents imposed rigorous ideological screening for their nominees. Moreover, with the exception of Clinton, these presidents were nonlawyers and all largely delegated responsibility for selecting judicial nominees to their attorneys general. To be sure, charges of cronyism leveled during the FDR–Truman years contributed to Eisenhower's bipartisan approach. And Ford, Carter, and Clinton were, for different reasons, institutionally constrained during their presidencies and would have confronted fierce confirmation battles had they tried to make more ideological appointments to the federal bench.

Finally, a third model—that of "Republican ideological judicial selection"— was inspired by Republican president Richard M. Nixon and perfected by Reagan. During his 1968 campaign, Nixon promised to return "law and order" to the country and to appoint justices and judges who would adhere to "judicial self-restraint." In short, federal judgeships were deemed symbols and instruments of presidential power: the administration's ideological and policy agenda was given top priority, even over rewarding party faithful with judgeships and their potential nominees' professional competence. Nixon, however, from the perspective of those later in Reagan's DoJ and White House, failed to follow through on his campaign pledges and specifically failed to adopt a rigorous enough judicial selection process.[5] And in that respect, the legacy of the Reagan administration was that of putting into place and fine-tuning a rigorous, ideological process for selecting federal judges.

REFORMING THE FEDERAL JUDICIAL SELECTION PROCESS

One among many of Reagan's great strengths was his ability to forge a broad coalition among traditional conservatives, moderate Republicans, and the new right or "movement conservatives." Like other presidents who have to deal with their special interest groups, once in office Reagan sought in symbolic and tangible ways to satisfy his new right supporters. Indeed, it was notably the new right's agenda, rather than traditional conservatives' concerns with judicial self-restraint and "law and order," that defined "Reagan justice" and his administration's politics of law. This led to some intra-party fighting over the appointment of a few lower court judges and badly divided the Republican legal establishment in the unsuccessful 1987 battle for Senate confirmation of Judge Robert H. Bork to the Supreme Court. Nonetheless, Reagan had an ambitious agenda for legal reform and put into place one of the most rigorous processes for selecting federal judges.

An Ambitious Agenda for Legal Reform. "No administration has thought longer and more deeply about law since that of FDR, and we have thought more deeply than that administration."[6] That was no immodest boast on the part of Terry Eastland, the Justice Department's director of public affairs.

Why? In retrospect, it appears the result of a combination of six factors. First, the Justice Department's agenda reflected both staffing and the political strategy of young "movement conservatives." They were attracted to the department and were recruited from the senatorial staff of Reagan Republicans and the ranks of former law clerks to leading conservative jurists, like Justice Rehnquist, as well as law professors elevated by Reagan to the federal bench, such as Robert H. Bork, Antonin Scalia, Richard Posner, and Ralph Winter. In addition, many were associated with the Federalist Society, a conservative legal fraternity founded in the early 1980s.

What they shared was a sense of being in the vanguard of a new conservative legal movement—a movement that went beyond older conservatives' opposition to the "liberal jurisprudence" of the Warren Court (1953–1969). They also defined the department's social-policy agenda largely in terms of the new right's opposition to rulings of the Burger Court (1969–1986) on abortion, affirmative action, busing, school prayer, and the like.

Admittedly, there were some divisions within the ranks of the DoJ and those associated with the Federalist Society. While many were concerned with federalism and returning power to the states, some were more libertarian, especially those associated with the "Chicago law and economics movement." Reagan appointed several of the leaders of the movement to the lower federal courts, including Robert H. Bork, Richard Posner, Frank Easterbook, and Douglas H. Ginsburg.[7] But that in turn on occasion resulted in some hasty or ill-considered judicial nominations and a breaking of ranks with cultural conservatives, notably with the defeat of two nominees who were closely associated with the law and economics movement: Judge Douglas H. Ginsburg on his nomination to the Supreme Court and Bernard Seigan to the federal appellate bench.

Second, the DoJ's promotion of the new right's social–civil rights positions and a free-market economic analysis of law was also politically strategic. During his first term, Reagan lent presidential prestige to proposals for constitutional amendments that would overturn the Supreme Court's 1973 abortion ruling in *Roe v. Wade* and to curb the jurisdiction of lower federal courts in other controversial areas, such as school prayer.[8] But within a couple of years, it was clear that Congress would not go along with that. Thereafter, Reagan offered politically symbolic support in speeches, but never really pushed the new right's agenda in Congress. Instead, the Justice Department pursued it through litigation and judicial selection.

Third, there was a greater appreciation than in prior administrations for the significance of the expanding number of judgeships and the changing role of courts in American politics. In the 1980s, with fifty or more judicial vacancies annually becoming available (due to the creation of new judgeships because of rising caseloads), the federal bench could quickly bear the imprint of a particular president. Because federal judges are basically guaranteed lifetime tenure, they are attractive vehicles for achieving a president's legal-policy goals. As the former associate deputy attorney general, Bruce Fein, observed, "The judiciary is a primary player in the formulation of public policy," and hence "it would be silly for an administration not to try to affect the direction of legal-policy" when filling vacancies on the federal bench.[9]

Fourth, as noted, the judges appointed by previous Republican administrations were largely viewed by the Justice Department as disappointing and representing lost opportunities. Quite simply, prior Republican administrations allowed political patronage and professional considerations to overshadow their own legal-policy goals in judicial selection. Stephen Markman, the assistant attorney general overseeing judicial selection in Reagan's second term, offered this critical assessment of prior Republican administrations' judicial appointments: "While many of the Nixon appointees were more conservative judicially than judges selected under earlier administrations, the ability of the Nixon Administration to affect the overall philosophy of the federal bench was ultimately frustrated by the concessions the Administration was forced (or chose) to make."

Judges picked during the Ford presidency were even more disappointing. In Markman's words, "The Ford Administration did not make significant changes in the judicial selection process," and "the weakness of the Ford Administration may be seen in the statistic that a record 21 percent of its district court appointments went to members of the opposing party." Both administrations, though, were constrained by a Democratic-controlled Congress, and the Watergate scandal had further eroded their bargaining power with the Senate. Still, in the view of Markman and others, Nixon and Ford failed to "view the philosophical grounding of [judicial] candidates to be as important" as did those in Reagan's Justice Department.[10]

Fifth, President Carter's "affirmative action" program for selecting judges inspired a reaction. Carter forged historic changes in the federal bench by seeking a more "representative judiciary" through the recruitment of blacks, women, and other minorities. For those in Reagan's Justice Department, his "affirmative action" program was irrelevant and sacrificed "judicial merit" for the political symbolism of a more "representative" federal bench.

Finally, as a result of the previous factors, during Reagan's presidency the Justice Department became more and more aggressive in defining and pushing its agenda in litigation and in judicial selection. This reflected incremental changes in the staffing and strategies of the DoJ during Reagan's two terms, as well as within the administration a growing synergism associated with waging the "Reagan Revolution."

In other words, during Reagan's first term, under Attorney General William French Smith, the department basically sought to establish what it was *against*. It wanted to overturn Warren Court precedents that had expanded protection for the rights of the accused, especially through enforcement of the exclusionary rule and *Miranda* warnings.[11] And it opposed the Burger Court's rulings permitting abortions and affirmative action as well as requiring what it regarded as a rigid separation of church and state.

In Reagan's second term, under Attorney General Edwin Meese, the DoJ aimed to broadly establish what Reagan justice stood *for*. Nothing symbolized this more (nor captured wider public attention) than Meese's call for a "return to a jurisprudence of original intention" and Judge Bork's defense of that view during his confirmation hearings.[12]

Reforming the Judicial Selection Process. The Reagan administration, in the words of Stephen Markman, put "in place what is probably the most thorough and comprehensive system for recruiting and screening federal judicial candidates of any administration ever. This administration has, moreover, attempted to assert the President's prerogatives over judicial selection more consistently than many of its predecessors."[13]

From the outset, it was clear that greater presidential control over judicial selection was necessary if the department was to reverse what it perceived as a trend toward appointing liberal to moderate judges. One of the first steps was the elimination of Carter's nominating commissions for appellate court judges. Moreover, Reagan also requested senators to submit three to five or more names for each district court vacancy in their home states. This gave the administration more flexibility and bargaining power over the nomination of lower federal court judges.

A number of other changes and reforms also contributed to forging a more rigorous and ideological process for recruiting federal judges. Presidential control over the judicial selection was enhanced by also abandoning Carter's policy of working with the National Bar Association—representing African American lawyers—and various women's organizations. These groups no longer had input into the department's judicial selection process. In addition, the department's relationship with the American Bar Association (ABA) deteriorated, particularly after some of Reagan's nominees ran into trouble.

Even more crucial was the reorganization of the judicial screening and selection process within the Reagan presidency. Primary responsibility shifted from the DoJ to the White House and became a larger staff operation. The attorney general no longer had total responsibility or solely relied on his deputy attorney general for assistance. Instead, the assistant attorney general for the Office of Legal Policy was put in charge of screening potential judicial candidates, subject to further review by the White House.

A White House Judicial Selection Committee was created to decide whom the president should nominate. It met weekly in the White House and included the attorney general; the deputy attorney general; the counselor to the president; and the assistant attorneys general for the Office of Legal Policy, personnel and legislative affairs; as well as other White House advisers, including the chief of staff.

This reorganization concentrated power, institutionalized the role of the White House, and better positioned the Reagan administration to combat senatorial patronage when filling lower court vacancies, as well as enabled rigorous ideological screening of potential judicial nominees.

In addition, an unprecedented screening process for potential judicial nominees was introduced. The White House Judicial Selection Committee considered judicial candidates only after they had undergone daylong interviews with DoJ officials. And the interviews took place only after candidates' records—containing speeches, articles, and opinions—were compared with hundreds of others in the department's computer data bank.

The interviews were unprecedented and controversial. Among those criticizing the practice were Eisenhower's attorney general, Herbert Brownell, and Carter's attorney general, Griffin Bell. Brownell termed the questioning of judicial candidates "shocking." In Bell's words, "It politicized the process badly. I don't believe that you should ask a judge his views [on specific issues] because he is likely to have to rule on that."[14]

No less controversial were some of the questions asked of candidates for judgeships. Some who made it to the bench and others who didn't told of being asked about their views on abortion, affirmative action, and criminal justice. National Public Radio correspondent Nina Totenberg reported that several contenders said "they were asked directly about their views on abortion."[15]

This screening and scrutiny of judicial nominees drew criticism from liberal senators and groups like the Alliance for Justice, created to monitor judicial nominations for a coalition of liberal organizations. Even some officials in past Republican administrations and leading conservative law professors, like Philip Kurland, were critical. Philip Lacovara, a former official in Nixon's Justice Department, even resigned as Reagan's representative on the nominating commission for the District of Columbia courts. He claimed that officials told him that he was "too liberal," "not politically reliable," and that he had failed the "litmus test for philosophical orthodoxy."[16]

Justice Department officials, however, repeatedly denied having a "litmus test." In White House counselor Fred Fielding's words, "no one factor was considered." Candidates, they contended, were asked about past rulings and hypothetical cases—dealing, admittedly, with heated issues like abortion—but that was to "see how they think through a case" and where they stood on the role of the courts. As Attorney General Meese further explained: "We do discuss the law with judicial candidates. . . . In discussing the law with lawyers there is really no way not to bring up cases—past cases—and engage in a dialogue over the reasoning and merits of particular decisions. But even here, our primary interest is how someone's mind works, whether they have powers of discernment and the scholarly grounding required of a good judge."[17] Others in the administration defended their screening process on the ground that a president who fails to scrutinize the legal philosophy of federal judicial nominees courts frustration of his own policy agenda.

Such explanations satisfied few critics and troubled moderate Republican senators. Indeed, it was the latter who had the toughest time with Reagan's Judicial Selection Committee. And that, perhaps, is one of the best measures of the extent to which the administration placed its own ideological and legal-policy goals above partisan patronage, and at times even above the professional qualifications of potential judicial nominees.

Prior administrations usually deferred to senators in their own party when filling lower court vacancies. This meant occasionally bargaining and sacrificing their own legal-policy goals. But Reagan's Justice Department was decidedly less willing to do so. That in turn led to delays in filling some judgeships and occasionally to rather bitter fighting within the Republican Party. In Pennsylvania, for example, six vacancies remained open for almost two years due to the DoJ's refusal to nominate James R. McGregor, a respected trial court judge supported by Pennsylvania's two Republican senators, Arlen Specter and John Heinz. McGregor was deemed too lenient on criminal justice matters, and only after Democrats regained the Senate in 1987 did the department finally agree to his nomination.

There were also instances when the Justice Department was forced into hard horse trading in order to win Senate confirmation for its judicial nominees. Daniel Manion's controversial confirmation for the U.S. Court of Appeals for the Seventh Circuit illustrates how far the Reagan presidency at times pressed its legal-policy goals and took a hard-line approach when dealing with moderate Republicans. Manion was narrowly confirmed by a vote of 48–46, but only after the Justice Department was forced to trade other judgeships for the votes of moderate Republican senators. Minnesota's Republican senator David Durenberger withdrew his opposition to Manion after the department relented on a yearlong veto of the nomination to a district court of his friend and past president of Minnesota's state bar association, David Doty. Then, Washington's Republican senator Slade Gorton shifted positions on Manion, casting a crucial vote for confirmation despite widespread criticism of the nominee by the legal profession and a sitting judge on the Seventh Circuit. He did so because the Justice Department finally approved, after nearly a year, William Dwyer for a district judgeship in his home state. (That well-publicized incident, however, became a campaign issue that contributed to his defeat for reelection, though he subsequently ran again and was reelected.)

Notably, in the case of Manion and a few other controversial judicial nominations, President Reagan made personal phone calls to pivotal senators that paid off and underscored his commitment to reforming the federal judiciary through his judicial appointments.[18]

In sum, the Reagan administration's meticulous screening of judicial nominees and hard-line positions with moderate Republicans challenged the norms of senatorial patronage. They nevertheless strengthened presidential control over judicial selection, even at the cost of some tough confirmation battles and a few setbacks. The nomination of Jefferson B. Sessions III to a district court in Alabama, for instance, was narrowly defeated by the Senate Judiciary Committee; this had happened only once before in the previous half century. Sherman Unger, the only Reagan nominee rated "not qualified" by the ABA, confronted stiff opposition but died before his confirmation. A few others also ran into trouble, and Reagan was forced to withdraw them from consideration. Some, like law school professors William Harvey, Bernard Seigan, and Lino Graglia, had received unfavorable ABA reports and met with strong opposition due to their positions on economic and constitutional rights. Still, considering the unrivaled number of appointments, Reagan achieved remarkable success, suffering really only one major defeat, his nomination of Judge Bork to the Supreme Court in 1987.

Winning Senate Confirmation. The main obstacle in appointing judges for Reagan, as for any president, was the Senate's power, under the advice and consent clause of Article 2, to reject judicial nominees. Yet, that power rarely poses a major threat, and whether it becomes a major obstacle depends on the level of judgeships, fluctuations in presidential strength, the chairman of the Senate Judiciary Committee, and, of course, the composition of the Senate. This is because there are usually few incentives for the Senate to do more than pass on the vast majority of judicial nominees. Supreme Court nominees are the exception; one out of four have been rejected or forced to withdraw from consideration.

During the first six years of Reagan's presidency, the chairman of the judiciary committee, South Carolina's Republican senator Strom Thurmond, proved an influential ally. Under Senator Thurmond, most nominees were quickly approved. By comparison with the committee under Massachusetts' Democratic senator Edward Kennedy (1979–1980), which passed on appellate court nominees after an average of sixty-six days and district court nominees after fifty-five days, Thurmond's committee referred nominees to the full Senate within twenty days of their nominations.[19]

Senator Thurmond's handling of Reagan judges during the Ninety-ninth Congress (1985–1986) remains illustrative. The judiciary committee considered 136 nominees, yet only 6 had more than one pro forma hearing. Only one, Jefferson Sessions, failed to make it out of the committee. Of those who had more than one hearing, two federal district court judges—Stanley Sporkin and George Revercomb—were later confirmed without a record vote. Four others—Alex Kozinski and Manion for the appellate bench, and Sessions and Sidney Fitzwater for district courts—encountered heated confirmation fights. None was rejected, however.

The importance of Thurmond's chairmanship and a Republican-controlled Senate for Reagan's success in winning confirmation for his judicial appointees is underscored by the record after Democrats regained a senatorial majority and Senator Joseph Biden (D-Del.) became chairman of the Senate Judiciary Committee in 1987. The committee was no longer disposed to quickly passing on Reagan's judges. Democrats immediately sought to ensure that by reducing the committee's size from eighteen to fourteen, thereby excluding North Carolina's Republican senator Jesse Helms. Biden also created a four-member panel, headed by Vermont's Democratic senator Patrick Leahy, to undertake additional screening of nominees. The Reagan administration in turn became slower at filling vacancies and named fewer controversial conservatives. Officials in the DoJ understood that the kinds of conservatives approved by Senator Thurmond's committee were not as likely to win confirmation, and hence not always worth the trouble of nominating or fighting battles for their confirmation.

Undeniably, the most dramatic consequence of the change in the control of the Senate came with the rejection of Supreme Court nominee Judge Bork, a leading conservative intellectual identified with the legal policies of the DoJ and the new right. Yet, that nomination was ill-fated because in 1986 Reagan had again made judgeships an issue of campaign politics. When campaigning for Republicans in ten Senate races, including five in the South, he asked voters to elect Republicans so that his judicial nominees would continue to win Senate confirmation. But all ten races were lost to Democrats. The conservative southern Democrats elected—due to receiving 90 percent of the black vote in their states—were especially not inclined to be counted as allies in any confirmation battle raising the issue of race and civil rights. And along with six moderate Republicans, they cast the crucial votes defeating Bork's confirmation in 1987.

REAGAN'S LOWER COURT JUDGES

In historical perspective, the striking feature of Reagan's lower court judges is that they were predominantly young, white, upper-middle-class males, with prior judicial or prosecutorial experience and reputations for legal conservatism established on the bench, in law schools, or in politics.

Reagan appointed few women, blacks, and other minorities. However, as shown in tables 14.2 and 14.3, his record in appointing women was second to that of Carter's, while the worst for African Americans since the Ford and Eisenhower administrations, when the pool of qualified African Americans was much smaller than in the 1980s. Reagan judges generally came from wealthy, upper-class backgrounds and from medium to large legal practices, the judiciary, or government. Close to half had a net worth exceeding $500,000, compared with barely a quarter of Carter's judges.

The Justice Department claimed to pay no attention to the religious backgrounds of its nominees. However, a comparison of lower court judges appointed by presidents from FDR to Reagan (in table 14.3) is revealing. Not since the JFK and LBJ administrations had a higher percentage of Catholics been appointed. Moreover, in Reagan's second term, almost 40 percent of the appellate judgeships went to Catholics. In addition, he was the first president to name two Catholics to the Supreme Court, Justices Scalia and Anthony M. Kennedy. Whether coincidentally or due to the DoJ's search for opponents of abortion, Reagan set a record in appointing more Catholics than any prior president, including FDR who rewarded them with judgeships because of their part in the New Deal coalition.

Finally, in terms of the ABA's ratings of professional qualifications, Reagan's judges on balance compare favorably with those appointed by prior administra-

Table 14.2. Number of Women Appointed to the Federal Bench Court and Appointing President

	Roosevelt (FDR)	Truman	Eisenhower	Kennedy	Johnson	Nixon	Ford	Carter	Reagan
Supreme Court									1
Courts of Appeals	1				1		1	11	4
District		1		1	2	1	1	29	24
Totals	1	1		1	3	1	1	40	29

Note: Based on data supplied by the Department of Justice. Reagan appointed two women to district courts and subsequently elevated them to the appellate bench; they are counted here only as appointments to the courts of appeals.

Table 14.3. Religion and Race/Ethnicity of Lower Federal Court Appointees

	Roosevelt (FDR)	Truman	Eisenhower	Kennedy/Johnson	Nixon/Ford	Carter	Reagan
Religion							
Protestant	130	70	128	177	195	134	188
Catholic	46	38	30	77	49	71	103
Jewish	7	13	11	30	23	33	38
Other/None		2	2	6	19	20	39
Race/Ethnicity							
White	183	122	171	273	273	203	344
Black		1		12	9	37	7
Hispanic				4	3	16	15
Asian				1	3	2	2

Note: Based on data from the Department of Justice. Several black judges were also women; one was named by Johnson, seven by Carter, and one by Reagan.

tions. This is so despite the fact that in the first half of his second term, Reagan's judges generally received low ABA ratings, and especially during 1985 through 1986, the ABA was sharply split on rating a large number "qualified." The ABA's split ratings partially reflected the DoJ's recruitment of younger nominees from law schools and from within its own ranks. Due to their age, they often lacked extensive legal experience and occasionally ran afoul of the ABA's requirement of twelve years of prior legal experience. There were also some, such as Judge Manion and Supreme Court nominee Judge Bork, on which the ABA committee split because of disagreements over their "judicial temperament." This angered new right senators and DoJ officials. Nonetheless, in terms of the ABA's ratings, Reagan's judges stand up well next to those named by prior administrations. Table 14.4 shows the ABA's rating of district and appellate judges appointed by presidents from Johnson through Reagan.[20]

REAGAN'S JUSTICES

While hugely successful in appointing close to half of all the judges in the lower federal courts, Reagan failed to turn the Supreme Court completely around or, by the end of his presidency at least, to win a majority over to his Justice Department's positions on abortion, affirmative action, and other hotly contested issues. This was so in spite of naming three associate justices and elevating Justice Rehnquist to the chief justiceship. A chance to turn the Court around, however, didn't come until Justice Lewis F. Powell, Jr., stepped down on June 28, 1987. Subsequently, the administration suffered its major setback. Judge Bork, the first nominee for Powell's seat, was defeated after a bitter confirmation battle.

Table 14.4. ABA Ratings of Lower Court Appointees from Johnson through Reagan (by percentage)

	Johnson	Nixon	Ford	Carter	Reagan
District Court Judges					
Number appointed	122	179	52	202	290
Exceptionally well qualified	7.4	4.8	0	4.0	4.5
Well qualified	40.9	40.4	46.1	47.0	49.0
Qualified	49.2	54.8	53.8	47.5	46.6
Not qualified	2.5	–	–	1.5	–
Appeals Court Judges					
Number appointed	40	45	12	57	78
Exceptionally well qualified	27.5	15.7	16.7	14.0	16.7
Well qualified	47.5	57.8	41.7	61.4	42.3
Qualified	20.0	26.7	33.3	24.6	41.0
Not qualified	2.5	–	–	–	–
No report made	2.5	–	–	–	–

The second, Judge Douglas H. Ginsburg, was forced to withdraw from consideration after controversies over his personal affairs led the new right to turn against him. Reagan's third nominee, Judge Kennedy, won easy confirmation, but this was due to his reputation for being open-minded and for his distance from the administration's hard-line legal-policy positions.

Justice Sandra Day O'Connor. Somewhat ironically, given his administration's opposition to affirmative action, Reagan's first appointee to the Court—Justice Sandra Day O'Connor—was chosen more for symbolic than for ideological reasons. During the 1980 election, Reagan promised to name the first woman to the Court. Specifically, in an October 1980 press release, then California governor Reagan announced "that one of the first Supreme Court vacancies in my administration will be filled by the most qualified woman I can possibly find. . . . It is time for a woman to sit among our highest jurists."[21]

Less than a year later in May 1981, Justice Potter Stewart privately told the president that he would retire at the end of the term. A two-month search concluded with a woman Reagan said shared his view "that the role of the courts is to interpret the law, not to enact new law by judicial fiat."[22] Among the other women considered were Michigan Supreme Court Chief Justice Mary Stallings Coleman and federal appellate court Judge Cornelia B. Kennedy, and to a lesser extent U.S. Court of Appeals for the Second Circuit Judge Amalya L. Kearse, as well as North Carolina Supreme Court Chief Justice Susie Marshall Sharp. But Coleman and Sharp were ruled out because of their age; both were in their sixties, whereas O'Connor had just turned fifty-one. Sixth Circuit Judge Kennedy was considered "a very strong candidate" but, like "the O'Connor woman," as one White House aide reported,[23] was opposed by Senator Donald Nickles (R.-Okla.) and pro-life leaders like Representative Henry Hyde (R.-Ill.). Hyde, though, was later persuaded to support Justice O'Connor's nomination.[24] So, too, did Senators Jesse Helms (R.-N.C.) and Steve Symms (R.-Idaho) initially oppose her nomination.[25] But O'Connor told DoJ officials that she personally opposed abortion and had never publicly taken either side of that controversy.[26] And Reagan embraced that position when defending her nomination and lobbying some Republican senators who had expressed reservations about her.[27]

Though conservative, O'Connor was not as doctrinaire as Reagan's subsequent appointees and had practical experience in state courts and politics. Not widely known in legal circles at the time of her nomination, O'Connor had risen through the ranks of Republican politics in her home state of Arizona. She had served as an assistant attorney general and in the state legislature, where she was majority leader, as well as on a municipal court, before former Democratic governor Bruce Babbitt appointed her to a state appellate court.

Nonetheless, O'Connor's confirmation hearings (the first ever to be televised and carried by the Public Broadcasting System) generated controversy among Reagan's pro-life supporters. In particular, the National Right to Life

Committee (NRLC) opposed her nomination because some of her votes in the Arizona legislature in the 1970s were viewed as too supportive of women's right to have abortions.[28] The NRLC and the Moral Majority, among others, attacked her not only for having voted for a "family planning" bill that would have repealed existing state statutes prohibiting abortions, but also for having favored the equal rights amendment.

During the judiciary committee's hearings, Iowa's Republican senators Charles E. Grassley and Roger W. Jepsen tried to extract concessions on how she might vote on the right to have an abortion and other heated issues. But O'Connor, as all earlier nominees, refused to give detailed answers or say much more than that she would uphold and apply settled law.[29] Her refusal to do so and vague answers to other questions disturbed some in the Justice Department and the new right. Still, the Senate voted overwhelmingly (99–0) for her confirmation.[30]

Chief Justice William H. Rehnquist. Reagan was handed a major opportunity to make an imprint on the Court in June 1986, when Chief Justice Burger announced that he would step down at the end of the October 1985–1986 term in order to head full-time the Commission on the Bicentennial of the Constitution. And the president shrewdly maximized it when filling the center chair on the high bench.

Actually, according to a memorandum written to record the sequence of events by Peter Wallison, who served at the time as White House counsel to the president, on May 27, 1986, Chief Justice Burger met with Reagan and then Chief of Staff Donald Regan, along with former White House counsel Fred Fielding, in the White House, where he told them of his decision to resign and head the Bicentennial Commission. At that time, he also provided a memo recommending as his replacement the following: Justice Rehnquist; Justice Byron White, who dissented along with Rehnquist in *Roe v. Wade* and generally voted conservatively on "law and order" issues but who had been named to the Court by Democratic president John F. Kennedy; U.S. Court of Appeals for the D.C. Circuit Judges Robert H. Bork and Antonin Scalia; U.S. Court of Appeals for the Ninth Circuit Judge J. Clifford Wallace, a Mormon and friend of the chief justice; and another friend, Judge Edward Re of the International Court of Trade.

Two days later, Regan, Meese, and Wallison met to discuss the process. They agreed to have files previously prepared on potential Supreme Court nominees by Assistant Attorney General William Bradford Reynolds to be sent to the White House for review. Those files focused attention on seven candidates: Justices O'Connor and Rehnquist; Judges Bork, Scalia, and Wallace, as the chief justice had also suggested; Judge Patrick Higginbotham, who Reagan had named in 1982 to the U.S. Court of Appeals for the Fifth Circuit and who was considered "conservative" but "somewhat unpredictable"; and Judge Ralph Winter, who Reagan named in 1982 to the U.S. Court of Appeals for the Second Circuit.

Others who had also been considered by DoJ lawyers and White House counsel included U.S. Court of Appeals for the Ninth Circuit Judge Cynthia Holcomb Hall, another Reagan appointee who was considered a solid conservative and was the second most senior woman (after Justice O'Connor) in the federal judiciary; Senator Orrin G. Hatch (R.-Utah), a reliable supporter of the administration but whose nomination would have entailed a significant loss of support in the Senate; Representative Henry Hyde, though he was considered too old at age sixty-three; and U.S. Court of Appeals for the Ninth Circuit Judge Anthony Kennedy, who was deemed by attorneys in the DoJ to be "bright and conservative" but, unlike Bork and Scalia, an "intellectual rather than practical [conservative], leading to an occasional anomalous result."[31]

Subsequently, on June 5, the list was narrowed to four leading candidates: Justices O'Connor and Rehnquist and Judges Bork and Scalia. Others were eliminated for the reasons mentioned earlier and for a variety of others; Judge Wallace, for instance, was considered conservative, but some of his public statements about his religion were thought to potentially invite unnecessary controversy, while Judge Winter was not as well known within the DoJ and, hence, was viewed as less predictable than Judges Bork and Scalia.

On June 9, President Reagan met with Regan, Meese, and Wallison to discuss Chief Justice Burger's replacement. Reagan indicated that he wanted to begin by meeting with Rehnquist, but also said he was intrigued by Judge Scalia, who impressed him because he was not only solidly conservative but also would become the first Italian American to sit on the high bench. Three days later, Reagan met with Rehnquist and offered him the position, which he immediately accepted. They then discussed the possibility of naming to his seat either Judge Bork or Scalia. Both were agreeable to Rehnquist. Although both were considered within the DoJ to be bright, predictable conservatives, and though both smoked, Scalia was ten years younger, reportedly smoked less, and was deemed more energetic and personable.

The decision to elevate Rehnquist from associate to chief justice and to appoint Judge Scalia to his seat could not have been more politically symbolic or strategic. Both were not merely sympathetic to the Reagan administration's legal-policy goals; they could claim to be intellectual architects of its agenda. Through their writings, they had largely defined the administration's positions on separation of powers, federalism, and the role of the judiciary. In addition, the White House knew that Rehnquist would prove controversial because of his long-standing, often extremely conservative views. Yet, naming him chief justice would symbolize Reagan's judicial legacy, and his elevation as a sitting justice made it even harder for the Senate to deny confirmation.

Rehnquist came to the Court in 1971 from Nixon's Department of Justice, where he served as an assistant attorney general. He had established his conservative credentials years earlier, initially as a law clerk for Justice Robert H. Jackson (1952–1953), and then as an Arizona attorney and supporter of Arizona senator Barry Goldwater's presidential candidacy. Like others in the 1950s and 1960s, he attacked the "liberal jurisprudence" of the Warren Court (1953–1969) for revolutionizing constitutional law and American society.

During the Burger Court years (1969–1986), there was no "constitutional counterrevolution," as some had predicted based on Nixon's four appointments. This was because the Burger court was fragmented and increasingly polarized, pulled in different directions by either its most liberal or its most conservative members. As chief justice, Burger was a disappointment for conservatives. For one thing, though a Republican, he came from the liberal wing of the party, in the mold of fellow Minnesotan Harold Stassen. For another, he could not lead the Court intellectually, and his personal style created tensions among the justices. As a result, there were only modest "adjustments," as Chief Justice Burger noted when announcing his retirement, in the jurisprudential house built by the Warren Court (though there were a few new additions, as with rulings on abortion, affirmative action, busing, and expanding the application of the equal protection clause to nonracial categories of discrimination).[32]

Within the Burger Court, it largely fell to Justice Rehnquist to stake out a conservative philosophy. And he articulated a well-developed view of the power of judicial review and for renewing the Court's defense of federalism and limiting congressional power. Less willing than others to compromise, Rehnquist appeared extreme, writing more solo dissents (fifty-four) than any of his colleagues in his fifteen years as an associate justice.

Justice Rehnquist's nomination as the sixteenth chief justice thus sparked a major controversy. Senator Kennedy led the attack, as he had when Rehnquist was first named to the Court, calling him "too extreme on race, too extreme on women's rights, too extreme on freedom of speech, too extreme on separation of church and state, too extreme to be Chief Justice." The confirmation hearings, Senator Hatch countered, threatened to become a "Rehnquisition."

The judiciary committee's televised hearings, however, were less enlightening than an occasion for speeches by supporters and attackers. Rehnquist was repeatedly asked about prior judicial opinions. But he refused to discuss them or how he might handle major issues in the future. He also confronted charges that as a law clerk in 1952 and 1953, he had supported segregated schools and later, in the 1960s as a poll worker, harassed minority voters at polling places.

In retrospect, about all that the Senate Judiciary Committee accomplished was a reassertion of its power to consider judicial philosophy when confirming appointees. Rehnquist was approved by the committee, with five Democrats voting against him and two joining Republicans in a 13–5 vote. He was subsequently confirmed by the Senate by a vote of 65–33, based on southern Democrats voting with Republicans and two Republicans siding with thirty-one Democrats in opposition.

Justice Antonin Scalia. In contrast to the scrutiny of Chief Justice Rehnquist, the Senate Judiciary Committee spent little time on Judge Scalia, and his hearings were quick and amicable. The differences are reflected in the committee's final reports on each: Chief Justice Rehnquist's runs 114 pages, while Justice Scalia's consists of 76 words. Justice Scalia was also unanimously recommended, and the full Senate, after barely five minutes of debate, voted (98–0) for confirmation.

Next to Rehnquist and Bork, no other jurist was closer to Reagan's Justice Department. In the 1970s, Scalia became connected with many who would assume positions of power within the Reagan administration. After graduating from Harvard Law School, he practiced law for six years before joining the University of Virginia Law School. Then, from 1971 to 1972 he took a one-year leave to work as general counsel in the Nixon administration. Two years later he was tapped by Ford's attorney general, Edward H. Levi, to head the Office of Legal Counsel in the Justice Department. When Ford left office, Levi returned to the University of Chicago Law School and persuaded Scalia to come along. Before going, however, Scalia spent perhaps the most crucial year of his early career at the American Enterprise Institute (AEI)—then the largest conservative think tank in Washington. Later, at Chicago, Scalia maintained his association with the AEI, serving as editor of its magazine, *Regulation,* as well as helping to found the Federalist Society.

In 1982, Reagan placed Scalia on the U.S. Court of Appeals for the D.C. Circuit. On the bench, Scalia continued to make his mark. He remained a prolific writer: almost two dozen articles and, in four years on the appellate court, more than eighty majority opinions and dozens of concurring and dissenting opinions. In addition, he was considered by some in the DoJ to be, even more so than Bork, "a superb technician on 'nuts and bolts' legal questions."[33]

The Battle over Judges Robert H. Bork and Douglas H. Ginsburg. The controversy over the nominations of Judges Bork and Ginsburg remains extraordinary. Instead of becoming the 104th justice, they became the 27th and 28th nominees to be rejected or forced to withdraw due to Senate opposition. Bork was opposed by the widest margin ever (58–42). Revelations about Ginsburg's private life—notably, that he had smoked marijuana as a Harvard Law School professor—forced him to withdraw after new right Republican senators turned against him. The controversy nevertheless underscores the extent to which judgeships were perceived as symbols of and instruments to ensure Reagan's legacy.

For a number of reasons, a political battle was virtually assured by the selection of Bork to replace Justice Powell. First, at the time, Justice Powell was not just the pivotal vote on the Court; in his last two terms the justices ruled 5–4 in eighty-one cases, and Powell repeatedly cast the crucial vote in cases rejecting the Reagan administration's positions on abortion, affirmative action, the death penalty, and some other issues.

Second, President Reagan chose, over more moderate Republicans and conservative jurists, one of the most outspoken critics of the Warren and Burger courts.[34] Moreover, he did so despite the Democrats having regained control of the Senate, which meant a battle over any nominee closely aligned with the new right.

In addition, the administration underestimated the extent of opposition. Yet, Bork had been passed over three times before, by Ford in 1975 and by Reagan in 1981 and again in 1986. And shortly after Justice Scalia's appointment to the Court, the White House had rumored that the next vacancy would go to Bork. Liberal interest groups, therefore, had studied his record and were prepared to fight against his confirmation.

Senators Kennedy and Biden immediately denounced Bork. More than eighty-three organizations followed. Calling him "unfit" to serve on the high bench, the American Civil Liberties Union (ACLU) abandoned its practice of not opposing Supreme Court nominees. The ACLU had only once before taken such a position; it opposed Rehnquist's nomination in 1971 but took no position on his elevation to chief justice.

It is worth recalling that new right organizations were no less active, although White House Chief of Staff Howard Baker initially discouraged them from strident public support. Over the objections of Meese and others in the Justice Department, the White House advanced the strategy of recasting Bork's conservative record in order to make opponents appear shrill and partisan. In a July 1987 speech, President Reagan equated his nominee with Justice Powell, in spite of Bork's past attacks on that justice's opinions. A 70-page White House briefing book was prepared, followed by a 240-page report released by the Justice Department, aimed at portraying Bork as a "mainstream" jurist.

The publicity was also extraordinary. Numerous reports from the left and the right analyzing Bork's record were distributed to editorial boards around the country. The staff of the Democratically controlled Senate Judiciary Committee issued its own 72-page study refuting the Reagan administration's "centrist" depiction of Bork. For political consultants and fund-raisers, Bork was a "bonanza." The People for the American Way launched a $2 million media campaign opposing the nomination, while the National Conservative Political Action Committee (NCPAC) committed over $1 million to lobbying for his confirmation.

What had far greater impact, though, was Bork's own role in the preconfirmation fray and in the confirmation proceedings. Even before the hearings began, Bork took the unusual step of granting an unrivaled number of newspaper interviews. Like Louis Brandeis in 1911, Bork faced charges of being a "radical." Unlike Brandeis and all prior Supreme Court nominees who let their records speak for themselves, Bork sought to explain, clarify, and amend his twenty-five-year record as a Yale Law School law professor, solicitor general in the Nixon administration at the time of Watergate, and federal judge. That broke with tradition and gave the appearance of a public relations campaign.[35]

During his five days of nationally televised testimony before the judiciary committee, Bork continued to give the appearance of refashioning himself into a moderate, even "centrist," jurist. A key consideration thus became, in Senator Leahy's words, one of "confirmation conversion"—whether Bork was "born-again." Besides deserting much of his past record, Bork's lengthy explanations were unprecedented in other ways. Since 1925, when Harlan F. Stone first appeared as a witness during his confirmation hearings, down to Reagan's previous appointees, all nominees had refused to talk about their views on specific cases, let alone discuss how they might vote on issues likely to come before the Court. But Bork gave unusual assurances on how he would vote, if confirmed.

Republican senator Arlen Specter and Arizona's Democratic senator Dennis DeConcini extracted promises (or concessions) on the First Amendment, the Fourteenth Amendment, the commerce clause, and on issues like abortion and gender-based discrimination. Although still finding fault with the reasoning in *Bolling v. Sharpe*,[36] which desegregated the schools in the District of Columbia, for instance, Bork said he "would never dream" of overturning that precedent, even though he disagreed with its underlying constitutional analysis. As much as anything else, Bork strove to assure all that he had "no ideological agenda" and had "great respect for precedent." That proved difficult because of his history of assailing so many watershed rulings and his repeated declarations that "in the field of constitutional law, precedent is not all that important."

By the time Bork finished thirty hours of testifying, he had contradicted much of what he had stood for. Noting the "considerable difference between what Judge Bork has written and what he has testified he will do if confirmed," Senator Specter observed: "I think that what many of us are looking for is some assurance of where you are."

Bork's testimony weighed far more than that of the 110 witnesses assembled for and against him in the following two weeks. Admittedly, they contributed to the atmosphere of campaign politics that surrounded the hearings. For the first time, a former president, Gerald Ford, introduced a Supreme Court nominee to the committee, while Carter subsequently sent a letter expressing his opposition. Nor have justices, especially sitting justices, ever before come out as allies of a nominee. Yet, retired Chief Justice Burger testified, and Justices John Paul Stevens and Byron White publicly endorsed Bork.

The strategies of members of the judiciary committee were also important. Bork's staunchest defenders, Senators Hatch and Alan K. Simpson (R-Wyo.), repeatedly decried the "campaign of distortion." Chairman Biden was measured and meticulously fair; he even won praise from Senators Hatch, Simpson, and Thurmond. Biden was also well advised by conservative law professor Philip Kurland, among others, to frame the debate broadly in terms of the Court's role in protecting individual rights—in particular, the right of privacy—rather than focusing on narrower, more divisive issues such as abortion and affirmative action. The debate, in Biden's words, was "not about Judge Bork but about the

Constitution." This was tactical and timely, since the hearings began two days before the bicentennial of the Constitution (on September 17).

The fundamental issue remained, after all, the constitutional views shared by Bork and the Reagan administration. That is what had already sown divisions with the legal establishment over the nomination of some lower court judges and broke open with the battle over Bork. It was reflected in the ABA's rating of Bork as "well qualified" but with a third of its committee opposed, and the broad opposition of the legal profession; 1,925 law professors (40 percent of the academic legal profession) signed letters opposing Bork, more than five times the number (300) that had opposed Nixon's ill-fated nomination of Harold Carswell to the Supreme Court.

Nonetheless, what captured attention at the end of three weeks of hearings were public opinion polls. A *Washington Post*/ABC News poll found that 52 percent of the public opposed Bork's confirmation. Another, *Atlanta Constitution,* poll of twelve southern states likewise found that 51 percent of its respondents were against Bork, including white conservatives. Bork and his supporters, not surprisingly, decried the influence of public opinion on the outcome.

But to attribute Bork's defeat entirely to public opinion polls would be wrong. Most senators and their staffs spent an entire summer examining Bork's record, reputation, and judicial philosophy. The Senate Judiciary Committee's hearings were more exhaustive than, perhaps, any before. It is no less wrong to solely credit or blame the pressure of civil rights groups for Bork's defeat. There was also, as noted, a campaign for Bork by the new right. That is why some senators delayed the Senate's final vote for two weeks, over the objections of Majority Leader Robert Byrd (D-W.Va.) and Minority Leader Robert Dole (R-Kans.), so that more money could be raised and certain senators targeted with letter-writing campaigns.[37]

To be sure, the publicity and pressure-group activities figured into the outcome. Within a couple of days of the judiciary committee's vote, seven conservative southern Democrats, led by Louisiana's senator J. Bennett Johnston, announced their opposition. This, along with similar announcements by Senators Specter and DeConcini, prodded the two remaining Democrats on the committee, Senators Byrd and Howell Heflin, to abandon their view that the committee ought not to make any recommendation to the full Senate. As a result, the vote was 9–5.

Ultimately, though, Bork was defeated because of his views and association with Reagan's Justice Department and the new right's legal-policy goals. That was what the debate over the Constitution during the committee's hearings was about. And it is what turned conservative southern Democrats and six moderate Republicans against Bork in the final vote on the Senate floor.

The defeat was a major setback for the Reagan presidency. Bork, Meese, and others in the DoJ were bitter and blamed White House staff for not pushing hard enough for confirmation. They were also vindictive and, thus, seeking revenge, persuaded Reagan to nominate Judge Ginsburg, rather than Judge Anthony M. Kennedy, a less controversial conservative.

Judge Ginsburg shared more with Bork than a nomination and a seat on the same appellate court. In many respects, he was Bork's protégé, twenty years younger but tracking a similar path back to law school days at the University of Chicago. After graduating, he followed Bork in specializing in antitrust and into an academic career. In 1983, Ginsburg joined the Reagan Justice Department as an assistant attorney general in the antitrust division. There, he was known for moving it in the direction long advocated by Bork and others of the Chicago school of thought. In 1985, he was promoted to chief of the division and a year later to the appellate bench, on the prestigious U.S. Court of Appeals for the D.C. Circuit.[38]

In its haste to find a suitable ideological successor to Bork, the White House and the Justice Department failed to fully investigate Ginsburg's background, however. And ten days after his nomination, Judge Ginsburg was forced to withdraw, amid disclosures about his personal life and growing concerns about his ethical conduct as an attorney in the Justice Department, as well as his lack of judicial experience.[39]

A few days later, Reagan nominated Judge Kennedy for the seat vacated by Justice Powell almost five months earlier. Judge Kennedy had been earlier considered and, on November 8, 1987, had a "no holds barred" three-hour interview with Chief of Staff Howard Baker, Attorney General Meese, and other White House and DoJ lawyers; he also met briefly the following day with President Reagan who, besides exchanging pleasantries, simply wanted to find out if there was anything in his background that might prove embarrassing or controversial.[40] He had been passed over in favor of Judge Ginsburg's nomination because he was deemed more of a tradition conservative, rather than an ideologically committed "movement conservative."

Justice Anthony M. Kennedy. The nomination of Kennedy met with immediate and generally bipartisan praise. New right senators and supporters remained rather disappointed, but the Democratically controlled Senate was in no mood for another bitter confirmation battle. And that was reflected in Kennedy's confirmation hearings in mid-December. They were reminiscent of most in the past; few reporters showed up, no commercial television network broadcast them (as they had Bork's), and only PBS, C-SPAN, and CNN offered coverage.

At the Senate Judiciary Committee's hearings, Kennedy's testimony was subdued and mild mannered. His answers were reserved and straightforward, often descriptive discourses on developing constitutional law. When pressed on heated issues, such as abortion, he claimed that he had "no fixed view." Kennedy also distanced himself from some of the Reagan administration's and Bork's controversial positions. For instance, he accepted the constitutional status of a right of privacy and expressly rejected the view that "a jurisprudence of original intention" provides a sure guide for constitutional interpretation. The latter, in his words, was a "necessary starting point" rather than a "methodology" and "doesn't tell us how to decide a case." While such responses troubled new right Republican senators, the Senate Judiciary Committee unanimously recommended confirmation.[41]

Kennedy's confirmation sparked no major controversy because he was a seasoned jurist. Appointed to the Ninth Circuit by Ford in 1975, he had for more than a decade before practiced commercial and constitutional law, after graduating from Harvard Law School. In the 1960s and 1970s, he was modestly active in Republican state politics, meeting then-governor Reagan and helping in 1973 to draft a state tax-cutting measure. In his twelve years on the court of appeals, Kennedy established a reputation as an old-time conservative jurist. As Bruce Fein observed, Kennedy was (and on the high bench proved to be) "a technician rather than a judicial philosopher," like Bork.[42]

REAGAN'S JUDICIAL LEGACY

Indubitably, Reagan had a major, lasting impact on the federal judiciary, both in his unrivaled number of judicial appointments and in reinvigorating judicial conservativism on the federal bench. Although encountering a few setbacks and failing to achieve as much as some in the Justice Department and the new right sought, Reagan's judges on balance reflected the consensus of the dominant national political coalition on the role of the federal courts in American politics in the 1980s.

Besides moving the Supreme Court and the federal judiciary in a decidedly more conservative direction through his judicial appointments,[43] Reagan and his Office of Legal Policy and White House Judicial Selection Committee fundamentally changed the politics of appointing federal judges. Each of his successors gave greater priority and closer scrutiny to the appointment of federal judges than did Reagan's predecessors. Within and outside of each of those administrations—from that of George Bush, to Bill Clinton, and to George W. Bush—potential judicial nominees have been subject to greater scrutiny. After the Reagan era, interest groups on the left and the right have remained mobilized and actively monitoring and lobbying for and against judicial nominees. As in Reagan's second term, Presidents Clinton and George W. Bush confronted majorities of the opposing party in control of the Senate, and consequently increasing delays and bitter battles over the confirmation of their judicial nominees.[44] In short, in making federal judgeships symbols and instruments of presidential power, Reagan transformed and polarized the politics of appointing federal judges.

Finally, permit an observation based solely on the records in the Ronald Reagan Presidential Library that bear on the administration's selection of federal judges. Unquestionably, as some commentators have observed, Reagan was a "detached" president. He was not personally or actively involved in picking his judicial appointees, but instead delegated and relied heavily on his White House staff and the DoJ. He knew few of his judicial appointees and only briefly met with those he named to the Supreme Court. He intervened and lobbied for his judicial nominees only on occasions when they ran into serious trouble in the Senate. Yet, for every judicial nominee there is a record in his presidential library of President Reagan making a personal, though highly scripted, telephone call to the nominee and offering the nomination.[45] In sum, as one of the most popular presidents in the twentieth century, Reagan governed as a detached president who nevertheless remained both devoted to the principles of his presidency and a master of "the personal touch."

NOTES

1. Quoted and discussed in David M. O'Brien, *Judicial Roulette: Report of the Twentieth Century Fund Task Force on the Appointment of Federal Judges* (New York: Priority Press, 1988), 61–64.

2. See, e.g., Sheldon Goldman, *Picking Federal Judges: Lower Court Selection from Roosevelt through Reagan* (New Haven, Conn.: Yale University Press, 1997), chap. 8; and Henry J. Abraham, *Justices, Presidents, and Senators: A History of the U.S. Supreme Court Appointments from Washington to Clinton* (Lanham, Md.: Rowman & Littlefield, 1999), chaps. 11 and 12.

3. Quoted by David M. O'Brien, "Meese's Agenda for Ensuring the Reagan Legacy," *Los Angeles Times,* September 28, 1986, M1.

4. For further discussion, see O'Brien, *Judicial Roulette,* 49–64; and Victor Navasky, *Kennedy Justice* (New York: Atheneum, 1974).

5. For further discussion, see David M. O'Brien, "The Reagan Judges: His Most Enduring Legacy? in *The Reagan Legacy: Promise and Performance,* ed. Charles O. Jones (Chatham, N.J.: Chatham House Publishers, 1988), 60–100. Factors for consideration in judicial selection are set forth in a "Memorandum for Fred F. Fielding" from Herbert E. Ellington, June 23, 1981, Fred Fielding Files, CFOA 941942, Ronald Reagan Library (hereafter RRL).

6. Stephen Markman, "Memorandum for Attorney General Meese: A Comparison of Judicial Selection Procedures" (unpublished memorandum made available to the author, September 8, 1986).

7. See David M. O'Brien, "Ginsburg and the Chicago School of Thought," *Los Angeles Times,* November 8, 1987, M1 and M6, reprinted in Michael Luis Principe, ed., *American Government, Policy, and Law* (Dubuque, Iowa: Kendall/Hunt Publishing, 2000), 126–27.

8. *Roe v. Wade,* 410 U.S. 113 (1973).

9. Quoted in O'Brien, *Judicial Roulette.*

10. Markman, "Memorandum for Attorney General Meese."

11. *Miranda v. Arizona,* 384 U.S. 436 (1966).

12. See Edwin Meese, "The Attorney General's View of the Supreme Court: Toward a

Jurisprudence of Original Intention," in Charles Wise and David M. O'Brien, eds., *Law and Public Affairs, Public Administration Review* 45 (special issue, 1985): 701–4.

13. Markman, "Memorandum for Attorney General Meese."

14. Based on interviews quoted and discussed in O'Brien, *Judicial Roulette*, 59–60.

15. Quoted in U.S. Congress, Senate, *Confirmation Hearings on Federal Appointments: Hearings before the Committee on the Judiciary*, 95th Cong., 1st sess. (Washington, D.C.: Government Printing Office, 1986), pt. 2, 430.

16. Philip Lacovara, "The Wrong Way to Pick Judges," *New York Times*, October 3, 1986, A35.

17. Edwin Meese, "Address before the Palm Beach County Bar Association," February 10, 1986, 6.

18. See, e.g., PR 007-02, 406100-406199, RRL.

19. Based on data supplied to the author by the Senate Judiciary Committee and further discussed in O'Brien, *Judicial Roulette*, 65–81.

20. Data from Johnson through Ford appointees come from Sheldon Goldman, "Carter's Judicial Appointments: A Lasting Legacy," *Judicature* 64 (October–November 1981): 344. The data on Carter and Reagan judges was supplied by the American Bar Association and is further discussed in O'Brien, *Judicial Roulette*, chap. 5.

21. Reagan-Bush Committee, News Release, Fred Fielding Files, OA 3489, RRL.

22. See "Judicial Selection Criteria," June 18, 1981, Fielding Files, OA 3489, RRL. See also White House, "Statement by the President," July 7, 1981, Fielding Papers, OA 3489, RRL.

23. Memorandum from Max Friedersdorf, July 6, 1981, Fielding Files, OA 3489, RRL.

24. See Memorandum from Max Friedersdorf, July 18, 1981, Edwin Meese Files, AO 2408, RRL.

25. Memorandum from Max Friedersdorf, July 6, 1981, Fielding Files, OA 3489, RRL. See also Memorandum to Edwin Meese from Michael Uhlmann, July 6, 1981, Meese Files, OA 2408, RRL.

26. See Memorandum from Kenneth W. Starr, July 7, 1981, Meese Files, OA 2408, RRL.

27. See "Recommended Telephone Call," from Max Friedersdorf, September 16, 1981, Meese Files, OA 2408, RRL. Notably, President Reagan noted that after the call, Senator Jeremiah Denton (R.-Ala.) "is with us."

28. See, e.g., Letter from John C. Willke, President, National Right to Life Committee, to President Reagan, July 3, 1981, Fielding Files, OA 3489, RRL.

29. See, U.S. Congress, Senate, *Nomination of Sandra O'Connor: Hearings before the Senate Committee on the Judiciary on the Nomination of Judge Sandra Day O'Connor of Arizona to Serve as an Associate Justice of the Supreme Court of the United States*, 97th Cong., 1st sess. (Washington, D.C.: Government Printing Office, 1981), 57–58.

30. See Grover Rees III, "Memorandum on the Proper Scope of Questioning Supreme Court Nominees at Senate Advice and Consent Hearings," September 1, 1981, Fielding Files, OA 3489, RRL.

31. All quotes are from "Proposed Nominees," Arthur (A. B.) Culvahouse Files, OA 15065, RRL.

32. This discussion draws on David M. O'Brien, "The Supreme Court: From Warren to Burger to Rehnquist," *PS* 20 (winter 1987): 12–20.

33. Wallison Files, OA 14286, RRL.

34. See David M. O'Brien and Ronald Collins, "Picking a S.Ct. Justice to Perpetuate the Reagan Legacy," *Los Angeles Times,* June 27, 1987, M1.

35. Much of the following discussion draws on Ronald Collins and David M. O'Brien, "Just Where Does Judge Bork Stand? *National Law Journal* (September 7, 1987): 13.

36. *Bolling v. Sharpe,* 347 U.S. 497 (1954).

37. For further discussion, see Elizabeth Drew, "Letter from Washington," *New Yorker,* November 2, 1987, 150. For a different view, see Robert H. Bork, *The Tempting of America: The Political Seduction of the Law* (New York: Free Press, 1990), 267–351.

38. See Jeffrey Lord, White House Political Affairs Associate Director, OA 15548, RRL.

39. See Kenneth Karpay, "Questions Linger as Ginsburg Returns to Circuit," *Legal Times* (November 16, 1987): 8.

40. See Culvahouse Files, OA 15065, RRL.

41. See Terrence Moran, "Conservatives Set to Challenge Kennedy," *Legal Times* (December 14, 1987): 6; and Ronald Collins and David M. O'Brien, "Kennedy Hearings as Bad as Bork Hearings—In Different Way," *Baltimore Sun,* December 20, 1987, E1.

42. Quoted by Paul Marcotte, "Bork to Ginsburg to Kennedy," *American Bar Association Journal* (January 1, 1988): 15.

43. See Goldman, *Picking Federal Judges,* 285–346; C. K. Rowland and Robert A. Carp, *Politics and Judgment in Federal District Courts* (Lawrence: University Press of Kansas, 1996), 47–56, 66–68; and Tinsley E. Yarbrough, *The Rehnquist Court and the Constitution* (New York: Oxford University Press, 2001).

44. See, e.g., David M. O'Brien, "Judicial Legacies: The Clinton Presidency and the Courts," in *The Clinton Legacy,* ed. Colin Campbell and Bert. A. Rockman (Chatham, N.J.: Chatham House, 2000), 96–117.

45. See, for instance, FG 052, 033000-034999, 037000-048499; and Fielding Files, CFOA 425, RRL.

Afterword: Legacies of the Reagan Years

James T. Patterson

Evaluating the not-so-distant presidency of Ronald Reagan necessarily leads to a number of tentative conclusions. On the one hand, a fairly clear scholarly consensus persists concerning three aspects of his presidency: the substance of his ideas, the nature of his personality, and the style of his leadership. On the other hand, scholars and others still argue heatedly over his legacy. Thanks to some key developments since his presidency—notably the end of the cold war and the return by the mid-1990s of widespread prosperity and of federal budget surpluses—his reputation among scholars may be marginally higher today than it was in 1989. But we are still too close to the Reagan years to reach assured judgments about his legacy.

Virtually all students of Reagan's ideas agree that long before his successful run for the presidency in 1980, he had been one of the nation's more ideologically committed political figures. Indeed, friends from the 1940s remember him carrying about copies of the *Congressional Record*.[1] At that time, and later, he professed great admiration for FDR, for whom he voted four times.[2] In 1948 he supported Truman, writing a friend after the election, "I'm sure Truman, with a Democratic congress, will do lots to make things better in every way, and what a landslide it was, the votes boy!"[3] In 1950 he backed Helen Gahagan Douglas in her race against Richard Nixon for a Senate seat from California. Thereafter, however, a series of developments—Reagan's anger at high income taxes, his marriage in 1952 to Nancy Davis, his work as traveling spokesman for the General Electric Company from 1952 to 1962—moved him politically to the right. Formally turning Republican in 1962, he served two terms as California governor between 1967 and 1975, and nearly overcame incumbent Gerald Ford in a race for the Republican presidential nomination in 1976.

By then, Reagan was well known as a highly conservative politician. Moreover, we now understand, thanks to the publication in 2001 of some 670 hand-

Thanks to Otis L. Graham, Jr., Gareth Davies, Daniel Williams, Michael Klarman, and Robert Collins for their help with this essay.

written radio addresses delivered in the late 1970s, how profoundly and ideologically engaged he continued to be in those years, mainly about a fairly small range of concerns.[4] As Godfrey Hodgson put it, "Reagan had a few big ideas, deeply held, and he was brilliantly successful at communicating them."[5]

These ideas were focused on economics and foreign policy. Though he had relished ridiculing hippies while governor of California, he was only sporadically a culture warrior, and his radio addresses after 1974—like his speeches as president—had relatively little to say about social matters such as race, immigration, or religion. These radio addresses are best described as earnest and fact-filled, revealing that he prepared carefully and that he could marshal arguments clearly—he was emphatically not the moron that opponents thought (or said) he was. These speeches were also ideologically predictable, for Reagan was consistent in his beliefs. Like many of his statements as president, they celebrated ideas taken from the well-traveled baggage of antistatist, anticommunist conservatism as set forward in his own time by leading Republicans such as Robert Taft and Barry Goldwater. Passionately, they asserted that the United States must carry out its historic, God-given mission of promoting freedom and liberty, both at home and abroad.

Reagan, indeed, was then and later a regular reader of the conservative publication, *Human Events*. Domestically, he aimed to cut back the size of government, abolish excessive regulation, and—above all—reduce taxes. As he expressed this approach (most famously) in his inaugural, "government is not the solution to our problem; government *is* the problem."[6] His foreign policy rested on building up the military so as to enable the United States to negotiate from a position of strength with the Soviet Union. But negotiations would have to follow the buildup. Meanwhile, Reagan repeatedly denounced the Soviet Union, most memorably in 1983 by branding it an "evil empire."

In one way his ideas about foreign and military policy featured a highly personal stamp: his attraction to biblical prophecies about apocalypse, which he foresaw as an outcome of the nuclear arms race. Frightened by the prospect of a nuclear war, he resolved to make America safe from Armageddon. The result was his call in 1983 for a Strategic Defense Initiative (SDI), or "Star Wars," which almost all knowledgeable officials concerned with defense policies found bizarre, except perhaps as a bargaining chip to use in future negotiations with the Soviet Union. As Frances FitzGerald has emphasized, SDI was "way out there in the blue."[7] This belief, and the passionate certitude that animated Reagan's worldview, placed his ideas solidly on the political right.

There is also consensus among scholars concerning Reagan's qualities as a person and as a presidential leader and administrator. It begins with agreement that he was a genial, kindly, and unpretentious man. Perhaps because he was the son of an alcoholic father, he grew up trying hard to please people. As speechwriter Peggy Noonan put it, for the rest of his life, "he thought it was his job to cheer people up."[8] He was unusually optimistic and upbeat—so much so, indeed, that he often came across as a Pollyanna. Garry Wills likened him to Mr. Magoo.[9] Maureen Reagan, irritated by her father's unfailing cheeriness, commented, "It's enough to drive you nuts."[10]

Virtually all students of Reagan have also identified a related personal trait: his remarkable self-assurance. Katharine Graham of the *Washington Post* observed that Reagan was perhaps the only modern president who did not worry much about what his critics—or hostile journalists—said about him. Reagan, she wrote, "was so successful [with the press] because he had supreme self-confidence."[11] Wills, too, has highlighted Reagan's self-assurance, noting that he was an oddity—a "cheerful conservative." "What must strike the candid observer," Wills wrote, "is the President's almost preternatural security, the lack of inner division that he maintains despite so much contained diversity."[12]

There is agreement also that Reagan consciously and eagerly sought to stamp this upbeat attitude into the minds of the American people. As a fan of science fiction, he was certain that the future would be better than the past. Again and again he insisted that nothing was impossible for the United States, which in his mind had always been a wonderful, exceptional civilization. Americans needed only to have confidence—in themselves and in the nation. "What I'd really like to do," he said in 1981, "is to go down in history as the president who made Americans believe in themselves again."[13]

Most observers also concur that Reagan's cheerful, buoyant demeanor, which contrasted sharply with the grimness of President Jimmy Carter, was a key to the popularity that he enjoyed for most of his years as president. In 1984 the political scientist Austin Ranney exclaimed, "Win, lose or draw, Reagan has made it at least possible for us to look at our leader with a feeling of uplift."[14] Lou Cannon, Reagan's discerning biographer, later added, "Because of his ability to reflect and give voice to the aspirations of his fellow citizens, Reagan succeeded in reviving national confidence at a time when there was a great need for inspiration. This was his great contribution as president."[15]

Scholarly observers tend to agree as well on other, less flattering personal traits of the president. One is his intellectual rigidity concerning most issues. Seventy years of age in February 1981, he was set in most of his ideas. After responding with extraordinary courage and good humor following John Hinckley's attempt to assassinate him in March 1981, he basked in an especially warm glow of popular affection. Thereafter, he seemed even more incurious than earlier, relying on his well-honed talents as a speaker and media presence to sustain his happy political relationship with the public. Friends as well as foes deplored this trait. Clark Clifford, a Democratic insider, memorably labeled him an "amiable dunce." Peggy Noonan added, "Beyond those warm eyes is a lack of curiosity that is, somehow, disorienting."[16] Edmund Morris, Reagan's official biographer, tells how he was warned that the president did not have "hidden depths": "what you see," Reagan's associates said, "is what you get." "Nevertheless," Morris added, "I could not believe how little one indeed 'got,' and how shallow those depths appeared to be."[17]

Both Thomas "Tip" O'Neill, Reagan's adversary as Democratic Speaker of the House, and James Baker, Reagan's top aide during the first presidential term, offered similar opinions. O'Neill commented that the president was "most of the time an actor reading lines, who didn't understand his own programs." Reagan, he cracked, "would have made a hell of a king."[18] Baker recalled the time in 1983 when he left Reagan a thick briefing book on the eve of an economic summit of the world's democratic leaders. The next morning Baker could see that the book lay unopened. He asked Reagan why he had not looked at it. "Well, Jim," the president replied calmly, *The Sound of Music* was on last night."[19]

Other Reagan officials were quick to complain of the president's inattentiveness and passivity. At meetings he was normally affable, but often—especially in his second term—he scarcely seemed to listen, and he frequently said nothing of substance when conferences came to a close. What had the president decided? aides wondered. As Martin Anderson later wrote, Reagan "made decisions like an ancient king or a Turkish pasha, passively letting his subjects serve him, selecting only those morsels of public policy that were especially tasty. Rarely did he ask searching questions and demand to know why someone had or had not done something. He just sat back in a supremely calm, relaxed manner and waited until important things were brought to him."[20]

Anderson, an adviser and admirer, contended that Reagan normally decided decisively and wisely. Other observers have added that Reagan's style of management, which depended heavily on the ability of loyal aides, usually worked adequately, at least in his first presidential term.[21] Many advisers, however, were even then dismayed.[22] Some resigned or (like Baker) sought government jobs outside the White House. Even before Reagan's presidency ended, ten ex-staffers had published memoirs testifying to their frustrations. Secretary of State Alexander Haig later complained to Cannon, "To me, the White House was as mysterious as a ghost ship; you heard the creak of the rigging and the groan of the timbers and sometimes even glimpsed the crew on the deck. But which of the crew had the helm? Was it [attorney general Edwin] Meese, was it Baker, was it someone else? It is impossible to know for sure."[23]

Members of Reagan's own family also confessed frustration with this curious passivity. To them as to others, it was if he were still on the silver screen, beguiling admirers with his performances but keeping a star's careful distance from his audience. As Nancy Reagan observed, "Although he loves people, he often seems remote, and he doesn't let anybody get too close. There's a wall around him."[24] His son Michael tells perhaps the most distressing—and perhaps best-known—story of this remoteness. After speaking at Michael's high school graduation, Reagan shook hands with some of the students. Facing Michael, who was dressed in cap and gown, he said, "My name is Ronald Reagan. What's yours?"[25]

Examples such as these bolster what is perhaps the most widely held view of Reagan the man and the leader: that he was so much the actor and performer as to be unfathomable as a person. Cannon subtitles his study of Reagan's presidency *The Role of a Lifetime.* The historian Gil Troy cites William Allen White's depiction of President William McKinley as applicable to Reagan: "Living thirty years in politics, McKinley became galvanized with a certain coating of publicity. He lost his private life and his private view. He walked among men a bronze statue, for thirty years determinedly looking for his pedestal."[26]

Seeking to discover the sources of Reagan's remoteness can plunge us into armchair psychology, some of which suggests that Reagan was fundamentally shy and therefore hard to reach. Other speculation has it that harsh life experiences—notably his father's alcoholism and the hurtful breakup of his first marriage—made him profoundly wary of closeness to others.[27] Whatever the roots of Reagan's remoteness, many people have agreed that he was especially "mysterious." No one, of course, has advanced this view more memorably than Edmund Morris, who spent years trying to crack Reagan's shell. When he finally published his "memoir" of Reagan, he complained of the president's "slabby, alabaster-like quality." At the close of the book, Morris confessed that "Dutch [Reagan's boyhood name] remained a mystery to me, and worse still . . . an apparent airhead."[28] Favorably reviewing Morris's book, Reagan's daughter Patti added, "I still don't fully understand my father. After all those years of exhaustive research, even Edmund says the man is a mystery."[29]

Except for a few loyal aides, most careful students of Reagan agree, finally, that as president he was laid-back.[30] Rejecting the workaholic style of Jimmy Carter, he refused to hold early morning staff meetings, and he normally left the Oval Office before five. Easily tired, he was known to doze at meetings in the afternoon. He spent almost a full year of days at his beloved ranch in California, as well as 183 weekends at Camp David. Using humor to disarm critics of these work habits, Reagan told reporters, "I am concerned about what is happening in government—and it's caused me many a sleepless afternoon." On another occasion he quipped, "It's true hard work never killed anyone but I figure, why take the chance?"[31]

Humor was indeed a major source—Cannon called it a "saving grace"—of Reagan's political success.[32] There was no doubt that he had a wonderful gift for telling jokes and stories. Some of these, ridiculing the excesses of Big Government, helped him score political points. He was also quick with one-liners, such as his disarming quip at the 1984 Gridiron dinner about the federal deficit. "I'm not worried about the deficit," he cracked. "It's big enough to take care of itself." Perhaps no quips were more memorable than those he tossed off following the attempt on his life in 1981. As he was being wheeled in for surgery, he joked with the surgeons, "Please assure me that you are all Republicans." Told that he would be happy to hear that the government was running smoothly while he was in the hospital (twelve days), he responded, "What makes you think I'd be happy about that?"[33]

About these matters—the nature of Reagan's ideas, personality, and style of leadership—I reiterate that scholars today do not much disagree. In many other ways, however, scholarly consensus has always remained elusive. Students of Reagan's presidency differ considerably now, as they did in the 1980s, about the legacy of many of his key initiatives—notably his economic and foreign policies. They also continue to disagree about the long-range impact of his ideas. Indeed, debates over the legacies of Reagan's presidency seem about as polarized today as they were in 1989.

This is not to say that polls of historians reveal large disagreement about Reagan's legacies. On the contrary, these polls expose considerable scholarly disenchantment with him. One survey, conducted between 1988 and 1990, elicited 481 responses, most of which were negative about the president. More than 18 percent of respondents judged him a flat failure, 44 percent rated him below average, slightly more than 20 percent said he was either above average or near great, and just under 1 percent scored him as great. Reagan's mean ranking left him in the below average category, between Zachary Taylor and John Tyler.[34]

Six years later, in late 1996, a poll of 33 historians organized by Arthur Schlesinger, Jr., reached similarly unflattering conclusions. The poll placed Reagan in an "average low" category, along with Gerald Ford, George Bush, Chester Arthur, Benjamin Harrison, and seven others. At the same time a poll of 719 historians ranked Reagan twenty-sixth among America's forty-one presidents, behind Bush (twenty-second) and Clinton (twenty-third). Schlesinger, criticized for polling liberals, pointed to the larger poll as evidence of negative scholarly consensus about Reagan. The 719 historians, he observed, placed Reagan in "roughly the same position as we found him."[35]

Over the years, other scholars have individually offered negative opinions of Reagan. Fred Greenstein, who had helped to rehabilitate the presidential reputation of Dwight Eisenhower, emphasizing that Ike had used a "hidden hand" to take charge of his administration, refused to credit Reagan with such control. Reagan's presidency, he said, featured "no hands" leadership. Stanley Kutler complained that Reagan did little "except to foster a residual distrust and suspicion of government." And in 1984 Robert Dallek concluded, "It is difficult to believe that a nation of 226 million people cannot find a more rational, thoughtful, and energetic leader with greater self-awareness and a better grip on national and international realities." Fifteen years later, Dallek added that Reagan's presidency "teaches that great leadership in a democratic society must rest not only on sentimental attachments but also on a considered agenda for meeting national and international dislocations."[36]

But unflattering assessments such as these by no means command universal support among historians. Indeed, seven of the thirty-three historians in Schlesinger's poll rated Reagan as "near-great," and eleven said he was "average." Some liberals, too, have had complimentary things to say about Reagan's presidency. Frank Freidel, biographer of FDR, said in 1989 that if Soviet-American relations continued to improve, "we're going to hail him as a man who grasped the opportunity when it was there." Alonzo Hamby, a sympathetic student of American liberalism, wrote in 1997, "When passions cool after a generation or so, Ronald Reagan will be widely accepted by historians as a near-great chief executive. . . . [He] uplifted a depressed national spirit with his rhetoric, revived a sick economy, and established a policy course that won the cold war. He may not end up on Mount Rushmore, but more than any other president since Truman, he will be a contender."[37]

Liberal political figures here and there have also conceded that Reagan had great gifts as president. O'Neill, hearing him speak after the *Challenger* tragedy in 1986, began to weep. Reagan, he said, "may not be much of a debater, but with a prepared text he's the best public speaker I've ever seen. . . . I'm beginning to think that in this regard he dwarfs both Roosevelt and Kennedy." Ted Kennedy added in 1989, "Ronald Reagan was a successful candidate and an effective president above all else because he stood for a set of ideas. . . . Ronald Reagan may have forgotten names but never his goals. He was a great communicator, not simply because of his personality or his TelePrompter, but mostly because he had something to communicate."[38]

Faced with conflicting evaluations such as these, we might throw up our hands in confusion. But a look at a few specific aspects of Reagan's presidency may help us move beyond grand generalizations. I will focus on the two concerns that most engaged Reagan himself: taxes and foreign policy.

No issue was closer to Reagan's heart than lowering income taxes. Donald Regan, Treasury secretary in his first term, helps explain why this was so by relating a story that Reagan told about his own experience. "When he was in Hollywood," Donald Regan said,

> he would make about three or four hundred thousand dollars per picture. It took about three months to complete a picture. Reagan would work for three months, and loaf for three months, so he was making between six and seven hundred thousand dollars per year. Between Uncle Sam and the state of California, over 91 percent of that was going in taxes. His question, asked rhetorically, was: "Why should I have done a third picture, even if it was *Gone with the Wind?* What good would it have done me?"
>
> So he loafed for a part of the year. And he said the same thing was happening throughout America. People would reach a certain peak, and they weren't willing to do the extra effort that was needed to keep us a first-class nation.[39]

As this story indicates, Reagan had strongly held personal reasons for his loathing of high taxes, and in the 1970s he became an ardent backer of some of the more extreme and populistic versions of supply-side economics. Various ideas within this movement, indeed, were then attracting considerable bipartisan support, for the American economy seemed to be in free fall at the time. By 1980, inflation was running at 13 percent and unemployment at 7 percent. The prime interest rate, averaging more than 15 percent for the year, peaked at over 21 percent in December. Many regulatory policies had come to seem counter-productive in the emergent global and high-tech economy. Popular unrest against high taxes broke out in California and many other places. Once promising "de-mand side" theories, such as Keynesianism, seemed to be in tatters.[40]

While advocates of supply-side economics differed among themselves, they agreed that tax cuts would stimulate entrepreneurial activity, investment, pro-duction, and—the key—economic growth. Most of them, notably Congress-man Jack Kemp of New York, were conservative Republicans. Senator Daniel Moynihan, observing this ideological ferment in Republican circles, warned in 1980, "Of a sudden, the GOP has become a party of ideas." But prominent Demo-crats, too, became true believers. Lloyd Bentsen, chairman of the Joint Economic Committee of Congress, declared in 1980 that America had entered "the start of a new era of economic thinking. For too long we have focused on short-run policies to stimulate spending, or demand, while neglecting supply—labor, savings, investment, and production. Consequently, demand has been over-stimulated and supply has been strangled."[41]

At the time, of course, many critics ridiculed the supply-side approach. George Bush, challenging Reagan for the GOP nomination, famously dismissed it as "Voodoo Economics." Reagan, however, insisted that tax cuts would actu-ally *reduce* government deficits in time, and he demanded sharp reductions in rates for all taxpayers, not just for the wealthy.[42] Thus he wasted no time in 1981 in urging an across-the-board 30 percent tax cut, to be accomplished over three years. In subsequent efforts for these cuts, he impressed Washington insiders with political maneuvering of a high order. Democratic leaders, seriously under-estimating his persistence in lobbying congressmen and his ability to articulate his case on television, were stunned. "I'm getting the shit whaled out of me," O'Neill complained. Jim Wright, the House majority leader, commented in a diary entry in June 1981, "I stand in awe . . . of [Reagan's] political skill. I am not sure that I have seen its equal."[43]

Thanks in no small part to Reagan's able leadership, which helped draw forty-eight Democratic congressmen to his side on the final vote, a significant tax bill passed in July 1981. It promised to cut taxes by 23 percent over three years, dropping the top marginal rate for individuals from 70 percent to 50 per-cent, as well as reducing marginal rates in lower brackets. It was estimated at the time that tax cuts over the next five years would amount to $750 billion.[44] On August 13 Reagan signed both the tax bill and a major budget measure that he said would reduce funding for social programs, especially Aid to Families with Dependent Children and Food Stamps, by some $130 billion over the next three years. Scaling back such programs had also been a major goal of Reagan's first year.

Veteran reporters lauded Reagan's leadership on these issues. Hedley Donovan wrote that these two acts represented the "most formidable domestic initiative any president has driven through since the Hundred Days of Franklin Roosevelt."[45] Donovan's praise was echoed again and again in the next few years, as scholars, journalists, and others welcomed Reagan's forceful, assured leadership, which they regularly contrasted with the ineptness that Carter had shown in dealing with Capitol Hill. At last, it seemed, America had a president who could oil the wheels of government.[46]

What many contemporary observers seemed happiest about was the ability of the president to take control of things. Their comments reflected a deep yearning, which had escalated during the troubled 1970s, for a show of presidential forcefulness. Then, and in later years, Reagan's reputation benefited from popular perceptions that he rescued the nation from political gridlock.

Reagan, to be sure, had dazzled Washington insiders, but it remained to be seen whether his economic policies were good for the country. Were they? Now as then, there is no sure answer to that question.[47] Defenders of Reaganomics maintain correctly that the economy grew uninterruptedly between 1983 and 1990. During his presidency, some seventeen million new jobs developed.[48] Thanks mainly to tight monetary policies in the early 1980s, sternly imposed (with Reagan's strong backing) by Federal Reserve Board chairman Paul Volcker, inflation dropped from 13 percent in 1980 to 4.4 percent in 1989. Unemployment fell from 7 percent to 5.5 percent. Statistics like these, jubilantly advertised by supporters of Reagan's policies, contributed greatly to Reagan's personal popularity.[49]

Even then, however, many students of Reagan's economic policies had their doubts. And these doubts have persisted over the years. For a start, the tax and budget acts of 1981 failed to prevent the nation from plunging into a sharp recession in 1981 and 1982, during which unemployment surged to 10 percent. Moreover, it became clear even in 1981 that the budgetary projections used by Reagan and his advisers bore almost no relation to reality. Congressional pork barreling sent these projections even farther off line. David Stockman, Reagan's budget director, famously confessed in late 1981, "None of us really understands what's going on with all these numbers."[50]

The most staggering "numbers," as it turned out, surfaced in the buckets of red ink of federal deficits during the Reagan years. Contrary to Reagan's beliefs, tax cuts did not lead to escalating government revenues. Whopping increases in spending on defense, on entitlements such as Social Security and Medicare, and on interest payments to cover federal borrowing accounted for perhaps two-thirds (tax cuts the other third) of deficits that became huge in every year of Reagan's presidency. Between the fiscal years 1980 and 1989, the national debt tripled from $914 billion to $2.7 trillion.[51] While congressional actions contributed to these deficits, the administration, which never submitted a balanced budget, was far and away the main source of them.[52] By 1989, alarm about deficits was mounting greatly. Lou Cannon concluded at the time, "The deficit is Reagan's great failure."[53]

By then, some people were beginning to suspect that the Reagan administration had deliberately fostered large deficits in order to make it more difficult for liberals to increase spending for social programs. This, they said, was "Reagan's Revenge."[54] Systematic, conspiratorial plotting of this sort cannot be documented. Still, the huge deficits amassed under his watch incited such widespread alarm by the early 1990s that ambitious social plans (such as Clinton's health care proposal in 1993) became politically difficult to sell.[55]

It is also clear that Reagan's economic policies helped to magnify inequality.[56] This was not the result of his tax cuts—income tax progressivity did not change in the 1980s.[57] Moreover, Reagan reluctantly took belated steps to moderate the deficits that the tax cuts of 1981 helped to enlarge, signing income tax increases in 1982 and 1984. In 1983 he approved a bipartisan agreement to hike payroll taxes for Social Security and Medicare. These taxes, regressive in nature, especially affected working-class people and exacerbated income inequality.

Thanks in part to the hike in payroll taxes, Reagan also did not reach his goal of lessening the overall federal tax burden. By 1988 it was estimated that the share of national income that went to the federal government in taxes was 19.3 percent, compared with 19.4 percent in 1980.[58]

Reaganomics also failed to achieve one of the most important goals of the supply-side vision: promoting more rapid economic growth. Real growth in GNP averaged 3.2 percent per year between 1971 and 1978, 3 percent during the worst years of stagflation under Carter, and 3 percent again under Reagan's watch.[59] What the tax cuts seemed to do, instead, was to bolster consumer demand in the short run. They did not appear to motivate many people to work harder, though by the 1990s they may have helped to stimulate the growth in productive investment that some of the supply-siders had anticipated.[60]

To say these things is not to conclude on an altogether negative note about Reagan's tax policies. For one thing, deficits had been growing earlier, promoted in part by decisions in the 1970s that led to large increases in spending on entitlements. Reagan, like his successors, dared not seriously tamper with the largest of these, Social Security and Medicare. Military spending had begun rising considerably in the last year of the Carter administration, though not so rapidly as it was to do under Reagan. Income inequality also started to accelerate before the 1980s, perhaps because of the long-term, disadvantageous effects of economic globalization on those American workers who were relatively unskilled and uneducated. Most of this inequality has shown in pretax incomes, which indicates that forces other than tax reduction have contributed importantly to it. Reagan's policies heightened inequality and delegitimated efforts to reverse it, but they were not the only sources of it.

It is also hard to know whether the huge deficits were an altogether bad thing. To be sure, they led to greatly increased interest payments, thereby diverting money that might have been used for other, more productive purposes. But the Keynesian-style deficits, mounting by the mid-1980s, may have been antirecessionary after 1982. They may therefore have helped significantly to promote the extended and fairly stable economic expansion of the mid- and late 1980s. And, of course, the federal government again managed to show surpluses (thanks in part to tax increases in the early 1990s) in the late 1990s and 2000. However frightening the Reagan era deficits seemed to be at the time, it is arguable that they did not cause great harm in the long run.

Some limitations of Reagan's economic ideas nonetheless stand out. Various of his supply-side aides came up with wildly inaccurate projections. Their most ambitious predictions—a much strengthened work ethic, a lower overall federal tax burden, considerably more rapid growth—were not met, at least not in the 1980s. Moving more cautiously after 1981, Reagan and his advisers shifted a few gears between 1982 and 1984, notably by accepting higher income and payroll taxes. In the second term, he worked with Congress to secure still lower income tax rates, as well as tax reforms. For the most part these lower rates have survived into the early 2000s, perhaps promoting voluntary compliance with the tax code. These are important legacies. But these efforts, too, did not represent serious changes in Reagan's supply-side ideas. By 1989 Reaganomics still commanded the loyalties of true believers. The president's supply-side ideas, however, remained controversial.

Aside from cutting taxes, Reagan cared most deeply about foreign policy and defense issues. And these issues, of course, dominated his second term, during which he revealed considerable strengths, offset by striking weaknesses.

Many of the weaknesses had been apparent in his first term. From the beginning, high-ranking aides were upset by what they considered to be his ignorance concerning important matters relating to foreign and military policy. In early 1983, Brent Scowcroft was astonished to realize that Reagan did not recognize that land-based Soviet ICBMs represented the major threat to United States security. A few months later the president staggered a group of congressmen by telling them that bombers and submarines did not carry nuclear missiles. Backing the Strategic Defense Initiative in 1983, he refused to listen to arguments that the policy of nuclear deterrence had helped to keep the peace, or to appreciate that America's submarine-based missiles offered a strong defense that could well make "Star Wars" unnecessary.[61]

His management of foreign policy also caused despair among top aides. Anxious not to offend people, Reagan was ordinarily unwilling to resolve conflicting viewpoints, notably those that divided Secretary of State George Shultz and Defense Secretary Caspar Weinberger. Richard Perle, an adviser, grumbled, "It never ceased to amaze me how inconclusive meetings at the highest levels were. They are almost never decisive."[62]

Reagan's handling of the National Security Council (NSC) especially revealed his weak managerial skills. Until Frank Carlucci became head of it in 1987, the NSC often floundered, mired in turf wars between strong-minded men like Shultz, Weinberger, and CIA Director William Casey. In December 1981, for instance, Reagan, Secretary of State Haig, Weinberger, Baker, Meese, Michael Deaver, and Vice President Bush met to discuss a plan of Casey's to aid the contras in Nicaragua. Most of those at the meeting did not think much of Casey's ideas, but they supported his plan as a way of avoiding *larger* support for the contras, in whom they had little confidence. As Cannon puts it, "A more negative consensus is hard to conceive." Reagan nonetheless set in motion the plan, which ultimately had huge political consequences.[63]

The sometimes chaotic nature of Reagan administration decision making concerning foreign policy matters was especially obvious in what became known as the Iran-Contra scandal. Here, Reagan was led astray by his deep personal yearning to arrange for the release of American hostages, by his predilection for covert operations, and—again—by poorly coordinated staff work, this time centering around NSC head Robert McFarlane and chief of staff Regan, who scarcely spoke to one another. Ignoring the views of Shultz and Weinberger (who for once agreed with each other), Reagan encouraged McFarlane to establish connections with so-called moderates in Iran and then to work out various arms-for-hostages deals. These deals were in fact harebrained, doing nothing to advance "moderation" in Iran and resulting in more hostages being taken than were released. When news leaked of the deals, Reagan, who had proudly proclaimed that he would never deal with terrorists, suffered a body blow to his personal popularity, which declined from 67 percent to 46 percent in November 1986.[64]

Reagan knew in advance of the arms-for-hostages deals. Whether he also knew of the activities of NSC aide Colonel Oliver North, who was funneling profits from the arms sales to the contras, remains unknown. In fact, Reagan did not want to engage American soldiers in aid of the contras. Privately denouncing advocates of direct American military intervention, he told his chief of staff in 1988, "Those sonsofbitches won't be happy until we have 25,000 troops in Managua, and I'm not going to do it."[65] But he obviously admired the contras, once calling them the "moral equivalent of our Founding Fathers." He had secretly sought to find money to aid them, notably from the Saudis.[66] North and others were fully aware that the president was eager to offer funding to the contras.

It may well be that Admiral John Poindexter, who succeeded McFarlane as NSC director, had told Reagan what he had authorized North and others to do, before the scandal broke in November 1986. It may also be, however, that Poindexter told the truth when he later fell on his sword and denied having informed the president. Or it may be that Poindexter had told him and that Reagan had forgotten about it. Any of these scenarios, of course, makes the president look bad. Either Reagan knowingly authorized secret payments, in violation of congressional direction, or he was no longer in control of his own administration. Perhaps he was suffering from the early ravages of Alzheimer's disease. Only his strong personal standing with the American people—and the absence of a smoking gun to prove that he had knowingly approved the diversion of profits—saved him from possible impeachment proceedings.

Among the events most helpful in bolstering Reagan's standing at that time, of course, were the fruitful series of meetings that he held with Soviet leader Mikhail Gorbachev between 1985 and 1988. These led to the signing in December 1987 (and Senate ratification in May 1988) of the historic Intermediate Nuclear Forces (INF) Treaty, whereby the Soviets and Americans agreed to scrap intermediate-range and short-range nuclear missiles. This was the first time that the two nations had accepted destruction of any nuclear weapons and the first pact approved to establish on-site monitoring. By the time Reagan left office in January 1989, the world was a little safer place.

The thaw that warmed Soviet-American relations in these years has come under near-endless scrutiny, leading many writers to acclaim Reagan as the man who ended the cold war.[67] Librarian of Congress James Billington, a historian of Russia, wrote in 1997, "President Ronald Reagan was the single most important political figure in ending the Cold War without either making concessions or incurring major loss of life on either side. It was an astonishing accomplishment."[68] Francis Loewenheim, a diplomatic historian, added, "Without firing a shot, Ronald Reagan brought down the house that Lenin, Stalin, Khrushchev and Brezhnev had built. . . . That certainly looks like a world-historical achievement."[69]

That Reagan, long an ardent cold warrior, could be lauded for helping to end the cold war could scarcely have been imagined during his first term. Misled by sometimes overheated CIA estimates of Soviet strength, he greatly escalated defense spending—this effort, Raymond Garthoff has written, was a "mindless spending spree."[70] In March 1983, he denounced the Soviet Union as the "focus of evil in the modern world." He then overruled virtually all his top advisers by calling for creation of the Strategic Defense Initiative. "Star Wars," they thought, was unnecessary, unworkable, and provocative. Shultz at first called the idea "lunacy."

Still, as Reagan's defenders point out, the president did prove flexible enough to change course, especially after Gorbachev came to power in 1985. Agreeing to a summit at Geneva in November 1985, he prepared with great thoroughness. Once at the summit, he worked effectively to establish good relations with Gorbachev. The strong personal bond created at Geneva enabled the two men to push ahead, notably at Reykjavik in 1986, for the INF Treaty. Moreover, the strong anticommunist credentials that Reagan enjoyed with the American people gave him the secure political base that he needed to sell his efforts at home. In this sense, his defense buildup had a domestic political payoff.[71] Most important, Reagan's admirers insist, the president's defiant support of SDI frightened Soviet leaders, who are said to have realized that they could no longer afford to keep up with the United States and therefore resolved to cut a deal.

Most scholars of Reagan's policy toward the Soviet Union nonetheless stop well short of giving him all, or even most, of the credit for relaxation of the cold war.[72] Instead, they point to the sad economic condition of the Soviet Union as of the early 1980s. Bleeding from a war in Afghanistan, reeling economically, the Soviet Union was simply in no position—SDI or no SDI—to engage in further expansion of the arms race against the United States. It had become an enormous Potemkin village that Gorbachev was determined to reform. Reagan's provocative insistence on going ahead with SDI—and on building up the military in general—may in fact have made it more difficult for Gorbachev, confronted with hard-liners at home, to be accommodating.[73]

To focus on Gorbachev's role is not to deny that Reagan played an important part in the relaxation of tensions. Indeed, this relaxation is the most notable legacy of his presidency. Still, it also seems clear that a key source of the thaw lay in the Soviet Union. Not everything that improves international relations has its origins in the United States.

Difficult though it is to pinpoint the still controversial legacies of Reagan's presidency, a few final stabs in that direction may make a start.

Those who are impressed with the size of Reagan's shadow often emphasize three general points. First, that he succeeded in resisting what had appeared to be an irreversible tide of Big Government. Second, that he shoved politics and political thinking toward the right. And third, that he heightened popular faith in the nation.

The first claim is inaccurate insofar as means-tested programs for the poor are concerned. Though stemmed in 1981, they increased again after 1984, and welfare spending was higher in 1989 than it had been in 1981.[74] In other ways, too, this claim is overstated. His own rhetoric to the contrary, Reagan was far too adept a politician to undertake any serious dismantling of large and popular social programs such as Social Security or Medicare. Although he talked repeatedly about the evils of federal regulation, he did not scrap important government agencies. Federal bureaucracy, which had swelled since the 1960s, emerged unscathed.[75] The number of federal employees increased more rapidly during his presidency than it had under Jimmy Carter. Federal government spending as a percentage of gross domestic product was slightly higher under Reagan than it was to become under Bill Clinton.[76]

Reagan also failed to overturn, or even seriously to challenge, a number of highly controversial practices, such as abortion or affirmative action, that he said he would fight hard against.[77] Though a supporter of school-directed prayers, he did little to bring them into being. In coping with these matters, as with popular programs of the New Deal, a politically careful Reagan took the path of least resistance. Knowing that ardent social conservatives would never support liberal Democrats, he gave only lip service to these social conservative causes. He played symbolic politics very well, enraging many conservatives in the process.[78]

Reagan also recognized, of course, that reversing existing practices concerning abortion and school prayer would require changes in judicial interpretation.

With that goal in mind, he was careful to name conservatives to the federal courts. Most observers think that these conservatives were well qualified.[79] But though he ended by naming nearly four hundred federal judges—almost half of the total on the bench—the courts moved more slowly to the right in later years than ardent conservatives had hoped. Most of the landmark liberal decisions of the 1960s and early 1970s—concerning school prayers, criminal rights, and reproductive rights—had not been overturned as of early 2003.

The second claim, that Reagan helped move politics and political thinking to the right, seemed to be valid in the early and mid-1980s. In 1980, Republicans captured the Senate for the first time since 1954. The GOP also seemed to be making headway in other ways. In 1980, for instance, polls showed that there was a considerable Democratic edge—of more than 20 percent—in the expressed partisan preference of voters. After Reagan's reelection, however, Republicans were approaching parity with Democrats.[80] The victory of George Bush in 1988 seemed to indicate that Reaganism was promoting a political realignment in the nation.

There is also little doubt that the resurgence of conservative thinking in the Reagan years placed liberal ideas on the defensive. In 1988 Bush effectively demonized the "l" word, liberalism. And Democrats, too, saw conservative handwriting on the wall. Under Bill Clinton, they moved to the right, especially in the areas of welfare and fiscal policy. The recentering of the Democratic Party under Clinton, who understood the force of Reagan's impact on political thinking, was probably a key to the revival of its fortunes in the 1990s.

Another pronounced political development of the 1990s was what Benjamin Ginsberg and Martin Shefter have called the "Reagan Diaspora." Many conservative activists, energized greatly by Reagan's victories in the 1980s, entered electoral politics, some of them leading the GOP electoral bonanza of 1994. They also strengthened a network of organizations—the Christian Coalition, the National Taxpayers Union, the National Rifle Association, various think tanks— that bolstered conservative ideas and pressure groups at all levels of government. On some issues both parties seemed to become more conservative after 1980 than they had been in the 1960s and 1970s.[81]

It was obvious by 2003, however, that Reagan failed to accomplish what FDR had done: create a major realignment of partisan preferences. Democrats maintained firm control of the House of Representatives until 1995, recaptured the Senate between 1987 and 1995, and regained the White House in 1993. In 2000, Al Gore and Ralph Nader won 52 percent of the popular vote for president. Nor is it accurate to credit Reagan alone for the resurgence of the Republican Party. Nixon, after all, had earlier paved the way for a GOP strategy that brought millions of disaffected Democrats, especially southerners, into the Republican column. And conservative intellectuals, founding journals and think tanks, had advanced impressively in the late 1960s and 1970s. As Martin Anderson has stressed, this conservative "Revolution," as he calls it, was well on its way before 1980. Reagan gave a substantial boost to many conservative ideas, to be sure, but he was a beneficiary as well as a mover of the rise of the right.[82]

What, then, of the final claim—that Reagan's greatest legacy was to make Americans feel good again about themselves and the future of the nation? If by this claim it is meant that Reagan—the avowed enemy of Big Government—ironically restored popular faith in the competence of Washington, that is true—to some extent—in two ways. First, as Morris has written, Reagan was "centered and purposeful, a man of unstoppable, slow, inexorable drive."[83] Unusually constant for a politician, he stuck with most of his strongly held convictions. In this sense he was more resolute than most men in public life and therefore personally admired. Second, Reagan was lucky to follow four presidents—LBJ, Nixon, Ford, and Carter—who had stumbled off the national stage with low popular ratings. By contrast, Reagan was fortunate to be president in an era of mostly improving prosperity, and he managed to keep the nation out of major wars. A professional actor whose final approval rating of 68 percent was the best since FDR's, he was a star whom many people applauded.

But Reagan's tenure did not mean that the majority of Americans came to love their government. (Nor, of course, would he have wanted them to love it.) They admired the star, not the play. For one thing, Iran-Contra strengthened a host of already anguished popular doubts about the evils of federal officialdom. For another, many followers of Reagan above all cherished his antigovernment message. We need not agree with Garry Wills that Reagan's antistatism prepared the ground for Rush Limbaugh, the Freemen, and extremists like Timothy McVeigh.[84] Still, polls since 1989 indicate that a majority of Americans have remained suspicious and distrustful of government.[85] Reagan's rhetoric not only fed these feelings; it also helped to kindle antistatist fires that blazed fiercely during the heyday of Newt Gingrich and other right-wing leaders of the mid-1990s.

The larger claim, that Reagan made Americans feel good about themselves and about their country, is in any solidly quantifiable sense unverifiable. But the claim is plausible. Like FDR, he was indeed an optimist and a booster who was fortunate politically in that he entered the White House at a somber time in United States history. Rejecting the notion that America had reached an Age of Limits, the Great Communicator told people again and again that they could still accomplish wonderful things and that the future would be better than the past.[86] In so preaching he made effective use of the bully pulpit of the White House. Though this was often "feel good" leadership, it helped him forge a bond with many Americans. Without this leadership, the malaise of the late 1970s might have persisted.

With the limited hindsight that we now enjoy, however, it is hard to claim too much for the legacy of Reagan's presidency. Though strong as a booster, he was a frequently negligent and incurious manager. Concerning many policy areas—race relations, urban affairs, immigration and population issues, health care, action against AIDS, education, environmental concerns—he was essentially uninterested. Excepting his efforts to lower income tax rates, and—more important—his contributions to the ending of the cold war, he did little in the way of developing new or effective approaches to key problems, some of which were allowed to fester.

To speak, therefore, of a "Reagan Revolution," or of an "Age of Reagan," seems excessive. Grand phrases such as these are best reserved for twentieth-century presidents like Theodore Roosevelt, who did much to promote the activist presidency of our own times; like Franklin Roosevelt, whose New Deal inaugurated the welfare state; or like Harry Truman, whose foreign policies established America's response to the Soviet Union for forty years or more. By contrast to these formidable figures, Ronald Reagan does not seem quite so tall. Still, his legacies in the realms that he cared most about—tax rates and Soviet-American relations—have been durable as well as significant. His large shadow remains.

NOTES

1. William E. Pemberton, *Exit with Honor: The Life and Presidency of Ronald Reagan* (Armonk, N.Y.: M. E. Sharpe, 1998), 28–29.

2. William Leuchtenburg, *In the Shadow of FDR: From Harry Truman to Bill Clinton* (Ithaca, N.Y.: Cornell University Press, 1989), 209–35; Philip Abbott, "Reagan's FDR: (Re)constructing the New Deal Memory," in Eric J. Schmerz et al., eds., *Ronald Reagan's America* (Westport, Conn.: Greenwood Press, 1997), 673–82.

3. Douglas Brinkley, "The President's Pen Pal," *New Yorker,* July 26, 1999, 33.

4. Kiron K. Skinner, Annelise Anderson, and Martin Anderson, eds., *Reagan, In His Own Hand* (New York: Free Press, 2001). For commentary on this volume, see William Safire, "Reagan Writes," *New York Times Magazine,* December 31, 2000, 38–42; and Jay Nordlinger, "Reagan in Full," *National Review,* February 19, 2001, 44–46.

5. Godfrey Hodgson, *The World Turned Right Side Up: A History of the Conservative Ascendancy in America* (Boston: Houghton Mifflin, 1996), 247.

6. *Public Papers of the Presidents of the United States: Ronald Reagan, 1981–1989* (Washington, D.C.: Government Printing Office, 1981), 1–4.

7. See Frances FitzGerald, *Way Out There in the Blue: Reagan, Star Wars, and the End of the Cold War* (New York: Simon & Schuster, 2000), especially 26–33. Also Bill Keller, "Missile Defense: The Untold Story," *New York Times,* December 29, 2001.

8. Cited in Michael Schaller, *Reckoning with Reagan: America and Its President in the 1980s* (New York: Oxford University Press, 1992), 6.

9. Garry Wills, "Mr. Magoo Remembers," *New York Review of Books,* December 20, 1990, 29; also Wills, *Reagan's America* (New York: Penguin Books, 2000), ix.

10. Cited in Pemberton, *Exit with Honor,* 17.

11. Katharine Graham, "The Press and the President," *Miller Center Report* 16, no. 1 (spring 2000) (Miller Center, University of Virginia), 6. See also Mike Wallace, "The Reagan Years: A Reporter's Notebook," in Schmerz et al., *Ronald Reagan's America,* 5–9.

12. Wills, *Reagan's America* (Garden City, N.Y.: Doubleday, 1988), 2.

13. *Washington Post,* January 22, 1984 (referring to an interview in 1981).

14. Ibid.

15. Lou Cannon, *President Reagan: The Role of a Lifetime* (New York: Simon & Schuster, 2000), 837.

16. Peggy Noonan, *What I Saw at the Revolution: A Political Life in the Reagan Era* (New York: Random House, 1990), 151.

17. Edmund Morris, *Dutch: A Memoir of Ronald Reagan* (New York: Random House, 1999), 579. See also Michael Korda, "Prompting the President," *New Yorker,* October 6, 1997, 88–95.

18. Cited in Pemberton, *Exit with Honor,* 111.

19. Cannon, *Role of a Lifetime,* 37.

20. Martin Anderson, *Revolution: The Reagan Legacy* (Stanford: Hoover Institution Press, 1990), 289–91.

21. See John Sloan, "President Reagan's Administrative Formula for Political Success," in Schmerz et al., *Ronald Reagan's America,* 535–46.

22. See the essays in this volume by Gareth Davies and by Martha Derthick and Steven Teles for documentation of Reagan's inattentiveness (concerning social policies) during his first term.

23. Cannon, *Role of a Lifetime,* 162.

24. Nancy Reagan, with Michael Novak, *My Turn, the Memoirs of Nancy Reagan* (New York: Random House, 1989), 106.

25. Michael Reagan, with Joe Hyams, *On the Outside Looking In* (New York: Kensington Publishing, 1988), 96.

26. Gil Troy, "It's a Strange Book on a Mystifying President," *Newsday,* October 13, 1999 (review of Morris, *Dutch*).

27. See Cannon, *Role of a Lifetime,* 194; Pemberton, *Exit with Honor,* 17–18.

28. Morris, *Dutch,* 4, 579.

29. *Washington Post,* October 10, 1999.

30. One top aide, Martin Anderson (*Revolution,* 138–39), maintains that Reagan was a "closet workaholic."

31. Pemberton, *Exit with Honor,* 112.

32. Cannon, *Role of a Lifetime,* 114.

33. See Cannon, *Role of a Lifetime,* 95–114, for an excellent chapter on Reagan's use of humor. Also Andrew Stark, "The Great Storyteller," *Times Literary Supplement,* November 12, 1999, 9–10.

34. Robert K. Murray and Tim H. Blessing, *Greatness in the White House: Rating the Presidents,* 2d ed. (University Park: Penn State University Press, 1994), 79–91.

35. Arthur Schlesinger, Jr., "The Ultimate Approval Rating," *New York Times Magazine,* December 15, 1996, 46–51; William J. Ridings and Stuart B. McIver, *Rating the Presidents* (Secaucus, N.J.: Carol Publishing Group, 1997). Schlesinger comment in *Washington Times,* February 6, 1997.

36. For Greenstein, see Cannon, *Role of a Lifetime,* 748. Also see Stanley Kutler, "Ronald Reagan: The Novel and the Movie," *Chicago Tribune,* October 3, 1999; and Robert Dallek, *Ronald Reagan: The Politics of Symbolism* (Cambridge: Harvard University Press, 1984), 194; reprint (Cambridge: Harvard University Press, 1999), xx.

37. Freidel in *Los Angeles Times,* July 28, 1989; Hamby in Alvin Felzenberg, "'There You Go Again': Liberal Historians and the *New York Times* Deny Reagan His Due," *Policy Review* 82 (March–April 1997), 53. The conservative editor William Buckley, also quoted in *Policy Review,* wrote, "Reagan belongs on Mount Rushmore, and he'll be there, after the carpers die off" (52).

38. O'Neill cited in Morris, *Dutch,* 586; Kennedy quoted in William C. Berman, *America's Right Turn: From Nixon to Bush* (Baltimore: Johns Hopkins University Press, 1994), 143.

39. Cited in Deborah Hart Strober and Gerald S. Strober, *Reagan: The Man and His Presidency* (Boston: Houghton Mifflin, 1998), 131.

40. For economic policies during the 1970s, see Otis L. Graham, Jr., *Losing Time: The Industrial Policy Debate* (Cambridge: Harvard University Press, 1992).

41. Moynihan cited in Robert M. Collins, *More: The Politics of Economic Growth in Postwar America* (New York: Oxford University Press, 2000), 189–90. See also Martin Feldstein, "American Economic Policy in the 1980s: A Personal View," in *American Economic Policy in the 1980s,* ed. Martin Feldstein (Chicago: University of Chicago Press, 1994), 1–80; Louis Galambos, "The United States Corporate Economy in the Twentieth Century," in *The Cambridge Economic History of the United States,* vol. 3, *The Twentieth Century,* ed. Stanley Engerman and Robert Gallman (Cambridge: Cambridge University Press, 2000), 927–68; and W. Elliot Brownlee, "The Public Sector," in ibid., 1013–60.

42. See essay by W. Elliot Brownlee and C. Eugene Steuerle in this volume.

43. Collins, *More,* 192. See also Presidential Telephone Files, in Presidential Handwriting File, Ronald Reagan Library (RRL), for evidence of Reagan's very active telephoning of congressional leaders during the months of struggle for the tax law of 1981.

44. Pemberton, *Exit with Honor,* 96–104; Berman, 89–98. See also Alonzo L. Hamby, *Liberalism and Its Challengers: From FDR to Bush,* 2d. ed. (New York: Oxford University Press, 1992), 362–72.

45. Hedley Donovan, "Reagan's First Two Hundred Days," *Fortune,* September 21, 1981, 63.

46. See *Washington Post,* September 3, 1983, for many such positive evaluations.

47. Among the many sources that explore Reaganomics are William A. Niskanen, *Reaganomics: An Insider's Account of the Policies and the People* (New York: Oxford University Press, 1988); John W. Sloan, *The Reagan Effect: Economics and Presidential Leadership* (Lawrence: University Press of Kansas, 1999); David A. Stockman, *The Triumph of Politics: Why the Revolution Failed* (New York: Harper & Row, 1986); C. Eugene Steuerle, *The Tax Decade: How Taxes Came to Dominate the Public Agenda* (Washington, D.C.: Urban Institute Press, 1992); and "Economists Assess the Presidency," in Schmerz et al., *Ronald Reagan's America,* 759–82.

48. Most of them were low paying, many of them taken by women, whose participation in the labor force continued to surge.

49. See Brownlee and Steuerle's essay in this volume for the argument that Reagan's across-the-board approach to tax reduction, together with loophole plugging and further tax reduction enacted in 1986, had the unintended and ironic effect of promoting greater popular support for the progressive federal income tax system.

50. William Greider, "The Education of David Stockman," *Atlantic Monthly* 248, December 1981, 27.

51. Collins, *More,* 203.

52. George Will, generally a supporter of Reagan, estimated that thirteen-fourteenths of the deficit stemmed from Reagan budgets. *Newsweek,* January 9, 1989, 29.

53. *Newsweek,* January 9, 1989.

54. See Daniel P. Moynihan, "Reagan's Bankrupt Budget," *New Republic,* December 26, 1983, 15–20; Moynihan, *Came the Revolution: Argument in the Reagan Era* (San Diego: Harcourt Brace Jovanovich, 1988), 21, 31; and Alan Brinkley, "Reagan's Revenge," *New York Times Magazine,* June 19, 1994, 37.

55. Clinton's plan had other political liabilities.

56. Sloan, *Reagan Effect,* 246–62.

57. Brownlee and Steuerle's essay, this volume.

58. *Los Angeles Times,* March 21, 1988.

59. Pemberton, *Exit with Honor,* 207.

60. Scholars have long questioned whether the tax cuts had such a beneficial impact on productive investment. Some, echoing liberals, have argued to the contrary—that the cuts stimulated unproductive investments, as in junk bonds. The "truth" is probably impossible to demonstrate through economic analysis.

61. Cannon, *Role of a Lifetime,* 249–51. For the story of Star Wars, see FitzGerald, *Way Out There in the Blue.*

62. Cannon, *Role of a Lifetime,* 294.

63. Cannon, *Role of a Lifetime,* 308–9.

64. See Cannon, *Role of a Lifetime,* 521–662; and Pemberton, *Exit with Honor,* 172–90, for balanced treatments of the Iran-Contra scandal. A sharp critique of Reagan's Central American policies is William M. LeoGrande, *Our Own Backyard: The United States in Central America, 1977–1992* (Chapel Hill: University of North Carolina Press, 1998).

65. Cannon, *Role of a Lifetime,* 291.

66. He was also anxious to keep the Saudi aid secret. "If such a story gets out," he told aides in 1984, "we'll all be hanging by our thumbs in front of the White House." *Washington Post,* March 11, 1989.

67. Among the many books on the subject are Raymond L. Garthoff, *The Great Transition: American-Soviet Relations and the End of the Cold War* (Washington, D.C.: Brookings Institution Press, 1994); John Lewis Gaddis, *The United States and the End of the Cold War: Implications, Reconsiderations, Provocations* (New York: Oxford University Press, 1992); Richard Ned Lebow and Janice Gross Stein, *We All Lost the Cold War* (Princeton: Princeton University Press, 1994); and FitzGerald, *Way Out There in the Blue,* especially 412–78.

68. Billington assessment, September 25, 1997, in Vertical File, Reagan Speeches and Articles, 1981–1989 (RRL).

69. *Cleveland Plain Dealer,* May 3, 1993. For lavish praise of Reagan's dealings with Gorbachev, see Noonan, *What I Saw at the Revolution,* 344.

70. For CIA estimates, see "What They Knew (Not!): Forty-four Years of CIA Secrets," *New York Times,* March 19, 2001; Garthoff, *Great Transition,* 758.

71. On this point, see Gaddis, *United States and the End of the Cold War,* 131; Garthoff, *Great Transition,* 765–77; and FitzGerald, *Way Out There in the Blue,* 473–78.

72. See the essay in this volume by Beth Fischer.

73. Lebow and Stein, *We All Lost the Cold War,* 370–76.

74. See essays by Davies and by Brownlee and Steuerle, this volume.

75. See Hugh Davis Graham, "Legacies of the 1960s," *Journal of Policy History* 10, no. 3 (1988): 267–88; and the essay by Ted McAllister in this volume.

76. Pemberton, *Exit with Honor,* 202.

77. As governor of California he had signed a liberal abortion law.

78. Jerome Himmelstein, "If They Did So Well, Why Do They Feel So Bad? The Right after the Reagan Years," in Schmerz et al., *Ronald Reagan's America,* 55–65.

79. David O'Brien, "The Reagan Revolution and the Federal Judiciary," in ibid., 359–77.

80. Sidney M. Milkis, *The President and the Parties: The Transformation of the American Party System Since the New Deal* (New York: Oxford University Press, 1993), 264–65.

81. Benjamin Ginsberg and Martin Shefter, *Politics by Other Means: Politicians, Prosecutors, and the Press from Watergate to Whitewater,* rev. ed. (New York: W. W. Norton, 1999), 66–68.

82. Anderson, *Revolution.*

83. Cited in *New York Times,* January 1, 2002.

84. Wills, *Reagan's America* (2000), xxiii.

85. See Robert Samuelson, *The Good Life and Its Discontents* (New York: Random House, 1997), 188–204, 263–64.

86. On Reagan's progressive view of history, see the essay by McAllister in this volume.

Contributors

TERRI BIMES is a lecturer and research scholar at the University of California, Berkeley. She has published articles on the presidency, divided government, and American political history.

W. ELLIOT BROWNLEE is Professor Emeritus at the University of California, Santa Barbara, and is at work on a history of the financing of World War I, and on a collaborative, comparative history of taxation in the United States and Japan in the twentieth century. His latest books on the history of public finance are *Funding the Modern American State, 1941–1995: The Rise and Fall of the Era of Easy Finance* (editor) and *Federal Taxation in America: A Short History.*

DONALD T. CRITCHLOW, Professor of History, Saint Louis University, is the author of eleven books, including most recently *Intended Consequences: Birth Control, Abortion, and the Federal Government; Studebaker: The Life and Death of an American Corporation;* and *Enemies of the State: Personal Stories from the Gulag* (editor).

GARETH DAVIES is University Lecturer in American History at Oxford University, England. He is the author of *From Opportunity to Entitlement: The Transformation and Decline of Great Society Liberalism,* which won the Organization of American Historians' Ellis W. Hawley Prize, and of a number of essays about the politics of social policy in twentieth-century America.

MARTHA DERTHICK retired in 1999 as the Julia Allen Cooper Professor of Government and Foreign Affairs at the University of Virginia. She is the author of *Policymaking for Social Security* and *Agency under Stress: The Social Security Administration in American Government,* among other works on American institutions and public policy.

BETH A. FISCHER is an assistant professor in the political science department at the University of Toronto, where she specializes in international security. She has written numerous articles on the Reagan administration's foreign policy, as well as *The Reagan Reversal: Foreign Policy Change and the End of the Cold War.* Dr. Fischer was a Senior Fellow at the Norwegian Nobel Institute in 2002, where she continued work on her forthcoming book on the ending of the cold war.

HUGH DAVIS GRAHAM was the Holland N. McTyeire Professor of History at Vanderbilt University. His book-length publications include *Southern Politics and the Second Re-*

construction; The Civil Rights Era: Origins and Development of National Policy, 1960–1972; The Uncertain Triumph: Federal Education Policy in the Kennedy and Johnson Years; Civil Rights and the Presidency; The Carter Presidency: Policy Choices in the Post–New Deal Era (coeditor); and *Collision Course: The Strange Consequence of Affirmative Action and Immigration Policy in America.*

OTIS L. GRAHAM, JR., is Professor Emeritus at the University of California, Santa Barbara, and Fellow at the Randall Library, University of North Carolina, Wilmington. He is the author of numerous works in modern American history, including most recently (with Roger Daniels) *Debating American Immigration, 1882 to Present.* He was the recipient of the 1999 Robert Kelley Memorial Award from the National Council on Public History.

HUGH HECLO is Robinson Professor of Public Affairs at George Mason University. He has won national academic book awards for his volumes *Modern Social Politics in Britain and Sweden, Comparative Public Policy,* and *A Government of Strangers: Executive Politics in Washington.* Most recently he is coauthor of *The Government We Deserve* and senior contributing editor of *Religion Reenters the Public Square: Faith and Policy in America.*

TED V. MCALLISTER is the Edward L. Gaylord Professor of Public Policy at Pepperdine University and is the author of *Revolt against Modernity: Leo Strauss, Eric Voegelin, and the Search for a Postliberal Order.*

DAVID M. O'BRIEN is Leone Reaves and George W. Spicer Professor at the University of Virginia. Among his numerous books is *Storm Center: The Supreme Court in American Politics,* which won the American Bar Association's Silver Gavel Award for contributing to public understanding of the law.

CHESTER J. PACH, JR., is a faculty member of the Department of History, Ohio University, and the author of *Arming the Free World: The Origins of the United States Military Assistance Program, 1945–1950* and *The Presidency of Dwight D. Eisenhower.* He was awarded the Stuart L. Bernath Article Prize of the Society for Historians of American Foreign Relations.

JAMES T. PATTERSON is Ford Foundation Professor of History (now emeritus) at Brown University. His publications include *Grand Expectations: The United States, 1945–1974,* which won the Bancroft Prize in History in 1997. His latest book is *Brown v. Board of Education: A Civil Rights Milestone and Its Troubled Legacy.*

C. EUGENE STEUERLE is a Senior Fellow at the Urban Institute and has served as president of the National Tax Association (2001–2002), deputy assistant secretary of the Treasury for Tax Analysis (1987–1989), economic coordinator for the Project for Fundamental Tax Reform that led to the Tax Reform Act of 1986 (1984–1986), and chair of the 1999 Technical Panel advising Social Security on its methods and assumptions. He is also the author, coauthor, or editor of ten books, more than 150 reports, articles, and congressional testimonies, and more than 650 columns for *Tax Notes Magazine,* the *Financial Times,* and the Urban Institute.

JEFFREY K. STINE is the Curator of Engineering and Environmental History at the National Museum of American History, Smithsonian Institution. His publications include *Mixing the Waters: Environment, Politics, and the Building of the Tennessee-Tombigbee Waterway* and *A History of Science Policy in the United States, 1940–1985.*

STEVEN M. TELES is Assistant Professor of Politics at Brandeis University and author of *Whose Welfare? AFDC and Elite Politics.* He is currently working on the evolution of conservative public policy institutions.

SAMUEL F. WELLS, JR., is Associate Director of the Woodrow Wilson International Center for Scholars in Washington, D.C. His major publications include *Economics and World Power: An Assessment of American Diplomacy Since 1789; The Challenges of Power: American Diplomacy, 1900–1921;* and *New European Orders, 1919 and 1991.*

Index

ABA. *See* American Bar Association
Abdnor, James, 247
Abortion, 10–11, 296–305, 309–12, 324n75
   1972 election and, 297–98
   conservatist movement and, 294
   federal funding for, 298, 300, 303, 306,
    307t, 310–11
   judicial appointments and, 304, 306, 308,
    325–26n94, 327, 334, 337
   legislation on, 11, 296–98, 302–4, 308–9,
    318n34
   medical effects of, 310
   Nixon and, 297–98, 317–18n28, 318n29
   O'Connor and, 306, 308, 341–42
   presidential campaigns and, 300–302,
    321n48, 321n50
   Supreme Court on, 11, 297–98, 303,
    309–10, 325n87
   undue burden doctrine and, 308
   women and, 297, 316–17n25
Abortion and the Conscience of the Nation
   (Reagan), 309
Abortion in America (Mohr), 303
Abstract reason, 42
Abzug, Bella, 318n34
Acid rain, 243–45
ACLU. *See* American Civil Liberties Union
Adarand decision, 289
Adolescent Family Life Act, 306
AEI. *See* American Enterprise Institute
AFDC. *See* Aid to Families with Dependent
   Children
Affirmative action, 10, 284–90
   corporations and, 284–85, 287–88, 290
   Executive Order 11246, 283–86, 290
   immigration and, 288–90
   judicial appointments and, 289, 332

   neoconservatives on, 47
   small business and, 285, 288, 290
Afghanistan, 92, 106–8, 114, 125, 134–35
African Americans
   affirmative action and, 288–89
   judicial appointments of, 337, 338t
   See also Civil rights
Agnew, Spiro, 69, 75
Agricultural workers, 265–67, 269, 271–72,
   278n15
Ahlstrom, Sidney, 23
Aid to Families with Dependent Children
   (AFDC), 7, 209, 211, 218, 221
   after Reagan, 225, 227
   cuts in, 212, 216, 219, 362
   state government and, 223
   waivers for, 213
*Akron v. Akron Center for Reproductive
   Health, Inc.,* 325n87
Alaskan offshore drilling, 238
Alexander, Lamar, 224
Allen, Richard, 134, 151n12
Allen, William B., 311–12
Alliance for Justice, 334
America
   belief in, 357
   Contract with, 56–57
   feeling good about, 370
   founding principles of, 21, 25, 32, 45, 48,
    50, 289
   freedom and, 20–21, 29, 50
   God blessing, 20–21, 33
   personality of, 25
   as the promised land, 20–21
   as the rescuer, 22
   traditions of, 43
   vision of, 50

American Bar Association (ABA), 335, 337, 340, 340t, 348
American Citizens Concerned for Life, 305
American Civil Liberties Union (ACLU), 274, 346
American College of Gynecologists, Thornburgh v., 309–10
American Dream, 51
American Enterprise Institute (AEI), 345
American GI Forum, 74
American Hospital Association, Bowen v., 324n81
American Revolution, 43
Americans for Democratic Action, 62
Ammunition, duties on, 249–50
Amnesty, 261, 263–69, 271–72
Anderson, Annelise, 286
Anderson, Martin
    on civil rights, 286
    on conservatism, 369–70
    on immigration, 265–67
    on Reagan's personality, 192, 358
    on Social Security reform, 182
    on tax reform, 157, 160
    on welfare, 210, 215, 226
Andropov, Yuri, 118
Antiballistic Missile Treaty of 1972, 103, 117
Appellate court judges, 333, 335–36, 340t
Approval ratings. *See* Public opinion polls
Archer, William, 186, 199
Archives, 2
Argentina, 98
Armageddon, 52, 356
Arms control negotiations, 17–18, 89, 117–19
    Antiballistic Missile Treaty of 1972, 103, 117
    defense spending and, 95–96
    Europe and, 136, 149
    Geneva summit, 126–27, 130n1, 136, 143–44, 146, 367
    Gorbachev and, 114, 143–45, 149–50
    INF treaty, 115, 135–36, 139–40, 143, 149, 367
    Reykjavik summit, 144–46, 367
    SDI and, 141
    Strategic Arms Limitations Talks, 89, 96, 136, 143, 146, 295

Arms race, 114, 120–21, 124
    cost of, 125–27, 129
Armstrong, William, 185–86, 199
Army Corps of Engineers, 247–48
Army for Civil Works, 247
Arnold, Douglas, 202
Aronson, Elliot, 74
Ashbrook, John, 295–96
Asian Americans, 289, 338t
Aspin, Les, 127, 210
Associated General Contractors, 284
Asylum, 263, 273–74
Atomic weapons. *See* Nuclear weapons
Authority, traditional, 32
Autocracy, 71
Autonomy, 53

Babbitt, Bruce, 341
Babbitt, Irving, 42
Baby Doe regulation, 324–25n81
Baker, Howard, 224–25, 346, 349
Baker, James A. III
    on abortion, 324n75
    on affirmative action, 10, 284
    appointment of, 225
    on Central America, 97
    on foreign policy, 134
    on immigration, 265
    influence of, 162, 216
    on Nicaragua, 97, 366
    on Reagan's personality, 358
    on Social Security reform, 185–86, 193, 197–99, 202
    on tax reform, 7–8, 165–66, 171, 179n46
    on welfare, 221–22
Bakke lawsuit, 287–88
Ball, Robert M., 188–89, 199–202
Ball, William, 223
Bancroft, George, 37–38n10
Bankruptcy, 4–5, 120–21
Barrier islands, 247
Bauer, Gary, 305, 308, 311
Beirut bomb attack, 35, 100–101
Beliefs, 20, 23, 32
Bellah, Robert, 23
Bell, Griffin, 334
Bell, Grove City College v., 311–12
Bennett, William J., 284, 310

Bentsen, Lloyd, 362
Berkowitz, Edward, 212
Berlin Wall, 147, 278n11
Berman, Larry, 2
Bible, 42
Biden, Joseph, 336, 346–47
Big business. *See* Corporations
Big government, 6, 368–69
    "Business, Ballots, and Bureaus" speech
        on, 65
    Clinton on, 57
    growth of, 29–31, 34, 45, 56
    populist appeals on, 3, 67, 70t, 71–72, 74
Billington, James, 36, 367
Bishop, Maurice, 99–100
Blacks. *See* African Americans
Blackwell, Morton, 303–5, 308
Block, John, 221
Bolingbroke (Henry St. John), 31
Bolling, Richard, 198
Bolling v. Sharpe, 347
Borjas, George, 272
Bork, Robert H.
    American Bar Association on, 340
    Hyde amendment and, 298
    on jurisprudence of original intention,
        332
    lower court appointment, 331
    nomination of, 326n94, 336, 345–49
    public opinion of, 348
    rejection of, 330, 337
    selection of, 342
Boschwitz, Rudy, 185
Boskin, Michael, 184, 187
Bowen, Otis, 11, 305–6, 310, 324–25n81
*Bowen v. the American Hospital
    Association,* 324n81
Bracket-creep taxes, 156, 175n6
Bradley, Bill, 164
Brandeis, Louis, 346
Brezhnev, Leonid I., 88–90, 124
Briggs, Vernon, 267, 272
Brock, William E., III, 10, 284–85
Broder, David, 66, 217–18
Brookings Institution, 260
Brownell, Herbert, 334
Brown, Harold, 94
Bryan, William Jennings, 61
Brzezinski, Zbigniew, 107

Buckley, James, 297
Buckley, William F., 44–45
Budget deficits. *See* Deficits
Budget, federal
    balanced, 92
    Congressional Budget Act and, 158
    new revenues for, 163–65
    populist appeals on, 69
    projections for, 92–93, 363
    for social services, 295
    supply-side economics and, 157, 164,
        167–68, 175n8
    See also Defense spending
Bureau of Land Management, 236
Bureau of Mines, 236
Bureau of Reclamation, 236
Burger, Warren, 325n94, 331, 342, 344,
    347
Burke, Sheila, 223
Burt, Richard, 136–38, 141, 147–49
Bush, George H. W.
    conservatist view of, 56
    deregulation and, 8
    election of, 369
    on environmental issues, 251
    European Community and, 150
    on immigration, 272
    judicial appointments by, 350
    on Nicaragua, 366
    oil industry and, 173
    policy agenda of, 4
    populist appeals of, 75t, 76
    scholarly consensus on, 360
    on supply-side economics, 362
    tax expenditures and, 174
    welfare and, 221, 227, 231n77
Bush, George W.
    judicial appointments by, 350
    Reagan revolution and, 12, 76–77
    Social Security reform and, 9, 203–4
    tax reform and, 173
"Business, Ballots, and Bureaus" speech,
    65
Byrd, Robert, 348

Cabaniss, Nabors, 310
Cabinet Council on Natural Resources and
    Environment, 236–37, 246, 248
Calhoun, John C., 174n2

California
  abortion legislation, 297
  immigration and, 262, 270
  minority set-aside program, 290
  offshore drilling proposals, 237–38
  Proposition 13, 157
California Environmental Quality Act, 234
California governor, Reagan as
  on abortion, 297
  campaign for, 63–64, 66–67
  conservatist view of, 28–29
  environment and, 233–34
  immigration and, 262
  populist appeals of, 66–67
  social policy of, 52
  tax reform and, 52, 156
  welfare and, 226
Call to Return, 3, 43, 45, 55
Camarota, Steven, 272
Campaigns
  1980 presidential, 53, 67–68, 184, 194,
    235, 301–2
  abortion and, 300–302, 321n48, 321n50
  for California governor, 63–64, 66–67
  environmental issues and, 235, 244–45
  populist appeals in, 67–68, 73–74, 73t, 75t
  Social Security reform and, 184, 194
Campbell, Carroll, 194
Canada, acid rain and, 243–44
Cannon, Lou
  on abortion, 304, 324n75
  on deficits, 363
  on environmental issues, 235
  on government, 65, 67
  on immigration, 263
  on the poor, 214
  on popularity polls, 223
  on Reagan's personality, 2, 357–59
  on tax reform, 155
Capital income, 159–60, 163, 166
Capitalism, 45, 49, 55–56, 213
Capra, Frank, 49–50
Carleson, Robert, 213
Carlucci, Frank, 365–66
Carpenter, Smith L., 63, 76, 78n15
Carswell, Harold, 308, 348
Carter, Jimmy
  on abortion, 300, 321n48
  on affirmative action, 287

  on Bork, 347
  debate with, 86
  on environmental issues, 235
  feminists and, 300, 321–22n51, 323n57
  on immigration, 261
  judicial appointments by, 328t, 329–30,
    332–33, 338t–40t
  on loopholes, 158
  on national security, 87, 89, 91–92
  personality of, 357
  policy agenda of, 4
  populist appeals of, 75–76, 75t
  presidential campaign (1980), 301–2
  social issues and, 301
  on Social Security reform, 184
  on water resources, 81n69, 246–47
Carter, Rosalyn, 321n50
Casey, William E., 97, 99, 134
Catholic Church
  1984 election and, 308–9
  on abortion, 297, 303–4, 312
  judicial appointments and, 337, 338t
  Republican Party and, 294, 301
CDC. See Centers for Disease Control
CDU. See Christian Democratic Union
CEA. See Council of Economic Advisers
Cecchini, Paolo, 148
Census Bureau, 272, 290
Center for Immigration Studies, 272
Centers for Disease Control (CDC), 241–42
Central America, 96–98, 261, 277–78n11
Central Intelligence Agency (CIA), 138–39,
    367
Centrist liberals, 55
Chafee, John, 219, 249
Chamber of Commerce, 284–85, 288
Chambers, Whittaker, 29, 43–44, 51
Chapman, Bruce, 170, 180n47
Chapman, Leonard, 261
Chapoton, John (Buck), 163, 166, 169
Charity, 217
Cheney, Dick, 215
Chernenko, Konstantin, 118
Chernyaev, Anatoly, 124–26, 128, 146
Chesterton, G.K., 33
Chicago Council of Foreign Relations, 90
Child nutrition programs, 214–15
China, 295
Chiswick, Barry, 272

Christian coalition, 11, 294, 369
Christian Democratic Union (CDU), 140
Christian fundamentalism, 47, 299
Christianity, practical, 20
CIA. *See* Central Intelligence Agency
Circuit court judges, 328t
Citizen politicians, 63–64, 76
Citizens for Tax Justice, 168
"City on a Hill" image, 21
Civil religion, 35–36
Civil rights, 283–92
   conservatist movement and, 46
   neoconservatives on, 47–48
   Republican Party on, 283, 285, 314n8
   standard account of, 285–86
   statistical enforcement programs for, 283
Civil Rights Act of 1964, 46, 286
Civil war, in Central America, 96–98
Clark, William P., 134, 138, 239
Class, race and, 40
Clay, Lucius, 314n8
Clean Air Act, 243
Clifford, Clark, 357
Clinton, Bill
   1992 election of, 56
   on big government, 57
   on civil rights, 289
   conservatism and, 369
   government shutdown and, 34
   government spending under, 368
   on immigration, 259
   judicial appointments by, 329–30, 350
   populist appeals of, 75t
   scholarly consensus on, 360
   tax reform and, 173–74
   welfare and, 222, 225–26
Coal-fired power plants, 243–44
Coastal Barrier Resources Act, 247
Coastal Zone Management Act, 238
Cold War, 113–32
   America's mission in, 27, 86
   Chambers on, 43–44
   end of, 5, 36, 113–16, 129–30, 130n1, 367–68
   Europe and, 133, 145–47
   Reagan Victory School theory of, 114–15,
   Soviet Union collapse and, 126–28

   See also Arms control negotiations; Soviet Union
Collectivism, 74
Commentary, 47
Commission on Immigration Reform, 259–60
Commission on Strategic Forces, 95
Common man, 52
Communication, 33, 61, 361, 370
Communism
   in Central America, 277–78n11
   conservatist view of, 51
   end of, 27
   expansionism of, 97
   vs. freedom, 43–44
   fusionist view of, 45
   motion picture industry and, 25
   threat of, 3–4, 26–27, 52, 65, 86, 120
Community Work Experience Programs (CWEP), 213, 226
Compassionate conservatism, 76–77
Comprehensive Environmental Response, Compensation and Liability Act of 1980, 240–41, 243
Conable, Barber, 186, 198–99
Congressional Budget Act (1975), 158
Congressional Politics of Immigration Reform, The (Gimpel and Edwards), 267
Conner, Roger, 271
Conservatism, 17, 40–60
   in the 1960s and 1970s, 46–49
   of Bush, George H. W., 56
   California governorship and, 28–29
   capitalism and, 55–56
   compassionate, 76–77
   conflict within, 54–58
   cultural, 35
   development of, 3, 355, 369–70
   emergence of (1950s–1960s), 44–46
   Europe and, 45
   freedom and, 43
   free market and, 44, 55
   fusionist philosophy of, 45, 47, 51–52, 54
   grassroots, 294, 296, 313
   intellectual origins of, 41–44
   legal agenda of, 331
   morality and, 46–47, 296

vs. neoconservatism, 48
postwar, 42–44
of Reagan, 49–54, 355
social issues and, 55, 293–95
social vs. economic, 46–47, 294, 312–13
women and, 294, 296, 313, 316–17n25
See also New Right
Conservatist Digest, 312
Conservative Action Committee, 217
Conservative Party, 297
Conspiracy theories, 25, 29
Constanza, Midge, 300
Constitutional minimalism, 289
Constitution of the United States, 48
Consumer culture, 55–56
Consumption taxes, 169, 176n10
Contract with America, 56–57
Conventional forces, 140, 142, 145
Cooke, Terence, 297
Coors, Holly, 217
Corporations
affirmative action and, 284–85, 287–88, 290
hazardous waste and, 241
immigration and, 288–89
profits of, 63
tax reform and, 159, 167–69, 173, 181n62
vs. workers, 63–64, 71
Corruption, 124
Council of Economic Advisers (CEA), 270
Council on Environmental Quality, 235–36
Criminal justice, 332
Croce, Benedetto, 36
Cronin, Thomas, 61
Cronkite, Walter, 265
Croson decision, 289
Cuba
Grenada and, 97, 100
Nicaragua and, 135
refugees from, 261, 263, 265
Cultural conservatism, 35
Culture
consumer, 55–56
popular, 57
social issues and, 294
Cuomo, Mario, 222
CWEP. See Community Work Experience Programs

Dallek, Robert, 61, 72, 360
Danforth amendment, 311–12
Danforth, John, 311
Daniels, Mitch, 222
Darman, Richard
on corporate taxes, 169
influence of, 216
Moynihan and, 224
on Reagan's advisors, 219–20
on Social Security reform, 8, 193, 197–99
on tax reform, 7, 165–68, 171, 179n46
on welfare, 211, 218, 221–22
Darmon, Richard, 163
Death benefits, 188
Deaver, Michael, 97, 134, 186, 216, 366
Declaration of Independence, 48
DeConcini, Dennis, 347–48
Defense, national. See National security
Defense spending, 4–5, 90–93
deficits and, 215–16
Gorbachev on, 126–27
increases in, 107–8, 117, 127–28, 135, 364, 367
presidential campaign (1980) and, 87
Soviet economy and, 114, 124, 126–29
tax reform and, 161
Deficit Reduction Act of 1984 (DEFRA), 167–69
Deficits
defense spending and, 215–16
increases in, 7, 93, 363–65
inflation and, 166
reduction plans, 163–65, 177n22
Social Security reform and, 163, 200
tax cuts and, 157, 159–61, 362
TEFRA and, 161–63
welfare and, 215
DEFRA. See Deficit Reduction Act of 1984
Democracy, 42, 48
Democratic globalism, 51, 53
Democratic Party
affirmative action and, 285
conservatist movement of, 369
environmental issues and, 243–44
family planning and, 306
immigration and, 276, 282n75
Reagan in, 62–63
social issues and, 301
Social Security reform and, 182, 194–95

Democratic Party *(continued)*
   Watt and, 238–39
   white southerners in, 46
   women and, 294, 312
Dense Pack system, 95
Denton, Jeremiah, 306
Department of Justice, 330–33,
Department of the Interior, 9, 236–39, 243,
   246
Depreciation, 159
Deregulation, 8–9, 251
Destler, I. M., 134
Détente, 89–90, 121, 134
Dewey, John, 32
Dewey, Thomas, 63
Dickenson, Russell E., 237
Dilley, Patricia E., 206n27
Dingell, John D., 241
Dingman, Dick, 308
Dioxin, 241–42
DiPietro, Aldona, 189–90
Disability benefits, 188–89, 193
Disarmament. *See* Arms control
   negotiations
Discrimination
   reverse, 284–85, 287–88
   sex, 311
District court judges, 328t, 333, 336, 340t
Diversity, 288–89
Divine election, 21
Dobrynin, Anatoly, 123, 131n13
Dole, Elizabeth, 10, 284, 303, 308
Dole, Robert
   on Bork, 348
   Social Security reform and, 195, 198–99,
      203
   tax reform and, 162, 164, 166
   welfare and, 215, 218
Domenici, Pete, 185, 203, 215
Donovan, Hedley, 362–63
Donovan, Raymond J., 284
Dos Rios Dam, 234
Doty, David, 335
Douglas, Helen Gahagan, 64, 355
Douglas, Stephen, 25
Dred Scott decision, 309
Dresser, Robert, 314n8
D'Sousa, Dinish, 311
Duberstein, Kenneth, 199

Duck stamps, 249
Dunlap, Louise, 239
Durenberger, David, 219, 335
Dwyer, William, 335

Early retirement, 184, 187, 190–91, 194–
   95, 201
Earned Income Tax Credit (EITC), 212, 222
Easterbook, Frank, 331
Eastern Europe, 147
Eastern Germany, 147
East, John P., 302–3
Eastland, Terry, 330
Economic globalization, 288, 364
Economic growth, 362, 364–65
Economic libertarianism, 49, 53
Economic policy, 5–6, 9, 361–65
   international, 147–50
   populist appeal of, 71–72
   See also Budget, federal; Supply-side
      economics; Tax reform
Economic Recovery Tax Act of 1981
   (ERTA), 159–62, 170
Economics, planned, 124
Edwards, James, 267, 273
Edwards, Jonathan, 22
EEOC. *See* Equal Employment Opportunity
   Commission
Ehrlichman, John, 318n29
Eisenhower, Dwight
   judicial appointments by, 327, 328t, 329,
      338t–39t
   leadership style of, 80–81n66
   popularity of, 44
   populist appeals of, 75t
EITC. *See* Earned Income Tax Credit
Elites
   government, 51–53, 64
   intellectual, 51, 66–67
   neoconservative, 57
Ellwood, David, 222
El Salvador, 96–97, 135, 261
Emergency Wetlands Resources Act, 249–50
Employee Retirement Income Security Act
   (ERISA), 288
Employees, rights of, 287–88
Employer sanctions, 261, 263, 265–69,
   271–72
Encounter groups, 293

Entin, Stephen J., 189–90
Entitlement spending, 162, 186. *See also* Welfare
Entrepreneurs, 285, 362
Environmental policy, 8–9, 233–56
  on acid rain, 243–45
  administrative appointments and, 235–36, 240, 242
  administrative fiat and, 233–34, 250
  campaign strategies and, 235, 244–45
  of deregulation, 251
  extremist, 242
  goals of, 233, 240
  on hazardous waste, 241–43, 250
  health and, 250
  industry and, 244
  markets and, 251
  public concern for, 250–51
  on water resources, 234, 246–50
Environmental Policy Institute, 239
Environmental Protection Agency (EPA), 9, 235–36, 239–40, 244–45
Equal Employment Opportunity Commission (EEOC), 284–85, 288–89
Equality, 48, 50, 53, 286, 293
Equal Rights Amendment (ERA), 11, 296, 298, 317n25, 319n36
  ratification of, 299–300, 321n50
ERISA. *See* Employee Retirement Income Security Act
Ermarth, Fritz, 139
ERTA. *See* Economic Recovery Tax Act of 1981
Ervin, Sam, 299
Essentialism, 42
Eurêka, 142
Europe, 133–52
  arms control negotiations and, 136, 149
  Cold War and, 133, 145–47
  conservatist view of, 45
  conventional forces in, 140, 142, 145
  exports to, 149
  integration of, 133, 147–50
  missile systems in, 135–37, 139–40, 144
  nuclear weapons in, 136, 144
  Soviet Union and, 135
  Strategic Defense Initiative and, 140–45, 149
  trade negotiations and, 147–48

European Community, 133, 147–50
European Union, 133
Evangelical Christians, 294, 296, 300–301, 312
Evangelical Protestantism, 25, 301, 315n19
Evil, 25–26, 33–34, 36
Evil empire speech, 26, 117, 125, 129, 356
Excise taxes, 216
Exclusionary rule, 332
Executive Order 11246, 283–86, 290
Executive privilege, 241
Experience, 32
Experts, 76
Exports, 149

FAIR. *See* Federation for American Immigration Reform
Fairness issue, 214–15, 221
Fairy-stories, 36–37
Falkland Islands crisis, 98
Family Assistance Plan, 212, 226, 295, 314n11
Family planning, 304–6, 307t, 342
Family Support Act of 1988, 8, 222–23
Family values, 70–71, 327
FAR. *See* Force d'Action Rapide
Farabundo Martí Front for National Liberation (FMLN), 96
FDP. *See* Free Democratic Party
Federal government *See* Government
Federalism, 331
Federalist Society, 331, 345
Federal judges. *See* Judicial appointments
Federal Water Pollution Control Act Amendments of 1972, 247
Federation for American Immigration Reform (FAIR), 270–71, 274, 278n15
Fein, Bruce, 331, 350
Feldstein, Martin, 149, 164, 166–68, 184
Feminist movement
  on abortion, 296–97
  Carter and, 300, 321–22n51, 323n57
  emergence of, 296
  gender gap and, 304, 312
  Reagan and, 305
Ferraro, Geraldine, 221
Fielding, Fred, 327, 334
Fink, Judy, 297
Fish and Wildlife Service, 236, 248

FitzGerald, Frances, 104
Fitzwater, Sidney, 336
Flat-rate taxes, 157–58, 163–66
Flood control projects, 247
FMLM. *See* Farabundo Martí Front for
    National Liberation
Food programs, 219–21
Food Research and Action Center, 214
Food stamps program, 211, 216, 218,
    220–21
Force d'Action Rapide (FAR), 139
Ford, Betty, 298–300
Ford, Gerald
    on abortion, 298–300
    on Bork, 347
    on the ERA, 299–300
    on foreign policy, 296
    on immigration, 261
    judicial appointments by, 328t, 329–30,
        332, 338t–40t
    populist appeals of, 75t
    social issues and, 296
    on welfare, 218
Foreign policy
    conservatists on, 48
    Europe and, 133, 138
    of Ford, 296
    goals of, 134–35
    leadership and, 4
    neoconservatives on, 48
    of Nixon, 295
    priorities of, 356
    staff members for, 133–34, 149
Forsythe, Edwin, 249
Fortas, Abe, 329
Fortune 500 companies, 285
Founding principles, 21, 25, 32, 45, 48,
    50, 289
France, 136, 142, 144
Franco-German brigade, 142
Frankel, Charles, 18, 32, 138–39
Fratricide, 95
Free Democratic Party (FDP), 140
Freedom
    as America's mission, 20–21, 26, 50
    vs. communism, 29, 43–44
    conservatism and, 43–44
    extinction of, 31
    fusionism on, 45

    goal of, 53
    God and, 33
    government and, 30–34, 36, 51
    markets and, 34, 49
    vs. order, 42–43
    private power and, 34
    property and, 55
    socialism and, 51
Free market
    conservatist view of, 55
    freedom and, 49
    vs. government collectivism, 28
    moral superiority of, 43
    poverty and, 217
    wheat sales and, 120
Freidel, Frank, 360
Fried, Charles, 309–10
Friedman, Milton, 156
Friends of the Earth, 239
Frum, David, 293
Fuller, Craig, 216, 249
Fundamentalist Christians. *See* Christian
    fundamentalism
Fund for Animals, 235
Fusionism, 45, 47, 51–52, 54

Gaddis, John Lewis, 107
Gag rule, 306
Garn amendment, 302
Garthoff, Raymond L., 139, 151n12, 367
Gas exploration, 237–38, 249
Gasper, Jo Ann, 310
GATT (General Agreement on Trade and
    Tariffs), 148
Gearhart bill, 63
Gender gap, 304, 312, 326n105
General Electric Company, 51, 65, 155–
    56
Geneva summit, 126–27, 130n1, 136, 143–
    44, 146, 367
Genscher, Hans-Dietrick, 140
Gephardt, Richard A., 164, 191
Germany, 136, 139, 139–42
Gerster, Carolyn, 297, 308
Gesell, Gerhard, 324–25n81
General Electric Theater, 65
Ghorbanifar, Manucher, 105, 107
Gianelli, William R., 247
Gimpel, James, 267, 273

Gingrich, Newt, 56–57, 101, 225–26
Ginsberg, Benjamin, 369
Ginsburg, Douglas H., 331, 341, 345, 349
Glasnost, 130n1
Glazer, Nathan, 212
Globalism, democratic, 51, 53
Globalization, economic, 288, 364
God, America and, 20–21, 33
Godlessness, 44
Goldberg, Arthur J., 329
Goldwater, Barry, 46, 62, 344
    Reagan's speech for, 66–67, 73, 156, 183
Gorbachev, Mikhail
    agenda of, 146
    arms control negotiations and, 114, 143–45, 149–50
    Dec. 17, 1987 Politburo speech, 146–47
    on defense spending, 126–27
    domestic reform policy, 114
    Geneva summit and, 126–27, 130n1, 136, 143–44, 146, 367
    on illegal immigrants, 277–78n11
    INF treaty and, 136
    "New Thinking" policy, 114–15, 123–26, 129, 130n1
    Reagan's meetings with, 4–5, 104, 146, 367
    Reykjavik summit and, 144–46, 367
    rise to power, 113
    on SDI, 128, 145
Gore, Al, 222, 369
Gorsuch, Anne M., 9, 240–43, 245
Gorton, Slade, 185, 335
Government
    domestic role of, 33–34
    elites, 51–53, 64
    faith in, 370
    federal vs. state, 27–28
    freedom and, 30–34, 36, 51
    growth of, 29–31, 34, 45, 56
    vs. individuals, 28–29
    innovation and, 32–33
    vs. nation, 27–29
    power of, 41–42
    rule by, 28–29
    shutdown of, 34
    the system of, 50
    vs. taxpayers, 64

threat of, 3, 25, 29, 65
World War II and, 41
See also Big government; Budget, federal; State government
Government regulation
    changes in, 368–69
    by government elites, 52–53
    markets and, 34
    populist appeals on, 69, 72
    private power and, 34
    of wetlands, 248
Governor. See California governor, Reagan as
Graglia, Lino, 335
Graham, Katharine, 357
Gramm, Phil, 187
Grassley amendment, 302
Grassley, Charles E., 342
Grassroots conservatism, 294, 296, 313
Great Britain, 98, 142, 144
Great Communicator, 61, 370
Great Society program, 5, 210, 212, 216
Greenspan, Alan, 160, 177n22
Greenspan Commission, 8, 163, 198
Greenstein, Fred, 360
Greenstein, Robert, 211
Greider, William, 185
Grenada, 99–100
Gromyko, Andrei, 128
Groups
    primacy of, 43, 55
    rights of, 289, 294
Grove City College v. Bell, 311–12
Guaranteed income, 212
Guatemalan refugees, 261
Guestworkers, 265–67, 269, 271–72, 278n15
Guns, duties on, 249–50

Habib, Philip, 98
Hadley, Arthur, 87
Haig, Alexander M., Jr.
    on communism, 97
    Falkland Islands crisis and, 98
    foreign policy and, 134
    on Nicaragua, 366
    pipeline sanctions and, 138
    on Reagan's personality, 358
Haines, Gerald K, 138

Haitian refugees, 261
Hall, Cynthia Holcomb, 343
Hamby, Alonzo, 360–61
Handicapped children, 324–25n81
Handlin, Oscar, 269
Harper, Edwin, 308
Harris v. McRae, 300
Harvey, William, 335
Hatch amendment, 302–3, 308
Hatch, Orrin, 302, 304, 343–44, 347
Hatfield, Mark, 303
Hayakawa, S. I., 304
Hayek, Friedrich von, 43
Hazardous waste, 241–43, 250
Health, environment and, 250
Health Services and Pregnancy Prevention
    and Care Act, 306
Heckler, Margaret, 11, 284, 305
Heclo, Hugh, 59n17
Heflin, Howell, 348
Hegel, Georg Wilhelm Friedrich, 22
Heinz, John, 335
Helms amendment, 302–5, 308
Helms, Jesse, 302, 336, 341
Heritage Foundation, 224
Hernandez, John, 240
Herrington, John, 284
Hesburgh, Theodore, 261, 263, 267, 270
HICCASP. *See* Hollywood Independent
    Citizens Committee of the Arts,
    Sciences and Profession
Higginbotham, Patrick, 342
Hinckley, John, 357
Hispanics. *See* Latinos
Hiss, Alger, 29
History
    contemporary, 36
    philosophy of, 17–19, 25, 35–36, 53
Hobbs, Charles, 222–24
Hodel, Donald, 284
Hodgson, Godfrey, 356
Hodsoll, Francis, 264
Hoff, Joan, 295
Hollywood Independent Citizens
    Committee of the Arts, Sciences and
    Profession (HICCASP), 62
"Hollywood Speech," 64
Honduras, 135
Hostages, 91, 100, 105–6, 134

Howard, Christopher, 222
Howe, Geoffrey, 100
Huddleston, Walter D., 264
Human Events, 51, 356
Human experience, 32
Human Life Review, 309
Human life statute, 302
Human nature, 48
Human resources departments, 287–88
Humor, 359
Humphrey, Hubert, 62, 317–18n28
Hunger issue, 220
Hyde amendment, 298, 318n34
Hyde, Henry J., 298, 341, 343
Hyland, William, 136

ICBMs. *See* Intercontinental ballistic
    missiles
Identification cards, 265–66, 273, 275
Ideology, 2–3, 355–56
    blind spots in, 33–36
    conservatism and, 42, 58n3
    development of, 33
    vs. interests, 46
    judicial appointments and, 329–30
    old-fashioned, 19, 32
    pragmatic, 224–25
    public philosophy and, 2–3, 17–39
    rigidity of, 276, 357
    vs. slogans, 19
    struggle about, 18
Idolatry, 35
Iklé, Fred, 134
Illegal immigrants, 10, 259–82
    amnesty for, 261, 263–69, 271–72, 275
    asylum for, 263, 273–74
    Commission on Immigration Reform on,
        259–60
    economic benefits of, 272
    employer sanctions and, 261, 263, 265–
        69, 271–72
    IRCA on, 267–72
    from Mexico, 262, 269–72, 277–78n11
    public opinion of, 264
    statistics on, 260–61, 267, 272
Immigration, 10, 259–82
    affirmative action and, 288–90
    corporations and, 288–89
    economic benefits of, 272, 274

identification cards and, 265–66, 273, 275
mass, 288–91
national origins system for, 260
naturalization and, 262
public opinion of, 259, 264, 274–75
sources of, 260–61
special interest groups and, 274
statistics on, 260–61, 272, 276
welfare and, 267
See also Illegal immigrants; Refugees
Immigration Act of 1965, 10, 276
Immigration and Naturalization Service,
267
Immigration Reform and Control Act
(IRCA), 10, 267–72, 276, 289
Imperialism, 48
Inaugural address, 68, 70t, 73t, 74, 75t
Income taxes. See Tax reform; Taxes
Individualism, 43, 50
Individuals
autonomy of, 53
vs. government, 28–29
liberation of, 58
moral integrity of, 43
primacy of, 43, 55
rights of, 289
Industry, 244. See also Corporations
INF. See Intermediate-range nuclear forces
(INF) treaty
Inflation, 156, 161, 166, 183, 363
Innocence, 24–27, 36
Innovation, 32–33
Insider books, 38n21
Integration, 46
Intercontinental ballistic missiles (ICBMs),
123, 365
Interests, vs. ideas, 46
Interior Department, 9, 236–39, 243, 246
Intermarriage, 290
Intermediate-range nuclear forces (INF)
treaty, 115, 135–36, 139–40, 143,
149, 367
International economic policy, 147–50
International Ladies Garment Workers
Union, 62–63
Iran
Afghan resistance and, 106–7
arms for, 104–6, 143, 145
hostages in, 91, 134

Iran-Contra scandal, 104–6, 143, 145
decision making and, 276, 366–67
legacy of, 370
public opinion of, 223
IRCA. See Immigration Reform and
Control Act
Irrigation projects, 246
Isolationism, 51
Israel, 98, 104–5

Jackson, Andrew, 61, 64
Jackson, Robert H., 343–44
Jefferson, Mildred, 297
Jencks, Christopher, 271, 276
Jepsen, Dee, 305
Jepsen, Roger W., 342
Jews, judicial appointments of, 338t
Jobs proposals, 213, 220
Joffe, Josef, 140
Johnson, Douglas, 304, 312
Johnson, Lyndon
election of, 66
Great Society program of, 5, 210, 212, 216
on immigration, 260
judicial appointments by, 328t, 329,
338t–40t
populist appeals of, 75t
Johnston, J. Bennett, 348
Jordan, Barbara, 259–60
Judicial appointments, 11–12, 327–53, 368–
69.
abortion and, 304, 306, 308, 325–26n94,
327, 334, 337
affirmative action and, 289, 332
appellate court, 333, 335–36, 340t
circuit court, 328t
considerations for, 306, 327–30
democratic model of, 329
district court, 328t, 333, 336, 340t
ideology and, 329–30
legacy of, 350–51
lower court, 327, 333–35, 337–40, 338t–
40t
of minorities, 333, 337, 339t
by president, 328t, 329–30, 338t–39t
pro-life, 304, 306, 308, 325–26n94, 327
Reagan's involvement with, 351
religion and, 337, 338t
selection process for, 330, 333–36

Judicial appointments *(continued)*
  Senate confirmation of, 336–37
  of women, 337, 338t
  See also Supreme court
Jurisprudence
  liberal, 331, 344
  of original intention, 332
Justice Department, 330–33,

Kampelman, Max, 144
Kant, Immanuel, 17–18
Katz, Michael, 210, 214
Kazin, Michael, 61, 68–69
Kearse, Amalya L., 341
Kemp, Jack, 156–58
Kennedy, Anthony M., 337, 341, 343, 349–50
Kennedy, Cornelia B., 341
Kennedy, Edward
  Gorbachev and, 144
  Grove City bill and, 311
  on immigration, 274
  judicial appointments and, 336, 344, 346
  on Reagan's personality, 361
Kennedy, John F., 328t, 329, 338t–39t
Kennedy, Robert, 75t
Khachigian, Ken, 68
Khrushchev, Nikita, 124
Kirkpatrick, Jeane, 97
Kirk, Russell, 43
Kissinger, Henry, 295–96
Kiwanis International Convention, 64
Kleinberg, David, 190
Kohl, Helmut, 139–40, 142
Koop, C. Everett, 305, 310
Kozinski, Alex, 336
Kraft, Michael E., 251
Kristol, William, 57
Kurland, Philip, 334, 347
Kutler, Stanley, 360

Labor force. *See* Workers
Labor unions, 63
Lacovara, Philip, 334
Laffer, Arthur, 175n8, 215
Laham, Nicholas, 263, 272–73, 286
Laird, Melvin R., 89
Land and Water Conservation Act, 249
Landers, Ann, 103

Langley, Edward, 65
Latinos
  affirmative action and, 289–90
  on immigration, 268, 274
  judicial appointments of, 338t
Laxalt, Paul, 94
Leadership Conference on Civil Rights, 285–86
Leadership style, 29–31, 276, 356–59, 363
  consensual, 71–74, 224–25
  rhetorical, 61
Leahy, Patrick, 336, 347
Lebanon, 35, 98–101, 105–6
Legacy, Reagan's, 355–75
Legal reform, 330–32
Leggett, Robert E., 138
Lemann, Nicholas, 38n21
Levi, Edward H., 345
Lew, Jack, 199
Liberalism, 33–35, 55, 276, 294, 369
Liberal jurisprudence, 331, 344
Liberation, 58, 294
Libertarianism, 44–45, 49, 53
Life Amendment Political Action Committee, 303
Light, Paul, 198
Limited Nuclear Test Ban Treaty, 95
Lincoln, Abraham, 25, 48
Livermore, Norman (Ike), 253n28
Loewenheim, Francis, 367
Lofton, John, 312
Logging industry, 237
Long, Russell, 161
"Looking Out a Window" speech, 52
Loopholes, 158, 162–63, 168, 170–71
Lott, Trent, 215
Lower court judges, 327, 333–35, 337–40, 338t–40t
Low Income Opportunity Advisory Board, 226–27
Lure of progress, 3, 43, 45, 55

Maastricht Treaty, 149
MacEachin, Douglas, 121–22, 139
MacIntyre, Alasdair, 17
MAD. *See* Mutual assured destruction
Maddox, Thomas, 267
Madison, James, 48
Majority, tyranny of, 42

Manhattan Project, 41
Manion, Daniel, 335–36, 340
Manpower Demonstration Research
    Corporation (MDRC), 214
March for Life, 303
Mariel boatlift, 263, 265
Markets
    environmental policy and, 251
    government regulation and, 34
    illegal labor and, 270
    See also Free market
Markman, Stephen, 332–33
Married women, vs. single, 294, 301–2,
    312, 326n105
Marshall, Thurgood, 329
Marshner, Connie, 308
masses, the, 52
Mass immigration, 288–91
Materialism, 55–56
Matlock, Jack, 119, 122
Mazzoli, Romano, 262, 264, 267–71, 273
McCloskey, Michael, 238
McFarlane, Robert C.
    on foreign policy, 134
    on Grenada, 99–100
    Iran-Contra scandal and, 105, 366
    on SDI, 123, 141
    on the Soviet Union, 119, 121–22
McGovern, George, 317–18n28
McGregor, James R., 335
McIntyre, James Francis, 297
McIntyre, Robert, 168
McKinley, William, 359
McLure, Charles, 166, 169
McRae, Harris v., 300
MDRC. See Manpower Demonstration
    Research Corporation
Mead, Lawrence, 222
Meanness, moral, 217–18
Mecklenburg, Marjory, 297, 305
Medicaid
    abortion and, 298, 300, 324n81
    cuts in, 215–16
    increases in, 212
    state government and, 218
Medicare, 324n81, 364
Meese, Edwin
    on abortion, 324n75
    on affirmative action, 284–85

on Anderson, Martin, 215–16
departure of, 219–20
on immigration, 265, 270, 272
influence of, 162, 216
judicial appointments and, 327, 334,
    342–44, 349
priorities of, 332
on Social Security reform, 186, 207n37
on tax reform, 164
on welfare, 210, 220–21
Melnick, R. Shep, 250
Memoirs, insider, 38n21
Memory, 35
Metzenbaum, Howard M., 311
Mexico
    guestworkers from, 265–67, 271–72,
        278n15
    illegal immigrants from, 262, 269–72,
        277–78n11
Meyer, Frank S., 3, 45, 52
Michel, Robert, 197, 202, 215, 239
Migratory Bird Conservation Fund,
    249
Military force
    conventional, 140, 142, 145
    superiority of, 26
    uses of, 96–102
    See also National security; Nuclear
        weapons
Military spending. See Defense spending
Miller, James C., III, 284
Milton, John, 30–31
Minimalism, constitutional, 289
Mining industry, 237
Minorities, judicial appointments of, 333,
    337, 339t
Minority preference policies, 286, 288–90
Miranda warnings, 332
Missile systems
    in Europe, 135–37, 139–40, 144
    intercontinental ballistic, 123, 365
    intermediate-range nuclear, 115, 135–36,
        139–40, 143, 149, 367
    MX, 94–96
    zero-option proposal, 136–37
    See also Arms control negotiations;
        Strategic Defense Initiative
Mitterrand, François, 136–37, 139
Mohr, James, 303

MOMI. *See* Mothers Outraged at the
    Murder of Innocents
Mondale, Walter
    defeat of, 226
    on the environment, 245
    on immigration, 269, 273
    tax reform and, 167, 169
Morality
    conservatist view of, 46–47, 296
    free market and, 43
    meanness of, 217–18
    vs. political problems, 33
    traditional, 23
Moral Majority, 342
Moran, Don, 190
Moretti, Robert, 225
Morris, Dick, 225, 357
Morris, Edmund, 359, 370
Mothers Outraged at the Murder of
    Innocents (MOMI), 297
Motion picture industry, 25, 64
Motives, 25
Mott, William Penn, Jr., 246
Mountain States Legal Foundation, 236
Moyers, Bill, 215
Moynihan, Daniel Patrick
    on deficits, 160
    Family Support Act and, 8
    on Social Security reform, 195, 199
    on supply-side economics, 362
    on welfare, 222–26, 231n77
Mr. Smith Goes to Washington, 49–50
Mujahideen, 106–7, 114, 135
Murphy, George, 143
Murphy, James M., 148–49
Muskie, Edmund, 105
Mutual assured destruction (MAD), 85, 88
MX missile, 94–95
Myers, Robert J., 189–90

Nader, Ralph, 369
NARAL. *See* National Abortion and
    Reproductive Rights Action League
Nathan, Richard, 213
Nation, 22, 27–29, 35
National Abortion and Reproductive Rights
    Action League (NARAL), 316–17n25
National Association of Manufacturers,
    284–85, 288

National Bar Association, 333
National Commission on Social Security
    Reform, 8, 163, 198
National Conference of Catholic Bishops,
    297, 303
National Conference of Christians and
    Jews, 217
National Conservative Political Action
    Committee (NCPAC), 346
National identification cards, 265–66, 273, 275
National Organization for Women, 311
National origins system, 260
National Park Service, 236–37, 246, 250
National Pro-Life Political Action
    Committee, 301, 303
National Review, 44–45, 51, 66
National Rifle Association, 369
National Right to Life Committee (NRLC)
    establishment of, 297
    on the Grove City bill, 311–12
    on the Hatch amendment, 303
    on the Helms amendment, 304
    on O'Connor, 341–42
    women and, 316–17n25
National security, 27, 85–112
    agenda for, 86–90
    legacy of, 365–68
    military force and, 96–102
    strengthening, 89–90
    See also Arms control negotiations;
        Defense spending; Military force
National Security Council (NSC), 134,
    365–66
National Security Decision Directive 166
    (NSDD 166), 107
National Security Decision Directive 75
    (NSDD 75), 95
National Taxpayers Union, 369
National Wildlife Federation, 237
National Wildlife Refuge System, 249–50
National Women's Party, 319n36
NATO (North Atlantic Treaty
    Organization), 135, 142
Naturalization, 262
Natural resources, 233–56. *See also*
    Environmental policy
Navigation projects, 246–47
NCPAC. *See* National Conservative
    Political Action Committee

Nelson, Alan, 269–70
Neoconservatism
    1980 presidential campaign and, 53
    vs. conservatism, 48
    definition of, 13n5
    evolution of, 47–48
    social policy and, 9–10
    vs. traditionalists, 54
    on virtue, 57
Neutralism, 139
New Deal
    belief in, 294
    creeping socialism of, 43
    purpose of, 41, 64, 209
    reforming, 5, 216
New Federalism proposal, 7, 211, 218–19,
    226
New Right
    on abortion, 10–11
    concerns of, 54
    definition of, 315n17
    vs. fusionism, 47
    judicial appointments and, 11, 330–31,
    348
    origins of, 296
    social policy and, 9–10, 12
    See also Conservatism
"New Thinking" policy, 114–15, 123–26,
    129, 130n1
Nicaragua
    aid to, 96–97, 366
    Iran-Contra scandal and, 104–6, 145,
    223
    Soviet Union and, 135
Nickles, Donald, 341
Niskanen, William, 190
Nitrogen control programs, 243
Nitze, Paul, 144
Nixon, Richard
    1968 convention and, 295
    on abortion, 297–98, 317–18n28, 318n29
    on affirmative action, 287–88
    on environmentalists, 79n39
    Family Assistance Plan and, 295, 314n11
    foreign policy of, 295–96
    judicial appointments by, 328t, 330, 332,
    338t–40t
    on the poor, 212
    populist appeals of, 69, 75, 75t, 81n67

    relationship with Reagan, 64, 226,
        232n79
    on social issues, 295
    Treaty of Fifth Avenue and, 46
Nofziger, Lyn, 215
Noonan, Peggy, 356–57
North American Aerospace Defense
    Command, 102
North Atlantic Treaty Organization
    (NATO), 135, 142
North, David, 273–75
North, Oliver, 105–6, 366
Norton, Eleanor Holmes, 289
NRLC. See National Right to Life
    Committee
NSC. See National Security Council
NSDD 75, 95, 166, 107
Nuclear deterrence, 140–41
Nuclear freeze movement, 103–4
Nuclear weapons
    development of, 41
    elimination of, 4–5, 103, 141, 145,
        356
    in Europe, 136, 144
    Soviet thinking on, 87–88, 127–28
    See also Arms control negotiations
Nunn Amendment of 1984, 140, 151n18
NWF. See National Wildlife Federation

OASI. See Old-Age and Survivors (OASI)
    trust fund
OBRA. See Omnibus Budget Reconciliation
    Act
Occupational Safety and Health
    Administration (OSHA), 284, 288
O'Connor, Sandra Day, 306, 308, 325n87,
    341–43
O'Donnell, Kirk, 197–98
OECS. See Organization of Eastern
    Caribbean States
OFCC. See Office of Federal Contract
    Compliance
Office of Federal Contract Compliance
    (OFCC), 284
Office of Legal Policy, 12, 333, 350
Offshore drilling, 237–38
Oil industry, 173, 237–38, 249
Old-Age and Survivors (OASI) trust fund,
    198

Omnibus Budget Reconciliation Act
    (OBRA), 196, 211–19, 222
O'Neill, Thomas P.
    1980 elections and, 302
    on immigration, 268–69, 273–74
    on Reagan's personality, 358, 361–62
    relationship with Reagan, 225
    Social Security reform and, 6, 8, 184,
        194, 197–99, 202–3
    on Watt, 239
    on welfare, 210–11, 220
Opinion polls. See Public opinion polls
Opportunity, equality of, 48
Order, vs. freedom, 42–43
Organization of Eastern Caribbean States
    (OECS), 99
Ortega, Daniel, 96
OSHA. See Occupational Safety and Health
    Administration

Packwood, Robert, 172, 303–4, 311
Paine, Thomas, 22, 53
Palestine Liberation Organization (PLO), 98
Paramount amendment, 302
Passivity, 358–59
Pasztor, Andy, 244–45
Paternalism, 51
Patrimony, 43, 48
Patriotism, 31
Patronage, political, 329, 335
Paul, Alice, 319n36
Peace, 26–27
Pearlman, Ronald, 169
Pear, Robert, 269
People for the American Way, 346
People Like Us, 215
Percy, Charles, 301
Perestroika, 130n1, 146
Perkins, Carl, 210
Perle, Richard, 136, 144, 365
Personality
    American, 25
    Reagan's, 24, 40, 220, 356–59
Personal Responsibility and Work
    Opportunity Reconciliation Act
    (PRWORA), 209, 214, 225–27
Personnel management, 287–88
Pfaelzer, Mariana, 238
Philadelphia Plan, 284

Philosophy
    of history, 17–19, 25, 35–36, 53
    public, 2–3, 17–39
Pickle, J. J. (Jake), 186, 191–92, 196–98,
    200–201
Pipeline sanctions, 137–39, 149
Pipes, Richard E., 88
Placeholder taxes, 164–65
Planned Parenthood, 305–6
Planned Parenthood Federation of America,
    310
Platonism, 42
PLO. See Palestine Liberation Organization
Poindexter, John, 106, 366
Poland, 136
Policy planning, 4, 6–7
Political Action Conference, 302
Politicians, citizen, 63–64, 76
Politics
    corporations and, 64, 71
    leadership and, 29–31
    vs. moral problems, 33
    patronage and, 329, 335
    religion and, 32
Polls. See Public opinion polls
Pomerance, Rafe, 239
Poor, the
    tax reform and, 169–70
    welfare and, 212–15, 221
    working, 212–13
Pope Pius XII, 22
Popular culture, 57
Populism, 3, 61–81
    in the 1980 presidential campaign, 67–68
    California governorship and, 67
    conservatist, 69, 75
    cultural, 68–69, 72
    definition of, 77n5
    development of, 62–67
    economic, 57, 68–72
    vs. expertise, 76
    legacy of, 75–77
    rhetorical specialization of, 66, 72–77
    specialization of, 72–77
    in speeches, 70t, 73–74, 73t, 75t
Populist Persuasian, The (Kazin), 61
Portillo, Lopez, 264
Portney, Paul R., 233–34
Positive polarization, 69

Posner, Richard, 331
Postwar conservatism, 42–44
Poverty, 7, 209, 217
POWDR. *See* Protect Our Wetlands and
    Duck Resources
Powell, Lewis F., Jr., 326n94, 340, 345–46,
    349
Practical Christianity, 20
Prayer, school, 11, 303, 331
Presidential campaigns. *See* Campaigns
Presidential Task Force on Regulatory
    Relief, 8, 248
Private sector giving, 217
Privatization, 9, 183
Problems, moral vs. political, 33
Pro-family movement, 300–301, 308–9
Profits, 63, 217
Program for Better Jobs and Income, 213
Progress, lure of, 3, 43, 45, 55
Project for Fundamental Reform, 169
Project on Food Assistance and Poverty,
    211
Promised land, 20–21
Property, 43, 55
Property taxes, 156–57
Proposition 13, 157
Prosperity, 53
Protect Our Wetlands and Duck Resources
    (POWDR), 248
Protestantism
    evangelical, 25, 301, 315n19
    judicial appointments and, 338t
Providence, 21
PRWORA. *See* Personal Responsibility and
    Work Opportunity Reconciliation Act
Public Health Service Act, 306
Public opinion polls
    on Bork, 348
    on Central America, 97–98
    on environmental policy, 250–51
    on illegal immigrants, 264
    on immigration, 259, 264, 274–75
    on the Iran-Contra scandal, 223
    on Reagan, 216, 216t, 218, 357
Public philosophy, 2–3, 17–39
Puritanism, 21

Qaddafi, Muammar, 102
Quotas, 285

Race, class and, 40
Radicalism, 68
Radio speeches, 22, 30, 52, 286–87, 356.
    See also Reagan, Ronald, speeches of
Rambo, First Blood, 96
Ranney, Austin, 357
Reagan coalition, 47–49
Reagan diaspora, 369
Reagan Republicans, 56
Reagan revolution, 1–13, 215, 225–26, 289,
    294, 332
Reagan, In His Own Hand (Reagan), 286–
    87
Reagan, Maureen, 357
Reagan, Michael, 358
Reagan, Nancy, 324n75, 358
Reagan, Nellie, 20
Reagan, Patti, 359
Reagan, Ronald
    *Abortion and the Conscience of the
        Nation,* 309
    administrative appointments of, 287,
        305–6
    administrative skills of, 287, 365–66
    administrative style of, 53–54, 133, 351,
        356–59
    advisors, 4, 219–20
    on America (*see* America)
    approval ratings of, 216, 216t, 218, 357
    "being Reagan", 289–90
    blind spots of, 33–36
    campaigns of (*see* Campaigns)
    communication skills of, 33, 61, 361, 370
    compromises by, 52
    as a consensus builder, 71–74, 77, 224–
        25
    conservatism of, 49–54, 355
    as a decision maker, 192
    as a Democrat, 62–63
    early career of, 25–26, 355
    early life of, 24–27, 64–65
    fusionism and, 51
    as General Electric spokesman, 51, 65,
        155–56
    as governor (*see* California governor,
        Reagan as)
    on history, 17–19, 24–25, 35–36, 53
    humor of, 359
    ideology of (*see* Ideology)

Reagan, Ronald *(continued)*
  incuriosity of, 276, 370–71
  insider books on, 38n21
  intellectual rigidity of, 276, 357
  judicial appointments by *(see* Judicial
    appointments)
  leadership style of, 29–33, 276, 356–59,
    363
  legacy of, 12–113, 355–75
  on the nation vs. the government, 27–29
  optimism of, 356–57
  the outdoors and, 234
  passivity of, 276, 358–59
  personality of, 24, 40, 220, 356–59
  personal taxes paid by, 51, 155, 361
  political views 1950s, 64–65
  populist appeal of *(see* Populism)
  priorities of, 51, 54, 286–87
  radio speeches by, 22, 30, 52, 286–87, 356
  Reagan, In His Own Hand, 286–87
  reelection of, 220–22, 244–45
  religion and, 50
  remoteness of, 24, 358–59
  Ronald Reagan: An American Life, 262
  scholarly consensus on, 360
  as a soft-sell spokesperson, 61–62, 72
  as a symbol, 56
  as a thinker, 18
  vision of, 17, 19–25, 28, 33–36, 59n17
  work habits of, 359
Reagan, Ronald, speeches of
  on abortion, 302, 304
  on American memory, 31
  on America's destiny, 21–23
  on arms control, 89
  "Business, Ballots, and Bureaus", 65
  on civil rights, 286–87
  on communism, 86, 120
  on deficit reduction, 157
  on destiny, 22
  on environmental issues, 245
  on evil, 26
  "evil empire", 26, 117, 125, 129, 356
  on freedom, 31
  on government growth, 30
  on government power, 28–29
  "Hollywood Speech", 64
  on immigration, 262, 266–67, 277–
    78n11, 278n13

  inaugural addresses, 68, 70t, 73t, 74, 75t
  "Looking Out a Window", 52
  populist appeals in, 70t, 73–74, 73t, 75t
  on the promised land, 20–21
  on refugees, 21–22
  on the rescuing redeemer nation, 21–23
  "Russian Wheat Deal", 120
  on SDI, 102, 141
  on the shining city, 20–21, 24, 35
  on social issues, 302
  specialization of, 72–77
  State of the Union address, 70t, 73t, 74,
    75t
  on superpower relations, 117–18
  on tax reform, 165, 171–72
  "the Speech," 66, 68, 73–74, 156, 183, 210
  on time, 22
Reagan Victory School theory, 114–15,
Reason, 42
Recessions, 47, 161, 163, 215, 363
Rediscovery, 29–33
Reductionism, 42
Re, Edward, 342
Reeves, Richard, 61
Refugees
  Mariel boatlift and, 263, 265
  rescuing, 21–22
  statistics on, 261, 273
  welfare for, 265
  See also Immigration
Regan, Donald
  on affirmative action, 285
  on foreign policy, 134
  on Iran-Contra, 104
  leadership ability of, 223–24
  on Reagan's leadership, 276
  on the Rosy Scenario, 161
  on Social Security reform, 189, 192
  on tax reform, 7, 161, 164–67, 169, 361
Regenstein, Lewis, 235
Rehnquist, William H.
  chief justice appointment of, 11, 325n94,
    340, 342–45
  on civil rights, 289
Reimer, David, 271
Religion
  America's role and, 50
  civil, 35–36
  as the foundation of politics, 32

judicial appointments and, 337, 338t
  traditions of, 23
Religious History of the American People
  (Ahlstrom), 23
Remembrance, 35
Reproductive rights, 10–11. *See also*
  Abortion
Republican Party
  in the 1950s-1960s, 44–46
  1968 convention, 295
  in the 1970s, 47
  1980 elections and, 301–2
  abortion and, 298, 300
  civil rights and, 283, 285, 314n8
  Contract with America and, 56–57
  Evangelical Christians and, 301
  grassroots activists and, 294
  immigration and, 275
  judicial appointments and, 327
  resurgence of, 369
  silent majority and, 47–48
  social issues and, 301, 312–13
  Social Security reform and, 182, 184,
    194, 202–3
  women and, 294, 312
Rescuer redeeming nation, 22
Resources for the Future, 233
Retirement age
  early, 6, 184, 187, 190–91, 194–95, 201
  normal, 196, 200–201
Return, call to, 3, 43, 45, 55
Revenues, 157, 163–65, 167–68, 175n8. *See*
  also Budget, federal; Tax reform
Revercomb, George, 336
Reverse discrimination, 284–85, 287–88
Reykjavik summit, 144–46, 367
Reynolds, William Bradford, 284–85, 342
Rhetorical specialization, 66, 72–77
Richardson, Elliot, 226
Rich, tax reform and the, 156, 158–59
Rights
  of employees, 287–88
  of groups, 289, 294
  of individuals, 289
  natural, 48
Right to Life League, 297
Right wing conservatism *See* Conservatism;
  New Right
Right-wing liberals, 55

Road to Serfdom, The (Hayek), 43
Robb, Charles, 222
Roberts, Paul Craig, 158, 160, 162, 189–90
Roberts, Steven, 210
Rockefeller, Nelson, 295–98, 318n29
Rockman, Bert, 61
Rodino, Peter, 270–71
Roe v. Wade, 11, 297–98, 304, 309–10, 331
Ronald Reagan: An American Life
  (Reagan), 262
Roosevelt, Franklin D.
  judicial appointments by, 327, 328t, 329,
    338t–39t
  legacy of, 1, 371
  populism of, 61, 64, 71, 75t
  Reagan and, 3, 5, 62, 225
  See also New Deal
Roosevelt, Theodore, 81n66, 371
Roots, 32
Rostenkowski, Dan, 172, 197–98
Rosy Scenario, 161
Roth, William, 195
Rowny, Edward L., 141
Rubin, Jerry, 293
Ruckelshaus, William D., 242–45, 251
Rusher, William, 296
"Russian Wheat Deal" speech, 120

Sacramental vision, 3, 19–24, 59n17
  blind spots in, 33–36
  threats to, 25, 28
Safire, William, 68
SALT *See* Strategic Arms Limitations Talks
Sandinista National Liberation Front, 96,
  135
Santa Maria Basin, 237–38
Scalia, Antonin, 325n94, 337, 342–43, 345
Schlafly, Phyllis, 295, 299–301, 320n42
Schlesinger, Arthur, Jr., 360
Schmidt, Helmut, 136, 139
School meals, 214
School prayer, 11, 303, 331
Schuck, Peter, 276
Schültze, Walter, 140
Schumer, Charles, 270–71
Schweiker, Richard
  appointment of, 11, 305
  Social Security reform and, 186–93, 195,
    197, 206n27

Science, 53
Scott, Dred, 309
Scowcroft, Brent, 95, 105, -365
SCRIP. *See* Select Commission on
    Immigration and Refugee Policy
SDI. *See* Strategic Defense Initiative
Second American Revolution, 69–70
Secularism, 44
Seigan, Bernard, 331, 335
Select Commission on Immigration and
    Refugee Policy (SCRIP), 261, 263–66
Self-confidence, 357
Self-employment, 200
Self-government, 51
September 11, 2001 terrorist attacks, 259,
    272, 275
Service, for the nation, 35
Sessions, Jefferson B., III, 335–36
Sex discrimination, 311
Shabecoff, Philip, 244
Shaknazarov, Georgy, 124
Shannon, Jim, 198
Sharpe, Bolling v., 347
Sharp, Susie Marshall, 341
Shefter, Martin, 369
Shevardnadze, Eduard, 125
Shining city, 20–21, 24, 35
Shultz, George P.
    on affirmative action, 10, 284
    European Community and, 147
    on Grenada, 99–101
    on INF treaty, 139–40
    Iran-Contra scandal and, 106
    on Lebanon, 98–99
    on pipeline sanctions, 138, 149
    on the Reykjavik summit, 104
    on SDI, 128, 149, 367
    on the Soviet Union, 121–23
    on tax reform, 164
    viewpoint of, 365
Sierra Club, 237–38
Silent majority, 46–47
Simpson, Alan
    on Bork, 347
    on immigration, 262, 264, 267–71, 273–
    74
Single European Act, 148–49
Sixties period, 23, 35, 44–49
Skipchenko, Vladimir, 124–25, 125–26

Skrentny, John David, 283
Slocombe, Walter, 136
Slogans, 19
Small Business Administration, 290
Small business, on affirmative action, 285,
    288, 290
Smeal, Eleanor, 300
Smith, Jefferson, 49–50
Smith, Martin, 243
Smith, William French
    on immigration, 263, 265–67, 272, 274
    priorities of, 332
Snyder, Mitch, 221
Social conservatives, 46–47
Social Democratic Party, 139
Social good, 49
Socialism, 29, 43, 51, 55, 65
Social issues, 9–10, 293–326, 368–71
    of the 1970s, 293–94
    administrative appointments and, 305–6
    conservatism and, 55, 293–95
    Democratic Party and, 301
    New Right and, 12
    Republican Party on, 301, 312–13
    tax reform and, 364
    women and, 293–326
Social Security Act Amendment of 1983, 8,
    200–201
Social Security cards, 265–66
Social Security reform, 6, 8, 165–66, 182–
    208
    campaign promises on, 184, 194
    Congress and, 185, 187, 194–97, 201–3
    consensus package for, 199–200
    cost-of-living increases and, 185, 199, 203
    deficits and, 163, 200
    de-welfarization for, 185, 196
    disability benefits and, 188, 193
    early retirement and, 6, 184, 187, 190–
    91, 194–95, 201
    Gearhart bill, 63
    inter-fund borrowing for, 198
    legacy of, 364
    minimum monthly payments and, 188
    need for, 183
    normal retirement age and, 196, 200–201
    privatization for, 183, 204
    student benefits and, 187–88, 201
    taxing benefits and, 200

Social services expenditures, 295
Soft-sell spokesperson, 61–62, 72
Solidarity, 136
Solomon, Richard, 144
Somoza, Anastasio, 96
Southeast Asia, 261, 295
Southerners, 46
Soviet Union, 4–5, 113–32
  bankruptcy of, 120–21
  CIA estimates of, 138–39, 367
  collapse of, 114, 116, 123, 126–29
  conservatist view of, 43–44
  corruption in, 124
  defense spending by, 114, 124, 126–29
  dialogue with, 117–20
  domestic problems, 114, 123–24, 128
  economic problems, 114–15, 120–22,
    124–25, 129, 139, 368
  Europe and, 135
  evil empire label, 26, 117, 125, 129, 356
  Grenada and, 100–101
  hard-line policy toward, 116–20, 129
  hard-liners, 115
  invasion of Afghanistan, 92, 106–8, 114,
    125, 134–35
  Lebanon and, 101
  military expansionism of, 86–87
  National Security Decision Directive 75
    on, 95
  nuclear strategy, 87–88, 127–28
  Poland and, 136
  policy toward, 113, 134–35, 360, 367–68
  on SDI, 117, 127–28, 130n8
  threat of, 26–27
  values of, 36
  See also Arms control negotiations; Cold
    War; Gorbachev, Mikhail
Space-based weapons, 145
Special interest groups, 71–74, 274
Specialization, rhetorical, 66, 72–77
Specter, Arlen, 335, 347–48
"Speech, The," 66, 68, 73–74, 156, 183,
  210
Spencer, Stuart, 179n46
Sporkin, Stanley, 336
SSI. See Supplemental Security Income
Stallings, Mary, 341
Standard of living, 156
Stand-by taxes, 165–66

Starr, Kenneth W., 308
Star Wars, 293
Stassen, Harold, 344
State government
  vs. federal, 27–28
  water resources policy and, 247
  welfare and, 218–19, 222–23, 226
State legislation, on abortion, 296–98, 309–
  10
State of the Union address, 70t, 73t, 74,
  75t
Statistics, 76
Steuerle, C. Eugene, 169–70
Stevens, John Paul, 347
Stewart, Potter, 341
Stockman, David
  on abortion, 305
  Congress and, 6
  on defense spending, 91–92,
  on deficits, 160, 167
  on flat-rate taxes, 164–65
  on Reagan ideology, 19, 224–25
  on Social Security reform, 182, 186–88,
    190–94, 196–97, 199, 207n36
  on tax reform, 166, 168
  on welfare, 213, 216, 218
Stone, Harlan F., 347
Stop-ERA, 299, 301, 312
Storey, James, 212
Storytelling, 18, 36, 36–37, 76
Strategic Arms Limitations Talks (SALT),
  89, 96, 136, 143, 146, 295
Strategic Defense Initiative (SDI), 4–5, 85,
  102–4, 356
  Europe and, 140–45, 149
  insistence on, 365, 367–68
  Soviet economy and, 114–15, 123
  Soviet response to, 117, 127–28, 130n8
Strauss, Leo, 57
Strength, innocence and, 24–27
Strip mining, 237
Stubbing, Richard A., 94
Suffering, 33
Sulphur control programs, 243
Sununu, John, 224
Superfund program, 240–41, 243
Superpower relations, 117–18, 129
Supplemental Security Income (SSI), 195–
  96

Supply-side economics, 5–6, 53
    deficits and, 157, 164, 167–68, 175n8
    development of, 361–62
    failure of, 165, 364
    tax cuts and, 160
Supreme Court
    on abortion, 11, 297–98, 303, 309–10,
        325n87
    appointments to, 12, 306, 308, 327, 328t,
        340–50
    on Baby Doe, 324–25n81
    considerations for appointment to, 329–30
    Senate confirmation of, 336–37
    See also specific justices
Svahn, John A., 190, 194–95, 213
Swoap, David, 187, 190, 213
Symbolism, 12, 56
Symms, Steve, 341
System, the, 50

Taft-Hartley law, 63
Taft, Robert, 44
Talbott, Strobe, 141
TANF. See Temporary Assistance to Needy
    Families
Tarasenko, Sergei, 125
Task Force on Immigration and Refugee
    Policy, 263, 265
Tattoos, 266
Tax credits, 162
Tax deductions, 158–59, 162
Tax Equity and Fiscal Responsibility Act
    (TEFRA), 161–63, 168
Taxes
    bracket-creep, 156, 175n6
    consumption, 169, 176n10
    excise, 216
    flat-rate, 157–58, 163–66
    increases in, 163
    motion picture industry and, 64
    negative income, 212
    placeholder, 164–65
    progressive income, 155–59
    property, 156–57
    socialism through, 29
    stand-by, 165–66
    value-added, 176n10
Tax exemptions, 162, 170
Tax expenditures, 158–59, 173–74

Tax reform, 5–9, 155–81, 361–65
    5-10-10 formula, 161
    10-10-10 formula, 156, 160
    base broadening plan, 159, 163, 166–68,
        170
    as California governor, 156
    corporations and, 159, 167–69, 173,
        181n62
    deficits and, 157, 159–61, 362
    failure of, 56
    family and, 70–71
    indexing plans, 161
    inequalities in, 364
    legacy of, 361–65
    loopholes in, 158, 162–63, 168, 170–71
    the poor and, 169–70
    populist appeal of, 69–70, 70t
    revenue increases and, 157, 167–68,
        175n8
    the rich and, 156, 158–59
    simplification plan, 167
    social issues and, 364
    Treasury I and II plans, 170–72
Tax Reform Act of 1986, 7–8, 71, 155,
    168–74, 222
Tax shelters, 158, 161, 166, 168, 174
Technology, 114, 124, 135, 141
TEFRA. See Tax Equity and Fiscal
    Responsibility Act
Teitelbaum, Michael, 274
Teles, Steen, 226–27
Temporary Assistance to Needy Families
    (TANF), 225
Terrorist attacks, 24, 259, 272, 275
Thatcher, Margaret, 100, 134, 136, 138, 141
Think tanks, 369
Thompson, Lawrence H., 187–88
Thompson, Tommy, 222
Thornburgh v. American College of
    Gynecologists, 309–10
Threats, external vs. internal, 3, 25–26, 29, 65
Thurmond, Strom, 295, 336, 347
Time, 22
Times Beach, Missouri, 241–43
Title IX, 311
Title X, 306
Tolkien, J.R.R., 36
Totenberg, Nina, 334
Tower Commission, 276

Tower, John, 105, 185
Toxic waste, 241–43, 250
Trade negotiations, 147–48
Traditionalists, 43, 45, 47, 54
Traditions, American, 23
Treasury I and II plans, 170–72
Treaty of Fifth Avenue, 46
Triumph of Politics, The (Stockman), 216
Troy, Gil, 359
Truman, Harry
    judicial appointments by, 328t, 329,
        338t–39t
    legacy of, 371
    populist appeals of, 62–64, 71, 74–75,
        75t
    Reagan and, 3, 61–62, 67, 355
Ture, Norman, 158, 160, 162, 192
Turnage, William, 239
Tyranny of the majority, 42

Uhlmann, Michael, 305, 309
Undeserving Poor, The (Katz), 210
Undue burden doctrine, 308
Unemployment, 220
Unger, Sherman, 335
Up from Dependency report, 211
U.S. Catholic Conference, 309
U.S. Court of Appeals, 335
U.S. Geological Survey, 236
U.S. Information Agency, 122
USS Midway, 21–22
USSR. *See* Soviet Union

Value-added taxes, 176n10
Values
    choosing, 32
    family, 70–71, 327
    inherited, 23
    sixties period and, 35
Veterans of Foreign Wars, 89
Vietnam, 96–98, 102, 261, 295
Viguerie, Richard, 312
Virtue, 45, 57
Vision, sacramental. *See* Sacramental vision
Volcker, Paul, 161, 177n22, 363
Voluntarism, 218–19

Wade, Richard, 269
Wade, Row v., 11, 297–98, 304, 309–10, 331

Waggoner, Joe D., Jr., 199
Waiver authority, 226–27
Walker, Charls, 159–60
Wallace, George, 61, 297
Wallace, J. Clifford, 342–43
Wallison, Peter, 342–44
Walsh, Lawrence E., 105
Walsh, W.H., 18
Warren, Earl, 331–32, 344
Watergate, 296
Water resources, 234, 246–50
Water Resources Council, 246
Watt, James G.
    appointment of, 9, 236–37
    Democrats and, 238–39
    on identification cards, 266
    on offshore drilling, 237–38
    reelection campaign and, 245
    on Ruckelshaus, 242–43
    on water resources, 247–49
Weakland, Rembert, 309
Wealth, 51
Weaver, Richard, 41, 43
Weaver, R. Kent, 227
Weber, Brian, 285
Weicker, Lowell, 195, 219, 311
Weil, Simone, 32
Weinberger, Caspar W.
    on defense spending, 91–92, , 135
    Iran-Contra scandal and, 106
    on Lebanon, 98–99
    on Nicaragua, 366
    on SDI, 142
    on the use of force, 101–2
    viewpoint of, 134, 365
Weinberger Doctrine, 102
Welfare, 7, 9, 73, 209–32, 363
    after Reagan, 225–27
    damage from, 209
    definition of, 228n17
    immigration and, 267
    New Deal and, 41
    reform 1983-1986, 219
    reform 1986-1988, 222–25
    for refugees, 265
    the Speech on, 66
    state government and, 218–19, 222–23,
        226
Western European Union, 139, 142

Wetlands Loan Act, 249
Wetlands management, 247–50
Weyrich, Paul, 308
Wheat sales, 120
White, Byron, 342, 347
White House Judicial Selection Committee,
    12, 333–34, 350
White, Joseph, 198, 202
White, William Allen, 359
Whose Welfare? (Teles), 226
Wildavsky, Aaron, 198, 202
Wilderness Area activities, 236
Wilderness Society, 237, 239
Williams, Bradford, 10
Wills, Gary, 357
Wilson, Pete, 203, 269
Winter, Jay, 274
Winter, Ralph, 342–43
Winthrop, John, 21, 35
Wirthlin, Richard B., 93
Witness (Chambers), 43–44, 51
Women
    abortion and, 297, 316–17n25
    conservatist activists, 294, 296, 313,
        316–17n25
    Democratic Party and, 294, 312
    Equal Rights Amendment and, 299
    gender gap and, 304, 326n105
    judicial appointments of, 337, 338t
    Republican Party and, 294, 312

right-wing, 294–95
single vs. married, 294, 301–2, 312,
    326n105
social issues and, 293–326
traditional, 317n25
voters, 301–2, 312
See also Feminist movement
Wood, Gordon, 25
Workers
    agricultural, 265–67, 269, 271–72, 278n15
    cheap, 272, 274–75
    vs. corporations, 63–64, 71
    guestworker programs for, 265–67, 269,
        271–72, 278n15
    identification cards for, 265–66, 273
    illegal, 261, 263, 268, 270
    immigration and, 260, 274, 288–89
Workfare programs, 213, 225
Work habits, 359
Working poor, 212–13
World Federalists, 62
Worldview, 33–36
World War II, 41
Wright, James, 196, 362
Wright, Joseph, 231n77

Yakovlev, Aleksandr, 127
Young Americans for Freedom, 46

Zero-option proposal, 136–37